Road Atlas
Spain · Portugal · Europe

Autoatlas Spanien · Portugal · Europa

Atlante stradale Spagna · Portogallo · Europa

Atlas de carreteras España · Portugal · Europa

Atlas de estradas Espanha · Portugal · Europa

Autoatlas Spanien · Portugal · Europa

Bilatas Spanje · Portugal · Europa

Autóatlas Španělsko · Portugalsko · Evropa

Autóatlas Španielsko · Portugalsko · Európa

Atlas samochodowy Hiszpania · Portugalia · Europa

1:400 000 · 1:3 500 000

freytag & berndt
www.freytagberndt.com
© FREYTAG-BERNDT u. ARTARIA KG, 1230 VIENNA, AUSTRIA, EUROPE

9th Edition

AA Media Limited 2017

ISBN: 978-0-7495-7876-3

A05497

1:3 500 000

1:400 000

Reykjavik  IS

N

S

Oslo

Stockholm

DK

København

IRL

Dublin

GB

London

Amsterdam

NL

Bruxelles

B

Luxembourg

L

Paris

Berlin

D

Praha

CZ

Wien

Brati

F

Bern

CH

Vaduz

FL

A

H

SLO

Ljubljana

Zagreb

HR

BiH

Monaco

MC

San Marino

RSM

Sara

Andorra

AND

Madrid

P

Lisboa

E

Roma

V

Podg

I

El Djazâ'ir

Rabat

Tunis

Valletta

M

TN

MA

DZ

Tripolis

LAR

FIN

Helsinki

Tallinn
EST

Riga   LV

LT
Vilnius
RUS
Minsk
BY

Warszawa
PL

Kyjiv

UA

Moskva
RUS

RUS

KZ

UZB

TM

SK
va
Budapest
RO

Bucureşti

Beograd
SRB
vo
Prishtinë   Sofia   BG
MNE
RKS
rica
Skopje
ranë   MK

AL
GR

Athina

MD
Chişinău

Ankara

TR

Lefkosia
CY

1:3 500 000

SYR

RL
Beirut   Damaskus
HKJ

Amman
Jerusalem

IL

ET
Kairo

LAR

GE   Tbilisi   AZ   Baki

Erevan
ARM

Teheran

IR

Baghdad

IRQ

KSA

KWT   Kuwait

LEGEND ·
Legende · Legenda · Leyenda · Legenda · Signaturforklaring · Legende · Vysvětlivky · Vysvetlivky · Legenda

Motorway / Autobahn / Autostrada / Autovía / Auto-Estrada / Motorvej / Autosnelweg / Dálnice / Diaľnica / Autostrady	E05 European route with road numbers / Europastraße mit Straßennummern / Strada Europea con numerazione delle strade / Via europea con su numeración / Estradas europeias - identificação da estrada / Europavej - vejnummer / Europaweg met wegnummers / Silnice s mezinárodním označením / Európska cesta s číslami ciest / Droga europejska z numeracją dróg
Primary route / Fernverkehrsstraße / Strada die grande comunicazione / Carretera nacional / Itinerário principal / Vigtig hovedvej / Autoweg / Dálková silnice / Diaľková cesta / Drogi główne	193 Distances in kilometres / Entfernungen in km / Distanze in km / Distancias en km / Distância em quilómetros (km) / Afstande i km / Afstanden in km / Vzdálenosti v km / Vzdialenosti v km / Odległości w km
Railway / Eisenbahn / Ferrovia / Ferrocarril / Caminho-de-Ferro / Jernbane / Spoor / Železnice / Železnica / Koleje	National boundary / Staatsgrenze / Confine die Stato / Frontera / Fronteira nacional / Statsgrænse / Staatsgrens / Státní hranice / Štátna hranica / Granica państwa

Country codes (right margin): IS, RKS, L, LT, LV, MC, MD, MK, MNE, N, NL, P, PL, RO, RSM, RUS, S, SRB, SK, SLO, TR, UA, V

6

STATE INFORMATION · STAATENINFORMATION · INFORMAZIONI DELLO STATO · INFORMACIÓN SOBRE LOS ESTADOS · INFORMAÇÃO SOBRE OS PAÍSES · LANDEFAKTA · INFORMATIE VAN DE STAAT · INFORMACEO STÁTECH · INFORMÁCIE O ŠTÁTOCH · INFORMACJE O PAŃSTWACH

		Country		Motorway	Expressway	Road	Built-up	Alcohol	Emergency
A		Austria — Österreich / Autriche / Austria / Austria	▦	130 km/h	100 km/h	100 km/h	50 km/h	0,5 ‰	133, 144
AL		Albania — Albanien / Albanie / Albania / Albania		110 km/h	90 km/h	80 km/h	40 km/h	0,0 ‰	00355/17, 19
AND		Andorra — Andorra / Andorre / Andorra / Andorra				50 km/h	40 km/h	0,5 ‰	110, 118
B		Belgium — Belgien / Belgique / Belgio / Bélgica		120 km/h	90 km/h	90 km/h	50 km/h	0,5 ‰	100, 101
BG		Bulgaria — Bulgarien / Bulgarie / Bulgaria / Bulgaria	▦	130 km/h	90 km/h	90 km/h	50 km/h	0,5 ‰	166, 150
BiH		Bosnia-Hercegovina — Bosnien-Herzegowina / Bosnie-Hercégovine / Bosnia-Hercegovina / Bosnia-Herzegovina	▦	100 km/h	100 km/h	80 km/h	50 km/h	0,5 ‰	92, 94
BY		Belarus — Weißrussland / Biélorussie / Russia Bianca / Bielorrusia	▦	110 km/h	90 km/h	90 km/h	60 km/h	0,0 ‰	02
CH		Switzerland — Schweiz / Suisse / Svizzera / Suiza	▦	120 km/h	100 km/h	80 km/h	50 km/h	0,5 ‰	117, 144
CY		Cyprus — Zypern / Chypre / Cipro / Chipre	▦	100 km/h	80 km/h	80 km/h	50 km/h	0,4 ‰	199
CZ		Czech Republic — Tschechische Republik / République Tchèque / Repubblica Ceca / República Checa	▦	130 km/h	130 km/h	90 km/h	50 km/h	0,0 ‰	112
D		Germany — Deutschland / Allemagne / Germania / Alemania		–	–	100 km/h	50 km/h	0,5 ‰	110
DK		Denmark — Dänemark / Danmark / Danimarca / Dinamarca		130 km/h	80 km/h	60 km/h	50 km/h	0,5 ‰	112
E		Spain — Spanien / Espagne / Spagna / España	▦	120 km/h	100 km/h	90 km/h	50 km/h	0,5 ‰	092, 112
EST		Estonia — Estland / Estonie / Estonia / Estonia		110 km/h	110 km/h	90 km/h	50 km/h	0,0 ‰	110, 112
F		France — Frankreich / France / Francia / Francia	▦	130 km/h	110 km/h	90 km/h	50 km/h	0,5 ‰	17, 15, 112
FIN		Finland — Finnland / Finlande / Finlandia / Finlandia		120 km/h	100 km/h	80 km/h	50 km/h	0,5 ‰	112
FL		Liechtenstein — Liechtenstein / Liechtenstein / Liechtenstein / Liechtenstein			100 km/h	80 km/h	50 km/h	0,8 ‰	117, 144, 112
GB		United Kingdom — Vereinigtes Königreich / Royaume Unie / Regno Unito / Reino Unido		112 km/h	112 km/h	96 km/h	48 km/h	0,8 ‰	99, 112
GR		Greece — Griechenland / Grèce / Grecia / Grecia	▦	120 km/h	110 km/h	90 km/h	50 km/h	0,5 ‰	100, 166 (Athina)
H		Hungary — Ungarn / Hongrie / Ungheria / Hungaría	▦	130 km/h	110 km/h	90 km/h	50 km/h	0,0 ‰	107, 104
HR		Croatia — Kroatien / Croatie / Croazia / Croacia	▦	130 km/h	110 km/h	90 km/h	50 km/h	0,0 ‰	112
I		Italy — Italien / Italie / Italia / Italia	▦	130 km/h	110 km/h	90 km/h	50 km/h	0,5 ‰	112, 118
IRL		Ireland — Irland / Irlande / Irlanda / Irlanda		120 km/h	80 km/h	80 km/h	50 km/h	0,8 ‰	112, 999
IS		Iceland — Island / Islande / Islanda / Islandia			90 km/h	90 km/h	50 km/h	0,5 ‰	112
L		Luxembourg — Luxemburg / Luxembourg / Lussemburgo / Luxemburgo		130 km/h	90 km/h	90 km/h	50 km/h	0,8 ‰	113, 112
LT		Lithuania — Litauen / Lithuanie / Lituania / Lithuania		110 km/h	110 km/h	90 km/h	50 km/h	0,49 ‰	112
LV		Latvia — Lettland / Lettonie / Lettonia / Letonia		100-130 km/h	100-130 km/h	90 km/h	50 km/h	0,4 ‰	112
M		Malta — Malta / Malte / Malta / Malta				80 km/h	50 km/h	0,8 ‰	191, 196, 112
MC		Monaco — Monaco / Monaco / Monaco / Mónaco		130 km/h	100 km/h	90 km/h	50 km/h	0,5 ‰	17, 15, 112
MD		Moldova — Moldawien / Moldavie / Moldavia / Moldavia		90 km/h	90 km/h	90 km/h	60 km/h	0,0 ‰	902, 903
MK		Macedonia — Mazedonien / Macédonie / Makedonia / Macedonia	▦	120 km/h	100 km/h	80 km/h	60 km/h	0,5 ‰	192, 194
MNE		Montenegro — Montenegro / Monténégro / Montenegro / Montenegro	▦	120 km/h	100 km/h	80 km/h	60 km/h	0,5 ‰	92, 94
N		Norway — Norwegen / Norvège / Norvegia / Noruega	▦	90 km/h	80 km/h	80 km/h	50 km/h	0,2 ‰	112, 113
NL		The Netherlands — Niederlande / Pays Bas / Paesi Bassi / Países Bajos		130 km/h	100 km/h	80 km/h	50 km/h	0,5 ‰	112
P		Portugal — Portugal / Portugal / Portugallo / Portugal	▦	120 km/h	100 km/h	90 km/h	50 km/h	0,5 ‰	112
PL		Poland — Polen / Pologne / Polonia / Polonia	▦	140 km/h	120 km/h	90 km/h	50 km/h	0,2 ‰	997, 999
RKS		Kosovo — Kosovo / Kosovo / Kosovo / Kósovo		–	100 km/h	80 km/h	60 km/h	0,5 ‰	–
RO		Romania — Rumänien / Roumanie / Romania / Rumanía	▦	120 km/h	90 km/h	90 km/h	50 km/h	0,0 ‰	955, 961
RSM		San Marino — San Marino / Saint-Marin / San Marino / San Marino		130 km/h	110 km/h	90 km/h	50 km/h	0,5 ‰	113, 118, 112
RUS		Russian Federation — Russische Föderation / Russie / Russia / Rusia		110 km/h	90 km/h	90 km/h	60 km/h	0,0 ‰	02, 03
S		Sweden — Schweden / Suède / Svezia / Suecia		110 km/h	110 km/h	70-90 km/h	50 km/h	0,2 ‰	112
SRB		Serbia — Serbien / Serbie / Serbia / Serbia	▦	120 km/h	100 km/h	80 km/h	60 km/h	0,5 ‰	92, 94
SK		Slovakia — Slowakei / République Slovaque / Repubblica Slovacca / Eslovaquia	▦	130 km/h	130 km/h	90 km/h	50 km/h	0,0 ‰	158, 155
SLO		Slovenia — Slowenien / Slovénie / Slovenia / Eslovenia	▦	130 km/h	100 km/h	90 km/h	50 km/h	0,5 ‰	113, 112
TR		Turkey — Türkei / Turquie / Turchia / Turquía	▦	130 km/h	90 km/h	90 km/h	50 km/h	0,0 ‰	155, 112
UA		Ukraine — Ukraine / Ukraine / Ucraina / Ucrania		130 km/h	110 km/h	90 km/h	60 km/h	0,0 ‰	112
V		Vatican City — Vatikan Stadt / Cité du Vatican / Città del Vaticano / Ciudad del Vaticano					30 km/h	0,5 ‰	112, 113

MAP OF EUROPE · Übersicht Europa · Panoramica d'Europa · Vista general de Europa ·
Europa – Visão geral · Oversigtskort Europa · Overzicht Europa ·
Přehled – Evropa · Prehľad – Evropa · Przeglądowa Europy . . . . 2 – 3

GENERAL MAP · Verkehrsübersicht · Carta sinottica · Vista general · Mapa geral de tráfego ·
Primære rejseruter · Overzichtskaart · Přehledná mapa · Prehľadná mapa · Przeglądowa . . . . 4 – 5

INFORMATION OF EUROPEAN STATES · Staateninformation Europa ·
Informazioni dello stato Europa · Información de los estados Europa ·
Informação sobre os países Europa · Landefakta Europa · Informatie van de Staat Europa ·
Informace o státech Evropa · Informácie o štátoch Evropa ·
Informacje o państwach Europy 6

SPAIN · Spanien · Spagna · España · Espanha ·
Spanien · Spanje · Španělsko · Španielsko · Hiszpania

KEY TO MAP PAGES/LEGEND · Blattübersicht/Legende · Tavola riassuntiva delle pagine/Legenda ·
Vista de la página/Leyenda · Visão geral dos mapas/Legenda ·
Inddeling i kortsider/Signaturforklaring · Bladoverzicht/Legende · Klad listů/Vysvětlivky ·
Prehľad kladu listov/Vysvetlivky · Skorowidz arkuszy/Legenda . . . . I – II

ROAD MAPS SPAIN 1:400 000 · Auto + Freizeitkarte Spanien ·
Carta stradale + turistica Spagna · Mapa de rutas + del ocio España ·
Mapa de Estradas + de lazer Espanha · Bil- og fritidskort Spanien ·
Auto + Vrije tijd kaart Spanje · Automapa + mapa pro volný čas Španělsko ·
Automapa + mapa pre voľný čas Španielsko · Mapa samochodowa i rekreacyjna Hiszpania . . . . 1 – 81

SPAIN – PLACENAME INDEX WITH POSTCODES · Ortsregister mit Postleitzahlen ·
Indice con codici postali · Índice con códigos postales ·
Indice de lugares com códigos postais · Stedregister med postnumre ·
Plaatsnamenregister met postcode · Rejstřík míst s PSČ ·
Zoznam obcí s PSČ · Indeks miejscowości z kod pocztowy . . . . 82 – 126

PORTUGAL · Portugal · Portugallo · Portugal · Portugal ·
Portugal · Portugal · Portugalsko · Portugalsko · Portugalia

KEY TO MAP PAGES/LEGEND · Blattübersicht/Legende · Tavola riassuntiva delle pagine/Legenda ·
Vista de la página/Leyenda · Visão geral dos mapas/Legenda ·
Inddeling i kortsider/Signaturforklaring · Bladoverzicht/Legende · Klad listů/Vysvětlivky ·
Prehľad kladu listov/Vysvetlivky · Skorowidz arkuszy/Legenda . . . . I – II

ROAD MAPS PORTUGAL 1:400 000 · Auto + Freizeitkarte Portugal ·
Carta stradale + turistica Portugallo · Mapa de rutas + del ocio Portugal ·
Mapa de Estradas + de lazer Portugal · Bil- og fritidskort Portugal ·
Auto + Vrije tijd kaart Portugal · Automapa + mapa pro volný čas Portugalsko ·
Automapa + mapa pre voľný čas Portugalsko · Mapa samochodowa i rekreacyjna Portugalia . . . . 1 – 18

PORTUGAL – PLACENAME INDEX WITH POSTCODES · Ortsregister mit Postleitzahlen ·
Indice con codici postali · Índice con códigos postales ·
Indice de lugares com códigos postais · Stedregister med postnumre ·
Plaatsnamenregister met postcode · Rejstřík míst s PSČ · Zoznam obcí s PSČ ·
Indeks miejscowości z kod pocztowy . . . . 19 – 31

CITY MAPS · Stadtpläne · Piante di città · Planos de la ciudad · Mapas da cidade ·
Bykort · Plattegronden · Plány měst · Plány miest · Plany miasta

KEY TO CITY MAPS/LEGEND · Blattübersicht/Legende · Tavola riassuntiva delle pagine/Legenda ·
Vista de la página/Leyenda · Visão geral dos mapas/Legenda ·
Inddeling i kortsider/Signaturforklaring · Bladoverzicht/Legende ·
Klad listů/Vysvětlivky · Prehľad kladu listov/Vysvětlivky ·
Skorowidz arkuszy/Legenda . . . . 1 – 2

Barcelona	3	Lisboa	6 – 7	Santiago de Compostalla	12
Bilbao	4	Madrid	9 – 11	Sevilla	13
Granada	5	Porto	8	Valencia	14

STREET INDEX · Straßenverzeichnis · Indice stradale · Callejero · Índice de ruas · Gadefortegnelse ·
Straatnamenregister · Rejstřík ulic · Register názvov ulíc a námestí · Skorowidz ulic . . . . 15 – 24

EUROPE · Europa · Europa · Europa · Europa ·
Europa · Europa · Europa · Evropa · Europa

KEY TO MAP PAGES/LEGEND · Blattübersicht/Legende · Tavola riassuntiva delle pagine/Legenda ·
Vista de la página/Leyenda · Visão geral dos mapas/Legenda ·
Inddeling i kortsider/Signaturforklaring · Bladoverzicht/Legende · Klad listů/Vysvětlivky ·
Prehľad kladu listov/Vysvetlivky · Skorowidz arkuszy/Legenda 1

ROAD MAPS EUROPE 1:3 500 000 · Autokarte Europa · Carta stradale Europa ·
Mapa de carreteras Europa · Mapa de estradas Europa · Bil- og fritidskort Europa ·
Autokaart Europa · Automapa Europa · Automapa Evropa · Mapa samochodowa Europa . . . . 2 – 23

EUROPE – PLACENAME INDEX · Ortsregister · Indice · Índice de localidades · Indice de lugares ·
Stedregister · Plaatsnamenregister · Rejstřík míst · Zoznam obcí · Indeks miejscowości . . . . 24 – 39

SPAIN · SPANIEN · SPAGNA · ESPAÑA
ESPANHA · SPANIEN · SPANJE
ŠPANĚLSKO · ŠPANIELSKO · HISZPANIA

1:400 000

0   5   10   20   30   40 km

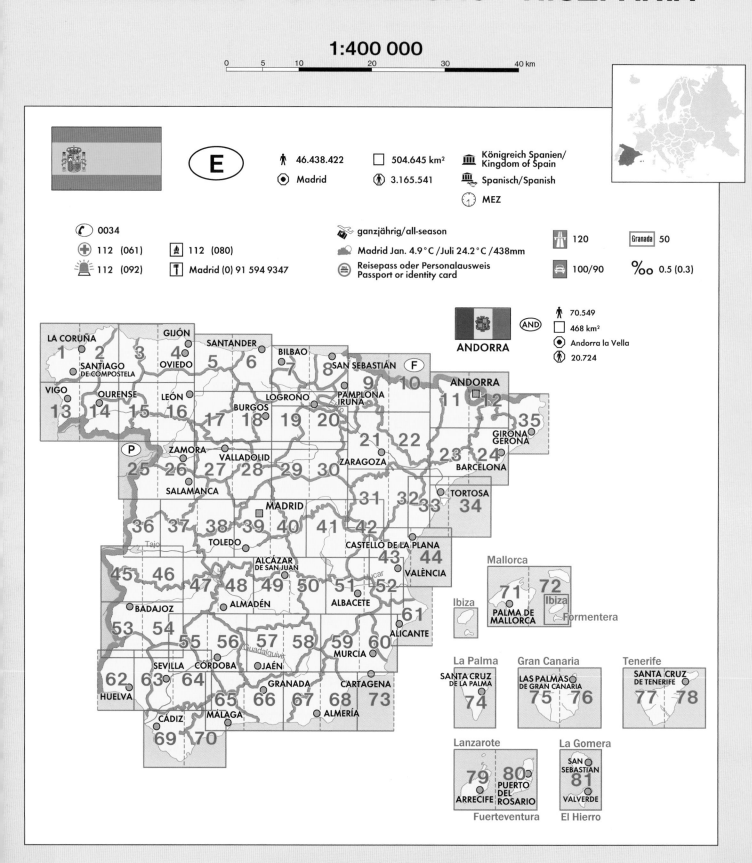

E	🚶 46.438.422	▢ 504.645 km²
	◉ Madrid	🚶 3.165.541

🏛 Königreich Spanien/ Kingdom of Spain
🏛 Spanisch/Spanish
🕐 MEZ

☎ 0034

✚ 112 (061)   🔥 112 (080)
🚨 112 (092)   ℹ Madrid (0) 91 594 9347

✈ ganzjährig/all-season
☁ Madrid Jan. 4.9°C /Juli 24.2°C /438mm
🛏 Reisepass oder Personalausweis
      Passport or identity card

🛣 120   Granada 50
🚗 100/90   ‰ 0.5 (0.3)

ANDORRA   AND
🚶 70.549
▢ 468 km²
◉ Andorra la Vella
🚶 20.724

LA CORUÑA
1   2   3   GIJÓN 4   SANTANDER   BILBAO   SAN SEBASTIÁN   F
SANTIAGO DE COMPOSTELA   OVIEDO   5   6   7   8   9   10   ANDORRA
VIGO   OURENSE   LEÓN   LOGROÑO   PAMPLONA IRUÑA   11   12
13   14   15   16   17   BURGOS 18   19   20   21   22   23   24   35   GIRONA GERONA
P   ZAMORA   VALLADOLID   ZARAGOZA   BARCELONA
25   26   27   28   29   30   31   32   33   34   TORTOSA
SALAMANCA   MADRID
36   37   38   39   40   41   42   CASTELLÓ DE LA PLANA
TOLEDO   43   44
ALCÁZAR DE SAN JUAN   VALÈNCIA   Mallorca
45   46   47   48   49   50   51   52   71   72   Ibiza
BADAJOZ   ALMADÉN   ALBACETE   61   Ibiza   PALMA DE MALLORCA   Formentera
53   54   55   56   57   58   59   60   ALICANTE
SEVILLA   CÓRDOBA   JAÉN   MURCIA
62   63   64   GRANADA   CARTAGENA   La Palma   Gran Canaria   Tenerife
HUELVA   65   66   67   68   73   SANTA CRUZ DE LA PALMA   LAS PALMAS DE GRAN CANARIA   SANTA CRUZ DE TENERIFE
CÁDIZ   MÁLAGA   ALMERÍA   74   75   76   77   78
69   70
Lanzarote   La Gomera
79   80   SAN SEBASTIÁN 81
ARRECIFE   PUERTO DEL ROSARIO   VALVERDE
Fuerteventura   El Hierro

Legend Legende Legenda Leyenda Legenda Legende
Signaturforklaring Vysvětlivky Vysvetlivky Legenda

Motorway; Projected motorway
Autobahn; Autobahn geplant
Autostrada; Autostrada in progetto
Autopista; Autopista en proyecto
Auto estrada; Auto-estrada em projecto
Autosnelweg; Autosnelweg in ontwerp
Motorvej; Motorvej projekteret
Dálnice; Plánovaná dálnice
Diaľnica; Plánovaná diaľnica
Autostrady; Autostrady projektowane

El Cuadrejón

Filling station; Service area - with overnight accomodation
Tankstelle; Autobahnraststation - mit Übernachtung
Distributore di benzina, Aera di servizio con motel
Gasolinera; Área de servicio - motel
Posto de gasolina; Área de serviço - hotel
Tankstation; Wegrestaurant met overnachting
Bensinstation; Motorvejsrestauration med hotel
Čerpací stanice; Dálniční odpočívadlo - s možností přenocování
Čerpacia stanica; Areál autoslužieb s možnosťou prenocovania
Stacja benzynowa; Miejsca obsługi podróżnych z noclegiem

2020

Motorway under construction with scheduled opening date
Autobahn in Bau mit Fertigstellungstermin
Autostrada in costruzione con data di apertura
Autopista en construcción (fecha de apertura)
Auto-estrada em construção com data de inauguração
Autosnelweg in aanleg (datum openstelling bekend)
Motorvej under opførsel med datum for indvielse
Dálnice ve stavbě s termínem dokončení
Rozostavaná diaľnica s termínom dokončenia
Autostrady w budowie z terminem otwarcia

Sanlucar

Motorway with interchange
Autobahn mit Anschlussstelle
Autostrada con raccordo
Autopista con conexión
Auto-estrada com ligação
Autosnelweg, aansluitingen volledig
Motorvej med komplet tilkørsel
Dálnice s nájezdem
Diaľnica s nájazdom
Autostrady z węzłami

Dual carriageway; Primary route
Fernverkehrsstraße, 4 - spurig; Fernverkehrsstraße
Strada di grande comunicazione a quattro corsie; Strada di grande comunicazione
Autovía de 4 carriles; Carretera nacional
Itnerário principal com 4 faixas; Estrada nacional
Autoweg, 4 rijstroken; Autoweg
Motortrafikvej med 4 baner; Fjerntrafikvej
Dálková silnice, čtyřproudová; Dálková silnice
Diaľková cesta štvorprúhová; Diaľková cesta
Drogi dwujezdniowe; Drogi główne

Main road; Secondary road
Hauptstraße; Nebenstraße
Strada principale; Strada secondaria
Carretera principal; Carretera secundaria
Estrada principal; Estrada secundária
Belangrijke verkeersader; Secundaire weg
Vigtig hovedvej; Hovedvej
Hlavní silnice; Vedlejší silnice
Hlavná cesta; Vedľajšia cesta
Drogi drugorzędne; Drogi lokalne

Roads under construction; Scenic route
Straßen in Bau; Landschaftlich besonders schöne Strecke
Strade in costruzione; Tratto di paesaggio particolarmente bello
Calles en construcción; Ruta panorámica
Estrada em construção; Caminho muito pitoresco
Straten in aanleg; Schilderachtig traject
Vej under opførselraten; Landskabelig smuk vejstrækknig
Silnice ve stavbě; Trasa vedoucí obzvlášť krásnou krajinou
Cesty vo výstavbe; Zvlášť pekná prírodná cesta
Drogi w budowie; Drogi piękne widokowo

XII-III

Road closed during the cold season (Primary routes class "A" & "B" roads)
Wintersperre (auf Fern - und Hauptstraßen)
Chiusura invernale (di strade di grande comunicazione e principali)
Carretera cerrada en invierno (carretera nacional y principal)
Impedimento de inverno (estrada nacional e principal)
In de winter afgesloten (auto- en hoofdwegen)
Spærret om vinteren (fjerntrafikvej, hovedvej)
Zimní uzavírka (na dálkových a hlavních silnicích)
Zimné uzávery (na diaľkových a hlavných cestách)
Drogi zamknięte zimą (główne i drugorzędne)

Camino de Santiago
15%-20%
10%-15%   30%

Toll road; Camino de Santiago; Gradient; Mountain pass
Mautstraße; Jakobsweg, Steigungen; Pass
Strada a pedaggio; Cammino di San Giacomo, Pendenze; Passo di montagna
Carretera de peaje; Camino de Santiago, Pendiente; Puerto de montaña
Estrada com portagem; Caminho do Santiago, Inclinação; Passo de montanha
Tolweg; Jacobsweg, Stijging; Bergpas
Toldvej; Jakobvej; Stigning; Bjergpas
Silnice s poplatkem; Svatojakubská cesta, Stoupání; Průsmyk
Cesta s mýtnym poplatkom; Cesta sv. Jakuba, Stúpania; Priesmyk
Drogi płatne; Droga św. Jakuba, Strome podjazdy, Przełęcz

8 4   4
4 8

Distances in kilometres
Entfernungen in km
Distanze in km
Distancias en km
Distância em quilómetros (km)
Afstanden in km
Afstand i km
Vzdálenosti v km
Vzdialenosti v km
Odległości w km

A7 E15
IP6 IC3
324 NIV
P-235 AC-552

Motorway; European route; Road numbers
Autobahn; Europastraße; Straßennummern
Autostrada; Strada europea; Numerazione delle strade
Autopista; Carretera europea; Número de la carretera
Autostrada; Strada europea; Identificação da estrada
Autosnelweg; Europese weg; Wegnummers
Motorvej; Europavej; Vejnummer
Dálnice; Evropská silnice; Číslo silnice
Diaľnica; Európska cesta; Číslo cesty
Numery autostrad; Dróg miedzynarodowych; Dróg krajowich

MADRID
MURCIA

Seat of the federal government; Provincial capital
Bundeshauptstadt; Landeshauptstadt
Capitale federale; Città-capoluogo
Capital federal; Capital de provincia
Capital; Capital de distrito
Hoofdstad; Provinciehoofdstad
Hovedstad; Administrationssæde
Hlavní město; Sídlo kraje
Hlavné mesto štátu; Krajské mesto
Stolice państw; Miasta wojewódzkie

Main - railway line; Subsidiary railway, Rack; Cable railway
Hauptbahn; Nebenbahn, Zahnradbahn; Seilschwebebahn
Linea ferrovia principale; Linea ferrovia secondaria; Ferrovia a cremagliera; Funivia
Línea férrea principal; - secundaria; Línea de cremallera; Funicular
Ferrovia principal; Ferrovia secundária; Elevador de cremalheira; Teleférico
Spoor; Zijspoor; Tandradspoor; Kabelbaan
Jernbane, hovedbane, sidebane; Tandhjulsbane; Tovbane
Hlavní železniční trať; Vedlejší železniční trať; Ozubená dráha; Lanovka
Hlavná železnica; Vedľajšia železnica; Ozubnicová železnica ; visutá lanová dráha
Koleje główne; Koleje drugorzędne; Koleje zebate; Koleje linowe

Car - ferry; Passenger - ferry
Autofähre; Personenfähre
Traghetto per il automobile; Traghetto per passeggeri
Transbordador para coches; Transbordador para pasajeros
Ferry-boat; Barco de passageiros
Autoveerboot; Personenveerboot
Bilfærge; Personfærge
Trajekt pro automobily; Převoz
Autokompa; Kompa
Promy samochodowe; Promy osobowe

Military reservation; Nature reserve
Truppenübungsplatz; Naturschutzgebiet
Campo di addestramento militare; Area naturale protetta
Campo de maniobras militares; Reserva natural
Área exercicio militar; Reserva ecológica
Militair oefenterrein; Natuureservaat
Spærret militærisk område; Nationalpark
Vojenské cvičiště; Přírodní rezervace
Vojenský cvičný priestor; Prírodná rezervácia
Poligon wojskowy; Rezerwat przyrody

National boundary; Provincial boundary
Staatsgrenze; Landesgrenze
Confine di Stato; Confine regionale
Frontera nacional; Límite de provincia
Fronteira; Limite de província
Staatsgrens; Provinciegrens
Statsgrænse; Amtsgrænse
Státní hranice; Krajská hranice
Štátna hranica; Hranica kraja
Granice państw; Granice województw

International airport; Airport
Internationaler Flughafen; Flugplatz
Aeroporto internazionale; Aeroporto
Aeropuerto Internacional; Aeropuerto
Aeroporto internacional; Aeroporto
Internationale vliegveld; Vliegveld
Intern. Lufthavn; Lufthavn
Mezinárodni letiště; Letiště
Medzinárodné letisko; Lisko
Porty lotnicze międzynarodowe; Lotniska

Monastery, church; Manor-house, castle; Ruin; Telecommunications tower
Kloster, Kirche; Schloss, Burg; Ruine; Sender
Convento, chiesa; Castello, fortezza; Rovine; Stazione transmittente
Monasterio, iglesia; Mansión, fortaleza; Ruinas; Torre de comunicaciones
Convento, igreja; Castelo, fortaleza; Ruinas; Retransmissor
Klooster, kerk; Kasteel, burcht; Ruïne; Zender
Kloster, kirke; Slot; Borgruin; Vysílač
Klášter, kostel; Zámek, hrad; Zřícenina; Vysílač
Kláštor, kostol; Zámok, hrad; Ruiny; Vysíelač
Klasztory, kościoły; Zamki; Ruiny; Maszty nadawcze

Place of particular interest; Monument; Look - out tower
Besonders sehenswertes Objekt; Denkmal; Aussichtsware
Località di grande interesse; Monumento; Torre panoramica
Lugar de interés; Monumento; Mirador
Local de interesse especial; Monumento; Vista panorâmica
Bijzondere bezienswaardigheden; Gedenkteken; Uitzichttoren
Seværdighed; Mindesmærke; Udsigtstårn
Obzvlášt zajímavý objekt; Pomník; Vyhlídkové místo
Mimoriadne pozoruhodný objekt; Pamätnik; Vyhliadková veža
Miejsca warte zwiedzenia; Pomniki; Wieże widokowe

Antique sites; Cave; Hotel, inn, mountain cabin
Antike Ruinenstätte; Höhle; Hotel, Gasthof, Schutzhütte
Luoghi con rovine; Grotta; Albergo, trattoria, rifugio
Yacimiento arqueológico; Cueva; Hotel, albergue, refugio
Sitio arqueológico; Gruta; Hotel, albergue, pousada
Antieke ruïne; Grot; Hotel, gasthuis, schuilhut
Ruiner, oldtidsminde; Hule; Hotel, krog bjerghytte
Antické zříceniny; Jeskyně (přístupná veřejnosti); Hotel, hostinec, horská chata
Antické zrúcaniny; Sprístupnená jaskyňa; Hotel, penzión, horská chata
Ruiny antyczne; Jaskinie; Hotele, zajazdy, schroniska górskie

Marina; Lighthouse; Camping site; Spa; Scenic viewpoint; Golf-course
Marina; Leuchtturm; Campingplatz; Heilbad; Schöner Ausblick; Golfplatz
Marina; Faro; Campeggio; Località termale; Vista panoramica; Campo da golf
Puerto deportivo; Faros; Camping; Estación termal; Vista panorámica; Campo de golf
Marina; Farol; Parque de campismo; Termas; Vista panorâmica; Campo de golfe
Jachthaven; Vuurtoren; Kampeerterrein; Kuurbad; Uitzichtpunt panorama; Golfterrein
Lystbådehavn; Fyrtårn; Campingplads; Kurbad; Udsigtspunkt; Golfbane
Přístav; Maják; Kemping; Lázně; Krásný výhled; Golfové hřiště
Prístav; Maják; Kemping; Kúpele; Pekny výhľad; Golfové ihrisko
Porty jachtowe; Latarnia morska; Campingi; Uzdrowiska; Punkty widokowe; Pola golfowe

Mulhacén
3481

Summit; Height; World Heritage
Gipfel; Höhe; Weltkulturerbe
Vertice; Altezza; Patrimoni dell'umanilà
Cumbre; Altura; Patrimonio de la Humanidad
Cúpula; Altura; Património Mundial
Top; Hoogte; Werelderfgoed
Topmøde; Højde; Verdensarvsliste
Vrcholek; Výška; Seznam světového dědictva
Vrchol; Výška; Lokalita svetového dedičstva
Jzczyt; Wysokość; Obiekty z listy dziedzictwa UNESCO

1:400 000

0   5   10   20   30 km

Alba de Cerrato · Población de Cerrato · Cubillas de Cerrato · Esguevillas de Esgueva · Amusquillo · Villaco · Castroverde de Cerrato · Fombellida · Castrillo de Don Juan · Encinas de Esgueva · Canillas de Esgueva · Villovela de Esgueva · Villatuelda · Terradillos de Esgueva · Olmedillo de Roa · Sotillo de la Ribera · Gumiel del Mercado · Santibáñez de Esgueva · Oquillas · Villalbilla de Gumiel · Tubilla · Gumiel de Izán · Quintana de Pidio · La Aguilera · Villanueva de Gumiel

VA-140 · Villafuerte · Castrillo-Tejeriego · Montecillo · Villavaquerín · Olivares de Duero · Valbuena de Duero · Conv. de S. Bernardo · Jaramiel de Arriba · Piñel de Abajo · Piñel de Arriba · San Llorente · Pesquera de Duero · Curiel de Duero · Valdearcos de la Vega · Guzmán · Villaescua de Roa · Boada de Roa · Pedrosa de Duero · Corrales de Duero · Quintanamanvirgo · La Horra · Anguix · Valcavado de Roa · Roa · Berlangas de Roa · La Cueva de Roa · Ventosilla · Quemada · Zazuar · San Ju

N-122 · Sardón de Duero · Traspinedo · Quintanilla de Onésimo · Quintanilla de Arriba · Padilla de Duero · Peñafiel · Manzanillo · Langayo · Olmos de Peñafiel · Castrillo de Duero · Mambrilla de Castejón · San Martín de Rubiales · Nava de Roa · Fuentecén · Haza · Campillo de Aranda · Castrillo de la Vega · Fresnillo de las Dueñas · Aranda de Duero · Vadocondes · La Vid · Fuentespina

Montemayor de Pililla · Cogeces del Monte · Fompedraza · Rábano · Canalejas de Peñafiel · Laguna de Contreras · Sacramenia · Convento de San Bernardo · Valtiendas · Hontangas · Adrada de Haza · Fuentemolinos · La Sequera de Haza · Moradillo de Roa · Torregalindo · Milagros · Fuentelcésped · Pardilla · Fuentenebro · Montejo de la Vega de la Serrezuela · Maluque · Villaverde de Montejo · Honrubia de la Cuesta · Valdevacas de Montejo · Moral de Hornuez · Valdevarnés · Maderuelo

VA-203 · Torrescárcela · Bahabón · Aldeasoña · Membibre de la Hoz · Calabazas · Fuentesoto · Torreadrada · Pradales · Ciruelos · Carabias · Fuentemizarra · Cilleruelo de San Mamés · Campo de

Viloria · San Miguel de Arroyo · A-601 · Fuentes de Cuéllar · Moraleja de Cuéllar · Vegafría · Fuentesaúco de Fuentidueña · Fuentidueña · Castro de Fuentidueña · Castroserracín · Navares de las Cuevas · Fresno de la Fuente · Bercimuel · Riag

Vallelado · CL-602 · San Cristóbal de Cuéllar · Cuéllar · Con. de Santa Clara · Dehesa Mayor · Olombrada · Fuentepiñel · San Miguel de Bernuy · Cobos de Fuentidueña · Navares de Enmedio · Navares de Ayuso · Encinas · Grajera · Pajarejos · Castiltierra · Mata de Cuéllar · Chañe · Arroyo de Cuéllar · Sanchonuño · Perosillo · Frumales · Adrados · Cozuelos de Fuentidueña · Torrecilla del Pinar · Carrascal del Río · Burgomillodo · Convento de La Hoz · Castrillo de Sepúlveda · Castillo morisco · Sepúlveda · Aldeonte · Boceguillas · Sequera de Spino · Fresn de Cante · Aldeanu del Mont · Turrubuelo · Barbolla

Fresneda de Cuéllar · Narros de Cuéllar · Chatún · Gomezserracín · Hontalbilla · Navalilla · Fuenterrebollo · Villar de Sobrepeña · Sto. María de la Peña · Duratón · El Olmo · Castillejo de Mesleón · Samboal · Mudrián · Pinarejos · Zarzuela del Pinar · Lastras de Cuéllar · Cantalejo · Sebúlcar · Castillo · Urueñas · Aldeonsancho · Aldealcorvo · Perorrubio · Duruelo · Cerezo de Arri · Sotillo · Vellosillo

Navas de Oro · Navalmanzano · Fuentepelayo · Sauquillo de Cabezas · Cabezuela · Valdesimonte · San Pedro de Gaíllos · Villafranca · Castroserna de Abajo · St. Marta del Cerro · Cerezo de Abajo · Sto. Tomé del Puerto · Pinarnegrillo · Aldea Real · Veganzones · Puebla de Pedraza · Rebollo · La Matilla · Ventosilla y Tejadilla · Casla · Siguero · Sigüeruelo

A-601 · Bernardos · Miguelañez · Carbonero el Mayor · Monzoncillo · Escalona del Prado · Turégano · Otones de Benjumea · Valdevacas · Arahuetes · La Velilla · Huerta · Prádena · N-110 · Somosierra · Robregordo

Domingo García · Miguel Ibáñez · Ortigosa de Pestaño · Tabanera la Luenga · Escarabajosa de Cabezas · Peñarrubias de Pirón · Torreiglesias · Caballar · Cubillo · Castillo de Velasco · Pedraza · Arcones · Colganzos · Horcajo de la Sierra

Nieva · Armuña · Cantimpalos · Escobar de Polendos · Carrascal · La Mata · Torre Val de S. Pedro · Gallegos · Matabuena · La Acebeda · Horcajuelo de la Sierra · Madarcos · Prádena del Rincón

Sta. María la Real de Nieva · Yanguas de Eresma · Cabañas de Polendos · Losana de Pirón · Pelayos del Arroyo · Ceguilla · Navafría · Collado Hermoso · Braojos · La Serna del Monte · Gascones · Piñuecar · Prádena del Rincón · Paredes de Buitrago

Pascuales · Pinilla-Ambroz · Carbonero de Ahusín · Roda de Eresma · Brieva · Basardilla · Sotosalbos · La Higuera · Villavieja del Lozoya · San Mamés · Pinilla de Buitrago · Buitrago del Lozoya · Cincovillas

Balisa · Aragoneses · Paradinas · Añe · Encinillas · Bernuy de Porreros · Espirdo · Los Neveros · Navarredonda · Gargantilla del Lozoya · Villoslada · Marazuela · CL-605 · Hontanares de Eresma · Garcillán · Torrecaballeros · Lozoya · Embalse de Riosequillo · Las Navas de Buitrago · Lozoyuela

Velagómez · Marazoleja · Anaya · Valverde del Majano · Zamarramala · La Lastrilla · San Cristóbal de Segovia · Trescasas · Parque Nacional de la Sierra de Guadarrama · El Tornillar · Pinilla de Buitrago · Cotos de Monterrey

Sangarcía · Martín Miguel · SEGOVIA · Catedral · Old Town and its Aqueduct · Perogordo · Palazuelos de Eresma · Palacio · S. Ildefonso · Oteruelo del Valle · Pinilla del Valle · Canencia · Sieteiglesias · Cobos de Segovia · Juarros de Riomoros · Abades · Madrona · Hontoria · Revenga · Palacio Jardines · Monast. de El Paular · Alameda del Valle · Valdemanco · Bustarviejo · El Berrueco

Muñopedro · Marugán · SG-322 · Fuentemilanos · Navas de Riofrío · La Losa · Pradera de Navalhorno · Rascafría · Miraflores de la Sierra · Navalafuente · Cabanillas de la Sierra · Torremoc de Jaram

Monterrubio · Otero de los Herreros · N-110 · N-603 · Peñalara · M-604 · Navalagamella · Redueña · Torrelaguna

Zarzuela del Monte · Valdeprados · AP-61 · La Mujer Muerta · Otero de · S. del Quintanar · Guadalix de la Sierra · M-608 · El Vellón · Venturada · Cabeza de Hierro · Villacastín · N-VI · Vegas de Matute · Prados · Yelmo

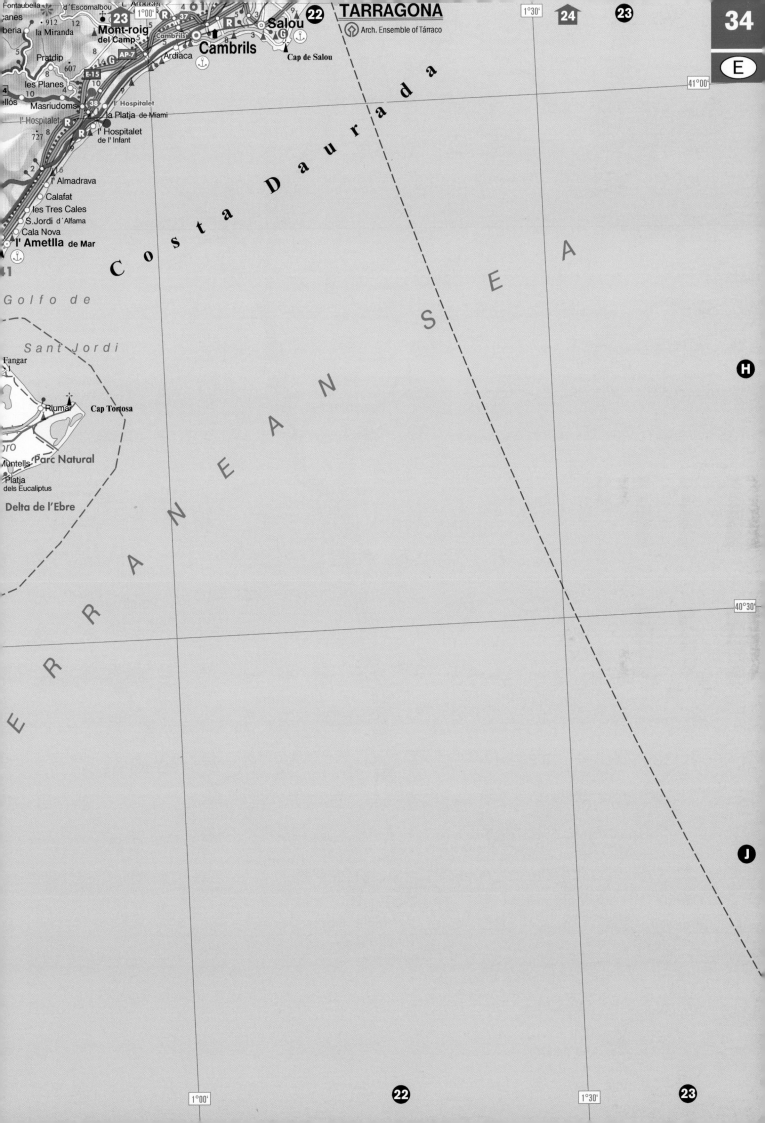

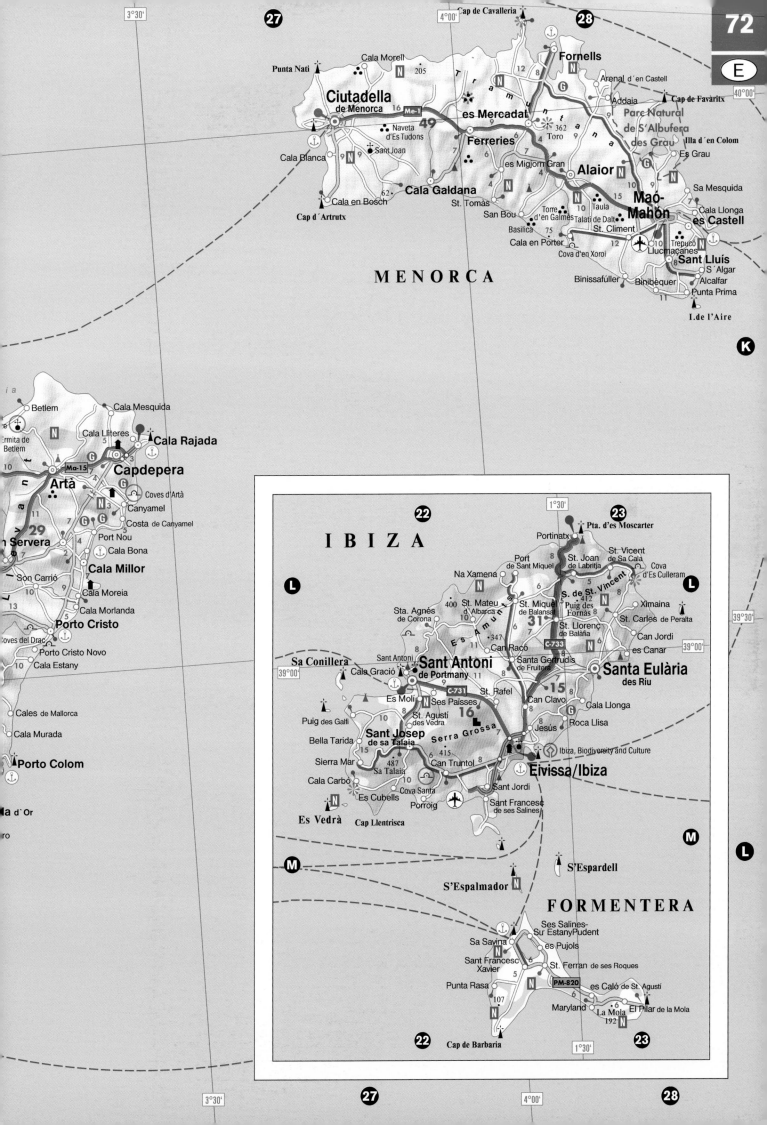

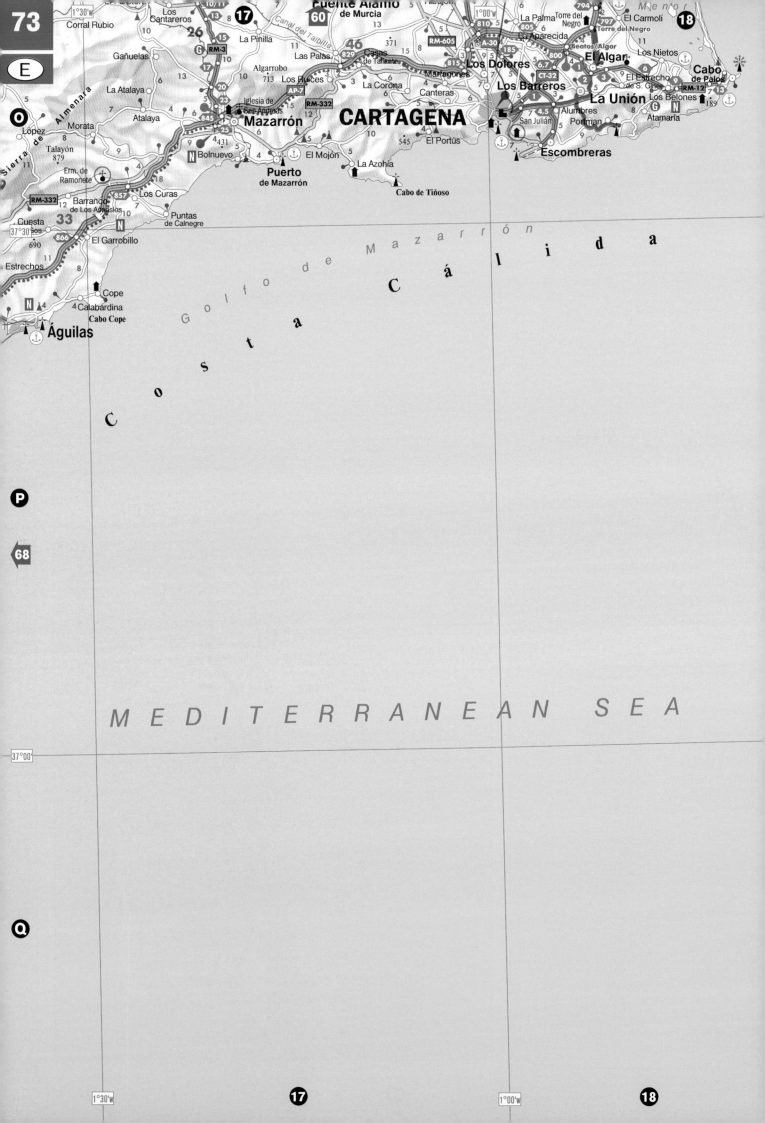

O

P

68

Q

MEDITERRANEAN SEA

Golfo de Mazarrón

C o s t a   C á l i d a

Corral Rubio
Los Cantareros
17
60 Fuente Álamo de Murcia
La Palma Torre del Negro
El Carmolí
18

La Pinilla
26
46
RM-605
El Algar
Los Nietos

Gañuelas
Las Palas
Casas de Tallante
Los Dolores
La Aparecida
La Unión
Cabo de Palos

Algarrobo
Los Ruices
La Corona
Los Barreros
El Estrecho de S. Ginés
Los Belones

La Atalaya
Iglesia de San Andrés
Canteras
San Julián
Alumbres
Portman
Atamaria

Atalaya
Mazarrón
CARTAGENA

Morata
Bolnuevo
El Mojón
El Portús
Escombreras

Talayón
Puerto de Mazarrón
La Azohía

Erm. de Ramonete
Cabo de Tiñoso

Barranco de Los Asensios
Los Curas
Puntas de Calnegre

Cuesta
El Garrobillo

Estrechos

Cope
Calabardina
Cabo Cope

Águilas

Punta de Sardina

Punta de Gáldar
Punta de Guanarteme
Puerto Nuevo

Puerto de la Caleta
Sardina
Gáldar
Puntas del

Puerto de Sardina
Santiago de las Caballeros
Guía/ Gáldar
8 9 10

Roque Partido
Gáldar
7

Barrial

Punta Marqués
San Isidro
Almagro 469
Santa María
de Guía de Gran Canaria

El Calabozo

Playa El Juncal
GC-2
Hoya Pineda

Puerto de las Nieves
Cueva de las Cruces
Pico de Viento 837
Paso María de Los Santos

El Dedo de Dios
Agaete
Verdejo

Playa de Guayedra
GC-2
Saucillo
Alfa 951
Lo

Guayedra
San Pedro
GC-220

Playa Segura
Caideros
Barranco del Pinar

La Laja del Risco
Casas del Camino
San Barto de Fonta

Playa del Risco 29
Casas de Tamadaba
El Hornillo
Fagajesto

Playa de la Virgen
El Risco
Tamadaba 1444
Embalse de Los Perez
San Barto

Punta de Gongora
Casas Las Hoyas
Lugarejos
Lan

GC-200
Cruz de la Virgen
El Tablado

Mirador del Balcón
Casas de Tirma
Moriscos 1771
Valse

Cuevas Negras
Altavista 1376
Artenara

Punta de la Aldea
GC-2
Acusa
El Rincón

Puerto de la Aldea
Embalse de El Parralillo
Cueva del Rey
Roque Ventaiga 1412
Tejeda

Las Marciegas
GC-200
El Chorrillo
GC-60

Roque Colorado
Casas de Pino Gordo
Embalse de El Siberio
El Espinillo
Roque Nublo 1813

La Aldea de San Nicolás
Embalse Caidero de la Niña
El Carrizal
22

Artejévez
El Fraile 1729

Playa de Güigüi Grande
Tocodomán
Montaña de Sándara 1583
Aya

Montaña de las Vacas 914
13

Playa de Güigüí Chico
Mirador de Tasártico 25
Embalse de Cueva de las Niñas
GC-200

Playa de Güigüí Grande
Tasártico
Tasarte
Embalse de El Mulato
San Ba

Punta de las Tetas
Mogarenes 892
Embalse de Soria
Cercados de Araña

Casas El Manatial
Las Casas de Veneguera
Embalse de Chira
Morro de la Hierba Huerta 1819

Punta Carpintera
Casas de La Huerta Nueva
El Pie de la Cuesta
Soria

Casas de la Vistilla
El Baranquillo Andrés
Casas de Chamoriscan

Punta de los Vallecillos
Casas El Sao
El Caidero
Santidad 1193

Playa de Tasarte
Casas El Inglés
Mogán
GC-505

Casas de la Postreragua de Veneguera
GC-200 10
Casas de Tauro Alto
Cercados de Espinos
Casas Taginos

Playa del Cerillo
Tabaibales 602
Los Navartos
El Horno

Veneguéra
El Palmita
Hoya del Salitre
Los Peñones

El Horno
Tabaibales
Tanigue
El Sao

Morgan/ Taurito
68
Monteleón

Punta del Castillete
67 Taurito

Puerto de Mogán
Taurito

Taurito

Playa del Diablito
62 **Puerto Rico**

La Playa del Tauro
GC-500 Tauro

Playa del Cura

GRAN CANARIA
Punto de la Hondura
Puerto Rico
Montaña de Ladata

Playa de Puerto Rico
T8
GC-1

0   2 km   4 km
Solobre Golf
10 **El Tablero**

Punta de los Inciensos
53 GC-1 **48**

Patalavaca
56
GC-500 14,5
Pasito Blanco

Arguineguín
50

Parchel
Bahía de Santa Agueda

Punta del Parchel
Puerto Deportivo de Pasito Blanco

Playa de las Meloneras

El Faro

Playa de

4   5   6   7

A

B

C

D

E

Punta del Hidalgo
Bajamar
Punta Gotera
Punta del Fraile
Punta de la Barranquera
Tejina
Valle Guerra
Tegueste
Casa de Carta
Punta del Viento
Mesa del Mar
Punta de la Mesa
La Caridad
Tacoronte
El Sauzal
La Matánza de Acentejo
Punta de Juan Blas
Punta del Sol
Ravelo
La Victoria
La Mantánza de Acentejo
La Esperanza
La Victoria de Acentejo
Lomo Pelado
Santa Ursula
Santa Ursula
La Orotava
La Cuesta
Pta. de la Cruz
La Orotava
La Florida
Pinoleris
El Bebedero
Aguamansa
Camino Chasna
Arafo
Güímar
El Tablero
Tabaiba Alta
el Rosario
Tabaiba Baja
Barranco Hondo
Igueste de Candelarias
Araya
Las Cuevecitas
Candelaria
Malpais
La Hidalga
Arafo
Valle de Güímar
El Socorro
Güímar
Pájara
La Medida
Lomo de Mena
El Escobonal
Agüerche
Fasnia
La Zarza
Chajaña
La Florida
Sabina Alta
Cruz del Roque
Las Eras
Arico Viejo
La Degollada
Sabinita
Arico
Los Gavilanes
El Río
imiche
Porís de Abona
Abades
La Listada
Jardín del Atlántico
La Jaca
Cueva Honda
San Miguel de Tajao
Chimiche El Río
Callao del Rio
Pol. Ind. Granadilla
Casas de las Montañas
Güirre
Punta de los Mejillones
nas del Mar
édano

Punta de los Troches
Playa de los Troches
Punta Fajana
Punta de Tamadite
Playa del Tamadite
Punta Poyata
Punta Poyata
Playa de El Draquillo
Playa de Benijo
Roque de Dentro
Playa del Junquillo
Faro de Anaga
Almáciga
Benijo
Chamorga
Punta El Jurado
Punta del Drago
Lomo de Las Bodegas
Punta de Anaga
Taborno
Afur
Taganana
Chinobre
Igueste de San Andrés
Batán de Abajo
Batán de Arriba
Valle Crispín
Valle Brosque
María Jiménez
Playa de las Gaviotas
Punta de Antequera
Playa de Jiuana
Las Carboneras
Pedro Alvarez
Mesa de Tejina
Las Canteras
Las Mercedes
Ramonal
San Andrés
Playa de las Teresitas
El Portezuelo
San Diego
San Benito
San Cristóbal de La Laguna
Puerto
Guamasa
Aeropuerto Tenerife Norte
San Bartolomé de Geneto
La Cuesta
Somesierra Cementerio
SANTA CRUZ DE TENERIFE
Los Naranjeros
Agua Garcia
El Ortigal
Los Baldios
Taco-La Cuesta
Taco
Taco-Ofra
Sobradillo
Llano el Moro
Barranco Grande
Santa Cruz/ Av. Maritima
Las Rosas
Santa Maria del Mar
Hoya Fria
Punta de la Encendida
Sta. Maria del Mar
Playa de Berruguette
Playa de la Nea
Radazul
Radazul
Punta de Guadamojete
Barr. Hondo
Punta del Morro
Igueste de Candelarias
Las Caletillas
Las Caletillas
Playa de Samarines
Playa de la Entrada
Puerto de Güímar
Punta Prieta La Caleta
Playa de Arriba
Playa de Abajo
Playa de la Caleta
Playa Barranco Arriba
Playa de la Margallera
El Tablado El Escabonal
El Tablado
Punta del Poris
Fasnia Los Roques
Cambio de Sentido
Punta de Honduras
Las Eras
Playa de Las Ceras
Punta del Rincón
Arico Poris de Abona
Punta La Ternera
Playa Grande
Punta de los Roquetes
P.I.R.S. Tajao
Playa de la Jaca
Playa del Río
Playa Los Tarajales
Playa del Tambor
Punta del Tanque del Vidrio

TF13
TF16
TF16
TF156
TF152
TF152
TF172
TF5
TF217
TF21
TF23
TF27
TF226
TF237
TF24
TF265
TF263
TF5
TF256
TF28
TF21
TF24
TF523
TF245
TF525
TF61
TF1
TF28
TF617
TF620
TF625
TF627
TF629
TF1
TF13
TF13
TF12
TF111
TF180
TF194
TF134
TF12
TF121
TF11

TENERIFFA

0   2 km   4 km

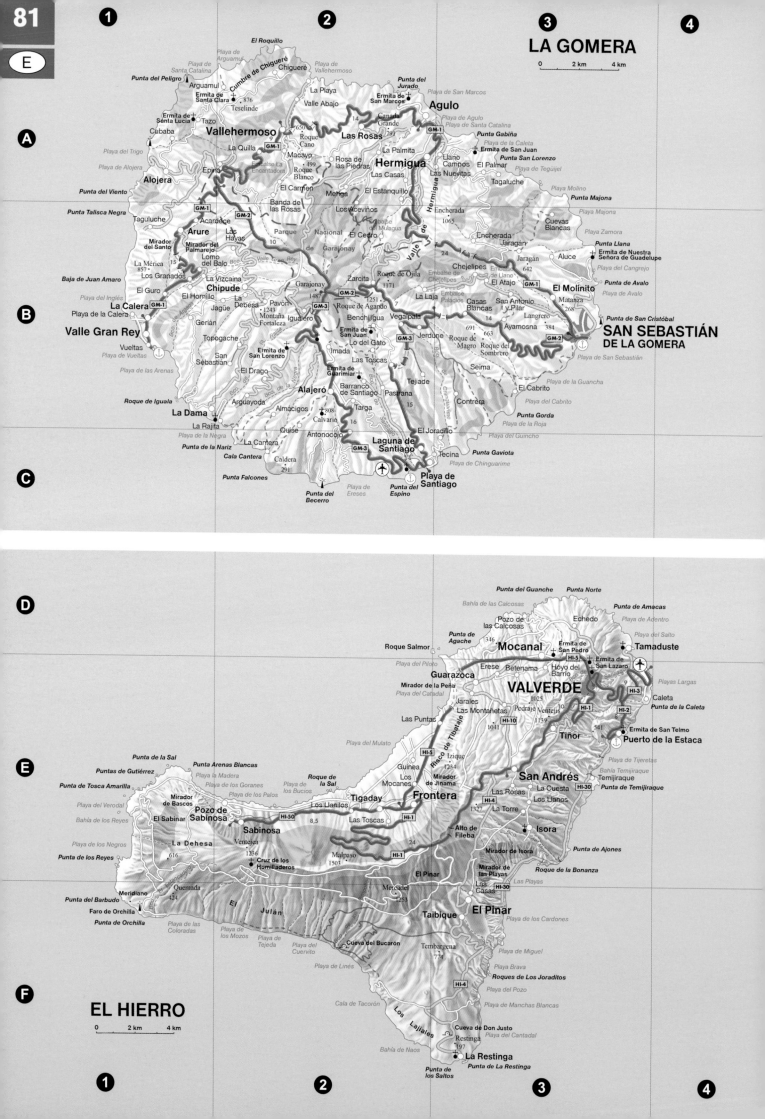

INDEX·ORTSREGISTER·INDICE·ÍNDICE·ÍNDICE·INDHOLDSFORTEGNELSE·
PLAATSNAMENREGISTER·REJSTŘÍK MÍST·ZOZNAM OBCÍ·INDEKS MIEJSCOWOŚCI

82

E

A Baiuca · E · **Alcantarilla** · E

A

15142 A Baiuca 1 C 3
27520 A Barrela 14 D 4
36880 A Caniza 13 E 3
15070 A Coruña-La Coruña
   1 C 3
27816 A Costa 2 C 4
27346 A Cruz de Incio 14 D 5
36856 A Chán 13 E 3
27796 A Devesa 3 B 5
32526 A Ermida 14 D 3
36680 A Estrada 13 D 3
27100 A Fonsagrada 3 C 5
32643 A Forxa 14 E 4
27124 A Frairía 3 C 5
36889 A Frangueira 13 E 3
36520 A Golada 2 D 3
36780 A Guardia 13 F 2
32540 A Gudina 15 E 5
15565 A Igrexa 2 B 4
36830 A Lama 13 E 3
15845 A Laracha 1 C 2
27133 A Lastra 3 C 5
36850 A Laxe 13 E 3
15593 A Mariña 2 B 3
32830 A Merca 14 E 4
32549 A Mezquita 15 E 5
36556 A Millarada 13 D 3
15838 A Peña 1 D 2
32150 A Peroxa 14 E 4
32703 A Piúca 14 E 4
32316 A Pobla 15 E 5
27656 A Pobra 3 D 5
32365 A Ponte 15 E 6
27720 A Pontenova 3 C 5
21730 A Praga 14 E 3
15883 A Ramallosa 1 D 2
27234 A Retorta 2 D 4
15819 A Riba 1 D 2
27654 A Ribeira 3 C 6
32350 A Rúa 15 E 5
32821 A Seara 14 E 3
32860 A Terrachá 14 F 3
32360 A Veiga 15 E 5
32311 A Veiga de Cascallá
   15 E 6
27112 A Veiga de Logares
   3 C 5
27418 A Vide 14 D 4
32858 A Vila 14 F 3
44155 Ababuj 32 H 18
15563 Abade 2 B 4
40141 Abades 28 H 11
10748 Abadía 37 J 8
27730 Abadín 2 C 5
31280 Abáigar 8 D 15
09141 Abajas 18 D 12
26339 Ábalos 7 D 14
33556 Abamia 5 C 9
19432 Abánades 30 H 15
42368 Abanco 29 G 14
30640 Abanilla 60 N 17
50375 Abanto 30 G 16
30550 Abarán 60 N 17
34338 Abarca de Campos
   17 E 10
32372 Abarxa 15 E 5
31178 Abárzuza 8 D 15
31692 Abaurregaina-Abaurrea
   Alta 9 D 17
31692 Abaurrepea-Abaurrea
   Baja 9 D 17
22713 Abay 10 D 18
42146 Abejar 19 F 14
44422 Abejuela 43 K 18
02439 Abejuela/Letur
   59 N 15
04691 Abejuela/Taberno
   68 O 16
32520 Abelenda 13 E 3
24145 Abelgas 4 D 8

25651 Abella de la Conca
   11 E 22
15685 Abella/Ordes 2 C 3
22472 Abella/Pont de Suert
   11 E 21
22622 Abellada 10 E 19
15290 Abelleira 1 D 1
22620 Abena 10 E 19
44565 Abenfigo 32 H 19
02250 Abengibre 51 L 16
22621 Abenilla 10 E 19
13180 Abenójar 48 M 11
01193 Aberasturi 8 D 14
10262 Abertura 46 L 8
49834 Abezames 27 F 9
16195 Abia de la Obispalía
   41 J 15
34491 Abia de las Torres
   18 E 11
39211 Abiada 6 C 11
22143 Abiego 22 E 19
31473 Abínzano 9 D 17
42127 Abión 30 F 15
39639 Abionzo 6 C 12
22392 Abizanda 22 E 20
04510 Abla 67 P 14
19442 Ablanque 30 H 15
31523 Ablitas 20 F 16
08630 Abrera 24 F 23
33774 Abres 3 C 5
04520 Abrucena 67 P 14
27546 Abuíme 14 D 4
37640 Abusejo 37 H 7
24996 Acebedo 5 C 9
36556 Acebeiro 13 D 3
10857 Acebo/Moraleja 36 J 6
24413 Acebo/Ponferrada
   15 E 7
06730 Acedera 47 L 8
31282 Acedo 8 D 15
10879 Acehuche 36 K 6
10666 Aceituna 36 J 7
33868 Acellana 4 C 7
34111 Acera de la Vega
   17 D 10
50347 Acered 31 G 16
32870 Aceredo 14 F 3
06207 Aceuchal 54 M 7
18131 Ácula 66 P 12
22612 Acumuer 10 D 19
22147 Adahuesca 22 E 19
39761 Adal 7 C 13
47129 Adalia 27 F 9
14430 Adamuz 56 N 10
05296 Adanero 27 H 10
46140 Ademuz 42 J 17
36979 Adina 13 E 2
39788 Adino 7 C 13
31448 Adoain 9 D 17
19325 Adobes 42 H 16
04770 Adra 67 Q 13
09462 Adrada de Haza
   28 F 12
40192 Adrada de Pirón
   28 G 11
42216 Adradas 30 G 15
24859 Adrados/Boñar 5 D 9
40354 Adrados/Cuéllar
   28 G 11
25797 Adrall 12 E 22
41728 Adriano 63 P 8
03786 Adsubia 61 M 19
03730 Aduanas 61 M 20
12006 Adzaneta 33 J 19
37510 Agallas 36 J 7
25691 Àger 11 E 21
50560 Agón 21 F 17
26509 Agoncillo 20 E 15
03698 Agost 60 N 18
02409 Agra 59 N 16
02490 Agramón 59 N 16
25310 Agramunt 23 F 22
42100 Agreda 20 F 16
03837 Agres 61 M 18
18132 Agrón 66 P 12

04149 Agua Amarga 68 Q 16
18640 Aguadero 66 P 12
04720 Aguadulce/Almería
   67 Q 14
41550 Aguadulce/Osuna
   64 P 10
15148 Agualada 1 C 2
50408 Aguarón 21 G 17
22141 Aguas 22 E 19
09593 Aguas Cándidas
   7 D 12
02070 Aguas Nuevas
   51 M 16
36854 Aguasantas/A Lama
   13 E 3
15911 Aguasantas/Dices
   1 D 2
27391 Aguasmestas
   14 E 5
44382 Aguatón 42 H 17
44566 Aguaviva 32 H 19
42258 Aguaviva de la Vega
   30 G 15
13410 Agudo 47 M 10
33844 Agüera 4 C 7
33814 Agüera del Coto 3 C 6
22808 Agüero 9 E 18
47418 Agüesal 27 G 10
40340 Aguilafuente 28 G 11
44156 Aguilar de Alfambra
   32 H 18
19283 Aguilar de Anguita
   30 G 15
09249 Aguilar de Bureba
   7 D 13
34800 Aguilar de Campoo
   6 D 11
47814 Aguilar de Campos
   17 F 9
31228 Aguilar de Codés
   8 D 15
14920 Aguilar de la Frontera
   65 O 10
30880 Águilas 68 P 16
09216 Aguillo 7 D 14
43429 Aguiló 24 F 22
22588 Aguinalíu 22 E 20
02611 Aguiño 13 D 1
17707 Agullana 35 E 25
46890 Agullent 52 M 18
09551 Ahedo del Butrón
   6 D 12
10650 Ahigal 37 J 7
37173 Ahigal de Villarino
   25 G 7
16176 Ahillas 42 K 18
06940 Ahillones 54 N 8
20809 Aia/Segura 8 D 15
31460 Aibar 9 D 17
25595 Aidí 11 D 22
46812 Aielo de Malferit
   52 M 18
25515 Aiguabella 11 E 21
17255 Aiguablava 35 F 26
08591 Aiguafreda 24 F 24
43815 Aiguamúrcia 24 G 22
17181 Aiguaviva/Anglès
   35 F 25
43714 Aiguaviva/Vilafranca
   del Penedès
   24 G 23
03569 Aigües 61 N 19
12222 Ain 43 K 19
25573 Ainet de Besan
   11 D 22
22623 Aineto 10 E 19
22330 Ainsa 10 E 20
31697 Aintziba 9 D 17
50570 Ainzón 21 F 16
22860 Aísa 10 D 18
25182 Aitona 23 G 20
25577 Aiueto 11 D 22
31172 Aizpún 8 D 16
39806 Aja 7 C 12
28864 Ajalvir 40 H 13

26133 Ajamil 20 E 15
39170 Ajo 6 C 12
45110 Ajofrín 48 K 12
48313 Akorda 7 C 14
44549 Alacón 31 G 18
50481 Aladrén 31 G 17
47510 Alaejos 27 G 9
50630 Alagón 21 F 17
07730 Alaior 72 K 28
01207 Alaiza 8 D 15
42368 Alalo 29 G 14
28130 Alalpardo 40 H 13
29530 Alameda 65 P 10
13690 Alameda de Cervera
   49 L 13
45240 Alameda de la Sagra
   39 J 12
28749 Alameda del Valle
   28 H 12
18520 Alamedilla 66 O 13
13413 Alamillo 56 M 10
45909 Alamín 39 J 11
19490 Alaminos 29 H 14
06840 Alange 54 M 7
41380 Alanís 54 N 8
46970 Alaquas 43 L 19
34480 Alar del Rey 18 D 11
37312 Alaraz 38 H 9
50345 Alarba 31 G 16
16214 Alarcón 51 K 15
07340 Alaró 71 K 25
25718 Alás 12 E 23
22760 Alastúey 9 D 18
02152 Alatoz 51 L 17
27207 Albá 2 D 4
34219 Alba de Cerrato
   18 F 11
34888 Alba de los Cardaños
   5 D 10
37800 Alba de Tormes
   26 H 8
37478 Alba de Yeltes 36 H 7
44395 Alba/Monreal del
   Campo 42 H 17
27813 Alba/Vilalba 2 C 4
02070 Albacete 51 M 16
46860 Albaida 61 M 18
41809 Albaida del Aljarafe
   63 P 7
09216 Albaina 7 D 14
10187 Albalá del Caudillo
   46 L 7
13340 Albaladejo 58 M 14
16111 Albaladejo del
   Cuende 41 K 15
46687 Albalat de la Ribera
   61 L 19
22534 Albalate de Cinca
   22 F 20
16841 Albalate de las
   Nogueras 41 J 15
19117 Albalate de Zorita
   40 J 14
44540 Albalate del Arzobispo
   32 G 18
22220 Albalatillo 22 F 19
27619 Albán 2 D 5
04857 Albánchez 68 P 15
23538 Albánchez de Úbeda
   57 O 13
17733 Albanyà 35 E 25
43360 Albarca 23 G 21
32514 Albarellos/Carballiño
   14 E 3
36516 Albarellos/Lalin
   14 D 3
19112 Albares 40 J 13
33830 Albariza 4 C 7
44100 Albarracín 42 J 17
45522 Albarreal de Tajo
   39 K 11
02653 Albatana 59 M 16
25171 Albàtàrrec 23 F 21
03340 Albatera 60 N 18
22558 Albelda 23 F 20

26120 Albelda de Iregua
   20 E 15
16812 Albendea 41 J 15
19275 Albendiego 29 G 13
14859 Albendín 65 O 11
44477 Albentosa 43 J 18
45695 Alberche del Caudillo
   38 K 10
32622 Alberguería 14 E 4
46260 Alberic 52 L 18
26141 Alberite 22 E 16
50529 Alberite de San Juan
   21 F 17
22112 Albero Alto 22 E 19
22255 Albero Bajo 22 E 19
22147 Alberuela de la Liena
   22 E 19
22212 Alberuela de Tubo
   22 F 19
25135 Albesa 23 F 21
50549 Albeta 21 F 17
09239 Albillos 18 E 12
43716 Albinyana 24 G 22
24293 Albires 17 E 9
12140 Albocácer 32 J 20
04531 Alboloduy 67 P 14
18220 Albolote 66 P 12
18708 Albondón 67 Q 13
17136 Albons 35 E 26
46369 Alborache 43 L 18
02215 Alborea 51 L 17
19264 Alboreca 30 G 14
15256 Alborés 1 D 2
50781 Alborge 22 G 19
05358 Albornos 27 H 10
04800 Albox 68 P 15
30190 Albudeite 60 N 17
30330 Albujón 60 O 17
18518 Albuñán 67 P 13
18700 Albuñol 67 Q 13
18659 Albuñuales 66 Q 12
06510 Alburquerque 45 L 6
45523 Alcabón 39 J 11
46290 Alcácer 43 L 19
02124 Alcadozo 59 M 16
04830 Alcaide 59 O 15
44792 Alcaine 31 H 18
12570 Alcalá de Chivert
   33 J 20
50691 Alcalá de Ebro 21 F 17
41500 Alcalá de Guadaira
   64 P 8
22282 Alcalá de Gurrea
   21 E 18
28800 Alcalá de Henares
   40 J 13
03788 Alcalá de la Jovada
   61 M 19
44432 Alcalá de la Selva
   32 J 18
16315 Alcalá de la Vega
   42 J 16
11180 Alcalá de los
   Gazules 69 R 8
50591 Alcalá de Moncayo
   20 F 16
02210 Alcalá del Júcar
   51 L 17
22135 Alcalá del Obispo
   22 E 19
41200 Alcalá del Río 63 O 8
23680 Alcalá la Real 66 P 12
03728 Alcalalí 61 M 19
22560 Alcampell 23 F 20
26509 Alcanadre 20 E 15
43530 Alcanar 33 H 20
43530 Alcanar Platje
   33 H 21
49500 Alcanices 26 F 7
44600 Alcañiz 32 G 19
45687 Alcañizo 38 K 9
25162 Alcanó 23 G 21
16290 Alcanozo 51 L 16
10980 Alcántara 45 K 6
30820 Alcantarilla 60 O 17

E

Alcàntera de Xúquer (E) **Alovera**

46293 Alcàntera de Xúquer 52 L 18
16812 Alcantud 41 H 15
14480 Alcaracejos 55 N 10
02300 Alcaraz 58 M 15
25180 Alcarràs 23 F 21
29711 Alcaucín 65 Q 11
23660 Alcaudete 66 O 11
45662 Alcaudete de la Jara 38 K 10
04769 Alcaudique 67 Q 14
18710 Alcázar 66 Q 13
13600 Alcázar de San Juan 49 L 13
16464 Alcázar del Rey 40 J 14
47238 Alcazarén 27 G 10
24649 Alcedo 4 D 8
13116 Alcoba 48 L 11
42351 Alcoba de la Torre 29 F 13
28100 Alcobendas 39 H 12
19125 Alcocer 41 J 14
03841 Alcocer de Planes 61 M 19
09258 Alcocero de Mola 19 E 13
16537 Alcohujate 41 J 14
13107 Alcolea de Calatrava 48 M 11
22410 Alcolea de Cinca 22 F 20
19277 Alcolea de las Peñas 29 G 14
45571 Alcolea de Tajo 38 K 9
19260 Alcolea del Pinar 30 G 15
41449 Alcolea del Río 64 O 8
14610 Alcolea/Cordoba 56 O 10
04480 Alcolea/Ugíjar 67 Q 14
03814 Alcoleja 61 M 19
25660 Alcoletge 23 F 21
10135 Alcollarín 46 L 8
42134 Alconaba 30 F 15
37329 Alconada 27 H 9
40529 Alconada de Maderuelo 29 G 13
06131 Alconchel 53 M 5
42269 Alconchel de Ariza 30 G 15
16433 Alconchel de la Estrella 50 K 14
04897 Alcontar 67 P 14
21130 Alcor 62 P 6
12006 Alcora 43 J 19
03699 Alcoraya 60 N 18
28920 Alcorcón 39 J 12
44550 Alcorisa 32 H 19
10515 Alcorneo 45 L 5
19310 Alcoroches 42 H 16
12570 Alcossebre 33 J 20
16176 Alcotas/Lliria 43 K 18
44422 Alcotas/Manzanera 43 J 18
43460 Alcover 23 G 22
03203 Alcoy-Alcoi 61 M 19
42320 Alcozar 29 F 13
02249 Alcozarejos 51 L 16
22251 Alcubierre 22 F 19
42351 Alcubilla de Avellaneda 29 F 13
42213 Alcubilla de las Peñas 30 G 14
49696 Alcubilla de Nogales 16 E 8
13391 Alcubillas 49 M 13
45521 Alcubillete 39 K 11
46172 Alcublas 43 K 18
07400 Alcúdia 71 K 26
18511 Alcudia de Guadix 67 P 13
04276 Alcudia de Monteagud 68 P 15
12222 Alcudia de Veo 43 K 19

10160 Alcuéscar 46 L 7
24207 Alcuetas 17 E 9
19264 Alcuneza 30 G 14
01117 Alda 8 D 15
31892 Aldaba 8 D 16
46960 Aldaia 43 L 19
36945 Aldán 13 E 2
48340 Aldana 7 C 14
31878 Aldatz 8 C 16
32848 Aldea de Arriba 14 E 4
39419 Aldea de Ebro 6 D 11
42345 Aldea de San Esteban 29 F 13
47160 Aldea de San Miguel 27 G 10
10253 Aldea de Trujillo 46 K 8
10163 Aldea del Cano 46 L 7
37488 Aldea del Obispo 36 H 6
09660 Aldea del Pinar 19 F 13
13380 Aldea del Rey 49 M 12
40292 Aldea Real 28 G 11
05153 Aldeabad de Mirón 37 H 9
10251 Aldeacentenera 47 K 8
37718 Aldeacipreste 37 J 8
48891 Aldeacueva 7 C 13
37250 Aldeadávila de la Ribera 25 G 6
42134 Aldealafuente 30 F 15
40513 Aldealázaro 29 G 13
40389 Aldealcorvo 28 G 12
37350 Aldealengua 26 H 8
05193 Aldealgordo 27 H 10
42180 Aldealices 20 F 15
42112 Aldealpozo 20 F 15
42180 Aldealseñor 20 F 15
40555 Aldealuenga de Santa María 29 G 13
47162 Aldeamayor de San Martín 27 F 10
45908 Aldeancabo de Escalona 38 J 11
19244 Aldeanueva de Atienza 29 G 13
45661 Aldeanueva de Barbarroya 38 K 9
26123 Aldeanueva de Cameros 19 E 14
26559 Aldeanueva de Ebro 20 E 16
37429 Aldeanueva de Figueroa 26 G 8
19152 Aldeanueva de Guadalajara 40 H 13
40532 Aldeanueva de la Serrezuela 28 G 12
37621 Aldeanueva de la Sierra 37 H 7
10440 Aldeanueva de la Vera 37 J 8
45575 Aldeanueva de San Bartolomé 47 K 9
10740 Aldeanueva del Camino 37 J 8
40462 Aldeanueva del Codonal 27 G 10
23215 Aldeaquemada 57 N 13
37110 Aldearrodrigo 26 G 8
37340 Aldearrubia 26 G 9
05212 Aldeaseca 27 G 10
37317 Aldeaseca de la Frontera 27 H 9
40235 Aldeasoña 28 G 11
37187 Aldeatejada 26 H 8
05193 Aldeavieja 38 H 11
40533 Aldehorno 28 F 12
10638 Aldehuela 36 J 7
42107 Aldehuela de Agreda 20 F 16

42193 Aldehuela de Calatañazor 29 F 14
37460 Aldehuela de la Bóveda 26 H 7
50374 Aldehuela de Liestos 30 G 16
42180 Aldehuela de Periáñez 20 F 15
37639 Aldehuela de Yeltes 36 H 7
40462 Aldehuela del Codonal 27 G 10
10671 Aldehuela del Jerte 36 J 7
19354 Aldehuela/Molina de Aragón 30 H 16
44158 Aldehuela/Montalbán 32 H 18
44192 Aldehuela/Teruel 42 J 17
18514 Aldeire 67 P 13
15108 Aldemunde 1 C 2
40380 Aldeonsancho 28 G 12
40531 Aldeonte 28 G 12
27611 Aldosende 14 D 4
43591 Aldover 33 H 21
33345 Alea 5 C 9
19237 Aleas 29 H 13
30859 Aledo 59 O 16
01240 Alegría-Dulantzi 8 D 14
42225 Alentisque 30 G 15
25736 Alentorn 23 F 22
22588 Aler 11 E 20
50679 Alera 9 E 17
22194 Alerre 22 E 19
26324 Alesanco 19 E 14
33111 Alesga 4 C 7
26315 Alesón 19 E 14
18170 Alfacar 66 P 12
46910 Alfafar 43 L 19
03838 Alfafara 52 M 18
50172 Alfajarín 21 F 18
44160 Alfambra 42 H 17
50461 Alfamén 21 G 17
22416 Alfántega 22 F 20
46148 Alfara de Algimia 43 K 19
43592 Alfara dels Ports 33 H 20
49177 Alfaraz 26 G 8
29194 Alfarnate 65 Q 11
29194 Alfarnatejo 65 Q 11
26540 Alfaro 20 E 16
46197 Alfarp 43 L 18
25120 Alfarràs 23 F 21
46893 Alfarrasí 61 M 19
25161 Alfés 23 F 21
50120 Alfocea 21 F 18
12609 Alfondeguilla 43 K 19
41150 Alfonso XIII 63 P 7
43365 Alforja 23 G 21
50783 Alforque 22 G 19
27639 Alfoz 3 D 5
24238 Algadefe 16 E 8
07210 Algaida 71 K 25
14439 Algallarín 56 N 11
41661 Algámitas 70 P 9
11639 Algar 69 Q 8
19332 Algar de Mesa 30 G 16
46593 Algar de Palancia 43 K 19
19116 Algarga 40 J 13
18280 Algarinejo 65 P 11
16338 Algarra 42 J 17
29750 Algarrobo 66 Q 11
29491 Algatocín 70 Q 9
11270 Algeciras 70 R 9
46680 Algemesí 61 L 19
25130 Algerri 23 F 21
28110 Algete 40 H 13
30157 Algezares 60 O 17
12414 Algimia de Almonacid 43 K 19

46230 Alginet 43 L 19
11680 Algodonales 70 Q 9
28310 Algodor 39 K 12
19268 Algora 29 H 14
03169 Algorfa 60 N 18
48990 Algorta 7 C 13
25125 Alguaire 23 F 21
30560 Alguazas 60 N 17
03668 Algueña 60 N 17
18518 Alguife 67 P 13
04567 Alhabia 67 Q 14
04400 Alhama de Almería 67 Q 14
50230 Alhama de Aragón 30 G 16
18120 Alhama de Granada 66 P 12
30840 Alhama de Murcia 60 O 17
13248 Alhambra 50 M 13
29130 Alhaurín de la Torre 65 Q 10
29120 Alhaurín el Grande 70 Q 10
18620 Alhendín 66 P 12
19132 Alhóndiga 40 H 14
10137 Alia 47 L 9
44150 Aliaga 32 H 18
16313 Aliaguilla 52 K 17
03200 Alicante-Alacant 61 N 18
04409 Alicún 67 Q 14
18539 Alicún de las Torres 67 O 13
18538 Alicún de Ortega 67 O 13
33782 Alienes 4 C 7
24761 Alija del Infantado 16 E 8
25574 Alins 11 D 22
22421 Alíns del Monte 22 E 20
43813 Alió 24 G 22
19129 Alique 41 H 14
10550 Aliseda 45 L 6
42132 Aliud 30 F 15
21110 Aljaraque 62 P 5
04629 Aljariz 68 P 16
02512 Aljube 59 M 16
06894 Aljucén 46 L 7
31797 Alkotz 8 C 16
25100 Almacelles 23 F 20
29718 Almáchar 65 Q 11
18829 Almaciles 59 O 15
13400 Almadén 47 M 10
41240 Almadén de la Plata 63 O 7
13480 Almadenejos 48 M 10
04150 Almadrava de Montelva 68 Q 15
19490 Almadrones 29 H 14
24374 Almagarinos 16 D 7
13270 Almagro 49 M 12
04650 Almajalejo 68 P 16
42180 Almajano 20 F 15
19390 Almallá 41 H 16
42258 Almaluez 30 G 15
31796 Almándoz 8 C 16
02640 Almansa 52 M 17
23470 Almansas 58 O 13
24170 Almanza 17 D 9
04815 Almanzora 68 P 15
42191 Almarail 30 F 15
10350 Almaraz 37 K 8
49180 Almaraz de Duero 26 G 8
29330 Almargen 70 P 9
42169 Almarza 20 F 15
26111 Almarza de Cameros 20 E 14
46132 Almàssera 43 K 19
12550 Almassora 44 K 19
25187 Almatret 23 G 20
29749 Almayate Bajo 65 Q 11

42200 Almazán 30 G 14
22148 Almazorre 22 E 20
42126 Almazul 30 F 15
12413 Almedíjar 43 K 19
13328 Almedina 58 M 14
14812 Almedinilla 66 P 11
18438 Almegíjar 66 Q 13
49210 Almeida 26 G 7
25126 Almenar 23 F 21
42130 Almenar de Soria 30 F 15
47419 Almenara de Adaja 27 G 10
37115 Almenara de Tormes 26 G 8
25331 Almenara/Agramunt 23 F 22
12590 Almenara/Vall d`Uxo 43 K 19
21730 Almendra 26 F 8
37176 Almendra 26 G 7
06171 Almendral 53 M 6
45631 Almendral de la Cañada 38 J 10
06200 Almendralejo 54 M 7
30893 Almendricos 68 P 16
16420 Almendros 40 K 14
41111 Almensilla 63 P 7
04070 Almería 67 Q 15
04711 Almerimar 67 Q 14
19225 Almiruete 29 G 13
44591 Almochuel 32 G 18
13580 Almodóvar del Campo 56 M 11
16215 Almodóvar del Pinar 51 K 16
14720 Almodóvar del Río 55 O 9
29150 Almogía 65 Q 10
19115 Almoguera 40 J 14
23392 Almohadilla 58 N 14
44369 Almohaja 42 H 17
10132 Almoharín 46 L 7
46723 Almoines 61 M 19
50133 Almonacid de la Cuba 31 G 18
50108 Almonacid de la Sierra 21 G 17
45420 Almonacid de Toledo 49 K 12
19118 Almonacid de Zorita 40 J 14
16431 Almonacid del Marquesado 40 K 14
21350 Almonaster la Real 62 O 6
18816 Almontaras 58 O 14
21730 Almonte 63 P 6
03160 Almoradí 60 N 18
11351 Almoraima 70 R 9
06614 Almorchón 55 M 9
45900 Almorox 39 J 11
43393 Almoster 23 G 22
22531 Almudafar 22 F 20
30410 Almudema 59 N 16
22270 Almudévar 22 E 18
22420 Almunia de San Juan 22 F 20
22255 Almuniente 22 F 19
33700 Almuña 3 B 6
18690 Almuñécar 66 Q 12
13760 Almuradiel 57 M 13
33843 Almurfe 4 C 7
46440 Almussafes 43 L 19
44134 Alobras 42 J 17
19125 Alocén 40 H 14
18350 Alomartes 66 P 12
10109 Alonso de Ojeda 46 L 8
48810 Alonsotegi 7 C 14
29500 Álora 70 Q 10
21520 Alosno 62 O 5
19208 Alovera 40 H 13

Alozaina   Ⓔ   **Arredondo**

Ⓔ

29567 Alozaina 70 Q 10
17538 Alp 12 E 23
29460 Alpandeire 70 Q 9
42213 Alpanseque 29 G 14
42218 Alparrache 30 F 15
50109 Alpartir 21 G 17
03788 Alpatro 61 M 19
28640 Alpedrete 39 H 11
19276 Alpedroches 29 G 14
44721 Alpeñés 31 H 17
08587 Alpens 12 E 24
02690 Alpera 52 M 17
25110 Alpicat 29 F 21
30152 Alporchones 68 O 16
46178 Alpuente 42 K 17
30580 Alquerias 60 N 17
22145 Alquézar 22 E 20
40510 Alquité 29 G 13
25632 Alsamora 11 E 21
04568 Alsodux 67 P 14
27230 Alta 2 C 4
03291 Altabix 60 N 18
09219 Altable 7 D 13
16780 Altarejos 41 K 15
03590 Altea 61 M 19
25289 Altés 12 E 22
22540 Altorricón 23 F 20
25567 Altron 11 E 22
31800 Altsasu-Alsasua
         8 D 15
12410 Altura 43 K 18
46389 Altury 43 L 18
50322 Aluenda 21 G 16
30351 Alumbres 73 O 18
19320 Alustante 42 H 16
27579 Alvidrón 2 D 4
46600 Alzira 61 L 19
31472 Alzórriz 9 D 17
32668 Allariz 14 E 4
44145 Allepuz 32 J 18
33578 Allés 5 C 10
31262 Allo 8 D 15
44509 Alloza 32 H 18
44492 Allueva 31 H 17
31715 Amaiur-Mala 9 C 17
31395 Amatriain 9 D 16
05560 Amavida 38 H 9
09136 Amaya 18 D 11
19332 Amayas 30 G 16
34485 Amayuelas de Ojeda
         6 D 11
33826 Ambás/Belmonte 4 C 7
33312 Ambás/Villaviciosa
         5 C 9
24150 Ambasaguas 5 D 9
24524 Ambasmestas 15 D 6
50546 Ambel 21 F 16
28580 Ambite 40 J 13
27865 Ambosores 2 B 4
15313 Ambroa 2 C 3
42230 Ambrona 30 G 14
15298 Ameixenda 1 D 1
17170 Amer 35 E 25
09219 Ameyugo 7 D 13
33558 Amieva 5 C 9
32520 Amiudal 14 E 3
36840 Amoedo 13 E 2
32170 Amoeiro 14 E 4
27579 Amoexa 2 D 4
48289 Amoroto 8 C 14
43870 Amposta 33 H 21
34191 Ampudia 17 F 10
39840 Ampuero 7 C 13
01470 Amurrio 7 C 13
34420 Amusco 18 E 11
47177 Amusquillo 28 F 11
44212 Anadón 31 H 18
40121 Anaya 28 H 11
37863 Anaya de Alba 37 H 9
33534 Anayo 5 C 9
19287 Anchuela del Campo
         30 G 15
19350 Anchuela del
         Pedregal/Molina
         de Aragón 30 H 16

19350 Anchuela del
         Pedregal/Tordellego
         42 H 16
13117 Anchuras 47 L 10
31281 Ancín 8 D 15
01439 Anda 7 D 14
42366 Andaluz 29 F 14
01439 Andatoia 7 D 14
49162 Andavias 26 F 8
33719 Andés 3 B 6
46170 Andilla 43 K 18
15684 Andoio 1 C 2
44500 Andorra 32 H 19
31261 Andosilla 20 E 16
07150 Andratx 71 K 24
33596 Andrín 5 C 10
23740 Andújar 57 N 11
50369 Anento 31 G 17
32825 Anfeoz 14 E 4
17160 Anglès 35 F 25
25320 Anglesola 23 F 21
25320 Anglesona 23 F 22
19245 Angon 29 G 14
26210 Anguciana 7 D 14
22123 Angüés 22 E 19
26322 Anguiano 19 E 14
19283 Anguita 30 G 15
09312 Anguix/Roa 28 F 12
19119 Anguix/Sacedón
         40 J 14
39727 Angustina 6 C 12
22162 Aniés 10 E 18
39571 Aniezo 5 C 10
50313 Aniñón 30 G 16
33719 Anleo 3 B 6
24488 Anllares del Sil 3 D 6
15110 Anllóns 1 C 2
27466 Anlo 14 E 4
46820 Anna 52 L 18
15149 Anós 1 C 2
31172 Anoz 8 D 16
19287 Anquela del Ducado
         30 H 15
27554 Ansar 14 D 4
25798 Anserall 12 E 22
22728 Ansó 9 D 18
04628 Antas 68 P 16
27570 Antas de Ulla 2 D 4
46266 Antella 52 L 18
29200 Antequera 65 P 10
15845 Antes 1 D 2
01220 Antezana 7 D 14
34248 Antigüedad 18 F 11
22133 Antillón 22 E 19
24281 Antoñan del Valle
         16 D 8
01128 Antoñana 8 D 15
15684 Anxeriz 1 C 2
25738 Anya 23 F 22
09215 Añastro 7 D 14
42108 Añavieja 20 F 16
40492 Añe 28 G 11
01477 Añes 7 C 13
50590 Añón 20 F 16
14450 Añora 56 N 10
31154 Añorbe 8 D 16
45250 Añover de Tajo
         39 K 12
37111 Añover de Tormes
         26 G 8
31430 Aoiz-Agoitz 9 D 17
25799 Aós/Andorra la Vella
         12 D 22
31481 Aós/Aoiz-Agoitz
         9 D 17
48291 Apatamonasterio
         8 C 14
22195 Apiés 22 E 19
01129 Apiñaniz 8 D 15
01439 Aprikano 7 D 14
50155 Aquilón 22 G 17
22625 Aquilué 10 E 19
22620 Ara 10 E 19
48498 Aracaldo 7 C 14
21200 Aracena 63 O 6

19344 Aragoncillo 30 H 15
40123 Aragoneses 28 G 11
19294 Aragosa 29 H 14
22720 Araguas del Solano
         9 D 18
22730 Aragüés del Puerto
         9 D 18
41600 Arahal 64 P 8
40173 Arahuetes 28 G 12
12119 Araia/Alcora 43 J 19
01250 Araia/Salvatierra
         8 D 15
24146 Aralla 4 D 8
25518 Aramunt 11 E 22
31271 Aranarache 8 D 15
33756 Arancedo 3 B 6
42180 Arancón 20 F 15
09400 Aranda de Duero
         28 F 12
50259 Aranda de Moncayo
         30 F 16
50266 Arándiga 21 F 17
09410 Arandilla 29 F 13
16812 Arandilla del Arroyo
         41 H 15
33128 Arango 4 C 7
28300 Aranjuez 39 J 12
31754 Arano 8 C 16
25762 Aranser 12 E 23
27714 Arante 3 C 5
31790 Arantza 8 C 16
20567 Arantzazu 8 D 15
12232 Arañuel 43 J 19
19141 Aranzueque 40 J 13
25573 Araós 11 D 22
20568 Araotz 8 D 15
37796 Arapiles 26 H 8
31239 Aras 20 D 15
46179 Aras de Alpuente
         42 K 17
22193 Arascués 22 E 19
09451 Arauzo de Miel
         19 F 13
09451 Arauzo de Salce
         19 F 13
09451 Arauzo de Torre
         19 F 13
19237 Arbancón 29 H 13
22121 Arbaniés 22 E 19
25140 Arbeca 23 F 21
19492 Arbeteta 41 H 15
31839 Arbizu 8 D 15
04660 Arboleas 68 P 15
33718 Arbón 3 C 6
17401 Arbúcies 35 F 25
42240 Arbujelo 30 G 15
23193 Arbuniel 66 O 12
36684 Arca 13 D 3
25799 Arcabell 12 E 22
24227 Arcabueja 16 D 9
36690 Arcade 13 E 2
33185 Arcallana 4 B 7
16123 Arcas 41 K 15
37429 Arcediano 26 G 8
15618 Arceo 2 C 3
30600 Archena 60 N 17
29300 Archidona/Antequera
         65 P 11
41899 Archidona/El
         Ronquillo 63 O 7
19411 Archilla 40 H 14
30195 Archivel 59 N 15
45182 Arcicóllar 39 J 11
09592 Arconada/Briviesca
         7 D 12
34449 Arconada/Villalcázar
         de Sigra 18 E 11
40164 Arcones 28 G 12
32500 Arcos (Santa María)
         14 E 3
42250 Arcos de Jalón 30 G 15
11630 Arcos de la Frontera
         69 Q 8
49699 Arcos de la
         Polvorosa 16 F 8

16141 Arcos de la Sierra
         41 J 15
44421 Arcos de las Salinas
         42 K 17
09195 Arcos/Burgos 18 E 12
15258 Arcos/Cée 1 D 1
27518 Arcos/Chantada
         14 D 4
22149 Arcusa 10 E 20
31697 Ardaitz 9 D 17
29550 Ardales 65 Q 10
36914 Ardán 13 E 2
15109 Ardaña 1 C 2
31421 Ardanaz 9 D 17
22474 Ardanúy 11 E 21
25287 Ardèvol 24 F 23
43850 Ardiaca 23 G 22
50614 Ardisa 21 E 18
33507 Ardisana 5 C 10
24232 Ardón 16 E 8
24251 Ardoncino 16 E 8
36313 Area 13 E 2
27578 Areás 2 D 4
48143 Areatza 7 C 14
31263 Arellano 8 D 15
22583 Arén 11 E 21
07740 Arenal d`en Castell
         72 J 28
18290 Arenales 66 P 12
13619 Arenales de San
         Gregorio 50 L 13
39450 Arenas de Iguña
         6 C 11
13679 Arenas de San Juan
         49 L 13
05400 Arenas de San Pedro
         38 J 9
18126 Arenas del Rey
         66 Q 12
33538 Arenas/Infiesta 5 C 9
29753 Arenas/Vélez-
         Málaga 66 Q 11
42368 Arenillas 29 G 14
09239 Arenillas de Muñó
         18 E 12
09107 Arenillas de
         Riopisuerga
         18 E 11
09133 Arenillas de Villadiego
         18 D 12
41640 Arenoso 64 P 9
44622 Arens de Lledó
         33 H 20
08350 Arenys de Mar 35 F 25
08358 Arenys de Munt
         35 F 25
26311 Arenzana de Abajo
         19 E 14
15624 Ares 2 C 3
12165 Ares del Maestre
         32 J 19
31876 Areso 8 C 16
01476 Arespalditza 7 C 13
01400 Areta 7 C 14
20550 Aretxabaleta 8 C 14
25575 Àreu 11 D 22
05153 Arevalillo 37 H 9
05200 Arévalo 27 G 10
42161 Arévalo de la Sierra
         20 F 15
14298 Argallón 55 N 9
15217 Argalo 1 D 2
13710 Argamasilla de Alba
         49 L 13
13440 Argamasilla de
         Calatrava 48 M 11
02328 Argamasón 51 M 15
28500 Arganda 40 J 13
49251 Arganín 26 G 7
24722 Argañoso 16 D 7
24546 Arganza/Ponferrada
         15 D 6
33875 Arganza/Tineo 3 C 7
22135 Argavieso 22 E 19
19196 Argecilla 29 H 14

17853 Argelaguer 35 E 25
12230 Argelita 43 J 19
08717 Argençola 24 F 22
44165 Argente 42 H 17
08310 Argentona 35 F 24
45122 Argés 39 K 11
01192 Argomaniz 8 D 14
27748 Argomoso 3 C 5
39197 Argoños 7 C 13
24989 Argovejo 5 D 9
27511 Argozón 14 D 4
31513 Arguedas 21 E 16
02484 Arguellite 58 N 15
33314 Argüero 5 B 9
39212 Argüeso 6 C 11
42169 Arguijo 20 F 14
22150 Arguís 10 E 19
16360 Arguisuelas 41 K 16
49716 Argujillo 26 G 8
31671 Aria 9 D 17
07529 Ariany 71 K 26
31671 Aribe 9 D 17
24132 Arienza 4 D 7
09570 Arija 6 D 12
15892 Aríns 1 D 2
44547 Ariño 32 G 18
25722 Aristot 12 E 23
31892 Aristregui 8 D 16
31448 Aristu 9 D 17
50220 Ariza 30 G 15
31292 Arizala 8 D 16
48970 Arizgoiti 7 C 14
31713 Arizkun 9 C 17
23760 Arjona 57 O 11
23750 Arjonilla 56 O 11
01192 Arkaute 7 D 14
09199 Arlanzón 19 E 13
33427 Arlós 4 C 8
01216 Arluzea 8 D 14
15689 Armada 2 C 3
19461 Armallones 41 H 15
31228 Armañanzas 20 D 15
37755 Armenteros 37 H 9
15144 Armentón 1 C 2
18100 Armilla 66 P 12
44742 Armillas 31 H 18
48620 Armintza 7 C 14
01220 Armiñón 7 D 14
24009 Armunia 16 D 8
40494 Armuña 28 G 11
04888 Armuña de Almanzora
         67 P 15
19135 Armuña de Tajuña
         40 H 13
26589 Arnedillo 20 E 15
26580 Arnedo/Calahorra
         20 E 15
09571 Arnedo/Reinosa
         6 D 12
43597 Arnes 33 H 20
03312 Arneva 60 N 18
32417 Arnoia 14 E 3
39195 Arnuezo 7 C 12
21240 Aroche 62 O 6
15121 Arou 1 C 1
49126 Arquillinos 26 F 8
29790 Arquillos/Campillos
         65 P 10
23230 Arquillos/Linares
         57 N 13
36970 Arra 13 E 2
36390 Arrabal/A Guardia
         13 E 2
44368 Arrabal/Cella 42 H 17
49696 Arrabalde 16 E 8
01120 Arraia-Maeztu 8 D 15
31174 Arraiza 8 D 16
31417 Arrako 9 D 18
16855 Arrancacepas 41 J 15
48498 Arrankudiaga 7 C 14
31866 Arrarats 8 C 16
48291 Arrazola 8 C 14
09572 Arreba 6 D 12
14191 Arrecife 56 O 10
39813 Arredondo 6 C 12

25551 Arres 11 D 21
22751 Arrés 9 D 18
25586 Arreu 11 D 22
29350 Arriate 70 Q 9
31891 Arribe 8 C 16
31438 Arrieta 9 D 17
48114 Arrieta-Libao 7 C 14
48480 Arrigorriaga 7 C 14
33540 Arriondas 5 C 9
22336 Arro 10 E 20
13193 Arroba de los
Montes 48 L 10
33314 Arroes 4 B 8
48370 Arronategi 7 C 14
31243 Arroniz 8 D 15
39419 Arroyal 6 D 11
47195 Arroyo 27 F 10
46140 Arroyo Cerezo
42 J 17
40215 Arroyo de Cuéllar
28 G 11
10900 Arroyo de la Luz
46 L 6
41889 Arroyo de la Plata
63 O 7
19238 Arroyo de las
Fraguas 29 G 13
09615 Arroyo de Salas
19 E 13
06850 Arroyo de San
Serván 54 M 7
23340 Arroyo del Ojanco
58 N 14
44123 Arroyofrío 42 J 17
10161 Arroyomolinos de la
Vera 37 J 8
21280 Arroyomolinos de
León 54 N 7
10161 Arroyomolinos de
Montánchez 46 L 7
28939 Arroyomolinos/
Móstoles 39 J 12
09549 Arroyuelo 7 D 13
31840 Arruazu 8 D 16
26509 Arrúbal 20 E 15
25799 Ars 12 E 22
25722 Arsèguel 12 E 23
11100 Arsenal de la
Carraca 69 R 7
07570 Artà 72 K 26
31422 Ártaiz 9 D 17
31481 Artajo 9 D 17
31140 Artajona 8 D 16
12257 Artana 43 K 19
31395 Artariáin 9 D 16
22390 Artasona 22 E 20
22283 Artasona del Llano
22 E 18
01428 Artatza/Subijana
7 D 14
01196 Artatza/Vitoria-
Gasteiz 7 D 14
48141 Artaun 7 C 14
31290 Artavia 8 D 15
31109 Artazu 8 D 16
02137 Arteaga de Arriba
59 M 15
25718 Artedó 12 E 23
33536 Artedosa 5 C 9
15108 Artes 1 C 2
08271 Artés 24 F 23
25150 Artesa de Lleida
23 F 21
25730 Artesa de Segre
23 F 22
31172 Arteta 8 D 16
31480 Artieda/Lumbier 9 D 17
50683 Artieda/Sos del Rei
Catolico 9 D 18
25599 Arties 11 D 21
20301 Artikutza 8 C 16
22620 Arto 10 E 19
01474 Artziniega 7 C 13
27612 Arxemil 2 D 5
32616 Arzádigos 14 F 5

15839 Arzón 1 D 2
15810 Arzúa 2 D 3
36638 As Covas 13 E 2
15613 As Neves/Ferrol 2 C 3
15332 As Neves/Ortigueira
2 B 4
36440 As Neves/Ponteareas
13 E 3
27677 As Nogais 3 D 5
15320 As Pontes de García
Rodriguez 2 C 4
22725 Ascara 9 D 18
09215 Ascarza 7 D 14
43791 Ascó 23 G 21
30535 Ascoy 60 N 17
31171 Asiáin 8 D 16
50619 Asín 21 E 17
22372 Asín de Broto 10 D 19
27516 Asma 14 D 4
22638 Aso de Sobremonte
10 D 19
39806 Asón 6 C 12
25151 Aspa 23 G 21
27157 Aspai 2 C 4
49124 Aspariegos 26 F 8
03680 Aspe 60 N 18
31454 Aspurz 9 D 17
50683 Asso Veral 9 D 18
20115 Astigarraga 8 C 16
31879 Astitz 8 D 16
17538 Astoll 12 E 23
24700 Astorga 16 E 7
31190 Astráin 8 D 16
39806 Astrana 7 C 12
34450 Astudillo 18 E 11
01426 Astulez 7 D 13
45642 Atalaya del Alberche
38 J 10
30878 Atalaya/Mazarrón
73 O 17
06329 Atalaya/Zafra 54 N 7
29688 Atalaya-Isdabe 70 R 9
30385 Atamaría 73 O 18
19153 Atanzón 40 H 14
09199 Atapuerca 19 E 12
47210 Ataquines 27 G 10
22700 Atarés 10 D 18
18230 Atarfe 66 P 12
42345 Atauta 29 F 13
50348 Atea 31 G 16
50200 Ateca 30 G 16
01423 Atiaga 7 D 13
19270 Atienza 29 G 14
11393 Atlanterra 69 R 8
04113 Atochares 68 Q 15
46891 Atzeneta d`Albaida
61 M 19
25537 Aubèrt 11 D 21
24796 Audanzas del Valle
16 E 8
01206 Audikana 8 D 15
04549 Aulago 67 P 14
48380 Aulesti 8 C 14
19130 Auñón 40 H 14
31640 Auritz-Burguete 9 D 17
31694 Aurizberri-Espinal
9 D 17
26513 Ausejo 20 E 15
42172 Ausejo de la Sierra
20 F 15
34191 Autilla del Pino 17 F 10
34338 Autillo de Campos
17 E 10
26560 Autol 20 E 15
31797 Auza 8 D 16
05357 Aveinte 27 H 10
10638 Avellanar 36 J 7
05580 Avellaneda 37 J 9
25714 Avellanet 12 E 22
09345 Avellanosa de Muñó
18 F 12
09131 Avellanosa del
Páramo 18 E 12
08610 Avià 12 E 23
05070 Ávila 38 H 10

30812 Avilés/Lorca 59 O 16
33400 Avilés/Oviedo 4 B 8
30592 Avileses 60 O 18
08279 Avinyó 24 F 23
17706 Avinyonet de
Puigventos
35 E 25
15552 Aviño 2 B 3
32520 Avión 14 E 3
21400 Ayamonte 62 P 5
31448 Ayechu 9 D 17
31240 Ayegui 8 D 15
22800 Ayerbe 21 E 18
31492 Ayesa 9 D 17
50152 Ayles 21 G 17
40520 Ayllón 29 G 13
02125 Ayna 59 M 15
12224 Ayódar 43 K 19
09145 Ayoluengo 6 D 12
33782 Ayones 4 C 7
49619 Ayóo de Vidriales
16 E 7
46620 Ayora 52 L 17
34473 Ayuela 17 D 10
09219 Ayuelas 7 D 13
12127 Azafranares 43 J 18
31560 Azagra 20 E 16
44560 Azaila 22 G 19
19492 Azañón 41 H 14
22421 Azanúy 22 F 20
31172 Azanza 8 D 16
22311 Azara 22 E 19
26289 Azarulla 19 E 13
42230 Azcamellas 30 G 15
01193 Azilu 8 D 15
22311 Azlor 22 E 19
41819 Aznalcázar 63 P 7
41870 Aznalcóllar 63 O 7
31439 Azparren 9 D 17
31891 Azpirotz 8 C 16
06920 Azuaga 54 N 8
50140 Azuara 31 G 18
12490 Azuébar 43 K 19
14447 Azuel 56 N 11
31228 Azuelo 8 D 15
19200 Azuqueca de
Henares 40 H 13
45571 Azután 38 K 9

B

27370 Baamonde 2 C 4
27417 Baamorto 14 D 4
24141 Babia 4 D 7
37330 Babilafuente 26 H 9
22462 Bacamorta 11 E 20
04889 Bacares 67 P 15
06070 Badajoz 53 M 6
08910 Badalona 24 G 24
39764 Bádames 7 C 13
26310 Badarán 19 E 14
44491 Badenas 31 G 17
07181 Badia de Palma
71 L 25
07609 Badia Gran 71 L 25
41570 Badolatosa 65 P 10
50491 Badules 31 G 17
22569 Baells 23 F 20
14850 Baena 65 O 11
23440 Baeza 57 O 13
08695 Bagà 12 E 23
44320 Báguena 31 G 17
25598 Baguergue 11 D 21
50685 Bagüés 9 D 18
47312 Bahabón 28 G 11
09350 Bahabón de Esgueva
18 F 12
30860 Bahía 73 O 17
29693 Bahía Dorada 70 R 9
34127 Bahíllo 17 E 10
19295 Baides 29 G 14
23710 Bailén 31 N 12
24740 Baíllo 15 E 7
09515 Baíllo 7 D 12
22760 Bailo 9 D 18
15127 Baíñas 1 C 1

15150 Baio 1 C 2
36300 Baiona 13 E 2
01118 Bajauri 8 D 14
31810 Bakaiku 8 D 15
48130 Bakio 7 C 14
25600 Balaguer 23 F 21
04713 Balanegra 67 Q 14
15110 Balarés 1 C 2
02320 Balazote 51 M 15
19281 Balbacil 30 G 15
05520 Balbarda 38 H 10
06195 Balboa/Badajoz 45 M 6
24525 Balboa/Pedrafita do
Cebreiro 15 D 6
36585 Balboa/Silleda 1 D 3
50366 Balconchán 31 G 17
19411 Balconete 40 H 14
32433 Balde 14 E 3
22571 Baldellou 23 F 21
25737 Baldomar 23 F 22
46178 Baldovar 42 K 17
32708 Baldrei 14 E 4
04712 Balerma 67 Q 14
40449 Balisa 28 G 11
48800 Balmaseda 7 C 13
33778 Balmonte 3 C 6
30630 Balneario de la
Fuensanta 59 O 16
22650 Balneario de Panticosa
10 D 19
36682 Baloira 1 D 2
03812 Balones 61 M 19
24433 Balouta 3 D 6
27817 Balsa 2 C 4
02214 Balsa de Ves 52 L 17
30332 Balsapintada 60 O 17
08660 Balsareny 24 F 23
30591 Balsicas 60 O 18
34240 Baltanás 18 F 11
15819 Baltar/Arzúa 2 D 3
27246 Baltar/Meira 3 C 5
32632 Baltar/Verin 14 F 4
22484 Ballabriga 11 E 21
12599 Ballestar 33 H 20
13428 Ballesteros 48 L 12
13432 Ballesteros de
Calatrava 48 M 12
22234 Ballobar 22 F 20
33158 Ballota 4 B 7
42212 Balluncar 30 G 14
15822 Bama 1 D 3
36618 Bamio 13 D 2
22713 Banaguás 10 D 18
22194 Banariés 22 E 19
22194 Banastás 22 E 19
22140 Bandalíes 22 E 19
32840 Bande 14 E 4
36570 Bandeira 2 D 3
15380 Bandoxa 2 C 3
33114 Bandujo 4 C 7
32813 Bangueses 14 E 3
42218 Baniel 30 F 15
03450 Banyeres de Mariola
52 M 18
43711 Banyeres del
Penedès 24 G 23
17820 Banyoles 35 E 25
07191 Bañalbufar 71 K 25
37271 Bañóbárez 25 H 6
44357 Bañón 31 H 17
01307 Baños de Ebro 19 D 14
31593 Baños de Fitero
20 E 16
46354 Baños de Fuente
Podrida 51 L 17
11580 Baños de Gigonza
69 Q 8
30420 Baños de Gilico
59 N 16
23711 Baños de la Encina
57 N 12
34878 Baños de la Peña
5 D 10
32701 Baños de Molgas
14 E 4

10750 Baños de Montemayor
37 J 8
26320 Baños de Río Tobía
19 E 14
26241 Baños de Rioja 19 D 14
19390 Baños de Tajo 41 H 16
02480 Baños de Tús 58 N 15
09450 Baños de Vadearados
19 F 12
18811 Baños de Zújar 67 O 14
19276 Bañuelos 29 G 14
09248 Bañuelos de Bureba
19 D 13
31272 Baquedano 8 D 15
34305 Baquerín de Campos
17 E 10
39575 Bárago 5 C 10
22714 Baraguas 10 D 19
42213 Barahona 29 G 14
31879 Baraibar 8 D 16
16410 Barajas de Melo
40 J 14
28042 Barajas/Madrid 39 J 12
05635 Barajas/Piedrahita
38 J 9
27680 Baralla 3 D 5
09569 Baranda 7 C 12
31395 Barásoain 8 D 16
32890 Barbadás 18 E 4
37440 Barbadillo 26 H 8
09615 Barbadillo de Herreros
19 E 13
09613 Barbadillo del Mercado
19 E 13
09614 Barbadillo del Pez
19 E 13
16196 Barbalimpia 41 K 15
22464 Barbaruéns 11 D 20
22300 Barbastro 22 E 20
11160 Barbate 69 R 8
19262 Barbatona 30 G 14
27113 Barbeitos 3 C 5
25262 Barbens 23 F 22
22637 Barbenuta 10 D 19
43422 Barberà de la Conca
23 G 22
08210 Barberà del Vallès
24 F 24
50297 Bárboles 21 F 17
40530 Barbolla 28 G 12
22255 Barbués 22 F 19
22132 Barbuñales 22 E 19
42210 Barca 29 G 14
22148 Barcabo 22 E 20
06160 Barcarrota 53 M 6
42318 Barcebal 29 F 13
42318 Barcebalejo 29 F 13
08070 Barcelona 24 G 24
09592 Bárcena de Bureba
7 D 12
34477 Bárcena de Campos
18 E 11
39249 Bárcena de Ebro
6 D 11
39420 Bárcena de Pié de
Concha 6 C 11
33874 Bárcena del Monasterio
3 C 6
39518 Bárcena Mayor 6 C 11
09566 Barcenas 7 C 12
39477 Barcenilla 6 C 12
09567 Barcenillas de
Cerezos 6 C 12
37217 Barceo 25 G 7
33787 Barcia/Luarca 3 B 6
36837 Barcia/Pontevedra
13 E 3
36878 Barciademera 13 E 3
47674 Barcial de la Loma
17 F 9
49760 Barcial del Barco
16 F 8
45525 Barcience 39 K 11
09212 Barcina del Barco
7 D 13

Barcones   (E)   Berzosa de los Hidalgos

42368 Barcones 29 G 14
16118 Barchín del Hoyo 51 K 15
50296 Bardallur 21 F 17
50694 Bárdena 21 E 17
45593 Bargas 39 K 11
31229 Bargota 20 D 15
31396 Bariáin 9 D 16
31523 Barillas 20 F 16
30648 Barinas 60 N 17
24239 Bariones de la Vega 16 E 8
15113 Barizo 1 C 2
24521 Barjas 15 D 6
22192 Barluenga 22 E 19
25593 Baro 11 E 22
01211 Barola 7 D 14
25692 Baronia de Sant Oísme 11 F 21
15979 Baroña 1 D 1
30179 Barqueros 60 O 17
10318 Barquilla de Pinares 37 J 9
12420 Barracas 43 J 18
44220 Barrachina 31 H 17
10696 Barrado 37 J 8
32430 Barral 14 E 3
30876 Barranco de Los Asensios 68 O 16
30412 Barranda 59 N 16
02639 Barrax 51 L 15
27124 Barreiros 3 D 5
33794 Barres 3 B 6
01423 Barrio 7 D 13
46390 Barrio Arroyo 52 K 17
39720 Barrio de Arriba 6 C 12
44132 Barrio de las Minas 42 J 17
09135 Barrio de San Felices 18 D 11
34810 Barrio de Santa Mária 6 D 11
39478 Barrio de Velo 6 C 12
44313 Barrio del Centro 42 H 16
44313 Barrio del Hospital 42 H 16
12591 Barrio Mar 44 K 19
09126 Barrio-Panizares 6 D 12
19490 Barriopedro 40 H 14
09199 Barrios de Colina 19 E 13
09124 Barrios de Villadiego 18 D 11
33595 Barro 5 C 10
05229 Barromán 27 G 10
33930 Barros/Langreo 4 C 8
39408 Barros/Los Corrales 6 C 11
37255 Barruecopardo 25 G 6
34820 Barruelo de Santullán 6 D 11
09124 Barruelo de Villadiego 18 D 11
47129 Barruelo/Tordesillas 27 F 9
09554 Barruelo/Villarcayo 7 D 12
25527 Barruera 11 D 21
46758 Barx 61 L 19
27391 Barxa de Lor 15 D 5
46667 Barxeta 61 L 19
33117 Bárzana 4 C 8
40180 Basardilla 28 G 11
17483 Bàscara 35 E 25
15685 Bascoi 2 C 3
09126 Basconcillos del Tozo 6 D 12
34406 Báscones de Ojeda 5 D 10
34813 Báscones de Valdivia 6 D 11
27146 Báscuas 2 C 5

16191 Bascuñana de San Pedro 41 J 15
01420 Basquiñuelas 7 D 14
25289 Bassella 11 E 22
22141 Bastarás 22 E 19
16420 Batán de San Pedro 40 K 14
43786 Batea 23 G 20
06659 Baterno 47 M 10
28979 Batres 39 J 12
18860 Baul 67 P 14
25549 Bausen 11 D 21
04479 Bayárcal 67 P 14
04888 Bayarque 67 P 15
33119 Bayo 4 C 7
42366 Bayubas de Abajo 29 F 14
42366 Bayubas de Arriba 29 F 14
18800 Baza 67 P 14
13739 Bazán 57 M 12
27258 Bazar/Castro de Rei 2 C 5
15847 Bazar/Santa Catalina de Armada 1 C 2
44492 Bea 31 G 17
32431 Beade/Ribadavia 14 E 3
36312 Beade/Vigo 13 E 2
16152 Beamud 41 J 16
15688 Beán 1 C 3
31179 Bearin 8 D 15
32520 Beariz 14 E 3
21630 Beas 62 P 6
18184 Beas de Granada 66 P 13
18516 Beas de Guadix 67 P 13
23280 Beas de Segura 58 N 14
27533 Beascós 14 D 4
15258 Beba 1 D 1
05610 Becedas 37 J 8
05153 Becedillas 38 H 9
44588 Beceite 33 H 20
27640 Becerreá 3 D 5
40510 Becerril 29 G 13
34310 Becerril de Campos 17 E 10
47670 Becilla de Valderaduey 17 E 9
04288 Bédar 68 P 16
48390 Bedia 7 C 14
23537 Bedmar 57 O 13
09568 Bedón 7 C 12
17867 Beget 35 E 24
23520 Begijar 57 O 12
27373 Begonte 2 C 4
08415 Begues 24 G 23
17255 Begur 35 F 26
15809 Beigondo 2 D 3
31753 Beintza-Labaien 8 C 16
31393 Beire 20 E 16
04458 Beires 67 P 14
32981 Beiro 14 E 4
37700 Béjar 37 J 8
12430 Bejís 43 K 18
12512 Bel 33 H 20
46620 Bel Horizonte 52 L 17
14280 Belalcázar 55 M 9
27612 Belante 2 D 5
31174 Belascoáin 8 D 16
09226 Belbimbre 18 E 11
50130 Belchite 21 G 18
27891 Belén/Cervo 2 B 5
10292 Belén/Trujillo 46 L 8
37789 Beleña 37 H 8
19237 Beleña de Sorbe 29 H 13
33557 Belén 5 C 9
33996 Belerda 5 C 9
36307 Belesar 13 E 2
46868 Bèlgida 61 M 19
25266 Belianes 23 F 22

22123 Belillas 22 E 19
16470 Belinchón 40 J 13
14240 Belmez 55 N 9
23568 Belmez de la Moraleda 57 O 13
50332 Belmonte de Calatayud 21 G 16
34306 Belmonte de Campos 17 F 10
44642 Belmonte de San José 32 H 19
28390 Belmonte de Tajo 40 J 13
33830 Belmonte/Grado 4 C 7
16640 Belmonte/Mota del Cuervo 50 K 14
16779 Belmontejo 41 K 15
09250 Belorado 19 E 13
42248 Beltejar 30 G 15
36939 Beluso 13 E 2
22533 Belver de Cinca 22 F 20
49830 Belver de los Montes 26 F 9
28862 Belvis 40 H 12
45660 Belvís de la Jara 38 K 10
10394 Belvís de Monroy 37 K 8
07469 Bella Tarida 72 M 22
25177 Bellaguarda 23 G 21
41014 Bellavista 63 P 8
25337 Bellclaire d`Urgell 23 F 21
22436 Bellestar 11 E 20
22196 Bellestar del Flúmen 22 E 19
25450 Bell-Lloc d` Urgell 23 F 21
25336 Bellmunt d`Urgell 23 F 21
33686 Bello/Cabañaquinta 4 C 8
44232 Bello/Calamocha 31 H 17
43421 Bellprat 24 F 22
25250 Bellpuig 23 F 22
43413 Belltall 23 F 22
46839 Bellús 61 M 19
43719 Bellvei del Penedès 24 G 23
25720 Bellver de Cerdanya 12 E 23
25142 Bellvís 23 F 21
24300 Bembibre/Ponferrada 16 D 7
15873 Bembibre/Santiago de Compostela 1 C 2
22580 Benabarre 11 E 20
41805 Benacazón 63 P 7
29493 Benadalid 70 Q 9
47880 Benafarces 27 F 9
12449 Benafer 43 K 18
12134 Benafigos 32 J 19
29738 Benagalbón 65 Q 11
46312 Benagéber 52 K 17
46180 Benaguasil 43 K 18
04410 Benahadux 67 Q 15
29679 Benahavís 70 Q 9
29790 Benajarafe 65 Q 11
29639 Benalmádena 70 Q 10
18510 Benalúa de Guadix 67 P 13
18564 Benalúa de las Villas 66 P 12
11190 Benalup 69 R 8
11679 Benamahoma 70 Q 9
29718 Benamargosa 65 Q 11
24233 Benamariel 16 E 8
18817 Benamaurel 67 O 14
14910 Benamejí 65 P 10
42230 Benamira 30 G 15
29719 Benamocarra 65 Q 11
25576 Benante 11 D 22

11612 Benaocaz 70 Q 9
29370 Benaoján 70 Q 9
29791 Benaque 65 Q 11
29490 Benarrabá 70 Q 9
12160 Benasal 32 J 19
03814 Benasau 61 M 19
22440 Benasque 11 D 21
23390 Benatae 58 N 14
25658 Benavent de al Conca 11 E 22
25132 Benavent de Segrià 23 F 21
22436 Benavente de Aragón 11 E 20
06519 Benavente/ Alburquerque 45 L 5
49600 Benavente/Zamoras 16 E 8
24280 Benavides de Orbigo 16 D 8
49123 Benegiles 26 F 8
03460 Beneixama 60 M 18
03390 Benejúzar 60 N 18
25555 Benès 11 E 21
03316 Benferri 60 N 18
33556 Benia de Onís 5 C 10
03788 Beniali 61 M 19
03778 Beniarbeig 61 M 20
46722 Beniarjó 61 M 19
03850 Beniarrés 61 M 19
46844 Beniatjar 61 M 19
12580 Benicarló 33 J 20
12560 Benicàssim 44 J 20
03794 Benichembla 61 M 19
46838 Benicolet 61 M 19
03500 Benidorm 61 M 19
30130 Beniel 60 N 17
46450 Benifaió 43 L 19
46511 Benifairó de les Valls 43 K 19
43512 Benifallet 33 H 21
03517 Benifato 61 M 19
46830 Benigánim 61 M 19
03178 Benijofar 60 N 18
03810 Benilloba 61 M 19
03827 Benillup 61 M 19
03516 Benimantell 61 M 19
03812 Benimassot 61 M 19
46291 Benimodo 52 L 18
46611 Benimuslem 61 L 19
04768 Beninar 67 Q 13
46469 Beniparrell 43 L 19
46181 Benisanó 43 K 18
03720 Benissa 61 M 20
43747 Benissanet 23 G 21
04276 Benitagla 68 P 15
04275 Benitorafe 68 P 15
05141 Benitos 38 H 10
04276 Benizalón 68 P 15
02438 Benizar y La Tercia 59 N 16
12181 Benlloch 33 J 20
25551 Benòs 11 D 21
10185 Benquerencia 46 L 7
06429 Benquerencia de la Serena 55 M 9
04569 Bentarique 67 Q 14
32890 Bentraces 14 E 4
22150 Bentué de Rasal 10 E 18
24389 Benuza 15 E 6
04647 Benzal 68 P 16
31483 Beortegui 9 D 17
39730 Beranga 6 C 12
48640 Berango 7 C 14
01211 Berantevilla 7 D 14
25510 Beranui o Brenni 11 E 21
22583 Beranúy 11 E 21
20492 Berastegi 8 C 16
42107 Beratón 30 F 16
31780 Bera-Vera de Bidasoa 8 C 16
22131 Berbegal 22 F 19

33346 Berbes 5 C 9
09569 Bercedo 7 C 13
26327 Berceo 19 E 14
47115 Bercero 27 F 9
47115 Berceruelo 27 F 9
18451 Bérchules 67 Q 13
40144 Bercial 28 H 11
05229 Bercial de Zapardiel 27 G 10
24252 Bercianos del Páramo 16 E 8
24325 Bercianos del Real Camino 17 E 9
40550 Bercimuel 28 G 12
50316 Berdejo 30 F 16
15151 Berdeogas 1 C 1
15884 Berdía 1 D 2
15128 Berdoias 1 C 1
33887 Berducedo 3 C 6
36850 Berducido 13 E 3
22770 Berdún 9 D 18
08600 Berga 12 E 23
01212 Bergantzu 7 D 14
22583 Berganúy 11 E 21
26588 Bergasa 20 E 15
26588 Bergasillas Bajera 20 E 15
44556 Berge 32 H 19
01423 Bergonda 7 D 13
22373 Bergua 10 D 19
31191 Beriáin 8 D 16
04760 Berja 67 Q 14
06930 Berlanga 54 N 8
42360 Berlanga de Duro 29 G 14
24438 Berlanga del Bierzo 15 D 6
09316 Berlangas de Roa 28 F 12
48370 Bermeo 7 C 14
36517 Bermés 14 D 3
03599 Bermia 61 M 19
33118 Bermiego 4 C 7
49510 Bermillo de Alba 26 F 7
49200 Bermillo de Sayago 26 G 7
15329 Bermui 2 C 4
48891 Bernales 7 C 13
40430 Bernardos 28 G 11
19133 Berninches 40 H 14
22711 Bernués 10 E 18
45693 Bérnuy 38 K 10
05211 Bernúy - Zapardiel 27 H 10
40190 Bernuy de Porreros 28 G 11
05195 Bernúy-Salinero 38 H 10
15687 Berreo 1 D 3
31195 Berrioplano 8 D 16
48240 Berriz 8 C 14
31790 Berrizaun 8 C 16
02329 Berro 59 M 15
21647 Berrocal 63 O 6
37609 Berrocal de Huebra 37 H 8
37795 Berrocal de Salvatierra 37 H 8
10392 Berrocalejo 37 K 9
05194 Berrocalejo de Aragona 38 H 10
31796 Berroeta 9 C 16
22373 Berroy 10 D 19
01194 Berroztegieta 7 D 14
47813 Berrueces 17 F 9
50373 Berrueco 31 H 17
15866 Bertamirans 1 D 2
31866 Beruete 8 C 16
10129 Berzocana 47 L 9
42351 Berzosa 29 F 13
09245 Berzosa de Bureba 7 D 13
34485 Berzosa de los Hidalgos 18 D 11

Berzosa de Lozoya　　　　　　E　　　　　　**Cabdella**

28194 Berzosa de Lozoya
　　　29 H 12
39250 Berzosilla　6 D 11
17850 Besalú　35 E 25
17162 Bescanó　35 F 25
25719 Bescaran　12 E 23
22133 Bespén　22 E 19
27379 Bestar　2 C 4
22362 Bestué　10 D 20
33815 Besullo　3 C 6
15300 Betanzos　2 C 3
31890 Betelu　8 C 16
46117 Bétera　43 K 19
22638 Betés　10 D 19
16870 Beteta　41 H 15
07579 Betlem　71 K 26
01510 Betolatza　7 D 14
22148 Betorz　22 E 20
25539 Betrén　11 D 21
12549 Betxí　43 K 19
17850 Beuda　35 E 25
31867 Beunza　8 D 16
09572 Bezana　6 D 12
26312 Bezares　19 E 14
44121 Bezas　42 J 17
18660 Béznar　66 Q 12
48890 Biañez　7 C 13
03410 Biar　60 M 18
46825 Bicorp　52 L 18
27569 Bidouredo　2 D 4
50619 Biel　9 E 18
22350 Bielsa　10 D 20
39550 Bielva　6 C 11
02380 Bienservida　58 M 14
13596 Bienvenida/Almadén
　　　56 M 10
06250 Bienvenida/Zafra
　　　54 N 7
22144 Bierge　22 E 19
22630 Biescas　10 D 19
01129 Bigara Goien　8 D 15
03380 Bigastro　60 N 18
31454 Bigüezal　9 D 17
50316 Bijuesca　30 F 16
41540 Bilbao　64 P 9
48070 Bilbao-Bilbo　7 C 14
48112 Billabaso　7 C 14
33818 Bimeda　3 C 6
33528 Bimenes　4 C 8
22510 Binaced　22 F 20
22500 Binefar　22 F 20
07143 Biniali　71 K 25
07101 Biniaraix　71 K 25
07711 Binibèquer　72 K 28
22773 Biniés　9 D 18
07711 Binissafúller　72 K 28
07350 Binissalem　71 K 25
25752 Biosca　24 F 22
50695 Biota　21 E 17
22470 Bisauri　11 E 21
25657 Biscarri　11 E 22
22807 Biscarrues　21 E 18
50561 Bisimbre　21 F 17
09554 Bisjueces　6 D 12
31695 Biskarreta-Gerendiain
　　　9 D 17
43510 Bítem　33 H 21
01130 Bitoriano　7 D 14
17723 Biure　35 E 25
31398 Biurrun　8 D 16
05540 Blacha　38 H 10
42193 Blacos　29 F 14
30540 Blanca　60 N 17
43411 Blancafort　23 G 22
02110 Blancares Nuevos
　　　51 L 15
44314 Blancas　31 H 17
17300 Blanes　35 F 25
05193 Blascoeles　38 H 11
05146 Blascomillán　27 H 9
05299 Blasconuño de
　　　Matacabras
　　　27 G 10
05290 Blascosancho　27 H 10
22133 Blecua　22 E 19

44790 Blesa　31 G 18
42128 Bliecos　30 F 15
42248 Blocona　30 G 15
37290 Boada　26 H 7
34305 Boada de Campos
　　　17 F 10
09314 Boada de Roa　28 F 12
17723 Boadella d`Empordà
　　　35 E 25
34349 Boadilla de Rioseco
　　　17 E 10
34468 Boadilla del Camino
　　　18 E 11
33720 Boal　3 C 6
15119 Boaño　1 C 1
47462 Bobadilla del Campo
　　　27 G 9
23669 Bobadilla/Alcaudete
　　　65 O 11
29540 Bobadilla/Antequera
　　　65 P 10
32514 Boborás　14 E 3
24911 Boca de Huérgano
　　　5 D 10
46880 Bocairent　52 M 18
40560 Boceguillas　28 G 12
47419 Bocigas　27 G 10
42329 Bocigas de Perales
　　　29 F 13
09553 Bocos　7 D 12
19276 Bochones　29 G 14
36598 Bodaño　2 D 3
46160 Bodega Vanacloig
　　　43 K 18
06394 Bodonal de la Sierra
　　　53 N 6
47151 Boecillo　27 F 10
34859 Boedo　5 D 10
15826 Boente　2 D 3
24312 Boeza　16 D 7
37291 Bogajo　25 H 6
02130 Bogarra　59 M 15
18562 Bogarre　66 P 13
27722 Bogo　3 C 5
06692 Bohonal　48 L 10
10320 Bohonal de Ibor　37 K 9
05690 Bohoyo　37 J 9
25528 Boí　11 D 21
33810 Boiro/A Fonsagrada
　　　3 D 6
15930 Boiro/Rianxo　13 D 2
24717 Boisan　16 E 7
25652 Boixols　11 E 22
12599 Bojar　33 H 20
13260 Bolaños de Calatrava
　　　49 M 12
47675 Bolaños de Campos
　　　17 E 9
46822 Bolbaite　52 L 18
25332 Boldú　23 F 22
22160 Bolea　22 E 18
48279 Bolibar/Markina-
　　　Xemein　8 C 14
01194 Bolibar/Vitoria-
　　　Gasteiz　7 D 14
30877 Bolnuevo　73 O 17
22340 Boltaña　10 E 20
03518 Bolulla　61 M 19
17539 Bolvir　12 E 23
16843 Bolvir　41 J 15
41110 Bollullos de la Mitación
　　　63 P 7
21710 Bollullos del Condado
　　　63 P 6
22486 Bonansa　11 E 21
11540 Bonanza　69 Q 7
24850 Boñar　5 D 9
43884 Bonastre　24 G 22
02691 Bonete　52 M 17
16311 Boniches　42 K 16
33426 Bonielles　4 C 8
16540 Bonilla　41 J 14
05514 Bonilla de la Sierra
　　　38 H 9
17164 Bonmatí　35 F 25

22487 Bono　11 D 21
33675 Boo　4 C 8
42193 Boos　29 F 14
50641 Boquiñeni　21 F 17
22860 Borau　10 D 18
42223 Borchicayada　30 G 15
50229 Bordalba　30 G 15
42367 Bordecorex　29 G 14
42216 Bordeje　30 G 14
17462 Bordils　35 E 25
25548 Bordius　11 D 21
44563 Bordón　32 H 19
25586 Borén　11 D 22
50540 Borja　21 F 16
42218 Borjabad　30 F 15
39699 Borleña　6 C 12
02249 Bormate　51 L 16
41930 Bormujos　63 P 7
15119 Borneiro　1 C 2
11640 Bornos　69 Q 8
42138 Borobia　30 F 16
45222 Borox　39 J 12
17770 Borrassà　35 E 25
36525 Borraxeiros　2 D 3
08619 Borredà　12 E 23
24443 Borrenes　15 E 6
33878 Borres　3 C 6
12190 Borriol　44 J 19
25550 Bòssost　11 D 21
43785 Bot　33 G 20
43772 Botarell　23 G 21
10185 Botija　46 L 7
50441 Botorrita　21 F 17
32520 Bouza　11 E 4
32110 Bouzas/Carballiño
　　　14 E 4
24414 Bouzas/Ponferrada
　　　15 E 6
27340 Bóveda　14 D 5
01427 Boveda　7 D 13
27233 Boveda (Santa Eulalia)
　　　2 D 4
09514 Bóveda de la Ribera
　　　7 D 13
37316 Bóveda del Río Almar
　　　27 H 9
25178 Bovera　23 G 21
09219 Bozoo　7 D 13
05357 Brabos　27 H 10
43812 Bràfim　24 G 22
47461 Brahojos de Medina
　　　27 G 9
27277 Brañas　2 C 4
15819 Brandeso　2 D 3
49513 Brandilanes　26 F 7
15859 Brandomil　1 C 2
15859 Brandoñas　1 C 2
33194 Brañes　4 C 8
34829 Brañosera　6 D 11
24360 Brañuelas　16 D 7
28737 Braojos　28 G 12
15818 Brates　2 C 3
27867 Bravos　2 B 4
09490 Brazacorta　29 F 13
13450 Brazatortas　56 M 11
39700 Brazomar　7 C 13
24716 Brazuelo　16 E 7
28596 Brea de Tajo　40 J 13
17400 Breda　35 F 25
27331 Brence　14 D 5
41320 Brenes　63 O 8
33775 Bres　3 C 5
32636 Bresmaus　14 E 4
49751 Bretó　16 F 8
49698 Bretocino　16 F 8
27286 Bretoña　3 C 5
25513 Bretui　11 E 22
42173 Bretún　20 E 15
36658 Briallos　13 D 2
42368 Brías　29 G 14
15669 Bribes　2 C 3
09572 Bricia　6 D 12
26324 Brieva de Cameros
　　　19 E 14
05194 Brieva/Ávila　38 H 10

40180 Brieva/Segovia
　　　28 G 11
19400 Brihuega　40 H 14
49629 Brime de Sog　16 E 7
26290 Briñas　7 D 14
37217 Brincones　26 G 7
26330 Briones　19 D 14
09610 Briongos　19 F 12
09240 Briviesca　19 D 13
09557 Brizuela　6 D 12
36526 Brocos　2 D 3
22370 Broto　10 D 19
10950 Brozas　45 K 6
17510 Brucs　12 E 24
32521 Brués　14 E 3
17533 Bruguera　12 E 24
09129 Brulles　18 D 12
28690 Brunete　39 J 12
17441 Brunyola　35 F 25
22665 Bubal　10 D 19
42132 Buberos　30 F 15
50239 Bubierca　30 G 16
18412 Bubión　66 Q 13
16851 Buciagas　41 J 15
19133 Budia　40 H 14
27779 Budián　2 B 5
16114 Buenache de Alarcón
　　　51 K 15
16192 Buenache de la Sierra
　　　41 J 16
37209 Buenamadre　26 H 7
28599 Buenamesón　40 J 13
29693 Buenas Noches　70 R 9
45673 Buenasbodas　47 K 10
45634 Buenaventura　38 J 10
34470 Buenavista de Valdavia
　　　17 D 10
37789 Buenavista/Alba de
　　　Tormes　26 H 8
03720 Buenavista/Moraira
　　　61 M 20
16512 Buendía　40 J 14
44394 Bueña　42 H 17
22375 Buerba　10 D 20
33990 Bueres　5 C 9
22375 Buesa　10 D 19
36930 Bueu　13 E 2
46891 Bufali　61 M 18
15866 Bugallido　1 D 2
46165 Bugarra　43 K 18
09293 Bugedo　7 D 13
07311 Búger　71 K 25
42162 Buitrago　20 F 15
28730 Buitrago de Lozoya
　　　28 H 12
14650 Bujalance　56 O 11
19247 Bujalaro　29 H 14
19266 Bujalcayado　29 G 14
50177 Bujaraloz　22 G 19
19263 Bujarrabal　30 G 14
05140 Bularros　38 H 10
50546 Bulbuente　21 F 16
30180 Bullas　59 N 16
09230 Buniel　18 E 12
07110 Bunyola　71 K 25
22196 Buñales　22 E 19
46360 Buñol　43 L 18
31540 Buñuel　21 F 17
01330 Buradon Gatzara
　　　7 D 14
44330 Burbáguena　31 G 17
24437 Burbia　3 D 6
22315 Burceat　22 E 20
09587 Burceña　7 C 13
27880 Burela　3 B 5
50547 Bureta　21 F 17
25595 Burg　11 D 22
49698 Burganes de Valverde
　　　16 F 8
27233 Burgo　2 D 4
05113 Burgohondo　38 J 10
40331 Burgomillodo　28 G 12
09070 Burgos　18 E 12
31412 Burgui　9 D 17
41220 Burguillos　63 O 8

45112 Burguillos de Toledo
　　　39 K 12
06370 Burguillos del Cerro
　　　53 N 6
27306 Buriz　2 C 4
46100 Burjassot　43 K 19
24994 Burón　5 C 9
15819 Burres　2 D 3
12530 Burriana　44 K 19
01138 Buruaga　7 D 14
45521 Burujón　39 K 11
15689 Buscás　1 C 3
33161 Busloñe　4 C 8
24521 Busmayor　15 D 5
33879 Busmeón　4 C 7
03111 Busot　61 N 19
18416 Busquístar　66 Q 13
39813 Bustablado　6 C 12
39292 Bustamante　6 C 11
33888 Bustantigo　3 C 6
19244 Bustares　29 G 13
39417 Bustarus　6 D 11
28720 Bustarviejo　28 H 12
15982 Bustelo　1 C 2
39417 Bustidoño　6 D 12
24172 Bustillo de Cea
　　　17 E 9
47608 Bustillo de Chaves
　　　17 E 9
34116 Bustillo de la Vega
　　　17 E 10
49831 Bustillo del Oro　26 F 9
24357 Bustillo del Páramo/
　　　Astorga　16 E 8
34129 Bustillo del Páramo/
　　　Corrión　17 E 10
09244 Busto de Bureba
　　　7 D 13
24793 Bustos　16 E 7
39593 Bustriguado　6 C 11
48350 Busturia　7 C 14
15873 Buxán　1 C 2
15151 Buxantes　1 D 1

C

07458 Ca`n Picafort　71 K 26
15996 Caamaño　13 D 1
44480 Caba Hero　43 J 18
15613 Cabalar　2 C 3
40182 Caballar　28 G 12
25748 Cabanabona　23 F 22
27868 Cabanas (San
　　　Pantaleón)　2 B 4
27868 Cabanas (Santa María)
　　　2 B 4
49709 Cabanas de Sayago
　　　26 G 8
17746 Cabanelles　35 E 25
17761 Cabanes/Figueres
　　　35 E 25
12180 Cabanes/Oropesa
　　　44 J 20
42225 Cabanillas　30 G 15
28721 Cabanillas de la Sierra
　　　28 H 12
19171 Cabanillas del Campo
　　　40 H 13
33686 Cabañaquinta　4 C 8
50638 Cabañas de Ebro
　　　21 F 17
40392 Cabañas de Polendos
　　　28 G 11
45312 Cabañas de Yepes
　　　40 K 12
10373 Cabañas del Castillo
　　　47 K 8
09198 Cabañas/Burgos
　　　19 E 13
15621 Cabañas/Pontedeume
　　　2 C 3
39584 Cabañes　5 C 10
09350 Cabañes de Esgueva
　　　18 F 12
43374 Cabassers　23 G 21
25515 Cabdella　11 E 21

Cabeza de Framontanos   (E)   **Candolías**

37174 Cabeza de Framontanos 25 G 7
06600 Cabeza del Buey 47 M 9
37214 Cabeza del Caballo 25 G 6
06293 Cabeza la Vaca 54 N 7
45890 Cabezamesada 40 K 13
13192 Cabezarados 48 M 11
13591 Cabezarrubias de Puerto 56 M 11
05217 Cabezas de Alambre 27 H 10
05514 Cabezas de Bonilla 38 H 9
05211 Cabezas del Pozo 27 G 10
05148 Cabezas del Villar 38 H 9
21580 Cabezas Rubias 62 O 5
30110 Cabezo de Torres 60 N 17
26135 Cabezón de Cameros 20 E 14
39500 Cabezón de la Sal 6 C 11
09612 Cabezón de la Sierra 19 F 13
39571 Cabezón de Liébana 5 C 10
33692 Cabezón/Pola de Lena 4 C 8
47260 Cabezón/Valladolid 27 F 10
40396 Cabezuela 28 G 12
10610 Cabezuela del Valle 37 J 8
09239 Cabia 18 E 12
28190 Cabida 29 G 13
05165 Cabizuela 27 H 10
25794 Cabó 11 E 22
30370 Cabo de Palos 73 O 18
24111 Caboalles de Arriba 4 D 7
50228 Cabolafuente 30 G 15
33792 Caborno 3 C 6
09191 Caborredonda 19 D 13
14940 Cabra 65 P 11
44409 Cabra de Mora 32 J 18
23550 Cabra de Santo Cristo 57 O 13
43811 Cabra del Camp 24 G 22
31227 Cabredo 8 D 15
27834 Cabreiros 2 C 4
42130 Cabrejas del Campo 30 F 15
42146 Cabrejas del Pinar 19 F 14
08349 Cabrera de Mar 35 F 24
37193 Cabrerizos 26 H 8
47832 Cabreros del Monte 17 F 9
24224 Cabreros del Río 16 E 8
26529 Cabretón 20 F 16
24142 Cabrillanes 4 D 7
37630 Cabrillas 37 H 7
08348 Cabrils 35 F 24
33829 Cabruñana 4 C 7
24540 Cacabelos 15 D 6
10070 Cáceres 46 L 7
33174 Caces 4 C 8
10881 Cachorrilla 36 K 6
01213 Caciedo Yuso 7 D 14
18129 Cacin 66 P 12
24517 Cadafresnas 15 D 6
09589 Cadagua 7 C 13
10865 Cadalso 36 J 6
28640 Cadalso de los Vidrios 39 J 11

17488 Cadaqués 35 E 26
33788 Cadavedo 4 B 7
32548 Cádavos 15 F 5
18440 Cádiar 67 Q 13
09549 Cadiñanos 7 D 13
11070 Cádiz 69 Q 7
31515 Cadreita 20 E 16
50420 Cadrete 21 F 18
07314 Caimari 71 K 25
24915 Caín 5 C 10
15105 Caión 1 C 2
22587 Cajigar 11 E 21
29792 Cajiz 65 Q 11
08276 Cal Riera 24 F 23
07769 Cala Blanca 72 K 27
07609 Cala Blava 71 L 25
07559 Cala Bona 72 K 26
07469 Cala Carbó 72 M 22
07713 Cala d`Alcaulfar 72 K 28
07811 Cala de Sant Vicenç 71 K 26
07660 Cala d'Or 71 L 26
07712 Cala en Porter 72 K 28
07659 Cala Figuera 71 L 26
07820 Cala Gració 72 M 22
07599 Cala Lliteres 72 K 26
07690 Cala Llombards 71 L 26
07849 Cala Llonga 72 M 23
07700 Cala Llonga/Mahón 72 K 28
07589 Cala Mesquida 72 K 26
07560 Cala Millor 72 K 26
07687 Cala Moreia 72 K 26
07760 Cala Morell 72 J 27
07687 Cala Morlanda 72 K 26
07688 Cala Murada 71 L 26
43860 Cala Nova 34 H 21
07639 Cala Pi 71 L 25
07590 Cala Ratjada 72 K 26
07689 Cala Romàntica 71 K 26
03509 Cala/Benidorm 61 M 19
21270 Cala/El Real de la Jara 63 O 7
30889 Calabardina 73 P 16
40356 Calabazas/Compaspero 28 G 11
47451 Calabazas/Olmedo 27 G 10
44610 Calaceite 33 G 20
22589 Caladrones 11 E 21
02880 Calaf 24 F 23
43860 Calafat 34 H 21
43820 Calafell 24 G 23
18730 Calahonda 66 Q 13
26500 Calahorra 20 E 16
34407 Calahorra de Boedo 18 D 11
45909 Calalberche 39 J 11
44200 Calamocha 31 H 17
06810 Calamonte 54 M 7
44570 Calanda 32 K 18
21300 Calañas 62 O 6
22514 Calasanz 11 E 20
30420 Calasparra 59 N 16
42193 Calatañazor 29 F 14
50300 Calatayud 30 G 16
50280 Calatorao 21 F 17
24170 Calaveras de Arriba 5 D 10
50268 Calcena 30 F 16
36650 Caldas de Reis 13 D 2
27210 Calde 2 D 4
22624 Caldearenas 10 E 19
15294 Caldebarcos 1 D 1
36460 Caldelas de Tui 13 E 2
08275 Calders 24 F 23
42112 Calderuela 20 F 15
17455 Caldes de Malavella 35 F 25
08140 Caldes de Montbui 24 F 24
24914 Caldevilla 5 C 10

33391 Caldones 4 C 8
33507 Caldueño 5 C 10
33995 Caleao 5 C 9
30810 Calebrina 59 O 16
08370 Calella 35 F 25
06292 Calera de León 54 N 7
45686 Calera y Chozas 38 K 10
09451 Caleruega 19 F 13
45589 Caleruela 38 K 9
07689 Cales de Mallorca 71 K 26
29751 Caleta de Vélez 66 Q 11
18290 Calicasas 66 P 12
12589 Cálig 33 J 20
50238 Calmarza 30 G 16
30876 Calnegre 73 O 17
15129 Calo 1 C 1
07872 Caló de St. Agustí 72 M 23
44126 Calomarde 42 J 16
08281 Calonge de Segarra 24 F 22
17251 Calonge/Palamós 35 F 26
07669 Calonge/Santanyi 71 L 26
03710 Calpe-Calp 61 M 20
42367 Caltojar 29 G 14
36770 Calvario 13 F 2
37181 Calvarrasa de Abajo 26 H 8
37191 Calvarrasa de Arriba 26 H 8
22485 Calvera 11 E 21
07184 Calvià 71 K 25
32849 Calvos 14 E 4
28600 Calypo 39 J 11
09244 Calzada de Bureba 7 D 13
13370 Calzada de Calatrava 57 M 12
37448 Calzada de Don Diego 26 H 8
34129 Calzada de los Molinos 17 E 10
37797 Calzada de Valdunciel 26 G 8
02249 Calzada de Vergara 51 L 16
24342 Calzada del Coto 17 E 9
10817 Calzadilla 36 J 6
34309 Calzadilla de la Cueza 17 E 10
06249 Calzadilla de los Barros 54 N 7
49331 Calzadilla de Tera 16 F 7
08506 Calldetenes 12 F 24
22255 Callén 22 F 19
33873 Calleras 4 C 7
46175 Calles 32 K 18
33411 Callezuela 4 B 8
36688 Callobre 13 D 3
03360 Callosa de Segura 60 N 18
03510 Callosa dU'En Sarrià 61 M 19
08262 Callús 24 F 23
39587 Camaleño 5 C 10
17465 Camallera 35 E 25
44167 Camañas 42 H 17
25613 Camarasa 23 F 21
45180 Camarena 39 J 11
44459 Camarena de la Sierra 42 J 17
45181 Camarenilla 39 J 11
44155 Camarillas 32 H 18
15123 Camariñas 1 C 1
28816 Camarma de Esteruelas 40 H 13
33554 Camarmeña 5 C 10

49332 Camarzana de Tera 16 F 7
41900 Camas 63 P 7
34849 Camasobres 6 C 11
36630 Cambados 13 D 2
15317 Cambás 2 C 4
32375 Cambela 15 E 5
32100 Cambeo 14 E 4
23120 Cambil 66 O 12
15112 Cambre/Malpica 1 C 2
15112 Cambre/Tarrlo 2 C 3
25283 Cambrils 12 E 22
43850 Cambrils de Mar 23 G 22
15121 Camelle 1 C 1
43894 Camerles 33 H 21
24883 Caminayo 5 D 10
39212 Camino 6 C 11
10620 Caminomorisco 36 J 7
44350 Caminreal 31 H 17
33312 Camoca 5 C 9
17834 Camós 35 E 25
07160 Camp de Mar 71 K 24
06460 Campanario 47 M 8
07310 Campanet 71 K 25
42290 Camparañón 30 F 14
47310 Campaspero 28 G 11
24221 Campazas 16 E 9
17530 Campdevànol 12 E 24
17534 Campelles 12 E 24
19223 Campillejo 29 G 13
16210 Campillo de Alto Buey 51 K 16
50214 Campillo de Aragón 30 G 16
09493 Campillo de Aranda 28 F 12
23130 Campillo de Arenas 66 O 12
37550 Campillo de Azaba 36 H 6
10329 Campillo de Deleitosa 47 K 8
19360 Campillo de Dueñas 30 H 16
02129 Campillo de la Virgen 51 M 16
02511 Campillo de las Doblas 51 M 16
06443 Campillo de Llerena 54 M 8
19223 Campillo de Ranas 29 G 13
23519 Campillo del Río 57 O 12
29320 Campillos 65 P 10
16311 Campillos-Paravientos 42 K 16
16316 Campillos-Sierra 42 J 16
09572 Campino 6 D 12
19275 Campisábalos 29 G 13
24699 Camplongo 4 D 8
17723 Campmany 35 E 25
22450 Campo 11 E 20
46352 Campo Arcis 52 L 17
15187 Campo da Feira 1 C 3
46178 Campo de Abajo 42 K 17
46178 Campo de Arriba 42 K 17
33990 Campo de Caso 5 C 9
13610 Campo de Criptana 49 L 13
39250 Campo de Ebro 6 D 12
03469 Campo de Mirra-El Camp de Mirra 60 M 18
40551 Campo de San Pedro 29 G 12
24225 Campo de Villavidel 16 E 8
15359 Campo do Hospital 2 B 4
36110 Campo Lameiro 13 D 2

30815 Campo López 68 O 16
10134 Campo Lugar 46 L 8
29649 Campo Mijas 70 Q 10
28510 Campo Real 40 J 13
02251 Campoalbillo 51 L 16
32626 Campobecerros 14 E 5
18815 Campocámara 58 O 14
21668 Campofrío 63 O 6
04110 Campohermoso 68 Q 15
09650 Campolara 19 E 13
15838 Campolongo 1 D 2
33620 Campomanes 4 C 8
24410 Camponaraya 15 D 6
47165 Camporredondo 27 G 10
34888 Camporredondo de Alba 5 D 10
22570 Camporrells 23 F 21
46330 Camporrobles 51 K 17
22395 Camporrotuno 10 E 20
30191 Campos del Río 60 N 17
33746 Campos y Salave 3 B 6
07630 Campos/Felanitx 71 L 26
44158 Campos/Montalbán 32 H 18
36596 Camposancos 2 D 3
43781 Camposines 23 G 21
18565 Campotéjar 66 P 12
43897 Camp-redó 33 H 21
17867 Camprodon 35 E 24
26311 Camprovín 19 E 14
45720 Camuñas 49 L 13
08589 Can Branques 12 E 24
07816 Can Fomet 72 M 22
07850 Can Jordi 72 L 23
43715 Can Llenas 24 G 22
07610 Can Pastilla 71 K 25
07714 Can Racó 72 L 22
07620 Can Ripoll 71 L 25
07839 Can Trontoll 72 M 22
27440 Canabal 14 E 4
02312 Canaleja 58 M 14
24170 Canalejas 5 D 10
47311 Canalejas de Peñafiel 28 F 11
16857 Canalejas del Arroyo 41 J 15
26326 Canales de la Sierra 19 E 13
19342 Canales de Molina 30 H 16
19432 Canales del Ducado 30 H 15
05212 Canales/Arévalo 27 G 10
24120 Canales/La Robla 16 D 8
12469 Canales/Segorbe 43 K 18
08718 Canaletes 24 G 23
46650 Canals 52 M 18
02490 Cancarix 59 N 16
27664 Cancelada/Becerreá 3 D 5
29688 Cancelada/Estepona 70 R 9
15107 Cances Grande 1 C 2
27832 Candamil 2 C 4
33314 Candanal 4 C 8
22889 Candanchú 10 D 18
24648 Candanedo de Fenar 4 D 8
33430 Candás 4 B 8
22591 Candasnos 22 F 20
32338 Candeda 15 E 6
37710 Candelario 37 J 8
05480 Candeleda 38 J 9
42134 Candilichera 30 F 15
24433 Candín 3 D 6
15286 Cando 1 D 2
39685 Candolías 6 C 12

89

E

I N D E X · O R T S R E G I S T E R · I N D I C E · Í N D I
P L A A T S N A M E N R E G I S T E R · R E J S T Ř Í K   M Í S

Canduela   E   **Casas de Ves**

34811 Canduela 6 D 11
27335 Canedo 14 D 5
25548 Caneján 11 D 21
25794 Canelles 12 E 22
23420 Canena 57 N 13
28743 Canencia 28 H 12
33787 Canero 4 B 7
08360 Canet de Mar 35 F 25
12350 Canet lo Roig 33 H 20
22880 Canfranc-Estación
         10 D 18
33550 Cangas de Onís 5 C 9
33800 Cangas del Narcea
         3 C 6
27892 Cangas/Burela 3 B 5
27437 Cangas/Monforte
         14 E 4
36940 Cangas/Vigo 13 E 2
09692 Canicosa de la Sierra
         19 F 13
18810 Caniles 67 P 14
29716 Canillas de Aceituno
         65 Q 11
29755 Canillas de Albaida
         66 Q 12
47185 Canillas de Esgueva
         18 F 11
26325 Canillas de Río Tuerto
         19 E 14
49128 Canizo 26 F 8
04450 Canjáyar 67 P 14
30838 Cánovas 60 O 17
19431 Canredondo 30 H 15
24838 Canseco 4 D 8
37716 Cantagallo 37 J 8
37400 Cantalapiedra 27 G 9
40320 Cantalejo 28 G 12
17708 Cantallops 35 E 25
22216 Cantalobos 22 F 19
37405 Cantalpino 27 G 9
42148 Cantalucía 29 F 14
37319 Cantaracillo 27 H 9
11179 Cantarranas 69 R 8
44140 Cantavieja 32 H 19
30393 Canteras 73 O 17
41320 Cantillana 64 O 8
40360 Cantimpalos 28 G 11
05211 Cantiveros 27 H 10
02214 Cantoblanco 52 L 17
32112 Cantoña 14 E 4
04850 Cantoria 68 P 15
08318 Canyamars 35 F 24
07589 Canyamel 72 K 26
17310 Canyelles/Lloret de Mar
         35 F 25
17480 Canyelles/Roses
         35 E 26
08811 Canyelles/Sant Pere
         de Ribes 24 G 23
17246 Canyet de Mar 35 F 25
03409 Cañada 60 M 18
23289 Cañada Catena
         58 N 14
44559 Cañada de Benatanduz
         32 H 18
13430 Cañada de Calatrava
         48 M 11
30414 Cañada de la Cruz
         59 N 15
41450 Cañada de la Jara
         55 O 8
23330 Cañada de la Madera
         58 N 14
14299 Cañada del Gamo
         55 N 9
16340 Cañada del Hoyo
         41 K 16
03657 Cañada del Trigo
         60 N 17
02326 Cañada Juncosa
         51 M 15
41439 Cañada Rosal 64 O 9
46178 Cañada Seca 42 K 18
44168 Cañada Vellida
         42 H 18

16720 Cañadajuncosa
         50 K 15
42220 Cañamaque 30 G 15
19276 Cañamares/Atienza
         29 G 14
16890 Cañamares/Priego
         41 J 15
13331 Cañamares/Villanueva
         de los Infantes
         50 M 14
10136 Cañamero 47 L 9
18418 Cáñar 66 Q 13
15175 Cañas 2 C 3
10820 Cañaveral 46 K 7
21388 Cañaveral de León
         54 N 6
16850 Cañaveras 41 J 15
16537 Cañaveruelas 41 J 14
39491 Cañeda 6 C 11
16300 Cañete 42 J 16
14660 Cañete de las Torres
         56 O 11
29340 Cañete la Real 70 Q 9
42315 Cañicera 29 G 13
49440 Cañizal 27 G 9
19197 Cañizar 40 H 13
09136 Cañizar de Amaya
         18 D 11
44707 Cañizar del Olivar
         32 H 18
16891 Cañizares 41 H 15
43364 Capafonts 23 G 22
31380 Caparroso 20 E 16
43776 Capçanes 23 G 21
07580 Capdepera 72 K 26
22212 Capdesaso 22 F 19
22480 Capella 11 E 20
08786 Capellades 24 F 23
12570 Capicorb 33 J 20
18413 Capileira 66 Q 13
06612 Capilla 47 M 9
34305 Capillas 17 E 10
08619 Capolat 12 E 23
30626 Caprés 60 N 17
28560 Carabaña 40 J 13
42126 Carabantes 30 F 16
40540 Carabias/Ayllón
         28 G 12
19266 Carabias/Sigüenza
         29 G 14
42311 Caracena 29 G 13
16540 Caracenilla 41 J 14
13191 Caracuel de Calatrava
         48 M 11
33114 Caranga 4 C 7
33557 Carangas 5 C 9
15121 Carantoña 1 C 1
19185 Caraquiz 29 H 13
39762 Carasa 7 C 13
18410 Carataunas 66 Q 13
30400 Caravaca de la Cruz
         59 N 16
09611 Carazo 19 F 13
24161 Carbajal de Rueda
         5 D 9
49160 Carbajales de Alba
         26 F 8
49347 Carbajales de la
         Encomienda
         15 E 7
10511 Carbajo 45 K 5
15115 Carballa 1 C 2
27370 Carballido/Guitiriz
         2 C 4
27110 Carballido/Lugo 3 C 5
27146 Carballido/Meira 2 C 5
27843 Carballido/Vilalba
         2 C 4
32500 Carballiño 14 E 3
33817 Carballo/Cangas del
         Narcea 3 C 7
32813 Carballo/Celanova
         14 E 4
27228 Carballo/Friol 2 C 4
15100 Carballo/Malpica 1 C 2

33936 Carbayín 4 C 8
49211 Carbellino 26 G 7
36582 Carbia 2 D 3
36511 Carboentes 14 D 4
42190 Carbonera de Frentes
         30 F 14
24608 Carbonera/La Pola
         de Gordón 4 D 8
34117 Carbonera/Saldaña
         17 D 10
04140 Carboneras 68 Q 16
16350 Carboneras de
         Guadazaón
         42 K 16
40491 Carbonero de Ahusín
         28 G 11
40270 Carbonero el Mayor
         28 G 11
23211 Carboneros 57 N 12
33707 Carboniella 3 C 6
10670 Carcaboso 36 J 7
14810 Carcabuey 65 P 11
46740 Carcaixnet 61 L 19
31579 Cárcar 20 E 16
31310 Carcastillo 9 E 17
33784 Carcedo 4 C 7
09193 Carcedo de Burgos
         18 E 12
02153 Carcelén 52 L 17
46294 Cárcer 52 L 18
23192 Carchelejo 66 O 12
15688 Cardama 1 D 3
34888 Cardaño de Arriba
         5 D 10
08440 Cardedeu 35 F 24
42138 Cardejón 30 F 15
14445 Cardeña 56 N 11
04009 Cárdenas/Almería
         67 Q 15
26311 Cárdenas/Najera
         19 E 14
16373 Cardenete 42 K 16
09194 Cardeñadijo 18 E 12
34309 Cardeñosa de
         Volpejera 17 E 10
05320 Cardeñosa/Ávila
         38 H 10
19269 Cardeñosa/Sigüenza
         29 G 14
25526 Cardet 11 E 21
45642 Cardiel de los Montes
         38 J 10
33449 Cardo 4 B 8
08261 Cardona 24 F 23
25594 Caregue 11 E 22
50212 Carenas 30 G 16
33314 Careñes 5 B 9
50400 Cariñena 21 G 17
15360 Cariño 2 B 4
24429 Cariseda 3 D 6
46240 Carlet 43 L 18
45531 Carmena 39 K 11
24838 Cármenes 4 D 8
25712 Carmenin 12 E 22
39558 Carmona/Cabezón
         de la Sal 6 C 11
41410 Carmona/Sevilla 64 P 8
06488 Carmonita 46 L 7
15121 Carnés 1 C 1
15169 Carnoedo 2 C 3
15293 Carnota 1 D 1
36856 Caroi 13 E 3
47470 Carpio 27 G 9
37497 Carpio de Azaba
         36 H 6
36659 Carracedo en
         Pontevedra 13 D 2
32547 Carracedo da Serra
         15 E 5
15175 Carral 1 C 3
18814 Carramaiza 67 O 14
33329 Carrandi 5 C 9
45216 Carranque 39 J 12
33590 Carranzo 5 C 10
40181 Carrascal 28 G 12

37451 Carrascal del Obispo
         26 H 8
40331 Carrascal del Río
         28 G 12
10331 Carrascalejo 47 K 9
16879 Carrascosa 41 H 15
42311 Carrascosa de Abajo
         29 G 13
42344 Carrascosa de Arriba
         29 G 13
16649 Carrascosa de Haro
         50 K 14
19247 Carrascosa de Henares
         29 H 13
42180 Carrascosa de la
         Sierra 20 F 15
19431 Carrascosa de Tajo
         41 H 15
16555 Carrascosa del Campo
         40 J 14
16500 Carrascosilla 41 J 14
29551 Carratraca 70 Q 10
15630 Carreira/Pontedeume
         2 C 3
15855 Carreira/Zas 1 C 2
33555 Carreña 5 C 10
09248 Carrias 19 E 13
39150 Carriazo 6 C 12
45532 Carriches 38 K 11
33492 Carrie 4 B 8
36610 Carril 13 D 2
15165 Carrio 2 C 3
13150 Carrión de Calatrava
         49 L 12
41820 Carrión de los
         Céspedes 63 P 7
34120 Carrión de los Condes
         17 E 10
24270 Carrizo de la Ribera
         16 D 8
13329 Carrizosa 50 M 14
24123 Carrocera 16 D 8
30200 Cartagena 73 O 18
29452 Cartajima 70 Q 9
29570 Cártama 65 Q 10
29250 Cartaojal 65 P 10
33719 Cartavio 3 B 6
21450 Cartaya 62 P 5
39311 Cartes 6 C 11
24442 Carucedo 15 E 6
29631 Carvajal 70 Q 10
07181 Cas Català 71 K 25
07208 Cas Concos 71 L 26
30335 Casa Blanca 59 N 15
02070 Casa Caballos 51 L 15
02070 Casa Capitán 51 L 15
13200 Casa de Calero
         49 M 13
11520 Casa de la Ballena
         69 Q 7
02070 Casa de la Cortesa
         51 M 16
03400 Casa de la Mina
         60 M 18
11140 Casa de Postas 69 R 7
19184 Casa de Uceda
         29 H 13
13427 Casa del Manojar
         48 L 11
39718 Casa del Monte 6 C 12
02070 Casa Grande 51 L 16
02110 Casa Matado 51 L 15
13432 Casa Santos 49 M 12
02612 Casa Vieja 50 L 14
29160 Casabermeja 65 Q 11
30559 Casablanca/Cieza
         60 N 17
41640 Casablanca/Osuna
         64 P 9
11400 Casablanca/Trebujena
         69 Q 7
37767 Casafranca 37 H 8
32337 Casaio (Santa María)
         15 E 6
26230 Casalarreina 19 D 14

45109 Casalgordo 48 K 12
32748 Casalta 14 E 4
10190 Casar de Cáceres
         46 K 7
10640 Casar de Palomero
         36 J 7
42148 Casarejos 19 F 13
10628 Casares de Las
         Hurdes 36 J 7
29690 Casares/Estepona
         70 R 9
15569 Casares/Ortigueira
         2 B 4
41580 Casariche 65 P 10
45950 Casarrubios del Monte
         39 J 11
28978 Casarrubuelos
         39 J 12
46147 Casas Altas 42 J 17
46146 Casas Bajas 42 J 17
13248 Casas Blancas
         50 M 14
16707 Casas de Benitez
         51 L 15
44114 Casas de Bucar
         42 J 16
30520 Casas de Cucharón
         60 N 17
10162 Casas de Don Antonio
         46 L 7
10818 Casas de Don Gómez
         36 J 6
18830 Casas de Don Juan
         58 O 15
06770 Casas de Don Pedro
         47 L 9
02690 Casas de Don Pedro
         52 L 17
50614 Casas de Esper
         21 E 18
46352 Casas de Eufemia
         52 L 17
16610 Casas de Fernando
         Alonso 50 L 15
16338 Casas de Garcimolina
         42 K 17
16708 Casas de Guijarro
         51 L 15
16611 Casas de Haro 50 L 15
02153 Casas de Juan Gil
         52 L 17
02151 Casas de Juan Núñez
         51 L 16
46620 Casas de la Undo
         52 L 17
44559 Casas de las Palomitas
         32 H 19
02329 Casas de Lázaro
         50 M 15
16612 Casas de los Pinos
         50 L 15
10592 Casas de Millán 36 K 7
10360 Casas de Miravete
         46 K 8
46310 Casas de Moya
         51 L 17
46354 Casas de Penen de
         Albosa 52 L 17
02600 Casas de Peña
         50 L 15
06445 Casas de Pila 54 N 8
11380 Casas de Porro 69 R 8
46310 Casas de Prada
         52 L 17
06960 Casas de Reina o
         Las Casas 54 N 8
16612 Casas de Roldán
         50 L 15
19246 Casas de San Galindo
         29 H 14
46199 Casas de Sotos
         52 L 17
30398 Casas de Tallante
         73 O 17
02212 Casas de Ves 52 L 17

Casas del Castañar   (E)   **Cebrones del Río**   E

10616 Casas del Castañar 37 J 8
02211 Casas del Cerro 51 L 17
10730 Casas del Monte 37 J 8
16238 Casas del Olmo 51 L 16
30529 Casas del Puerto 60 N 17
46356 Casas del Río 52 L 17
02200 Casas Ibáñez 51 L 17
16430 Casas Luján 40 K 14
16318 Casas Nuevas/Hoyal del Peral 42 J 17
30176 Casas Nuevas/Pliego 59 O 16
03190 Casas Rebate 60 O 18
02070 Casas Viejas 51 M 16
19129 Casasana 41 H 14
45124 Casasbuenas 39 K 11
49151 Casaseca de las Chanas 26 G 8
16239 Casasimarro 51 L 15
32679 Casasoá 14 E 4
47110 Casasola de Arión 27 F 9
05140 Casasola/Ávila 38 H 10
02124 Casasola/Ayna 59 M 15
24917 Casasuertes 5 C 10
10520 Casatejada 37 K 8
05450 Casavieja 38 J 10
22142 Casbas de Huesca 22 E 19
09280 Cascajares de Bureba 7 D 13
09640 Cascajares de la Sierra 19 E 13
42294 Cascajosa 29 F 14
31520 Cascante 20 E 16
44191 Cascante del Río 42 J 17
22395 Cascojuela de Sobrarbe 10 E 20
31490 Cáseda 9 D 17
32435 Caseiro 13 E 3
43787 Caseres 33 G 20
46810 Caserío Benali 52 L 18
02640 Caserío de Campillo 52 M 17
13248 Caserío del Allozo 50 M 14
16143 Caserío Embid 41 J 15
22589 Caserras del Castillo 11 E 21
03649 Cases del Senyor 60 N 18
50620 Casetas 21 F 17
02327 Casica del Madroño 51 M 15
42367 Casillas de Berlanga 29 G 14
10818 Casillas de Coria 36 K 6
37541 Casillas de Flores 36 J 6
02694 Casillas de Marín de Abajo 52 M 17
02694 Casillas de Marín de Arriba 52 M 17
16321 Casillas de Renera 42 K 17
05428 Casillas/Piedralaves 38 J 10
19276 Casillas/Sigüenza 29 G 14
46171 Casinos 43 K 18
40590 Casla 28 G 12
33681 Casomera 4 C 8
50700 Caspe 32 G 19
19412 Caspueñas 40 H 14
17244 Cassà de la Selva 35 F 25
08693 Casserres 12 E 23

25714 Cassovall 11 E 22
04760 Castala 67 Q 14
03420 Castalla 60 M 18
22474 Castanesa 11 E 21
10340 Castañar de Ibor 47 K 9
09199 Castañares 18 E 12
26240 Castañares de Rioja 19 D 14
33813 Castañedo 3 C 6
21290 Castaño del Robledo 63 O 6
18439 Cástaras 66 Q 13
22486 Castarné 11 E 21
50346 Castejón de Alarba 31 G 16
22121 Castejón de Arbaniés 22 E 19
50211 Castejón de las Armas 30 G 16
22222 Castejón de Monegros 22 F 19
22394 Castejón de Sobrarbe 10 E 20
22466 Castejón de Sos 11 D 20
44231 Castejón de Tornos 31 H 17
50612 Castejón de Valdejasa 21 F 18
42130 Castejón del Campo 30 F 15
22310 Castejón del Puente 22 F 20
31590 Castejón/Alfaro 20 E 16
16856 Castejón/Priego 41 J 14
44706 Castel de Cabra 31 H 18
25712 Castelbò 12 E 22
22215 Castelflorite 22 F 19
44592 Castelnou 32 G 19
15175 Castelo/Cambre 1 C 3
27559 Castelo/Taboada 14 D 4
44630 Castelseras 32 H 19
17249 Castell d`Aro 35 F 26
12319 Castell de Cabres 32 H 20
03793 Castell de Castells 61 M 19
18740 Castell de Ferro 66 Q 13
17211 Castella de Palafrugell 35 F 26
08671 Castelladral 24 F 23
15316 Castellana 2 C 3
24343 Castellanos 17 E 9
09227 Castellanos de Castro 18 E 11
37439 Castellanos de Moriscos 26 G 8
37797 Castellanos de Villiquera 26 G 8
05229 Castellanos de Zapardiel 27 G 10
25795 Castellar 12 E 22
11350 Castellar de la Frontera 70 R 9
19328 Castellar de la Muela 30 H 16
25289 Castellar de la Ribera 12 E 22
08696 Castellar de n`Hug 12 E 24
13750 Castellar de Santiago 57 M 13
23260 Castellar de Santisteban 58 N 13
08619 Castellar del Riu 12 E 23
08211 Castellar del Vallès 24 F 24

08755 Castellbisbal 24 G 23
25154 Castelldans 23 G 21
08860 Castelldefels 24 G 23
08729 Castellet 24 G 23
17856 Castellfollit de la Roca 35 E 25
08255 Castellfollit del Boix 24 F 23
08281 Castellfollit del Riubregós 24 F 22
12159 Castellfort 32 J 19
08297 Castellgali 24 F 23
25632 Castellnou de Montsec 11 E 21
25265 Castellnou de Seana 23 F 21
12413 Castellnovo 43 K 19
17486 Castelló d`Empúries 35 E 26
25136 Castelló de Farfanya 23 F 21
12070 Castelló de la Plana 44 K 19
46841 Castelló de Rugat 61 M 19
25526 Castelló de Tor 11 E 21
08719 Castellolí 24 F 23
44560 Castellote 32 H 19
25334 Castellserá 23 F 21
08183 Castellterçol 24 F 24
08619 Castelltort 12 E 23
43392 Castellvell del Camp 23 G 22
46141 Castielfabib 42 J 17
22710 Castiello de Jaca 10 D 18
22587 Castigaleu 11 E 21
14815 Castil de Campos 65 P 11
09248 Castil de Carrias 19 E 13
09592 Castil de Lences 7 D 12
09258 Castil de Peones 19 E 13
42128 Castil de Tierra 30 F 15
34306 Castil de Vela 17 F 10
06680 Castilblanco 47 L 9
19246 Castilblanco de Henares 29 H 14
41230 Castilblanco de los Arroyos 63 O 8
09259 Castildelgado 19 E 13
24206 Castilfale 17 E 9
19127 Castilforte 41 H 15
42180 Castilfrío de la Sierra 20 F 15
50696 Castiliscar 9 E 17
19413 Castilmimbre 40 H 14
19391 Castilnuevo 30 H 16
42113 Castilruiz 20 F 15
40518 Castiltierra 29 G 12
22313 Castillazuelo 22 E 20
18818 Castillejar 58 O 14
28311 Castillejo 39 K 12
16250 Castillejo de Iniesta 51 K 16
37592 Castillejo de Martín Viejo 36 H 6
40593 Castillejo de Mesleón 28 G 12
42328 Castillejo de Robledo 29 F 13
16541 Castillejo del Romeral 41 J 15
16141 Castillejo-Sierro 41 J 15
45641 Castillo de Bayuela 38 J 10
11350 Castillo de Castellar 70 R 9

45910 Castillo de Escalona 39 J 11
16623 Castillo de Garcimuñoz 50 K 15
23670 Castillo de Locubín 66 O 12
18329 Castillo de Tajarda 66 P 12
28598 Castillo de Tajo 40 J 13
12123 Castillo de Villamalefa 43 J 19
45215 Castillo del Olmo 39 J 12
16854 Castillo-Albarañez 41 J 15
27438 Castillón 14 D 4
22572 Castillonroy 23 F 21
31454 Castillo-Nuevo 9 D 17
39699 Castillo-Pedroso 6 C 12
32558 Castineira 15 E 5
44192 Castralvo 42 J 17
37494 Castraz 36 H 7
34492 Castrecias 6 D 11
47512 Castrejón 27 G 9
34850 Castrejón de la Peña 5 D 10
15128 Castrelo 1 C 1
21730 Castrelo de Abajo 15 F 5
32625 Castrelo do Val 14 F 5
21730 Castrelos 15 F 6
18816 Castril 58 O 14
34246 Castrillo de Don Juan 18 F 11
47318 Castrillo de Duero 28 F 11
49419 Castrillo de la Guareña 27 G 9
09691 Castrillo de la Reina 19 F 13
24721 Castrillo de la Valduerna 16 E 7
09391 Castrillo de la Vega 28 F 12
09109 Castrillo de Murcia 18 E 11
34219 Castrillo de Onielo 18 F 11
24163 Castrillo de Porma 17 D 9
09108 Castrillo de Riopisuerga 18 D 11
09141 Castrillo de Rucios 18 D 12
40317 Castrillo de Sepúlveda 28 G 12
39250 Castrillo de Valdelomar 6 D 11
24327 Castrillo de Valderaduey 17 D 10
34478 Castrillo de Villavega 18 E 11
39418 Castrillo del Haya 6 D 11
09193 Castrillo del Val 18 E 12
47329 Castrillo Tejeriego 28 F 11
09107 Castrillo-Matajudíos 18 E 11
33727 Castrillón 3 C 6
15848 Castriz 1 C 2
32760 Castro Caldelas 14 E 5
27576 Castro de Amarante 2 D 4
04212 Castro de Filabres 67 P 15
40315 Castro de Fuentidueña 28 G 12
27776 Castro de Ouro 3 B 5
27250 Castro de Rei/Meira 2 C 5

27611 Castro de Rei/Vilamaior 14 D 4
14840 Castro del Río 56 O 11
27527 Castro/Chantada 14 D 4
27269 Castro/Lugo 2 C 5
42315 Castro/Retortillo de Soria 29 G 13
15147 Castro/San Roque 1 C 2
09514 Castrobarto 7 C 13
47689 Castrobol 17 E 9
24760 Castrocalbón 16 E 8
24735 Castrocontrigo 16 E 7
47192 Castrodeza 27 F 10
49660 Castrogonzalo 16 F 8
09110 Castrojeriz 18 E 11
40315 Castrojimeno 28 G 12
27845 Castromaior 2 C 4
47882 Castromembibre 27 F 9
34305 Castromocho 17 E 10
47641 Castromonte 17 F 9
24171 Castromudarra 17 D 9
49127 Castronuevo 26 F 8
47171 Castronuevo de Esgueva 27 F 10
47520 Castronuño 27 G 9
24569 Castropetre 15 D 6
24314 Castropodame 15 D 7
33760 Castropol 3 B 5
47664 Castroponce 17 E 9
40318 Castroserna de Abajo 28 G 12
40315 Castroserracín 28 G 12
24323 Castrotierra 17 E 9
24765 Castrotierra de la Valduerna 16 E 8
39700 Castro-Urdiales 7 C 13
33747 Castrovaselle 3 C 6
27120 Castroverde 3 C 5
49110 Castroverde de Campos 17 F 9
47182 Castroverde de Cerrato 18 F 11
09613 Castrovido 19 E 13
26315 Castroviejo 19 E 14
06420 Castuera 47 M 8
46196 Catadau 43 L 18
46470 Catarroja 43 L 19
12513 Catí 32 J 20
36612 Catoira 13 D 2
03158 Catral 60 N 18
44396 Caudé 42 J 17
46315 Caudete de las Fuentes 52 K 17
12440 Caudiel 43 K 18
18564 Cauro 66 P 12
25722 Cava 12 E 23
32749 Caxide 14 E 4
33586 Cayarga 5 C 9
33428 Cayés 4 C 8
09239 Cayuela 18 E 12
45683 Cazalegas 38 J 10
23628 Cazalilla 57 O 12
41370 Cazalla de la Sierra 64 O 8
24796 Cazanuecos 16 E 8
27824 Cazás 2 C 4
33557 Cazo 5 C 9
23470 Cazorla 58 O 13
32130 Cea/Carballiño 14 E 4
24174 Cea/Sahagún 17 E 9
36617 Cea/Vilagarcía de Arousa 13 D 2
49512 Ceadea 26 F 7
48144 Ceanuri-Elexondo 7 C 14
24892 Cebanico 5 D 9
45680 Cebolla 38 K 10
09515 Cebolleros 7 D 13
09348 Cebrecos 18 F 12
05260 Cebreros 39 J 11
24796 Cebrones del Río 16 E 8

Ceceda

Constantí

33582 Ceceda 5 C 9
10870 Ceclavín 36 K 6
15350 Cedeira 2 B 3
10513 Cedillo 45 K 5
40550 Cedillo de la Torre 28 G 12
45214 Cedillo del Condado 39 J 12
12123 Cedramán 43 J 19
44147 Cedrillas 32 J 18
15270 Cée 1 D 1
24889 Cegoñal 5 D 10
40162 Ceguilla 28 G 12
30430 Cehegín 59 N 16
47692 Ceinos de Campos 17 E 9
39232 Cejancas 6 D 12
27666 Cela 3 D 6
24395 Celada 16 E 7
09591 Celada de la Torre 18 E 12
34846 Celada de Roblecedo 6 D 11
09226 Celada del Camino 18 E 12
44194 Celadas 42 J 17
09140 Celadilla-Sotobrín 18 E 12
32800 Celanova 14 E 4
27863 Celeiro 2 B 4
32786 Celeiros 14 E 5
39553 Celis 6 C 11
44370 Cella 42 J 17
25631 Cellers 11 E 21
26212 Cellorigo 7 D 14
33595 Celorio 5 C 10
17460 Celrà 35 E 25
15339 Céltigos 2 B 4
24231 Cembranos 16 E 8
30848 Cenajo 59 N 16
27840 Cendán 2 C 4
19245 Cendejas de Enmedio 29 H 14
19245 Cendejas de la Torre 29 H 14
19245 Cendejas del Padrastro 29 H 14
18190 Cenes de la Vega 66 P 12
26350 Cenicero 19 E 14
28650 Cenicientos 38 J 11
02247 Cenizate 51 L 16
08540 Centelles 24 F 24
42211 Centenera de Andaluz 29 F 14
42216 Centenera del Campo 30 G 14
22830 Centenera/Graus 11 E 20
19151 Centenera/Guadalajara 40 H 13
22830 Centenero 9 E 18
05132 Cepeda la Mora 38 J 9
37656 Cepeda/Béjar 37 J 7
36817 Cepeda/Redondela 13 E 2
36684 Cequiril 13 D 2
42181 Cerbón 20 F 15
19269 Cercadillo 29 G 14
27163 Cercéda 2 D 4
15823 Cerceda/Arzúa 1 D 3
28412 Cerceda/Moralzarzal 39 H 12
28470 Cercedilla 39 H 11
36139 Cercedo 13 D 3
08698 Cercs 12 E 23
46813 Cerdà 52 M 18
08290 Cerdanyola del Vallès 24 G 24
32526 Cerdeira 14 E 3
39798 Cerdigo 7 C 13
39860 Cereceda/Ampuero 7 C 13

33815 Cereceda/Arriondas 5 C 9
09559 Cereceda/Oña 7 D 13
19128 Cereceda/Saedón 41 H 14
49640 Cerecinos de Campos 16 F 9
49125 Cerecinos del Carrizal 26 F 8
22623 Ceresola 10 E 19
37253 Cerezal de Penahorcada 25 G 6
10663 Cerezo 36 J 7
40591 Cerezo de Abajo 28 G 12
40592 Cerezo de Arriba 28 G 12
09270 Cerezo de Riotirón 19 E 13
22449 Cerler 11 D 21
49325 Cernadilla 15 E 7
09141 Cernégula 18 D 12
15147 Cero 1 C 2
36152 Cerponzóns 13 E 2
15112 Cerqueda 1 C 2
29569 Cerralba 70 Q 10
37291 Cerralbo 25 H 6
09292 Cerratón de Juarros 19 E 13
32164 Cerreda 14 E 4
33812 Cerredo 3 D 7
28210 Cerro Alarcón 39 J 11
41389 Cerro del Hierro 55 O 8
02511 Cerro Lobo 51 M 16
14350 Cerro Muriano 56 N 10
41409 Cerro Perea 64 O 10
39213 Cervatos 6 D 11
34309 Cervatos de la Cueza 17 E 10
27342 Cervela 14 D 5
08758 Cervelló 24 G 23
25200 Cervera 23 F 22
50312 Cervera de la Cañada 30 G 16
45637 Cervera de los Montes 38 J 10
34840 Cervera de Pisuerga 6 D 11
16444 Cervera del Llano 41 K 15
12578 Cervera del Maestre 33 J 20
44720 Cervera del Rincón 42 H 18
26520 Cervera del Río Alhama 20 E 16
50368 Cerveruela 31 G 17
25588 Cervi 11 D 22
25460 Cervià de les Garrigues 23 G 21
17464 Cervià de Ter 35 E 25
47494 Cervillego de la Cruz 27 G 10
27891 Cervo 3 B 5
36693 Cesantes 13 E 2
09553 Céspedes 7 D 12
37750 Cespedosa de Tormes 37 H 8
15391 Cesuras 2 C 3
50292 Cetina 30 G 16
30562 Ceutí 60 N 17
34218 Cevico de la Torre 18 F 11
34247 Cevico Navero 18 F 11
39250 Cezura 6 D 11
31867 Cía 8 D 16
09228 Ciadoncha 18 E 12
31799 Ciáurriz 8 D 16
33817 Cibea 4 C 7
39790 Cícero 7 C 13
26291 Cidamón 19 E 14
42145 Cidones 19 F 14
28350 Ciempozuelos 39 J 12

33116 Cienfuegos 4 C 8
30530 Cieza 60 N 17
19420 Cifuentes 41 H 14
24166 Cifuentes de Rueda 17 D 9
47270 Cigales 17 F 10
42113 Cigudosa 20 F 15
09556 Ciguenza 6 D 12
47191 Ciguñuela 27 F 10
42126 Cihuela 30 G 16
18339 Cijuela 66 P 12
31194 Cildoz 8 D 16
31639 Cilveti 9 D 17
34829 Cillamayor 6 D 11
05149 Cillán 38 H 10
19339 Cillas 30 H 16
39697 Cillero 6 C 12
10895 Cilleros 38 H 6
02315 Cilleruelo 59 M 15
09349 Cilleruelo de Abajo 18 F 12
09349 Cilleruelo de Arriba 18 F 12
09572 Cilleruelo de Bezana 6 D 12
40551 Cilleruelo de San Mamés 28 G 12
32679 Cima de Vila 14 E 4
24239 Cimanes de la Vega 16 E 8
24272 Cimanes del Tejar 16 D 8
50213 Cimballa 30 G 16
13720 Cinco Casas 49 L 13
50182 Cinco Olivas 22 G 19
19277 Cincovillas/Atienza 29 G 14
28754 Cincovillas/Torrelaguna 28 H 12
12318 Cinctorres 32 H 19
15389 Cinés 2 C 3
31592 Cintruénigo 20 E 16
24660 Ciñera 4 D 8
49563 Cional 16 F 7
37216 Cipérez 26 H 7
36587 Cira 1 D 3
12231 Cirat 43 J 19
31131 Cirauqui 8 D 16
42138 Ciria 30 F 16
31174 Ciriza 8 D 16
42367 Ciruela 29 G 14
19197 Ciruelas 40 H 13
09610 Ciruelos de Cervera 19 F 12
19281 Ciruelos del Pinar 30 G 15
40540 Ciruelos/Aranda de Duero 28 G 12
45314 Ciruelos/Ocaña 39 K 12
26258 Cirueña 19 E 14
44158 Cirugeda 32 H 18
22589 Ciscar 11 E 21
05212 Cisla 27 H 9
34320 Cisneros 17 E 10
17741 Cistella 35 E 25
24800 Cistierna 5 D 9
13070 Ciudad Real 49 M 12
37500 Ciudad Rodrigo 36 H 6
07760 Ciutadella de Menorca 72 J 27
25341 Ciutadilla 23 F 22
25799 Civís 12 E 22
22484 Claravalls/Pont de Suert 11 E 21
25353 Claravalls/Tàrrega 23 F 22
19281 Clares 30 G 15
50314 Clarés de Ribota 30 F 16
08729 Clariana 24 F 22
26130 Clavijo 20 E 15
33795 Coaña 3 B 6
33756 Coba 3 C 6

02614 Cobatillas/Alcaraz 50 M 14
02400 Cobatillas/Elche de la Sierra 59 N 16
44157 Cobatillas/Montalbán 32 H 18
04858 Cóbdar 68 P 15
45291 Cobeja 39 J 12
28863 Cobeña 40 H 12
19443 Cobeta 30 H 15
45111 Cobisa 39 K 11
34248 Cobos de Cerrato 18 E 12
40332 Cobos de Fuentidueña 28 G 12
40144 Cobos de Segovia 28 H 11
39520 Cóbreces 6 C 11
49396 Cobreros 15 E 6
36142 Cobres (Santa Cristina) 13 E 2
40480 Coca 27 G 10
37830 Coca de Alba 27 H 9
03820 Cocentaina 61 M 19
09129 Coculina 18 D 12
19281 Codes 30 G 15
36684 Codeseda 13 D 3
15881 Codeso 1 D 3
50132 Codo 21 G 18
50326 Codos 31 G 17
27181 Coeses 2 D 4
24857 Cofiñal 5 C 9
22417 Cofita 22 F 20
46625 Cofrentes 52 L 17
47440 Cogeces de Íscar 27 G 10
47313 Cogeces del Monte 28 F 11
19490 Cogollor 29 H 14
09320 Cogollos 18 E 12
18518 Cogollos de Guadix 67 P 13
18197 Cogollos Vega 66 P 12
19230 Cogolludo 29 H 13
46749 Cogullada 61 L 19
39450 Cohiño 6 C 12
29100 Coín 70 Q 10
36947 Coiro 13 E 2
15316 Coirós de arriba 2 C 3
17496 Colera 35 E 26
49623 Colinas de Trasmonte 16 E 8
46192 Colinas de Venta Cabrera 43 L 18
24313 Colinas del Campo de Martín Moro 16 D 7
39750 Colindres 7 C 13
39584 Colio 5 C 10
29170 Colmenar 65 Q 11
28190 Colmenar de la Sierra 29 G 13
37711 Colmenar de Montemayor 37 J 8
28380 Colmenar de Oreja 40 J 13
28213 Colmenar del Arroyo 39 J 11
28770 Colmenar Viejo 39 H 12
28270 Colmenarejo 39 H 11
33590 Colombres 5 C 10
18564 Colomera 66 P 12
17144 Colomers 35 E 25
46367 Colonia Cinto de los Albates 43 L 18
07579 Colònia de Sant Pere 71 K 26
30812 Colonia de Santa Teresa 59 O 16
22283 Colonia de Tormos 21 E 18

46169 Colonia la Marinense 43 K 18
46392 Colonia La Peraleja 43 L 18
07638 Colònia Sant Jordi 71 L 25
39518 Colsa 6 C 11
33320 Colunga 5 C 9
22148 Colungo 22 E 20
25793 Coll de Nargó 11 E 22
07070 Coll dU'en Rabassa 71 K 25
39407 Collado 6 C 11
05309 Collado de Contreras 27 H 10
46360 Collado de Umán 43 L 18
05153 Collado del Mirón 37 H 9
40170 Collado Hermoso 28 G 12
28430 Collado Mediano 39 H 11
44211 Collados/Calamocha 31 H 17
16143 Collados/Cuenca 41 J 15
33680 Collanzo 4 C 8
34407 Collazos de Boedo 18 D 11
08293 Collbató 24 F 23
25739 Collderat 23 F 22
33568 Collera 5 C 9
25739 Collfred 23 F 22
33549 Collía 5 C 9
16194 Colliga 41 J 15
16194 Colliguilla 41 J 15
29195 Comares 65 Q 11
43880 Coma-ruga 24 G 23
36993 Combarro 13 E 2
24715 Combarros 16 D 7
39520 Comillas 6 C 11
29754 Cómpeta 66 Q 12
24414 Compludo 15 E 7
33556 Con 5 C 9
25212 Concabella 23 F 22
22808 Concilio 9 E 18
44397 Concud 42 J 17
19287 Concha/Molina de Aragón 30 G 16
48891 Concha/Ramales de la Victoria 7 C 13
18659 Cónchar 66 Q 12
22414 Conchel 22 F 20
09559 Condado 7 D 12
19275 Condemios de Abajo 29 G 13
19275 Condemios de Arriba 29 G 13
27235 Condes 2 D 4
43427 Conesa 23 F 22
27728 Conforto 3 C 5
03517 Confrides 61 M 19
34470 Congosto de Valdavia 5 D 10
09124 Congosto/Aguilar de Campoo 18 D 11
24398 Congosto/Ponferrada 15 D 6
19243 Congostrina 29 G 14
11140 Conil de la Frontera 69 R 7
08280 Conill 24 F 22
42230 Conquezuela 30 G 14
14448 Conquista 56 N 10
10240 Conquista de la Sierra 46 L 8
06410 Conquista del Guadiana 46 L 7
07330 Consell 71 K 25
15314 Consistorio/Betanzos 2 C 3
36430 Consistorio/Pinteareas 13 E 3
43120 Constantí 23 G 22

Constantina   (E)   **Chía**   E

41450 Constantina 55 O 8
05217 Constanzana 27 H 10
45700 Consuegra 49 L 12
09613 Contreras 19 E 13
39408 Cóo 6 C 11
30889 Cope 73 P 17
01138 Copegi 7 D 14
19292 Copernal 29 H 13
08281 Copons 24 F 23
12599 Corachar 33 H 20
44193 Corbalán 42 J 18
44721 Corbatón 31 H 17
32847 Corbelle 14 E 3
46612 Corbera 61 L 19
08757 Corbera Alta 24 G 23
24225 Corbillos de los Oteros 17 E 9
25137 Corbins 23 F 21
17121 Corçà 35 F 26
25692 Corçà/Tamarite de Litera 11 E 21
15111 Corcoesto 1 C 2
19127 Córcoles 41 J 14
46178 Corcolilla 42 K 17
39294 Corconte 6 C 12
47280 Corcos 17 F 10
41599 Corcoya 65 P 10
15130 Corcubión 1 D 1
06011 Corchuela 53 M 5
27892 Cordido 3 B 5
14070 Córdoba 56 O 10
14500 Cordobilla 65 P 10
06487 Cordobilla de Lácara 46 L 7
34259 Cordovilla la Real 18 E 11
37337 Cordovilla/Salamanca 27 H 9
02513 Cordovilla/Tobarra 59 M 16
26311 Cordovín 19 E 14
19341 Corduente 30 H 16
31591 Corella 20 E 16
26144 Corera 20 E 15
15110 Cores 1 C 2
49530 Coreses 26 F 8
10800 Coria 36 K 6
41100 Coria del Río 63 P 7
33129 Corias 4 C 7
41780 Coripe 70 Q 9
15114 Corme-Aldea 1 C 2
26526 Cornago 20 E 15
15281 Cornanda 1 D 2
15807 Corneda 2 D 3
15837 Corneira 1 D 2
09568 Cornejo 6 C 12
17844 Cornellà de Terri 35 E 25
25717 Cornellana/La Seu d'Urgell 12 E 23
33850 Cornellana/Salas 4 C 7
24980 Corniero 5 D 9
34879 Cornón de la Peña 5 D 10
43360 Cornudella de Montsant 23 G 21
09246 Cornudilla 7 D 13
33310 Coro 5 C 9
28811 Corpa 40 J 13
24740 Corporales/Ponferrada 15 E 7
26259 Corporales/Santo Domingo de la Calzada 19 E 14
45880 Corral de Almaguer 49 K 13
40529 Corral de Ayllón 29 G 13
13190 Corral de Calatrava 48 M 11
30850 Corral Rubio 60 O 16
49700 Corrales 26 G 8
47317 Corrales de Duero 28 F 11
02693 Corral-Rubio 51 M 17

01322 Correbusto 20 D 15
24849 Correcillas 5 D 9
15819 Corredoiras 2 C 3
39518 Correpoco 6 C 11
27188 Cortapezas 2 D 4
06196 Corte de Peleas 53 M 6
32200 Cortegada/Melón 14 E 3
32636 Cortegada/Xinzo 14 E 4
06196 Cortegana/ Almendralejo 53 M 6
21230 Cortegana/Aracena 62 O 6
21208 Cortelazor 63 O 6
31530 Cortes 21 F 17
44791 Cortes de Aragón 31 H 18
12127 Cortes de Arenoso 43 J 18
18814 Cortes de Baza 67 O 14
29380 Cortes de la Frontera 70 Q 9
46199 Cortes de Pallás 43 L 18
19261 Cortes de Tajuña 30 H 15
24412 Cortiguera/Ponferrada 15 D 6
39350 Cortiguera/Suances 6 C 11
13427 Cortijos de Abajo 48 L 11
02156 Cortijos de San Isidro 51 L 16
18820 Cortijos Nuevos de la Sierra 58 O 14
05289 Cortos/Ávila 38 H 10
42180 Cortos/Soria 20 F 15
24515 Corullón 15 D 6
29753 Corumbela 66 Q 11
09410 Coruña del Conde 19 F 13
27690 Corvelle 3 D 5
30153 Corvera 60 O 17
30329 Corverica 60 O 17
32839 Corvillón 14 E 4
27845 Corvite 2 C 5
27749 Corvoeira 3 C 5
32369 Corzos 15 E 5
44358 Cosa 31 H 17
25318 Coscó 23 F 22
22312 Coscojuela de Fontova 22 E 20
22141 Coscullano 22 E 19
42216 Coscurita 30 G 15
39582 Cosgaya 5 C 10
39559 Cosío 6 C 11
24143 Cospedal 4 D 7
07589 Costa de Canyamel 72 K 26
22312 Costeán 22 E 20
07144 Costitx 71 K 25
12119 Costur 44 J 19
50409 Cosuenda 21 G 17
27299 Cotá 2 C 4
49639 Cotanes del Monte 17 F 9
02461 Cotillas 58 N 14
39451 Cotillo 6 C 11
11649 Coto de Bornos 69 Q 8
23290 Coto-Rios 58 N 14
28729 Cotos de Monterrey 28 H 12
15125 Coucieiro 1 C 1
36511 Couso 14 D 4
27556 Couto 14 D 4
27712 Couxela 14 D 4
15339 Couzadoiro 2 B 4
32786 Cova 15 E 5
33589 Covadonga 5 C 9
42157 Covaleda 19 F 14

09143 Covanera 6 D 12
42212 Covarrubias/Almazán 30 G 14
09346 Covarrubias/Lerma 19 E 12
32141 Covas/Carballiño 14 E 4
15541 Covas/Ferrol 2 B 3
32311 Covas/O Barco 15 E 6
27861 Covas/Viveiro 2 B 4
36872 Covelo 13 E 3
25653 Covet 11 E 22
03560 Coveta Fumá 61 N 19
03350 Cox 60 N 18
30812 Coy 59 O 16
13345 Cózar 58 M 13
40354 Cozuelos de Fuentidueña 28 G 11
34486 Cozuelos de Ojeda 6 D 11
18659 Cozvíjar 66 Q 12
36420 Crecente 14 E 3
22315 Cregenzán 22 E 20
43839 Creixel de Mar 24 G 22
24980 Crémenes 5 D 9
17832 Crespià 35 E 25
05300 Crespos 27 H 10
44623 Cretas 33 H 20
03330 Crevillente 60 N 18
09512 Criales 7 D 13
01308 Cripan 8 D 14
06479 Cristina 54 M 7
21730 Cristinade 13 E 2
37684 Cristóbal 37 J 8
44557 Crivillén 32 H 18
32515 Cruceiro 14 E 3
15980 Cruces/Dices 1 D 2
15816 Cruces/Sobrado 2 C 3
17116 Cruilles 35 F 26
13428 Cruz de Piedra 49 L 12
10430 Cuacos de Yuste 37 J 8
12070 Cuadro Santiago 44 J 20
24620 Cuadros 16 D 8
32689 Cualedro 14 F 4
22197 Cuarte 22 E 19
50410 Cuarte de Huerva 21 F 18
37891 Cuatro Calzadas 26 H 8
02249 Cubas/Alcalá del Júcar 51 L 16
28978 Cubas/Griñón 39 J 12
50376 Cubel 31 G 16
08880 Cubelles 24 G 23
25737 Cubells 23 F 21
42148 Cubilla/Abejar 29 F 14
09211 Cubilla/Miranda de Ebro 7 D 13
24688 Cubillas de Arbas 4 D 8
34219 Cubillas de Cerrato 18 F 11
24224 Cubillas de los Oteros 16 E 8
24940 Cubillas de Rueda 17 D 9
47290 Cubillas de Santa Marta 17 F 10
19263 Cubillas del Pinar 30 G 14
19362 Cubillejo de la Sierra 30 H 16
19363 Cubillejo del Sitio 30 H 16
40185 Cubillo 28 G 12
09620 Cubillo del Campo 18 E 12
49730 Cubillos 26 F 8
09514 Cubillos de Losa 7 C 13
09572 Cubillos del Rojo 6 D 12

24492 Cubillos del Sil 15 D 6
44191 Cubla 42 J 17
49327 Cubo de Benavente 16 E 7
42134 Cubo de Hogueras 30 F 15
42167 Cubo de la Sierra 20 F 15
42191 Cubo de la Solana 30 F 15
44491 Cucalón 31 G 17
39575 Cucayo 5 C 10
02329 Cucharal 50 M 15
39318 Cuchía 6 C 11
09215 Cucho 7 D 14
32103 Cudeiro 14 E 4
33150 Cudillero 4 B 7
49717 Cuelgamures 26 G 8
28209 Cuelgamuros 39 H 11
40200 Cuéllar 28 G 11
24917 Cuénabres 5 C 10
47650 Cuenca de Campos 17 E 9
14297 Cuenca/Granja de Torrehermosa 55 N 8
16070 Cuenca/Taracón 41 J 15
44495 Cuencabuena 31 G 17
33813 Cueras 3 C 6
33537 Cuerrias 5 C 9
45126 Cuerva 48 K 11
23043 Cuesta de Gos 68 O 16
48880 Cueto/Balmaseda 7 C 13
39012 Cueto/Santander 6 C 12
09558 Cueva 6 C 12
42107 Cueva de Agreda 20 F 16
09198 Cueva de Juarros 19 E 12
09558 Cueva de Manzanedo 6 D 12
16879 Cueva del Hierro 41 H 15
12410 Cueva Santa 43 K 18
33843 Cuevas 4 C 7
29220 Cuevas Bajas 65 P 11
44169 Cuevas de Almudén 32 H 18
09136 Cuevas de Amaya 18 D 11
42342 Cuevas de Ayllón 29 G 13
44562 Cuevas de Cañart 32 H 19
44730 Cuevas de Portalrubio 31 H 18
40239 Cuevas de Provanco 28 F 12
09346 Cuevas de San Clemente 18 E 12
29210 Cuevas de San Marcos 65 P 11
16542 Cuevas de Velasco 41 J 15
12005 Cuevas de Vinromá 33 J 20
04610 Cuevas del Almanzora 68 P 16
29470 Cuevas del Becerro 70 Q 9
18813 Cuevas del Campo 67 O 14
05414 Cuevas del Valle 38 J 9
05414 Cuevas del Valle 39 J 11
19392 Cuevas Labradas 30 H 15
19392 Cuevas Minadas 30 H 15
15332 Cuiña 2 B 4

16843 Culebras 41 J 15
03658 Culebrón 60 N 18
16163 Culla 32 J 19
18194 Cúllar Vega 66 P 12
18850 Cúllar-Baza 67 O 14
46400 Cullera 61 L 19
46900 Cumbres de Calicanto 43 L 18
21387 Cumbres de Enmedio 53 N 6
21386 Cumbres de San Bartolomé 53 N 6
46640 Cumbres de Valencia 52 M 18
21380 Cumbres Mayores 53 N 6
24738 Cunas 16 E 7
50513 Cunchillos 20 F 16
15149 Cundíns 1 C 2
43881 Cunit 24 G 23
15148 Cuns 1 C 2
36670 Cuntis 13 D 2
22269 Curbe 22 F 19
15937 Cures 1 D 2
47316 Curiel de Duero 28 F 11
24732 Curillas 16 E 7
27544 Currelos 14 D 4
36692 Curro 13 D 2
24127 Curueña 4 D 8
32530 Cusanca 14 D 3
44210 Cutanda 31 H 17
29718 Cútar 65 Q 11
09490 Cuzcurrita 29 F 13
26214 Cuzcurrita de Río Tirón 19 D 14

Ch

15238 Chacín 1 D 2
37861 Chagarcía-Medianero 37 H 9
05309 Chaherrero 27 H 10
22233 Chalamera 22 F 20
05141 Chamartín 38 H 10
27169 Chamoso (San Cristovo) 2 D 5
32372 Chandoiro 15 E 5
40216 Chañe 28 G 11
27500 Chantada 14 D 4
27242 Chao de Pousadoiro 3 C 5
42259 Chaorna 30 G 15
29649 Chaparral/Fuengirola 70 Q 10
18290 Chaparral/Peligros 66 P 12
36811 Chapela 13 E 2
28694 Chapinería 39 J 11
18511 Charches 67 P 14
11400 Charco de los Hurones 69 Q 8
13428 Charco del Tamujo 49 L 12
23687 Charilla 66 P 12
22336 Charo 10 E 20
40241 Chatún 28 G 11
18330 Chauchina 66 P 12
42153 Chavaler 20 F 15
27544 Chave 14 D 4
27864 Chavín 2 B 4
19310 Checa 42 H 16
06105 Cheles 53 M 5
46821 Chella 52 L 18
46176 Chelva 42 K 18
36413 Chenlo 13 E 2
19310 Chequilla 41 H 16
19353 Chera/Molina de Aragón 30 H 16
46350 Chera/Utiel 52 K 18
42222 Chercoles 30 G 15
04859 Chercos Nuevo 68 P 16
18494 Cherín 67 Q 13
12340 Chert 33 H 20
46380 Cheste 43 L 18
22465 Chía 11 D 20

93

I N D E X · O R T S R E G I S T E R · I N D I C E · Í N D I
P L A A T S N A M E N R E G I S T E R · R E J S T Ř Í K   M Í S

E

Chiclana de la Frontera — (E) — El Molar

11130 Chiclana de la Frontera 69 R 7
23264 Chiclana de Segura 58 N 13
12592 Chilches/Nules 44 K 19
29790 Chilches/Rincón de la Victoria 65 Q 11
19160 Chiloeches 40 H 13
16190 Chillarón de Cuenca 41 J 15
19128 Chillarón del Rey 40 H 14
13412 Chillón 47 M 10
23477 Chilluevar 58 N 13
18329 Chimeneas 66 P 12
22194 Chimillas 22 E 19
15357 Chimparra 2 B 3
02520 Chinchilla de Monte Aragón 51 M 16
28370 Chinchón 40 J 13
50792 Chiprana 32 G 19
04825 Chirivel 68 O 15
46370 Chiva 43 L 18
50269 Chodes 21 G 17
12005 Chodos 43 J 19
12499 Chovar 43 K 19
24392 Chozas de Abajo 16 D 8
45960 Chozas de Canales 39 J 11
21891 Chucena 63 P 7
45113 Chueca 49 K 12
46167 Chulilla 43 K 18
16216 Chumillas 41 K 15
15313 Churío 2 C 3
29140 Churriana 65 Q 10

D

32536 Dadín 14 E 3
28814 Daganzo de Arriba 40 H 13
13250 Daimiel 49 L 12
46710 Daimús 61 M 19
04750 Dalías 67 Q 14
27375 Damil 2 C 4
17722 Darnius 35 E 25
50360 Daroca 31 G 17
26373 Daroca de Rioja 20 E 14
04768 Darrical 67 Q 13
18181 Darro 66 P 13
17538 Das 12 E 23
42108 Débanos 20 F 16
33812 Degaña 3 D 6
03189 Dehesa de Campoamor 60 O 18
34844 Dehesa de Montejo 6 D 10
34406 Dehesa de Romanos 18 D 11
40230 Dehesa Mayor 28 G 11
18538 Dehesas de Guadix 67 O 13
18567 Dehesas Viejas 66 P 12
18570 Deifontes 66 P 12
01468 Delika 7 D 14
36967 Dena 13 E 2
03700 Dénia 61 M 20
22474 Denúy 11 E 21
48160 Derio 7 C 14
03296 Derramador 60 N 18
42153 Derroñadas 19 F 14
10866 Descargamaria 36 J 7
31229 Desojo 8 D 15
24730 Destriana 16 E 7
32235 Deva 14 E 3
15339 Deveso 2 B 4
15332 Devesos 2 B 4
15177 Dexo 2 C 3
07179 Deyà 71 K 25
42126 Deza 30 G 15
31263 Dicastillo 8 D 15
15911 Dices 1 D 2
05151 Diego Alvaro 38 H 9

18180 Diezma 66 P 13
18152 Dílar 66 P 12
27548 Diomondi 14 D 4
37478 Dios le Guarde 36 H 7
27822 Distriz 2 C 4
42172 Diustes 20 E 15
32520 Doade 14 E 5
09551 Dobro 6 D 12
33731 Doiras 3 C 6
18512 Dólar 67 P 14
03150 Dolores 60 N 18
36957 Domaio 13 E 2
42153 Dombellas 20 F 14
46174 Domeño Antiguo 52 K 18
46174 Domeño/Lliria 43 K 18
31454 Domeño/Lumbier 9 D 17
40495 Domingo García 28 G 11
18567 Domingo Pérez/ Campotéjar 66 P 12
45544 Domingo Pérez/ Cebolla 38 K 10
06820 Don Álvaro 54 M 7
06400 Don Benito 46 M 8
23509 Donado 57 O 13
27373 Donalbai 2 C 4
31750 Donamaria 8 C 16
36388 Donas 13 E 2
01117 Done Bikendi Harana 8 D 15
49323 Doney de la Requejada 15 E 6
31740 Doneztebe-Santesteban 8 C 16
40469 Donhierro 27 G 10
27667 Donís 3 D 6
05217 Donjimeno 27 H 10
36948 Donón 13 E 2
20070 Donostia-San Sebastián 8 C 16
05215 Donvidas 27 G 10
04530 Doña María Ocaña 67 P 14
14860 Doña Mencía 65 O 11
14248 Doña Rama 55 N 9
09451 Doña Santos 19 F 13
37130 Doñinos de Ledesma 26 G 7
37120 Doñinos de Salamanca 26 H 8
15807 Dormeá 2 D 3
44367 Dornburg 42 H 16
15178 Dorneda 2 C 3
31829 Dorrao-Torrano 8 D 15
17536 Dòrria 12 E 24
46198 Dos Aguas 43 L 18
41700 Dos Hermanas 63 P 8
36945 Dos Torres 56 N 10
44562 Dos Torres de Mercader 32 H 19
45311 Dosbarrios 40 K 13
08319 Dosrius 35 F 24
19116 Driebes 40 J 13
42134 Duañez 30 F 15
25527 Ducro 11 E 21
18192 Dúdar 66 P 13
34210 Dueñas 17 F 10
43773 Duesaigües 23 G 21
15151 Dumbría 1 C 1
17257 Dunas 35 E 26
01520 Durana 7 D 14
48200 Durango 7 C 14
40312 Duratón 28 G 12
18650 Dúrcal 66 Q 12
19143 Durón 40 H 14
01118 Durruma Kanpezu 8 D 15
40312 Dueruelo 28 G 12
42158 Duruelo de la Sierra 19 F 14
36599 Duxame 2 D 3

E

48287 Ea 8 C 14
31396 Echagüe 9 D 16
31174 Echarri 8 D 16
41400 Écija 64 O 9
22451 Egea 11 E 20
01207 Egilehor 8 D 15
01193 Egileta 8 D 14
01260 Egino 8 D 15
31486 Egües 9 D 16
01207 Eguilaz 8 D 15
36527 Eidián 2 D 3
21730 Eidos 13 E 2
15856 Eirón 1 D 2
50600 Ejea de los Caballeros 21 E 17
37891 Ejeme 26 H 8
22438 Ejep 22 E 20
44559 Ejulve 32 H 18
16412 El Acebrón 40 K 14
05370 El Ajo 27 H 9
28607 El Álamo 39 J 12
28219 El Alcor 39 H 11
13114 El Alcornocal 48 L 11
30366 El Algar 73 O 18
04619 El Alhanchete 68 P 16
10136 El Alisillo 47 L 9
04559 El Almendral 67 P 14
46192 El Alt 43 L 18
03195 El Altet 61 N 18
05416 El Arenal/Arenas de San Pedro 38 J 9
40176 El Arenal/Pedraza 28 G 12
04149 El Argamasón 68 Q 16
39610 El Astillero 6 C 12
28189 El Atazar 29 H 13
02695 El Bachiller 51 M 17
08784 El Badorc 24 G 23
02614 El Ballestero 50 M 15
05600 El Barco de Ávila 37 J 8
05110 El Barraco 38 J 10
28610 El Barro 39 J 11
50694 El Bayo 21 E 17
18515 El Bejarín 67 P 13
45571 El Bercial 38 K 9
41240 El Berrocal 63 O 7
28192 El Berrueco/ Torrelaguna 28 H 12
23649 El Berrueco/ Villardompardo 57 O 12
28413 El Boalo 39 H 12
37520 El Bodón 36 J 6
05165 El Bohodón 27 H 10
13129 El Bonal 48 L 11
02610 El Bonillo 50 M 14
29718 El Borge 65 Q 11
11670 El Bosque 69 Q 9
46409 El Brosquil 61 L 19
08294 El Bruc 24 F 23
08553 el Brull 35 F 24
11390 El Bujeo 69 R 8
13129 El Bullaque 48 L 11
29420 El Burgo 70 Q 10
50730 El Burgo de Ebro 21 F 18
42300 El Burgo de Osma 29 F 13
24343 El Burgo Ranero 17 E 9
50548 El Buste 21 F 16
37621 El Cabaco 37 H 7
30860 El Cabezo 59 N 16
04150 El Cabo de Gata 68 Q 15
14290 El Cabril 55 N 9
14709 El Calonge 64 O 9
19070 El Calvín 40 H 13
03560 El Campello 61 N 19
01308 El Campillar 20 D 14
47460 El Campillo 27 G 9

45578 El Campillo de la Jara 47 K 9
41870 El Campillo/Aznalcóllar 63 O 7
23269 El Campillo/Chiclana de Segura 58 N 13
21650 El Campillo/Nerva 63 O 6
44121 El Campillo/Teruel 42 J 17
50800 El Campillo/Zuera 21 F 18
44131 El Campo 42 J 17
37317 El Campo de Peñaranda 27 H 9
25218 el Canós 23 F 22
04825 El Cantal 68 O 15
30648 El Cantón 60 N 18
02435 El Cañal 59 N 16
16738 El Cañavate 50 K 15
33909 El Carbayo 4 C 8
30520 El Carche 60 N 17
28190 El Cardoso de la Sierra 29 G 13
30368 El Carmolí 60 O 18
14620 El Carpio 56 O 11
45533 El Carpio de Tajo 38 K 11
06894 El Carrascalejo 46 L 7
19170 El Casar 40 H 13
45542 El Casar de Escalona 38 J 10
45614 El Casar de Talavera 38 K 10
12006 El Castell 43 J 19
44409 El Castellar 32 J 18
24132 El Castillo 16 D 7
49543 El Castillo de Alba 26 F 7
41890 El Castillo de las Guardas 63 O 7
43764 El Catllar de Gaià 24 G 22
13129 El Cebero 48 L 11
23214 El Centenillo 57 N 12
23487 El Cerrillo 58 O 13
37720 El Cerro 37 J 8
21320 El Cerro de Andévalo 62 O 6
04760 El Cid 67 Q 14
04648 El Cocón 68 P 16
25152 El Cogul 23 G 21
46178 El Collado/La Yesa 42 K 17
42172 El Collado/Soria 20 F 15
11149 El Colorado 69 R 7
11630 El Concejo 69 Q 8
04825 El Contador 68 O 15
05380 El Convento de Duruelo 27 H 9
41760 El Coronil 64 P 8
04639 El Cortijo Grande 68 P 16
28749 El Cuadrón 28 H 12
19186 El Cubillo de Uceda 29 H 13
02340 El Cubillo/Alcaraz 50 M 15
16315 El Cubillo/Teruel 42 J 17
37281 El Cubo de Don Sancho 26 H 7
49710 El Cubo de la Tierra del Vino 26 G 8
04661 El Cucador 68 P 15
44134 El Cuervo 42 J 17
41749 El Cuervo de Sevilla 69 Q 7
18818 El Cura 58 O 14
04271 El Chive 68 P 15
29552 El Chorro 65 Q 10
46390 El Derramador 52 L 17
34306 El Deseo 17 E 10
46408 El Dosel 61 L 19

04700 El Ejido 67 Q 14
45480 El Emperador 49 L 12
14249 El Entredicho 55 N 9
30333 El Escobar 60 O 17
28280 El Escorial 39 H 11
28722 El Espartal 40 H 11
40400 El Espinar 39 H 11
46409 El Estany 61 L 19
30381 El Estrecho de San Gines 73 O 18
22640 El Formigal 10 D 19
50610 El Frago 21 E 18
50320 El Frasno 21 G 17
05197 El Fresno 38 H 10
24718 El Ganso 16 E 7
14100 El Garabato 64 O 10
41888 El Garrobo 63 O 7
11687 El Gastor 70 Q 9
25717 El Ges 12 E 22
02125 El Ginete 59 M 15
28760 El Goloso 39 H 12
10392 El Gordo 37 K 9
22390 El Grado 22 E 20
21594 El Granado 62 O 5
12593 El Grao 44 K 19
46700 El Grau 61 M 19
12530 El Grau de Burriana 44 K 19
12100 El Grau de Castelló 44 K 20
02139 El Grego 59 M 15
05268 El Herradón 38 H 10
16290 El Herrumblar 51 L 16
14979 El Higueral 65 P 11
04898 El Hijate 67 P 14
16441 El Hito 40 K 14
46178 El Hontanar/La Yesa 42 K 17
46178 El Hontanar/Torrebaja 42 J 17
02314 El Horcajo 58 M 15
05415 El Hornillo 38 J 9
05250 El Hoyo de Pinares 39 H 11
14209 El Hoyo/Belmez 55 N 9
13594 El Hoyo/La Carolina 57 N 12
22394 El Humo de Muro 10 E 20
02340 El Jardín 50 M 15
04619 El Largo 68 P 16
11391 El Lentiscal 69 R 8
04114 El Lentiscar 68 P 15
43894 el Ligallo de Ganguil 33 H 21
13248 El Lobillo 50 M 13
05692 El Losar 37 J 8
33774 El Llano 3 C 5
25211 el Llor 24 F 22
49719 El Maderal 26 G 8
29678 El Madroñal 70 Q 9
37621 El Maíllo 37 H 7
17178 el Mallol 35 E 24
37171 El Manzano 26 G 7
04271 El Marchal 68 P 15
18851 El Margen 67 O 14
23412 El Mármol 57 N 13
25340 el Mas de Bondia 23 F 22
08320 El Masnou 35 G 24
43736 El Masroig 23 G 21
45663 El Membrillo 38 K 10
39727 El Mercadillo 6 C 12
43143 el Milà 23 G 22
25287 El Miracle 24 F 23
19119 El Mirador 40 J 13
43718 El Mirador del Penedès 24 G 22
05154 El Mirón 37 H 9
30868 El Mojón/Mazarrón 73 O 17
30740 El Mojón/San Pedro del Pinatar 60 O 18
43736 El Molar 23 G 21

El Molar/Torrelaguna
(E)
Escúllar
E

28710 El Molar/Torrelaguna 39 H 12
18180 El Molinillo/Diezma 66 P 13
13194 El Molinillo/Menasalbas 48 L 11
30413 El Moral 59 N 15
30412 El Moralejo 59 O 15
29793 El Morche 66 Q 12
43760 El Morell 23 G 22
43893 el Munts 24 G 22
40510 El Muyo 29 G 13
18560 El Navazuelo 66 O 13
19133 El Olivar 40 H 14
19141 El Olmillo 40 J 13
40530 El Olmo 28 G 12
19244 El Ordial 29 G 13
05164 El Oso 27 H 10
02611 El Ossero 50 M 14
47169 El Otero 27 F 10
29689 El Padrón 70 R 9
46410 El Palmar 43 L 19
41719 El Palmar de Troya 64 P 8
30120 El Palmar/Murcia 60 O 17
11159 El Palmar/Vejer de la Frontera 69 R 7
03360 El Palmera 61 N 18
30589 El Pañero 60 O 18
08754 el Papiol 24 G 24
28048 El Pardo 39 H 12
30858 El Paretón 60 O 17
05146 El Parral 27 H 10
23290 El Parralejo 58 N 14
30648 El Partidor 60 N 17
43550 El Pas 11 D 21
37524 El Payo 36 J 6
16638 El Pedernoso 50 L 14
19327 El Pedregal/Monreal de Campo 42 H 16
33877 El Pedregal/Tineo 4 C 7
41360 El Pedroso 64 O 8
37410 El Pedroso de la Armuña 27 G 9
18520 El Peñón 67 O 13
16240 El Peral 51 K 16
16192 El Percher 41 J 16
49720 El Perdigón 26 G 8
46420 El Perelló/Sueca 43 L 19
43519 El Perelló/Tortosa 33 H 21
46410 El Perellonet 43 L 19
04829 El Piar de Abajo 68 O 15
16211 El Picazo 51 L 15
04271 El Pilar 68 P 15
28296 El Pimpollar 39 H 11
47153 El Pinar 27 F 10
43594 El Pinell de Bray 33 G 21
49715 El Pinero 26 G 8
41370 El Pintado 63 O 8
28649 El Piquillo 39 J 11
25114 el Pla de la Font 23 F 20
43714 el Pla de Manlleu 24 G 23
25796 el Pla de Sant Tirs 12 E 22
43810 El Pla de Santa Maria 24 G 22
08733 el Pla del Penedès 24 G 23
03726 El Poble Nou de Benitatxel 61 M 20
43549 El Poblenou del Delta 33 H 21
44155 El Pobo 32 H 18
19326 El Pobo de Dueñas 42 H 16
04271 El Pocico 68 P 15

43817 El Pont d`Armentera 24 G 22
25723 El Pont de Bar 12 E 23
25517 el Pont de Claverol 11 E 21
08254 El Pont de Vilomara 24 F 23
23239 El Porrosillo 57 N 13
17489 El Port de la Selva 35 E 26
12530 El Port/Burriana 44 K 19
46500 El Port/Sagunto-Sagunt 43 K 19
11596 El Portal 69 Q 7
21459 El Portil 62 P 5
30393 El Portús 73 O 17
49524 El Poyo 15 F 7
44392 El Poyo del Cid 31 H 17
04117 El Pozo de los Frailes 68 Q 15
18770 El Pozuelo/Adra 67 Q 13
02125 El Pozuelo/Ayna 59 M 15
16812 El Pozuelo/Priego 41 H 15
08820 el Prat de Llobregat 24 G 24
41440 El Priorato 55 O 9
16670 El Provencio 50 L 14
45570 El Puente del Arzobispo 38 K 9
39788 El Puente/Ampuero 7 C 13
49350 El Puente/Puebla de Sanabria 15 E 6
04693 El Puertecico 68 O 16
33840 El Puerto 4 C 7
11500 El Puerto de Santa María 69 Q 7
22338 El Pueyo de Araguás 10 E 20
22662 El Pueyo de Jaca 10 D 19
33315 El Puntal 5 B 9
25723 El Quer Foradat 12 E 23
42156 El Quintanarejo 19 F 14
03739 El Rafalet 61 M 20
26124 El Rasillo de Cameros 19 E 14
05489 El Raso 37 J 9
08711 el Raval 24 F 23
41250 El Real de la Jara 63 O 7
45640 El Real de San Vicente 38 J 10
46391 El Rebollar 52 L 17
19492 El Recuenco 41 H 15
26146 El Redal 20 E 15
46300 El Remedio 52 K 17
10690 El Rincón 47 L 9
14100 El Rinconcillo 65 O 10
04270 El Río de Aguas 68 P 15
28810 El Robledal 40 J 13
13114 El Robledo 48 L 11
21750 El Rocío 63 P 7
45770 El Romeral 49 K 13
21459 El Rompido 62 P 5
41880 El Ronquillo 63 O 7
29600 El Rosario 70 Q 10
02129 El Royo/Ayna 59 M 15
42153 El Royo/Soria 19 F 14
41568 El Rubio 64 P 10
50617 El Sabinar/Ejea de los Caballeros 21 E 17
30441 El Sabinar/Moratella 59 N 15
02127 El Sahuco 59 M 15
37510 El Sahugo 36 J 6

46910 El Saler 43 L 19
14814 El Salobral/Alcaudete 65 O 11
02140 El Salobral/Chinchilla de Monte Aragón 51 M 16
04694 El Saltador 68 P 16
17811 el Sallent 35 E 25
22583 El Sas 11 E 21
41650 El Saucejo 64 P 9
18850 El Saúco 67 O 15
16709 El Simarro 50 L 15
14250 El Soldado 55 N 9
25163 El Soleràs 23 G 21
14815 El Solvito 66 O 11
13429 El Sotillo/Porzuna 48 L 11
19491 El Sotillo/Sigüenza 29 H 14
28412 El Soto 39 H 12
25331 el Tarrós 23 F 22
14915 El Tejar 65 P 10
05270 El Tiemblo 38 J 11
11370 El Tiradero 69 R 8
16879 El Tobar 41 H 15
45820 El Toboso 50 K 14
39517 El Tojo 6 C 11
41719 El Torbiscal 63 P 8
22215 El Tormillo 22 F 19
12232 El Tormo 43 J 19
17830 El Torn Ventajol 35 E 25
37765 El Tornadizo 37 H 8
28739 El Tornillar 28 H 12
11594 El Torno/La Barca de la Florida 69 Q 8
10617 El Torno/Plasencia 37 J 8
13194 El Torno/Porzuna 48 L 11
12429 El Toro 43 K 18
06717 El Torviscal 54 L 8
13129 El Trincheto 48 L 11
41727 El Trobal 63 P 8
18370 El Turro 66 P 12
14320 El Vacar 56 N 10
46140 El Val de la Sabina 42 J 17
24315 El Valle/Bembibre 16 D 7
23479 El Valle/Cazorla 58 O 14
44123 El Vallecillo 42 J 16
18613 El Varadero 66 Q 12
28722 El Vellón 39 H 12
43700 el Vendrell 24 G 23
16340 El Ventorro 41 J 16
09589 El Vigo 7 C 13
25794 el Vilar 11 E 22
25457 el Vilosell 23 G 21
26511 El Villar de Arnedo 20 E 15
24138 El Villar de Santiago 4 D 7
26586 El Villar/Arnedillo 20 E 15
21349 El Villar/Nerva 62 O 6
13597 El Villar/Puertollano 57 M 11
44120 El Villarejo 42 J 16
14470 El Viso 56 N 10
45215 El Viso de San Juan 39 J 12
41520 El Viso del Alcor 64 P 8
02214 El Viso/Albacete 51 L 16
02214 El Viso/Alcalá de Júbar 52 L 17
48310 Elantxobe 7 C 14
31700 Elbete 9 C 16
01340 Elciego 19 D 14
02430 Elche de la Sierra 59 N 15
02127 Elche/Elx 60 N 18

03600 Elda 60 N 18
20493 Elduain 8 C 16
48940 Elexalde 7 C 14
48650 Elexalde 7 C 14
31744 Elgorriaga 8 C 16
31700 Elizondo (Baztan) 9 C 16
10891 Eljas 36 J 6
48230 Elorrio 8 C 14
01170 Elosu 7 D 14
25221 Els Alamús 23 F 21
25795 Els Castells 11 E 22
43153 els Garidells 23 G 22
43777 Els Guiamets 23 G 21
08781 els Hostalets de Pierola 24 F 23
25795 Els Hostalets/La Seu d`Urgell 12 E 22
17730 Els Hostalets/Torelló 35 E 24
12182 Els Ivarsos 33 J 19
17256 els Masos de Pals 35 F 26
12163 Els Montllats 32 J 19
43879 Els Muntells 33 H 21
25412 els Omellons 23 F 21
43449 Els Omells de Na Gaia 23 G 22
43151 els Pallaresos 24 G 22
08281 Els Prats de Rei 24 F 23
43527 Els Reguers 33 H 20
12182 Els Rosildos 32 J 19
43559 Els Valentins 33 H 20
31797 Eltzaburu 8 C 16
01309 Elvillar 20 D 14
15008 Elviña 1 C 3
29600 Elviria 70 R 10
19339 Embid 30 H 16
50239 Embid de Ariza 30 G 16
22740 Embún 9 D 18
31415 Enaquesa 9 D 18
22312 Enate 22 E 20
48392 Encina de Muxika 7 C 14
37114 Encina de San Silvestre 26 G 7
50470 Encinacorba 31 G 17
14711 Encinarejo de Córdoba 56 O 10
40531 Encinas 28 G 12
37893 Encinas de Abajo 26 H 9
47186 Encinas de Esgueva 18 F 11
14913 Encinas Reales 65 P 11
21390 Encinasola 53 N 6
37256 Encinasola de los Comendadores 25 G 6
24745 Encinedo 15 E 6
40391 Encinillas 28 G 11
09219 Encio 7 D 13
26586 Enciso 20 E 15
32748 Endrada 14 E 4
37766 Endrinal 37 H 8
31153 Enériz 8 D 16
15900 Enfesta/Padrón 1 D 2
15884 Enfesta/Sigüeiro 1 D 3
46810 Enguera 52 M 18
16372 Enguidanos 51 K 16
04729 Enix 67 Q 14
15821 Enquerentes 1 D 3
25586 Ensil o Gil 11 D 22
39577 Enterríes 5 C 10
15236 Entís (San Ourente) 1 D 2
49721 Entrala 26 G 8
09585 Entrambasaguas 7 C 13
39682 Entrambasmestas 6 C 12
09568 Entrambosrios 6 C 12

32552 Entrecinsa 15 E 5
15109 Entrecruces 1 C 2
26375 Entrena 20 E 14
19131 Entrepeñas 40 H 14
06197 Entrín Bajo 53 M 6
50290 Épila 21 F 17
31748 Eratzun 8 C 16
31290 Eraul 8 D 15
15147 Erbecedo 1 C 2
31867 Erbedeiro 14 D 4
01207 Erdoñana 8 D 15
20128 Ereñozu 8 C 16
20211 Ergoiena 8 D 15
31867 Erice 8 D 16
25528 Erill-La-Val 11 D 21
25516 Erinyà 11 E 21
22148 Eripol 22 E 20
22469 Eriste 11 D 20
50611 Erla 21 E 18
27320 Ermida 15 E 5
23686 Ermita Nueva 66 P 12
48260 Ermua 8 C 14
31714 Erratzu 9 C 17
31891 Errazkin 8 C 16
31698 Errea 9 D 17
31868 Errotz 8 D 16
45540 Erustes 38 K 11
25551 Es Bòrdes 11 D 21
07850 Es Canar 72 M 23
07196 Es Capdellà 71 K 24
07720 Es Castell 72 K 28
07839 Es Cubells 72 M 22
07690 Es Llombards 71 L 26
07740 Es Mercadal 72 K 28
07749 Es Migjorn Gran 72 K 28
07820 Es Molí 72 M 22
07690 Es Palmer 71 L 26
07160 Es Port 71 K 24
07871 Es Pujols 72 M 22
43816 Esblada 24 G 22
27540 Escairón 14 D 4
09145 Escalada 6 D 12
39795 Escalante 7 C 12
19390 Escalera 41 H 15
25596 Escaló 11 D 22
40350 Escalona del Prado 28 G 11
22363 Escalona/Ainsa 10 D 20
45910 Escalona/Torrijos 39 J 11
05289 Escalonilla/Cardeñosa 38 H 10
45517 Escalonilla/Torrijos 39 K 11
19127 Escamilla 41 H 14
09557 Escaño 6 D 12
23657 Escañuela 57 O 11
40291 Escarabajosa de Cabezas 28 G 11
15992 Escarabote 13 D 2
19119 Escariche 40 J 13
32696 Escarnobois 14 E 4
22760 Escarrilla 10 D 19
50790 Escatrón 22 G 19
50682 Escó 9 D 17
09559 Escobados de Abajo 6 D 12
24341 Escobar de Campos 17 E 10
40393 Escobar de Polendos 28 G 11
42223 Escobosa de Almazán 30 G 15
30350 Escombreras 73 O 18
19119 Escopete 40 J 13
14480 Escorial 56 N 10
44161 Escorihuela 42 H 18
18293 Escoznar 66 P 12
44193 Escriche 42 J 18
22362 Escuaín 10 D 20
44770 Escucha 31 H 18
22636 Escuer 10 D 19
04532 Escúllar 67 P 14

95

I N D E X · O R T S R E G I S T E R · I N D I C E · Í N D I
P L A A T S N A M E N R E G I S T E R · R E J S T Ř Í K   M Í S

E

21730 Esculqueira 15 F 5
24397 Escuredo/Puela de
            Sanabria 16 D 8
49323 Escuredo/Rioseco
            de Tapia 15 E 6
10133 Escurial 46 L 8
37762 Escurial de la Sierra
            37 H 8
36636 Escusa 13 D 2
18130 Escúzar 66 P 12
22482 Esdolomada 11 E 20
36470 Esfarrapada 13 E 2
32720 Esgos 14 E 4
47176 Esguevillas de Esgueva
            18 F 11
20540 Eskoriatza 8 C 14
31494 Eslava 9 D 17
39694 Esles 6 C 12
12528 Eslida 43 K 19
31697 Esnotz 9 D 17
49342 Espadanedo 16 E 7
37148 Espadaña 26 G 7
12230 Espadilla 43 J 19
25795 Espaén 11 E 22
06860 Esparragalejo 46 M 7
06620 Esparragosa 47 M 9
08292 Esparreguera 24 F 23
41807 Espartinas 63 P 7
31191 Esparza 8 D 16
31453 Esparza de Salazar
            9 D 17
15339 Espasante 2 B 4
37497 Espeja 36 H 6
42142 Espeja de San
            Marcelino 19 F 13
14830 Espejo 65 O 10
42142 Espejón 19 F 13
23628 Espeluy 57 N 12
11648 Espera 69 Q 8
31119 Esperun 9 D 16
22472 Espés 11 E 21
14220 Espiel 55 N 9
22351 Espierba 10 D 20
22611 Espín 10 E 19
17868 Espinabell 35 E 24
39588 Espinama 5 C 10
33537 Espinaredo 5 C 9
17405 Espinelves 35 F 24
39211 Espinilla 6 C 11
37419 Espino de la Orbada
            26 G 9
09610 Espinosa de Cervera
            19 F 13
19292 Espinosa de Henares
            29 H 13
05296 Espinosa de los
            Caballeros
            27 G 10
09560 Espinosa de los
            Monteros 7 C 12
34491 Espinosa de
            Villagonzalo
            18 E 11
09258 Espinosa del Camino
            19 E 13
09268 Espinosa del Monte
            19 E 13
45650 Espinoso del Rey
            48 K 10
27738 Espiñarcao 2 C 5
15324 Espiñaredo 2 C 4
40191 Espirdo 28 H 11
19445 Esplegares 30 H 15
22451 Espluga 11 E 20
22535 Esplús 22 F 20
17753 Espolla 35 E 26
17832 Esponella 35 E 25
07190 Esporles 71 K 25
22860 Esposa 10 D 18
25597 Espot 11 D 22
31228 Espronceda 8 D 15
22714 Espuéndolas 10 D 19
25515 Espui 11 E 21
22810 Esquedas 22 E 18
41209 Esquivel 63 O 8

45221 Esquivias 39 J 12
01220 Estabelu 7 D 14
19287 Establés 30 G 15
07120 Establiments 71 K 25
36679 Estacas 13 D 2
29580 Estación Cártama
            65 Q 10
41380 Estación de Alanís
            54 O 8
23590 Estación de Cabra
            66 O 13
41370 Estación de Cazalla
            y Constantina
            64 O 8
02520 Estación de Chinchilla
            51 M 16
23590 Estación de Huelma
            66 O 13
14350 Estación de Obejo
            56 N 10
29315 Estación de Salinas
            65 P 11
22424 Estada 22 E 20
22423 Estadilla 22 E 20
25597 Estaís 11 D 22
22625 Estallo 10 E 19
25719 Estamariu 12 E 23
25725 Estana 12 E 23
22589 Estaña 11 E 21
25214 Estaràs 24 F 22
11593 Estella del Marques
            69 Q 7
31200 Estella-Lizarra 8 D 15
07192 Estellenchs 71 K 24
27740 Estello 2 C 5
46300 Estenas 52 K 17
41560 Estepa 65 P 10
42180 Estepa de San Juan
            20 F 15
09230 Estépar 18 E 12
29680 Estepona 70 R 9
42130 Esteras de Lubia
            30 F 15
42230 Esteras de Medinaceli
            30 G 15
44558 Estercuel 32 H 18
15848 Esternande 1 C 2
25580 Esterri d` Àneu
            11 D 22
25571 Esterri de Cardós
            11 D 22
22412 Estiche de Cinca
            22 F 20
32680 Estivadas 14 E 4
46590 Estivella 43 K 19
26328 Estollo 19 E 14
22589 Estopiñán 11 F 21
28595 Estremera 40 J 13
19262 Estriégana 30 G 14
46817 Estubeny 52 L 18
31281 Etayo 8 D 15
09267 Eterna 19 E 13
40134 Etreros 28 H 11
01138 Etxaguen 7 D 14
31798 Etxain 9 D 16
31760 Etxalar 8 C 16
31486 Etxalaz 9 D 16
31869 Etxaleku 8 D 16
48340 Etxano 7 C 14
31174 Etxauri 8 D 16
31638 Eugi 9 D 16
31271 Eulate 8 D 15
28514 Eurovillas 40 J 13
07800 Evissa/Ibiza 72 M 22
31820 Extarri-Aranatz 8 D 15
09549 Extramiana 7 D 13
26280 Ezcaray 19 E 13
31690 Ezcároz 9 D 17
31749 Ezkurra 8 C 16

F

50793 Fabara 32 G 20
24420 Fabero 15 D 6
31670 Fábrica de Orbaitzeta
            9 C 17

41360 Fábrica del Pedroso
            64 O 8
03813 Facheca 61 M 19
11391 Facinas 69 R 8
33159 Faedo 4 B 7
15325 Faeira 2 C 4
36537 Fafián 14 D 4
22729 Fago 9 D 18
01216 Faidu 7 D 14
31370 Falces 20 E 16
17831 Falgons 35 E 25
08259 Fals 24 F 23
43730 Falset 23 G 21
22375 Fanlo 10 D 19
33325 Fano 4 C 8
12230 Fanzara 43 J 19
22135 Fañanás 22 E 19
15822 Fao 2 D 3
29461 Faraján 70 Q 9
49141 Faramontanos de
            Tábara 16 F 8
50619 Farasdues 21 E 17
43459 Farena 23 G 22
49213 Fariza 26 G 7
50163 Farlete 22 F 18
15912 Faro/Dices 1 D 2
27863 Faro/Viveiro 2 B 4
24133 Fasgar 4 D 7
33879 Fastias 4 C 7
18816 Fátima 58 O 14
46512 Faura 43 K 19
46614 Favara 61 L 19
50795 Fayón 23 G 20
27789 Fazouro 3 B 5
32523 Feás/Carballiño
            14 E 3
15317 Feás/Ponte Aranga
            2 C 3
32699 Feces de Abaixo
            14 F 5
31580 Féculas 20 E 15
15899 Fecha (San Xoán)
            1 D 2
07200 Felanitx 71 L 26
24760 Felechares de la
            Vadería 16 E 7
24858 Felechas 5 D 9
33688 Felechosa 4 C 8
15563 Felgosas 3 B 4
33637 Felgueras 4 C 8
04730 Félix 67 Q 14
24837 Felmín 4 D 8
27205 Felpós 2 D 4
30627 Fenazar 60 N 17
15500 Fene 2 C 3
02436 Férez 59 N 15
06390 Feria 53 M 6
27377 Feria do Monte 2 C 4
14520 Fernán Núñez 65 O 10
04116 Fernán Pérez 68 Q 15
13140 Fernancaballero
            49 L 12
27770 Ferreira/Foz 2 B 5
27430 Ferreira/Monforte
            14 D 4
27206 Ferreira/Palas de Rei
            2 D 4
27816 Ferreira/Vilalba 2 C 4
49335 Ferreras de Abajo
            16 F 7
49335 Ferreras de Arriba
            16 F 7
27335 Ferrería 15 D 5
07750 Ferreries 72 K 28
44490 Ferreruela de
            Huerva 31 G 17
49550 Ferreruela de Tábara
            26 F 7
46171 Ferriol 43 K 18
15315 Ferrol 2 C 3
15316 Fervenzas 2 C 3
08590 Figaró 35 F 24
25794 Fígols d'Organya
            12 E 22

25634 Fígols de la Conca
            11 E 21
08698 Fígols/Berga 12 E 23
33794 Figueras 3 B 5
17600 Figueres 35 E 25
25655 Figuerola d`Orcau
            11 E 21
43811 Figuerola del Camp
            24 G 22
12122 Figueroles 43 J 19
49520 Figueruela de Arriba
            15 F 7
50639 Figueruelas 21 F 17
36490 Filgueira 14 E 3
24733 Filjel 16 E 7
04500 Fiñana 67 P 14
04869 Fines 68 P 15
03509 Finestrat 61 M 19
27418 Fiolleda 14 D 4
33548 Fíos 5 C 9
22373 Fiscal 10 E 19
15155 Fisterra 1 D 1
27328 Fisteus 15 E 5
31593 Fitero 20 E 16
32767 Fitoiro 14 E 5
32618 Flariz 14 F 4
43750 Flix 23 G 21
32616 Florderrei 14 F 5
25211 Florejacs 23 F 22
05370 Flores de Ávila 27 H 9
37129 Florida de Liébana
            26 G 8
46134 Foios 43 K 19
17132 Foixà 35 E 25
27145 Folgosa 3 D 5
36558 Folgoso 13 D 3
27325 Folgoso de Courel
            15 D 5
24311 Folgoso de la Ribera
            16 D 7
27861 Folgueiro 2 B 4
08519 Folgueroles 35 F 24
24608 Folledo 4 D 8
47184 Fombellida/Peñafiel
            18 F 11
39213 Fombellida/Reinosa
            6 D 11
50491 Fombuena 31 G 17
47311 Fompedraza 8 F 11
47492 Foncastín 27 G 9
26211 Foncea 7 D 13
24722 Foncebadón 16 E 7
22474 Fonchanina 11 D 21
25244 Fondarella 23 F 21
32870 Fondevila 14 F 3
04460 Fondón 67 Q 14
18515 Fonelas 67 P 13
27113 Fonfría/A Fonsagrada
            3 C 6
44492 Fonfría/Calamocha
            31 H 17
49510 Fonfría/Zamora
            26 F 7
08259 Fonollosa 24 F 23
12160 Font d`En-Segures
            32 J 19
23486 Fontanar/Pozo Alcón
            67 O 14
19290 Fontanar/Yunquera
            de Henares
            40 H 13
13193 Fontanarejo 48 L 10
46635 Fontanars dels Alforins
            52 M 18
27133 Fontaneira 3 C 5
25751 Fontanet 24 F 22
24291 Fontanil de los Oteros
            17 E 9
17257 Fontanilles 35 E 26
13473 Fontanosas 48 M 10
27698 Fontaror 3 D 5
17833 Fontcoberta 35 E 25
25611 Fontdepou 23 F 21
01423 Fontecha/Miranda
            de Ebro 7 D 13

39212 Fontecha/Reinosa
            6 C 11
24250 Fontecha/Valdevimbre
            16 E 8
15822 Fonte-Díaz 2 D 3
32626 Fontefría 14 E 5
31512 Fontellas 21 E 16
27278 Fonteo 3 C 5
39212 Fontibre 6 C 11
47609 Fontihoyuelo 17 E 9
09349 Fontioso 18 F 12
05310 Fontiveros 27 H 10
25615 Fontllonga 23 F 21
24434 Fontoria 15 D 6
43813 Fontscaldes 23 G 22
22422 Fonz 22 E 20
26211 Fonzaleche 7 D 13
25737 Foradada 23 F 22
22452 Foradada de Toscar
            10 E 20
12310 Forcall 32 H 19
36550 Forcarei 13 D 3
43425 Forès 23 G 22
03179 Formentera del
            Segura 60 N 18
44440 Formiche Alto 32 J 18
44441 Formiche Bajo 32 J 18
22336 Formigales 10 E 20
24124 Formigones 16 D 8
24746 Forna 15 E 6
07109 Fornalutx 71 K 25
27518 Fornas 14 D 4
27768 Fórnea 3 C 5
27334 Fornelas 14 D 5
07748 Fornells 72 J 28
17458 Fornells de la Selva
            35 F 25
17255 Fornells de Mar
            35 F 26
36455 Fornelos 13 E 3
18127 Fornes 66 Q 12
22415 Fornillos 22 F 20
49513 Fornillos de Aliste
            26 F 7
49232 Fornillos de Fermoselle
            26 G 7
44650 Fórnoles 32 H 20
25717 Fórnols del Cadí
            12 E 23
15807 Foro 2 C 3
01196 Foronda 7 D 14
46418 Fortaleny 61 L 19
44143 Fortanete 32 H 18
17469 Fortià 35 E 26
30620 Fortuna 60 N 17
36853 Forzáns 13 E 3
22452 Fosado 10 E 20
36685 Foxo 13 D 3
27780 Foz 3 B 5
44579 Foz-Calanda 32 H 19
49519 Fradellos 26 F 7
37766 Frades de la Sierra
            37 H 8
22268 Fraella 22 F 19
22520 Fraga 23 F 20
22377 Fragén 10 D 19
10627 Fragosa 36 J 7
23690 Frailes 66 P 12
27569 Frameán 2 D 4
32418 Francelos 14 E 3
40514 Francos 29 G 13
09230 Frandovinez 18 E 12
34306 Frechilla 17 E 10
42216 Frechilla de Almazán
            30 G 14
12599 Fredes 33 H 20
06340 Fregenal de la Sierra
            53 N 6
43558 Freginals 33 H 21
18812 Freila 67 O 14
15861 Freixeiro 1 C 2
25290 Freixenet 24 F 23
15576 Freixo/As Pontes de
            Garcia Rodriguez
            2 B 4

Freixo/Samos · (E) · **Garrobillo**

27620 Freixo/Samos 15 D 5
50562 Fréscano 21 F 17
09259 Fresmeña 19 E 13
21730 Fresnadillo 26 G 7
01426 Fresneda 7 D 13
16781 Fresneda de Altarejos 41 K 15
40217 Fresneda de Cuéllar 28 G 11
16141 Fresneda de la Sierra 41 J 15
09267 Fresneda de la Sierra Tirón 19 E 13
24429 Fresnedelo 3 D 6
05427 Fresnedilla/Sotillo de la Adrada 38 J 10
23300 Fresnedilla/Villacarillo 58 N 14
28214 Fresnedillas 39 J 11
39806 Fresnedo/Ramales de la Victoria 7 C 13
24492 Fresnedo/Toreno 15 D 6
10328 Fresnedoso de Ibor 47 K 8
09491 Fresnillo de las Dueñas 28 F 12
37789 Fresno Alhándiga 37 H 8
40516 Fresno de Cantespino 29 G 13
42311 Fresno de Caracena 29 G 13
40540 Fresno de la Fuente 28 G 12
49693 Fresno de la Polvorosa 16 E 8
49318 Fresno de la Ribera 26 F 8
24223 Fresno de la Vega 16 E 8
09272 Fresno de Riotirón 19 E 13
09290 Fresno de Rodilla 19 E 13
49216 Fresno de Sayago 26 G 8
28815 Fresno de Torote 40 H 13
34889 Fresno del Río 5 D 10
47480 Fresno el Viejo 27 G 9
27777 Frexulfe 2 B 5
09211 Frías 7 D 13
44126 Frías de Albarracín 42 J 16
21730 Friera de Valverde 16 F 8
29788 Frigiliana 66 Q 12
27220 Friol 2 C 4
27638 Frollais 14 D 5
34440 Frómista 18 E 11
27437 Frontón 14 E 4
22269 Frula 22 F 19
40298 Frumales 28 G 11
19390 Fuembellida 41 H 16
46199 Fuen Vich 52 L 17
50619 Fuencalderas 9 E 18
42141 Fuencaliente de El Burgo 29 F 13
09127 Fuencaliente de Lucio 6 D 11
42230 Fuencaliente de Medinaceli 30 G 15
13130 Fuencaliente/ Conquista 56 N 11
13429 Fuencaliente/El Sotillo 48 L 11
19237 Fuencemillán 29 H 13
22452 Fuendecampo 10 E 20
50529 Fuendejalón 21 F 17
50142 Fuendetodos 21 G 18
44741 Fuenferrada 31 H 17

29640 Fuengirola 70 Q 10
06660 Fuenlabrada de los Montes 47 L 10
02329 Fuenlabrada/Alcaraz 59 M 15
28940 Fuenlabrada/Madrid 39 J 12
13333 Fuenllana 50 M 14
26360 Fuenmayor 20 E 14
47194 Fuensaldaña 27 F 10
45510 Fuensalida 39 J 11
02129 Fuensanta 51 L 15
23610 Fuensanta de Martos 66 O 12
42134 Fuensaúco 20 F 15
30320 Fuente Alamo 60 O 17
46197 Fuente Almaguer 43 L 19
18530 Fuente Caldera 67 O 13
18314 Fuente Camacho 65 P 11
39588 Fuente Dé 5 C 10
06240 Fuente de Cantos 54 N 7
21609 Fuente de la Corcha 62 P 6
16411 Fuente de Pedro Naharro 40 K 13
29520 Fuente de Piedra 65 P 10
40496 Fuente de Santa Cruz 27 G 10
02430 Fuente de Táif 59 N 15
06980 Fuente del Arco 54 N 8
14978 Fuente del Conde 65 P 11
28708 Fuente del Fresno 39 H 12
06360 Fuente del Maestre o la Fuente 54 M 7
30528 Fuente del Pino 60 M 17
13680 Fuente el Fresno 49 L 12
40359 Fuente el Olmo de Fuentidueña 28 G 12
40218 Fuente el Olmo de Iscar 27 G 11
28140 Fuente el Saz de Jarama 40 H 12
05212 Fuente el Seuz 27 H 10
47494 Fuente el Sol 27 G 10
49618 Fuente Encalada 16 E 8
02449 Fuente Higuera 59 N 15
14260 Fuente la Lancha 55 N 9
12428 Fuente la Reina 43 J 18
30178 Fuente Librilla 60 O 17
14290 Fuente Obejuna 55 N 9
47418 Fuente Olmedo 27 G 10
14120 Fuente Palmera 55 O 9
23290 Fuente Segura 58 N 14
18340 Fuente Vaqueros 66 P 12
02651 Fuente-Álamo 60 M 17
02260 Fuentealbilla 51 L 16
42141 Fuentearmegil 29 F 13
11500 Fuentebravía 69 Q 7
42342 Fuentecambrón 29 F 13

42162 Fuentecantos 20 F 15
42317 Fuentecatales 29 F 14
09315 Fuentecén 28 F 12
42214 Fuentegelmes 29 G 14
37540 Fuenteguinaldo 36 J 6
21292 Fuenteheridos 63 O 6
19182 Fuentelahiguera de Albatages 40 H 13
42291 Fuentelaldea 29 F 14
49410 Fuentelapeña 27 G 9
42294 Fuentelárbol 29 F 14
42211 Fuentelcarro 30 F 14
09471 Fuentelcesped 28 F 12
19144 Fuentelencina 40 H 14
16647 Fuentelespino de Haro 50 K 14
16311 Fuentelespino de Moya 42 K 17
37291 Fuenteliante 25 H 6
42220 Fuentelmonge 30 G 15
19287 Fuentelsaz 30 G 16
42162 Fuentelsaz de Soria 20 F 15
19144 Fuentelviejo 40 H 14
40153 Fuentemilanos 28 H 11
40552 Fuentemizarra 28 G 12
09315 Fuentemolinos 28 F 12
09461 Fuentenebro 28 F 12
19113 Fuentenovilla 40 J 13
09124 Fuenteodra 6 D 11
40260 Fuentepelayo 28 G 11
42294 Fuentepinilla 29 F 14
40358 Fuentepiñel 28 G 11
40330 Fuenterrebollo 28 G 12
37768 Fuenterroble de Salvatierra 37 H 8
46314 Fuenterrobles 51 K 17
44340 Fuentes Claras 31 H 17
42107 Fuentes de Agreda 20 F 16
41420 Fuentes de Andalucía 64 P 9
05212 Fuentes de Año 27 G 10
12225 Fuentes de Ayódar 43 J 19
37790 Fuentes de Béjar 37 H 8
24206 Fuentes de Carbajal 17 E 9
18295 Fuentes de Cesna 65 P 11
40232 Fuentes de Cuéllar 28 G 11
50740 Fuentes de Ebro 22 F 18
50390 Fuentes de Jiloca 31 G 16
19412 Fuentes de la Alcarria 40 H 14
06280 Fuentes de León 53 N 6
34337 Fuentes de Nava 17 E 10
37480 Fuentes de Oñoro 36 H 6
49670 Fuentes de Ropel 16 E 8
44415 Fuentes de Rubielos 43 J 18
34419 Fuentes de Valdepero 18 E 11
33817 Fuentes/Carballo 4 C 7
16193 Fuentes/Cuenca 41 K 15

45574 Fuentes/La Estrella 47 K 9
49400 Fuentesaúco 26 G 9
40355 Fuentesaúco de Fuentidueña 28 G 11
16843 Fuentesbuenas 41 J 15
44711 Fuentes-Calientes 42 H 18
16191 Fuentesclaras del Chillarón 41 J 15
40314 Fuentesoto 28 G 12
44587 Fuentespalda 33 H 20
09471 Fuentespina 28 F 12
42113 Fuentestrún 20 F 15
42134 Fuentetecha 30 F 15
42190 Fuentetoba 20 F 14
14815 Fuente-Tójar 65 O 11
42366 Fuentetovar 29 G 14
09125 Fuente-Urbel 18 D 12
28597 Fuentidueña de Tajo 40 J 13
40357 Fuentidueña/Calabazas 28 G 12
14859 Fuentidueña/Valenzuela 56 O 11
23180 Fuerte de Rey 57 O 12
16890 Fuertescusa 41 J 15
25411 Fulleda 23 G 22
31360 Funes 20 E 16
27527 Furco 14 D 4

G

22470 Gabás 11 E 20
22514 Gabasa 11 E 20
48313 Gabika 7 C 14
04560 Gádor 67 Q 15
04277 Gafarillos 68 P 15
08672 Gaià 24 F 23
12415 Gaibiel 43 K 19
27373 Gaioso 2 C 4
19192 Gajanejos 29 H 14
37874 Gajates 27 H 9
28260 Galapagar/El Escorial 39 H 11
23100 Galapagar/Jaén 57 O 12
42315 Galapagares 29 G 14
19174 Galápagos 40 H 13
09199 Galarde 19 E 13
21291 Galaroza 63 O 6
31283 Galbarra 8 D 15
09247 Galbarros 19 D 13
26212 Galbárruli 7 D 14
48191 Galdames 7 C 13
27867 Galdo 2 B 4
27285 Galegos/Meira 3 C 5
27693 Galegos/Sarria 3 D 5
49360 Galende 15 E 6
18840 Galera 58 O 14
07195 Galilea/Calviá 71 K 25
26144 Galilea/Ribafrecha 20 E 15
37785 Galinduste 37 H 8
10691 Galisteo 36 K 7
39160 Galizano 6 C 12
48319 Gallartu 7 C 14
40162 Gallegos 28 G 12
05141 Gallegos de Altamiros 38 H 10
37497 Gallegos de Argañán 36 H 6
47134 Gallegos de Hornija 27 F 9
05147 Gallegos de Sobrinos 38 H 9
37751 Gallegos de Solmirón 37 H 9
21730 Gallegos del Campo 15 F 7
49539 Gallegos del Pan 26 F 8
37450 Galleguillos 27 H 9

09146 Gallejones 6 D 12
08146 Gallifa 24 F 24
42161 Gallinero 20 F 15
26122 Gallinero de Cameros 19 E 14
17468 Galliners 35 E 25
31493 Gallipienzo 9 D 17
31493 Gallipienzo-Nuevo 9 D 17
50373 Gallocanta 31 G 16
31451 Gallués 9 D 17
50650 Gallur 21 F 17
44168 Galve 32 H 18
19275 Galve de Sorbe 29 G 13
45164 Gálvez 48 K 11
34815 Gama/Aguilar de Campoo 6 D 11
39790 Gama/Santoña 7 C 12
48113 Gamiz-Fika 7 C 14
39682 Gamonal/Puente 6 C 12
45613 Gamonal/Talavera de la Reina 38 K 10
13117 Gamonoso 47 L 10
15818 Gándara 2 C 3
43780 Gandesa 33 G 20
46700 Gandia 61 M 19
41500 Gandul-Marchenilla 64 P 8
31241 Ganuza 8 D 15
30877 Gañuelas 73 O 17
16312 Garaballa 42 K 17
48200 Garai 7 C 14
31672 Garaioa 9 D 17
11500 Garanina 69 Q 7
24120 Garaño 16 D 8
19283 Garbajosa 30 G 15
06690 Garbayuela 47 L 10
43749 Garcia 23 G 21
10250 Garcíaz 47 L 8
23539 Garciez 57 O 13
37810 Garcihernández 26 H 9
40120 Garcillán 28 H 11
16510 Garcinarro 40 J 14
45643 Garciotún 38 J 10
37460 Garcirrey 26 H 7
31414 Garde 9 D 18
24160 Garfín 5 D 9
06711 Gargáligas 47 L 8
44558 Gargallo 32 H 18
28743 Garganta de los Montes 28 H 12
05134 Garganta del Villar 38 J 9
10412 Garganta la Olla 37 J 8
13414 Gargantiel 48 M 10
28739 Gargantilla del Lozoya 28 H 12
10749 Gargantilla/Hervás 37 J 8
45671 Gargantilla/La Nava de Ricomalillo 47 K 10
19459 Gárgoles de Abajo 41 H 14
19459 Gárgoles de Arriba 41 H 14
10696 Gargüera 37 J 8
31291 Garísoain 8 D 16
06656 Garlitos 47 M 9
25539 Garòs 11 D 21
24891 Garrafe de Torío 16 D 8
31693 Garralda 9 D 17
50190 Garrapinillos 21 F 17
42162 Garray 20 F 15
17476 Garrigàs 35 E 25
17466 Garrigoles 35 E 26
17780 Garriguella 35 E 26
30889 Garrobillo 73 P 16

Garrovillas　　　　　　　　　　　　　E　　　　　　　　　　　　**Higuera de la Sierra**

10940 Garrovillas 46 K 6
04630 Garrucha 68 P 16
10333 Garvín 47 K 9
25736 Gàrzola 23 F 22
28737 Gascones 28 G 12
16532 Gascueña 41 J 14
19243 Gascueña de Bornova
　　　29 G 13
31283 Gastiáin 8 D 15
10860 Gata 36 J 6
03740 Gata de Gorgos
　　　61 M 20
48110 Gatika 7 C 14
47606 Gatón de Campos
　　　17 E 10
46169 Gátova 43 K 18
29480 Gaucín 70 Q 9
01193 Gauna 8 D 15
08850 Gavà 24 G 24
46267 Gavarda 52 L 18
25793 Gavarra 11 E 22
25588 Gavàs 11 D 22
25639 Gavet de la Conca
　　　11 E 21
05460 Gavilanes 38 J 10
09569 Gayangos 7 C 12
01206 Gebara 8 D 14
30848 Gebas 60 O 17
33811 Gedrez 3 C 6
37114 Gejuelo del Barro
　　　26 G 7
12412 Geldo 43 K 19
08790 Gelida 24 G 23
50786 Gelsa 22 G 19
41120 Gelves 63 P 7
05197 Gemuño 38 H 10
29492 Genalguacil 70 Q 9
23392 Genave 58 N 14
24792 Genestacio 16 E 8
24144 Genestosa 4 C 7
33817 Genestoso 4 C 7
31227 Genevilla 8 D 15
24837 Genicera 4 D 9
07014 Gènova 71 K 25
46894 Genovés 61 M 19
17539 Ger 12 E 23
33875 Gera 3 C 7
24608 Geras 4 D 8
25614 Gerb 23 F 21
22339 Gerbe 10 E 20
41860 Gerena 63 O 7
01207 Gereñu 8 D 15
04550 Gérgal 67 P 14
47131 Geria 27 F 10
45518 Gerindote 39 K 11
48300 Gernika-Lumo 7 C 14
22622 Gésera 10 E 19
25598 Gessa 11 D 21
46166 Gestalgar 43 K 18
24568 Gestoso/Ponferrada
　　　15 D 5
33776 Gestoso/Villanueva
　　　de Oscos 3 C 5
28900 Getafe 39 J 12
09612 Gete 19 F 13
39809 Gibaja 7 C 13
11630 Gibalbín 69 Q 8
21500 Gibraleón 62 P 6
09585 Gijano 7 C 13
33200 Gijón/Xixón 4 B 8
21342 Gil Márquez 62 O 6
05619 Gilbuena 37 J 8
41564 Gilena 65 P 10
46149 Gilet 43 K 19
01139 Gilierna 7 D 14
25112 Gimenells 23 F 20
05380 Gimialcón 27 H 9
01426 Ginea 7 D 13
41960 Gines 63 P 7
43748 Ginestar d`Ebre
　　　33 G 21
12123 Giraba de Arriba
　　　43 J 19
17070 Girona/Gerona
　　　35 F 25

08680 Gironella 12 E 23
22367 Gistaín 10 D 20
09512 Gobantes 7 D 13
18563 Gobernador 66 P 13
43516 Godall 33 H 20
46388 Godelleta 43 L 18
50238 Godojos 30 G 16
36873 Godóns 13 E 3
44221 Godos/Calamocha
　　　31 H 17
36615 Godos/Caldas de Reis
　　　13 D 2
15325 Goente 2 C 4
27614 Goián 2 D 5
36512 Goiás 14 D 3
27840 Goiriz 2 C 4
48215 Goiuria 7 C 14
31754 Goizueta 8 C 16
18150 Gójar 66 P 12
15819 Golán 2 D 3
39590 Golbardo 6 C 11
15145 Golmar 1 C 2
42190 Golmayo 20 F 14
25241 Golmes 23 F 21
02253 Golosalvo 51 L 16
37170 Golpejas 26 H 8
42120 Gómara 30 F 15
17531 Gombreny 12 E 24
27164 Gomean 2 D 5
37420 Gomecello 26 G 8
47493 Gomeznarro 27 G 10
40518 Gómeznarro 29 G 13
40240 Gomezserracín
　　　28 G 11
36990 Gondar 13 E 2
36380 Gondomar 13 E 2
27363 Gondrame 2 D 4
27188 Gonzar 2 D 4
31172 Goñi 8 D 16
27346 Goo 14 D 5
18870 Gor 67 P 14
18890 Gorafe 67 P 13
24325 Gordaliza del Pino
　　　17 E 9
48192 Gordexola 7 C 13
01208 Gordoa 8 D 15
24294 Gordoncillo 17 E 9
03811 Gorga 61 M 19
17527 Gorguja 12 E 24
48630 Gorliz Elexalde 7 C 14
42313 Gormaz 29 G 13
01427 Gorostiaga 7 D 13
08697 Gósol 12 E 23
05163 Gotarrendura 27 H 10
50257 Gotor 30 F 16
02489 Goutar 58 N 15
28339 Gozquez de Arriba
　　　39 J 12
36549 Graba 14 D 3
24160 Gradefes 17 D 9
33820 Grado 4 C 7
40512 Grado del Pico
　　　29 G 13
18517 Graena 67 P 13
16339 Graja de Campalbo
　　　42 K 17
16251 Graja de Iniesta
　　　51 K 16
24340 Grajal de Campos
　　　17 E 9
40569 Grajera 28 G 12
34846 Gramedo 6 D 11
25217 Gramuntell 23 F 22
50450 Gran Torrubia 21
18070 Granada 66 P 12
13360 Granátula de Calatrava
　　　49 M 12
33730 Grandas 3 C 6
05357 Grandas 38 H 10
24858 Grandoso 5 D 9
49740 Granja de Moreruela
　　　16 F 8
03348 Granja de Rocamora
　　　60 N 18

06910 Granja de
　　　Torrehermosa
　　　55 N 8
50213 Granja Llumes 30 G 16
08400 Granollers 35 F 24
49621 Granucillo 16 E 8
25218 Granyanella 23 F 22
25160 Granyena de les
　　　Garrigues
　　　23 G 21
25217 Granyena de Segarra
　　　23 F 22
15110 Graña 1 C 2
15339 Grañas 2 B 4
22260 Grañén 22 F 19
26259 Grañón 19 E 13
43737 Gratallops 23 G 21
22430 Graus 22 E 20
26587 Grávalos 20 E 16
11610 Grazalema 70 Q 9
44110 Grea de Albarracín
　　　42 J 17
09142 Gredilla de Sedano
　　　6 D 12
44114 Griegos 42 J 16
09128 Grijalba 18 E 11
34192 Grijota 17 E 10
28971 Griñón 39 J 12
50513 Grisel 20 F 16
50297 Grisén 21 F 17
15845 Grixoa 1 C 2
31292 Grocin 8 D 16
32850 Grou 14 F 3
24346 Grulleros 16 D 8
33829 Grullos 4 C 7
33840 Gúa 4 C 7
18560 Guadahortuna
　　　66 O 13
41339 Guadajoz 64 O 8
19070 Guadalajara/Madrid
　　　40 H 13
50730 Guadalajara/Zaragoza
　　　21 F 18
44115 Guadalaviar 42 J 16
41390 Guadalcanal 54 N 8
14130 Guadalcázar 56 O 10
03517 Guadalest 61 M 19
23519 Guadalimar del Caudillo
　　　57 N 12
28794 Guadalix de la Sierra
　　　28 H 12
29004 Guadalmar-San Julián
　　　65 Q 11
13490 Guadalmez 47 M 10
29678 Guadalmina 70 R 10
10140 Guadalupe/Logrosán
　　　47 L 9
23400 Guadalupe/Úbeda
　　　57 N 13
28690 Guadamonte 39 J 12
45160 Guadamur 39 K 11
37590 Guadapero 36 H 7
28440 Guadarrama 39 H 11
46839 Guadasequies
　　　61 M 19
46610 Guadassuar 61 L 19
06186 Guadiana 45 M 6
11311 Guadiaro 70 R 9
09135 Guadilla de Villamar
　　　18 D 11
10137 Guadisa 47 L 9
18500 Guadix 67 P 13
37219 Guadramiro 25 G 7
18195 Guájar Alto 66 Q 12
18195 Guájar Faragüit
　　　66 Q 12
08474 Gualba 35 F 25
19459 Gualda 40 H 14
17257 Gualta 35 E 26
25747 Gualter 23 F 22
03140 Guardamar del Segura
　　　60 N 18
04715 Guardias Viejas
　　　67 Q 14
25748 Guardiola 23 F 22

08694 Guardiola de Berguedà
　　　12 E 23
08694 Guardiola de Font-rubí
　　　24 G 23
34880 Guardo 5 D 10
06470 Guareña 54 M 7
39611 Guarnizo 6 C 12
49156 Guarrate 26 G 9
23210 Guarromán 57 N 12
22714 Guasa 10 D 18
22349 Guaso 10 E 20
34306 Guaza de Campos
　　　17 E 10
04647 Guazamara 68 P 16
44433 Gudar 32 J 18
18160 Güéjar-Sierra 66 P 13
48840 Güeñes 7 C 13
25590 Guerri de la Sal
　　　11 E 22
31452 Güesa 9 D 17
33779 Guiar 3 C 5
14413 Guijo 56 N 10
10815 Guijo de Coria 36 J 7
10816 Guijo de Galisteo
　　　36 J 7
10665 Guijo de Granadilla
　　　37 J 7
10459 Guijo de Santa
　　　Bárbara 37 J 8
42141 Guijosa/El Borgo de
　　　Osma 19 F 13
19263 Guijosa/Sigüenza
　　　30 G 14
37770 Guijuelo 37 H 8
36868 Guillada 13 E 3
27154 Guillar 2 C 4
36720 Guillarei 13 E 2
41210 Guillena 63 O 7
17528 Guils de Cerdanya
　　　12 E 23
25714 Guils del Cantó
　　　11 E 22
24429 Guimara 3 D 6
25341 Guimerà 23 F 22
31448 Guindano 9 D 17
09219 Guinicio 7 D 13
31291 Guirguillano 8 D 16
15165 Guisamo 2 C 3
05417 Guisando 38 J 9
25210 Guissona 23 F 22
27300 Guitiriz 2 C 4
48289 Guizaburuaga 8 C 14
36417 Guizán 13 E 2
27416 Gullade 14 E 4
09370 Gumiel de Hizán
　　　18 F 12
09440 Gumiel del Mercado
　　　18 F 12
27469 Gundibós 14 E 4
27623 Gundriz 15 D 5
32634 Guntín 14 F 4
27211 Guntín de Pallarés
　　　2 D 4
08503 Gurb 12 F 24
22280 Gurrea de Gállego
　　　21 E 18
24209 Gusendos de los
　　　Oteros 17 E 9
23339 Gutar 58 N 14
05296 Gutierrez - Muñoz
　　　27 H 10
26530 Gutur 20 F 16
32868 Guxinde 14 F 3
09314 Guzmán 18 F 12

H

09611 Hacinas 19 F 13
09613 Haedo 19 F 13
09573 Haedo de las Pueblas
　　　6 C 12
09557 Haedo de Linares
　　　6 C 12
26200 Haro 7 D 14
49833 Hayn 26 F 9
09316 Haza 28 F 12

23713 Haza Alta 58 N 14
18750 Haza del Trigo
　　　66 Q 13
39738 Hazas de Cesto
　　　6 C 12
22720 Hecho 9 D 18
06613 Helechal 55 M 9
06692 Helechosa 47 L 10
39569 Helgueras 6 C 10
02400 Hellín 59 M 16
16312 Henarejos 42 K 17
30890 Henares 68 O 16
19491 Henche 40 H 14
39805 Herada 7 C 13
19197 Heras de Ayuso
　　　40 H 13
12317 Herbés 32 H 19
09571 Herbosa 6 D 12
26584 Herce 20 E 15
01206 Heredia 8 D 15
13640 Herencia 49 L 13
10230 Herguijuela 46 L 8
37762 Herguijuela del Campo
　　　37 H 8
34247 Hérmedes de Cerrato
　　　18 F 11
49572 Hermisende 15 F 6
09246 Hermosilla 7 D 13
18880 Hernán Valle 67 P 13
20120 Hernani 8 C 16
10868 Hernán-Pérez 36 J 7
05164 Hernansancho
　　　27 H 10
26213 Herramélluri 19 D 13
10512 Herrera de Alcántara
　　　45 K 5
47161 Herrera de Duero
　　　27 F 10
39509 Herrera de Ibio 6 C 11
13200 Herrera de La Mancha
　　　49 L 13
50150 Herrera de los Navarros
　　　31 G 17
34400 Herrera de Pisuerga
　　　18 D 11
42148 Herrera de Soria
　　　19 F 13
34259 Herrera de Valdecañas
　　　18 E 11
06670 Herrera del Duque
　　　47 L 9
41567 Herrera/Puente Genil
　　　65 P 10
23315 Herrera/Villacarillo
　　　57 N 13
19342 Herrería 30 H 16
42145 Herreros 19 F 14
24767 Herreros de Jamuz
　　　16 E 8
24161 Herreros de Rueda
　　　17 D 9
05146 Herreros de Suso
　　　27 H 9
10560 Herreruela 45 L 6
34846 Herreruela de
　　　Castillería 6 D 11
45588 Herreruela de
　　　Oropesa 38 K 9
48143 Herriiko Plaza 7 C 14
47607 Herrín de Campos
　　　17 E 10
10700 Hervás 37 J 8
25212 Hestalfrancs 23 F 22
19242 Hiendelaencina
　　　29 G 14
09549 Hierro 7 D 13
10359 Higuera 47 K 8
23746 Higuera de Arjona
　　　57 O 12
23611 Higuera de Calatrava
　　　56 O 11
06441 Higuera de la Serena
　　　54 M 8
21220 Higuera de la Sierra
　　　63 O 7

Higuera de las Dueñas　　　　　Ⓔ　　　　　**Jeres del Marquesado**　　Ⓔ

05427 Higuera de las Dueñas
　　　　38 J 10
06445 Higuera de Llerena
　　　　54 N 8
06132 Higuera de Vargas
　　　　53 N 6
06350 Higuera la Real 53 N 6
04887 Higueral 67 P 15
12449 Higueras 43 K 18
02694 Higueruela 51 M 17
46170 Higueruelas 43 K 18
44530 Híjar 32 G 19
02410 Híjar 59 M 15
19276 Hijes 29 G 14
09119 Hinestrosa 18 E 11
10192 Hinojal 46 K 7
21388 Hinojales 53 N 6
30816 Hinojar 68 O 16
09454 Hinojar del Rey
　　　　19 F 13
23486 Hinojares 58 O 14
21740 Hinojos 63 P 7
19334 Hinojosa 30 G 16
37230 Hinojosa de Duero
　　　　25 H 6
44157 Hinojosa de Jarque
　　　　32 H 18
45645 Hinojosa de San
　　　　Vicente 38 J 10
42112 Hinojosa del Campo
　　　　30 F 15
14270 Hinojosa del Duque
　　　　55 N 9
06226 Hinojosa del Valle
　　　　54 N 7
13590 Hinojosas de Calatrava
　　　　56 M 11
36945 Hio 13 E 2
04768 Hirmes 67 Q 14
19248 Hita 29 H 13
10829 Holguera 36 K 7
19328 Hombrados 30 H 16
03688 Hondón de las Nieves
　　　　60 N 18
03689 Hondón de los Frailes
　　　　60 N 18
47219 Honquilana 27 G 10
16730 Honrubia 50 K 15
40541 Honrubia de la Cuesta
　　　　28 F 12
16118 Hontacillas 51 K 15
40353 Hontalbilla 28 G 11
45159 Hontanar 48 K 10
40490 Hontanares de Eresma
　　　　28 H 11
05418 Hontanares/Arenas
　　　　de San Pedro
　　　　38 J 10
19413 Hontanares/Brihuega
　　　　29 H 14
09227 Hontanas 18 E 11
16421 Hontanaya 50 K 14
09462 Hontangas 28 F 12
19119 Hontoba 40 J 13
09141 Hontomín 18 D 12
34209 Hontoria de Cerrato
　　　　18 F 11
09620 Hontoria de la Cantera
　　　　18 E 12
09450 Hontoria de
　　　　Valdearados
　　　　29 F 12
33593 Hontoria/Ribadesella
　　　　5 C 10
40195 Hontoria/San Ildefonso
　　　　o La Granja
　　　　28 H 11
16162 Horcajada de la Torre
　　　　41 J 14
28755 Horcajo de la Sierra
　　　　28 G 12
05210 Horcajo de las Torres
　　　　27 G 9
13110 Horcajo de los Montes
　　　　48 L 10

37712 Horcajo de Montemayor
　　　　37 J 8
16410 Horcajo de Santiago
　　　　40 K 13
28755 Horcajuelo de la Sierra
　　　　28 G 12
19140 Horche 40 H 13
09230 Hormaza 18 E 12
09129 Hormazuela 18 D 12
45919 Hormigos 39 J 11
26123 Hormilla 19 E 14
26223 Hormilleja 19 E 14
02529 Horna/Chinchilla de
　　　　Monte Aragón
　　　　51 M 16
19264 Horna/Sigüenza
　　　　30 G 14
06228 Hornachos 54 M 7
14740 Hornachuelos 55 O 9
39716 Hornedo 6 C 12
41640 Hornia 64 P 9
30413 Hornico 59 N 15
24515 Hornija 15 D 6
09568 Hornillayuso 6 C 12
47438 Hornillos 27 G 10
26133 Hornillos de Cameros
　　　　20 E 15
34249 Hornillos de Cerrato
　　　　18 F 11
09230 Hornillos del Camino
　　　　18 E 12
23292 Hornos 58 N 14
43596 Horta de Sant Joan
　　　　33 H 20
42366 Hortezuela 29 G 14
19445 Hortezuela de Océn
　　　　30 H 15
09610 Hortezuelos 19 F 13
39549 Hortigal 6 C 11
09640 Hortigüela 19 E 13
16195 Hortizuela 41 J 15
25290 Hortoneda de Cardener
　　　　12 F 23
25517 Hortoneda de la Conca
　　　　11 E 22
46357 Hortunas 52 L 17
24286 Hospital de Orbigo
　　　　16 E 8
22621 Hostal de Ipiés
　　　　10 E 19
17450 Hostalric 35 F 25
02310 Hoya Conejo 50 M 14
44421 Hoya de la Carrascosa
　　　　42 J 17
03111 Hoya de los Patos
　　　　61 N 19
30559 Hoya del Campo
　　　　60 N 17
02696 Hoya Gonzalo
　　　　51 M 16
16318 Hoyal del Peral
　　　　42 J 17
09316 Hoyales de Roa
　　　　28 F 12
28240 Hoyo de Manzanares
　　　　39 H 12
05123 Hoyocasero 38 J 10
10850 Hoyos 36 J 6
05132 Hoyos de Miguel
　　　　Muñoz 38 J 9
05634 Hoyos del Collado
　　　　38 J 9
40136 Hoyuelos 28 G 11
42311 Hoz de Abajo 29 G 13
39794 Hoz de Anero 6 C 12
09572 Hoz de Arreba 6 D 12
42311 Hoz de Arriba 29 G 13
22312 Hoz de Barbastro
　　　　22 E 20
22662 Hoz de Jaca 10 D 19
09559 Hoz de Valdivielso
　　　　7 D 13
09593 Hozabejas 7 D 12
39716 Hoznayo 6 C 12
31620 Huarte 9 D 16

45511 Huecas 39 J 11
10849 Huélaga 36 J 6
18540 Huélago 66 P 13
16152 Huélamo 42 J 16
23560 Huelma 66 O 13
21070 Huelva 62 P 6
16465 Huelves 40 J 14
18512 Huéneja 67 P 14
04230 Huércal de Almería
　　　　67 Q 15
04600 Huercal-Overa
　　　　68 P 16
26314 Huércanos 19 E 14
24356 Huerga de Frailes
　　　　16 E 8
24143 Huergas 4 D 7
16311 Huérguina 42 J 16
09150 Huérmeces 18 D 12
19295 Huérmeces del Cerro
　　　　29 G 14
50336 Huérmeda 21 G 16
22194 Huerrios 22 E 19
09614 Huerta de Abajo
　　　　19 E 13
09614 Huerta de Arriba
　　　　19 E 13
16195 Huerta de la Obispalía
　　　　41 K 15
45750 Huerta de
　　　　Valdecarábanos
　　　　39 K 12
22313 Huerta de Vero
　　　　22 E 20
16316 Huerta del Marquesado
　　　　42 J 16
09430 Huerta del Rey
　　　　19 F 13
40164 Huerta/Pedraza
　　　　28 G 12
37338 Huerta/Salamanca
　　　　26 H 9
19441 Huertahernando
　　　　30 H 15
19461 Huertapelayo 41 H 15
10514 Huertas de Cansa
　　　　45 L 5
13779 Huertezuelas 57 M 12
22210 Huerto 22 F 19
46192 Huerto de la Rabasa
　　　　43 L 18
23487 Huesa 58 O 13
44213 Huesa del Común
　　　　31 G 18
22070 Huesca 22 E 19
18830 Huéscar 58 O 14
16500 Huete 40 J 14
18183 Huetor-Santillán
　　　　66 P 12
18360 Huétor-Tájar 66 P 11
18198 Huétor-Vega 66 P 12
19429 Huetos 41 H 14
19119 Hueva 40 J 14
41830 Huévar 63 P 7
09124 Humada 18 D 11
19220 Humanes 29 H 13
28970 Humanes de Madrid
　　　　39 J 12
29531 Humilladero 65 P 10
09191 Hurones 18 E 12
42174 Hurteles 20 E 15
05147 Hurtumpascual
　　　　38 H 9
34419 Husillos 17 E 10

I

10280 Ibahernando 46 L 8
01160 Ibarra/Aretxabaleta
　　　　8 C 14
48419 Ibarra/Llodio 7 C 14
48311 Ibarrangelua 7 C 14
50236 Ibdes 30 G 16
09198 Ibeas de Juarros
　　　　19 E 12
03440 Ibi 61 M 18
22122 Ibieca 22 E 19

09259 Ibrillos 19 E 13
23450 Ibros 57 N 12
31473 Idocin 9 D 17
31452 Igal 9 D 17
31790 Igantzi 8 C 16
26525 Igea 20 E 15
09640 Iglesiapinta 19 E 13
09345 Iglesiarrubia 18 F 12
09227 Iglesias 18 E 12
48140 Igorre 7 C 14
36851 Igrexa 13 E 3
15510 Igrexafeita 2 C 4
22193 Igriés 22 E 19
08700 Igualada 24 F 23
29440 Igualeja 70 Q 9
24312 Igueña 16 D 7
31241 Igúzquiza 8 D 15
31850 Ihabar 8 D 16
31869 Ihaben 8 D 16
22415 Ilche 22 F 20
32869 Illa 14 F 3
36600 Illa de Arousa 13 D 2
45681 Illán de Vacas 38 K 10
19119 Illana 40 J 14
33734 Illano 3 C 6
04431 Illar 67 Q 14
33411 Illas 4 C 8
33718 Illaso 3 C 6
45200 Illescas 39 J 12
18260 Íllora 66 P 12
50250 Illueca 21 F 16
31699 Ilurdotz 9 D 16
31448 Imirizaldu 9 D 17
19269 Imón 29 G 14
07300 Inca 71 K 25
09558 Incinillas 6 D 12
31421 Induráin 9 D 17
42345 Inés 29 F 13
26531 Inestrillas 20 F 16
33530 Infiesto 5 C 9
16235 Iniesta 51 L 16
19283 Iniéstola 30 H 15
37609 Iñigo 37 H 8
50323 Inogés 21 G 17
01450 Inoso 7 C 14
04430 Instinción 67 Q 14
15339 Ínsua 2 B 4
36599 Insua/Arzua 2 D 3
36826 Insua/Ponte Caldelas
　　　　13 E 2
27556 Insua/Taboada 14 D 4
31891 Intza 8 C 16
22621 Ipiés 10 E 19
31639 Iragi 9 D 16
31849 Irañeta 8 D 16
31680 Irati 9 D 17
09219 Ircio 7 D 14
24148 Irede de Luna 4 D 8
24125 Irián 16 D 8
31879 Iribas 8 D 16
19150 Iriépal 40 H 13
32530 Irixo 14 D 3
32530 Irixo de Arriba 14 D 3
42269 Iruecha 30 G 15
37217 Iruelos 26 G 7
19143 Irueste 40 H 14
31730 Irurita 9 C 16
31448 Irurozqui 9 D 17
31860 Irurtzun 8 D 16
09587 Irús 7 C 13
39691 Iruz 6 C 12
31417 Isaba 9 D 18
09130 Isar 18 E 12
25586 Isavarre 11 D 22
47420 Iscar 27 G 10
22612 Isín 10 D 19
39195 Isla 6 C 12
21410 Isla Cristina 62 P 5
21449 Islantilla 62 P 5
39798 Islares 7 C 13
04118 Isleta de Arráez
　　　　68 Q 15
24855 Isoba 5 C 9
25650 Isona 11 E 22
17539 Isòvol 12 E 23

48288 Ispaster 8 C 14
02420 Isso 59 N 16
29611 Istán 70 Q 10
50687 Isuerre 9 E 17
34468 Itero de la Vega
　　　　18 E 11
09107 Itero del Castillo
　　　　18 E 11
18612 Ítrabo 66 Q 12
37551 Ituero de Azaba 36 J 6
02314 Ituero/Alcaraz
　　　　50 M 15
42191 Ituero/Soria 30 F 15
31745 Ituren 8 C 16
31176 Iturgoyen 8 D 16
31810 Iturmendi 8 D 15
48215 Iturreta 8 C 14
25260 Ivars d`Urgell 23 F 21
25122 Ivars de Noguera
　　　　23 F 21
25216 Ivorra 24 F 22
24293 Izagre 17 E 9
31451 Izal 9 D 17
31689 Izalzu 9 D 17
42291 Izana 29 F 14
01194 Izarza 8 D 14
18660 Izbor 66 Q 12
14970 Iznájar 65 P 11
18550 Iznalloz 66 P 12
23338 Iznatoraf 58 N 13
01479 Izoria 7 C 13
31868 Izurdiaga 8 D 16

J

16194 Jabaga 41 J 15
16512 Jabalera 40 J 14
44122 Jabaloyas 42 J 17
23712 Jabalquinto 57 N 12
21290 Jabugo 62 O 6
22700 Jaca 10 D 18
03310 Jacarilla 60 N 18
19240 Jadraque 29 H 14
23070 Jaén 57 O 12
17143 Jafre 35 E 26
44566 Jaganta 32 H 19
46624 Jalance 52 L 17
03727 Jalón 61 M 19
26134 Jalón de Cameros
　　　　20 E 15
49191 Jambrina 26 G 8
23658 Jamilena 57 O 12
22371 Jánovas 10 E 19
50237 Jaraba 30 G 16
46623 Jarafuel 52 L 17
46311 Jaraguas 51 K 17
10380 Jaraicejo 46 K 8
10400 Jaraíz de la Vera
　　　　37 J 8
09640 Jaramillo de la Fuente
　　　　19 E 13
09640 Jaramillo Quemado
　　　　19 E 13
11510 Jarana 69 Q 7
10450 Jarandilla de la Vera
　　　　37 J 8
42132 Jaray 30 F 15
33816 Jarceley 4 C 7
10728 Jarilla 37 J 7
22714 Jarlata 10 D 19
50258 Jarque 30 F 16
18127 Jatar 66 Q 12
44592 Jatiel 32 G 19
14911 Jauja 65 P 10
50141 Jaulín 21 G 18
31866 Jauntsarats 8 C 16
31691 Jaurrieta 9 D 17
03730 Jávea-Xàbia 61 M 20
31411 Javier 9 D 17
22750 Javierregay 9 D 18
22624 Javierrelatre 10 E 18
18127 Jayena 66 Q 12
11620 Jédula 69 Q 8
40135 Jemenuño 27 H 11
18518 Jeres del Marquesado
　　　　67 P 13

11470 Jerez de la Frontera 69 Q 7
06380 Jeréz de los Cabaleros 53 N 6
12450 Jérica 43 K 18
10612 Jerte 37 J 8
07819 Jesús 72 M 22
43870 Jesús i Maria 33 H 21
03749 Jésus Pobre 61 M 20
18699 Jete 66 Q 12
13420 Jétor 49 L 12
03100 Jijona-Xixona 61 M 18
23530 Jimena 57 O 13
11339 Jimena de la Frontera 70 R 9
24767 Jiménez de Jamuz 16 E 8
29392 Jimera de Líbar 70 Q 9
19245 Jirueque 29 H 14
17176 Joanetes 35 E 24
24326 Joara 17 E 10
24324 Joarilla de las Matas 17 E 9
23500 Jodar 57 O 13
42216 Jodra de Cardos 30 G 14
01439 Jokano 7 D 14
33629 Jomezana 4 C 8
18492 Jorairátar 67 Q 13
08719 Jorba 24 F 23
44156 Jorcas 32 H 18
02248 Jorquera 51 L 16
44792 Josa 31 H 18
11579 José Antonio 69 Q 8
40130 Juarros de Riomoros 28 H 11
40445 Juarros de Voltoya 27 G 10
26131 Jubera 20 E 15
29492 Jubrique 70 Q 9
42259 Judes 30 G 15
30520 Jumilla 60 N 17
25165 Juncosa 23 G 21
25430 Juneda 23 F 21
21730 Junqueira 25 G 6
11620 Junta de los Ríos 69 Q 8
22142 Junzano 22 E 19
22588 Juseu 11 E 20
50015 Juslibol 21 F 18
49340 Justel 16 E 7
18452 Juviles 66 Q 13
37115 Juzbado 26 G 8

K

01118 Kintana 8 D 15
01117 Kontrasta 8 D 15
01129 Korres 8 D 15

L

08592 l`Abella 24 F 24
43479 l`Albiol 23 G 22
43381 l`Aleixar 23 G 22
25794 l`Alzina 12 E 22
25218 l`Aranyó 23 F 22
43720 l`Arboc 24 G 23
17472 l`Armentera 35 E 26
17258 l`Escala 35 E 26
17421 l`Esparra 35 F 25
08614 l`Espunyola 12 E 23
08148 l`Estany 24 F 24
17258 L`Estartit 35 E 26
17258 L`Estartit 35 E 26
25155 L`Albagés 23 G 21
25450 L`Albi 23 G 21
46250 l`Alcudia 61 L 18
43896 l`Aldea 33 H 21
03581 L`Alfàs del Pi 61 M 19
43890 L`Almadrava 34 H 21
43890 L`Almadrava 34 H 21
03829 L`Alqueria d`Asnar 61 M 19
43860 L`Ametlla de Mar 34 H 21

25692 L`Ametlla de Montsec 11 E 21
43895 L`Ampolla 33 H 21
43312 L`Arbocet 23 G 21
43773 L`Argentera 23 G 21
08480 l`Atmella del Vallès 24 F 24
12513 L`Avellà 32 H 20
46810 L`Eliana 43 K 18
46183 L`Eliana 52 M 18
46669 L`Ènova 61 L 19
25410 L`Espluga Calba 23 G 22
43440 L`Espluga de Francolí 23 G 22
12319 L`Herbeset 32 H 19
43890 L`Hospitalet de l`Infant 34 H 21
08900 L`Hospitalet de Llobregat 24 G 24
17854 l`Hostalnou de Bianya 35 E 24
03590 L`Olla 61 M 19
28755 La Acebeda 28 G 12
05430 La Adrada 38 J 10
09370 La Aguilera 28 F 12
37497 La Alameda de Gardón 36 H 6
13379 La Alameda/Calzada de Calatrava 57 M 12
42126 La Alameda/Deza 30 F 15
37554 La Alamedilla 36 J 6
05160 La Alamedilla del Berrocal 38 H 10
37624 La Alberca 37 J 7
16620 La Alberca de Záncara 50 K 15
37555 La Alberguería de Argañán 36 J 6
06170 La Albuera 53 M 6
04778 La Alcazaba 67 Q 13
41899 La Alcornocosa 63 O 7
34240 La Aldea 18 F 11
09211 La Aldea del Portillo de Busto 7 D 13
28380 La Aldehuela/Aranjuez 40 J 13
05593 La Aldehuela/El Barco de Ávila 37 J 9
04830 La Alfahuara 59 O 15
02448 La Alfera 59 M 15
41980 La Algaba 63 P 7
11549 La Algaida 69 Q 7
44562 La Algecira 32 H 19
04770 La Alguería 67 Q 14
16740 La Almarcha 50 K 15
46178 La Almeza 42 K 18
50178 La Almolda 22 F 19
50100 La Almunia de Doña Godina 21 G 17
30528 La Alquería 60 M 17
24796 La Antigua 16 E 8
39849 La Aparecida/Ampuero 7 C 13
30395 La Aparecida/Los Dolores 73 O 18
03311 La Aparecida/Orihuela 60 N 17
37591 La Atalaya/Ciudad 36 H 7
29311 La Atalaya/Villanueve de Algaidas 65 P 11
30868 La Azohía 73 O 17
14220 La Ballesta 56 N 10
24746 La Bana 15 E 6
24750 La Baneza 16 E 8
19269 La Barbolla 29 G 14
11570 La Barca de la Florida 69 Q 8
12193 La Barona 33 J 19
24441 La Barosa 15 E 6
03420 La Barraca 61 M 18
04450 La Barriada de Alcora 67 Q 14

11139 La Barrosa 69 R 7
37621 La Bastida 37 H 7
08476 la Batllória 35 F 25
19192 La Beltraneja 29 H 14
28240 La Berzosa 39 H 12
17421 la Bisbal d`Empordà 35 F 26
43372 La Bisbal de Falset 23 G 21
43717 La Bisbal del Penedès 24 G 22
19278 La Bodera 29 G 14
23485 La Bodera 58 O 14
17474 la Bomba 35 E 26
22300 La Boquera 22 E 20
25551 La Bordeta 23 F 21
37488 La Bouza 25 H 6
49155 La Bóveda de Toro 27 G 9
28339 La Boyeriza 40 J 12
33757 La Braña/Boal 3 C 6
24845 La Braña/Boña 5 D 9
24520 La Braña/Pedrafita do Cebreiro 15 D 6
37777 La Cabeza de Béjar 37 H 8
46199 La Cabezuela 52 L 17
28751 La Cabrera 28 H 12
43364 La Cadeneta 23 G 22
29649 La Cala 70 R 10
10137 La Calena 47 K 9
13248 La Calera 50 M 13
18680 La Caleta-Guardia 66 Q 12
37714 La Calzada de Béjar 37 J 8
45580 La Calzada de Oropesa 38 K 9
30813 La Campana/Águilas 68 P 16
41429 La Campana/Lora del Río 64 O 9
14400 La Canaleja 56 N 10
03689 La Canalosa 60 N 18
41350 La Cantera 64 O 8
17857 La Canya 35 E 24
05294 La Cañada 38 H 11
04839 La Cañada de Cañepla 59 O 15
04120 La Cañada de San Urbano 67 Q 15
44643 La Cañada de Verich 32 H 19
46330 La Cañada/Minglanilla 51 K 17
46351 La Cañada/Utiel 52 K 17
39723 La Carcova 6 C 12
06929 La Cardenchosa/Azuaga 55 N 8
14299 La Cardenchosa/Fuente Obejuna 55 N 9
33750 La Caridad 3 B 6
14100 La Carlota 65 O 10
23200 La Carolina 57 N 12
23614 La Carrasca 66 O 12
05620 La Carrera 37 J 8
43870 la Carroba 33 H 21
22213 La Cartuja de Monegros 22 F 19
39720 La Cavada 6 C 12
30520 La Celia 60 N 17
17165 la Cellera de Ter 35 F 25
09514 La Cerca 7 D 13
44651 La Cerollera 32 H 19
23190 La Cerradura 66 O 12
44422 La Cervera 43 K 18
16340 La Cierva/Cuenca 41 J 16
41510 La Cierva/Sevilla 64 P 8
11650 La Cierva/Villamartin 69 Q 8

47193 La Cisterniga 27 F 10
44640 La Codoñera 32 H 19
06518 La Codosera 45 L 5
05192 La Colilla 38 H 10
25284 la Coma 12 E 23
14816 La Concepción 65 P 11
39728 La Concha 6 C 12
23730 La Condesa 57 N 12
30189 La Copa 59 N 16
30396 La Corona 73 O 17
14298 La Coronada/Fuente Obejuna 55 N 9
06469 La Coronada/Villanueva de la Serena 47 M 8
33458 La Corrada 4 B 7
39292 La Costana 6 C 11
30849 La Costera 60 O 17
42192 La Cuenca 29 F 14
42173 La Cuesta 20 E 15
24141 La Cueta 4 C 7
09315 La Cueva de Roa 28 F 12
04149 La Cueva del Pájaro 68 P 16
02510 La Cueva/Chinchilla de Monte Aragón 51 M 16
16192 La Cueva/Cuenca 41 J 16
46178 La Cuevarruz 42 K 18
10270 La Cumbre 46 L 8
14100 La Chica Carlota 55 O 10
29692 La Chullera 70 R 9
02139 La Dehesa/Ayna 59 M 15
02459 La Dehesa/Letur 59 N 15
25317 la Donzell 23 F 22
46758 La Drova 61 L 19
29692 La Duquesa 70 R 9
37515 La Encina/Ciudad Rodrigo 36 H 6
03408 La Encina/Villena 52 M 18
41730 La Encinilla 69 Q 8
24870 La Ercina 5 D 9
44424 La Escaleruela 43 J 18
33877 La Espiña 4 C 7
34840 La Estación/Cervera de Pisuerga 6 D 11
41320 La Estación/Los Rosales 64 O 8
45574 La Estrella 47 K 9
08585 La Farga de Belvie 12 E 24
25799 La Farga de Moles 12 E 22
43781 La Fatarrella 23 G 20
02156 La Felipa 51 L 16
33708 La Figal 3 B 6
43736 La Figuera de Falset 23 G 21
25351 la Figuerosa 23 F 22
25413 La Floresta 23 F 21
46717 La Font d`En Carròs 61 M 19
46630 La Font de la Figuera 52 M 18
10516 La Fontañera 45 L 5
33193 La Foz 4 C 8
37220 La Fregeneda 25 H 6
44596 La Fresneda/Alcañiz 33 H 20
45651 La Fresneda/Los Navalucillos 47 K 10
16144 La Frontera 41 J 15
14111 La Fuencubierta 55 O 10
02129 La Fuensanta 59 M 15
19268 La Fuensaviñán 30 H 14
04647 La Fuente 68 P 16

37200 La Fuente de San Esteban 26 H 7
25332 la Fuliola 23 F 22
43515 La Galera del Pla 33 H 20
09612 La Gallega 19 F 13
41370 La Ganchosa 63 O 8
30629 La Garapacha 60 N 17
10759 La Garganta 37 J 8
08530 La Garriga 35 F 24
06870 La Garrovilla 46 M 7
02211 La Gila 51 L 17
44643 La Ginebrosa 32 H 19
02110 La Gineta 51 L 16
41600 La Gironda 64 P 8
23740 La Goleta 57 N 12
14730 La Graja 64 O 9
02480 La Gralla 59 N 15
08792 la Granada 24 G 23
21668 La Granada de Riotinto 63 O 6
25177 La Granadella 23 G 21
10711 La Granja 37 J 8
25185 la Granja d`Escarp 23 G 20
14207 La Granjuela 55 N 9
25331 la Guàrdia 23 F 22
25795 la Guàrdia d`Ares 11 E 22
23170 La Guardia de Jaén 57 O 12
25632 La Guardia de Tremp 11 E 21
17732 La Guardia/Fugueres 35 E 25
45760 La Guardia/Tembleque 40 K 13
44195 La Guea 42 J 17
14547 La Guijarrosa 65 O 10
25597 la Guingueta d`Áneu 11 D 22
06714 La Haba 54 M 8
41730 La Harinosa 69 Q 8
10591 La Herguijuela/Malpartida de Plasencia 37 K 8
05631 La Herguijuela/Piedrahita 38 J 9
39580 La Hermida 5 C 10
18697 La Herradura 66 Q 12
30176 La Herreña 59 O 16
02162 La Herrera 51 M 15
14129 La Herrería/Posadas 55 O 9
02124 La Herrería/Villarejo 59 M 15
02693 La Higuera/Almansa 51 M 17
40191 La Higuera/Segovia 28 G 11
05131 La Hija 38 H 10
49192 La Hiniesta 26 F 8
42142 La Hinojosa/Burgo de Osma 19 F 13
16435 La Hinojosa/San Lorenzo de la Parrillar 50 K 15
28191 La Hiruela 29 G 13
05695 La Horcajada 37 J 9
09311 La Horra 28 F 12
28297 La Hoya/Las Navas del Marqués 39 H 11
37716 La Hoya/Piedrahita 37 J 8
02314 La Hoz 58 M 15
44791 La Hoz de la Vieja 31 H 18
04289 La Huelga 68 P 15
19238 La Huerce 29 G 13
45633 La Iglesuela 38 J 10
44142 La Iglesuela del Cid 32 J 19
11595 La Ina 69 Q 7
12340 La Jana 33 H 20
17700 La Jonquera 35 E 25

La Joya · E · **Ladrillal**

29260 La Joya 65 Q 10
50692 La Joyosa 21 F 17
30800 La Juncosa 59 O 16
30412 La Junquera 59 O 15
46339 La Laberuela 52 K 17
23740 La Lancha 57 N 12
06391 La Lapa 54 N 6
05630 La Lastra del Cano
          37 J 9
40196 La Lastrilla 28 H 11
11300 La Línea de la
          Concepción
          70 R 9
19441 La Loma 30 H 15
39211 La Lomba 6 C 11
40420 La Losa 28 H 11
42181 La Losilla 20 F 15
41430 La Luisiana 64 O 9
08779 La Llacuna 24 G 23
08120 la Llagosta 24 F 24
25288 la Llena 12 E 22
25615 La Maçana 23 F 21
30878 La Majada 73 O 17
24144 La Majúa 4 D 7
18750 La Mamola 66 Q 13
28330 La Maranosa 39 J 12
33536 La Marea 5 C 9
03194 La Marina 60 N 18
12124 La Masada 43 J 19
22215 La Masadera 22 F 19
37130 La Mata de Ledesma
          26 G 8
44557 La Mata de los Olmos
          32 H 18
24887 La Mata de
          Monteagudo 5 D 9
12312 La Mata de Morella
          32 H 19
40170 La Mata/Pedraza
          28 G 12
11520 La Mata/Rota 69 Q 7
45534 La Mata/Torrijos
          39 K 11
40175 La Matilla 28 G 12
37780 La Maya 37 H 8
16193 La Melgosa 41 J 15
04149 La Mesa Roldán
          68 Q 16
02312 La Mesta 58 M 15
22811 La Mezquita 21 E 18
19225 La Mierla 29 H 13
43559 La Miliana 33 H 20
19278 La Miñosa 29 G 14
10849 La Moheda 36 J 6
30849 La Molata 60 O 17
17537 La Molina 12 E 23
09591 La Molina de Ubierna
          18 D 12
08281 la Molsosa 24 F 23
46174 La Monrabana 43 K 18
33734 La Montana 3 C 6
14549 La Montiela 65 O 10
12428 La Monzona 43 J 18
25211 la Morana 23 F 22
41670 La Morena 70 P 9
06176 La Morera 53 M 6
43361 La Morera de Montsant
          23 G 21
11690 La Mota 70 Q 9
47630 La Mudarra 17 F 10
42294 La Muela/El Burgo de
          Osma 29 F 14
50196 La Muela/Épila
          21 F 17
11689 La Muela/Puerto
          Serrano 70 Q 9
11150 La Muela/Vejer de la
          Frontera 69 R 8
04618 La Mulería 68 P 16
03315 La Murada 60 N 18
30153 La Murta 60 O 17
45670 La Nava de Ricomalillo
          47 K 10
06486 La Nava de Santiago
          46 L 6

41380 La Nava/Alanís 55 N 8
21291 La Nava/Cortegana
          53 O 6
28260 La Navara 39 H 12
24792 La Nora 16 E 8
03530 La Nucía 61 M 19
33909 La Nueva 4 C 8
09125 La Nuez de Arriba
          18 D 12
36945 La Ñora 60 O 17
19266 La Olmeda de
          Jadraque 29 G 14
42313 La Olmeda/El Burgo de
          Osma 29 F 13
16336 La Olmeda/Landete
          42 K 17
42112 La Omeñaca 20 F 15
37428 La Orbada 26 G 9
30812 La Paca 59 O 16
30593 La Palma 60 O 18
43370 La Palma d`Ebre
          23 G 21
21700 La Palma del Condado
          63 P 6
08717 La Panadella 24 F 22
28297 La Paradilla 39 H 11
33681 La Paraya 4 C 8
02213 La Pared 52 L 17
16113 La Parra de las Vegas
          41 K 15
04770 La Parra/Adra 67 Q 13
05400 La Parra/Arenas de
          San Pedro 38 J 9
06176 La Parra/Fuente del
          Maestre o la
          Fuente 53 M 6
11591 La Parra/Jerez de la
          Frontera 69 Q 7
47328 La Parrilla 27 F 10
09133 La Parte 18 D 12
09249 La Parte de Bureba
          7 D 13
14100 La Paz 65 O 10
47196 La Pedraja de Portillo
          27 G 10
23688 La Pedriza 66 P 12
39728 La Pedrosa 6 C 12
12193 La Pelejaneta 33 J 19
37214 La Pena/Vitigudino
          25 G 8
39691 La Penilla 6 C 12
33617 La Peña/Oviedo 4 C 8
11380 La Peña/Tarife 69 R 8
33414 La Peral 4 C 8
16532 La Peraleja 41 J 14
33877 La Pereda 4 C 7
42315 La Perera 29 G 13
10649 La Pesga 37 J 7
16269 La Pesquera 51 K 16
18517 La Peza 66 P 13
09125 La Piedra 18 D 12
30335 La Pinilla 73 O 17
43460 La Plana 23 G 22
25510 la Plana de Mont-ros
          11 E 21
43882 La Platja de Calafell
          24 G 23
12550 La Platja de la Torre
          44 K 19
43892 La Platja de Miami
          34 G 21
43549 La Platja dels
          Eucaliptus 33 H 21
41620 La Platosa 64 P 9
33111 La Plaza 4 C 7
44562 La Pobla d`Alcolea
          32 H 18
12599 la Pobla de Benifassà
          33 H 20
43429 la Pobla de Carivenys
          24 F 22
25471 La Pobla de Cérvoles
          23 G 21
08787 La Pobla de Claramunt
          24 F 23

46139 La Pobla de Farnals
          43 K 19
08696 La Pobla de Lillet
          12 E 23
43783 La Pobla de Massaluca
          23 G 20
43761 la Pobla de Montornès
          24 G 22
25500 La Pobla de Segur
          11 E 21
46185 La Pobla de Valbona
          43 K 18
46840 La Pobla del Duc
          61 M 19
46670 La Pobla Llarga
          61 L 19
13197 La Poblachuela
          48 M 12
39293 La Población 6 C 12
46170 La Pobleta 43 K 18
25513 la Pobleta de Bellveí
          11 E 21
24600 La Pola de Gordón
          4 D 8
23269 La Porrosa 58 N 14
25134 la Portella 23 F 21
44589 La Portellada 32 H 20
46357 La Portera 52 L 17
04619 La Portilla 68 P 16
42169 La Poveda de Soria
          20 E 14
25214 la Prenyanosa
          24 F 22
45840 La Puebla de
          Almoradiel
          49 K 13
09294 La Puebla de Arganzón
          7 D 14
22435 La Puebla de Castro
          22 E 20
41540 La Puebla de Cazalla
          64 P 9
22437 La Puebla de Fantova
          11 E 20
44510 La Puebla de Híjar
          32 G 19
41479 La Puebla de los
          Infantes 55 O 9
45516 La Puebla de
          Montalbán 39 K 11
22482 La Puebla de Roda
          11 E 21
34470 La Puebla de Valdavia
          17 D 10
44450 La Puebla de Valverde
          42 J 18
22588 La Puebla del Mon
          11 E 20
41130 La Puebla del Río
          63 P 7
45690 La Pueblanueva
          38 K 10
19492 La Puerta 41 H 14
23360 La Puerta de Segura
          58 N 14
42126 La Quiñonería
          30 F 15
39418 La Quintana 6 D 11
25271 La Rabassa 24 F 22
18760 la Rábita 62 Q 13
31383 La Rada 9 E 16
04271 La Rambla Aljibe
          68 P 15
44730 La Rambla de Martín
          31 H 18
02127 La Rambla/Albacete
          51 M 15
14540 La Rambla/Montilla
          65 O 10
25617 la Rapita 23 F 21
08730 la Rápita 24 G 23
42310 La Rasa 29 F 13
02249 La Recueja 51 L 17
37247 La Redonda 25 H 6
12004 La Renegà 44 J 20

42291 La Revilla de
          Calatañazor
          29 F 14
39860 La Revilla/Ampuero
          7 C 13
09613 La Revilla/Salas de los
          Infantes 19 E 13
39547 La Revilla/San Vincente
          de la Barquere
          6 C 11
43450 La Riba 23 G 22
42368 La Riba de Escalote
          29 G 14
09127 La Riba de Valdelucio
          6 D 11
24567 La Ribera 15 D 6
33841 La Riera 4 C 7
43762 la Riera de Gaià
          24 G 22
05278 La Rinconada/El
          Tiemblo 38 J 10
41309 La Rinconada/Sevilla
          63 P 8
39293 La Riva 6 C 12
24640 La Robla 16 D 8
06190 La Roca de la Sierra
          45 L 6
08430 la Roca del Vallès
          35 F 24
41590 La Roda de Andalucía
          65 P 10
33747 La Roda/Castropol
          3 B 6
02630 La Roda/Villarrobledo
          51 L 15
03669 La Romana 60 N 18
41530 La Romera 64 P 9
42162 La Rubia 20 F 15
37465 La Sagrada 37 H 7
02139 La Sarguilla 59 M 15
11330 La Sauceda 69 Q 8
07870 La Savina 72 M 22
24630 La Seca/La Robla
          16 D 8
47491 La Seca/Rueda
          27 G 10
43765 la Secuita 24 G 22
17489 la Selva de Mar
          35 E 26
43470 La Selva del Camp
          23 G 22
25617 La Sentiu de Sió
          23 F 21
41740 La Señuela 69 Q 7
09462 La Sequera de Haza
          28 F 12
34128 La Serna 17 E 10
28737 La Serna del Monte
          28 G 12
43746 La Serra d`Almos
          23 G 21
05192 La Serrada 38 H 10
25700 la Seu d` Urgell 12 E 22
02450 La Sierra 58 M 14
02127 La Solana/Ayna
          51 M 15
13240 La Solana/Manzanares
          49 M 13
34240 La Tablada 18 F 11
37752 La Tala 37 H 8
17134 la Tallada 35 E 26
18814 La Teja 67 O 14
46191 La Teulada 43 K 18
19243 La Toba/Brihuega
          29 H 14
23297 La Toba/Santiago de la
          Espada 58 N 14
25515 la Torre de Cabdella
          11 E 21
45920 La Torre de Esteban
          Hambrán 39 J 11
43774 La Torre de Foutaubella
          23 G 21
43792 La Torre de`l Espanyol
          23 G 21

05540 La Torre/Blacha
          38 H 10
30530 La Torre/Cieza 60 N 16
03530 La Torre/Pilar de la
          Horadada 60 O 18
46313 La Torre/Utiel 52 K 17
19268 La Torresaviñán
          30 H 14
50210 La Tranquera 30 G 16
21207 La Umbría 63 O 7
30360 La Unión 73 O 18
47670 La Unión de Campos
          17 E 9
24127 La Urz 4 D 8
17707 la Vajol 35 E 25
12513 La Vallivana 33 H 20
24840 La Vecilla 5 D 9
24888 La Vega de Almanza
          5 D 9
33529 La Vega/Nava 4 C 8
33193 La Vega/Oviedo 4 C 8
39577 La Vega/Poles 5 C 10
03180 La Veleta 60 O 18
40173 La Velilla 28 G 12
37427 La Vellés 26 G 8
18860 La Venta/Gor 67 P 14
33193 La Venta/Oviedo 4 C 8
14112 La Ventilla 55 O 9
16843 La Ventosa 41 J 15
14140 La Victoria 65 O 10
09471 La Vid 29 F 13
09249 La Vid de Bureba
          7 D 13
34485 La Vid de Ojeda
          18 D 11
43375 la Vilella Alta 23 G 21
43374 La Vilella Baixa
          23 G 21
45850 La Villa de Don
          Fadrique 49 K 13
50219 La Vilueña 30 G 16
44431 La Virgen de la Vega
          32 J 18
24198 La Virgen del Camino
          16 D 8
46178 La Yesa 42 K 18
02161 La Yunquera 50 M 15
19361 La Yunta 30 H 16
03408 La Zafra 52 M 18
50784 La Zaida 22 G 19
37253 La Zarza de Pumareda
          25 G 6
30529 La Zarza/Alcantarilla
          60 O 17
30529 La Zarza/Algueña
          60 N 17
02327 La Zarza/Ayna
          51 M 15
47452 La Zarza/Olmedo
          27 G 10
11393 La Zarzuela 69 R 8
03189 La Zenia 60 O 18
44707 La Zoma 32 H 18
40146 Labajos 27 H 10
39595 Labarces 6 C 11
01330 Labastida/Bastida
          7 D 14
22142 Labata 22 E 19
31192 Labiano 9 D 16
18540 Laborcillas 66 P 13
33556 Labra 5 C 9
27307 Labrada/Guitiriz 2 C 4
27737 Labrada/Londoñedo
          2 C 5
01322 Labraza 20 D 15
19333 Labros 30 G 16
19333 Labros 30 G 16
22360 Labuerda 10 E 20
18514 Lacalahorra 67 P 13
50615 Lacorvilla 21 E 18
18327 Lachar 66 P 12
33993 Ladines/Pola de
          Laviana 5 C 9
33194 Ladines/Posada 4 C 8
10625 Ladrillal 36 J 7

44562 Ladruñán 32 H 19
22364 Lafortunada 10 D 20
45567 Lagartera 38 K 9
34347 Lagartos 17 E 10
50134 Lagata 31 G 18
33886 Lago 3 C 6
27287 Lagoa 3 C 5
27693 Lagos/Becerreá 3 D 5
29760 Lagos/Torre del Mar
66 Q 11
01300 Laguardia 20 D 14
22587 Laguarres 11 E 20
22623 Laguarta 10 E 19
44492 Lagueruela 31 G 17
24248 Laguna Dalga 16 E 8
26135 Laguna de Cameros
20 E 14
40236 Laguna de Contreras
28 G 11
47140 Laguna de Duero
27 F 10
24234 Laguna de Negrillos
16 E 8
16316 Laguna del
Marquesado
42 J 16
40136 Laguna-Rodrigo
28 H 11
22131 Lagunarrota 22 F 19
16878 Lagunaseca 41 H 15
37724 Lagunilla 37 J 8
26131 Lagunilla del Jubera
20 E 15
01427 Lahoz 7 D 13
15981 Laiño (San Xulián)
1 D 2
31830 Lakuntza 8 D 15
01427 Lalastra 7 D 13
46250 L'Alcúdia 61 L 18
36500 Lalín 14 D 3
22125 Laluenga 22 E 19
22214 Lalueza 22 F 19
27339 Lamaigrexa 14 D 5
32366 Lamalonga 15 E 6
27117 Lamas de Moreira
3 C 5
15562 Lamas/Neda 2 B 3
27632 Lamas/Samos 15 D 5
15150 Lamas/Zas 1 C 2
22393 Lamata 22 E 20
39573 Lamedo 6 C 11
22250 Lanaja 22 F 19
15839 Lañas 1 D 2
22621 Lanave 10 E 19
27367 Láncara 3 D 5
39293 Lanchares 6 C 12
01308 Lanciego 20 D 14
16330 Landete 42 K 17
27866 Landrove 2 B 4
48895 Lanestosa 7 C 13
05213 Langa 27 G 10
42320 Langa de Duero
29 F 13
50367 Langa del Castillo
31 G 17
01520 Langara Ganboa
8 D 14
47314 Langayo 28 F 11
42159 Langosto 19 F 14
33900 Langreo 4 C 8
40556 Languilla 29 G 13
18420 Lanjarón 66 Q 13
34468 Lantadilla 18 E 11
36657 Lantañón 13 D 2
01478 Lantatxu 7 C 13
18518 Lanteira 67 P 13
31798 Lantz 8 D 16
15685 Lanzá 2 C 3
05490 Lanzahita 38 J 10
48892 Lanzas Agudas
7 C 13
27816 Lanzós 2 C 4
44491 Lanzuela 31 G 17
09216 Laño 7 D 14
22126 Laperdiguera 22 F 19

01306 Lapuebla de Labarca
20 E 14
09651 Lara de los Infantes
19 E 13
19268 Laranueva 30 H 14
26140 Lardero 20 E 15
39770 Laredo 7 C 13
15292 Lariño 1 D 1
33813 Larna 3 C 6
32632 Laroá 14 E 4
18494 Laroles 67 P 13
33813 Larón 3 D 6
32358 Larouco 15 E 5
04868 Laroya 68 P 15
48195 Larrabetzu 7 C 14
31251 Larraga 20 D 16
31797 Larrainzar 8 D 16
31270 Larraona 8 D 15
22666 Lárrede 10 D 19
22612 Larrés 10 D 19
31290 Larrión 8 D 15
37865 Larrodrigo 37 H 9
22761 Larúes 9 D 18
31892 Larumbe 8 D 16
23591 Larva 57 O 13
04558 Las Alcubillas Altas
67 P 14
42173 Las Aldehuelas
20 F 15
44423 Las Alhambras 43 J 18
22144 Las Almunias 22 E 19
04638 Las Alparatas 68 P 16
19128 Las Anclas 40 H 14
02512 Las Anorias 51 M 16
33554 Las Arenas 5 C 10
48190 Las Barrientas 7 C 13
03292 Las Bayas 60 N 18
14850 Las Beatas 65 O 11
22149 Las Bellostas 10 E 19
05162 Las Berlanas 27 H 10
19128 Las Brisas 40 H 14
41730 Las Cabezas de San
Juan 69 Q 8
39460 Las Caldas de Besaya
6 C 11
30817 Las Canales 59 O 16
12592 Las Casas/Chilches
44 K 19
42190 Las Casas/Soria
20 F 15
09150 Las Celadas 18 E 12
47639 Las Cortas de Blas
17 F 10
04839 Las Covatillas 59 O 15
50373 Las Cuerlas 31 H 16
46313 Las Cuevas 52 K 17
04160 Las Cuevas de los
Medinas 68 Q 15
04130 Las Cuevas de los
Ubedas 68 Q 15
42291 Las Cuevas de Soria
29 F 14
16878 Las Chorretas 41 J 16
02214 Las Eras 51 L 17
42192 Las Fraguas 29 F 14
02690 Las Fuentes 52 L 17
18110 Las Gabias 66 P 12
19120 Las Gaviotas 40 J 14
45664 Las Herencias 38 K 10
04116 Las Hortichuelas
67 Q 14
13118 Las Huertas del
Sauceral 48 L 10
45675 Las Hunfrías 47 K 10
28312 Las Infantas/Aranjuez
39 J 12
23639 Las Infantas/Villagordo
57 O 12
19491 Las Inviernas 29 H 14
41360 Las Jarillas 64 O 8
04830 Las Juntas 59 O 15
13660 Las Labores 49 L 12
29640 Las Lagunas 70 Q 10
14817 Las Lagunillas 65 P 11
24526 Las Lamas 15 D 6

10519 Las Lanchuelas 45 L 5
48192 Las Llanas 7 C 13
11179 Las Lomas 69 R 8
50830 Las Lomas del Gállego
21 F 18
16142 Las Majadas 41 J 15
07610 Las Maravillas 71 K 25
28290 Las Matas 39 H 12
24442 Las Médulas 15 E 6
04890 Las Menas 67 P 14
16650 Las Mesas/Las
Pedroñeras
50 L 14
10694 Las Mesas/Torrejón El
Rubio 46 K 7
30809 Las Minas/Hellín
59 N 16
44710 Las Minas/Montalban
42 H 18
02139 Las Mohedas 59 M 15
41600 Las Monjas/Arahal
64 P 8
46310 Las Monjas/Requena
52 L 17
30420 Las Murtas 59 N 16
14800 Las Navas 65 P 11
28754 Las Navas de Buitrago
28 H 12
19244 Las Navas de Jadraque
29 G 13
41460 Las Navas de la
Concepción
55 O 9
05230 Las Navas del Marqués
39 H 11
45121 Las Navillas 48 K 11
04116 Las Negras 68 Q 15
45191 Las Nieves 39 K 12
13739 Las Norias 57 M 12
04716 Las Norias/El Ejido
67 Q 14
04690 Las Norias/Huercal-
Overa 68 P 16
30813 Las Norias/Puerto
Lumbreras
68 O 16
24273 Las Omañas 16 D 8
41219 Las Pajanosas 63 O 7
30334 Las Palas 73 O 17
44566 Las Parras de
Castellote 32 H 19
44769 Las Parras de Martín
31 H 18
14270 Las Patudas 55 N 9
16660 Las Pedroñeras
50 L 14
50612 Las Pedrosas 21 E 18
28620 Las Picadas 39 J 11
14950 Las Piedras 65 P 11
44563 Las Planas 32 H 19
04813 Las Pocicas 68 P 15
13428 Las Povedillas 48 L 11
33692 Las Puentes 4 C 8
09515 Las Quintanillas
18 E 12
13129 Las Ravinadas 48 L 11
39416 Las Rozas 6 D 11
28230 Las Rozas de Madrid
39 J 12
24990 Las Salas 5 D 9
04740 Las Salinas 67 Q 14
13345 Las Terceras 58 M 13
30812 Las Terreras 59 O 16
13128 Las Tiñosillas 48 L 11
30565 Las Torres de Cotillas
60 N 17
37217 Las Uces 25 G 7
45691 Las Vegas y San
Antonio 38 K 10
37454 Las Veguillas 37 H 8
44477 Las Venta 43 J 18
45127 Las Ventas con Peña
Aguilera 48 K 11
45183 Las Ventas de
Retamosa 39 J 11

45568 Las Ventas de San
Julián 38 J 9
18859 Las Vertientes 67 O 15
09249 Las Vesgas 7 C 13
02639 Las Villas Nuevas
51 L 15
30850 Las Vinas 59 O 16
18880 Las Viñas 67 P 13
03409 Las Virtudes 60 M 18
13738 Las Virtudes/Santa
Cruz de Mudela
57 M 13
22622 Lasaosa 10 E 19
22196 Lascasas 22 E 19
22124 Lascellas 22 E 19
22471 Laspaúles 11 E 21
22361 Laspuña 10 D 20
22586 Lasquarri 11 E 21
22215 Lastanosa 22 F 19
40352 Lastras de Cuéllar
28 G 11
09510 Lastras de la Torre
7 C 13
09514 Lastras de las Eras
7 C 13
40142 Lastras del Pozo
28 H 11
33330 Lastres 5 B 9
31869 Latasa/Irurtzun 8 D 16
31799 Latasa/Pamplona-Iruña
8 D 16
21730 Latedo 25 F 6
22349 Latorrecilla 10 E 20
22620 Latrás 10 E 19
22624 Latre 10 E 19
04470 Laujar de Andarax
67 Q 14
48110 Laukiz 7 C 14
44700 Lavaderos 31 H 18
33418 Laviana 4 B 8
33891 Lavio 4 C 7
08775 Lavit 24 G 23
15117 Laxe/Carballa 1 C 1
27512 Laxe/Chantada 14 D 4
50679 Layana 21 E 17
42240 Layna 30 G 15
45123 Layos 39 K 11
32620 Laza 14 E 5
24136 Lázado 4 D 7
31588 Lazagurría 20 E 15
31460 Leache 9 D 17
34847 Lebanza 5 D 10
39583 Lebeña 5 C 10
15809 Leboreiro 2 D 4
36519 Lebozán 14 D 3
19392 Lebrancón 41 H 15
33756 Lebredo 3 C 6
41740 Lebrija 69 Q 7
50131 Lécera 31 G 18
33347 Leces 5 C 9
22148 Lecina 22 E 20
50160 Leciñena 22 F 18
18656 Lecrín 66 Q 12
44495 Lechago 31 H 17
50369 Lechón 31 G 17
16237 Ledaña 51 L 16
19196 Ledanca 29 H 14
37100 Ledesma 26 G 7
26321 Ledesma de la Cogolla
19 E 14
42127 Ledesma de Soria
30 F 15
34347 Ledigos 17 E 10
37730 Ledrada 37 J 8
42173 Ledrado 20 E 15
28910 Leganes 39 J 12
16461 Leganiel 40 J 14
31133 Legarda 8 D 16
01170 Legutiano 7 D 14
33845 Leiguarda 4 C 7
20530 Leintz-Gatzaga 8 D 14
33818 Leiro 14 E 3
31880 Leitza 8 C 16
48280 Lekeitio 8 C 14

48330 Lemoa 7 C 14
15864 Lens 1 D 2
18699 Lentejí 66 Q 12
41630 Lentejuela 64 P 9
32372 Lentellais 15 E 5
24070 León 16 D 8
33390 Leorio 4 C 8
31395 Leoz 9 D 16
21440 Lepe 62 P 5
31639 Leranotz 9 D 16
36156 Lérez 13 E 2
31494 Lerga 9 D 17
31260 Lerín 20 E 16
09340 Lerma 18 E 12
01195 Lermanda 7 D 14
09141 Lermilla 18 D 12
25540 Lés 11 D 21
03700 Les Arenetes 61 M 20
25612 Les Avellanes 23 F 21
25400 Les Borges Blanques
23 F 21
43350 Les Borges del Camp
23 G 22
25528 Les Caldes de Boí
11 D 21
43569 Les Cases d'Alcanar
33 H 21
43569 Les Cases d'Alcanar
71 K 26
12570 Les Fonts 33 J 20
17515 les Llosses 12 E 24
25793 Les Masies 11 E 22
43596 Les Montcades
33 H 20
25214 Les Olugues 24 F 22
43817 Les Ordes 24 G 22
25212 les Pallargues 23 F 22
07609 Les Palmeres 71 L 25
46419 Les Palmeres/Sueca
43 L 19
43428 Les Piles de Gaià
24 F 22
17172 les Planes 34 G 21
17854 les Planes d' Hostoles
35 E 25
12004 Les Platgetes 44 J 20
43815 les Pobles 24 G 22
17178 Les Preses 35 E 24
03700 Les Rotes 61 M 20
17164 Les Serres 35 E 25
43860 Les Tres Cales
34 H 21
12118 Les Useres 44 J 19
43558 les Ventalles 33 H 20
25316 Les Ventoses 23 F 22
31770 Lesaka 8 C 16
15212 Lesende 1 D 2
27216 Lestedo/Palas de Rei
2 D 4
15881 Lestedo/Sales (San
Julián) 1 D 3
02424 Letur 59 N 15
50136 Letux 31 G 18
27688 Lexo 3 D 5
01309 Leza 7 D 14
26132 Leza de Río Leza
20 E 15
01450 Lezama/Amurrio
7 C 14
48196 Lezama/Arizgoiti
7 C 14
31177 Lezáun 8 D 16
02160 Lezuza 50 M 15
39527 Liandres 6 C 11
39692 Liaño 6 C 12
33325 Libardón 5 C 9
27664 Liber 3 D 5
11158 Libreros 69 R 8
30892 Librilla 60 O 17
44132 Libros 42 J 17
42341 Liceras 29 G 13
44164 Lidón 42 H 17
31487 Liédena 9 D 17
24994 Liegos 5 C 9
33580 Lieres 4 C 8

Lierta　　　　　　　　Ⓔ　　　　　　　　**Llesp**

22161 Lierta 22 E 19
2410 Liétor 59 M 16
42342 Ligos 29 G 13
22372 Ligüerre de Ara 10 E 19
04859 Líjar 68 P 15
45870 Lillo 49 K 13
24428 Lillo del Bierzo 15 D 6
39820 Limpias 7 C 13
15839 Linaio 1 D 2
49593 Linarejos 15 F 7
21207 Linares de la Sierra 63 O 6
44412 Linares de Mora 32 J 18
37760 Linares de Riofrio 37 H 8
23700 Linares/Bailén 57 N 12
33890 Linares/Pola de Altande 3 C 6
39580 Linares/Poles 5 C 10
33867 Linares/Salas 4 C 7
22378 Linás de Broto 10 D 19
22809 Linás de Marcuello 9 E 18
33116 Lindes 4 C 8
27742 Lindín 3 C 5
31696 Lintzoain 9 D 17
25240 Linyola 23 F 21
32520 Liñares/Bouza 14 E 3
27671 Liñares/Las Lamas 15 D 5
15292 Lira 1 D 1
15139 Lires 1 D 1
22466 Liri 11 D 21
50582 Litago 20 F 16
22585 Litera 11 E 21
49334 Litos 16 F 7
50581 Lituénigo 20 F 16
31829 Lizarraga/Altsasu-Alsasua 8 D 15
31421 Lizarraga/Pamplona-Iruña 9 D 17
31799 Lizaso 8 D 16
22809 Loarre 10 E 18
50687 Lobera de Onsella 9 E 17
06498 Lobón 53 M 6
30331 Lobosillo 60 O 17
18449 Lobras 67 Q 13
18820 Lobrega 58 O 15
42248 Lodares 30 G 15
42313 Lodares de Osma 29 F 13
42212 Lodares del Monte 30 G 14
33846 Lodón 4 C 7
31580 Lodosa 20 E 15
09131 Lodoso 18 E 12
28890 Loeches 40 J 13
26070 Logroño 20 E 15
10120 Logrosán 47 L 9
15339 Loiba 2 B 4
24991 Lois 5 D 9
48180 Loiu 7 C 14
18300 Loja 65 P 11
18270 Lojilla 66 P 11
09213 Lomana 7 D 13
34449 Lomas 17 E 10
24388 Lomba 15 E 6
39572 Lomeña 5 C 10
45212 Lominchar 39 J 12
47494 Lomoviejo 27 G 10
50460 Longares 21 G 17
50688 Longás 9 E 18
32160 Loña do Monte 14 E 4
14820 Lope Amargo 56 O 10
23780 Lopera 56 O 11
18517 Lópera 66 P 13
22192 Loporzano 22 E 19
41564 Lora de Estepa 65 P 10
41440 Lora del Río 64 O 8
19141 Loranca de Tajuña 40 J 13

16550 Loranca del Campo 40 J 14
09272 Loranquillo 19 E 13
31292 Lorca/Estella-Lizarra 8 D 16
30800 Lorca/Puerto Lombreras 68 O 16
03860 Lorcha 61 M 19
33682 Loredo/Oviedo 4 C 8
39160 Loredo/Santander 6 C 12
24122 Lorenzana 16 D 8
34848 Lores 5 D 10
18328 Loreto 66 P 12
33191 Loriana 4 C 8
46393 Loriguilla 43 L 18
30564 Lorquí 60 N 17
44563 Los Alagones 32 H 19
04640 Los Alamos 68 O 15
45138 Los Alares 48 L 10
04116 Los Albaricoques 68 Q 15
30710 Los Alcázares 60 O 18
02448 Los Alejos 59 M 15
14740 Los Ángeles/Alcolea 56 O 10
11339 Los Ángeles/Jimena de la Frontera 70 R 9
02140 Los Anguijes 51 M 16
31210 Los Arcos 20 D 15
30889 Los Arejos 68 P 16
41430 Los Arenales/Fuentes de Andalucía 64 P 9
14029 Los Arenales/Santa María de Trassierra 56 O 10
11179 Los Baladejos 69 R 8
09119 Los Balbases 18 E 11
03186 Los Balcones 60 O 18
30193 Los Baños de Mula 60 N 17
30310 Los Barreros 73 O 17
11170 Los Barrios 69 R 9
09246 Los Barrios de Bureba 7 D 13
24148 Los Barrios de Luna 4 D 8
30358 Los Belones 73 O 18
14208 Los Blázquez 55 N 9
21730 Los Cabezodos 63 P 6
30178 Los Calderones 60 O 17
12428 Los Calpes 43 J 18
30369 Los Camachos 60 O 18
11159 Los Caños de Meca 69 R 7
33592 Los Carriles 5 C 10
29533 Los Carvajales 65 P 10
04278 Los Castaños 68 P 15
02137 Los Catalmerejos 59 M 15
30817 Los Cautivos 59 O 16
44400 Los Cencerrosos 43 J 18
44422 Los Cerezos 43 J 18
45682 Los Cerralbos 38 K 10
04813 Los Cerricos 68 O 15
41510 Los Claveles 64 P 8
46354 Los Cojos 52 L 17
02449 Los Collados 59 N 15
41657 Los Corrales/Martín 64 P 10
39400 Los Corrales/Torrelavega 6 C 11
46313 Los Corrales/Utiel 52 K 17
13427 Los Cortijos/Porzuna 48 L 11
16318 Los Cortijos/Teruel 42 J 17
30876 Los Curas 73 O 17
04810 Los Chacones 68 P 15

41728 Los Chapatales 63 P 8
30810 Los Chillidos 59 O 16
14817 Los Chirimeros 65 P 11
02340 Los Chospes 50 M 15
30310 Los Dolores 73 O 17
46352 Los Duque 52 L 17
23740 Los Escoriales 57 N 12
04118 Los Escullos 68 Q 15
30880 Los Estrechos 68 P 16
50513 Los Fayos 20 F 16
04280 Los Gallardos 68 P 16
11139 Los Gallos 69 R 7
04820 Los Gázquez 68 O 16
04289 Los Giles 68 P 15
06713 Los Guadalperales 47 L 8
18614 Los Gualchos 66 Q 13
30333 Los Guerreros 60 O 17
04647 Los Guiraos 68 P 16
16417 Los Hinojosos 50 K 14
30510 Los Hitos 52 M 17
28810 Los Hueros 40 J 13
04490 Los Huertos 28 G 11
42291 Los Llamosos 30 F 14
02070 Los Llanos 51 M 16
57023 Los Llanos de Ignacio 69 Q 8
39450 Los Llares 6 C 11
46310 Los Marcos 52 L 17
30156 Los Martinez 60 O 17
44479 Los Mases 43 J 18
13739 Los Mirones 57 M 12
41750 Los Molares 64 P 8
04858 Los Molinas 68 P 15
22338 Los Molinos/Ainsa 10 E 20
28460 Los Molinos/Cercedilla 39 H 11
29600 Los Monteros 70 Q 10
03187 Los Montesinos 60 N 18
18564 Los Morales 66 P 12
14299 Los Morenos 55 N 9
18440 Los Morenos 67 Q 13
44479 Los Moyas 43 J 18
45140 Los Navalmorales 48 K 10
45130 Los Navalucillos 48 K 10
11158 Los Naveros 69 R 8
28409 Los Negrales 39 H 11
30390 Los Nietos/El Algar 73 O 18
04117 Los Nietos/Retamar 68 Q 15
41620 Los Ojuelos 64 P 9
44557 Los Olmos/Andorra 32 H 19
18810 Los Olmos/Caniles 67 P 14
44557 Los Olmos/Manzanera 43 J 18
14730 Los Ortegas 55 O 9
16340 Los Oteros 41 J 16
41720 Los Palacios y Villafranca 63 P 8
14249 Los Pánchez 55 N 9
02320 Los Partidores 51 M 15
23350 Los Pascuales 58 N 14
46355 Los Pedrones 52 L 17
28250 Los Peñascales 39 H 12
04619 Los Perdigones 68 P 16
41599 Los Pérez 65 P 10
14511 Los Piedros 65 P 10
10137 Los Pinos 47 L 9
02129 Los Pocicos 51 M 16
13179 Los Pozuelos de Calatrava 48 M 11
14800 Los Prados 65 P 11
02612 Los Puercos 50 L 14
13428 Los Quiles 48 L 12
42191 Los Rábanos 30 F 15

28791 Los Rancajales 39 H 12
41330 Los Rosales 64 O 8
30411 Los Royos 59 O 15
06929 Los Rubios 55 N 8
26145 Los Ruedas de Ocón 20 E 15
30334 Los Ruices/Mazarrón 73 O 17
46353 Los Ruices/Requena 52 L 17
37768 Los Santos 37 H 8
28817 Los Santos de la Humosa 40 H 13
06230 Los Santos de Maimona 54 N 7
46354 Los Sardineros 52 L 17
18418 Los Tablones 66 Q 13
39518 Los Tojos 6 C 11
29130 Los Tomillares 65 Q 10
04827 Los Tonosas 68 O 15
09150 Los Tremellos 18 D 12
30858 Los Tuelas 60 O 17
09125 Los Valcárceles 18 D 12
30627 Los Valientes 60 N 17
28500 Los Villares 40 J 13
23160 Los Villares/Andújar 57 N 12
23160 Los Villares/Jaén 66 O 12
45470 Los Yébenes 49 K 12
02070 Los Yesares 51 L 16
46168 Losa del Obispo 43 K 18
49541 Losacino 26 F 7
24318 Losada 15 D 7
24746 Losadilla 15 E 6
40192 Losana de Pirón 28 G 11
10460 Losar de la Vera 37 J 8
22809 Loscorrales 22 E 18
44493 Loscos 31 G 17
36876 Lougares 13 E 3
15310 Lourdes 2 C 3
15822 Loureda 1 D 3
27865 Loureiro 2 B 4
36779 Lourenza 13 F 2
27760 Lourenzá (San Adriano) 3 C 5
36647 Louro/Enfesta 13 D 2
15291 Louro/Muros 1 D 1
27185 Lousada (Santabaia) 2 D 4
15214 Lousame 1 D 2
28742 Lozoya 28 H 12
28752 Lozoyuela 28 H 12
33440 Luanco 4 B 8
33700 Luarca 3 B 6
42290 Lubia 30 F 14
49570 Lubián 15 E 6
04271 Lubrín 68 P 15
04210 Lucainena de las Torres 68 P 15
04887 Lúcar 67 P 15
14900 Lucena 65 P 11
50294 Lucena de Jalón 21 F 17
12120 Lucena del Cid 43 J 19
50640 Luceni 21 F 17
32688 Lucenza 14 F 4
33328 Luces 5 B 9
15883 Luci 1 D 2
13108 Luciana 48 M 11
24271 Lucillo 16 E 7
45684 Lucillos 38 K 10
44563 Luco de Bordón 32 H 19
44391 Luco de Jiloca 31 H 17
12123 Luco de Jiloca 43 J 19
49215 Luelmo 26 G 7
50619 Luesia 9 E 17
50151 Luesma 31 G 17
39594 Luey 6 C 11

46668 Lugar Nuevo de Fenollet 61 L 19
27070 Lugo 2 C 4
18516 Lugros 66 P 13
24843 Lugueros 5 D 9
32160 Luintra 14 E 4
33156 Luiña 4 B 7
18614 Lújar 66 Q 13
01139 Lukiao 7 D 14
24140 Lumajo 4 D 7
31440 Lumbier 9 D 17
37240 Lumbrales 25 H 6
26126 Lumbreras 19 E 14
32764 Lumeares 14 E 5
42368 Lumias 29 G 14
50295 Lumpiaque 21 F 17
50610 Luna/Ejea de los Caballeros 21 E 18
01439 Luna/Urcabustaiz 7 D 14
21730 Luneda 13 E 3
15883 Luou 1 D 2
19142 Lupiana 40 H 13
22811 Lupiñén 22 E 18
23526 Lupión 57 O 12
14880 Luque 65 O 11
31243 Luquin 8 D 15
24568 Lusio 15 D 6
01408 Luxaondo 7 C 14
24717 Luyego 16 E 7
19261 Luzaga 30 H 15
31660 Luzaide-Valcarlos 9 C 17
22585 Luzás 11 E 21
39509 Luzmela 6 C 11
19285 Luzón 30 G 15

Ll
43320 Llaberia 23 G 21
17745 Lladó 35 E 25
25576 Lladorre 11 D 22
25576 Lladrós 11 D 22
25283 Lladurs 12 E 23
17211 Llafranc 35 F 26
17240 Llagostera 35 F 25
22474 Llagunas 11 E 21
25566 Llagunes 11 E 22
24271 Llamas de la Ribera 16 D 8
24161 Llamas de Rueda 17 D 9
33816 Llamas del Mouro 4 C 7
33829 Llamero 4 C 7
33591 Llames 5 C 10
17869 Llanars 35 E 24
24912 Llanaves de la Reina 5 C 10
17490 Llança 35 E 26
46814 Llanera de Ranes 52 M 18
33500 Llanes 5 C 10
09127 Llanillo 6 D 11
39416 Llano 6 D 12
30161 Llano de Brujas 60 N 17
09246 Llano de Bureba 7 D 13
47418 Llano de Olmedo 27 G 10
13220 Llanos del Caudillo 49 L 13
33117 Llanuces 4 C 8
25186 Llardecans 23 G 21
46613 Llaurí 61 L 19
25595 Llavorsí 11 E 22
44624 Lledó 33 H 20
25070 Lleida 23 F 21
06227 Llera 54 N 7
33546 Llerandi 5 C 9
06900 Llerena 54 N 7
17730 Llers 35 E 25
22451 Llert 11 E 20
25726 Lles 12 E 23
25526 Llesp 11 E 21

Llesui · E · **Matute**

25567 Llesui 11 E 22
03729 Llíber 61 M 20
08186 Lliçà d`Amunt 24 F 24
25639 Llimiana 11 E 21
25217 Llinars 12 E 22
08450 Llinars del Vallès
35 F 24
46160 Llíria 43 K 18
17527 Llívia 12 E 23
43737 Lloà 23 G 21
25794 Llobera/La Seu d`Urgell
12 E 22
25281 Llobera/Solsona
24 F 22
46726 Llocnou de Sant Jeroni
61 M 19
01400 Llodio 7 C 14
07124 Llofriu 35 F 26
46195 Llombai 43 L 18
24609 Llombera 4 D 8
33578 Llonín 5 C 10
17152 Llora 35 E 25
43427 Llorac 24 F 22
25657 Llordà 11 E 22
39694 Lloreda 6 C 12
25267 Llorenç de Vallbona
23 F 22
43712 Llorenç del Penedès
24 G 23
09511 Llorengoz 7 D 13
17310 Lloret Blau 35 F 25
17310 Lloret de Mar 35 F 25
07518 Lloret de Vista Alegre
71 K 25
17170 Lloret Salvatge 35 F 25
46815 Llosa de Ranes
52 L 18
07360 Lloseta 71 K 25
33795 Llosoiro 3 C 6
07430 Llubí 71 K 26
07315 Lluc 71 K 25
08514 Lluçà 12 E 24
07749 Llucalari 72 K 28
07179 Llucalcari 71 K 25
07620 Llucmajor 71 L 25
46838 Llutxent 61 M 19

M
17843 Ma Mota 35 E 25
04867 Macael 68 P 15
17720 Maçanet de Cabrenys
35 E 25
17412 Maçanet de la Selva
35 F 25
46368 Macastre 43 L 18
32700 Maceda/Montederramo
14 E 4
27163 Maceda/Puebla de San
Xulián 2 D 5
36873 Maceira 13 E 3
36518 Maceiras 14 D 3
15937 Macenda 1 D 2
32231 Macendo 14 E 3
34131 Macintos 17 E 10
30648 Macisvenda 60 N 17
37310 Macotera 27 H 9
37893 Machacón 26 H 8
28755 Madarcos 28 G 12
32534 Madarnás 14 E 3
40554 Maderuelo 29 G 12
17462 Madremanya 35 F 25
28070 Madrid 39 J 12
45710 Madridejos 49 L 12
19277 Madrigal 29 G 14
10480 Madrigal de la Vera
37 J 9
05220 Madrigal de las Altas
Torres 27 G 10
09320 Madrigal del Monte
18 E 12
10110 Madrigalejo 47 L 8
09390 Madrigalejo del Monte
18 E 12
40510 Madriguera 29 G 13
02230 Madrigueras 51 L 16

40154 Madrona 28 H 11
10210 Madroñera 46 L 8
42315 Madruedano 29 G 13
50710 Maella 32 G 20
05291 Maello 27 H 10
25317 Mafet 23 F 22
06468 Magacela 54 M 8
50520 Magallón 21 F 17
45590 Magán 39 K 12
42181 Magaña 20 F 15
24396 Magaz de Cepeda
16 D 7
05216 Magazos/Arévalo
27 G 10
27850 Magazos/Viveiro
2 B 4
06939 Maguilla 54 N 8
09228 Mahamud 18 E 12
49522 Mahide 16 F 7
02240 Mahora 51 L 16
30649 Mahoya 60 N 17
17851 Maià de Montcal
35 E 25
25179 Maials 23 G 21
44791 Maicas 31 H 18
50368 Mainar 31 G 17
27742 Maior 3 C 5
18494 Mairena 67 P 13
41510 Mairena del Alcor
64 P 8
41927 Mairena del Aljarafe
63 P 7
28220 Majadahonda 39 J 12
10529 Majadas 37 K 8
19223 Majaelrayo 29 G 13
42225 Maján 30 G 15
22771 Majones 9 D 18
18130 Malá 66 P 12
25215 Malacara 24 F 22
19413 Malacuera 40 H 14
29070 Málaga 65 Q 11
19219 Málaga del Fresno
40 H 13
13420 Malagón 49 L 12
19219 Malaguilla 29 H 13
50315 Malanquilla 30 F 16
32161 Malburguete 14 E 4
11179 Malcocinado/Benalup
69 R 8
06928 Malcocinado/
Guadalcanal
54 N 8
25266 Maldà 23 F 22
50549 Malejàn 21 F 16
08380 Malgrat de Mar 35 F 25
39600 Maliaño 6 C 12
24339 Malillos 17 E 9
08519 Malla 24 F 24
48269 Mallabia 8 C 14
46117 Mallaetes 43 K 19
33866 Mallecina 4 C 7
50550 Mallén 21 F 17
33866 Malleza 4 C 7
50511 Malón 20 F 16
37313 Malpartida 38 H 9
10910 Malpartida de Cáceres
46 L 6
05153 Malpartida de Corneja
37 H 9
06440 Malpartida de la Serena
55 M 8
10680 Malpartida de Plasencia
37 K 7
25529 Malpàs 11 E 21
15113 Malpica 1 C 2
50695 Malpica de Arba
21 E 17
45692 Malpica de Tajo 38 K 10
50340 Maluenda 31 G 16
40554 Maluque 28 F 12
49832 Malva 26 F 9
05298 Mamblas 27 G 9
09511 Mambliga 7 D 13
09317 Mambrilla de Castejón
28 F 12

09640 Mambrillas de Lara
19 E 13
50696 Mamillas 9 E 17
09612 Mamolar 19 F 13
07500 Manacor 71 K 26
48212 Mañaria 7 C 14
37315 Mancera de Abajo
27 H 9
05146 Mancera de Arriba
27 H 9
50366 Manchones 31 G 17
09133 Manciles 18 E 12
07312 Mancor de la Vall
71 K 25
23100 Mancha Real 57 O 12
06478 Manchita 54 M 7
19294 Mandayona 29 H 14
15595 Mandiá 2 B 3
32698 Mandín 14 F 5
49130 Manganeses de la
Lampreana 26 F 8
49694 Manganeses de la
Polvorosa 16 E 8
29691 Manilva 70 R 9
46980 Manises 43 L 19
05145 Manjabálago 38 H 9
24722 Manjarín 16 E 7
26315 Manjarrés 19 E 14
28754 Manjirón 28 H 12
08560 Manlleu 12 F 24
08240 Manresa 24 F 23
09150 Mansilla de Burgos
18 E 12
26329 Mansilla de la Sierra
19 E 14
24210 Mansilla de las Mulas
17 D 9
24217 Mansilla Mayor 17 D 9
19128 Mantiel 41 H 14
34889 Mantinos 5 D 10
46660 Manuel 61 L 19
01138 Manurga 7 D 14
32548 Manzalvos 15 F 5
49594 Manzanal de Arriba
15 F 7
49317 Manzanal de los
Infantes 16 E 7
13200 Manzanares 49 M 13
28410 Manzanares el Real
39 H 12
24891 Manzaneda de Torío
16 D 8
24738 Manzaneda/Destriana
16 E 7
33669 Manzaneda/Oviedo
4 C 8
32781 Manzaneda/Puebla de
Trives 15 E 5
09558 Manzanedo 6 D 12
45460 Manzaneque 49 K 12
44420 Manzanera 43 J 18
16339 Manzaneruela 42 K 17
21890 Manzanilla 63 P 7
47314 Manzanillo 28 F 11
13130 Mañeru 8 D 16
15339 Mañón 2 B 4
07700 Maó/Mahón 72 K 28
45515 Maqueda 39 J 11
33315 Mar 5 B 9
50331 Mara 31 G 16
18200 Maracena 66 P 12
19280 Maranchón 30 G 15
24996 Maraña 5 C 9
13720 Marañón/Alcázar de
San Juan 49 L 13
31227 Marañón/Logroño
8 D 15
09216 Marauri 7 D 14
40130 Marazoleja 28 H 11
42213 Marazovel 29 G 14
40133 Marazuela 28 H 11
29600 Marbella 70 Q 10
43775 Marça 23 G 21
31193 Marcalain 8 D 16
22268 Marcén 22 F 19

10662 Marchagaz 36 J 7
19180 Marchamalo 40 H 13
41620 Marchena 64 P 9
11339 Marchenilla 70 R 9
31340 Marcilla 20 E 16
34469 Marcilla de Campos
18 E 11
27164 Marei 2 D 5
33811 Marentes 3 C 6
46419 Mareny Blau 43 L 19
46419 Mareny de Barraquetes
43 L 19
46408 Mareny de Vilxes
43 L 19
46408 Mareny Sant Llorenç
43 L 19
30393 Marfagones 73 O 17
43371 Margalef de Montsant
23 G 21
33547 Margolles 5 C 9
04838 María 59 O 15
50430 María de Huerva
21 F 18
07519 María de la Salud
71 K 26
16143 Mariana 41 J 15
41727 Maribáñez 63 P 8
01260 Marieta 8 D 14
21647 Marigenta 63 O 6
02252 Marimínguez 51 L 17
36900 Marín 13 E 2
41569 Marinaleda 64 P 10
46169 Marines 43 K 18
27308 Mariz 2 C 4
45479 Marjaliza 49 K 12
01139 Markina 7 D 14
01216 Markiz 8 D 14
05140 Marlín 38 H 10
09131 Marmellar de Abajo
18 E 12
09131 Marmellar de Arriba
18 E 12
23770 Marmolejo 56 N 11
29787 Maro 66 Q 12
15256 Maroñas 1 D 2
01479 Maroño 7 C 13
50616 Marracos 21 E 18
45636 Marrupe 38 J 10
22772 Martes 9 D 18
37510 Martiago 36 J 7
42134 Martialay 30 F 15
27276 Martín 3 C 5
41658 Martín de la Jara
64 P 10
37494 Martín de Yeltes
26 H 7
44750 Martín del Río 31 H 18
23210 Martín Malo 57 N 12
40130 Martín Miguel 28 H 11
40466 Martín Muñoz de la
Dehesa 27 G 10
40446 Martín Muñoz de las
Posadas 27 H 10
37891 Martinamor 26 H 8
25724 Martinet 12 E 23
05151 Martínez 37 H 9
33527 Martinporra 4 C 8
08760 Martorell 24 G 23
08107 Martorelles 24 F 24
23600 Martos 57 O 12
33777 Martul 3 C 5
40142 Marugán 28 H 11
48112 Maruri 7 C 14
07872 Maryland 72 M 23
17493 Marza 35 E 26
47133 Marzales 27 F 9
24133 Marzan 16 D 7
12119 Mas d`Avall 44 J 19
43514 Mas de Barberans
33 H 20
12191 Mas de Flors 44 J 19
44132 Mas de la Cabrera
42 J 17
44566 Mas de las Altas
32 H 19

44564 Mas de las Matas
32 H 19
12165 Mas de les Solanes
32 J 19
12469 Mas de los Pérez
43 K 18
12135 Mas de Pesetes
32 J 19
46140 Mas del Olmo 42 J 17
44430 Mas del Señor 43 J 18
12190 Mas Vilarrelo 44 J 19
09142 Masa 18 D 12
12469 Masada del Sordo
43 K 18
46292 Masalavés 52 L 18
17763 Masarac 35 E 25
45430 Mascaraque 49 K 12
43878 Masdenverge 33 H 21
16878 Masegosa 41 H 15
02136 Masegosillo 58 M 15
19490 Masegoso de Tajuña
29 H 14
02314 Masegoso/Alcaraz
59 M 15
44123 Masegoso/Toril 42 J 16
17538 Masella 12 E 23
12120 Masia del Moro 43 J 19
32570 Maside 14 E 3
43718 Masllorenç 24 G 22
43382 Maspujols 23 G 22
08783 Masquefa 24 F 23
43891 Masriudoms 34 G 21
25184 Massalcoreig 23 G 20
46560 Massalfasar 43 K 19
46130 Massamagrell 43 K 19
17452 Massanes 35 F 25
25211 Massoteres 24 F 22
37251 Masueco 25 G 6
39409 Mata 6 C 11
10970 Mata de Alcántara
45 K 6
40214 Mata de Cuéllar
28 G 11
39418 Mata de Hoz 6 D 11
40163 Matabuena 28 G 12
24291 Matadeón de los Oteros
17 E 9
08230 Matadepera 24 F 24
24495 Matalavilla 4 D 7
42113 Matalebreras 20 F 15
09198 Matalindo 19 E 13
24836 Matallana de Torío
4 D 8
24357 Matalobos del Páramo
16 E 8
28492 Matalpino 39 H 12
17515 Matamala 12 E 24
42211 Matamala de Almazßn
29 F 14
39200 Matamorosa 6 D 11
24207 Matanza 17 E 9
42351 Matanza de Soria
29 F 13
39410 Mataporquera 6 D 11
47230 Matapozuelos 27 G 10
08300 Mataró 35 F 24
24460 Matarrosa 15 D 6
19237 Matarrubia 29 H 13
42175 Matasejún 20 F 15
12415 Matet 43 K 19
18859 Matián 67 O 15
39812 Matienzo/Colindres
6 C 12
48891 Matienzo/Ramalesa de
la Victoria 7 C 13
49692 Matilla de Arzón
16 E 8
47114 Matilla de los Caños
27 F 10
37450 Matilla de los Caños del
Río 26 H 8
49590 Matilla la Seca 26 F 9
19294 Matillas 29 H 14
27375 Mato 2 C 4
26321 Matute 19 E 14

Matute de Almazán   (E)   **Montcada i Reixac**   E

42211 Matute de Almazán 29 G 14
48391 Mauma 7 C 14
32880 Maus de Salas 14 F 4
34492 Mave 6 D 11
49718 Mayalde 26 G 8
47680 Mayorga 17 E 9
21130 Mazagón 62 P 6
44621 Mazaleón 33 G 20
42130 Mazalvete 30 F 15
45114 Mazarambroz 48 K 11
19286 Mazarete 30 G 15
34170 Mazariegos 17 E 10
30870 Mazarrón 73 O 17
16510 Mazarulleque 40 J 14
42126 Mazaterón 30 F 15
09114 Mazueco 19 E 13
19114 Mazuecos 40 J 13
34306 Mazuecos de Valdeginate 17 E 10
09228 Mazuela 18 E 12
09239 Mazuelo de Muñó 18 E 12
48115 Meakaur 7 C 14
09215 Meana 7 D 14
12133 Meanes 32 J 19
15145 Meáns 1 C 2
36557 Meavia 13 D 3
09346 Mecerreyes 18 E 12
18450 Mecina-Bombarón 67 Q 13
28880 Meco 40 H 13
32368 Meda 15 E 5
32618 Medeiros 14 F 4
06411 Medellín 46 M 8
50135 Mediana de Aragón 21 G 18
05194 Mediana de Voltoya 38 H 10
06320 Medina de las Torres 54 N 7
09500 Medina de Pomar 7 D 13
47800 Medina de Rioseco 17 F 9
47400 Medina del Campo 27 G 10
11170 Medina Sidonia 69 R 8
42240 Medinaceli 30 G 15
05619 Medinilla 37 J 8
08773 Mediona 24 G 23
19246 Medranda 29 H 14
26374 Medrano 20 E 14
34208 Megaz de Pisuerga 18 F 11
47440 Megeces 27 G 10
19315 Megina 41 H 16
27296 Meilán 3 C 5
27240 Meira/Castro de Rei 3 C 5
36955 Meira/Moaña 13 E 2
15550 Meirás 2 B 3
27558 Meixonfrío 2 D 4
45622 Mejorada 38 J 10
28840 Mejorada del Campo 40 J 13
02070 Melegriz 51 M 16
33528 Melendreros 4 C 8
47687 Melgar de Abajo 17 E 9
47686 Melgar de Arriba 17 E 9
09100 Melgar de Fernamental 18 E 11
49626 Melgar de Tera 16 F 7
34259 Melgar de Yuso 18 E 11
46133 Meliana 43 K 19
32711 Melias 14 E 4
18750 Melicena 66 Q 13
31382 Mélida 9 E 16
15800 Melide 2 D 3
32411 Melón 14 E 3
49512 Mellanes 26 F 7

24165 Mellanzos 17 D 9
40234 Membibre de la Hoz 28 G 11
13230 Membrilla 49 M 13
19247 Membrillera 29 H 14
21647 Membrillo Alto 63 O 6
10580 Membrío 45 K 5
25139 Menàrguens 23 F 21
45128 Menasalbas 48 K 11
48382 Mendata 7 C 14
31587 Mendavia 20 E 15
31282 Mendaza 8 D 15
31150 Mendigorría 8 D 16
32789 Mendoia 15 E 5
01191 Mendoza 7 D 14
34305 Meneses de Campos 17 F 10
06413 Mengabril 46 M 8
05131 Mengamuñoz 38 J 9
23620 Mengibar 57 O 12
41600 Menjillán 64 P 8
01477 Menoio 7 C 13
39812 Mentera-Barruelo 7 C 13
45930 Méntrida 39 J 11
31481 Meoz 9 D 17
50170 Mequinenza 23 G 20
27233 Mera/Lugo 2 D 4
15349 Mera/Ortigueira 2 B 4
17539 Merange 12 E 23
05154 Mercadillo/Piedrahita 37 H 9
48190 Mercadillo/Santurtzi 7 C 13
02510 Mercadillos de Abajo 51 M 16
33508 Meré 5 C 10
33779 Meredo 3 C 5
06800 Mérida 46 M 7
39728 Merilla 6 C 12
27866 Merille 2 B 4
27205 Merlán 2 D 4
22482 Merli 11 E 20
33579 Merodio 5 C 10
24141 Meroy 4 D 7
33686 Mérujal 4 C 8
36580 Merza 2 D 3
11590 Mesas de Asta 69 Q 7
45541 Mesegar 38 K 10
05514 Mesegar de Corneja 38 H 9
15685 Mesía 2 C 3
32516 Mesiego 14 E 3
32691 Mesón de Calvos 14 E 4
15689 Mesón do Vento 1 C 3
50267 Mesones de Isuela 21 F 16
02449 Mesones/Riópar 58 N 15
19185 Mesones/Torrelaguna 40 H 13
48903 Mespelerreka 7 C 13
13592 Mestanza 57 M 11
33507 Mestas 5 C 10
48120 Mesterika 7 C 14
31241 Metauten 8 D 15
50152 Mezalocha 21 G 17
42213 Mezquetillas 30 G 14
44169 Mezquita de Jarque 32 H 18
44493 Mezquita de Loscos 31 G 17
10100 Miajadas 46 L 8
50683 Mianos 9 D 18
49624 Micereces de Terra 16 F 8
34485 Micieces de Ojeda 6 D 11
50330 Miedes 31 G 17
19276 Miedes de Atienza 29 G 14
39310 Miengo 6 C 12
17830 Mieres 35 E 25

33600 Mieres del Camino-Mieres del Camín 4 C 8
37254 Mieza 25 G 6
45830 Miguel Esteban 50 K 13
40494 Miguel Ibáñez 28 G 11
40441 Migueláñez 28 G 11
13170 Miguelturra 49 M 12
01211 Mijancas 7 D 14
05461 Mijares 38 J 10
29650 Mijas 70 Q 10
31320 Milagro 20 E 16
09460 Milagros 28 F 12
37256 Milano 25 G 6
19287 Milmarcos 30 G 16
19127 Millana 41 H 14
10394 Millanes 37 K 8
46199 Millares 43 L 18
03812 Millena 61 M 19
49699 Milles de la Polvorosa 16 F 8
21270 Minas de Cala 63 O 7
14449 Minas de Horcajo 56 M 11
21660 Minas de Riotinto 63 O 6
45672 Minas de Santa Quiteria 47 L 10
02499 Minateda 59 N 16
02620 Minaya 50 L 15
16260 Minglanilla 51 K 16
02409 Mingogil 59 N 16
05280 Mingorria 38 H 10
13592 Minos Diógenes 56 M 11
42126 Miñana 30 F 15
34127 Miñanes 17 E 10
01510 Miñao Barren 7 D 14
42230 Miño de Medinaceli 30 G 14
42328 Miño de San Esteban 29 F 13
09513 Miñón 18 E 12
15218 Miñortos 1 D 2
27865 Miñotos 2 B 4
01427 Mioma 7 D 13
22393 Mipanas 22 E 20
16393 Mira 51 K 17
10540 Mirabel 36 K 7
19268 Mirabueno 29 H 14
28210 Mirador del Romero 39 J 11
03779 Miraflor 61 M 20
11369 Miraflores 69 Q 7
28792 Miraflores de la Sierra 28 H 12
31219 Mirafuentes 8 D 15
25242 Miralcamp 23 F 21
02070 Miralcampo 51 L 16
19246 Miralrío 29 H 14
22529 Miralsot 22 F 20
44141 Mirambel 32 H 19
27144 Miranda 3 D 5
31253 Miranda de Arga 20 E 16
37187 Miranda de Azán 26 H 8
42191 Miranda de Duero 30 F 15
42213 Miranda de Ebro 7 D 14
37660 Miranda del Castañar 37 J 8
23213 Miranda del Rey 57 N 12
06891 Mirandilla 46 M 7
24147 Mirantes 4 D 8
09280 Miraveche 7 D 13
43747 Miravet 33 G 21
44159 Miravete de la Sierra 32 H 18
27833 Miraz 2 C 4
05191 Mironcillo 38 H 10
39725 Mirones 6 C 12

05146 Miruena de los Infanzones 38 H 9
33758 Miudes 3 B 6
33583 Miyares 5 C 9
36950 Moaña 13 E 2
15686 Moar 2 C 3
45270 Mocejón 39 K 12
18247 Moclín 66 P 12
41440 Mochales/Lora del Rio 64 O 8
19332 Mochales/Maranchón 30 G 15
24815 Modino 5 D 9
09620 Modúbar de la Emparedada 18 E 12
09194 Modúbar de San Cibrián 18 E 12
37610 Mogarraz 37 J 7
36911 Mogor 13 E 2
39310 Mogro 6 C 12
21800 Moguer 62 P 6
02600 Moharras 50 L 15
45576 Mohedas de la Jara 47 K 9
19226 Mohernando 29 H 13
16193 Mohorte 41 J 15
08180 Moià 24 F 24
46640 Moixent-Mogente 52 M 18
04638 Mojácar 68 P 16
47250 Mojados 27 G 10
19264 Mojares 30 G 14
49120 Molacillos 26 F 8
33769 Moldes 3 B 5
49521 Moldones 15 F 7
49327 Molezuelas de la Carballeda 16 E 7
12135 Moli Azor 32 J 19
19300 Molina de Aragón 30 H 16
30500 Molina de Segura 60 N 17
24413 Molinaseca 15 D 6
02440 Molinicos 59 N 15
01213 Molinilla 7 D 14
37683 Molinillo 37 J 8
11180 Molino Castro 69 R 8
22623 Molino de Villobas 10 E 19
44556 Molinos 32 H 19
42156 Molinos de Duero 19 F 14
16192 Molinos de Papel 41 J 15
42165 Molinos de Razón 20 F 14
08750 Molins de Rei 24 G 24
39430 Molledo 6 C 11
25230 Mollerussa 23 F 21
08100 Mollet del Vallès 24 F 24
29532 Mollina 65 P 10
48879 Mollinedo 7 C 13
17868 Molló 35 E 24
18611 Molvízar 66 Q 12
27378 Momán/Feira do Monte 2 C 5
27826 Momán/Vilalba 2 C 4
42225 Momblona 30 G 15
49310 Mombuey 16 E 7
09512 Momediano 7 D 13
18193 Monachil 66 P 12
09613 Monasterio de la Sierra 19 E 13
09292 Monasterio de Rodilla 19 E 13
47688 Monasterio de Vega 17 E 9
42291 Monasterio/Izana 29 F 14
19239 Monasterio/Veguillas 29 H 13
01194 Monasterioguren 7 D 14

46113 Moncada 43 K 19
39791 Moncalián 7 C 12
09691 Moncalvillo 19 F 13
16520 Moncavillo del Huete 40 J 14
03149 Moncayo 60 N 18
27730 Moncelos 2 C 5
12003 Moncófar 44 K 19
29110 Monda 70 Q 10
36890 Mondareiz Balneario 13 E 3
36870 Mondariz 13 E 3
19110 Mondéjar 40 J 13
27748 Mondoñedo 3 C 5
24892 Mondreganes 5 D 9
27271 Mondriz 2 C 5
50164 Monegrillo 22 F 19
17721 Monells 35 F 26
09515 Moneo 7 D 13
22587 Monesma/Graus 11 E 21
22587 Monesma/Monzón 22 F 20
06260 Monesterio 54 N 7
50144 Moneva 31 G 18
49121 Monfarracinos 26 F 8
15618 Monfero (Santa Xuliana) 2 C 3
22111 Monflorite 22 E 19
27400 Monforte 14 D 4
44493 Monforte de Moyuela 31 G 17
03670 Monforte del Cid 60 N 18
08275 Monistrol de Calders 24 F 24
08691 Monistrol de Montserrat 24 F 23
37765 Monleón 37 H 8
37171 Monleras 26 G 7
03115 Monnegre 61 N 19
03640 Monovar/Monover 60 N 18
31471 Monreal 9 D 16
50291 Monreal de Ariza 30 G 15
44300 Monreal del Campo 31 H 17
16649 Monreal del Llano 50 K 14
10194 Monroy 46 K 7
44652 Monroyo 32 H 19
37532 Monsagro 36 H 7
05163 Monsalupe 38 H 10
46192 Monserrat 43 L 18
22482 Mont de Roda 11 E 21
46892 Montaberner 61 M 19
17855 Montagut 35 E 25
44700 Montalbán 31 H 18
14548 Montalbán de Córdoba 65 O 10
16434 Montalbanejo 50 K 15
16440 Montalbo 41 K 14
43421 Montalegre 24 G 22
02638 Montalvos 51 L 15
49149 Montamarta 26 F 8
25795 Montan 12 E 22
12447 Montán 43 J 18
10170 Montánchez 46 L 7
12448 Montanejos 43 J 18
22487 Montanuy 11 E 21
22584 Montañana/Tremp 11 E 21
50003 Montañana/Zaragoza 21 F 18
25738 Montargull 23 F 22
19229 Montarrón 29 H 13
42174 Montaves 20 E 15
43400 Montblanc 23 G 22
43425 Montbrió de la Marca 24 G 22
43340 Montbrió del Camp 23 G 22
08110 Montcada i Reixac 24 G 24

105

I N D E X · O R T S R E G I S T E R · I N D I C E · Í N D I
P L A A T S N A M E N R E G I S T E R · R E J S T Ř Í K   M Í S

Montclar   E   **Narboneta**

08614 Montclar 12 E 23
25317 Montclar d'Urgell
         23 F 22
47359 Monte Alto 28 F 11
19170 Monte Calderón
         40 H 13
27210 Monte de Meda 2 D 4
19237 Monte Hueco 29 H 13
22536 Monte Julia 22 F 20
23615 Monte López Álvarez
         56 O 11
22351 Monte Perdido 10 D 20
28596 Monte Robledal
         40 J 13
46389 Monte Tesoro 43 L 18
27879 Monte/Cervo 2 B 5
15560 Monte/Gandara 2 B 3
15839 Monte/Negreira 1 D 2
31522 Monteagudo 20 F 16
16360 Monteagudo de las
         Salinas 41 K 16
42220 Monteagudo de las
         Vicarías 30 G 15
44146 Monteagudo del
         Castillo 32 J 18
47816 Montealegre 17 F 10
02650 Montealegre del
         Castillo 52 M 17
14740 Montealto 55 O 9
45685 Montearagón 38 K 10
39250 Montecillo 6 D 12
29430 Montecorto 70 Q 9
27128 Montecubeiro 3 C 5
32750 Montederramo 14 E 4
18270 Montefrío 66 P 11
27390 Montefurado 15 E 5
10810 Montehermoso 36 J 7
29360 Montejaque 70 Q 9
18561 Montejícar 66 O 12
37795 Montejo 37 H 8
40468 Montejo de Arévalo
         27 G 10
09571 Montejo de Bricia
         6 D 12
28190 Montejo de la Sierra
         29 G 12
40542 Montejo de la Vega de
         la Serrezuela
         28 F 12
42341 Montejo de Tiermes
         29 G 13
41770 Montellano/Puerto
         69 Q 8
48191 Montellano/Santurtzi
         7 C 13
47320 Montemayor de Pililla
         28 F 11
37727 Montemayor del Río
         37 J 8
02329 Montemayor/Alcaraz
         59 M 15
14530 Montemayor/Montilla
         65 O 10
06291 Montemolín 54 N 7
25594 Montenartró 11 E 22
26127 Montenegro de
         Cameros 19 E 14
50213 Monterde 30 G 16
44368 Monterde de Albarracín
         42 H 17
32228 Monterredondo 14 E 3
32611 Monterrei 14 F 5
27560 Monterroso 2 D 4
40142 Monterrubio 28 H 11
09615 Monterrubio de
         Demanda 19 E 13
06427 Monterrubio de la
         Serena 55 M 9
37788 Monterrubio de la
         Sierra 26 H 8
33584 Montes 5 C 9
24415 Montes de Valdueza
         15 E 6
46692 Montesa 52 M 18
45620 Montesclaros 38 J 10

08585 Montesquiu 12 E 24
22269 Montesusín 22 F 19
25711 Montferrer 12 E 22
43812 Montferri 24 G 22
25616 Montgai 23 F 21
25598 Montgarri 11 D 22
08390 Montgat 35 G 24
17130 Montgó 35 E 26
09588 Montiano 7 C 13
46842 Montichelvo 61 M 19
13326 Montiel 58 M 14
06480 Montijo 45 M 6
14550 Montilla 65 O 10
18564 Montillana 66 O 12
17472 Montiró 35 E 26
23266 Montizón 58 N 13
25738 Montmagastre 11 F 22
08717 Montmaneu 24 F 22
08160 Montmeló 24 F 24
22811 Montmesa 21 E 18
17242 Montnegre 35 F 25
32765 Montoedo 14 E 5
25172 Montoliu de Lleida
         23 F 21
50391 Montón 31 G 16
09125 Montorio 18 D 12
25340 Montornès de Segarra
         23 F 22
14600 Montoro 56 N 11
44559 Montoro de Mezquita
         32 H 18
34486 Montoro de Ojeda
         6 D 11
46250 Montortal 61 L 18
27737 Montouto/Abadin
         2 C 4
15318 Montouto/Cesuras
         2 C 3
33839 Montovo 4 C 7
15359 Montoxo (San Román)
         2 B 4
15359 Montoxo (San Xulián)
         2 B 4
25271 Montpalau 24 F 22
25568 Montradit de Baix
         11 E 22
43364 Mont-ral 23 G 22
17253 Mont-ras 35 F 26
46193 Montroi 43 L 18
43892 Mont-roig del Camp
         23 G 21
08460 Montseny 35 F 24
42259 Montuenga de Soria
         30 G 15
40464 Montuenga/Arévalo
         27 G 10
09390 Montuenga/Burgos
         18 E 12
07230 Montuïri 71 K 25
14930 Monturque 65 P 10
50120 Monzalbarba 21 F 18
22400 Monzón 22 F 20
34410 Monzón de Campos
         18 E 11
40250 Monzoncillo 28 G 11
42218 Moñux 30 F 15
27776 Mor 2 B 5
45400 Mora 49 K 12
43740 Mora d'Ebre 23 G 21
44400 Mora de Rubielos
         43 J 18
43770 Móra la Nova 23 G 21
09462 Moradillo de Roa
         28 F 12
09142 Moradillo de Sedano
         6 D 12
09143 Moradillo del Castillo
         6 D 12
15125 Moraime 1 C 1
03724 Moraira 61 M 20
24155 Moral 17 D 9
13350 Moral de Calatrava
         49 M 12
40542 Moral de Horneuz
         28 G 12

47691 Moral de la Reina
         17 F 9
49254 Moral de Sayago
         26 G 7
18370 Moraleda de Zafayona
         66 P 12
10840 Moraleja 36 J 6
40461 Moraleja de Coca
         27 G 10
40233 Moraleja de Cuéllar
         28 G 11
28950 Moraleja de Enmedio
         39 J 12
47454 Moraleja de las
         Panaderas
         27 G 10
05299 Moraleja de
         Matacabras
         27 G 10
49177 Moraleja de Sayago
         26 G 7
49150 Moraleja del Vino
         26 G 8
42366 Morales 29 G 14
47811 Morales de Campos
         17 F 9
49810 Morales de Toro 27 F 9
49697 Morales de Valverde
         16 F 8
49190 Morales del Vino
         26 G 8
49253 Moralina 26 G 7
28411 Moralzarzal 39 H 12
19491 Moranchel 29 H 14
36667 Moraña (San Lourenzo)
         13 D 2
05350 Morañuela 27 H 10
27876 Moras 2 B 5
37590 Morasverdes 36 H 7
30878 Morata 73 O 17
50260 Morata de Jalón
         21 G 17
50344 Morata de Jiloca
         31 G 16
28530 Morata de Tajuña
         40 J 13
30440 Moratalla/Caravaca de
         la Cruz 59 N 16
14749 Moratalla/Posadas
         55 O 9
19144 Moratila de los Meleros
         40 H 14
34349 Moratinos 17 E 10
49622 Moratones 16 E 8
10811 Morcillo 36 J 7
42340 Morcuera 29 G 13
01322 Moreda de Alava
         20 D 15
33670 Moreda/Cabañaquinta
         4 C 8
18540 Moreda/Piña 66 P 13
32637 Moreiras 14 E 4
12300 Morella 32 H 19
19328 Morenilla 30 H 16
14659 Morente 56 O 11
49731 Moreruela de los
         Infanzones 26 F 8
49148 Moreruela de Tßbara
         16 F 8
50240 Morés 21 G 16
09219 Moriana 7 D 13
24136 Morias de Paredes
         4 D 7
14510 Moriles 65 P 10
22415 Morilla 22 F 20
37183 Morille 26 H 8
19492 Morillejo 41 H 15
22336 Morillo de Monclús
         10 E 20
31491 Moriones 9 D 17
05122 Morisco 38 J 10
37340 Moriscos 26 G 8
24736 Morla 16 E 7
42223 Morón de Almazán
         30 G 15

41530 Morón de la Frontera
         64 P 9
37258 Moronta 25 H 7
02485 Moropeche 58 N 15
25632 Moror 11 E 21
50215 Moros 30 G 16
15124 Morquitián 1 C 1
22141 Morrano 22 E 19
24397 Morriondo 16 D 8
07460 Mortitxet 71 K 25
36415 Mos 13 E 2
27364 Moscán 2 D 5
44124 Moscardón 42 J 16
07314 Moscari 71 K 25
36843 Moscoso 13 E 2
27861 Mosende 2 B 4
08470 Mosqueroles 35 F 24
44410 Mosqueruela 32 J 19
27270 Mosteiro/Meira 3 C 5
36637 Mosteiro/Pontevedra
         13 D 2
28930 Móstoles 39 J 12
16780 Mota de Altarejos
         41 K 15
16630 Mota del Cuervo
         50 K 14
47120 Mota del Marqués
         27 F 9
16200 Motilla del Palancar
         51 K 16
02220 Motilleja 51 L 16
19320 Motos 42 H 16
18600 Motril 66 Q 12
27185 Mougán 2 D 4
36309 Mougás 13 E 2
36437 Mourentán 13 E 3
32556 Mourisca 15 E 5
33827 Moutas 4 C 7
49514 Moveros 26 F 7
16337 Moya 42 K 17
50143 Moyuela 31 G 18
37796 Mozárbez 26 H 8
24172 Mozos de Cea 17 D 9
50440 Mozota 21 G 17
47194 Mucientes 27 F 10
34839 Mudá 6 D 11
40295 Mudrián 28 G 11
19196 Muduex 29 H 14
50450 Muel 21 G 17
49341 Muelas de los
         Caballeros 16 E 7
49167 Muelas del Pan 26 F 8
31219 Mues 8 D 15
31176 Muez 8 D 16
49212 Muga de Sayago
         26 G 7
15620 Mugardos 2 C 3
32930 Mugares 14 E 4
27377 Muimenta/Castro de
         Rei 2 C 5
36514 Muimenta/Lalin 14 D 3
32880 Muinos 14 F 4
30170 Mula 60 N 17
31192 Multiva Baja 8 D 16
02142 Mullidar 59 M 16
31172 Munárriz 8 D 16
48360 Mundaka 7 C 14
50219 Munebrega 30 G 16
02612 Munera 50 L 15
48100 Mungia 7 C 14
44780 Munesia 31 G 18
26586 Munilla 20 E 15
48381 Munitibar-Arbatzegi
         8 C 14
08505 Muntanyola 24 F 24
33873 Muñalén 3 C 6
05540 Muñana 38 H 9
33884 Muñás 4 C 7
42142 Muñecas 19 F 13
05540 Múñez 38 H 10
05145 Muñico 38 H 9
27652 Muñis 3 D 6
33519 Muñó 4 C 8
05520 Muñochas 38 H 10
05530 Muñogalindo 38 H 10

05309 Muñogrande 27 H 10
33628 Muñón-Cimero 4 C 8
40145 Muñopedro 28 H 11
05192 Muñopepe 38 H 10
05380 Muñosancho 27 H 9
05357 Muñoyerro 38 H 10
37493 Muñoz 26 H 7
08278 Mura 24 F 23
27836 Muras 2 C 4
31521 Murchante 20 E 16
30070 Murcia 60 O 17
50366 Murero 31 G 17
23686 Mures 66 P 12
24127 Murias de Ponjos
         16 D 7
24718 Murias de Rechivaldo
         16 E 7
33676 Murias/Cabañaquinta
         4 C 8
27652 Murias/Poboa 3 D 6
39600 Muriedas 6 C 12
19225 Muriel 29 H 13
42193 Muriel de la Fuente
         29 F 14
47219 Muriel de Zapardiel
         27 G 10
42148 Muriel Viejo 19 F 14
31280 Murieta 8 D 15
31292 Murillo de Gállego
         22808 Murillo de Gállego
         9 E 18
26143 Murillo de Río Leza
         20 E 15
31391 Murillo el Cuende
         20 E 16
31313 Murillo el Fruto 9 E 17
03792 Murla 61 M 19
42108 Muro de Agreda
         20 F 16
26587 Muro de Aguas
         20 E 15
03830 Muro de Alcoy
         61 M 19
26134 Muro en Cameros
         20 E 14
07440 Muro/Sa Pobla
         71 K 26
22363 Muro/San Martín
         10 E 19
33138 Muros/Cudillero 4 B 7
15250 Muros/Noia 1 D 1
18490 Murtas 67 Q 13
48394 Murueta 7 C 14
31152 Muruzábal 8 D 16
31152 Muruzábal de Andión
         8 D 16
01129 Musitu 8 D 15
31867 Muskitz 8 D 16
03110 Mutxamel 61 N 19
15124 Muxía 1 C 1

N

21730 N Castromil 15 E 6
07815 Na Xamena 72 L 22
04540 Nacimiento 67 P 14
22569 Nachá 23 F 20
27569 Nadela 2 D 4
01170 Nafarrete 8 D 14
42141 Nafría de Ucero
         29 F 13
42193 Nafría la Llana 29 F 14
19278 Naharros/Atiernza
         29 G 14
16162 Naharros/Cuenca
         41 J 14
26300 Nájera 19 E 14
31422 Najurieta 9 D 17
26190 Nalda 20 E 15
25341 Nalec 23 F 22
45190 Nambroca 39 K 12
31454 Napal 9 D 17
46119 Náquera 43 K 19
33874 Naraval 3 C 6
01208 Narbaxa 8 D 15
16371 Narboneta 51 K 17

Nardues-Andurra ⓔ **Olmillos de Sasamón** Ⓔ

31448 Nardues-Andurra 9 D 17
27226 Narla 2 C 4
27649 Narón/Becerreá 3 D 5
27213 Narón/Monterroso 2 D 4
05160 Narrillos de San Leonardo 38 H 10
42189 Narros 20 F 15
40443 Narros de Cuéllar 28 G 11
37609 Narros de Matalayegua 37 H 8
05358 Narros de Saldueña 27 H 10
05370 Narros del Castillo 27 H 9
05131 Narros del Puerto 38 H 10
02409 Nava Campana 59 N 16
02142 Nava de Abajo 59 M 16
05216 Nava de Arévalo 27 H 10
02142 Nava de Arriba 59 M 16
37776 Nava de Béjar 37 J 8
40450 Nava de la Asunción 27 G 11
09586 Nava de Ordunte 7 C 13
09318 Nava de Roa 28 F 12
23479 Nava de San Pedro 58 O 14
05697 Nava del Barco 37 J 8
47500 Nava del Rey 27 G 9
33520 Nava/Infiesto 4 C 8
17536 Nava/Ribes de Freser 12 E 24
05633 Navacepeda de Tormes 38 J 9
05571 Navacepedilla de Corneja 38 J 9
13189 Navacerrada/ Almodóvar del Campo 48 M 11
28491 Navacerrada/Cercedilla 39 H 11
10613 Navaconcejo 37 J 8
05134 Navadijos 38 J 9
24156 Navafría/León 17 D 9
40161 Navafría/Pedraza 28 G 12
45150 Navahermosa/ Menasalbas 48 K 11
29329 Navahermosa/Sierra de Yeguas 65 P 10
13114 Navajarra 48 L 11
12470 Navajas 43 K 18
26533 Navajún 20 F 15
22320 Naval 22 E 20
05134 Navalacruz 38 J 10
28729 Navalafuente 28 H 11
28212 Navalagamella 39 J 11
42290 Navalcaballo 30 F 14
45610 Navalcán 38 J 9
28600 Navalcarnero 39 J 11
14249 Navalcuervo 55 N 9
02329 Navalengua 59 M 15
42149 Navalero 19 F 13
37882 Navales 26 H 9
05697 Navalguijo 37 J 8
40331 Navalilla 28 G 12
40280 Navalmanzano 28 G 11
13180 Navalmedio de Morales 48 M 10
05120 Navalmoral 38 J 10
37794 Navalmoral de Béjar 37 J 8
10300 Navalmoral de la Mata 37 K 8
45573 Navalmoralejo 47 K 9

46811 Navalón/Almansa 52 M 18
16190 Navalón/Cuenca 41 J 15
05123 Navalosa 38 J 10
05240 Navalperal de Pinares 39 H 11
05631 Navalperal de Tormes 38 J 9
13193 Navalpino 48 L 10
19268 Navalpotro 30 H 14
28292 Navalquejigo 39 H 11
13114 Navalrincón 48 L 11
05132 Navalsauz 38 J 9
26586 Navalsaz 20 E 15
45677 Navaltoril 48 K 10
05100 Navaluenga 38 J 10
10341 Navalvillar de Ibor 47 K 9
06760 Navalvillar de Pela 47 L 9
37749 Navamorales 37 J 9
45630 Navamorcuende 38 J 10
05120 Navandrinal 38 J 10
05122 Navaquesera 38 J 10
08270 Navarcles 24 F 23
50686 Navardún 9 D 17
30410 Navares 59 N 16
40531 Navares de Ayuso 28 G 12
40532 Navares de Enmedio 28 G 12
40532 Navares de las Cuevas 28 G 12
01309 Navaridas 19 D 14
05635 Navarredonda de Gredos 38 J 9
37607 Navarredonda de la Rinconada 37 H 7
41659 Navarredonda/El Saucejo 64 P 9
28739 Navarredonda/ Torrelaguna 28 H 12
05120 Navarredondilla 38 J 10
46823 Navarrés 52 L 18
26370 Navarrete 20 E 14
44496 Navarrete del Río 31 H 17
05115 Navarrevisca 38 J 10
22452 Navarri 11 E 20
33400 Navarro 4 B 8
09249 Navas de Bureba 7 D 13
13194 Navas de Estena 48 L 10
02246 Navas de Jorquera 51 L 16
40470 Navas de Oro 28 G 11
40420 Navas de Riofrío 28 H 11
23240 Navas de San Juan 57 N 13
10930 Navas del Madroño 45 K 6
42142 Navas del Pinar 19 F 13
28695 Navas del Rey 39 J 11
14511 Navas del Selpillar 65 P 10
08670 Navàs/Sallent 24 F 23
08670 Navàs/Solsona 12 F 23
22714 Navasa 10 D 19
31450 Navascués 9 D 17
37542 Navasfrías 36 J 6
17744 Navata 35 E 25
05122 Navatalgordo 38 J 10
10331 Navatrasierra 47 K 9
33873 Navelgas 3 C 7
34405 Naveros de Pisuerga 18 E 11
10374 Navezuelas 47 K 9
33710 Navia 3 B 6

31282 Nazar 8 D 15
41520 Neblines 64 P 8
15978 Nebra 1 D 2
09348 Nebreda 18 F 12
15510 Neda 2 B 3
19245 Negredo 29 G 14
15830 Negreira 1 D 2
46145 Negrón 42 J 17
27113 Negueira 3 C 6
42223 Neguillas 30 G 15
09679 Neila 19 E 14
27111 Neiro 3 C 5
33449 Nembro 4 B 8
15124 Nemiña 1 C 1
42218 Nepas 30 F 15
22375 Nerín 10 D 20
29780 Nerja 66 Q 12
02530 Nerpio 59 N 15
21670 Nerva 63 O 6
27212 Nespereira 2 D 4
34810 Nestar 6 D 11
26110 Nestares 19 E 14
21840 Niebla 62 P 6
26124 Nieva de Cameros 19 E 14
32435 Nieva/Ribadavia 13 E 3
40447 Nieva/Segovia 28 G 11
36684 Nigoi 13 D 3
36350 Nigrán 13 E 2
18657 Nigüelas 66 Q 12
50269 Nigüella 21 F 16
04100 Níjar 68 Q 15
24395 Nistal 16 E 7
18197 Nívar 66 P 12
31110 Noain 8 D 16
23140 Noalejo 66 O 12
36990 Noalla 13 E 2
45350 Noblejas 40 K 13
09569 Noceco 7 C 13
27675 Noceda/As Nogais 15 D 5
27796 Noceda/Ribadeo 3 B 5
24319 Noceda/Torena 16 D 7
09142 Nocedo 6 D 12
32624 Nocedo do Val 14 E 5
27812 Noche 2 C 4
39780 Nocina 7 C 13
22622 Nocito 10 E 19
42193 Nodalo 29 F 14
27229 Nodar 2 C 4
45162 Noez 48 K 11
09515 Nofuentes 7 D 13
34128 Nogal de las Huertas 17 E 10
06173 Nogales 53 M 6
24744 Nogar 15 E 6
24734 Nogarejas 16 E 7
42315 Nograles 29 G 14
01426 Nograro 7 D 13
32526 Nogueira 14 E 3
27515 Nogueira de Miño 14 D 4
33730 Nogueirón 3 C 6
44113 Noguera 42 J 16
44414 Nogueras 31 G 17
22587 Noguero 11 E 21
23669 Noguerones 65 O 11
44414 Nogueruelas 43 J 18
16191 Noheda 41 J 15
15200 Noia 1 D 2
15104 Noicela 1 C 2
27893 Nois 3 B 5
39180 Noja 7 C 12
42223 Nolay 30 F 15
45917 Nombela 38 J 11
50369 Nombrevilla 31 G 17
42128 Nomparedes 30 F 15
50794 Nonaspe 32 G 20
33180 Noreña 4 C 8
33590 Noriega 5 C 10
25574 Norís 12 D 22
15171 Nos 2 C 3
22113 Novales/Huesca 22 E 19

39526 Novales/Santillana de Mar 6 C 11
50510 Novallas 20 F 16
03660 Novelda 60 N 18
06183 Novelda del Guadiana 45 M 6
33157 Novellana 4 B 7
25795 Noves de Segre 12 E 22
22712 Novés/Jaca 10 D 18
45519 Novés/Torrijos 39 J 11
42341 Noviercas 29 G 13
42132 Noviergas 30 F 15
50530 Novillas 21 F 17
33416 Nubledo 4 B 8
22193 Nueno 22 E 19
44220 Nueros 31 H 17
33592 Nueva 5 C 10
29660 Nueva Andalucía 70 Q 10
14857 Nueva Carteya 65 O 11
50210 Nuévalos 30 G 16
47464 Nuevavilla de las Torres 27 G 9
28514 Nuevo Baztán 40 J 13
49516 Nuez 15 F 6
50173 Nuez de Ebro 21 F 18
12520 Nules 44 K 19
27677 Nullán 15 D 5
43887 Nulles 24 G 22
45230 Numancia de la Sagra 39 J 12
45644 Nuño Gómez 38 J 10
10626 Nuñomoral 36 J 7

O
32300 O Barco 15 E 6
32370 O Bolo 15 E 5
27130 O Cádabo 3 C 5
27777 O Cadramón 2 C 5
32774 O Campo 15 E 5
36546 O Castro 14 D 3
27670 O Cebreiro 15 D 5
27163 O Corgo 2 D 5
32539 O Desterro 14 D 3
36980 O Grove 13 E 2
15821 O Pedrouzo 1 D 3
15296 O Pindo 1 D 1
15821 O Pino 1 D 3
36740 O Seixo 13 F 2
33811 Oballo 3 C 6
06730 Obando 47 L 9
31151 Obanos 8 D 16
01118 Obécuri 8 D 14
14310 Obejo 56 N 10
44792 Obón 31 H 18
33874 Obona 3 C 7
39690 Obregón 6 C 12
45300 Ocaña 40 K 12
19432 Ocentejo 41 H 15
24439 Ocero 15 D 6
31281 Oco 8 D 15
26144 Ocón 20 E 15
31680 Ochagavía 9 D 17
14129 Ochavillo del Río 55 O 9
25283 Odèn 12 E 22
08711 Òdena 24 F 23
31879 Oderitz 8 D 16
24742 Odollo 15 E 6
44233 Odón 31 H 16
24566 Oencia 15 D 6
39812 Ogarrio 7 C 12
17861 Ogassa 12 E 24
18151 Ogíjares 66 P 12
04459 Ohanes 67 P 14
01449 Oiardo 7 D 14
31720 Oieregi 8 C 16
32613 Oímbra 14 F 5
15819 Oíns 2 D 3
01320 Oion 20 D 15
27749 Oirán 3 B 5
27775 Oirás 2 C 5
50297 Oitura 21 F 17

31751 Oitz 8 C 16
17856 Oix 35 E 25
26270 Ojacastro 19 E 14
29610 Ojén 70 Q 10
30612 Ojós 60 N 17
05193 Ojos Albos 38 H 10
44313 Ojos Negros 42 H 17
42130 Ojuel 30 F 15
14299 Ojuelos Altos 55 N 9
01194 Okia 8 D 14
22135 Ola 22 E 19
31638 Olaberri 9 C 17
31798 Olagüe 8 D 16
31439 Olaldea 9 D 17
44211 Olalla 31 H 17
01450 Olamendi 7 C 14
31799 Olave 9 D 16
31481 Olaverri 9 D 17
31809 Olazti-Olazagutía 8 D 15
44479 Olba 43 J 18
31398 Olcoz 8 D 16
39418 Olea 6 D 11
34407 Olea de Boedo 18 D 11
15993 Oleiros/Puable de Caramiñal 13 D 1
15173 Oleiros/Sadra 2 C 3
27812 Oleiros/Vilalba 2 C 4
31281 Olejua 8 D 15
32869 Olelas 14 F 3
08795 Olesa de Bonesvalls 24 G 23
08640 Olesa de Montserrat 24 F 23
25790 Oliana 12 E 22
29197 Olías 65 Q 11
45280 Olías del Rey 39 K 12
44548 Oliete 32 H 18
25749 Oliola 23 F 22
31390 Olite 20 E 16
25286 Olius 12 E 23
46780 Oliva 61 M 19
06120 Oliva de la Frontera 53 N 6
06475 Oliva de Mérida 54 M 7
10667 Oliva de Plasencia 37 J 7
22636 Oliván 10 D 19
41804 Olivares 63 P 7
47359 Olivares de Duero 28 F 11
16760 Olivares del Júcar 41 K 15
36862 Oliveira 13 E 3
08818 Olivella 24 G 23
06100 Olivenza 53 M 5
19444 Olmeda de Cobeta 30 H 15
28515 Olmeda de las Fuentes 40 J 13
19413 Olmeda del Extremo 40 H 14
16216 Olmeda del Rey 41 K 15
16118 Olmedilla de Alarcón 51 K 15
16853 Olmedilla de Eliz 41 J 15
16550 Olmedilla del Campo 40 J 14
19264 Olmedillas 30 G 14
09311 Olmedillo de Roa 18 F 12
47410 Olmedo 27 G 10
37292 Olmedo de Camaces 25 H 6
16852 Olmedo de la Cuesta 41 J 15
42345 Olmillos 29 F 13
49147 Olmillos de Castro 26 F 8
09228 Olmillos de Muñó 18 E 12
09123 Olmillos de Sasamón 18 E 11

49450 Olmo de la Guareña
27 G 9
47173 Olmos de Esgueva
27 F 10
09133 Olmos de la Picaza
18 E 12
34486 Olmos de Ojeda
6 D 11
47318 Olmos de Peñafiel
28 F 11
46169 Olocau 43 K 18
12312 Olocau del Rey
32 H 19
40220 Olombrada 28 G 11
31396 Olóriz 8 D 16
08516 Olost 12 F 24
17800 Olot 35 E 24
22394 Olson 22 E 20
04212 Olula de Castro
67 P 15
04860 Olula del Río
68 P 15
08611 Olvan 12 E 23
27579 Olveda 14 D 4
42110 Ólvega 20 F 16
15127 Olveiroa 1 D 1
22439 Olvena 22 E 20
11690 Olvera 70 Q 9
50341 Olvés 30 G 16
31171 Olza 8 D 16
26220 Ollauri 19 D 14
31494 Olleta 9 D 16
31172 Ollo 8 D 16
24134 Omañon 4 D 7
15608 Ombre 2 C 3
27299 Ombreiro 2 C 4
39793 Omoño 6 C 12
42172 Oncala 20 F 15
02694 Oncebreros 51 M 17
12200 Onda 43 K 19
31448 Ongoz 9 D 17
03430 Onil 60 M 18
33816 Onón 4 C 7
42216 Ontalvilla de Almazán
30 G 14
39680 Ontaneda 6 C 12
45340 Ontígola 39 J 12
50810 Ontinar del Salz
21 F 18
22232 Ontiñena 22 F 20
46870 Ontinyent 52 M 18
39706 Onton 7 C 13
02652 Ontur 60 M 16
24231 Onzonilla 16 D 8
09530 Oña 7 D 13
01207 Opakua 8 D 15
01477 Opellora 7 C 13
09350 Oquillas 18 F 12
24113 Orallo 4 D 7
02510 Orán 51 M 16
03790 Orba 61 M 19
31670 Orbaitzeta 9 D 17
09192 Orbaneja-Riopico
18 E 12
09145 Orbanejo del Castillo
6 D 12
31671 Orbara 9 D 17
05296 Orbita 27 G 10
50366 Orcajo 31 G 17
25655 Orcau 11 E 21
18858 Orce 58 O 15
23370 Orcera 58 N 14
31160 Orcoyen 8 D 16
08739 Ordal 24 G 23
33979 Ordaliego 4 C 8
09124 Ordejón de Abajo o
Santo María
18 D 11
15680 Ordes 1 C 3
22376 Ordesa 10 D 19
17773 Ordis 35 E 25
15837 Ordoeste 1 D 2
22622 Ordovés 10 E 19
48460 Orduña 7 D 13
19311 Orea 42 H 16

06750 Orellana de la Sierra u
Orellanita 47 L 9
06740 Orellana la Vieja 47 L 8
50331 Orera 31 G 17
50619 Orés 21 E 17
17488 Orfes 35 E 25
25794 Organyà 12 E 22
45450 Orgaz 49 K 12
18400 Orgiva 66 Q 13
04810 Oria 68 P 15
31194 Oricain 8 D 16
07349 Orient 71 K 25
03300 Orihuela 60 N 18
44366 Orihuela del Tremedal
42 H 16
42142 Orillares 19 F 13
22213 Orillena 22 F 19
39780 Oriñón 7 C 13
31395 Orísoain 9 D 16
08518 Oristà 12 F 24
03679 Orito 60 N 18
33990 Orlé 5 C 9
22620 Orna de Gállego
10 E 19
31866 Orokieta 8 C 16
09219 Orón 7 D 14
31697 Orondritz 9 D 17
31451 Oronz 9 D 17
12594 Oropesa/Benicassim
44 J 20
45560 Oropesa/Talavera de la
Reina 38 K 9
31171 Ororbia 8 D 16
27204 Orosa 2 D 4
32520 Oroso 13 E 3
31439 Oroz-Betelu 9 D 17
48410 Orozko 7 C 14
31650 Orreaga-Roncesvalles
9 C 17
44161 Orrios 42 H 18
22583 Orrit 11 E 21
08317 Órrius 35 F 24
12311 Ortélls 32 H 19
26124 Ortigosa de Cameros
19 E 14
40495 Ortigosa de Pestaño
28 G 11
05145 Ortigosa de Rioalmar
38 H 9
15365 Ortigueira 2 B 4
33716 Ortiguera 3 B 6
22811 Ortilla 22 E 18
22611 Orús 10 E 19
28570 Orusco 40 J 13
03579 Orxeta 61 M 19
24839 Orzónaga 4 D 8
15280 Os Ánxeles 1 D 2
32634 Os Blancos 14 E 4
25610 Os de Balaguer
23 F 21
32440 Os Peares 14 E 4
16423 Osa de Vega 50 K 14
31193 Osacar 8 D 16
15141 Oseiro/A Coruña/La
Coruña 1 C 3
32136 Oseiro/Chantada
14 D 4
50258 Oseja 30 F 16
24916 Oseja de Sajambre
5 C 9
50175 Osera 22 F 18
31869 Oskotz 8 D 16
01426 Osma 7 D 13
42294 Osona 29 F 14
42291 Osonilla 29 F 14
17161 Osor 35 F 25
34468 Osornillo 18 E 11
34460 Osorno 18 E 11
02611 Ossa de Montiel
50 M 14
22532 Osso de Cinca 22 F 20
25318 Ossó de Sió 23 F 22
31799 Ostiz 8 D 16
41640 Osuna 64 P 9
39707 Otañes 7 C 13

31250 Oteiza 8 D 16
09512 Oteo/Medina de Pomar
7 C 13
01117 Oteo/Vitoria-Gasteiz
8 D 15
19431 Oter 41 H 15
49336 Otero de Bodas 16 F 7
34888 Otero de Guardo
5 D 10
40422 Otero de los Herreros
28 H 11
21730 Otero de Sariegos
16 F 8
33869 Otero/Salas 4 C 7
45533 Otero/Torrijos 38 J 10
28749 Oteruelo del Valle
28 H 12
42190 Oteruelos 20 F 14
19356 Otilla 42 H 16
31219 Otiñano 8 D 15
18698 Otívar 66 Q 12
22370 Oto 10 D 19
01191 Oto Goien 7 D 14
40394 Otones de Benjumea
28 G 11
46844 Otos/Albaida 61 M 19
02438 Otos/Socovos 59 N 15
33792 Otur 3 B 6
18630 Otura 66 P 12
48210 Otxandio 7 C 14
48860 Otxaran 7 C 13
36635 Oubiña 13 D 2
15167 Ouces 2 C 3
27392 Oural 14 D 5
32070 Ourense/Orense
14 E 4
33775 Ouria 3 C 5
27865 Ourol 2 B 4
27150 Outeiro de Rei 2 C 4
15280 Outeiro/Noia 1 D 2
32651 Outeiro/Ourense/
Orense 14 E 4
27328 Outeiro/Quiroga 15 D 5
32824 Outomuro 14 E 3
27113 Ouviaño 4 C 6
33070 Oviedo 4 C 8
24853 Oville 5 D 9
33156 Oviñana 4 B 7
15380 Oza/Betanzos 2 C 3
15107 Oza/Carballo 1 C 2
01206 Ozeta 8 D 15
15126 Ozón 1 C 1
24415 Ozuela 15 E 6

P

27611 Pacios (Paradela)
2 D 4
27136 Pacios/A Fonsagrada
3 C 5
27256 Pacios/Meira 3 C 5
27372 Pacios/Rábade 2 C 4
27146 Paderne 2 C 5
32112 Paderne de Allariz
14 E 4
09109 Padilla de Abajo
18 E 11
09108 Padilla de Arriba
18 E 11
47314 Padilla de Duero
28 F 11
19246 Padilla de Hita 29 H 14
19445 Padilla del Ducado
30 H 15
27670 Padornelo/Pedrafita
15 D 5
49574 Padornelo/Sanabria
15 E 6
15848 Padreiro 1 C 2
15900 Padrón 1 D 2
09593 Padrones de Bureba
7 D 12
36866 Padróns 13 E 2
18640 Padul 66 P 12
04458 Padules 67 Q 14
18400 Pago 66 Q 13

01211 Pagoeta 7 D 14
40567 Pajarejos/Boceguillas
28 G 12
05571 Pajarejos/Piedrahita
38 H 9
05292 Pajares de Adaja
27 H 10
49142 Pajares de la
Lampreana 26 F 8
24209 Pajares de los Oteros
16 E 9
19413 Pajares/Brihuega
40 H 14
16145 Pajares/Cuenca
41 J 15
33693 Pajares/Pola de Lena
4 C 8
28293 Pajares/Valdemorillo
39 H 11
16390 Pajarón 42 K 16
16390 Pajaroncillo 42 K 16
24891 Palacio de Torío 16 D 8
09130 Palacios de Benaver
18 E 12
05215 Palacios de Goda
27 G 10
09680 Palacios de la Sierra
19 F 13
24764 Palacios de la
Valduerna 16 E 8
09107 Palacios de
Riopisuerga
18 E 11
49322 Palacios de Sanabria
15 E 6
34490 Palacios del Alcor
18 E 11
37111 Palacios del Arzobispo
26 G 8
24495 Palacios del Sil 4 D 7
05216 Palacios Rubios
27 G 10
37406 Palaciosrubios 27 G 9
08389 Palafolls 35 F 25
17200 Palafrugell 35 F 26
17230 Palamós 35 F 26
19225 Palancares 29 G 13
12311 Palanques 32 H 19
27200 Palas de Rei 2 D 4
25633 Palau de Noguera
11 E 21
25747 Palau de Torà 24 F 22
17256 Palau-Sator 35 F 26
17495 Palau-Saverdera
35 E 26
08184 Palau-solità i
Plegamans
24 F 24
24839 Palazuela 4 D 9
49592 Palazuela da las
Cuevas 16 F 7
06717 Palazuelo 46 L 8
47812 Palazuelo de Vedija
17 F 9
10590 Palazuelo-Empalme
37 K 7
19266 Palazuelos 29 G 14
40194 Palazuelos de Eresma
28 H 11
09198 Palazuelos de la Sierra
19 E 13
09226 Palazuelos de Muñó
18 E 12
09124 Palazuelos de
Villadiego 18 D 11
34070 Palencia 17 E 10
37799 Palencia de Negrilla
26 G 8
14914 Palenciana 65 P 10
34257 Palenzuela 18 E 11
46724 Palma de Gandía
61 M 19
07070 Palma de Mallorca
71 K 25
14700 Palma del Río 55 O 9

07181 Palma Nova 71 K 25
19245 Pálmaces de Jadraque
29 G 14
07193 Palmanyola 71 K 25
17514 Palmerola 12 E 24
11379 Palmones 70 R 9
22337 Palo 10 E 20
17843 Palol de Revardit
35 E 25
44708 Palomar de Arroyos
31 H 18
11500 Palomar/El Puerto de
Santa María
69 Q 7
14512 Palomar/Puente Genil
65 P 10
04618 Palomares 68 P 16
37893 Palomares de Alba
26 H 8
41928 Palomares del Río
63 P 7
06476 Palomas 54 M 7
45213 Palomeque 39 J 12
16192 Palomera 41 J 15
16160 Palomeras del Campo
41 K 14
10660 Palomero 36 J 7
21810 Palos de la Frontera
62 P 6
25211 Palou de Sanaüja
23 F 22
17256 Pals 35 F 26
06907 Pallarés 54 N 7
22221 Pallaruelo de Monegros
22 F 19
08780 Pallejà 24 G 23
22583 Pallerol 11 E 21
18411 Pampaneira 66 Q 13
09220 Pampliega 18 E 12
31070 Pamplona-Iruña 8 D 16
39718 Panames 6 C 12
09280 Pancorvo 7 D 13
44720 Pancrudo 42 H 17
33529 Pandenes 5 C 9
48891 Pando/Balmaseda
7 C 13
33195 Pando/Oviedo 4 C 8
33316 Pando/Villaviciosa
5 C 9
33570 Panes 5 C 10
22438 Panillo 22 E 20
50480 Paniza 31 G 17
09559 Panizares 7 D 13
43870 Panizos 33 H 21
22438 Pano 22 E 20
10697 Pantano de Navabuena
37 K 8
13710 Pantano Peñarroya
50 L 13
22661 Panticosa 10 D 19
45290 Pantoja 39 J 12
22141 Panzano 22 E 19
26121 Panzares 20 E 14
42368 Paones 29 G 14
05358 Papatrigo 27 H 10
16373 Paracuellos 51 K 16
50342 Paracuellos de Jiloca
30 G 16
50299 Paracuellos de la
Ribera 21 G 16
37129 Parada de Arriba
26 H 8
37419 Parada de Rubiales
26 G 9
32740 Parada/Castro Caldelas
14 E 4
32651 Parada/Maside 14 E 4
41610 Paradas 64 P 9
32786 Paradaseca 14 E 5
27135 Paradavella 3 C 5
27611 Paradela/Poboa 3 D 5
36685 Paradela/Sales (San
Yulián) 1 D 3
24510 Paradeseca 15 D 6
40123 Paradinas 28 G 11

Paradinas de San Juan   (E)   **Pinedillo**

37318 Paradinas de San Juan 27 H 9
24512 Paradiña 15 D 6
18160 Paradollano 66 P 13
32788 Paraisás 15 E 5
28210 Paraiso 39 H 11
44422 Paraiso Alto 43 J 18
44422 Paraiso Bajo 43 J 18
33815 Parajas 3 C 6
09515 Paralacuesta 7 D 13
33776 Paramios 3 C 5
33111 Páramo 4 C 7
34407 Páramo de Boedo 18 D 11
24470 Páramo del Sil 3 D 7
15872 Paramos 1 D 2
29451 Parauta 70 Q 9
03792 Parcent 61 M 19
24457 Pardamaza 15 D 7
24820 Pardavé 16 D 8
32311 Pardellán 15 E 6
27235 Pardellas 2 C 4
24848 Pardesivil 5 D 9
09462 Pardilla 28 F 12
22484 Pardinella 11 E 21
17534 Pardines 12 E 24
19336 Pardos 30 H 16
28196 Paredes de Buitrago 28 G 12
45908 Paredes de Escalona 39 J 11
34300 Paredes de Nava 17 E 10
19277 Paredes de Sigüenza 29 G 14
33785 Paredes/Luarca 3 C 7
32750 Paredes/Monterramo 14 E 5
16465 Paredes/Tarancón 40 J 14
42132 Paredesroyas 30 F 15
19129 Pareja 41 H 14
08150 Parets del Vallès 24 F 24
27305 Parga (San Salvador) 2 C 4
27380 Parga (Santo Estevo) 2 C 4
28980 Parla 39 J 12
17133 Parlarà 35 E 26
33717 Parlero 3 C 6
28935 Parque Coímbra 39 J 12
18290 Parque de Cubillas 66 P 12
19170 Parque de las Castillas 40 H 13
45900 Parque Romillo 39 J 11
33509 Parres 5 C 10
45611 Parrillas 38 J 9
04810 Partaloa 68 P 15
22365 Parzán 10 D 20
20110 Pasai Donibane 8 C 16
10411 Pasaron de la Vera 37 J 8
05150 Pascualcobo 38 H 9
40122 Pascuales 28 G 11
43425 Passanant 23 F 22
37510 Pastores 36 H 6
27287 Pastoriza 3 C 5
19100 Pastrana/Sacedón 40 J 14
11311 Pastrana/Sanlúcar de Barrameda 69 Q 7
50195 Pastriz 21 F 18
46980 Paterna 43 K 19
11178 Paterna de Rivera 69 Q 8
21880 Paterna del Campo 63 P 7
02136 Paterna de la Madera 59 M 15
04479 Paterna del Río 67 P 14
31190 Paternáin 8 D 16

28189 Patones 29 H 13
28189 Patones de Abajo 29 H 13
21649 Patrás 62 O 6
17494 Pau 35 E 26
48890 Paules 7 C 13
22149 Paúles de Sarsa 10 E 20
09345 Paúles del Agua 18 E 12
43593 Paüls dels Ports 33 H 20
12449 Pavías 43 K 19
21560 Paymogo 62 O 5
34485 Payo de Ojeda 6 D 11
15313 Pazo de Irixoa 2 C 3
32515 Pazos/Carballiño 14 E 3
32980 Pazos/Orense 14 E 4
15112 Pazos/Ponte Ceso 1 C 2
36841 Pazos/Recondela 13 E 2
26226 Pazuengos 19 E 14
09559 Peadas de Burgos 6 D 12
23460 Peal de Becerro 58 O 13
04250 Pechina 67 Q 15
39594 Pechón 6 C 11
15365 Pedra 2 B 4
27389 Pedrafita 2 C 4
27695 Pedrafita de Camporredondo 3 D 5
27670 Pedrafita do Cebreiro 15 D 5
42391 Pedraja de San Esteban 29 F 13
42190 Pedrajas 20 F 14
47430 Pedrajas de San Esteban 27 G 10
46164 Pedralba 43 K 18
40172 Pedraza 28 G 12
37882 Pedraza de Alba 37 H 9
36139 Pedre 13 D 3
03750 Pedreguer 61 M 20
15807 Pedreira 2 D 3
39130 Pedreña 6 C 12
41566 Pedrera 65 P 10
28723 Pedrezuela 39 H 12
14630 Pedro Abad 56 O 11
02534 Pedro Andrés 58 N 15
05470 Pedro Bernardo 38 J 10
16337 Pedro Izquierdo 42 K 17
18530 Pedro Martínez 66 O 13
13620 Pedro Muñoz 50 L 14
05155 Pedro Rodríguez 27 H 10
14412 Pedroche 56 N 10
50690 Pedrola 21 F 17
09314 Pedrosa de Duero 28 F 12
34116 Pedrosa de la Vega 17 E 10
09239 Pedrosa de Muñó 18 E 12
09549 Pedrosa de Tobalina 7 D 13
09127 Pedrosa de Valdelucio 6 D 11
09133 Pedrosa del Páramo 18 E 12
09119 Pedrosa del Príncipe 18 E 11
47112 Pedrosa del Rey 27 F 9
09131 Pedrosa del Río Urbel 18 E 12
37871 Pedrosillo de Alba 27 H 9

37788 Pedrosillo de los Aires 37 H 8
37427 Pedrosillo el Ralo 26 G 8
10829 Pedroso de Acim 36 K 7
26321 Pedroso/Baños de Río Toba 19 E 14
33556 Pedroso/Cangas de Onis 5 C 10
15865 Pedrouzos/Negreira 1 D 2
32768 Pedrouzos/Puebla de Trives 14 E 5
33115 Pedroveya 4 C 8
23110 Pegalajar 57 O 12
25286 Pegaroles 12 F 23
03780 Pego 61 M 19
07160 Peguera 71 K 24
45918 Pelahustán 38 J 10
37209 Pelarrodríguez 26 H 7
37787 Pelayos 37 H 8
28696 Pelayos de la Presa 39 J 11
40170 Pelayos del Arroyo 28 G 12
49880 Peleagonzalo 26 G 9
19268 Pelegrina 29 G 14
33810 Peliceira 3 D 6
18210 Peligros 66 P 12
06679 Peloche 47 L 9
33686 Pelúgano 4 C 8
39582 Pembes 5 C 10
27129 Pena 3 C 5
21730 Penadiz 14 E 4
03815 Penàguila 61 M 19
27659 Penamil 3 D 5
27697 Penarrubia 3 D 5
27568 Penas 2 D 4
49178 Penausende 26 G 8
24699 Pendilla 4 C 8
33997 Pendones 5 C 9
33598 Pendueles 5 C 10
24469 Penedela 15 D 6
27414 Penela 14 E 5
25335 Penelles 23 F 21
24437 Penoselo 15 D 6
33778 Penzol 3 C 6
30629 Peña Zafra de Abajo 60 N 17
01212 Peñacerrada 7 D 14
47011 Peñafiel 28 F 11
47640 Peñaflor de Hornija 27 F 10
33829 Peñaflor/Grado 4 C 7
41470 Peñaflor/Palma del Río 55 O 9
50193 Peñaflor/Villanueva de Gállego 21 F 18
33739 Peñafuente 3 C 6
09591 Peñahorada 18 E 12
19128 Peñalagos 40 H 14
22592 Peñalba 22 G 19
05163 Peñalba de Avila 38 H 10
09454 Peñalba de Castro 19 F 13
28190 Peñalba de la Sierra 29 G 13
24142 Peñalba de los Cilleros 4 D 7
42345 Peñalba de San Esteban 29 F 13
24415 Peñalba de Santiago 15 E 6
19462 Peñalén 41 H 15
14129 Peñalosa 55 O 9
06610 Peñalsordo 47 M 9
19134 Peñalver 40 H 14
37523 Peñaparda 36 J 6
37300 Peñaranda de Bracamonte 27 H 9
09410 Peñaranda de Duero 29 F 13

37820 Peñarandilla 27 H 9
44586 Peñarróya de Tastavins 32 H 20
14200 Peñarroya-Pueblonuevo 55 N 9
44709 Peñarroyas 31 H 18
02314 Peñarrubia/Alcaraz 50 M 15
02486 Peñarrubia/Elche de la Sierra 59 N 15
02120 Peñas de San Pedro 58 M 15
02313 Peñascosa 58 M 15
40393 Peñasrrubias de Pirón 28 G 11
12598 Peñíscola 33 J 20
45638 Pepino 38 J 10
49318 Peque 16 E 7
44369 Peracense 42 H 17
08589 Perafita 12 E 24
43152 Perafort 24 G 22
09342 Peral de Arlanza 18 E 11
17491 Peralada 35 E 26
25736 Peralbà 11 F 21
10335 Peraleda de la Mata 37 K 9
10334 Peraleda de San Román 37 K 9
06919 Peraleda del Zaucejo 55 N 8
28211 Peralejo 39 H 11
44162 Peralejos 42 J 17
37216 Peralejos de Abajo 25 G 7
19313 Peralejos de Las Truchas 41 H 16
42315 Peralejos de los Escuderos 29 G 13
34429 Perales 17 E 10
28540 Perales de Tajuña 40 J 13
44162 Perales del Alfambra 42 H 17
10896 Perales del Puerto 36 J 6
28902 Perales del Río 39 J 12
31350 Peralta 20 E 16
22210 Peralta de Alcofea 22 F 19
22513 Peralta de la Sal 11 F 20
22311 Peraltilla 22 E 19
19493 Peralveche 41 H 15
13140 Peralvillo 49 L 12
25591 Peramea 11 E 22
25790 Peramola 11 E 22
24429 Peranzanes 3 D 6
22460 Perarrúa 11 E 20
17113 Peratallada 35 F 26
34486 Perazancas 6 D 11
15609 Perbes 2 C 3
33300 Perceyo 4 B 8
42218 Perdices 30 G 15
50161 Perdiguera 22 F 18
27533 Pereira/Chantada 14 D 4
15859 Pereira/Santa Catalina de Armada 1 D 2
15138 Pereiriña 1 D 1
15563 Pereiro/Neda 2 B 4
32548 Pereiro/Verín 15 E 5
37175 Perena de la Ribera 25 G 6
49280 Pereruela 26 G 8
09512 Perex 7 D 13
29710 Periana 65 Q 11
49145 Perilla de Castro 26 F 8
40154 Perogordo 28 H 11
37791 Peromingo 37 J 8

40310 Perorrubio 28 G 12
40354 Perosillo 28 G 11
22132 Pertusa 22 E 19
39572 Pesaguero 5 C 10
10882 Pescueza 36 K 6
02314 Pesebre 58 M 15
27516 Pesqueiras 14 E 4
47315 Pesquera de Duero 28 F 11
09146 Pesquera de Ebro 6 D 12
24815 Pesquera/Cistierna 5 D 9
39491 Pesquera/Reinosa 6 C 11
25518 Pessonada 11 E 22
39548 Pesués 6 C 11
50686 Petilla de Aragón 9 E 17
32356 Petín 15 E 5
07520 Petra 71 K 26
03610 Petrer 60 N 18
46500 Petrés 43 K 19
02692 Pétrola 51 M 16
03725 Peva/Vila Nova da Paiva 61 M 20
33735 Pezos 3 C 6
28812 Pezuela de las Torres 40 J 13
33778 Piantón 3 C 5
49580 Pías 15 E 6
46210 Picanya 43 L 19
46220 Picassent 43 L 19
13196 Picón 48 L 11
14298 Piconcillo 55 N 9
27207 Pidre 2 D 4
13100 Piedrabuena 48 L 11
24838 Piedrafita 4 C 8
05500 Piedrahita/El Barco de Ávila 38 J 9
44212 Piedrahita/Fonfria 31 G 17
13129 Piedralá 48 L 11
05440 Piedralaves 38 J 10
31219 Piedramillera 8 D 15
10991 Piedras Albas 36 K 6
33450 Piedras Blancas 4 B 8
34849 Piedrasluengas 6 C 11
50616 Piedratajada 21 E 18
08784 Piera 24 F 23
09246 Piérnigas 7 D 13
33842 Pigüeña 4 C 7
04648 Pilar de Jaravia 68 P 16
03190 Pilar de la Horadada 60 O 18
07872 Pilar de la Mona 72 M 23
41840 Pilas 63 P 7
46712 Piles 61 M 19
33456 Pillarno 4 B 8
36586 Piloño 2 D 3
22589 Pilzán 11 E 20
12429 Pina de Montalgrao 43 J 18
50750 Pina/Fuentes 22 G 18
07220 Pina/Palma de Mallorca 71 K 25
45900 Pinar de Almorox 39 J 11
18830 Pinar de la Vidriera 58 N 14
16622 Pinarejo 50 K 15
40296 Pinarejos 28 G 11
40294 Pinarnegrillo 28 G 11
16541 Pineda de Cigüela 41 J 14
09199 Pineda de la Sierra 19 E 13
08397 Pineda de Mar 35 F 25
17255 Pineda Pals 35 F 26
37712 Pinedas 37 J 8
09349 Pineda-Trasmonte 18 F 12
09345 Pinedillo 18 E 12

25286 Pinell de Solsonès
   12 F 22
46838 Pinet 61 M 19
28739 Pinilla de Buitrago
   28 H 12
49231 Pinilla de Fermoselle
   25 G 7
19246 Pinilla de Jadraque
   29 G 14
09612 Pinilla de los Barruecos
   19 F 13
09613 Pinilla de los Moros
   19 E 13
19312 Pinilla de Molina
   41 H 16
49850 Pinilla de Toro 27 F 9
42112 Pinilla del Campo
   30 F 15
42214 Pinilla del Olmo
   30 G 14
28749 Pinilla del Valle
   28 H 12
02310 Pinilla/Alcaraz 50 M 14
02512 Pinilla/Chinchilla de
   Monte Aragón
   51 M 16
40122 Pinilla-Ambroz 28 G 11
09610 Pinilla-Trasmonte
   18 F 12
26111 Pinillos 20 E 14
09350 Pinillos de Esgueva
   18 F 12
49514 Pino 26 F 7
28210 Pino Alto 39 H 11
09246 Pino de Bureba
   7 D 13
34110 Pino del Río 17 D 10
15238 Pino do Val 1 D 2
10630 Pinofranqueado 36 J 7
25287 Pinós 24 F 23
24144 Pinos 4 D 8
18191 Pinos-Genil 66 P 12
03650 Pinoso 60 N 17
18240 Pinos-Puente 66 P 12
50298 Pinseque 21 F 17
50694 Pinsoro 21 E 17
50685 Pintano 9 D 17
28320 Pinto 39 J 12
33534 Pintueles 5 C 9
33392 Pinzales 4 C 8
41728 Pinzón 63 P 7
34430 Piña de Campos
   18 E 11
47175 Piña de Esgueva
   28 F 11
18568 Piñar 66 P 13
27135 Piñeira/A Fonsagrada
   3 C 5
27318 Piñeira/San Clodio
   15 E 5
32693 Pineira/Xinzo de Limia
   14 E 4
27833 Piñeiro/Al Pontes de
   Garcia Ródriguez
   2 C 4
36191 Piñeiro/Caldas de Reis
   13 D 2
27248 Piñeiro/Meira 3 C 5
36873 Piñeiro/Mondariz
   13 E 3
15864 Piñeiro/Santiago de
   Compostela 1 D 2
47316 Piñel de Abajo 28 F 11
47316 Piñel de Arriba 28 F 11
33685 Piñeres 4 C 8
32135 Piñor 14 E 4
28737 Piñuecar 28 G 12
24916 Pío 5 C 9
10615 Piornal 37 J 8
21730 Piornedo 14 E 5
19162 Pioz 40 J 13
01118 Pipaón 7 D 14
42342 Piquera de San
   Esteban 29 F 13
19325 Piqueras 42 H 16

16118 Piqueras del Castillo
   51 K 15
27242 Piquín (Santabaia)
   3 C 5
43423 Pira 23 G 22
22268 Piracés 22 E 19
39696 Pisueña 6 C 12
44559 Pitarque 32 H 18
32510 Piteira 14 E 3
37490 Pitiegua 26 G 9
31392 Pitillas 20 E 16
18414 Pitres 66 Q 13
27294 Piúgos 2 D 4
29560 Pizarra 70 Q 10
37795 Pizarral 37 H 8
28210 Pizarrera 39 H 11
46750 Pla dels Corrals
   61 L 19
32785 Placin 15 E 5
22367 Plan 10 D 20
03828 Planes 61 M 19
17535 Planoles 12 E 24
10600 Plasencia 37 J 7
50296 Plasencia de Jalón
   21 F 17
88210 Plasencia del Monte
   22 E 18
10271 Plasenzuela 46 L 7
17250 Platja d`Aro 35 F 26
46713 Platja de Bellreguard
   61 M 19
46139 Platja de la Pobla de
   Farnals 43 K 19
12520 Platja de Nules
   44 K 19
46780 Platja de Oliva 61 M 19
46712 Platja de Piles 61 M 19
46540 Platja de Puig 43 K 19
46530 Platja de Puzol
   43 K 19
46760 Platja de Tavernes
   61 L 19
50700 Playas de Chacón
   32 G 19
50297 Pleitas 21 F 17
50143 Plenas 31 G 18
48620 Plentzia 7 C 14
30176 Pliego 60 O 16
44213 Plou 31 H 18
01420 Pobes 7 D 14
12191 Pobla Tornesa 44 J 19
39230 Población de Abajo
   6 D 12
34347 Población de Arroyo
   17 E 10
34449 Población de Campos
   18 E 11
34219 Población de Cerrato
   18 F 11
46199 Poblado Cortes La
   Muela 43 L 18
18126 Poblado del Embalse/
   Alhama de
   Granada 66 Q 12
14709 Poblado del Embalse/
   Hornachuelos
   55 O 9
24724 Pobladura de la Sierra
   15 E 7
24249 Pobladura de Pelayo
   García 16 E 8
49780 Pobladura del Valle
   16 E 8
13195 Poblete 48 M 12
43376 Poboleda 23 G 21
33418 Pobra 4 B 8
36994 Poio 13 E 2
33880 Pola de Allande 3 C 6
33980 Pola de Laviana 4 C 8
33630 Pola de Lena 4 C 8
33510 Pola de Siero 4 C 8
33840 Pola de Somiedo 4 C 7
33687 Pola del Pino 4 C 8
45161 Polán 39 K 11
22216 Poleñino 22 F 19

34846 Polentinos 5 D 10
18516 Polícar 66 P 13
39220 Polientes 6 D 12
08213 Polinyà 24 F 24
46688 Polinyà de Xúquer
   61 L 19
03520 Polop 61 M 19
04114 Polopos/Níjar 68 P 15
18710 Polopos/Torvizcón
   66 Q 13
18567 Poloria 66 P 12
24995 Polvoredo 5 C 9
07460 Pollença 71 K 26
47116 Pollos 27 G 9
39660 Pomaluengo 6 C 12
34813 Pomar de Valdivia
   6 D 11
39787 Pomar/Castro-Urdiales
   7 C 13
22413 Pomar/Monzón
   22 F 20
24389 Pombriego 15 E 6
50259 Pomer 30 F 16
22196 Pompenillo 22 E 19
24400 Ponferrada 15 D 6
24127 Ponjos 16 D 7
17706 Pont de Molins
   35 E 25
25520 Pont de Suert 11 E 21
15317 Ponte-Aranga 2 C 3
15110 Ponte-Ceso 1 C 2
32704 Ponte Ambía 14 E 4
32810 Ponte Barxas 14 E 3
36829 Ponte Caldelas 13 E 3
15887 Ponte Carreira 2 C 3
15286 Ponte Nafonso 1 D 2
36860 Ponteareas 13 E 2
15600 Pontedeume 2 C 3
24838 Pontedo 4 D 8
15683 Pontepedra 1 C 2
15883 Pontevea 1 D 2
36070 Pontevedra 13 E 2
33718 Ponticiella 3 C 6
23291 Pontones 58 N 14
08738 Pontons 24 G 23
17773 Pontós 35 E 25
25740 Ponts 23 F 22
22124 Ponzano 22 E 19
33555 Poo 5 C 10
24511 Porcarizas 15 D 6
33891 Porciles 3 C 6
23790 Porcuna 56 O 11
07839 Poroig 72 M 22
09551 Porquera del Butrón
   6 D 12
17834 Porqueres 35 E 25
11180 Porquerizas 69 R 8
24397 Porqueros 16 D 7
43739 Porrera 23 G 21
07260 Porreres 71 K 26
36400 Porrino 13 E 2
33509 Porrúa 5 C 10
07740 Port d`Addaia 72 J 28
07410 Port d`Alcúdia
   71 K 26
07157 Port d`Andratx
   71 K 24
07470 Port de Pollença
   71 K 26
07108 Port de Sóller 71 K 25
07190 Port des Canonge
   71 K 25
07559 Port Nou 72 K 26
10883 Portaje 36 K 6
44730 Portalrubio 31 H 17
16522 Portalrubio de
   Guadamajud
   41 J 14
07181 Portals Nous 71 K 25
07181 Portals Vells 71 L 25
50800 Portazgo 21 F 18
17497 Portbou 35 E 26
36938 Portela/Bueu 13 E 2
36539 Portela/Chantada
   14 D 4

36692 Portela/Pontevedra
   13 D 2
42167 Portelárbol 20 F 15
25216 Portell 24 F 22
12318 Portell de Morella
   32 H 19
10828 Portezuelo 36 K 7
30510 Portichuelo 60 M 17
16141 Portilla 41 J 15
24149 Portilla de Luna 4 D 8
34114 Portillejo 17 E 10
42138 Portillo de Soria
   30 F 15
45512 Portillo de Toledo
   39 J 11
47160 Portillo/Mojados
   27 G 10
39549 Portillo/San Vincente de
   la Barquera 6 C 11
07820 Portinax 72 L 23
17488 Port-Lligat 35 E 26
30364 Portman 73 O 18
49583 Porto 15 E 6
07680 Porto Cristo Novo
   72 K 26
27712 Porto de Abaixo 3 C 5
27795 Porto de Rinlo 3 B 5
15337 Porto do Barqueiro
   3 B 5
15970 Porto do Son 1 D 2
32626 Portocamba 14 E 5
27877 Portocelo 2 B 4
07670 Portocolom 71 L 26
07680 Portocristo 72 K 26
27179 Portomarín 2 D 4
15871 Portomouro 1 D 2
36970 Portonovo 13 E 2
07691 Portopetro 71 L 26
15999 Portosín 1 D 2
48920 Portugalete 7 C 13
18415 Pórtugos 66 Q 13
15319 Porzomillos 2 C 3
13120 Porzuna 48 L 11
24915 Posada de Valdeón
   5 C 10
33594 Posada/Llanes 5 C 10
33424 Posada/Oviedo 4 C 8
14730 Posadas/Almodóvar
   55 O 9
26289 Posadas/Ezcaray
   19 E 13
14248 Posadilla 55 N 9
39313 Posadillo 6 C 11
15948 Posmarcos 13 D 2
39570 Potes 5 C 10
46721 Potries 61 M 19
15818 Pousada/Sobrado
   2 C 3
27760 Pousada/Vilanova de
   Lourenzá 3 C 5
05560 Poveda 38 H 9
16195 Poveda de la Obispalía
   41 K 15
19463 Poveda de la Sierra
   41 H 15
37406 Poveda de las Cintas
   27 G 9
02311 Povedilla 58 M 14
05492 Poyales del Hoyo
   38 J 9
16878 Poyatos 41 J 15
09246 Poza de la Sal 7 D 12
34111 Poza de la Vega
   17 D 10
47450 Pozal de Gallinas
   27 G 10
47220 Pozaldez 27 G 10
42112 Pozalmuro 20 F 15
22313 Pozán de Vero 22 E 20
05292 Pozanco 27 H 10
19265 Pozancos 29 G 13
23485 Pozo Alcón 58 O 14
03679 Pozo Blanco 60 N 18
21420 Pozo Camino 62 P 5
02510 Pozo Cañada 51 M 16

19112 Pozo de Almoguera
   40 J 13
19161 Pozo de Guadalajara
   40 J 13
04647 Pozo de la Higuera
   68 P 16
02529 Pozo de la Peña
   51 M 16
13390 Pozo de la Serna
   49 M 13
34347 Pozo de Urama
   17 E 10
04648 Pozo del Esparto
   68 P 16
30594 Pozo Estrecho 60 O 18
16708 Pozoamargo 51 L 15
49835 Pozoantiguo 27 F 9
14400 Pozoblanco 56 N 10
02141 Pozohondo 59 M 16
02154 Pozo-Lorente 51 L 16
44368 Pozondón 42 H 17
16414 Pozorrubio 40 K 14
37216 Pozos de Hinojo
   25 H 7
16212 Pozoseco 51 K 16
42220 Pozuel de Ariza
   30 G 15
44315 Pozuel del Campo
   42 H 16
02327 Pozuelo 51 M 15
28223 Pozuelo de Alarcón
   39 J 12
50529 Pozuelo de Aragón
   21 F 17
13179 Pozuelo de Calatrava
   49 M 12
47831 Pozuelo de la Orden
   17 F 9
49148 Pozuelo de Tábara
   16 F 8
10813 Pozuelo de Zarzón
   36 J 7
28813 Pozuelo del Rey
   40 J 13
32368 Prada 15 E 5
40540 Pradales 28 G 12
09248 Prádanos de Bureba
   19 D 13
34486 Prádanos de Ojeda
   6 D 11
26510 Pradejón 20 E 15
40165 Prádena 28 G 12
19243 Prádena de Atienza
   29 G 13
28191 Prádena del Rincón
   29 G 12
40100 Pradera de Navalhorno
   28 H 11
43364 Prades 23 G 21
33889 Pradiella 3 C 6
50668 Pradilla de Ebro
   21 F 17
26122 Pradillo 19 E 14
24893 Prado de la Guzpeña
   5 D 9
11660 Prado del Rey 69 Q 8
36873 Prado/A Cañiza 13 E 3
33344 Prado/Colunga 5 C 9
36512 Prado/Silleda 14 D 3
49638 Prado/Villalpando
   17 F 9
21730 Pradoalvar 15 E 5
32560 Pradocabalos 15 E 5
09260 Pradollengo 19 E 13
32368 Pradolongo 15 E 5
02161 Pradorredondo
   50 M 15
24714 Pradorrey 16 E 7
19352 Prados Redondos
   42 H 16
30410 Prados/Caravaca de la
   Cruz 59 N 16
40410 Prados/El Espinar
   39 H 11
05560 Pradosegar 38 H 9

Prágdena   (E)   **Ramiro**   E

14029 Prágdena 56 O 11
43595 Prat de Comte 33 H 20
43320 Pratdip 23 G 21
25721 Prats 12 E 23
08513 Prats de Lluçanès 12 E 24
39739 Praves 6 C 12
33120 Pravia 4 C 7
25263 Preixana 23 F 22
25316 Preixens 23 F 22
26589 Préjano 20 E 15
8330 Premià de Mar 35 G 24
33438 Prendes 4 B 8
48891 Presa 7 C 13
22807 Presa del Gállego 21 E 18
15318 Presedo 2 C 3
09228 Presencio 18 E 12
15822 Prevediños 1 D 3
32710 Prexigueiros 14 E 4
24721 Priaranza de la Valduerna 16 E 7
24448 Priaranza del Bierzo 15 D 6
49143 Priedrahita de Castro 26 F 8
16800 Priego 41 J 15
14800 Priego de Córdoba 65 P 11
33867 Priero 4 C 7
33316 Priesca 5 C 9
24885 Prioro 5 D 10
39211 Proaño 6 C 11
33114 Proaza 4 C 7
15391 Probaos 2 C 3
32611 Progo 15 F 5
27860 Progreso 2 B 4
33129 Pronga 4 C 7
25727 Prullans 12 E 23
41670 Pruna 70 Q 9
33192 Pruvia 4 C 8
46530 Puçol 43 K 19
50137 Puebla de Albortón 21 G 18
06630 Puebla de Alcocer 47 M 9
06717 Puebla de Alcollarín 46 L 8
50171 Puebla de Alfindén 21 F 18
16421 Puebla de Almenara 40 K 14
37553 Puebla de Azaba 36 J 6
19229 Puebla de Beleña 29 H 13
18820 Puebla de Don Fadrique 58 O 15
13109 Puebla de Don Rodrigo 48 L 10
42222 Puebla de Eca 30 G 15
21550 Puebla de Guzmán 62 O 5
06490 Puebla de la Calzada 53 M 6
06477 Puebla de la Reina 54 M 7
28190 Puebla de la Sierra 29 G 13
24855 Puebla de Lillo 5 C 9
06191 Puebla de Obando 45 L 6
40184 Puebla de Pedraza 28 G 12
46140 Puebla de San Miguel 42 J 17
27360 Puebla de San Xulián 2 D 5
49300 Puebla de Sanabria 15 E 6
06310 Puebla de Sáncho Pérez 54 N 7
32780 Puebla de Trives 15 E 5

19225 Puebla de Valles 29 H 13
37606 Puebla de Yeltes 37 H 7
15950 Puebla del Caramiñal 13 D 2
06906 Puebla del Maestre 54 N 7
13342 Puebla del Príncipe 58 M 14
06229 Puebla del Prior 54 M 7
16269 Puebla del Savador 51 K 16
49171 Pueblica de Campean 26 G 8
04117 Puebloblanco 68 Q 15
06184 Pueblonuevo del Guadiana 45 M 6
24380 Puente de Domingo Flórez 15 E 6
23350 Puente de Genave 58 N 14
22584 Puente de Montañana 11 E 21
39530 Puente de San Miguel 6 C 11
02150 Puente de Torres 51 L 16
16892 Puente de Vadillos 41 H 15
37748 Puente del Congosto 37 J 8
23529 Puente del Obispo 57 O 12
39250 Puente del Valle 6 D 11
23659 Puente del Villar 57 O 12
18830 Puente Duda 58 O 14
47152 Puente Duero-Esparragal 27 F 10
14500 Puente Genil 65 P 10
39571 Puente Hojedo 5 C 10
22753 Puente la Reina 9 D 18
31100 Puente la Reina-Gares 8 D 16
39556 Puente Pumar 6 C 11
23100 Puente Tabla 57 O 12
09557 Puentedey 6 D 12
09347 Puentedura 18 E 12
39554 Puentenansa 6 C 11
39670 Puente-Viesgo 6 C 12
21730 Puercas 26 F 7
37159 Puertas 26 G 7
14512 Puerto Alegre 65 P 10
23196 Puerto Alto 66 O 12
23692 Puerto Blanco 66 P 12
05621 Puerto Castilla 37 J 8
31473 Puerto de Loiti 9 D 17
30860 Puerto de Mazarrón 73 O 17
45577 Puerto de San Vicente 47 K 9
10261 Puerto de Santa Cruz 46 L 8
33790 Puerto de Vega 3 B 6
04630 Puerto del Rey 68 P 16
06428 Puerto Hurraco 55 M 8
13650 Puerto Lápice 49 L 13
18249 Puerto López 66 P 12
30890 Puerto Lumbreras 68 O 16
21209 Puerto Moral 63 O 7
11510 Puerto Real 69 Q 7
45672 Puerto Rey 47 L 9
37488 Puerto Seguro 25 H 6
11659 Puerto Serrano 69 Q 8
22362 Puértolas 10 D 20
13500 Puertollano 56 M 11
44411 Puertomingalvo 32 J 19
31394 Pueyo 8 D 16
22135 Pueyo de Fañanás 22 E 19

22416 Pueyo de Santa Cruz 27 F 20
22161 Puibolea 22 E 18
46540 Puig 43 K 19
07469 Puig de Delfi 72 M 22
17520 Puigcerdà 12 E 23
08797 Puigdàlber 24 G 23
25420 Puiggròs 23 F 21
44660 Puig-Moreno 32 G 19
43812 Puigpelat 24 G 22
07194 Puigpunyent 71 K 25
08692 Puig-reig 12 F 23
25318 Puigverd d`Agramunt 23 F 22
25153 Puigverd de Lleida 23 F 21
50810 Puilatos 21 F 18
08282 Pujalt 24 F 22
39420 Pujayo 6 C 11
29450 Pujerra 70 Q 9
45125 Pulgar 48 K 11
18197 Pulianas 66 P 12
04640 Pulpí 68 P 16
18859 Pulpite 67 O 14
39507 Pumalverde 6 C 11
39584 Pumareña 5 C 10
32338 Pumares 15 E 6
17220 Punta Brava 35 F 26
07713 Punta Prima/Mahón 72 K 28
03189 Punta Prima/Torrevieja 60 O 18
07811 Punta Rasa 72 M 22
21100 Punta Umbría 62 P 6
43421 Puntills 24 G 22
32456 Punxin 14 E 4
47419 Puras 27 G 10
09258 Puras de Villafranca 19 E 13
04870 Purchena 68 P 15
18193 Purchil 66 P 12
30813 Purias 68 O 16
50247 Purroy 21 G 16
22589 Purroy de la Solana 11 E 20
50268 Purujosa 30 F 16
18519 Purullena 67 P 13
03296 Pusol 60 N 18
22363 Puyarruego 10 D 20

Q

17242 Quart 35 F 25
46510 Quart de les Valls 43 K 19
46930 Quart de Poblet 43 L 19
46510 Quartell 43 K 19
46837 Quatretonda 61 M 19
03811 Quatretondeta 61 M 19
09559 Quecedo 7 D 12
41140 Queipo de Llano 63 P 7
15998 Queiruga 13 D 1
17538 Queixans 12 E 23
15186 Queixas 1 C 3
27162 Queizán/O Corgo 2 D 5
27651 Queizán/Poboa 3 D 5
39195 Quejo 6 C 12
26570 Quel 20 E 15
09454 Quemada 28 F 12
19209 Quer 40 H 13
17534 Queralbs 12 E 24
19269 Querencia 29 G 14
45790 Quero 49 K 13
43816 Querol 24 G 22
33539 Ques 5 C 9
46824 Quesa 52 L 18
23480 Quesada 58 O 13
22191 Quicena 22 E 19
39590 Quijas 6 C 11
28693 Quijorna 39 J 11
15295 Quilmas 1 D 1
09510 Quincoces de Yuso 7 D 13

27662 Quindous 3 D 6
32411 Quines 14 E 3
24319 Quintana de Fuseros 16 D 7
06450 Quintana de la Serena 47 M 8
09370 Quintana de Pidio 18 F 12
24397 Quintana del Castillo 16 D 7
24762 Quintana del Marco 16 E 8
24930 Quintana del Monte 17 D 9
34250 Quintana del Puente 18 E 11
09213 Quintana María 7 D 13
09210 Quintana -Martín Galíndez 7 D 13
42291 Quintana Redonda 29 F 14
24767 Quintana y Congosto 16 E 7
33836 Quintana/Belmonte 4 C 7
39806 Quintana/Puente-Viesgo 6 C 12
39699 Quintana/Ramales de la Victoria 6 C 12
09246 Quintanabureba 7 D 13
09197 Quintanadueñas 18 E 12
09244 Quintanaelez 7 D 13
09248 Quintanaloranco 19 E 13
09314 Quintanamanvirgo 28 F 12
09593 Quintanaopio 7 D 13
09140 Quintanaortuño 18 E 12
09290 Quintanapalla 19 E 12
45800 Quintanar de la Orden 50 K 13
09670 Quintanar de la Sierra 19 F 13
16220 Quintanar del Rey 51 L 16
09454 Quintanarraya 19 F 13
09141 Quintanarruz 18 D 12
42313 Quintanas de Gormaz 29 F 14
09127 Quintanas de Valdelucio 6 D 11
42345 Quintanas Rubias de Abajo 29 G 13
42345 Quintanas Rubias de Arriba 29 G 13
34485 Quintanatello de Ojeda 6 D 11
09292 Quintanavides 19 E 13
39550 Quintanila 6 C 11
09514 Quintanilla 7 C 13
47360 Quintanilla de Arriba 28 F 11
24733 Quintanilla de Florez 16 E 7
09349 Quintanilla de la Mata 18 F 12
09620 Quintanilla de las Viñas 19 E 13
24208 Quintanilla de los Oteros 17 E 9
24743 Quintanilla de Losada 15 E 6
47350 Quintanilla de Omesimo 28 F 11
39232 Quintanilla de Rucandio 6 D 12
42351 Quintanilla de Tres Barrios 29 F 13
47283 Quintanilla de Trigueros 17 F 10
09614 Quintanilla de Urrilla 19 E 13

49622 Quintanilla de Urz 16 E 8
24738 Quintanilla de Yuso 16 E 7
09347 Quintanilla del Agua 18 E 12
09348 Quintanilla del Coco 19 F 12
24285 Quintanilla del Monte/ Astorga 16 D 8
49639 Quintanilla del Monte/ Villalpando 17 F 9
49638 Quintanilla del Olmo 17 F 9
09568 Quintanilla del Rebollar 6 C 12
09271 Quintanilla San García 19 D 13
09249 Quintanillabón 7 D 13
09640 Quintanilla-Cabrera 19 E 13
09125 Quintanilla-Pedro Abarca 18 D 12
09141 Quintanilla-Sobresierra 18 D 12
09140 Quintanilla-Vivar 18 E 12
27258 Quintela 2 C 5
32814 Quintela de Leirado 14 E 3
33314 Quintes 4 B 8
50770 Quinto 22 G 18
33314 Quintueles 4 B 8
22810 Quinzano 22 E 18
36116 Quireza 13 D 3
27320 Quiroga 15 E 5
49622 Quiruelas de Vidriales 16 E 8
45514 Quismondo 39 J 11

R

27370 Rábade 2 C 4
39550 Rábago 6 C 11
32767 Rabal/Puebla de Trives 14 E 5
32698 Rabal/Verín 14 F 5
24722 Rabanal del Camino 16 E 7
49519 Rabanales 26 F 7
26133 Rabanera 20 E 15
42191 Rabanera del Campo 30 F 15
09660 Rabanera del Pinar 19 F 13
47319 Rábano 28 F 11
49515 Rábano de Aliste 25 F 7
09268 Rábanos 19 E 13
09349 Rabé de los Escuderos 18 F 12
17753 Rabós 35 E 26
16649 Rada de Haro 50 K 14
22145 Radiquero 22 E 19
42213 Radona 30 G 15
03369 Rafal 60 N 18
44589 Ráfales 32 H 20
46666 Rafelguaraf 61 L 19
03769 Ráfol de Almunia 61 M 19
46843 Ráfol de Salem 61 M 19
37318 Rágama 27 H 9
25111 Raimat 23 F 20
32652 Rairiz de Veiga 14 E 4
08256 Rajadell 24 F 23
02486 Rala 59 N 15
05418 Ramacasteñas 38 J 9
39800 Ramales de la Victoria 7 C 13
22467 Ramastué 11 D 20
30628 Rambla Salada 60 N 17
32558 Ramilo 15 E 6
32810 Ramirás 14 E 3
47453 Ramiro 27 G 10

111

I N D E X · O R T S R E G I S T E R · I N D I C E · Í N D I
P L A A T S N A M E N R E G I S T E R · R E J S T Ř Í K   M Í S

E

32646 Randín 14 F 4
33829 Rañeces 4 C 7
09212 Ranedo 7 D 13
09211 Ranera 7 D 13
48891 Ranero 7 C 13
24391 Raneros 16 D 8
22337 Rañín 10 E 20
33459 Ranón 4 B 7
27652 Rao 3 D 6
40466 Rapariegos 27 G 10
22821 Rasal 10 E 18
28740 Rascafría 28 H 12
39860 Rasines 7 C 13
30657 Raspay 60 N 17
03690 Raspeig 61 N 18
02480 Raspilla 58 N 15
43513 Rasquera 33 G 21
05298 Rasueros 27 G 9
43529 Raval de Crist 33 H 20
43590 Raval de Jesús
       33 H 21
36992 Raxó 13 E 2
19229 Razbona 29 H 13
15107 Razo 1 C 2
32102 Readegos 14 E 4
46194 Real de Montroi
       43 L 18
34844 Rebanal de las Llantas
       5 D 10
27346 Reboiró 15 D 5
33989 Rebollada 4 C 8
10617 Rebollar/Plasencia
       37 J 8
42165 Rebollar/Soria 20 F 14
34492 Rebolledo de la Torre
       6 D 11
40184 Rebollo 28 G 12
42210 Rebollo de Duero
       29 G 14
19197 Rebollosa de Hita
       40 H 13
19245 Rebollosa de Jadraque
       29 G 14
27813 Rebordaos 2 C 4
15618 Rebordelo 2 C 3
36989 Reboredo 13 E 2
26509 Recajo 20 E 15
27777 Recaré 2 B 5
45211 Recas 39 J 12
27726 Rececende (San
       Estevo) 3 C 5
42313 Recuerda 29 G 14
09270 Redecilla del Campo
       19 E 13
31482 Redín 9 D 17
24855 Redipollos 5 C 9
24844 Redipuertas 5 C 9
30813 Redón 68 O 16
15137 Redonda 1 D 1
36800 Redondela 13 E 2
03370 Redován 60 N 18
28721 Redueña 28 H 12
36542 Refoxos 14 D 3
32432 Regadas 14 E 3
17214 Regencós 35 F 26
33814 Regla 3 C 6
25692 Règola 11 F 21
36415 Reguengo 13 E 2
24763 Regueras de Arriba
       16 E 8
09693 Regumiel de la Sierra
       19 F 14
27333 Rei 14 D 5
27266 Reigosa 3 C 5
16390 Reillo 41 K 16
06970 Reina 54 N 8
27794 Reinante 3 B 5
39200 Reinosa 6 C 11
39418 Reinosilla 6 D 11
09248 Reinoso 19 D 13
34208 Reinoso de Cerrato
       18 F 11
27544 Reiriz 14 D 4
42320 Rejas de San Esteban
       29 F 13

42141 Rejas de Ucero
       29 F 13
24339 Reliegos 17 E 9
30627 Rellano 60 N 17
33873 Rellanos 3 C 6
36547 Rellas 14 D 3
03578 Relleu 61 M 19
08299 Rellinars 24 F 23
42368 Rello 29 G 14
27359 Remesar 14 D 4
24990 Remolino 5 D 9
50637 Remolinos 21 F 17
40216 Remondo 28 G 11
06715 Rena 46 L 8
19432 Renales 30 H 14
43886 Renau 24 G 22
27627 Renche 15 D 5
34473 Renedo de Valdavia
       17 D 10
39511 Renedo/Cabezón de la
       Sal 6 C 11
39470 Renedo/Torrelavega
       6 C 12
47170 Renedo/Valladolid
       27 F 10
19145 Renera 40 J 13
42189 Renieblas 20 F 15
20100 Rentería 8 C 16
02316 Reolid 58 M 14
32160 Requeixo 14 E 4
39312 Requejada 6 C 11
49394 Requejo/Puebla de
       Sanabria 15 E 6
39291 Requejo/Reinosa
       6 C 11
46340 Requena 52 L 17
34469 Requena de Campos
       18 E 11
17708 Requesen 35 E 25
39681 Resconorio 6 C 12
34844 Resoba 5 D 10
34870 Respenda de la Peña
       5 D 10
18658 Restábal 66 Q 12
33827 Restiello 4 C 7
06442 Retamal 54 M 8
04131 Retamar/Almería
       68 Q 15
13598 Retamar/Puertollano
       56 M 11
45652 Retamoso 48 K 10
50367 Retascón 31 G 17
19225 Retiendas 29 H 13
42315 Retortillo de Soria
       29 G 14
09342 Retortillo/Ciudad
       Rodrigo 18 E 11
37495 Retortillo/Lerma 25 H 7
09347 Retuerta 19 E 12
13194 Retuerta del Bullaque
       48 L 11
24917 Retuerto 5 C 9
43200 Reus 23 G 22
34447 Revenga de Campos
       18 E 11
40195 Revenga/San Ildefonso
       la Granja 28 H 11
09228 Revenga/Villaverde del
       Monte 18 E 12
22364 Revilla 10 D 20
34407 Revilla de Collazos
       18 D 10
09194 Revilla del Campo
       19 E 12
09348 Revilla-Cabriada 19 E 12
09620 Revillarruz 18 E 12
34260 Revilla-Vallegera
       18 E 11
24856 Reyero 5 D 9
09108 Rezmondo 18 D 11
41226 Reznos 30 F 15
40529 Riaguas de San
       Bartolomé 29 G 13
15874 Rial/Bembibre 1 C 2

36691 Rial/Redondela 13 E 2
15981 Rial/Rianxo 13 D 2
25594 Rialp 11 E 22
39809 Riancho 7 C 13
15920 Rianxo 13 D 2
24900 Riaño/Guardo 5 D 9
33920 Riaño/Langreo 4 C 8
40500 Riaza 29 G 13
39815 Riba 7 C 12
27686 Riba de Neira 3 D 5
19441 Riba de Saelices
       30 H 15
19269 Riba de Santiuste
       29 G 14
01213 Ribabellosa 7 D 14
32400 Ribadavia 14 E 3
49362 Ribadelago 15 E 6
27700 Ribadeo 3 B 5
33560 Ribadesella 5 C 9
31550 Ribaforada 21 F 16
26130 Ribafrecha 20 E 15
16144 Ribagorda 41 J 15
43790 Riba-roja d`Ebre
       23 G 20
46190 Riba-roja de Turia
       43 K 18
19441 Ribarredonda 30 H 15
42134 Ribarroya 30 F 15
21730 Ribarteme 13 E 3
34429 Ribas de Campos
       17 E 10
27181 Ribas de Miño 2 D 4
27349 Ribas Pequeñas
       14 D 5
27410 Ribasaltas 14 D 5
15996 Ribasieira 13 D 2
16145 Ribatajada 41 J 15
16145 Ribatajadilla 41 J 15
28815 Ribatejada 40 H 13
27206 Ribeira 2 D 4
27260 Ribeiras de Lea 2 C 4
01427 Ribera 7 D 13
25576 Ribera de Cardós
       11 D 22
06225 Ribera del Fresno
       54 M 7
33127 Riberas 4 B 7
34309 Riberos de la Cueza
       17 E 10
17534 Ribes de Freser
       12 E 24
12210 Ribesalbes 43 J 19
40513 Ribota 29 G 13
09587 Ribota de Ordunte
       7 C 13
33116 Ricabo 4 C 8
50270 Ricla 21 F 17
49165 Ricobayo 26 F 8
30610 Ricote 60 N 17
24794 Riego de la Vega
       16 E 8
24127 Riello 16 D 8
17404 Riells 35 F 25
45524 Rielves 39 K 11
19269 Rienda 29 G 14
33592 Riensena 5 C 9
22808 Riglos 9 E 18
27879 Rigueira 2 B 5
41580 Rigüelo 65 P 10
44710 Rillo 42 H 18
19340 Rillo de Gallo 30 H 16
23311 Rincón 58 N 14
29730 Rincón de la Victoria
       65 Q 11
26550 Rincón de Soto
       20 E 16
02400 Rincón del Moro
       59 M 16
05145 Rinconada 38 H 9
25290 Riner 24 F 23
27691 Río 3 D 5
45159 Río Cedena 48 K 10
09566 Río de la Sía 6 C 12
09512 Río de Losa 7 D 13
11519 Rio San Pedro 69 Q 7

27868 Ríobarba 2 B 4
05164 Riocabado 27 H 10
09615 Riocavado de la Sierra
       19 E 13
09191 Riocerezo 18 E 12
49348 Rioconejos 15 E 7
44133 Riodeva 42 J 17
33537 Riofabar 5 C 9
49591 Riofrío de Aliste 16 F 7
40515 Riofrío de Riaza
       29 G 13
19269 Riofrío del Llano
       29 G 14
24285 Riofrío/Astorga 16 D 8
05190 Riofrío/Ávila 38 H 10
29180 Riogordo 65 Q 11
04260 Rioja 67 Q 15
10693 Riolobos 27 G 9
10693 Riolobos 36 K 7
49521 Riomanzanas 15 F 6
49326 Ríonegro del Puente
       16 E 7
39232 Ríopanero 6 D 12
02450 Riópar 58 N 15
12469 Ríos de Abajo 43 K 18
33193 Riosa 4 C 8
19269 Riosalido 29 G 14
24139 Ríoscuro 4 D 7
42193 Rioseco de Soria
       29 F 14
24275 Ríoseco de Tapia
       16 D 8
33993 Ríoseco/Ladines 5 C 9
39491 Ríoseco/Pesquera
       6 C 11
24890 Ríosequino de Torío
       16 D 8
09591 Rioserras 18 E 12
31799 Ripa 8 D 16
31448 Rípodas 9 D 17
17500 Ripoll 12 E 24
08291 Ripollet 24 G 24
39180 Ris 7 C 12
06657 Risco 47 M 9
43430 Riudabella 23 G 22
17421 Riudarenes 35 F 25
17179 Riudaura 35 E 24
43771 Riudecanyes 23 G 21
43390 Riudecols 23 G 21
17457 Riudellots de la Selva
       35 F 25
43330 Riudoms 23 G 22
25352 Riudovelles 23 F 22
43870 Riumar 34 H 21
28529 Rivas Vaciamadrid
       40 J 12
40421 Rivera de los Molinos
       28 H 11
22583 Rivera del Vall 11 E 21
39409 Rivero 6 C 11
05309 Rivilla de Barajas
       27 H 10
27274 Rixoán 3 C 5
09300 Roa 28 F 12
47673 Roales 16 E 9
47131 Robladillo 27 F 10
34127 Robladillo de Ucieza
       17 E 10
37521 Robleda/Ciudad
       Rodrigo 36 J 6
49321 Robleda/Puebla de
       Sanabria 15 E 6
45160 Robledal 39 K 11
10867 Robledillo de Gata
       36 J 7
28194 Robledillo de la Jara
       29 H 12
10493 Robledillo de la Vera
       37 J 8
19227 Robledillo de
       Mohernando
       29 H 13
10269 Robledillo de Trujillo
       46 L 8

05130 Robledillo/Ávila
       38 H 10
45676 Robledillo/Los
       Navalucillos
       47 K 10
24730 Robledino 16 E 7
24146 Robledo de Caldas
       4 D 8
28294 Robledo de Chavela
       39 J 11
19243 Robledo de Corpes
       29 G 14
24458 Robledo de las
       Traviesas 15 D 7
45138 Robledo del Buey
       48 K 10
45674 Robledo del Mazo
       47 K 10
02340 Robledo/Alcaraz
       50 M 15
33534 Robledo/Arriondas
       5 C 9
33730 Robledo/Grandas
       3 C 6
49393 Robledo/Puebla de
       Sanabria 15 E 6
32312 Robledo/Rubiá 15 E 6
19223 Roblelacasa 29 G 13
19223 Robleluengo 29 G 13
37130 Robliza de Cojos
       26 H 8
09591 Robredo-Termiño
       18 E 12
28755 Robregordo 28 G 12
22252 Robres 22 F 19
26131 Robres del Castillo
       20 E 15
07819 Roca Llisa 72 M 22
46111 Rocafort 43 K 19
43426 Rocafort de Queralt
       24 G 22
25344 Rocafort de Vallbona
       23 F 22
31409 Rocaforte 9 D 17
39250 Rocamundo 6 D 12
21720 Rociana del Condado
       63 P 6
11149 Roche 69 R 7
30739 Roda 60 O 18
43883 Roda de Berà 24 G 22
40290 Roda de Eresma
       28 G 11
22482 Roda de Isábena
       11 E 21
08510 Roda de Ter 35 F 24
04115 Rodalquilar 68 Q 15
36530 Rodeiro 14 D 4
22144 Rodellar 22 E 19
44310 Ródenas 42 H 16
26222 Rodezno 19 D 14
33876 Rodical 4 C 7
24134 Rodicol 3 C 7
24837 Rodillazo 4 D 8
43812 Rodonyà 24 G 22
27744 Rodrigas 3 C 5
24715 Rodrigatos de la
       Obispalía 16 D 7
30658 Rodriguillo 60 N 17
49211 Roelos 26 G 7
27229 Roimil 2 C 4
01129 Roitegui 8 D 15
39593 Roiz 6 C 11
03170 Rojales 60 N 18
43415 Rojals 23 G 22
09246 Rojas 7 D 13
30709 Roldán 60 O 17
42165 Rollamienta 20 F 14
37447 Rollán 26 H 8
19411 Romancos 40 H 14
19276 Romanillos de Atienza
       29 G 14
42213 Romanillos de
       Medinaceli
       30 G 14
19143 Romanones 40 H 14

Romanos   (E)   **San Esteve de Litera**   E

50491 Romanos 31 G 17
17240 Romanya de la Selva
       35 F 25
27737 Romariz 2 C 5
31415 Roncal 9 D 18
29400 Ronda 70 Q 9
25594 Roní 11 E 22
15288 Roo 1 D 2
24791 Roperuelos del Páramo
       16 E 8
04740 Roquetas de Mar
       67 Q 14
43520 Roquetes 33 H 21
09150 Ros 18 E 12
10391 Rosalejo 37 K 9
09514 Rosales 7 D 13
12511 Rosell 33 H 20
27548 Rosende 14 D 4
17480 Roses 35 E 26
49322 Rosinos de la
       Requejada 15 E 6
09514 Rosío 7 D 13
25124 Rosselló 23 F 21
11520 Rota 69 Q 7
46816 Rotglá y Corbera
       52 L 18
46725 Rotóva 61 M 19
47316 Roturas 28 F 11
27835 Roupar 2 C 4
02125 Royo-Odrea 59 M 15
44125 Royuela 42 J 16
09344 Royuela de Río Franco
       18 E 12
33729 Rozadas/Boal 3 C 6
33313 Rozadas/Villaviciosa
       4 C 8
39559 Rozadío 6 C 11
16452 Rozalén del Monte
       40 K 14
39808 Rozas 7 C 13
28649 Rozas de Puerto Real
       38 J 11
36875 Rua 13 E 3
27889 Rúa 3 B 5
39232 Ruanales 6 D 12
10189 Ruanes 46 L 7
39727 Rubalcaba 6 C 12
39719 Rubayo 6 C 12
09199 Rubena 18 E 12
07144 Ruberts 71 K 25
08191 Rubí 24 G 24
47494 Rubí de Bracamonte
       27 G 10
32310 Rubiá 15 E 6
06445 Rubiales/Berlanga
       54 N 8
44121 Rubiales/Teruel
       42 J 17
27350 Rubián 14 D 5
36619 Rubiáns 13 D 2
32558 Rubiás 15 E 5
27191 Rubiás 2 C 5
16212 Rubielos Altos 51 L 15
16212 Rubielos Bajos 51 L 15
44166 Rubielos de la Cérida
       42 H 17
44415 Rubielos de Mora
       43 J 18
25213 Rubinat 24 F 22
25737 Rubió/Artesa de Segre
       23 F 21
08719 Rubió/Igualada
       24 F 23
25737 Rubió/La Seu d`Urgell
       11 E 22
18711 Rubite 66 Q 13
09592 Rublacedo de Abajo
       19 D 13
09592 Rublacedo de Arriba
       19 D 12
09593 Rucandio/Oña 7 D 12
39232 Rucandio/Reinosa
       6 D 12
06412 Ruecas 46 L 8
47490 Rueda 27 G 10

50295 Rueda de Jalón
       21 F 17
19339 Rueda de la Sierra
       30 H 16
33576 Ruenes 5 C 10
39513 Ruente 6 C 11
39231 Ruerrero 6 D 12
50331 Ruesca 31 G 17
46842 Rugat 61 M 19
13249 Ruidera 50 M 14
17469 Ruimors 35 E 26
39528 Ruiseñada 6 C 11
17131 Rupià 35 E 26
23430 Rus 57 N 13
14960 Rute 65 P 11
09341 Ruyales del Agua
       18 E 12
09150 Ruyales del Páramo
       18 D 12

S
17248 S`Agaro 35 F 26
07713 S`Algar 72 K 28
07691 S`Alqueria Blanca
       71 L 26
07199 S`Aranjassa 71 K 25
07600 S`Arenal 71 K 25
07159 S`Arracó 71 K 24
07193 S`Esgleieta 71 K 25
07669 S`Horta 71 L 26
07700 S`Ullastrar 72 K 28
36516 Sa 14 D 3
07141 Sa Cabaneta 71 K 25
07100 Sa Calobra 71 K 25
07458 Sa Colònia 71 K 26
07011 Sa Indioteria 71 K 25
07409 Sa Marina 71 K 25
07420 Sa Pobla 71 K 26
07639 Sa Ràpita 71 L 25
17255 Sa Riera 35 F 26
07640 Sa Vall 71 L 26
07011 Sa Vileta 71 K 25
27336 Saa 14 D 5
08200 Sabadell 24 F 24
27517 Sabadelle 14 D 4
15280 Sabardes 1 D 2
27163 Sabarei 2 D 5
24810 Sabero 5 D 9
02611 Sabinares 50 M 14
22600 Sabiñánigo 10 D 19
23410 Sabiote 57 N 13
36581 Sabrexo 2 D 3
32821 Sabucedo/Celanova
       14 E 4
36559 Sabucedo/Forcarei
       13 D 3
15891 Sabugueira 1 D 3
12469 Sacañet 43 K 18
19432 Sacecorbo 30 H 15
24744 Saceda 15 E 6
16532 Saceda del Río 41 J 14
16463 Saceda-Trasierra
       40 J 14
19120 Sacedón 40 J 14
13414 Saceruela 48 M 10
36121 Sacos 13 D 2
40237 Sacramenia 28 G 12
15160 Sada/Carrio 2 C 3
31491 Sada/Sangüesa 9 D 17
50670 Sádaba 21 E 17
16430 Saelices 40 K 14
19443 Saelices de la Sal
       30 H 15
47689 Saelices de Mayorga
       17 E 9
24920 Saelices de Payuelo
       17 D 9
24172 Saelices del Río 17 D 9
49594 Sagallos 15 F 7
22572 Saganta 23 F 20
08517 Sagás 12 E 23
31486 Sagaseta 9 D 16
42259 Sagides 30 G 15
46500 Sagunto-Sagunt
       43 K 19

24320 Sahagún 17 E 9
37592 Sahelices el Chico
       36 H 6
22468 Sahun 11 D 20
39517 Saja 6 C 11
26212 Sajazarra 7 D 14
27206 Salaia 2 D 4
37070 Salamanca 26 H 8
18310 Salar 66 P 11
25598 Salardu 11 D 21
29714 Salares 66 Q 11
33860 Salas 4 C 7
22314 Salas Altas 22 E 20
22314 Salas Bajas 22 E 20
09593 Salas de Bureba
       7 D 13
24384 Salas de la Ribera
       15 E 6
24414 Salas de los Barrios
       15 D 6
09600 Salas de los Infantes
       19 E 13
25696 Salàs de Pallars
       11 E 21
09556 Salazar 6 D 12
09136 Salazar de Amaya
       18 D 11
49211 Salcé 26 G 7
24132 Salce 4 D 7
34829 Salcedillo/Barruelo
       6 D 11
44793 Salcedillo/Montalbán
       31 H 17
33117 Salcedo 4 C 8
34100 Saldaña 17 D 10
40514 Saldaña de Ayllón
       29 G 13
37259 Saldeana 25 G 6
08697 Saldes 12 E 23
31747 Saldias 8 C 16
44122 Saldón 42 J 17
42156 Salduero 19 F 14
46843 Salem 61 M 19
15885 Sales (San Xulián)
       1 D 2
15127 Salgueiros/Dumbría
       1 C 1
27568 Salgueiros/Vilanova
       2 D 4
09198 Salguero de Juarros
       19 E 13
17320 Salianç 35 F 25
04813 Saliente Alto 68 O 15
24495 Salientes 4 D 7
22110 Salillas 22 F 19
50294 Salillas de Jalón
       21 F 17
01426 Salinas de Añana
       7 D 14
22312 Salinas de Hoz
       22 E 20
31473 Salinas de Ibargoiti
       9 D 17
22822 Salinas de Jaca 9 E 18
42240 Salinas de Medinaceli
       30 G 15
31175 Salinas de Oro 8 D 16
34830 Salinas de Pisuerga
       6 D 11
22366 Salinas de Sín 10 D 20
16317 Salinas del Manzano
       42 J 16
33400 Salinas/Avilés 4 B 8
03638 Salinas/Elda 60 M 18
09247 Salinillas de Bureba
       19 D 13
08650 Sallent 24 F 23
22640 Sallent de Gállego
       10 D 19
30890 Salmerón/Calasparra
       59 N 16
19126 Salmerón/Sacedón
       41 H 15
16813 Salmeroncillos de Abajo
       41 H 14

37314 Salmoral 27 H 9
08269 Salo 24 F 23
05520 Salobral 38 H 10
05530 Salobralejo 38 H 10
02316 Salobre 58 M 14
18680 Salobreña 66 Q 12
43885 Salomó 24 G 22
10570 Salorino 45 L 5
43840 Salou 23 G 22
12186 Salsadella 33 J 20
17190 Salt 35 F 25
41909 Salteras 63 P 7
19119 Salto de Bolarque
       40 J 14
49513 Salto de Castro 26 F 7
46199 Salto de Millares
       43 L 18
16318 Salvacañete 42 J 17
05380 Salvadiós 27 H 9
47219 Salvador de Zapardiel
       27 G 10
06174 Salvaleón 53 M 5
06174 Salvaleón 53 M 6
25748 Salvanera 23 F 22
01200 Salvatierra 8 D 15
50684 Salvatierra de Escá
       9 D 17
06175 Salvatierra de los
       Barros 53 N 6
37779 Salvatierra de Tormes
       37 H 8
33119 Sama 4 C 7
01307 Samaniego 19 D 14
27842 Samarugo 2 C 4
40442 Samboal 28 G 11
27203 Sambreixo 2 D 4
33558 Sames 5 C 9
36992 Samieira 13 E 2
22394 Samitier 10 E 20
27620 Samos 15 D 5
22452 Samper 10 E 20
44520 Samper de Calanda
       32 G 19
50134 Samper del Salz
       31 G 18
36519 Samprizón 14 D 3
31570 San Adrián 20 E 16
09198 San Adrián de Juarros
       19 E 13
24797 San Adrián del Valle
       16 E 8
28750 San Agustín de
       Guadalix 39 H 12
49135 San Agustín del Pozo
       16 F 8
04716 San Agustín/Almerimar
       67 Q 14
44480 San Agustín/Segorbe
       43 J 18
32515 San Amaro 14 E 3
19237 San Andrés del
       Congosto 29 H 13
24070 San Andrés del
       Rabanedo 16 D 8
19143 San Andrés del Rey
       40 H 14
39687 San Andrés/
       Entrambasmestas
       6 C 12
39573 San Andrés/Potes
       5 C 10
42169 San Andrés/Soria
       20 F 15
26126 San Andrés/Villanueva
       de Cambreros
       20 E 14
33810 San Antolín 3 C 6
36194 San Antoniño 13 D 2
46390 San Antonio 52 K 17
46184 San Antonio de
       Benagéber
       43 K 18
26340 San Asensio 19 E 14
05516 San Bartolomé de
       Corneja 37 J 9

21510 San Bartolomé de la
       Torre 62 P 5
45654 San Bartolomé de las
       Abiertas 38 K 10
05267 San Bartolomé de
       Pinares 38 H 10
03314 San Bartolomé/Rafal
       60 N 18
26131 San Bartolomé/
       Ribafrecha
       20 E 14
06106 San Benito de la
       Contienda 53 M 5
46621 San Benito/Almansa
       52 M 17
13413 San Benito/Santa
       Eufemia 56 M 10
11648 San Bernardino 69 Q 8
21730 San Blas 15 F 7
44195 San Blás 42 J 17
14749 San Calixto 55 O 9
13247 San Carlos del Valle
       49 M 13
30592 San Cayetano 60 O 18
34429 San Cebrián de
       Campos 17 E 10
47129 San Cebrián de Mazote
       27 F 9
34839 San Cebrián de Mudá
       6 D 11
32559 San Cibrao 15 E 5
32911 San Cibráo das Viñas
       14 E 4
24857 San Cibrián de la
       Somoza 5 D 9
49359 San Ciprián 15 E 6
27888 San Ciprián 2 B 5
33191 San Claudio 4 C 8
33810 San Clemente/Poboa
       3 D 6
16600 San Clemente/Sisante
       50 L 15
27310 San Clodio 15 E 5
27124 San Cosme 3 B 5
09515 San Cristóbal de
       Almendres 7 D 13
34491 San Cristóbal de Boedo
       18 D 11
40212 San Cristóbal de
       Cuéllar 28 G 11
49690 San Cristóbal de
       Entrevinas 16 E 8
24359 San Cristóbal de la
       Polantera 16 E 8
40465 San Cristóbal de la
       Vega 27 G 10
09259 San Cristóbal del Monte
       19 E 13
39248 San Cristóbal del Monte
       6 D 11
33425 San Cucao 4 C 8
33885 San Emiliano/Pezos
       3 C 6
24144 San Emiliano/Pinos
       4 D 8
11312 San Enrique 70 R 9
48191 San Esteban de
       Galdames 7 C 13
42330 San Esteban de
       Gormaz 29 F 13
37671 San Esteban de la
       Sierra 37 H 8
05289 San Esteban de los
       Patos 38 H 10
24760 San Esteban de
       Nogales 16 E 8
05229 San Esteban de
       Zapardiel
       27 G 10
49650 San Esteban del Molar
       16 F 8
05412 San Esteban del Valle
       38 J 10
22512 San Esteve de Litera
       22 F 20

San Facundo/Carballiño (E) Sant Agnès de Corona

32139 San Facundo/ Carballiño 14 E 3
24378 San Facundo/ Ponferrada 16 D 7
09145 San Felices 6 D 12
37240 San Felices de los Gallegos 25 H 6
03158 San Felipe Neri 60 N 18
22470 San Feliú de Veri 11 E 21
33875 San Félix 3 C 6
11100 San Fernando 69 R 7
28830 San Fernando de Henares 40 J 12
06109 San Francisco de Olivenza 53 M 5
03177 San Fulgencio 60 N 18
05146 San García de Ingelmos 27 H 9
46160 San Gerardo 43 K 18
02690 San Gregorio 52 M 17
25271 San Guim de Freixenet 24 F 22
28292 San Ignacio 39 H 11
41209 San Ignacio del Viar 63 O 8
40100 San Ildefonso o La Granja 28 H 11
04117 San Isidro 68 Q 15
46116 San Isidro de Benagéber 43 K 19
31312 San Isidro del Pinar 9 E 17
30730 San Javier 60 O 18
25799 San Joan Fumat 12 E 22
22283 San Jorge/Almudévar 22 F 18
12320 San Jorge/Vinaròs 33 H 20
30559 San José Artesano 60 N 17
41300 San José de la Rinconada 63 P 8
11510 San José del Pedroso 69 Q 8
11580 San José del Valle 69 Q 8
04118 San José/Almería 68 Q 15
03550 San Juan de Alicante 61 N 19
41920 San Juan de Aznalfarache 63 P 7
05358 San Juan de la Encinilla 27 H 10
24545 San Juan de la Mata 15 D 6
04648 San Juan de los Terreros 68 P 16
50820 San Juan de Mozarrifar 21 F 18
33417 San Juan de Nieva 4 B 8
33159 San Juan de Piñera 4 B 7
22367 San Juan de Plan 10 D 20
39451 San Juan de Raicedo 6 C 11
22213 San Juán del Flúmen 22 F 19
05120 San Juan del Molinillo 38 J 10
09490 San Juan del Monte 29 F 12
05145 San Juan del Olmo 38 H 9
09199 San Juan/Burgos 18 E 12
46390 San Juan/Requena 52 K 17

22192 San Julián de Banzo 22 E 19
49358 San Justo 15 E 6
24710 San Justo de la Vega 16 E 7
41729 San Leandro 63 P 8
42140 San Leonardo de Yagüe 19 F 13
47317 San Llorente 28 F 11
34405 San Llorente de la Vega 18 E 11
24415 San Lorenzo 15 D 6
13779 San Lorenzo de Calatrava 57 N 12
28200 San Lorenzo de El Escorial 39 H 11
22212 San Lorenzo de Flúmen 22 F 19
16770 San Lorenzo de la Parrilla 41 K 15
22338 San Lorién 10 E 20
29692 San Luis de Sabinillas 70 R 9
28739 San Mamés 28 H 12
09125 San Mamés de Abar 6 D 11
39764 San Mamés de Aras 7 C 12
09230 San Mamés de Burgos 18 E 12
34127 San Mamés de Campos 17 E 10
39192 San Mamés de Meruelo 7 C 12
15176 San Marco 2 C 3
16370 San Martín de Boniches 42 K 16
49361 San Martín de Castaneda 15 E 6
09212 San Martín de Don 7 D 13
39231 San Martín de Elines 6 D 12
09217 San Martín de Galvarín 7 D 14
24688 San Martín de la Tercia 4 D 8
28330 San Martín de la Vega 39 J 12
05133 San Martín de la Vega del Alberche 38 J 9
50584 San Martín de la Virgen del Moncayo 20 F 16
09574 San Martín de las Ollas 6 D 12
45165 San Martín de Montalbán 48 K 11
33777 San Martín de Oscos 3 C 6
45170 San Martín de Pusa 38 K 10
09317 San Martín de Rubiales 28 F 12
49540 San Martín de Tábara 26 F 8
10892 San Martín de Trevejo 36 J 6
31495 San Martin de Unx 9 D 16
28680 San Martín de Valdeiglesias 39 J 11
47129 San Martín de Valderaduey 16 F 9
47209 San Martín de Valveni 17 F 10
22470 San Martín de Veri 11 E 21
37659 San Martín del Castañar 37 H 7
34407 San Martín del Monte 18 D 11

05132 San Martín del Pimpollar 38 J 9
44390 San Martín del Río 31 G 17
09558 San Martín del Rojo 6 D 12
11340 San Martín del Tesorillo 70 R 9
31272 San Martin/Eulate 8 D 15
22372 San Martín/Jánovas 10 E 19
32767 San Martiño/Castro Caldelas 14 E 5
32689 San Martino/Verín 14 F 4
50840 San Mateo de Gállego 21 F 18
15887 San Mauro 2 C 3
39491 San Miguel de Aguayo 6 C 11
39766 San Miguel de Aras 7 C 12
47164 San Miguel de Arroyo 28 G 11
40332 San Miguel de Burnuy 28 G 12
05514 San Miguel de Corneja 38 J 9
39687 San Miguel de Luena 6 C 12
39192 San Miguel de Meruelo 6 C 12
37659 San Miguel de Robledo 37 H 7
03193 San Miguel de Salinas 60 O 18
05150 San Miguel de Serrezuela 38 H 9
37763 San Miguel de Valero 37 H 8
47132 San Miguel del Pino 27 F 10
49680 San Miguel del Valle 16 E 9
28380 San Miguel/Aranjuez 40 J 12
33677 San Miguel/ Cabañaquinta 4 C 8
22413 San Miguel/Lleida 22 F 20
32792 San Miguel/Petin 15 E 5
23469 San Miguel/Úbeda 57 O 13
01427 San Milán de San Zadornil 7 D 13
26216 San Milán de Yécora 19 D 13
09640 San Millán de Jara 19 E 13
09198 San Millán de Juarros 19 E 12
26326 San Millán de la Cogolla 19 E 14
24237 San Millán de los Cabelleros 16 E 8
32688 San Millao 14 F 4
37208 San Muñoz 26 H 7
41388 San Nicolás del Puerto 54 O 8
11320 San Pablo de Buceite 70 R 9
47219 San Pablo de la Moraleja 27 G 10
45120 San Pablo de los Montes 48 K 11
32633 San Paio de Abades 14 F 4
09512 San Pantaleón de Losa 7 D 13
05164 San Pascual 27 H 10
29670 San Pedro de Alcántara 70 R 9

24252 San Pedro de Bercianos 16 E 8
34889 San Pedro de Cansoles 5 D 10
49628 San Pedro de Ceque 16 E 7
40389 San Pedro de Gaíllos 28 G 12
24329 San Pedro de las Dueñas 17 E 9
47851 San Pedro de Latarce 27 F 9
06893 San Pedro de Mérida 46 M 7
24436 San Pedro de Olleros 15 D 6
37183 San Pedro de Rozados 26 H 8
24328 San Pedro de Valderaduey 17 E 10
05350 San Pedro del Arroyo 27 H 10
30740 San Pedro del Pinatar 60 O 18
39686 San Pedro del Romeral 6 C 12
37170 San Pedro del Valle 26 G 8
42174 San Pedro Manrique 20 E 15
16813 San Pedro Palmiches 41 J 15
20110 San Pedro/Donostia-San Sebastian 8 C 16
02326 San Pedro/Hellín 51 M 15
28595 San Pedro/Tarancón 40 J 13
48130 San Pelaio 7 C 14
47129 San Pelayo 27 F 9
37110 San Pelayo de Guarena 26 G 8
34492 San Quirce del Río Pisuerga 18 D 11
12510 San Rafael del Río 33 H 20
03200 San Rafael/Alcoy/Alcoi 61 M 19
40410 San Rafael/El Espinar 39 H 11
11650 San Rafael/Villamartín 69 Q 8
22609 San Román de Basa 10 E 19
26133 San Román de Cameros 20 E 15
47530 San Román de Hornija 27 G 9
34347 San Román de la Cuba 17 E 10
45646 San Román de los Montes 38 J 10
27664 San Román/Becerreá 3 D 5
33828 San Román/Grullos 4 C 7
39012 San Román/Santander 6 C 12
33596 San Roque del Acebal 5 C 10
15147 San Roque/Carballo 1 C 2
32226 San Roque/Crecente 14 E 3
11360 San Roque/La Línea de la Concepción 70 R 9
39525 San Roque/Santillana de Mar 6 C 11
34847 San Salvador de Cantamuda 6 D 11
39554 San Sebastián de Garabandal 6 C 11

14150 San Sebastián de los Ballesteros 65 O 10
28700 San Sebastián de los Reyes 39 H 12
21591 San Silvestre de Guzmán 62 P 5
21330 San Telmo 62 O 6
32428 San Tomé 14 E 3
26291 San Torcuato 19 E 14
06500 San Vicente de Alcantara 45 L 5
05217 San Vicente de Arévalo 27 H 10
49592 San Vicente de la Cabeza 16 F 7
24154 San Vicente del Condado 17 D 9
47493 San Vincente del Palacio 27 G 10
03690 San Vicente del Raspeig 61 N 18
09268 San Vicente del Valle 19 E 13
41728 San Vicente Ferrer 63 P 7
12126 San Vicente/Alcora 43 J 19
15863 San Vicente/Negreira 1 D 2
32348 San Vicente/Rubiá 15 E 5
36989 San Vicenzo 13 E 2
26339 San Vincente 19 D 14
39540 San Vincente de la Barquera 6 C 11
39450 San Vincente de León 6 C 11
39699 San Vincente de Toranzo 6 C 12
39592 San Vincente del Monte 6 C 11
49523 San Vitero 16 F 7
01427 San Zadornil 7 D 13
25753 Sanaüja 24 F 22
24439 Sancedo 15 D 6
06655 Sancti-Spiritus/Cabeza de Buey 47 M 9
37470 Sancti-Spíritus/Ciudad Rodrigo 36 H 7
05290 Sanchidrián 27 H 10
50669 Sancho Abarca 1 F 17
37217 Sanchón de la Ribera 25 G 7
37466 Sanchón de la Sagrada 37 H 7
40297 Sanchonuño 28 G 11
05141 Sanchorreja 38 H 10
32823 Sande 14 E 3
32692 Sandiás 14 E 4
49594 Sandín 15 E 7
37468 Sando 26 H 7
09124 Sandoval de la Reina 18 D 11
03769 Sanet y Negrals 61 M 19
42113 Sanfelices 20 F 15
40134 Sangarcía 28 H 11
22100 Sangarrén 22 E 19
30833 Sangonera la Verde 60 O 17
31400 Sangüesa 9 D 17
11540 Sanlúcar de Barrameda 69 Q 7
21595 Sanlúcar de Guadiana 62 P 5
41800 Sanlúcar la Mayor 63 P 7
31448 Sansoáin/Aoiz-Agoitz 9 D 17
31494 Sansoáin/Tafalla 9 D 16
31220 Sansol 20 D 15
08930 Sant Adrià de Besòs 24 G 24
07828 Sant Agnès de Corona 72 L 22

Sant Agustí de Lluçanès E **Santa Margalida** E

08586 Sant Agustí de
Lluçanès 12 E 24
07839 Sant Agustí des Vedrà
72 M 22
25712 Sant Andreu 11 E 22
08740 Sant Andreu de la
Barca 24 G 23
08392 Sant Andreu de
Llavaneres
35 F 24
17455 Sant Andreu Salou
35 F 25
17154 Sant Aniol de Finestres
35 E 25
25213 Sant Antolí i Vilanova
24 F 22
17252 Sant Antoni de Calonge
35 F 26
07820 Sant Antoni de
Potmany 72 M 22
08459 Sant Antoni de
Vilamajor 35 F 24
08519 Sant Bartomeu del
Grau 12 F 24
08830 Sant Boi de Llobregat
24 G 24
08589 Sant Boi de Lluçanès
12 E 24
43540 Sant Carles de la
Ràpita 33 H 21
07850 Sant Carles de Peralta
08396 Sant Cebrià de Vallata
35 F 25
08470 Sant Celoni 35 F 24
07712 Sant Climent 72 K 28
08849 Sant Climent de
Llobregat 24 G 24
17751 Sant Climent Sessebes
35 E 25
17810 Sant Cristofol les Fonts
35 E 24
08190 Sant Cugat del Vallès
24 G 24
08798 Sant Cugat
Sesgarrigues
24 G 23
07159 Sant Elm 71 K 24
25632 Sant Esteve de la
Sarga 11 E 21
17154 Sant Esteve de
Llémana 35 E 25
08461 Sant Esteve de
Palautordera
35 F 24
08635 Sant Esteve Sesroirres
24 G 23
07818 Sant Fancesc
72 M 22
17451 Sant Feliu de Buixalleu
35 F 25
08182 Sant Feliu de Codines
24 F 24
17220 Sant Feliu de Guíxols
35 F 26
08980 Sant Feliu de Llobregat
24 G 24
17174 Sant Feliu de Pallerols
35 E 25
08274 Sant Feliu Sasserra
12 F 24
07871 Sant Ferran de ses
Roques 72 M 22
07769 Sant Francesc 72 K 27
07608 Sant Francesc de
Formentera
72 M 22
43479 Sant Francisc 23 G 22
08272 Sant Fruitós de Bages
24 F 23
17320 Sant Grau 35 F 25
17150 Sant Gregori 35 F 25
25211 Sant Guim de la Plana
24 F 22
17403 Sant Hilari Sacalm
35 F 25

08512 Sant Hipòlit de Voltregà
12 E 24
07730 Sant Jaume 72 K 28
73877 Sant Jaume d`Enveja
33 H 21
08619 Sant Jaume de
Frotanyà 12 E 24
17854 Sant Jaume de Llierca
35 E 25
43713 Sant Jaume dels
Domenys 24 G 23
07810 Sant Joan de Labritja
72 L 23
17860 Sant Joan de les
Abadesses
12 E 24
17463 Sant Joan de Mollet
35 E 25
12130 Sant Joan de Moró
44 J 19
08250 Sant Joan de
Vilatorrada
24 F 23
07769 Sant Joan Gran
72 K 27
17857 Sant Joan les Fonts
35 E 25
12550 Sant Joan/Almassora
44 K 19
07240 Sant Joan/Manacor
71 K 26
07817 Sant Jordi 72 M 22
17464 Sant Jordi Desvalls
35 E 25
07199 Sant Jordi/Algaida
71 K 25
07469 Sant Josef de sa Talaia
72 M 22
08694 Sant Julià de
Cerdanyola
12 E 23
08504 Sant Julià de Vilatorta
35 F 24
25287 Sant Just-Joval
12 F 23
17531 Sant Llorenç 35 F 25
08791 Sant Llorenç d`Hortons
24 G 23
07812 Sant Llorenc de Balàfia
72 L 22
17732 Sant Llorenç de la
Muga 35 E 25
25613 Sant Llorenç de
Montgai 23 F 21
25282 Sant Llorenç de
Morunys 12 E 23
08212 Sant Llorenç Savall
24 F 24
07710 Sant Lluís 72 K 28
08515 Sant Martí d`Albars
12 E 24
17861 Sant Martí d`Ogassa
12 E 24
25639 Sant Martí de
Bacedana 11 E 21
17153 Sant Martí de Llémena
35 E 25
25344 Sant Marti de Maldà
23 F 22
08712 Sant Martí de Tous
24 F 23
08731 Sant Martí Sarroca
24 G 23
08282 Sant Martí Sesgueioles
24 F 22
17746 Sant Martí Sesserres
35 E 25
17462 Sant Martí Vell 35 E 25
12170 Sant Mateu 33 J 20
07815 Sant Mateu d`Eubarca
72 L 22
17242 Sant Mateu de
Montnegre 35 F 25
17475 Sant Miguel de Fluvià
35 E 25

07815 St. Miquel 72 L 22
08818 Sant Miquel d`Olérdola
24 G 23
17831 Sant Miquel de
Campmajor
35 E 25
17467 Sant Mori 35 E 25
12140 Sant Pau 32 J 19
08739 Sant Pau d`Ordal
24 G 23
17864 Sant Pau de Seguries
35 E 24
08810 Sant Pere de Ribes
24 G 23
08776 Sant Pere de
Ruidebitlles
24 G 23
08572 Sant Pere de Torelló
12 E 24
08458 Sant Pere de Vilamajor
35 F 24
43070 Sant Pere i Sant Pau
24 G 22
17470 Sant Pere Pescador
35 E 26
08395 Sant Pol de Mar
35 F 25
17178 Sant Privat duren Bas
35 E 24
08777 Sant Quintí de Mediona
24 G 23
08580 Sant Quirze de Besora
12 E 24
08189 Sant Quirze Safaja
24 F 24
07816 Sant Rafel 72 M 22
07816 Sant Rafel de sa Creu
72 M 22
25215 Sant Ramon
24 F 22
25656 Sant Romà d`Abella
11 E 22
08770 Sant Sadurní d`Anoia
24 G 23
08519 Sant Sadurní de
Osormont 35 F 24
25638 Sant Salvador de Toló
11 E 22
25689 Sant Serni 11 E 21
07749 Sant Tomàs 72 K 28
08295 Sant Vicenç de
Castellet 24 F 23
08394 Sant Vicenç de Montalt
35 F 25
07811 Sant Vicent de sa Cala
72 L 23
08571 Sant Vicenç de Torelló
12 E 24
08620 Sant Vicenç dels Horts
24 G 24
17151 Santa Afra 35 F 25
06410 Santa Amalia 46 L 7
45653 Santa Ana de Pusa
38 K 10
21359 Santa Ana la Real
62 O 6
23692 Santa Ana/Alcalá la
Real 66 P 12
49518 Santa Ana/Alcanices
25 P 7
10189 Santa Ana/Ana 46 L 8
24394 Santa Ana/Astorga
16 E 8
02328 Santa Ana/AYna
59 M 15
02070 Santa Ana/Hellín
51 M 16
24394 Santa Ana/Ponferrada
15 D 6
50617 Santa Anastasia
21 E 17
21570 Santa Bárbara de Casa
62 O 5
43570 Santa Bàrbara/Amposta
33 H 20

12530 Santa Bárbara/Burriana
44 K 19
04662 Santa Bárbara/Huercal-
Overa 68 P 16
08773 Santa Cándia 24 F 23
15841 Santa Catalina de
Armada 1 C 2
34191 Santa Cecilia del Alcor
17 F 10
09341 Santa Cecilia/Lerma
18 E 12
42173 Santa Cecilia/Yanguas
20 E 15
22141 Santa Cilia 22 E 19
22791 Santa Cilia de Jaca
9 D 18
14280 Santa Clara 55 M 9
17430 Santa Coloma de
Farners 35 F 25
08920 Santa Coloma de
Gramanet 24 G 24
43420 Santa Coloma de
Queralt 24 F 22
26315 Santa Coloma/Bezares
19 E 14
33778 Santa Coloma/Illano
3 C 6
24848 Santa Colomba de
Curueño 5 D 9
24722 Santa Colomba de
Somoza 16 E 7
25712 Santa Creu de
Castellbò 11 E 22
17310 Santa Cristina 35 F 25
17246 Santa Cristina d`Aro
35 F 25
49620 Santa Cristina de la
Polvorose 16 E 8
24290 Santa Cristina de
Valmadrigal 17 E 9
49626 Santa Croya de Tera
16 F 8
21730 Santa Cruz de Abranes
15 F 6
39100 Santa Cruz de Bezana
6 C 12
34491 Santa Cruz de Boedo
18 D 11
50324 Santa Cruz de Grío
21 G 17
09198 Santa Cruz de Juarros
19 E 13
09471 Santa Cruz de la
Salceda 28 F 12
22792 Santa Cruz de la Serós
9 D 18
10260 Santa Cruz de la Sierra
46 L 8
45370 Santa Cruz de la Zarza
40 K 13
13327 Santa Cruz de los
Cánamos 58 M 14
50513 Santa Cruz de
Moncayo 20 F 16
16336 Santa Cruz de Moya
42 K 17
13730 Santa Cruz de Mudela
57 M 13
44493 Santa Cruz de
Nogueras 31 G 17
10661 Santa Cruz de
Paniagua 36 J 7
18129 Santa Cruz del Alhama
o del Comercio
66 P 12
34477 Santa Cruz del Monte
18 D 11
09125 Santa Cruz del Tozo
18 D 12
05413 Santa Cruz del Valle
38 J 9
09268 Santa Cruz del Valle
Urbión 19 E 13
04568 Santa Cruz/Aloboluduy
67 P 14

14820 Santa Cruz/Espejo
56 O 10
33612 Santa Cruz/Pola de
Lena 4 C 8
33427 Santa Cruz/Posada
4 C 8
42173 Santa Cuz de Yagüas
20 E 15
23213 Santa Elena 57 N 12
24762 Santa Elena de Jamuz
16 E 8
50669 Santa Engracia 21 F 17
22751 Santa Engracia de Jaca
9 D 18
26131 Santa Engracia de
Jubera 20 E 15
14491 Santa Eufemia
56 M 10
47811 Santa Eufemia del
Arroyo 17 F 9
08507 Santa Eugènia de
Berga 24 F 24
17006 Santa Eugenia/Girona/
Gerona 35 F 25
07220 Santa Eugènia/Palma
de Mallorca
71 K 25
33192 Santa Eulalia 4 C 8
26585 Santa Eulalia Bajera
20 E 15
24745 Santa Eulalia de
Cabrera 15 E 6
22806 Santa Eulalia de
Gállego 21 E 18
33776 Santa Eulalia de Oscos
3 C 5
08505 Santa Eulàlia de
Riuprimer 24 F 24
08187 Santa Eulàlia de
Ronçana 24 F 24
07840 Santa Eulàlia des Ríu
72 M 23
22192 Santa Eulalia la Mayor
22 E 19
44360 Santa Eulalia/Cella
42 H 17
39557 Santa Eulália/Potes
6 C 11
33310 Santa Eulália/
Villaviciosa 5 C 9
03630 Santa Eulalia/Villena
60 M 18
18320 Santa Fe 66 P 12
04420 Santa Fe de Mondújar
67 Q 14
09571 Santa Gadea 6 D 12
09219 Santa Gadea del Cid
7 D 13
07750 Santa Galdana
72 K 27
07814 Santa Gertrudis de
Fruitera 72 M 22
41620 Santa Iglesi 64 P 9
09390 Santa Inés 18 E 12
50003 Santa Isabel 21 F 18
01110 Santa Kurutze Kanpezu
8 D 15
22411 Santa Lecina 22 F 20
22461 Santa Liestra y San
Quílez 11 E 20
25612 Santa Linya 23 F 21
24415 Santa Lucía de
Valdueza 15 E 6
36660 Santa Lucía/Galdas de
Reis 13 D 2
24650 Santa Lucía/La Pola de
Gordón 4 D 8
26144 Santa Lucía/Pradejón
20 E 15
07700 Santa Madrona
72 K 28
12597 Santa Magdalena de
Pulpis 33 J 20
07450 Santa Margalida
71 K 26

Santa Margarida de Montbui · E · **Serén**

08710 Santa Margarida de Montbui 24 F 23
08730 Santa Margarida i els Monjos 24 G 23
08717 Sta. Maria Cami 24 F 22
08273 Santa Maria d`Oló 24 F 24
39491 Santa Maria de Aguayo 6 C 11
08584 Santa Maria de Besora 12 E 24
39694 Santa María de Cayón 6 C 12
08511 Santa Maria de Corcó 35 E 24
42260 Santa María de Huertas 30 G 15
28296 Santa María de la Alameda 39 H 11
24795 Santa María de la Isla 16 E 8
49696 Santa Maria de la Vega 16 E 8
42141 Santa María de las Hoyas 19 F 13
10318 Santa María de las Lomas 37 J 8
16639 Santa María de los Llanos 50 L 14
34492 Santa María de Mave 6 D 11
25736 Santa María de Meià 11 F 21
09453 Santa María de Mercadillo 18 F 12
08517 Santa María de Merlès 12 E 23
06908 Santa María de Nava la Zapatera 54 N 7
04693 Santa María de Nieva 68 P 16
24276 Santa María de Ordás 16 D 8
08460 Santa Maria de Palautordera 35 F 24
34849 Santa María de Redondo 6 D 11
40594 Santa María de Riaza 29 G 13
37468 Santa María de Sando 26 H 7
14011 Santa María de Trassierra 56 O 10
04710 Santa María del Aguila 67 Q 14
05530 Santa María del Arroyo 38 H 10
05510 Santa María del Berrocal 37 H 9
07320 Santa María del Camí 71 K 25
09342 Santa María del Campo 18 E 12
16621 Santa María del Campo Rus 50 K 15
19283 Santa Maria del Espino 30 H 15
09292 Santa María del Invierno 19 E 13
24343 Santa María del Monte de Cea 17 E 9
24240 Santa María del Páramo 16 E 8
42211 Santa María del Prado 29 G 14
24344 Santa María del Río 17 D 9
05429 Santa María del Tiétar 38 J 10
16876 Santa María del Val 41 H 15
40440 Santa María la Real de Nieva 28 G 11

23740 Santa María/Andújar 57 N 11
22820 Santa María/Jaca 9 E 18
09219 Santa María-Ribarredonda 7 D 13
32557 Santa Marina da Ponte 15 E 5
24393 Santa Marina del Rey 16 D 8
24493 Santa Marina del Sil 15 D 6
26132 Santa Marina/Arnedillo 20 E 15
46740 Santa Marina/Carcaixnet 61 L 19
10198 Santa Marta de Magasca 46 K 7
37900 Santa Marta de Tormes 26 H 8
40310 Santa Marta del Cerro 28 G 12
06150 Santa Marta/Amendralejo 53 M 6
02639 Santa Marta/La Roda 50 L 15
09588 Santa Olaja 7 C 13
24813 Santa Olaja de la Varga 5 D 9
34112 Santa Olaja de la Vega 17 D 10
45530 Santa Olalla 39 J 11
09292 Santa Olalla de Bureba 19 E 13
21260 Santa Olalla del Cala 63 O 7
43710 Santa Oliva 24 G 23
17811 Santa Pau 35 E 25
17244 Santa Pellaia 35 F 25
43421 Santa Perpètua de Gaià 24 G 22
08130 Santa Perpètua de Mogoda 24 F 24
07180 Santa Ponça 71 K 24
13115 Santa Quiteria 48 L 11
29591 Santa Rosalía-Maqueda 65 Q 10
15848 Santa Sabiña 1 C 2
17240 Santa Seclina 35 F 25
02529 Santa Susanna 12 F 23
07748 Santa Teresa 72 J 28
27830 Santabaia 2 C 4
31314 Santacara 9 E 16
14546 Santaella 65 O 10
19269 Santamera 29 G 14
34878 Santana 5 D 10
39070 Santander 6 C 12
07769 Santandria 72 K 27
07650 Santanyí 71 L 26
24330 Santas Martas 17 E 9
27766 Sante 3 C 5
50373 Santed 31 G 16
09574 Santelices 6 C 12
47609 Santervás de Campos 17 E 9
34112 Santervás de la Vega 17 D 10
43815 Santes Creus 24 G 22
10510 Santiago de Alcßntara 45 K 5
47160 Santiago de Arroyo 27 G 10
23612 Santiago de Calatrava 56 O 11
15770 Santiago de Compostela 1 D 2
23290 Santiago de la Espada 58 N 14
37311 Santiago de La Puebla 27 H 9
30720 Santiago de la Ribera 60 O 18

10191 Santiago del Campo 46 K 7
05592 Santiago del Collado 37 J 9
24732 Santiago Millas 16 E 7
33791 Santiago/Luarca 3 B 6
33314 Santiago/Villaviciosa 5 B 9
33569 Santianes/Ribadesella 5 C 9
33876 Santianes/Tineo 4 C 7
39649 Santibáñez 6 C 12
40512 Santibáñez de Ayllón 29 G 13
37740 Santibáñez de Béjar 37 J 8
34486 Santibáñez de Ecla 6 D 11
09350 Santibáñez de Esgueva 18 F 12
34870 Santibáñez de la Peña 5 D 10
33676 Santibáñez de Murias 4 C 8
34844 Santibáñez de Resoba 5 D 10
49625 Santibáñez de Tera 16 F 8
47331 Santibáñez de Valcorva 28 F 11
49610 Santibáñez de Vidriales 16 E 7
09348 Santibáñez del Val 19 F 13
10859 Santibáñez el Alto 36 J 6
10666 Santibáñez el Bajo 36 J 7
09150 Santibáñez-Zarzaguda 18 E 12
32314 Santigoso 15 E 6
09347 Santillán 18 E 12
34126 Santillán de la Vega 17 E 10
34469 Santillana de Campos 18 E 11
39330 Santillana de Mar 6 C 11
27422 Santiorxo 14 E 4
41970 Santiponce 63 P 7
23250 Santisteban del Puerto 57 N 13
39490 Santiurde de Reinosa 6 C 11
39699 Santiurde de Toranzo 6 C 12
40460 Santiuste de San Juan Bautista 27 G 10
42193 Santiuste/El Burgo de Osma 29 F 14
19245 Santiuste/Sigüenza 29 G 14
37110 Santiz 26 G 8
30151 Santo Angel 60 O 17
28708 Santo Domingo 39 H 12
26250 Santo Domingo de la Calzada 19 E 14
05292 Santo Domingo de las Posadas 27 H 10
16337 Santo Domingo de Moya 42 K 17
40180 Santo Domingo de Pirón 28 G 12
09610 Santo Domingo de Silos 19 F 13
45519 Santo Domingo-Caudilla 39 J 11
23311 Santo Tomé 58 N 13
05357 Santo Tomé de Zabarcos 27 H 10
44560 Santolea 32 H 19
30140 Santomera 60 N 17
39740 Santoña 7 C 13
04692 Santopétar 68 P 15
22583 Santorens 11 E 21

39555 Santotis 6 C 11
09549 Santotís 7 D 13
24391 Santovenia de la Valdoncina 16 D 8
09199 Santovenia de Oca 19 E 13
47155 Santovenia de Pisuerga 27 F 10
49750 Santovenia/Benavente 16 F 8
40135 Santovenia/Segovia 27 H 11
34490 Santoyo 18 E 11
08251 Santpedor 24 F 23
33190 Santulano 4 C 8
39706 Santullán 7 C 13
33611 Santullano 4 C 8
26260 Santurde de Rioja 19 E 14
26261 Santurdejo 19 E 14
33394 Santurio 4 B 8
48980 Santurtzi 7 C 13
36960 Sanxenxo 13 E 2
36390 Sanxián 13 F 2
32764 Sanxurxo 15 E 5
49152 Sanzoles 26 G 8
05289 Saornil de Voltoya 38 H 10
22583 Sapeira 11 E 21
15886 Sarandón (San Pedro) 1 D 3
09216 Saraso 7 D 14
01468 Saratxo 7 C 13
22366 Saravillo 10 D 20
39555 Sarceda 6 C 11
22613 Sardás 10 D 19
47340 Sardón de Duero 28 F 11
37172 Sardón de los Frailes 26 G 7
27891 Sargadelos 3 B 5
09145 Sargentes de la Lora 6 D 12
24121 Sariegos 16 D 8
22200 Sariñena 22 F 19
42174 Sarnago 20 E 15
39639 Saro 6 C 12
39620 Sarón 6 C 12
09620 Sarracín 18 E 12
43424 Sarral 23 G 22
12184 Sarratella 32 J 20
32631 Sarreaus 14 E 4
27600 Sarria 2 D 5
31451 Sarriés 9 D 17
44460 Sarrión 43 J 18
25555 Sarroca de Bellera 11 E 21
25175 Sarroca de Lleida 23 G 21
25554 Sarroqueta 11 E 21
22809 Sarsamarcuello 9 E 18
31589 Sartaguda 20 E 15
45632 Sartajada 38 J 10
22374 Sarvisé 10 D 19
32794 Sas de Penelas 14 E 5
22192 Sasa del Abadiado 22 E 19
22714 Sasal 10 D 19
09123 Sasamón 18 E 11
27791 Sasdónigas 2 C 5
09216 Sáseta 8 D 14
50780 Sástago 22 G 19
19262 Saúca 30 G 14
10390 Saucedilla 37 K 8
37257 Saucelle 25 G 6
42138 Sauquillo de Alcázar 30 F 15
42218 Sauquillo de Boñices 30 F 15
40351 Sauquillo de Cabezas 28 G 11
42315 Sauquillo de Paredes 29 G 14
42216 Sauquillo del Campo 30 G 15

17467 Saus 35 E 25
43427 Savalla de Comtat 24 F 22
50299 Saviñán 21 G 16
03630 Sax 60 M 18
29752 Sayalonga 66 Q 11
19119 Sayatón 40 J 14
32358 Seadur 15 E 5
27328 Seara 15 D 5
33769 Seares 3 C 5
40380 Sebúlcor 28 G 12
24273 Secarejo 16 D 8
22439 Secastilla 22 E 20
09142 Sedano 6 D 12
50334 Sediles 21 G 16
27545 Segán 14 D 4
46592 Segart 43 K 19
02487 Sege 59 N 15
12400 Segorbe 43 K 19
40070 Segovia 28 H 11
27419 Seguín 14 E 4
08280 Segur 24 F 22
43882 Segur de Calafell 24 G 23
23379 Segura de la Sierra 58 N 14
06270 Segura de León 54 N 6
44793 Segura de los Baños 31 H 18
10739 Segura de Toro 37 J 8
45621 Segurilla 38 J 10
22463 Seira 11 E 20
15339 Seixas 2 B 4
36835 Seixido 13 E 3
36913 Seixo 13 E 2
27229 Seixón 2 C 4
49515 Sejas de Aliste 25 F 7
39687 Sel de la Carrera 6 C 12
19346 Selas 30 H 15
39696 Selaya 6 C 12
33128 Selgas 4 C 7
22415 Selgua 22 F 20
03579 Sella 61 M 19
46295 Sellent 52 L 18
33316 Selorio 5 B 9
07313 Selva 71 K 25
19237 Semillas 29 G 13
22230 Sena 22 F 19
24145 Sena de Luna 4 D 8
43440 Senant 23 G 22
07140 Sencelles 71 K 25
01439 Sendadiano 7 D 14
15818 Sendelle 2 D 3
22666 Senegüé 10 D 19
04213 Senés 68 P 15
22253 Senés de Alcubierre 22 F 19
25553 Senet 11 D 21
44561 Seno 32 H 19
25514 Senterada 11 E 21
08181 Sentmenat 24 F 24
22450 Senz 11 E 20
39778 Seña 7 C 13
42216 Señuela 30 G 15
32766 Seoane Vello 14 E 4
27117 Seoane/A Fonsagrada 3 C 5
27324 Seoane/Pedrafita do Cebreiro 15 D 5
27659 Seón 3 D 5
37638 Sepulcro-Hilario 37 H 7
40300 Sepúlveda 28 G 12
27329 Sequeiros 15 E 5
40517 Sequera del Fresno 29 G 12
15861 Ser 1 C 2
33726 Serandinas 3 C 6
33749 Serantes/Castropol 3 B 6
15808 Serantes/Melide 2 D 3
32428 Serantes/Ribadavia 14 E 3
27299 Serén 2 C 4

Serinyà (E) **Tamarit de Mar** E

17852 Serinyà 35 E 25
25739 Seró 23 F 22
33810 Seroiro 3 C 6
04890 Serón 67 P 14
42127 Serón de Nájima 30 F 15
25183 Seròs 23 G 20
46118 Serra 43 K 19
46118 Serra de Daro 35 E 26
15230 Serra de Outes 1 D 2
28815 Serracines 40 H 13
47239 Serrada 27 G 10
28195 Serrada de la Fuente 29 H 12
25516 Serradell 11 E 21
02200 Serradiel 51 L 17
10530 Serradilla 37 K 7
37531 Serradilla del Arroyo 36 H 7
37530 Serradilla del Llano 36 J 7
22483 Serraduy 11 E 21
05115 Serranillos 38 J 10
28979 Serranillos del Valle 39 J 12
45646 Serranillos Playa 38 J 10
08673 Serrateix 12 F 23
29471 Serrato 70 Q 10
10528 Serrejón 37 K 8
15259 Serres 1 D 1
22625 Serué 10 E 19
22366 Serveto 10 D 20
32626 Servoi 14 E 5
07815 Ses Oliveres 72 L 22
07820 Ses Païsses 72 M 22
07748 Ses Salines 72 M 22
07640 Ses Salines/Santanyí 71 L 26
22110 Sesa 22 F 19
24434 Sésamo 15 D 6
45223 Seseña 39 J 12
45224 Seseña Nuevo 39 J 12
46140 Sesga 42 J 17
31293 Sesma 20 E 15
49550 Sesnandez de Tábara 16 F 7
50248 Sestrica 21 G 16
22467 Sesué 11 D 20
17869 Setcases 12 E 24
41440 Setefilla 55 O 9
27615 Séteventos 3 D 5
19324 Setiles 42 H 16
08553 Seva 35 F 24
33584 Sevares 5 C 9
41070 Sevilla 63 P 8
28609 Sevilla la Nueva 39 J 11
45671 Sevilleja de la Jara 47 K 10
29592 Sexmo 65 Q 10
07700 Shangril-la 72 K 28
25222 Sidamon 23 F 21
02513 Sierra 59 M 16
04259 Sierra Alhamilla 67 Q 15
10181 Sierra de Fuentes 46 L 7
50612 Sierra de Luna 21 E 18
29328 Sierra de Yeguas 65 P 10
12182 Sierra Engacerrán 32 J 19
07820 Sierra Mar 72 M 22
04878 Sierro 67 P 15
06650 Sieruela 47 M 9
22142 Sieso de Huesca 22 E 19
22624 Sieso de Jaca 10 E 18
22120 Siétamo 22 E 19
46392 Siete Aguas 43 L 18
37892 Siete Iglesias de Tormes 37 H 8

47511 Siete Iglesias de Trabancos 27 G 9
28330 Siete Villas 40 J 12
28753 Sieteiglesias 28 H 12
15884 Sigüeiro 1 D 3
19250 Sigüenza 29 G 14
40590 Siguero 28 G 12
40590 Sigueruelo 28 G 12
50682 Sigües 9 D 17
24388 Sigüeya 15 E 6
27837 Silán 2 B 4
09219 Silanes 7 D 13
14813 Sileras 66 P 11
23380 Siles 58 N 14
39438 Silió 6 C 11
46460 Silla 43 L 19
18181 Sillar Alta 66 P 13
36540 Silleda 14 D 3
21300 Silos de Calañas 62 O 6
17410 Sils 35 F 25
33783 Silvamayor 4 B 7
27228 Silvela 2 C 4
15240 Silvosa 1 D 2
36826 Silvoso 13 E 2
47130 Simancas 27 F 10
46750 Simat de la Valdigna 61 L 19
22366 Sín 10 D 20
46320 Sinarcas 52 K 17
07510 Sineu 71 K 26
44382 Singra 42 H 17
05215 Sinlabajos 27 G 10
09450 Sinovas 28 F 12
22860 Sinués 9 D 18
22141 Sipán 22 E 19
22790 Siresa 9 D 18
15106 Sísamo 1 C 2
50227 Sisamón 30 G 15
16700 Sisante 51 L 15
27377 Sistallo 2 C 4
33812 Sisterna 3 D 6
32765 Sistín 14 E 5
27865 Sisto 2 B 4
08870 Sitges 24 G 23
17469 Siurana 35 E 25
19269 Slenes 29 G 14
22611 Sobás 10 E 19
27150 Sobrada 2 C 4
32330 Sobradelo 15 E 6
50629 Sobradiel 21 F 17
37246 Sobradillo 25 H 6
15813 Sobrado/Melide 2 C 3
27150 Sobrado/O Corgo 3 D 5
33875 Sobrado/Pola de Allande 3 C 6
24567 Sobrado/Rubiá 15 D 6
36150 Sobral 13 E 2
33996 Sobrecastiello 5 C 9
33557 Sobrefoz 5 C 9
32140 Sobreira 14 E 4
39550 Sobrelapeña 6 C 10
08589 Sobremunt 12 E 24
24127 Socil 16 D 8
02435 Socovos 59 N 16
13630 Socuéllamos 50 L 14
15108 Sofán 1 C 2
50696 Sofuentes 9 E 17
33193 Sograndio 4 C 8
26376 Sojuela 20 E 14
12070 Sol y Mar 44 J 20
16893 Solan de Cabras 41 H 15
05621 Solana de Ávila 37 J 8
06209 Solana de los Barros 54 M 6
13593 Solana del Pino 56 N 11
09127 Solanas de Valdelucio 6 D 11
02314 Solanilla/Alcaraz 58 M 14

22392 Solanilla/Sabiñánigo 10 E 19
19491 Solanillos del Extremo 40 H 14
09348 Solarana 18 F 12
31395 Solchaga 8 D 16
09249 Solduengo 7 D 13
23569 Solera 66 O 13
16216 Solera de Gabaldón 51 K 16
42223 Soliedra 30 G 15
22337 Solipueyo 10 E 20
33470 Solís 4 B 8
43412 Solivella 23 G 22
46430 Sollana 43 L 19
07100 Sóller 71 K 25
07312 Solleric 71 K 25
39738 Solórzano 6 C 12
05130 Solosancho 38 H 10
25280 Solsona 12 F 23
42257 Somaen 30 G 15
22752 Somanes 9 D 18
33200 Somio 4 B 8
19275 Somolinos 29 G 13
04877 Somontín 67 P 15
48550 Somorrostro 7 C 13
28756 Somosierra 28 G 12
28756 Somosierra 28 G 12
25589 Son 11 D 22
07458 Son Bauló 71 K 26
07769 Son Carrió 72 K 26
44712 Son del Puerro 42 H 18
07190 Son Ferrandell 71 K 25
07509 Son Macià 71 K 26
07769 Son Olivar Vell 72 K 27
07120 Son Sardina 71 K 25
07550 Son Servera 72 K 26
09572 Soncillo 6 D 12
12480 Soneja 43 K 19
45100 Sonseca 48 K 12
04638 Sopalmo 68 P 16
22583 Sopeira 11 E 21
48600 Sopelana 7 C 14
39513 Sopeña/Cabezón de la Sal 6 C 11
39776 Sopeña/Laredo 7 C 13
22583 Soperún 11 E 21
08588 Sora 11 E 24
31194 Sorauren 8 D 16
04270 Sorbas 68 P 15
24478 Sorbeda 3 D 6
09128 Sordillos 18 E 11
42070 Soria 20 F 15
25566 Soriguera 11 E 22
23270 Sorihuela del Guadalimar 58 N 13
31219 Sorlada 8 D 15
25587 Sorpe 11 D 22
15980 Sorribas 1 D 2
08697 Sorribes 12 E 22
24649 Sorribos de Alba 16 D 8
25560 Sort 11 E 22
18713 Sorvilán 66 Q 13
26191 Sorzano 20 E 14
50680 Sos del Rey Católico 9 E 17
24139 Sosas de Laciana 4 D 7
24132 Sosas del Cumbral 4 D 7
25181 Soses 23 F 20
46168 Sot de Chera 43 K 18
12489 Sot de Ferrer 43 K 19
05198 Sotalvo 38 H 10
25654 Soterranya 11 E 21
26371 Sotés 20 E 14
21309 Sotiel Coronada 62 O 6
33639 Sotiello 4 C 8
40311 Sotillo 28 G 12
42344 Sotillo de Caracena 29 G 13

05420 Sotillo de la Adrada 38 J 10
09441 Sotillo de la Rivera 18 F 12
45635 Sotillo de las Palomas 38 J 10
42165 Sotillo del Rincón 20 F 14
21730 Sotillo deSanabria 15 E 6
45919 Soto Alberche 38 J 11
26132 Soto de Cameros 20 E 15
34209 Soto de Cerrato 18 F 11
39110 Soto de la Marina 6 C 12
24768 Soto de la Vega 16 E 8
33869 Soto de los Infantes 4 C 7
33156 Soto de Luiña 4 B 7
33172 Soto de Ribera 4 C 8
42345 Soto de San Esteban 29 F 13
28760 Soto de Viñuelas 39 H 12
28791 Soto del Real 39 H 12
28529 Soto Pajares 40 J 12
24125 Soto y Amio 16 D 8
33126 Soto/Avilés 4 B 7
39211 Soto/Reinosa 6 C 11
34407 Sotobañado y Priorato 18 D 11
19429 Sotoca del Tajo 41 H 14
19445 Sotodosos 30 H 15
11310 Sotogrande 70 R 9
09140 Sotopalacios 18 E 12
16143 Sotos 41 J 15
42318 Sotos del Burgo 29 F 13
40170 Sotosalbos 28 G 12
37657 Sotoserrano 37 J 7
09135 Sotovellanos 18 D 11
24195 Sotovenia del Monte 17 D 9
09197 Sotragero 18 E 12
33554 Sotres 5 C 10
09135 Sotresgudo 18 D 11
33950 Sotrondio 4 C 8
02612 Sotuélamos 50 L 14
24249 Sougillo del Páramo 16 E 8
36560 Soutelo 13 D 3
15635 Souto/Betanzos 2 C 3
36684 Souto/Cuntis 13 D 3
15806 Souto/Melide 2 D 4
32236 Souto/Melón 14 E 3
32617 Soutochao 15 F 5
36519 Soutolongo 14 D 3
25287 Su 24 F 23
39340 Suances 6 C 11
39213 Suano 6 D 11
24433 Suarbol 3 D 6
01428 Subilana 7 D 14
30590 Sucina 60 O 18
25113 Sucquets 23 F 20
25173 Sudanell 23 F 21
46410 Sueca 61 L 19
27279 Suegos 3 C 5
42189 Suellacabras 20 F 15
12223 Sueras 43 K 19
24713 Sueros de Cepeda 16 D 7
24433 Suertes 3 D 6
39150 Suesa 6 C 12
15140 Suevos 1 C 3
48395 Sukarrieta 7 C 14
46295 Sumacarcer 52 L 18
31791 Sunbilla 8 C 16
25174 Sunyer 23 F 21
32622 Suotelo Verde 14 E 5
08260 Súria 24 F 23

24489 Susañe del Sil 3 D 7
09133 Susinos del Páramo 18 E 12
32530 Suvirol 14 D 3

T
34257 Tabanera de Cerrato 18 E 11
34473 Tabanera de Valdavia 17 D 10
40291 Tabanera La Luenga 28 G 11
02200 Tabaqueros 51 L 17
31449 Tabar 9 D 17
49140 Tábara 16 F 8
37130 Tabera de Abajo 26 H 7
04200 Tabernas 67 P 15
22196 Tabernas de Isuela 22 E 19
04692 Taberno 68 P 15
28480 Tablada 39 H 11
09143 Tablada del Rudrón 6 D 12
24722 Tabladillo/Astorga 16 E 7
19129 Tabladillo/Sacedón 41 H 14
33874 Tablado 4 C 7
09514 Tablíega 7 C 13
27555 Taboada dos Freires 14 D 4
27550 Taboada/Chantada 14 D 4
36543 Taboada/Silleda 14 D 3
32690 Taboadela 14 E 4
36448 Taboexa 13 E 3
50547 Tabuenca 21 F 16
24721 Tabuyo del Monte 16 E 7
31300 Tafalla 20 D 16
08593 Tagamanent 24 F 24
49836 Tagarabuena 27 F 9
09108 Tagarrosa 18 E 11
04275 Tahal 68 P 15
11392 Tahivilla 69 R 8
33111 Taja 4 C 7
42112 Tajahuerce 30 F 15
42366 Tajueco 29 F 14
15289 Tal 1 D 1
08278 Talamanca 24 F 23
28160 Talamanca de Jarama 40 H 12
50546 Talamantes 30 F 16
09126 Talamillo del Tozo 18 D 12
25630 Talarn 11 E 21
06640 Talarrubias 47 L 9
10193 Talaván 46 K 7
02410 Talave 59 M 16
25213 Talavera 24 F 22
45600 Talavera de la Reina 38 K 10
45694 Talavera la Nueva 38 K 10
06140 Talavera la Real 53 M 6
10491 Talaveruela de la Vera 37 J 8
10310 Talayuela 37 K 8
16320 Talayuelas 42 K 17
12221 Tales 43 K 19
06133 Táliga 53 M 5
15216 Tállara 1 D 2
15981 Tallós 4 B 8
25211 Talteüll 24 F 22
42148 Talveila 19 F 14
39584 Tama 5 C 10
19222 Tamajón 29 G 13
37600 Tamames 37 H 7
34490 Támara de Campos 18 E 11
07769 Tamarinda 72 K 27
43070 Tamarit de Mar 24 G 22

117

I N D E X · O R T S R E G I S T E R · I N D I C E · Í N D I
P L A A T S N A M E N R E G I S T E R · R E J S T Ř Í K   M Í S

E

Tamarite de Litera — Torrelobatón

22550 Tamarite de Litera 23 F 20
47815 Tamariz de Campos 17 F 9
09227 Tamarón 18 E 12
21730 Tameirón 15 E 5
06658 Tamurejo 47 M 10
33994 Tanes 5 C 9
42174 Taniñe 20 E 15
39316 Tanos 6 C 11
09124 Tapia 18 D 11
33740 Tapia de Casariego 3 B 6
17721 Tàpies 35 E 25
49639 Tapioles 16 F 9
19193 Taracena 40 H 13
08552 Taradell 35 F 24
15985 Taragoña 13 D 2
19227 Taragudo 29 H 13
11369 Taraguilla 70 R 9
33775 Taramundi 3 C 5
16400 Tarancón 40 J 13
42315 Tarancueña 29 G 13
33557 Taranes 5 C 9
24887 Taranilla 5 D 10
19314 Taravilla 41 H 16
50500 Tarazona 20 F 16
37409 Tarazona de Guareña 27 G 9
02100 Tarazona de la Mancha 51 L 16
03518 Tàrbena 61 M 19
37429 Tardáguila 26 G 8
09130 Tardajos 18 E 12
42191 Tardajos de Duero 30 F 15
42294 Tardelcuende 29 F 14
22240 Tardienta 22 F 18
34209 Tariego de Cerrato 18 F 11
11380 Tarifa/Algeciras 69 R 8
18859 Tarifa/Cullar-Baza 67 O 15
44480 Tarin Nuevo y Viejo 43 J 18
21510 Tariquejos 62 P 5
33997 Tarna 5 C 9
42216 Taroda 30 G 15
43070 Tarragona 23 G 22
30412 Tarragoya 59 O 15
25300 Tàrrega 23 F 22
25480 Tarrés 23 G 22
15189 Tarrio 1 C 3
25212 Tarroja de Segarra 23 F 22
19333 Tartanedo 30 H 16
25528 Taüll 11 D 21
25795 Taús 11 E 22
50660 Tauste 21 F 17
46760 Tavernes Blanques 43 K 19
46760 Tavernes de la Valldigna 61 L 19
08519 Tavèrnoles 35 F 24
08511 Tavertet 35 F 24
25577 Tavescan 11 D 22
02437 Tazona 59 N 16
33315 Tazones 5 B 9
29327 Teba 65 Q 10
16710 Tebar 51 K 15
33816 Tebongo 3 C 6
36746 Tebra 13 E 2
27635 Teivilide 14 D 5
15314 Teixeiro/Guitiriz 2 C 3
27191 Teixeiro/Lugo 2 C 5
08329 Tejà 35 F 24
09348 Tejada 19 F 12
16317 Tejadillos 42 J 16
42128 Tejado 30 F 15
24433 Tejado de Ancares 3 D 6
24732 Tejados 16 E 7
10420 Tejeda de Tiétar 37 J 8
37607 Tejeda y Segoyuela 37 H 7

24497 Tejedo del Sil 4 D 7
24511 Tejera 15 D 6
24885 Tejerina 5 D 9
22364 Tella 10 D 20
33628 Telledo 4 C 8
45780 Tembleque 49 K 12
19134 Tendilla 40 H 14
37590 Tenebrón 36 H 7
36120 Tenorio 13 E 2
12469 Teresa 43 K 18
46620 Teresa de Cofrentes 52 L 17
33211 Termañes 4 B 8
25670 Térmens 23 F 21
09591 Termiño 19 E 12
09593 Terminón 7 D 13
19390 Teroleja 30 H 16
17731 Terrades 35 E 25
09350 Terradillos de Esgueva 18 F 12
09142 Terradillos de Sedano 18 D 12
08220 Terrassa 24 F 24
46842 Terrateig 61 M 19
19392 Terraza 30 H 16
09246 Terrazos 7 D 13
50293 Terrer 30 G 16
44120 Terriente 42 J 16
13341 Terrinches 58 M 14
26132 Terroba 20 E 15
44070 Teruel 42 J 17
19312 Terzaga 41 H 16
09511 Teza 7 D 13
39649 Tezanos 6 C 12
21520 Tharsis 62 O 5
08391 Tiana 35 G 24
03109 Tibi 61 M 18
04459 Tices 67 P 14
31398 Tiebas 8 D 16
47870 Tiedra 27 F 9
28550 Tielmes 40 J 13
33554 Tielve 5 C 10
18248 Tiena 66 P 12
50269 Tierga 21 F 16
42344 Tiermes 29 G 13
22336 Tierrantona 10 E 20
22192 Tierz 22 E 19
19390 Tierzo 41 H 16
10319 Tiétar del Caudillo 37 J 9
04880 Tíjola 67 P 15
25288 Timoneda 12 E 22
16522 Tinajas 41 J 14
02070 Tinajeros 51 L 16
33870 Tineo 4 C 7
15127 Tines 1 C 2
09198 Tinieblas 19 E 13
05165 Tiñosillos 27 H 10
33989 Tiraña 4 C 8
31154 Tirapu 8 D 16
26211 Tirgo 19 D 14
02161 Tiriez 50 M 15
12179 Tirig 33 J 20
13192 Tirteafuera 48 M 11
25595 Tírvia 11 D 22
14512 Tiscar 65 P 10
23489 Tiscar-Don Pedro 58 O 13
46178 Titaguas 42 K 17
28359 Titulcia 39 J 12
43511 Tivenis 33 H 21
43746 Tivissa 33 G 21
09559 Toba de Valdivielso 7 D 12
09133 Tobar 18 E 12
02500 Tobarra 59 M 16
30510 Tobarrilla Baja 52 M 17
50325 Tobed 21 G 17
01211 Tobera 7 D 14
09591 Tobes/Burgos 18 D 12
19269 Tobes/Sigüenza 29 G 14
26321 Tobía 19 E 14
01427 Tobillas 7 D 13
19286 Tobillos 30 H 15

41340 Tocina 64 O 8
18380 Tocón/La Peza 66 P 13
18380 Tocón/Villanueva de Mesía 66 P 12
12312 Todolella 32 H 19
14815 Todosaires 65 O 11
32930 Toén 14 E 4
27593 Toiriz/Escairón 14 D 4
36597 Toiriz/Vila de Cruces 2 D 3
05289 Tolbaños 38 H 10
09614 Tolbaños de Arriba 19 E 13
27639 Toldaos 3 D 5
42190 Toledillo 20 F 14
45070 Toledo 39 K 11
24845 Tolibia de Arriba 5 D 9
21730 Tolilla 26 F 7
33826 Tolinas 4 C 7
33986 Tolivia 4 C 8
03813 Tollos 61 M 19
25638 Toló 11 E 22
40467 Tolocirio 27 G 10
25723 Toloriu 12 E 23
02211 Tolosa/La Gila 51 L 17
29109 Tolox 70 Q 10
22585 Tolva 11 E 21
19411 Tomellosa 40 H 14
13700 Tomelloso 50 L 13
36158 Tomeza 13 E 2
08551 Tona 24 F 24
16191 Tondos 41 J 15
24699 Tonín 4 C 8
37799 Topas 26 G 8
04839 Toperas 59 O 15
25574 Tor/Andorra la Vella 12 D 22
17134 Tor/Torroella de Montgrí 35 E 26
25750 Torà 24 F 22
24237 Toral de los Guzmanes 16 E 8
31228 Toralba del Río 8 D 15
12431 Torás 43 K 18
33535 Torazo 5 C 9
27317 Torbeo 14 E 5
47830 Tordehumos 17 F 9
19325 Tordellego 42 H 16
19276 Tordelloso 29 G 14
19351 Tordelpalo 30 H 15
19277 Tordelrábano 29 G 14
08490 Tordera 35 F 25
47100 Tordesillas 27 F 10
19323 Tordesilos 42 H 16
37840 Tordillos 27 H 9
09341 Tordómar 18 E 12
09347 Tordueles 18 E 12
08570 Torelló 12 E 24
24450 Toreno 15 D 6
19392 Toreré 30 H 15
19190 Torija 40 H 13
10520 Toril/Navalmoral de la Mata 37 K 8
44123 Toril/Teruel 42 J 17
22376 Torla 10 D 19
42220 Torlengua 30 G 15
33812 Tormaleo 3 D 6
26213 Tormantos 19 E 13
09555 Torme 6 C 12
05697 Tormellas 37 J 8
44134 Tormón 42 J 17
25331 Tornabous 23 F 22
09320 Tornadijo 18 E 12
05215 Tornadizos de Arévalo 27 G 10
05196 Tornadizos de Ávila 38 H 10
10611 Tornavacas 37 J 8
32895 Torneiros/Fondevila 14 F 3
27280 Torneiros/Meira 3 C 5
24733 Torneros de Jamuz 16 E 7
24736 Torneros de la Valdería 16 E 7

33557 Tornín 5 C 9
44230 Tornos 31 H 17
49800 Toro 27 F 9
17474 Toroella de Fluvià 35 E 26
36779 Torona 13 E 2
11630 Toronjil 69 Q 8
34230 Torquemada 18 E 11
16842 Torralba 41 J 15
22254 Torralba de Aragón 22 F 18
42132 Torralba de Arciel 30 F 15
13160 Torralba de Calatrava 49 L 12
42193 Torralba de El Burgo 29 F 14
50374 Torralba de los Frailes 30 G 16
44359 Torralba de los Sisones 31 H 17
50311 Torralba de Ribota 30 G 16
42230 Torralba del Moral 30 G 15
12225 Torralba del Pinar 43 K 19
50368 Torralbilla 31 G 17
42342 Torraño 29 G 13
27558 Torre 14 D 4
11691 Torre Alháquime 70 Q 9
12165 Torre Beltrans 32 J 19
18563 Torre Cardela 66 O 13
12161 Torre D`en Besora 32 J 19
44653 Torre de Arcas 32 H 19
24143 Torre de Babia 4 D 7
10864 Torre de Don Miguel 36 J 6
12184 Torre de Endomenech 33 J 20
13344 Torre de Juan Abad 58 M 13
41209 Torre de la Reina 63 O 7
12595 Torre de la Sal 44 J 20
44709 Torre de las Arcas 31 H 18
06172 Torre de Miguel Sesmero 53 M 6
12004 Torre de Sant Vicent 44 J 20
50730 Torre del Barracón 21 F 18
24370 Torre del Bierzo 16 D 7
19197 Torre del Burgo 29 H 13
44597 Torre del Compte 33 H 20
29740 Torre del Mar 65 Q 11
14857 Torre del Puerto 65 O 10
26134 Torre en Cameros 20 E 14
22483 Torre la Ribera 11 E 21
44358 Torre los Negros 31 H 17
11592 Torre Melgarejo 69 Q 7
30700 Torre Pacheco 60 O 18
46630 Torre Tallada 52 M 18
40171 Torre Val de San Pedro 28 G 12
40313 Torreadrada 28 G 12
30579 Torreagüera 60 O 17
42294 Torreandaluz 29 F 14
42161 Torrearévalo 20 F 15
46143 Torrebaja 42 J 17
19229 Torrebeleña 29 H 13
25176 Torrebesses 23 G 21
42193 Torreblacos 29 F 14
12596 Torreblanca 33 J 20
41017 Torreblanca de los Caños 63 P 8

23510 Torreblascopedro 57 N 12
16771 Torrebuceit 41 K 14
25738 Torrec 11 F 22
40160 Torrecaballeros 28 H 11
14410 Torrecampo 56 N 10
11595 Torrecera 69 Q 8
44640 Torrecilla de Alcañiz 32 H 19
47114 Torrecilla de la Abadesa 27 G 9
45651 Torrecilla de la Jara 48 K 10
47513 Torrecilla de la Orden 27 G 9
10869 Torrecilla de los Angeles 36 J 7
50139 Torrecilla de Valmadrid 21 F 18
09390 Torrecilla del Monte 18 E 12
40359 Torrecilla del Pinar/ Cuéllar 28 G 11
19392 Torrecilla del Pinar/ Molina 30 H 15
44222 Torrecilla del Rebollar 31 H 17
47509 Torrecilla del Valle 27 G 9
26100 Torrecilla en Cameros 19 E 14
14600 Torrecilla/Montoro 56 N 11
16145 Torrecilla/Priego 41 J 15
10252 Torrecillas de la Tiesa 46 K 8
24133 Torrecillo 16 D 7
09345 Torrecitores 18 F 12
22391 Torreciudad 22 E 20
19491 Torrecuadrada de los Valles 30 H 14
19355 Torrecuadrada de Molina 41 H 16
19431 Torrecuadradilla 30 H 14
12232 Torrechiva 43 J 19
23640 Torredelcampo 57 O 12
43830 Torredembarra 24 G 22
25281 Torredenegó 24 F 22
23650 Torredonjimeno 57 O 12
25123 Torrefarrera 23 F 21
25212 Torrefeta 23 F 22
06410 Torrefresneda 46 M 7
09493 Torregalindo 28 F 12
49252 Torregamones 26 G 7
11100 Torregorda 69 R 7
25141 Torregrossa 23 F 21
11312 Torreguadiaro 70 R 9
42269 Torrehermosa 30 G 15
40192 Torreiglesias 28 G 11
28850 Torrejón de Ardoz 40 J 13
28991 Torrejón de la Calzada 39 J 12
28990 Torrejón de Velasco 39 J 12
10694 Torrejón El Rubio 46 K 7
10830 Torrejoncillo 36 K 7
16161 Torrejoncillo del Rey 41 J 14
44382 Torrelacarcel 42 H 17
28180 Torrelaguna 29 H 12
03188 Torrelamata 60 N 18
25138 Torrelameu 23 F 21
50316 Torrelapaja 30 F 16
09194 Torrelara 19 E 12
39300 Torrelavega 6 C 11
16414 Torrelengua 40 K 14
47134 Torrelobatón 27 F 9

Torrelodones

E

Valdealcón

E

28250 Torrelodones 39 H 12
50512 Torrellas 20 F 16
03320 Torrellano 61 N 18
08737 Torrelles de Foix 24 G 23
03108 Torremanzanas-La Torre de les Maçanes 61 M 19
06880 Torremayor 46 M 6
06210 Torremegía 54 M 7
03313 Torremendo 60 O 18
10184 Torremocha 46 L 7
42342 Torremocha de Ayllón 29 G 13
19245 Torremocha de Jadraque 29 G 14
28189 Torremocha de Jarama 29 H 13
19268 Torremocha del Campo 29 H 14
19345 Torremocha del Pinar 30 H 15
19391 Torremochuela 41 H 16
26359 Torremontalbo 19 E 14
34305 Torremormojón 17 F 10
12596 Torrenostra 33 J 20
17123 Torrent/Begur 35 F 26
46900 Torrent/Valencia 43 L 19
22590 Torrente del Cinca 23 G 20
18720 Torrenueva/Motril 66 Q 13
13740 Torrenueva/Santa Cruz de Mudela 57 M 13
10182 Torreorgaz 46 L 7
09345 Torrepadre 18 E 12
23320 Torreperogil 57 N 13
23638 Torrequebradilla 57 O 12
10183 Torrequemada 46 L 7
23540 Torres 57 O 12
14820 Torres Cabrera 56 O 10
23391 Torres de Albánchez 58 N 14
44111 Torres de Albarracín 42 J 16
22132 Torres de Alcanadre 22 F 19
22255 Torres de Barbués 22 F 19
50693 Torres de Berrellén 21 F 17
28813 Torres de la Almeda 40 J 13
22134 Torres de Montes 22 E 19
25170 Torres de Segre 23 F 21
49122 Torres del Carrizal 26 F 8
22588 Torres del Obispo 11 E 20
31229 Torres del Río 20 D 15
46148 Torres Torres 43 K 19
50333 Torres/Calatayud 21 G 16
31119 Torres/Pamplona-Iruña 9 D 16
09310 Torresandino 18 F 12
47313 Torrescárcela 28 G 11
25131 Torre-serona 23 F 21
37110 Torresmenudas 26 G 8
24144 Torrestio 4 C 7
42344 Torresuso 29 G 13
44641 Torrevelilla 32 H 19
42315 Torrevicente 29 G 14
03180 Torrevieja 60 O 18
45752 Torrico 38 K 9
44421 Torrijas 42 J 18
50217 Torrijo 30 G 16
44393 Torrijo del Campo 31 H 17

45500 Torrijos 39 K 11
17257 Torroella de Montgrí 35 E 26
43737 Torroja de Priorat 23 G 21
19127 Torronteras 41 H 14
29770 Torrox 66 Q 12
29793 Torrox-Costa 66 Q 12
42138 Torrubia de Soria 30 F 15
16413 Torrubia del Campo 40 K 14
16739 Torrubia del Castillo 50 K 15
14447 Torrubia/Cardeña 56 N 11
19337 Torrubia/Molina de Aragón 30 H 16
44162 Tortajada 42 J 17
17853 Tortellà 35 E 25
16122 Tórtola 41 K 15
19198 Tórtola de Henares 40 H 13
09312 Tórtoles de Esgueva 18 F 11
05514 Tórtoles/Piedrahita 38 H 9
50514 Tórtoles/Tarazona 20 F 16
19261 Tortonda 30 H 14
43500 Tortosa 33 H 21
19338 Tortuera 30 H 16
19225 Tortuero 29 H 13
18430 Torvizcón 66 Q 13
09258 Tosantos 19 E 13
18820 Toscana Nueva 58 O 15
32646 Tosende 14 F 4
17536 Toses 12 E 24
50154 Tosos 21 G 17
33546 Tospe 5 C 9
17320 Tossa 35 F 25
29197 Totalán 65 Q 11
30850 Totana 60 O 16
45163 Totanés 48 K 11
46590 Totxar 43 K 19
36141 Toural 13 E 2
15124 Touriñán 1 C 1
36828 Tourón 13 E 2
46269 Tous 52 L 18
27843 Touzas 2 C 4
33793 Tox 3 B 6
23460 Toya 58 O 13
42112 Tozalmoro 30 F 15
18249 Tózar 66 P 12
15119 Traba 1 C 1
27765 Trabada 3 C 5
24523 Trabadelo 15 D 6
37173 Trabanca 25 G 7
49516 Trabazos 25 F 7
16150 Tragacete 41 J 16
25790 Trago de Segre 11 E 22
31315 Traibuenas 20 E 16
19312 Traid 41 H 16
12330 Traiguera 33 H 20
44112 Tramacastilla 42 J 16
22663 Tramacastilla de Tena 10 D 19
22268 Tramaced 22 F 19
44133 Tramascastiel 42 J 17
23292 Tranco 58 N 14
48510 Trapagaran 7 C 13
15391 Trasanquelos 2 C 3
24429 Trascastro/Degaña 3 D 6
27347 Trascastro/Samos 15 D 5
09126 Trashaedo 6 D 12
06909 Trasierra 54 N 8
48879 Traslaviña 7 C 13
32695 Trasmiras 14 E 4
15864 Trasmonte/Ordes 1 C 3
15864 Trasmonte/Santiago de Compostela 1 D 2

50583 Trasmoz 20 F 16
50268 Trasobares 30 F 16
33114 Traspeña 4 C 7
47330 Traspinedo 28 F 11
01191 Trasponte 7 D 14
27363 Trebolle 2 D 4
11560 Trebujena 69 Q 7
39592 Treceño 6 C 11
25598 Tredòs 11 D 21
49359 Trefacio 15 E 6
17869 Tregurà de Dalt 12 E 24
33796 Trelles 3 C 6
37148 Tremedal de Tormes 26 G 7
24377 Tremor de Arriba 16 D 7
25620 Tremp 11 E 21
28760 Tres Cantos 39 H 12
39557 Tresabuela 6 C 11
33576 Trescares 5 C 10
16422 Tresjuncos 50 K 14
09540 Trespaderne 7 D 13
42113 Trévago 20 F 15
18417 Trevélez 66 P 13
26215 Treviana 19 D 13
33780 Trevías 4 B 7
26132 Trevijano 20 E 15
09215 Treviño 7 D 14
27630 Triacastela 15 D 5
16452 Tribaldos 40 K 14
21620 Trigueros 62 P 6
47282 Trigueros del Valle 17 F 10
19192 Trijueque 40 H 14
19450 Trillo 41 H 14
34844 Triollo 5 D 10
22820 Triste 9 E 18
24010 Trobajo del Camino 16 D 8
15886 Trobe 1 D 2
27112 Trobo/A Fonsagrada 3 C 5
27375 Trobo/Rábade 2 C 4
22438 Troncedo/Graus 10 E 20
33878 Troncedo/Tineo 3 C 6
44141 Tronchón 32 H 19
33100 Trubia 4 C 8
24740 Truchas 15 E 7
24740 Truchillas 15 E 7
48880 Trucios 7 C 13
06892 Trujillanos 46 M 7
10200 Trujillo 46 L 8
09143 Tubilla del Agua 6 D 12
09453 Tubilla del Lago 18 F 12
09146 Tubilleja 6 D 12
39555 Tudanca 6 C 11
31500 Tudela 16 E 16
47320 Tudela de Duero 27 F 10
25739 Tudela de Serge 23 F 22
26512 Tudelilla 20 E 15
46177 Tuejar 42 K 17
36700 Tui 13 E 2
33935 Tuilla 4 C 8
25717 Tuixén 12 E 23
33628 Tuiza 4 C 8
31522 Tulebras 20 F 16
33876 Tuña 4 C 7
15822 Turces 2 D 3
24285 Turcia 16 D 8
40730 Turégano 28 G 11
46389 Turís 43 L 18
01213 Turisu 7 D 14
45789 Turleque 49 K 12
19287 Turmiel 30 G 15
18491 Turón/Berja 67 Q 13
33610 Turón/Cabañaquinta 4 C 8
04639 Turre 68 P 16
02530 Turrilla 59 N 15
04211 Turrillas 68 P 15

40560 Turrubuelo 28 G 12
26587 Turruncún 20 E 15

U

27286 Úbeda 3 C 5
23400 Úbeda/Baeza 57 N 13
03658 Úbeda/Pinoso 60 N 18
39360 Ubiarco 6 C 11
48145 Ubidea 7 C 14
09141 Ubierna 18 E 12
11600 Ubrique 70 Q 9
31154 Ucar 8 D 16
19187 Uceda 29 H 13
24369 Ucedo 16 D 7
42317 Ucero 29 F 13
39513 Ucieda de Abajo 6 C 11
16452 Uclés 40 K 14
02409 Uchea 59 M 16
39850 Udalla 7 C 13
33119 Udrion 4 C 8
48490 Ugao-Miraballes 7 C 14
48141 Ugarana 7 C 14
45217 Ugena 39 J 12
18480 Ugíjar 67 Q 13
31840 Uharte-Arakil 8 D 16
31891 Uitzi 8 C 16
19276 Ujados 29 G 13
31496 Ujué 9 D 17
30612 Ulea/Archena 60 N 17
30612 Ulea/Moratalla 59 N 16
04279 Uleila del Campo 68 P 15
31283 Ulibarri 8 D 15
17140 Ullà 35 E 26
08231 Ullastrell 24 F 23
17114 Ullastret 35 E 26
43550 Ulldecona 33 H 20
43363 Ulldemolins 23 G 21
17133 Ultramort 35 E 26
19238 Umbralejo 29 G 13
13739 Umbría de Fresneda 57 M 12
05693 Umbrías 37 J 8
49327 Una de Quintana 16 E 7
25588 Unarre 11 D 22
48110 Unbe 7 C 14
50678 Uncastillo 9 E 17
31422 Unciti 9 D 16
50689 Undués de Lerda 9 D 17
48144 Undurraga 7 C 14
01449 Untzaga 7 D 14
31396 Unzué 8 D 16
16152 Uña 41 J 16
12500 Urbanització El Almendro 33 H 21
09125 Urbel del Castillo 18 D 12
33613 Urbiés 4 C 8
01110 Urbisu 8 D 15
01440 Urcabustaiz 7 D 14
04691 Urcal 68 P 16
45480 Urda 49 L 12
31698 Urdaitz 9 D 16
26289 Urdanta 19 E 14
31711 Urdax-Urdazuli 9 C 16
31810 Urdiain 8 D 15
24248 Urdiales del Páramo 16 E 8
15281 Urdilde 1 D 2
22732 Urdués 9 D 18
48610 Urdulitz 7 C 14
19265 Ures de Arriba 29 G 14
42240 Ures de Medina 30 G 15
48419 Urigoiti 7 C 14
43870 Uriola 33 H 21
31438 Uriz 9 D 17
22466 Urmella 11 D 21
20130 Urnieta 8 C 16
47671 Urones de Castroponce 17 E 9
04879 Urracal 68 P 15

05195 Urraca-Miguel 38 H 10
44593 Urrea de Gaén 32 G 19
50296 Urrea de Jalón 21 F 17
48860 Urrestieta 7 C 13
09199 Urrez 19 E 13
09515 Urría 7 D 13
50685 Urriés 9 D 17
32664 Urros 14 E 4
31752 Urroz/Elizondo 8 C 16
31420 Urroz/Pamplona-Iruña 9 D 17
01170 Urrunaga 7 D 14
31639 Urtasun 9 D 16
01118 Urturi 8 D 14
17538 Urtx 12 E 23
47862 Urueña 27 F 9
40317 Urueñas 28 G 12
26313 Uruñuela 19 E 14
17538 Urús 12 E 23
31416 Urzainqui 9 D 18
06290 Usagre 54 N 7
22339 Usana 10 E 20
19182 Usanos 40 H 13
31451 Uscarrés 9 D 17
50374 Used 31 G 16
31193 Usi 8 D 16
22210 Usón 22 F 19
31451 Ustés 9 D 17
31454 Usún 9 D 17
19196 Utande 29 H 14
50180 Utebo 21 F 18
31133 Uterga 8 D 16
46300 Utiel 52 K 17
41710 Utrera 64 P 8
42258 Utrilla 30 G 15
44760 Utrillas 31 H 18
09217 Uzguiano 7 D 14
01449 Uzkiano 7 D 14
39556 Uznayo 6 C 11
31418 Uztárroz 9 D 18

V

08233 Vacarisses 24 F 23
09559 Vadenoceda 6 D 12
22192 Vadiello 22 E 19
42148 Vadillo 19 F 13
49420 Vadillo de la Guareña 27 G 9
05560 Vadillo de la Sierra 38 H 9
26133 Vadillos 20 E 15
09491 Vadocondes 28 F 12
14912 Vadofresno 65 P 11
23713 Vadollano 57 N 13
14859 Vadomojón 65 O 11
19429 Val de San García 30 H 14
24717 Val de San Lorenzo 16 E 7
50372 Val de San Martín 31 G 17
44191 Valacloche 42 J 17
15239 Valadares 1 D 2
50617 Valareña 21 E 17
44430 Valbona 43 J 18
09119 Valbonilla 18 E 11
47359 Valbuena de Duero 28 F 11
34259 Valbuena de Pisuerga 18 E 11
34117 Valcabadillo 17 D 10
22511 Valcarca 22 F 20
09317 Valcavado de Roa 28 F 12
14029 Valchillón 56 O 10
34886 Valcovero 5 D 10
42328 Valdanzo 29 F 13
42328 Valdanzuelo 29 F 13
28594 Valdaracete 40 J 13
19141 Valdarachas 40 H 13
10614 Valdastillas 37 J 8
24171 Valdavida 17 D 9
09145 Valdeajos 6 D 12
42141 Valdealbín 29 F 13
24160 Valdealcón 17 D 9

119

I N D E X · O R T S R E G I S T E R · I N D I C E · Í N D I
P L A A T S N A M E N R E G I S T E R · R E J S T Ř Í K   M Í S

E

Valdealgorfa — Vejer de la Frontera

44594 Valdealgorfa 32 H 19
42193 Valdealvillo 29 F 14
09453 Valdeande 19 F 12
24330 Valdearcos 17 E 9
47317 Valdearcos de la Vega 28 F 11
19196 Valdearenas 29 H 14
19412 Valdeavellano 40 H 14
42165 Valdeavellano de Tera 20 F 14
42317 Valdeavellano de Ucero 29 F 13
28816 Valdeavero 40 H 13
19174 Valdeaveruelo 40 H 13
828 91 Valdeazogues 56 M 11
45139 Valdeazores 48 L 10
06194 Valdebotoa 45 M 6
34191 Valdebustos 17 F 10
06689 Valdecaballeros 47 L 9
16146 Valdecabras 41 J 15
16542 Valdecabrillas 41 J 15
34249 Valdecañas de Cerrato 18 F 11
14810 Valdecañas/Cabra 65 P 11
16843 Valdecañas/Cuenca 41 J 15
37881 Valdecarros 26 H 9
05143 Valdecasa 38 H 9
24853 Valdecastillo 5 D 9
23469 Valdecazorla 58 O 13
44193 Valdecebro 42 J 17
39724 Valdecilla 6 C 12
16541 Valdecolmenas de Abajo 41 J 15
19132 Valdeconcha 40 J 14
44779 Valdeconejos 31 H 18
44122 Valdecuenca 42 J 17
33615 Valdecuna 4 C 8
49882 Valdefinjas 26 G 9
24415 Valdefrancos 15 E 6
24228 Valdefresno 16 D 9
10180 Valdefuentes 46 L 7
37680 Valdefuentes de Sangusín 37 J 8
02150 Valdeganga 51 L 16
16122 Valdeganga de Cuenca 41 K 15
42112 Valdegeña 20 F 15
19412 Valdegrudas 40 H 13
26529 Valdegutur 20 F 16
13428 Valdehierro 48 L 11
50371 Valdehorna 31 G 17
06410 Valdehornillo 46 L 8
24854 Valdehuesa 5 D 9
10393 Valdehúncar 37 K 8
24288 Valdeiglesias 16 E 8
14290 Valdeinfierno 55 N 8
06185 Valdelacalzada 53 M 6
37791 Valdelacasa 37 H 8
10332 Valdelacasa de Tajo 47 K 9
37724 Valdelageve 37 J 8
42113 Valdelagua del Cerro 20 F 15
19459 Valdelagua/Brihuega 40 H 14
28750 Valdelagua/San Sebastián de los Reyes 39 H 12
28391 Valdelaguna 40 J 13
24459 Valdelaloba 15 D 6
21330 Valdelamusa 62 O 6
02161 Valdelaras de Abajo 51 M 15
02161 Valdelaras de Arriba 51 M 15
21291 Valdelarco 63 O 6
28049 Valdelatas 39 H 12
42175 Valdelavilla 20 F 15
19269 Valdelcubo 29 G 14
44413 Valdelinares 32 J 18
37799 Valdelosa 26 G 8
44620 Valdeltormo 33 H 20
26532 Valdemadera 20 F 15

42318 Valdemaluque 29 F 13
28729 Valdemanco 28 H 12
13411 Valdemanco del Esteras 47 M 10
28295 Valdemaqueda 39 H 11
23370 Valdemarín 58 N 14
16152 Valdemeca 42 J 16
24206 Valdemora 17 E 9
10329 Valdemoreno 37 K 8
24293 Valdemorilla 17 E 9
28210 Valdemorillo 39 H 11
16340 Valdemorillo de la Sierra 42 J 16
28340 Valdemoro 39 J 12
16521 Valdemoro del Rey 41 J 14
16316 Valdemoro-Sierra 42 J 16
42193 Valdenarros 29 F 14
42313 Valdenebro 29 F 14
47816 Valdenebro de los Valles 17 F 10
19197 Valdenoches 40 H 13
19185 Valdenuño Fernández 40 H 13
10672 Valdeobispo 36 J 7
16813 Valdeolivas 41 H 15
34239 Valdeolmillos 18 E 11
28130 Valdeolmos 40 H 13
33746 Valdepares 3 B 6
13300 Valdepeñas 49 M 13
23150 Valdepeñas de Jaén 66 O 12
19184 Valdepeñas de la Sierra 29 H 13
21730 Valdeperdices 26 F 8
26527 Valdeperillo 20 E 15
24847 Valdepiélago 5 D 9
28170 Valdepiélagos 40 H 13
19238 Valdépinillos 29 G 13
24930 Valdepolo 17 D 9
39419 Valdeprado del Río 6 D 11
42181 Valdeprado/Cervera de Río Alhamo 20 F 15
24489 Valdeprado/Degaña 3 D 6
39574 Valdeprado/Potes 6 C 11
40423 Valdeprados 28 H 11
24220 Valderas 17 E 9
39232 Valderías 6 D 12
34473 Valderrábano 17 D 10
09211 Valderrama 7 D 13
19490 Valderrebollo 29 H 14
24793 Valderrey 16 E 7
44580 Valderrobres 33 H 20
42294 Valderrodilla 29 F 14
37256 Valderrodrigo 25 G 6
18250 Valderrubio 66 P 12
42294 Valderrueda/Berlanga de Duero 29 F 14
24882 Valderrueda/Guardo 5 D 10
29738 Valdés 65 Q 11
10164 Valdesalor 46 L 7
24127 Valdesamario 16 D 8
19412 Valdesaz 40 H 14
40389 Valdesimonte 28 G 12
19225 Valdesotos 29 H 13
42191 Valdespina/Almazán 30 F 15
34419 Valdespina/Fuentes de Nepero 18 E 11
24207 Valdespino Cerón 17 E 9
24717 Valdespino de Somoza 16 E 7
47240 Valdestillas 27 G 10
24837 Valdeteja 5 D 9
06474 Valdetorres 46 M 7
28150 Valdetorres de Jarama 40 H 12
40185 Valdevacas 28 G 12

40185 Valdevacas de Montejo 28 F 12
40553 Valdevarnés 28 G 12
45572 Valdeverdeja 38 K 9
24230 Valdevimbre 16 E 8
09318 Valdezate 28 F 12
26289 Valdezcaray 19 E 14
41020 Valdezorras 63 P 8
28511 Valdilecha 40 J 13
32369 Valdín 15 E 6
06720 Valdivia 46 L 8
09320 Valdorros 18 E 12
33190 Valduno 4 C 7
47672 Valdunquillo 17 E 9
24165 Valduvieco 17 D 9
21730 Valeixe 13 E 3
46070 València 43 L 19
25587 Valéncia d` Àneu 11 D 22
10050 Valencia de Alcántara 45 L 5
24200 Valencia de Don Juan 16 E 8
06444 Valencia de las Torres 54 N 7
06134 Valencia del Mombuey 53 N 5
06330 Valencia del Ventoso 54 N 7
41907 Valencina de la Concepción 63 P 7
30420 Valentín 59 N 16
14670 Valenzuela 56 O 11
13279 Valenzuela de Calatrava 49 M 12
16216 Valera de Arriba 41 K 15
16216 Valeria 41 K 15
22223 Valfarta 22 F 19
19196 Valfermoso de las Monjas 29 H 14
19411 Valfermoso de Tajuña 40 H 14
22255 Valfonda de Santa Ana 22 F 19
36646 Valga 13 D 2
26288 Valgañón 19 E 13
19390 Valhermoso 41 H 16
16214 Valhermoso de la Fuente 51 K 15
44595 Valjunquera 32 H 20
12194 Vall d`Alba 33 J 19
12600 Vall d`Uxó 43 K 19
12414 Vall de Almonacid 43 K 19
03791 Vall de Laguart 61 M 19
46961 Vallada 52 M 18
42257 Valladares 30 G 15
47010 Valladolid 27 F 10
30154 Valladolises 60 O 17
46145 Vallanca 42 J 17
09245 Vallarta de Bureba 7 D 13
12230 Vallat 43 J 19
25268 Vallbona de les Mongues 23 F 22
08699 Vallcebre 12 E 23
43439 Vallclara 23 G 21
25793 Valldarques 11 E 22
07170 Valldemosa 71 K 25
29240 Valle de Abdalajís 65 Q 10
34209 Valle de Cerrato 18 F 11
06458 Valle de la Serena 54 M 8
06177 Valle de Matamoros 53 N 6
06178 Valle de Santa Ana 53 N 6
40331 Valle de Tabladillo 28 G 12
30590 Valle del Sol 60 O 17
39510 Valle/Cabezón de la Sal 6 C 11

33783 Valle/Luarca 4 C 7
33438 Valle/Nubledo 4 B 8
33840 Valle/Pola de Somiedo 3 C 7
39815 Valle/Ramales de la Victoria 7 C 12
33887 Valledor 3 C 6
34260 Vallegera 18 E 11
09589 Vallejo de Mena 7 C 13
40213 Vallelado 28 G 11
49326 Valleluengo 16 E 7
34260 Valles de Palenzuela 18 E 11
34115 Valles de Valdavia 17 D 10
49450 Vallesa de la Guareña 27 G 9
25680 Vallfogona de Balaguer 23 F 21
17862 Vallfogona de Ripollès 12 E 24
43427 Vallfogona de Riucorb 23 F 22
08470 Vallgorguina 35 F 25
07639 Vallgornera 71 L 25
12315 Vallibona 32 H 20
33791 Vallín 3 B 6
08759 Vallirana 24 G 23
25738 Vall-llebrera 23 F 22
17253 Vall-Llobrega 35 F 26
25287 Vallmanya 24 F 23
43144 Vallmoll 23 G 22
43800 Valls 23 G 22
01427 Valluerca 7 D 13
09219 Valluércanes 7 D 13
50138 Valmadrid 21 G 18
09268 Valmala 19 E 13
39575 Valmeo 5 C 10
45940 Valmojado 39 J 11
44661 Valmuel 32 G 19
22533 Valonga 22 F 20
18470 Válor 67 Q 13
34815 Valoria de Aguilar 6 D 11
47200 Valoria la Buena 17 F 10
50615 Valpalmas 21 E 18
49318 Valparaiso 16 F 7
16550 Valparaíso de Abajo 41 J 14
16550 Valparaíso de Arriba 41 J 14
24878 Valporquero de Rueda 5 D 9
24837 Valporquero de Torío 4 D 8
22283 Valsalada 22 E 18
19390 Valsalobre/Molina de Aragón 30 H 16
19490 Valsalobre/Priego 41 H 15
24495 Valseco 4 D 7
24620 Valsemana 16 D 8
14206 Valsequillo 55 N 9
19492 Valtablado del Río 41 H 15
42181 Valtajeros 20 F 15
40314 Valtiendas 28 G 12
31514 Valtierra 20 E 16
09108 Valtierra de Riopisuerga 18 E 11
50219 Valtorres 30 G 16
42220 Valtueña 30 G 15
42315 Valvenedizo 29 G 13
25261 Valverd 23 F 21
26529 Valverde 20 F 16
26528 Valverde de Agreda 20 F 16
06378 Valverde de Burguillos 54 N 6
16100 Valverde de Júcar 50 K 15
24911 Valverde de la Sierra 5 D 10

10490 Valverde de la Vera 37 J 9
24391 Valverde de la Virgen 16 D 8
06130 Valverde de Leganés 53 M 6
06927 Valverde de Llerena 54 N 8
19224 Valverde de los Arroyos 29 G 13
06890 Valverde de Mérida 46 M 7
21600 Valverde del Camino 62 O 6
10890 Valverde del Fresno 36 J 6
40140 Valverde del Majano 28 H 11
03139 Valverde/Alicante 61 N 18
09410 Valverde/Aranda de Duero 29 F 13
34240 Valverde/Baltanás 18 F 11
44211 Valverde/Calamocha 31 H 17
13195 Valverde/Ciudad Real 48 M 11
24292 Valverde-Enrique 17 E 9
16214 Valverdejo 51 K 15
24837 Valverdín 4 D 8
40514 Valvieja 29 G 13
43891 Vandellós 34 G 21
16709 Vara del Rey 50 L 15
15826 Varelas 2 D 3
39679 Vargas 6 C 12
32515 Varón 14 E 3
08289 Veciana 24 F 22
37450 Vecinos 26 H 8
15885 Vedra 1 D 3
39630 Vega 6 C 12
34485 Vega de Bur 6 D 11
24430 Vega de Espinareda 15 D 6
24346 Vega de Infanzones 16 E 8
10317 Vega de Mesillas 37 J 8
39685 Vega de Pas 6 C 12
33519 Vega de Poia 4 C 8
33813 Vega de Rengos 3 C 6
47609 Vega de Ruiponce 17 E 9
49331 Vega de Tera 16 F 7
24520 Vega de Valcarce 15 D 6
47139 Vega de Valdetronco 27 F 9
21730 Vega del Castillo 16 E 7
24836 Vegacervera 4 D 8
33770 Vegadeo 3 C 5
40220 Vegafría 28 G 11
33814 Vegalagar 3 C 6
49542 Vegalatrave 26 F 7
40395 Veganzones 28 G 12
24152 Vegaquemada 5 D 9
02448 Vegarella 59 M 15
06731 Vegas Altas 47 L 8
41470 Vegas de Almenara 55 O 9
10623 Vegas de Coria 37 J 7
40423 Vegas de Matute 28 H 11
24153 Vegas del Condado 5 D 9
10848 Vegaviana 36 J 6
39808 Veguilla 7 C 12
19238 Veguillas 29 H 13
44134 Veguillas de la Sierra 42 J 17
15189 Veiga 1 C 3
33840 Veigas 4 C 7
11150 Vejer de la Frontera 69 R 8

Velada ⒠ Villadepalos

45612 Velada 38 K 10
40134 Velagómez 28 H 11
42210 Velamazán 29 G 14
47463 Velascálvaro 27 G 10
05292 Velayos 27 H 10
04212 Velefique 67 P 15
04830 Vélez Blanco 68 O 15
18670 Vélez de Benaudalla 66 Q 12
04820 Vélez Rubio 68 O 15
29700 Vélez-Málaga 65 Q 11
22528 Velilla de Cinca 22 F 20
50760 Velilla de Ebro 22 G 19
50343 Velilla de Jiloca 31 G 16
42189 Velilla de la Sierra 20 F 15
42225 Velilla de los Ajos 30 G 15
42257 Velilla de Medinaceli 30 G 15
42320 Velilla de San Esteban 29 F 13
34869 Velilla de Tarilonte 5 D 10
34886 Velilla del Río Carrión 5 D 10
47114 Vellila 27 F 9
24392 Vellila de la Reina 16 D 8
16510 Vellisca 40 J 14
47131 Velliza 27 F 10
40312 Vellosillo 28 G 12
22549 Vencillón 23 F 20
46700 Venecia 61 M 19
49153 Venialbo 26 G 8
23688 Venta de Agramaderos 66 P 12
18567 Venta de Ándar 66 P 12
22210 Venta de Ballerías 22 F 19
34200 Venta de Baños 18 F 11
12005 Venta de Blanco 33 J 20
13768 Venta de Cárdenas 57 N 13
50150 Venta de Herrera 31 G 18
11638 Venta de la Perdiz 69 Q 8
43559 Venta de la Punta 33 H 20
23265 Venta de los Santos 58 N 13
04200 Venta de los Yesos 68 P 15
30530 Venta de Olivio 60 N 17
14446 Venta del Charco 56 N 11
30811 Venta del Coronel 68 O 16
06260 Venta del Culebrín 54 N 7
18640 Venta del Fraile 66 Q 12
46310 Venta del Moro 51 L 17
18891 Venta del Peral 67 O 14
18858 Venta Micena 58 O 15
46392 Venta Quemada/Buñol 43 L 18
18859 Venta Quemada/Cúllar-Baza 67 O 15
17473 Ventalló 35 E 26
34844 Ventanilla 5 D 10
26131 Ventas Blancas 20 E 15
32610 Ventas da Barreira 15 F 5

31797 Ventas de Arraiz 8 C 16
18131 Ventas de Huelma 66 P 12
44780 Ventas de Muniesa 31 G 18
18312 Ventas de Santa Bárbara 65 P 11
18128 Ventas de Zafarraya 65 Q 11
18312 Ventorros de Balerma 65 P 11
42291 Ventosa de Fuentepinilla 29 F 14
47239 Ventosa de la Cuesta 27 G 10
42161 Ventosa de la Sierra 20 F 15
42174 Ventosa de San Pedro 20 E 15
42230 Ventosa del Ducado 30 G 14
37329 Ventosa del Río Almar 27 H 9
36529 Ventosa/A Golada 14 D 4
19392 Ventosa/Molina de Aragón 30 H 16
40165 Ventosilla y Tejadilla 28 G 12
09443 Ventosilla/Aranda de Duero 28 F 12
23639 Ventosilla/Mengibar 57 O 12
26325 Ventrosa 19 E 14
28729 Venturada 28 H 12
12222 Veo 43 K 19
04620 Vera 68 P 16
50580 Vera de Moncayo 20 F 16
16540 Verdelpino de Huete 41 J 14
34846 Verdeña 6 D 11
29011 Verdiales 65 Q 11
33448 Verdicio 4 B 8
25340 Verdú 23 F 22
13459 Veredas 56 M 11
34839 Vergaño 6 D 11
17142 Verges 35 E 26
25271 Vergos Guerrejat 24 F 22
32600 Verín 14 F 5
33211 Veriña 4 B 8
34219 Vertavillo 18 F 11
41729 Vetaherrado 63 P 8
49840 Vezdemarbán 27 F 9
22585 Viacamp 11 E 21
31230 Viana 20 D 15
27513 Viana (San Pedro) 14 D 4
47150 Viana de Cega 27 F 10
42218 Viana de Duero 30 F 15
19295 Viana de Jadraque 29 G 14
19492 Viana de Mondejar 41 H 14
32550 Viana do Bolo 15 E 5
02315 Vianos 58 M 14
39511 Viaña 6 C 11
15687 Viaño Pequeno 1 C 2
36121 Viascón 13 E 2
04240 Viator 67 Q 15
33750 Viavélez 3 B 6
08500 Vic 12 F 24
28032 Vicálvaro 39 J 12
04738 Vícar 67 Q 14
27860 Vicedo 2 B 4
22190 Vicién 22 E 19
27157 Vicinte 2 C 4
05194 Vicolozano 38 H 10
02439 Vicorto 59 N 15
24815 Vidanes 5 D 9

31413 Vidángoz 9 D 17
49135 Vidayanes 16 F 8
49541 Vide de Alba 26 F 7
32613 Videferre 14 F 4
49164 Videmala 26 F 7
17411 Vidrieres 35 F 25
43844 Vidrieros 5 D 10
33718 Vidural 3 B 6
33558 Viego 5 C 9
25530 Vielha 11 D 21
09588 Viergol 7 C 13
50513 Vierlas 20 F 16
39315 Viérnoles 6 C 11
33869 Viescas 4 C 7
24722 Viforcos 16 D 7
33827 Vigaña 4 C 7
36200 Vigo 13 E 2
26121 Viguera 20 E 14
25537 Vila 11 D 21
15337 Vila de Bares 2 B 4
36590 Vila de Cruces 2 D 3
43814 Vila-Rodona 24 G 22
27122 Vilabade 3 C 5
43886 Vilabella del Camp 24 G 22
17760 Vilabertran 35 E 25
17180 Vilablareix 35 F 25
15543 Vilaboa/Cedeira 2 B 3
27724 Vilaboa/Rodrigas 3 C 5
27114 Vilabol 3 C 6
25537 Vilac 11 D 21
27770 Vilacampa 2 B 4
27663 Vilachá/Becerreá 3 D 5
27413 Vilachá/Quiroga 14 E 5
15872 Vilacova 1 D 2
08613 Vilada 12 E 23
17137 Viladamat 35 E 26
17464 Viladasens 35 E 25
15819 Viladavil 2 D 3
08840 Viladecans 24 G 24
08232 Viladecavalls 24 F 23
17468 Vilademuls 35 E 25
36309 Viladesuso 13 E 2
27259 Viladonga 3 C 5
17406 Viladrau 35 F 24
27699 Vilaesteva 3 D 5
27891 Vilaestrofe 3 B 5
12192 Vilafamés 44 J 19
17740 Vilafant 35 E 25
27299 Vilafiz 2 D 4
27767 Vilaformán 3 C 5
27797 Vilaframil 3 B 5
07250 Vilafranca de Bonany 71 K 26
08720 Vilafranca del Penedès 24 G 23
36600 Vilagarcía de Arousa 13 D 2
25330 Vilagrassa 23 F 22
17493 Vilajuiga 35 E 26
27800 Vilalba 2 C 4
27367 Vilaleo 2 D 5
27349 Vilalpape 14 D 5
27299 Vilalvite 2 C 4
25552 Vilaller 11 E 21
17529 Vilallobent 12 E 23
17176 Vilallonga de Ter 12 E 24
43141 Vilallonga del Camp 23 G 22
17869 Vilallonga/Campodron 35 E 24
17474 Vilamacolum 35 E 26
27613 Vilamaior 14 D 4
32633 Vilamaior de Boullosa 14 F 4
27233 Vilamaior de Negral 2 D 4
17469 Vilamalla 35 E 25
27663 Vilamane 3 D 5
17781 Vilamaniscle 35 E 26
17534 Vilamanya 12 E 24
27796 Vilamar 3 C 5
17468 Vilamarí 35 E 25
32101 Vilamarín 14 E 4

32340 Vilamartín de Valdeorras 15 E 5
46191 Vilamarxant 43 K 18
15638 Vilamateo 2 C 3
32895 Vilameá 14 F 3
36748 Vilameán 13 E 2
25654 Vilamitjana 11 E 21
27325 Vilamor 15 D 5
25551 Vilamòs 11 D 21
25566 Vilamur 11 E 22
17600 Vilanora de la Muga 35 E 26
12183 Vilanova d'Alcolea 33 J 20
43311 Vilanova d'Escornalbou 23 G 21
36620 Vilanova de Arousa 13 D 2
25264 Vilanova de Bellpuig 23 F 21
25749 Vilanova de L'Aguda 23 F 22
25690 Vilanova de la Barca 23 F 21
25613 Vilanova de les Avellanes 23 F 21
27760 Vilanova de Lourenzá 3 C 5
25735 Vilanova de Meià 11 F 22
43439 Vilanova de Prades 23 G 21
80519 Vilanova de Sau 35 F 24
25133 Vilanova de Segrià 23 F 21
08788 Vilanova del Camí 24 F 23
08800 Vilanova i la Geltrú 24 G 23
27215 Vilanova/Monterroso 2 D 4
32366 Vilanova/O Barco 15 E 6
27720 Vilaodriz 3 C 5
27614 Vilapedre/Sarria 2 D 5
27816 Vilapedre/Vilalba 2 C 4
43380 Vilaplana del Camp 23 G 22
27666 Vilapún 3 D 5
27531 Vilaquinte/Chantada 14 E 4
27659 Vilaquinte/Poboa 3 D 6
32702 Vilar de Barrio 14 E 4
32616 Vilar de Cervos 14 F 5
32412 Vilar de Condes 14 E 3
27240 Vilar de Mouros 3 C 5
32650 Vilar de Santos 14 E 4
32646 Vilar/Randín 14 F 4
36815 Vilar/Redondela 13 E 2
27328 Vilarbacú 15 D 5
27518 Vilarbasín 2 D 4
32152 Vilarchao 14 E 4
32616 Vilardevós 14 F 5
12540 Vila-real de los Infantes 44 K 19
27665 Vilarello 15 D 6
27307 Vilares 2 C 4
04618 Vilaricos 68 P 16
17741 Vilarig 35 E 25
36633 Vilariño 13 D 2
32557 Vilarino de Conso 15 E 5
27113 Vilarmeán 3 C 5
32555 Vilarmeao 15 E 5
27724 Vilarmide 3 C 5
27788 Vilaronte 3 B 5
27346 Vilarxoán 15 D 5
22451 Vilas del Turbón 11 E 21
25245 Vila-sana 23 F 21
15807 Vilasantar 2 C 3
17600 Vila-Saura 35 E 26
43480 Vilaseca de Solcina test 23 G 22

32555 Vilaseco 15 E 5
36879 Vilasobroso 13 E 3
27390 Vilaster 15 E 5
36519 Vilatuxe 14 D 3
17483 Vilaür 35 E 25
32549 Vilavella 15 E 5
43490 Vilaverd 23 G 22
32811 Vilavidal 14 E 3
32618 Vilaza 14 F 5
23220 Vilches 57 N 12
42311 Vilde 29 G 13
36539 Vilela/A Golada 14 D 4
15105 Vilela/Laracha 1 C 2
27714 Vilela/Ribadeo 3 B 5
27596 Vilela/Taboada 14 D 4
09249 Vileña 7 D 13
17832 Vilert 35 E 25
27747 Viloalle 3 C 5
17483 Vilopriu 35 E 25
09259 Viloria de Rioja 19 E 13
31283 Viloria/Estella-Lizarra 8 D 15
47166 Viloria/Güellar 28 G 11
15806 Vilouriz 2 D 4
17185 Viloví d'Onyar 35 F 25
37255 Vilvestre 25 G 6
42153 Vilviestre de los Nabos 19 F 14
09690 Vilviestre del Pinar 19 F 13
14640 Villa de Río 56 O 11
02213 Villa de Ves 52 L 17
10814 Villa del Campo 36 J 7
28630 Villa del Prado 39 J 11
10960 Villa del Rey 45 K 6
47329 Villabáñez 27 F 10
47607 Villabaruz de Campos 17 E 10
09510 Villabasil 7 C 13
34475 Villabasta de Valdavia 17 D 10
34406 Villabermudo 18 D 11
21590 Villablanca 62 P 5
24100 Villablino 4 D 7
33480 Villabona/Posada 4 C 8
47820 Villabrágima 17 F 9
24206 Villabraz 17 E 7
33826 Villabre 4 C 7
01307 Villabuena de Alava 19 D 14
49820 Villabuena del Puente 27 G 9
24548 Villabuena/Cacabelos 15 D 6
42290 Villabuena/Soria 29 F 14
19274 Villacadima 29 G 13
45860 Villacañas 49 K 13
22483 Villacarlí 11 E 21
47609 Villacarralón 17 E 9
39640 Villacarriedo 6 C 12
23300 Villacarrillo 58 N 13
40150 Villacastín 28 H 11
09511 Villacián 7 D 13
33818 Villacibrán 3 C 6
47607 Villacid de Campos 17 E 9
34349 Villacidaler 17 E 10
24161 Villacidayo 5 D 9
42192 Villaciervos 19 F 14
24344 Villacintor 17 E 9
47181 Villaco 28 F 11
34247 Villaconancio 18 F 11
16860 Villaconejos de Trabaque 41 J 15
40512 Villacorta 29 G 13
19269 Villacorza 29 G 14
47609 Villacreces 17 E 9
34340 Villada 17 E 10
24392 Villadangos del Párano 16 D 8
24530 Villadecanes 15 D 6
24565 Villadepalos 15 D 6

49250 Villadepera 26 F 7
09120 Villadiego 18 D 11
24127 Villadiego de Cea
    17 D 10
49129 Villádiga 16 F 9
50490 Villadoz 31 G 17
34475 Villaeles de Valdavia
    17 D 10
09314 Villaescua de Roa
    28 F 11
16647 Villaescusa de Haro
    50 K 14
19493 Villaescusa de
    Palositos 41 H 14
09559 Villaescusa del Butrón
    6 D 12
09292 Villaescusa la Sombría
    19 E 13
49430 Villaescusa/
    Fuentesaúco
    26 G 9
39213 Villaescusa/Reinosa
    6 D 11
41339 Villaesparra 64 O 8
47811 Villaesper 17 F 9
09650 Villaesposa 19 E 13
24791 Villaestrigo 16 E 8
49136 Villafáfila 16 F 8
24162 Villafañé 17 D 9
50391 Villafeliche 31 G 16
49695 Villaferruena 16 E 8
21730 Villaflor 26 F 8
05357 Villaflor 38 H 10
37406 Villaflores 27 G 9
47606 Villafrades de Campos
    17 E 10
14420 Villafranca de Córdoba
    56 O 10
47529 Villafranca de Duero
    27 G 9
50174 Villafranca de Ebro
    22 F 18
05571 Villafranca de la Sierra
    38 J 9
06220 Villafranca de los
    Barros 54 M 7
45730 Villafranca de los
    Caballeros 49 L 13
24500 Villafranca del Bierzo
    15 D 6
44394 Villafranca del Campo
    42 H 17
12150 Villafranca del Cid
    32 J 19
40318 Villafranca/Pedraza
    28 G 12
31330 Villafranca/San Adrián
    20 E 16
09257 Villafranca-Montes de
    Oca 19 E 13
41140 Villafranco del
    Guadalquivir
    63 P 7
47810 Villafrechos 17 F 9
09192 Villafría/Burgos 18 E 12
33129 Villafría/Pravia 4 B 7
09344 Villafruela 18 F 12
47180 Villafuerte 28 F 11
09339 Villafuertes 18 E 12
39638 Villafufre 6 C 12
09268 Villagalijo 19 E 13
47840 Villagarcía de Campos
    17 F 9
06950 Villagarcía de la Torre
    54 N 7
16236 Villagarcía del Llano
    51 L 16
47608 Villagómez la Nueva
    17 E 9
06473 Villagonzalo 54 M 7
37893 Villagonzalo de Tormes
    26 H 9
09195 Villagonzalo-
    Pedernales
    18 E 12

23630 Villagordo 57 O 12
09230 Villagutiérrez 18 E 12
34257 Villahán 18 E 11
14210 Villaharta 56 N 10
13332 Villahermosa 50 M 14
44494 Villahermosa del
    Campo 31 G 17
12124 Villahermosa del Río
    43 J 19
09125 Villahernando 18 D 12
34469 Villaherreros 18 E 11
09339 Villahizán 18 E 12
09128 Villahizán de Treviño
    18 E 11
09343 Villahoz 18 E 12
03570 Villajoyosa-La Vila
    Joíosa 61 M 19
34259 Villalaco 18 E 11
09514 Villalacre 7 C 13
47675 Villalán de Campos
    17 E 9
22822 Villalangua 9 E 18
33819 Villalar 3 C 7
47111 Villalar de los
    Comuneros 27 F 9
49158 Villalazán 26 G 8
42223 Villalba 30 G 15
44161 Villalba Alta 42 H 18
44162 Villalba Baja 42 J 17
47238 Villalba de Adaja
    27 G 10
13739 Villalba de Calatrava
    57 M 12
09443 Villalba de Duero
    28 F 12
34889 Villalba de Guardo
    5 D 10
47689 Villalba de la Loma
    17 E 9
16140 Villalba de la Sierra
    41 J 15
47639 Villalba de los Alcores
    17 F 10
06208 Villalba de los Barros
    54 M 6
37451 Villalba de los Llanos
    26 H 8
09511 Villalba de Losa 7 D 13
50333 Villalba de Perejil
    21 G 16
26292 Villalba de Rioja 7 D 14
21860 Villalba del Alcor
    63 P 7
16535 Villalba del Rey
    41 J 14
43782 Villalba dels Arcs
    23 G 20
47113 Villalbarsa 27 F 9
09197 Villalbilla de Burgos
    18 E 12
09370 Villalbilla de Gumiel
    18 F 12
09124 Villalbilla de Villadiego
    18 D 12
28810 Villalbilla/Alcalá de
    Hernares 40 J 13
16840 Villalbilla/Cuenca
    41 J 15
09141 Villalbilla-Sopresierra
    18 D 12
49166 Villalcampo 26 F 7
34449 Villalcázar de Sirga
    17 E 10
34347 Villalcón 17 E 10
09227 Villaldemiro 18 E 12
24426 Villalebrín 17 E 10
50216 Villalengua 30 G 16
02636 Villalgordo del Júcar
    51 L 15
16646 Villalgordo del
    Marquesado
    50 K 14
09390 Villalmanzo 18 E 12
26256 Villalobar de Rioja
    19 E 14

34419 Villalobón 17 E 11
49134 Villalobos 16 F 9
47600 Villalón de Campos
    17 E 9
46720 Villalonga 61 M 19
09001 Villalonquéjar 18 E 12
49860 Villalonso 27 F 9
49630 Villalpando 17 F 9
16270 Villalpardo 51 L 16
09559 Villalta 6 D 12
45520 Villaluenga de la Sagra
    39 J 12
16111 Villaluenga del Rosario
    70 Q 9
34307 Villalumbroso 17 E 10
09192 Villalval 19 E 12
33695 Villallana 4 C 8
34815 Villalobos 6 D 11
02270 Villamalea 51 L 16
12224 Villamalur 43 K 19
24234 Villamanán 16 E 8
24236 Villamandos 16 E 8
01426 Villamañe 7 D 13
24680 Villamanín 4 D 8
13343 Villamanrique 58 M 14
41850 Villamanrique de la
    Condesa 63 P 7
28598 Villamanrique de Tajo
    40 J 13
28610 Villamanta 39 J 11
28609 Villamantilla 39 J 11
47132 Villamarciel 27 F 10
24345 Villamarco 17 E 9
01427 Villamardones 7 D 13
33826 Villamarín 4 C 7
11650 Villamartín 69 Q 8
34170 Villamartín de Campos
    17 E 10
24344 Villamartín de Don
    Sancho 17 D 9
09568 Villamartín de
    Sotoscueva 6 C 12
09124 Villamartín de Villadiego
    18 D 11
13595 Villamayor de Calatrava
    48 M 11
49131 Villamayor de Campos
    17 F 9
09339 Villamayor de los
    Montes 18 E 12
31242 Villamayor de
    Monjardín 8 D 15
16415 Villamayor de Santiago
    50 K 14
09128 Villamayor de Treviño
    18 E 11
24155 Villamayor del Condado
    17 D 9
09259 Villamayor del Río
    19 E 13
33583 Villamayor/Infiesto
    5 C 9
37185 Villamayor/Salamanca
    26 G 8
50162 Villamayor/Zaragoza
    21 F 18
34347 Villambrán de Cea
    17 E 10
01423 Villambrosa 7 D 13
24397 Villameca 16 D 7
34239 Villamediana 18 E 11
26142 Villamediana de Iregua
    20 E 15
34260 Villamedianilla
    18 E 11
24711 Villamejil 16 D 7
33114 Villamejín 4 C 7
34477 Villameriel 18 D 11
10263 Villamesias 46 L 8
10893 Villamiel 36 J 6
09198 Villamiel de la Sierra
    19 E 13
45594 Villamiel de Toledo
    39 K 11
45440 Villaminaya 49 K 12

24344 Villamizar 17 D 9
24175 Villamol 17 E 9
24766 Villamontán de la
    Valduerna 16 E 8
09512 Villamor 7 D 13
49211 Villamor de Cadozos
    26 G 7
24339 Villamoratiel de las
    Matas 17 E 9
34126 Villamoronta 17 E 10
09269 Villamudria 19 E 13
45749 Villamuelas 39 K 12
34309 Villamuera de la Cueza
    17 E 10
24344 Villamuñío 17 E 9
47814 Villamuriel de Campos
    17 F 9
47131 Villán de Tordesilla
    27 F 10
09258 Villanasur-Río de Oca
    19 E 13
49697 Villanázar 16 F 8
09339 Villangómez 18 E 12
22467 Villanova 11 D 20
22710 Villanovilla 10 D 19
22870 Villanúa 10 D 18
47620 Villanubla 27 F 10
34879 Villanueva de Abajo
    5 D 10
45810 Villanueva de Alcardete
    50 K 13
19460 Villanueva de Alcorón
    41 H 15
29310 Villanueva de Algaidas
    65 P 11
09130 Villanueva de Argaño
    18 E 12
19246 Villanueva de Argecilla
    29 H 14
05114 Villanueva de Ávila
    38 J 10
45410 Villanueva de Bogas
    49 K 12
26123 Villanueva de Cameros
    19 E 14
37799 Villanueva de Canedo
    26 G 8
09611 Villanueva de Carazo
    19 F 13
46669 Villanueva de Castellón
    61 L 18
29230 Villanueva de Cauche
    65 Q 11
14440 Villanueva de Córdoba
    56 N 10
47239 Villanueva de Duero
    27 F 10
13310 Villanueva de Franco
    49 M 13
50830 Villanueva de Gállego
    21 F 18
05164 Villanueva de Gómez
    27 H 10
42311 Villanueva de Gormaz
    29 G 13
16532 Villanueva de
    Guadamajud
    41 J 14
09450 Villanueva de Gumiel
    28 F 12
34811 Villanueva de Henares
    6 D 11
50153 Villanueva de Huerva
    21 G 17
50370 Villanueva de Jiloca
    31 G 17
28691 Villanueva de la
    Cañada 39 J 11
29230 Villanueva de la
    Concepción
    65 Q 10
47608 Villanueva de la
    Condesa 17 E 9
13330 Villanueva de la Fuente
    58 M 14

34859 Villanueva de la Peña
    5 D 10
39509 Villanueva de la Peña/
    Cabezón de la Sal
    6 C 11
23730 Villanueva de la Reina
    57 N 12
06700 Villanueva de la Serena
    46 M 8
10812 Villanueva de la Sierra
    36 J 7
10470 Villanueva de la Vera
    37 J 9
24225 Villanueva de las
    Manzanas 16 E 9
49333 Villanueva de las Peras
    16 F 8
18539 Villanueva de las Torres
    67 O 13
19311 Villanueva de las Tres
    Fuentes 42 J 16
47850 Villanueva de los
    Caballeros 17 F 9
21540 Villanueva de los
    Castillejos 62 O 5
16194 Villanueva de los
    Escuderos 41 J 15
13320 Villanueva de los
    Infantes/Valde-
    peñas 50 M 13
47174 Villanueva de los
    Infantes/Valladolid
    28 F 11
09593 Villanueva de los
    Montes 7 D 13
18369 Villanueva de Mesía
    66 P 11
39250 Villanueva de Nía
    6 D 11
09128 Villanueva de Odra
    18 D 11
33777 Villanueva de Oscos
    3 C 6
28609 Villanueva de Perales
    39 J 11
09125 Villanueva de Puerta
    18 D 12
13379 Villanueva de San
    Carlos 57 M 12
41660 Villanueva de San Juan
    64 P 9
47813 Villanueva de San
    Mancio 17 F 9
22231 Villanueva de Sigena
    22 F 19
29315 Villanueva de Tapia
    65 P 11
12428 Villanueva de Viver
    43 J 18
05212 Villanueva del Aceral
    27 G 10
24197 Villanueva del Arbol
    16 D 8
23330 Villanueva del
    Arzobispo
    58 N 13
05591 Villanueva del Campillo
    38 H 9
49708 Villanueva del Campo
    17 F 9
37658 Villanueva del Conde
    37 H 7
14250 Villanueva del Duque
    55 N 10
06110 Villanueva del Fresno
    53 N 5
34115 Villanueva del Monte
    17 D 10
28229 Villanueva del Pardillo
    39 J 12
34309 Villanueva del Rebollar
    17 E 10
44223 Villanueva del Rebollar
    de la Sierra
    31 H 17

Villanueva del Rey/Belmez (E) **Vírgen de la Columna** E

14230 Villanueva del Rey/
    Belmez 55 N 9
41409 Villanueva del Rey/
    Écija 64 O 9
30613 Villanueva del Río
    Segura 60 N 17
41350 Villanueva del Río y
    Minas 64 O 8
29312 Villanueva del Rosario
    65 Q 11
29313 Villanueva del Trabuco
    65 P 11
33559 Villanueva/Cangas de
    Onis 5 C 9
33719 Villanueva/Navia 3 B 6
33111 Villanueva/Oviedo
    4 C 8
09239 Villanueva-Matamala
    18 E 12
09214 Villanueva-Soportilla
    7 D 13
34477 Villanuño de Valdavia
    17 D 10
24719 Villaobispo de Otero
    16 D 7
24222 Villaornate 16 E 8
39291 Villapaderne 6 C 11
24940 Villapadierna 5 D 9
02350 Villapalacios 58 M 14
33793 Villapedre 3 B 6
34491 Villaprovedo 18 D 11
24235 Villaquejida 16 E 8
24080 Villaquilambre 16 D 8
09119 Villaquirán de la Puebla
    18 E 11
09226 Villaquirán de los
    Infantes 18 E 11
24511 Villar de Acero 15 D 6
37497 Villar de Argañán
    36 H 6
16433 Villar de Cañas
    41 K 14
12162 Villar de Canes 32 J 19
16709 Villar de Cantos
    50 L 15
02695 Villar de Chinchilla
    51 M 16
37488 Villar de Ciervo 25 H 6
19444 Villar de Cobeta
    30 H 15
05516 Villar de Corneja
    37 J 9
16840 Villar de Domingo
    García 41 J 15
37320 Villar de Gallimazo
    27 H 9
16648 Villar de la Encina
    50 K 14
37488 Villar de la Yegua
    25 H 6
50156 Villar de los Navarros
    31 G 17
42173 Villar de Maya
    20 E 15
16196 Villar de Olalla
    41 J 15
46351 Villar de Olmos
    52 K 17
37147 Villar de Peralonso
    26 G 7
10720 Villar de Plasencia
    37 J 7
02070 Villar de Pozo Rubio
    51 L 16
06716 Villar de Rena 46 L 8
37217 Villar de Samaniego
    25 G 7
40317 Villar de Sobrepeña
    28 G 12
46351 Villar de Tejas 52 K 17
26325 Villar de Torre 19 E 14
33842 Villar de Vildas 4 C 7
16161 Villar del Aguila
    41 K 14
42165 Villar del Ala 20 F 14

46170 Villar del Arzobispo
    43 K 18
42112 Villar del Campo
    20 F 15
44114 Villar del Cobo 42 J 16
16162 Villar del Horno 41 J 15
16370 Villar del Humo
    42 K 16
16813 Villar del Infantado
    41 J 15
16542 Villar del Mestre
    41 J 15
28512 Villar del Olmo 40 J 13
10330 Villar del Pedroso
    47 K 9
13431 Villar del Pozo
    48 M 12
06192 Villar del Rey 45 L 6
44311 Villar del Salz 42 H 17
16123 Villar del Saz de Arcas
    41 K 15
16190 Villar del Saz de
    Navalón 41 J 15
24368 Villar/Bembibre 16 D 7
33829 Villar/Grullos 4 C 7
49159 Villaralbo 26 G 8
14490 Villaralto 55 N 10
09550 Villarcayo 6 D 12
49562 Villardeciervos 16 F 7
49132 Villardefallavés 17 F 9
47860 Villardefrades 27 F 9
49250 Villardiegua de la
    Ribera 26 F 7
23659 Villardompardo
    57 O 11
49871 Villardondiego 27 F 9
06107 Villareal 53 M 5
16432 Villarejo de Fuentes
    40 K 14
16541 Villarejo de la Peñuela
    41 J 15
19445 Villarejo de Medina
    30 H 15
45179 Villarejo de Montalbán
    38 K 10
24358 Villarejo de Orbigo
    16 E 8
28590 Villarejo de Salvamés
    40 J 13
16195 Villarejo Seco 41 K 15
16195 Villarejo Sobrehuerta
    41 J 15
02139 Villarejo/Ayna 59 M 15
40590 Villarejo/Pedraza
    28 G 12
26325 Villarejo/San Milán de
    la Cogolla 19 E 14
16771 Villarejo-Periesteban
    41 K 15
24217 Villarente 17 D 9
19244 Villares de Jadraque
    29 G 13
37184 Villares de la Reina
    26 G 8
37267 Villares de Yeltes
    25 H 7
16442 Villares del Saz
    41 K 14
33812 Villares/Degaña 3 D 6
02439 Villares/Elche de la
    Sierra 59 N 15
46317 Villargordo del Cabriel
    51 K 17
24144 Villargusán 4 D 8
09513 Villarias 7 D 12
09195 Villariezo 18 E 11
24741 Villarino 15 E 6
37160 Villarino de los Aires
    25 G 7
49518 Villarino Tras La Sierra
    25 F 7
24525 Villariños 15 D 6
44559 Villarluengo 32 H 18
37130 Villarmayor 26 G 8
33817 Villarmental 3 C 7

34447 Villarmentero de
    Campos 18 E 11
47172 Villarmentero de
    Esgueva 27 F 10
37217 Villarmuerto 25 G 7
50310 Villaroya de la Sierra
    30 G 16
33887 Villarpedre 3 C 6
44380 Villarquemado
    42 H 17
34113 Villarrabé 17 E 10
34340 Villarramiel 17 E 10
21850 Villarrasa 63 P 6
42181 Villarraso 20 F 15
50490 Villarreal de Huerva
    31 G 17
22771 Villarreal de la Canal
    9 D 18
10695 Villarreal de San Carlos
    37 K 7
49137 Villarrín de Campos
    16 F 8
02600 Villarrobledo 50 L 14
23393 Villarrodrigo 58 N 14
34113 Villarrodrigo de la Vega
    17 E 10
17004 Villarroja 35 F 25
24273 Villarroquel 16 D 8
26187 Villarroya 20 E 15
44144 Villarroya de los
    Pinares 32 H 18
50368 Villarroya del Campo
    31 G 17
14710 Villarrubia 56 O 10
13670 Villarrubia de los Ojos
    49 L 12
45360 Villarrubia de Santiago
    40 K 13
16420 Villarrubio 40 K 14
06678 Villarta de los Montes
    48 L 10
13210 Villarta de San Juan
    49 L 13
16280 Villarta/Minglanar
    51 L 16
45910 Villarta/Torrijos 39 J 11
26259 Villarta-Quintana
    19 E 13
16441 Villas Viejas 40 K 14
09580 Villasana de Mena
    7 C 13
09109 Villasandino 18 E 11
09569 Villasante 7 C 13
08339 Villasar de Dalt
    35 F 24
34491 Villasarracino 18 E 11
42214 Villasayas 29 G 14
37256 Villasbuenas 25 G 6
10858 Villasbuenas de Gata
    36 J 6
37468 Villasdardo 26 G 7
42132 Villaseca de Arciel 3
    0 F 15
19294 Villaseca de Henares
    29 H 14
45260 Villaseca de la Sagra
    39 K 12
24140 Villaseca de Laciana
    4 D 7
19184 Villaseca de Uceda
    29 H 13
14720 Villaseca/Posadas
    55 O 9
16144 Villaseca/Priego
    41 J 15
24144 Villasecino 4 D 7
49181 Villaseco 26 G 8
37114 Villaseco de los
    Gamitos 26 G 7
37150 Villaseco de los Reyes
    26 G 7
24344 Villaselán 17 D 9
45740 Villasequilla de Yepes
    39 K 12
39698 Villasevil 6 C 12

09123 Villasidro 18 E 11
34475 Villasila de Valdavia
    17 D 10
09109 Villasilos 18 E 11
44190 Villaspesa 42 J 17
37522 Villasrubias 36 J 6
44130 Villastar 42 J 17
34115 Villasur 17 D 10
09199 Villasur de Herreros
    19 E 13
39451 Villasuso 6 C 11
33817 Villategil 3 C 6
45310 Villatobas 40 K 13
09006 Villatoro/Burgos
    18 E 12
05560 Villatoro/Piedrahita
    38 H 9
02215 Villatoya 52 L 17
33879 Villatresmil 4 C 7
09310 Villatuelda 18 F 12
24226 Villaturiel 16 D 9
34192 Villaumbrales 17 E 10
09125 Villaute 18 D 12
33128 Villavaler 4 C 7
02154 Villavaliente 51 L 17
47329 Villavaquerín 28 F 11
09124 Villavedón 18 D 11
26329 Villavelayo 19 E 14
47883 Villavellid 27 F 9
49870 Villavendimio 27 F 9
09510 Villaventín 7 C 13
21730 Villaverde 16 E 7
24171 Villaverde de Arcayos
    17 D 9
02460 Villaverde de
    Guadalimar
    58 N 14
40219 Villaverde de Iscar
    27 G 10
47465 Villaverde de Medina
    27 G 9
40542 Villaverde de Montejo
    28 F 12
39793 Villaverde de Pontones
    6 C 12
26321 Villaverde de Rioja
    19 E 14
19261 Villaverde del Ducado
    30 G 15
09339 Villaverde del Monte/
    Burgos 18 E 12
42145 Villaverde del Monte/
    Soria 19 F 14
41318 Villaverde del Río
    63 O 8
16111 Villaverde y Pasaconsol
    41 K 15
33836 Villaverde/Cangas del
    Narcea 3 C 6
33316 Villaverde/Gijón/Xixón
    5 B 8
09226 Villaverde-Mogina
    18 E 11
31481 Villaveta/Aoiz-Agoitz
    9 D 17
09109 Villaveta/Melgar de
    Fernamental
    18 E 11
47676 Villavicencio de los
    Caballeros 17 E 9
14300 Villaviciosa de Córdoba
    55 N 9
28670 Villaviciosa de Odón
    39 J 12
19413 Villaviciosa de Tajuña
    40 H 14
05130 Villaviciosa/Ávila
    38 H 10
33300 Villaviciosa/Colunga
    5 C 9
12526 Villavieja 44 K 19
28739 Villavieja de Lozoya
    28 G 12
09239 Villavieja de Muñó
    18 E 12

37260 Villavieja de Yeltes
    25 H 7
47113 Villavieja del Cerro
    27 F 9
34249 Villaviudas 18 F 11
47134 Villaxesmir 27 F 9
33717 Villayón 3 C 6
24126 Villayuste 16 D 8
24763 Villazala 16 E 8
24328 Villazanzo de
    Valderaduey
    17 D 10
33868 Villazón 4 C 7
09226 Villazopeque 18 E 11
09128 Villegas 18 E 11
02512 Villegas o Mardos
    59 M 16
40496 Villeguillo 27 G 10
44131 Villel 42 J 17
19332 Villel de Mesa
    30 G 16
34492 Villela 6 D 11
34349 Villelga 17 E 10
03400 Villena 60 M 18
34305 Villerías 17 F 10
15896 Villestro 1 D 2
24324 Villeza 17 E 9
24163 Villimer 17 D 9
24250 Villivañe 16 E 8
34259 Villodre 18 E 11
34257 Villodrigo 18 E 11
34131 Villoldo 17 E 10
24218 Villomar 17 D 9
12311 Villores 32 H 19
33986 Villoria/Pola de Laviana
    4 C 8
37330 Villoria/Salamanca
    27 H 9
37338 Villoruela 27 G 9
40449 Villoslada 28 H 11
26125 Villoslada de Cameros
    19 E 14
34127 Villota del Duque
    17 E 10
34112 Villota del Páramo
    17 D 10
34129 Villotilla 17 E 10
09310 Villovela de Esgueva
    18 F 12
09348 Villoviado 18 F 12
34449 Villovieco 18 E 11
43430 Vimbodí 23 G 22
15129 Vimianzo 1 C 1
44591 Vinaceite 32 G 18
05216 Viñaderos 27 G 10
25440 Vinaixa 23 G 21
43517 Vinallop 33 H 21
12500 Vinaròs 33 J 20
49517 Vinas 15 F 7
16812 Vindel 41 H 15
43792 Vinebre 23 G 21
26325 Viniegra de Abajo
    19 E 14
26325 Viniegra de Arriba
    19 E 14
36687 Vinseiro 13 D 3
49177 Vinuela de Sayago
    26 G 8
42150 Vinuesa 19 F 14
22487 Viñal 11 D 21
05147 Viñegra 38 H 9
05309 Viñegra de Moraña
    27 H 10
39584 Viñón/Poles 5 C 10
33310 Viñón/Villaviciosa
    5 C 9
13460 Viñuela/Almodóvar del
    Campo 56 M 11
29712 Viñuela/Benamargosa
    65 Q 11
19184 Viñuelas 29 H 13
33448 Viodo 4 B 8
33449 Vioño 4 B 8
50730 Vírgen de la Columna
    21 F 18

15689 Visantoña   2 C 3
44164 Visiedo   42 H 17
36693 Viso   13 E 2
13770 Viso del Marqués
    57 M 12
50482 Vistabella   31 G 17
12135 Vistabella del
    Maestrazgo
    32 J 19
11500 Vistahermosa   69 Q 7
27328 Visuña   15 D 5
05146 Vita   27 H 9
37210 Vitigudino   25 G 7
01070 Vitoria-Gasteiz   7 D 14
22450 Viu   10 E 20
25556 Viu de Llevata   11 E 21
09587 Vivanco de Mena
    7 C 13
09140 Vivar del Cid   18 E 12
06412 Vivares   46 L 8
27850 Viveiró/Mondoñedo
    2 C 4
27850 Viveiro/Ortigueira
    2 B 4
44740 Vivel del Río Martín
    31 H 18
50249 Viver de la Sierra
    30 G 16
08673 Viver/Puig-reig
    12 F 23
12460 Viver/Segorbe   43 K 18
24137 Vivero   4 D 7
02310 Viveros   50 M 14
02536 Vizcable   59 N 15
09613 Vizcaínos   19 E 13
42173 Vizmanos   20 E 15
18179 Viznar   66 P 12
24444 Voces   15 E 6
42107 Vozmediano   20 F 16
24859 Voznuevo   5 D 9
17111 Vulpellac   35 F 26

W

47190 Wamba   27 F 10

X

15685 Xanceda   2 C 3
32365 Xares   15 E 6
46800 Xàtiva   61 M 18
46770 Xeraco   61 L 19
25555 Xerallo   11 E 21
46760 Xeresa   61 L 19
27833 Xermade   2 C 4
27377 Xermar   2 C 4
43592 Xerta   33 H 20
36835 Xesta/A Lama   13 E 3
36515 Xesta/Lalin   14 D 3
15186 Xesteda   1 C 2
32930 Xestosa   14 E 4
27227 Xiá   2 C 4
07850 Ximaina   72 L 23
32630 Xinzo de Limia   14 E 4
46950 Xirivella   43 L 19
32688 Xironda   14 F 4
27870 Xove   2 B 4
27877 Xuances   2 B 4
32459 Xubín   14 E 3
27720 Xudán   3 C 5
15995 Xuño   13 D 1
32670 Xunqueira de Ambía
    14 E 4
32730 Xunqueira de
    Espadañedo
    14 E 4
27377 Xustás   2 C 5

Y

42172 Yanguas   20 E 15
40493 Yanguas de Eresma
    28 G 11
22141 Yaso   22 E 19
18448 Yátor   67 Q 13
46367 Yátova   43 L 18
22375 Yeba   10 D 20
19141 Yebes   40 H 13

19111 Yebra   40 J 14
22610 Yebra de Basa
    10 E 19
30510 Yecla   60 M 17
37219 Yecla de Yeltes   25 H 7
01322 Yecora   20 D 15
30193 Yéchar   60 N 17
18460 Yegen   67 Q 13
19413 Yela   29 H 14
19143 Yélamos de Abajo
    40 H 14
19143 Yélamos de Arriba
    40 H 14
06411 Yelbes   46 M 7
45220 Yeles   39 J 12
42230 Yelo   30 G 14
16373 Yémeda   42 K 16
45313 Yepes   39 K 12
22193 Yéqueda   22 E 19
39685 Yera   6 C 12
24386 Yeres   15 E 6
31410 Yesa   9 D 17
22659 Yésero   10 D 19
02480 Yeste   59 N 15
02536 Yetas   59 N 15
45529 Yuncler   39 J 12
45591 Yunclillos   39 J 12
45210 Yuncos   39 J 12
29410 Yunquera   70 Q 10
19210 Yunquera de Henares
    40 H 13

Z

31448 Zabalza/Aoiz-Agoitz
    9 D 17
31174 Zabalza/Pamplona-
    Iruña   8 D 16
24396 Zacos   16 D 7
09339 Zael   18 E 12
18128 Zafarraya   65 Q 11
06300 Zafra   54 N 7
16771 Zafra de Záncara
    41 K 14
16317 Zafrilla   42 J 16
18311 Zagra   65 P 11
14816 Zagrilla   65 P 11
11688 Zahara   70 Q 9
11393 Zahara de los Atunes
    69 R 8
06129 Zahinos   53 N 6
11159 Zahora   69 R 7
22530 Zaidín   22 F 20
01120 Zaita   8 D 14
01138 Zaitegi   7 D 14
06430 Zalamea de la Serena
    55 M 8
21640 Zalamea la Real
    63 O 6
31484 Zalba   9 D 17
48250 Zaldibar   8 C 14
26289 Zaldierna   19 E 13
09199 Zalduendo   19 E 13
01208 Zalduondo   8 D 15
29569 Zalea   70 Q 10
48860 Zalla   7 C 13
42128 Zamajón   30 F 15
37591 Zamarra   36 H 7
40196 Zamarramala   28 H 11
37110 Zamayón   26 G 8
14950 Zambra   65 P 11
01212 Zambrana   7 D 14
23560 Zamora/Huelma
    66 O 13
49070 Zamora/Toro   26 F 8
14814 Zamoranos   65 O 11
48170 Zamudio   7 C 14
19495 Zaorejas   41 H 15
05154 Zapardiel de la Cañada
    37 H 9
05631 Zapardiel de la Ribera
    37 J 9
02315 Zapateros   58 M 14
42127 Zarabes   30 F 15
50070 Zaragoza   21 F 18
47610 Zaratán   27 F 10

30810 Zarcilla de Ramos
    59 O 16
46621 Zarra   52 L 17
26291 Zarratón   19 D 14
06611 Zarza Capilla   47 M 9
06830 Zarza de Alange
    54 M 7
10710 Zarza de Granadilla
    37 J 7
10189 Zarza de Montánchez
    46 L 7
16470 Zarza de Tajo   40 J 13
10880 Zarza la Mayor   36 K 6
30814 Zarzadilla de Totana
    59 O 16
28293 Zarzalejo   39 H 11
26586 Zarzosa   20 E 15
09108 Zarzosa de Riopisuerga
    18 D 11
16146 Zarzuela   41 J 15
19237 Zarzuela de Jadraque
    29 G 13
40152 Zarzuela del Monte
    28 H 11
40293 Zarzuela del Pinar
    28 G 11
15850 Zas   1 C 2
42351 Zayas de Bascones
    29 F 13
42329 Zayas de Torres
    29 F 13
42351 Zayuelas   29 F 13
09490 Zazuar   29 F 12
20215 Zegama   8 D 15
30588 Zeneta   60 N 18
31796 Ziga   9 C 16
31809 Ziordia   8 D 15
31180 Zizur Mayor-Zizur
    Nagusia   8 D 16
48499 Zollo   7 C 14
27627 Zoó   3 D 5
32703 Zorelle   14 E 4
10130 Zorita   47 L 8
37408 Zorita de la Frontera
    27 G 9
19119 Zorita de los Canes   40
    J 14
12311 Zorita del Maestrazgo
    32 H 19
48340 Zornotza   7 C 14
26288 Zorraquín   19 E 13
24791 Zotes del Páramo
    16 E 8
18140 Zubia   66 P 12
48499 Zubialde   7 C 14
31241 Zubielqui   8 D 15
31746 Zubieta   8 C 16
31630 Zubiri   9 D 16
12125 Zucaina   43 J 19
31272 Zudaire   8 D 15
50800 Zuera   21 F 18
21210 Zufre   63 O 7
31710 Zugarramurdi   9 C 16
48391 Zugaztieta   7 C 14
01430 Zuhatzu Koartango
    7 D 14
14870 Zuheros   65 O 11
18291 Zujaira   66 P 12
18811 Zújar   67 O 14
02214 Zulema   51 L 17
31470 Zulueta   7 D 14
01195 Zumeltzu   7 D 14
31484 Zunzarren   9 D 17
09245 Zuñeda   7 D 13
31284 Zúñiga   8 D 15
09294 Zurbitu   7 D 14
33629 Zureda   4 C 8
04650 Zúrgena   68 P 15
22569 Zurita   11 F 20
22728 Zuriza   9 D 18
01130 Zuya   7 D 14
09491 Zúzones   29 F 13

FUERTEVENTURA

35638 Agua de Bueyes
    80 C 6
35637 Aguas Verdes
    80 C 6
35628 Ajuy   80 C 5
35630 Antigua   80 C 6
35650 Arriba   80 A 6

35627 Bahía Calma
    80 E 5
35628 Bárgeda   80 C 6
35637 Betancuria   80 C 6
35625 Butihondo   80 E 4

35649 Caldereta   80 B 7
35627 Cardón   80 D 5
35625 Casas Risco del
    Paso   80 E 5
35628 Casilla Blanca
    80 D 6
35640 Casilla de Costa
    80 A/B 7
35611 Casillas del Angel
    80 B 6
35610 Castillo de la Caleta
    de Fustes   80 C 7
35625 Ciervo   80 E 4
35625 Cofete   80 E 4
35611 Colonia de García
    Escámez   80 B 6
35660 Corralejo   80 A 7
35627 Costa Calma
    80 D 5
35625 Cueva de la Negra
    79 E 4

35627 Chilegua   80 D 5

35627 Diego Alonso
    80 D 6

35637 El Almacigo   80 C 6
35628 El Alto   80 D 6
35640 El Cantil   80 B 7
35639 El Cortijo   80 C 6
35650 El Cotillo   80 A 6
35610 El Matorral   80 C 7
35639 El Sadadillo
    80 C/D 6
35640 El Tarajalito   80 B 7
35613 El Time   80 B 7
35640 El Tío Machín
    80 B 7
35625 Esquinzo   80 E 4
35628 Ezquen   80 D 6

35628 Fayagua   80 D 5
35610 Finca del Vicario
    80 C 7

35629 Giniginámar
    80 D 6
35620 Gran Tarajal
    80 D 6
35625 Gran Valle   80 E 4
35612 Guisguey   80 B 7

35628 Jacomar   80 D 7
35625 Jorós   80 E 4

35637 La Ampuyenta
    80 C 6
35613 La Asomada   80 B 7
35628 La Cañada de
    Teguital   80 D 6
35650 La Costilla   80 A 6
35628 La Florida   80 D 6
35610 La Guirra   80 C 7
35613 La Herradura
    80 B 7
35627 La Lajita   80 D 5
35613 La Matilla   80 B 6
35640 La Oliva   80 B 6

35627 La Pared   80 D 5
35640 La Tía Cristina
    80 B 7
35650 Lajares   80 A 6
35628 Las Casitas
    80 D 6
35627 Las Hermosas
    80 D 5
35640 Las Llanadas
    80 B 7
35629 Las Playitas   80 D 6
35638 Las Pocetas   80 C 6
35610 Las Salinas
    80 C 7
35628 Las Salinas
    80 D 5
35640 Los Apartaderos
    80 A 7
35625 Los Canarios de
    Abajo   80 E 5
35650 Los Lagos   80 A 6
35611 Los Molinos
    80 B 6
35600 Los Pozos   80 C 7
35627 Los Verodes
    80 E 5

35637 Llanos de la
    Concepcion
    80 C 6

35639 Majada Blanca
    80 C 6
35613 Majadas   80 B 7
35650 Majanicho   80 A 6
35625 Mal Nombre
    80 E 4
35625 Marabú   80 E 5
35627 Matas Blancas
    80 D 5
35625 Matorral   80 E 4
35628 Mézquez   80 C 5
35627 Montaña Hendida
    80 D 5
35638 Morales   80 C 6
35625 Morro Jable
    80 E 4

35629 Pablo Sánchez
    80 D 6
35628 Pájara   80 C 6
35625 Pecenescal
    80 E 5
35640 Peña Azul   80 A 7
35600 Playa Blanca
    80 C 7
35639 Pozo Negro
    80 C 7
35625 Puerto de la Cruz
    79 E 3/4
35640 Puerto de la Oliva
    80 B 7
35628 Puerto de la Peña
    80 C 5
35600 Puerto del Rosario
    80 B 7
35612 Puerto Lajas
    80 B 7

35650 Roque   80 A 6
35612 Rosa de la Monja
    80 B 7

35660 Solyplayas   80 A 7

35649 Taca   80 B 6
35627 Tamaretilla   80 D 5
35627 Tarajalejo   80 D 6
35611 Tefía   80 B 6
35628 Teguital   80 D 6
35627 Tesejerague
    80 D 6
35611 Tesjuates   80 B 6
35613 Tetir   80 B 6
35649 Tindaya   80 B 6

Tiscamanita   FUERTEVENTURA · GRAN CANARIA · EL HIERRO · LA GOMERA   **Arguamul**

35638 Tiscamanita
        80 C 6
35628 Tonicosquey
        80 D 6
35650 Tostón 80 A 6
35628 Toto 80 C 6
35639 Triquivijate 80 C 6
35628 Tuineje 80 C 6

35627 Ugán 80 D 5

35613 Valhondo 80 B 7
35637 Valle de Santa Inéz
        80 C 6
35649 Vallebrón 80 B 6
35638 Valles de Ortega
        80 C 6
35637 Vega de Rio Palmas
        80 C 6
35627 Vegueta 80 D 6
35640 Villaverde 80 B 7
35629 Violante 80 D 6

GRAN CANARIA

35350 Acusa 75 C 3
35480 Agaete 75 B 3
35299 Agualatente
        76 C 4
35260 Agüimes 76 C/D 5
35119 Aldea Blanca
        76 D 5
35197 Almatriche 76 B 5
35120 Arguineguín
        75 E 3
35118 Arinaga 76 D 6
35328 Arinez 76 B 4
35400 Arucas 76 B 5
35108 Arteara 76 D 4
35478 Artejévez 75 C 2
35478 Artenara 75 B 4
35369 Ayacata 75 C 4

35107 Bahia Feliz 76 E 5
35414 Bañaderos
        76 A 4/5
35421 Barranco del Pinar
        75 B 4
35469 Barrial 75 A 3
35009 Barrio de La Isleta
        76 A 5
35107 Besudo 76 E 4

35422 Cabo Verde
        76 A 4
35468 Caideros 75 B 4
35107 Caleta 76 D 5
35329 Camaretas 76 C 4
35190 Cardones 76 A 5
35240 Carrizal 76 C 5/6
35191 Casa Ayala
        76 A/B 5
35229 Casa Quemada
        76 B 4
35431 Casablanca 76 A 4
35280 Casas Blancas
        76 D 4
35149 Casas El Inglés
        75 D 3
35250 Casas de Aguatona
        76 C 5
35109 Casas de Ayagaures
        Alto 75 D 4
35109 Casas de Chamoriscan
        75 D 4
35421 Casas de El Tablero
        76 B 4
35149 Casas de La Huerta
        Nueva 75 D 3
35149 Casas de la
        Postreragua de
        Veneguera 75 D 3
35140 Casas de la Vistilla
        75 D 3

35280 Casasde los Sitios
        de Abaje 76 D 4
35211 Casas de Pasadilla
        76 C 5
35470 Casas de Pino Gordo
        75 C 3
35118 Casas de Risco Verde
        76 D 6
35109 Casas de Taginastal
        75 D 4
35350 Casas de Tamadaba
        75 B 3
35139 Casas de Tauro Alto
        75 D 3
35308 Casas de Tirma
        75 B 3
35489 Casas del Camino
        75 B 3
35478 CasasEl Manatial
        75 C 3
35149 Casas El Sao 75 D 3
35350 Casas Las Hoyas
        75 B 3
35200 Casas Nuevas 76 C 6
35107 Castillo del Romeral
        76 D 5
35211 Cazadores
        76 C 5
35369 Cercados de Araña
        75 C 4
35128 Cercados de Espinos
        75 D 4
35005 Ciudad Jardin
        6 B 5
35413 Costa 76 A 4
35191 Costa Ayala 76 A 5
35118 Cruce de Arinaga
        76 D 5
35218 Cruz de Gallinas
        76 B 5
35197 Cuesta Blanca
        76 B 5
35329 Cueva Grande
        76 C 4
35308 Cuevas Negras
        75 B 3

35193 Dragonal 76 B 5

35128 El Baranquillo
        Andrés 75 D 3
35128 El Caidero 75 D 3
35458 El Calabozo
        75 A/B 4
35240 El Carrizal 75 C 3
35216 El Cerón 76 C 5
35479 El Cruce 76 D 5
35229 El Chorrillo 75 C 3
35110 El Doctoral
        76 C 5
35368 El Espinillo 75 C 4
35379 El Estanco 76 D 5
35215 El Goro 76 C 6
35412 El Guincho 76 D 5
35216 El Helechal
        76 C 5
35468 El Hornillo 75 B 3
35149 El Horno 75 D 2
35128 El Horno 75 D 3
35259 El Mondragón
        76 C 5
35280 El Morisco 76 C 4
35140 El Palmita 75 D 3
35218 El Palmital 76 B 5
35140 El Pie de la Cuesta
        75 D 3
35360 El Rincón 75 C 4
35489 El Risco 75 B 3
35128 El Sao 75 D 3
35350 El Tablado 75 B 4
35109 El Tablero 75 E 4
35199 El Toscón 76 B 5
35100 El Veril 76 E 4
35349 El Zunracal
        76 B 4

35119 Era del Cardón
        76 D 5

35468 Fagajesto 75 B 4
35108 Fataga 76 D 4
35430 Firgas 76 B 4
35457 Frontón 76 A/B 4

35460 Gáldar 75 A 4
35119 Gallegos 76 D 5
35219 Gando 76 C 6
35489 Guayedra 75 B 3

35468 Hoya Pineda
        75 B 4
35308 Hoya de Gamonal
        76 C 4
35140 Hoya del Salitre
        75 D 3
35412 Huerta del Pinar
        76 B 4

35250 Ingenio 76 C 5
35280 Ingenio di Santa Lucia
        76 D 4

35220 Jinámar 76 B 5
35107 Juan Grande
        76 D 5
35400 Juan XXIII 76 B 5

35470 La Aldea de San
        Nicolas 75 C 2
35309 La Angostura
        76 B 5
35307 La Atalaya 76 B 5
35329 La Bodeguilla
        76 C 5
35211 La Breña 76 C 5
35432 La Caldera 76 B 4
35211 La Colomba
        76 C 5
35368 La Culata 76 C 4
35299 La Culata 75 C 4
35280 La Fortaleza
        76 D 5
35212 La Garita 76 C 6
35218 La Gavia 76 B 5
35329 La Lechuza 76 C 4
35138 La Playa del Tauro
        75 D 3
35218 La Solana 76 C 5
35328 La Vedra 76 B/C 4
35423 Lance 76 B 4
35340 Lanzarote 76 B 4
35006 Las Alcaravaneras
        76 B 5
35149 Las Casas de
        Veneguera
        75 C 3
35191 Las Coloradas
        76 A 5
35212 Las Huesas 76 C 5
35280 Las Lagunas
        76 C/D 4
35328 Las Lagunetas
        76 C 4
35479 Las Marciegas
        75 C 2
35199 Las Mesas Bajas
        76 B 5
35070 Las Palmas de Gran
        Canaria 76 A/B 5
35190 Las Torres 76 B 5
35216 Las Vegas 76 C 5
35219 Lazareto de Gando
        76 C 6
35192 Lomo Blanca 76 B 5
35196 Los Altos 76 B 5
35211 Los Arenales 76 B 5
35423 Los Caserones
        76 B 4
35218 Los Caserones
        76 C 5

35260 Los Corralillos
        76 D 5
35432 Los Dolores
        76 A 4
35229 Los Hoyes 76 B 5
35217 Los Llanetes
        76 C 5
35140 Los Navartos 75 D 3
35128 Los Penoñes
        75 D 3/4
35280 Los Sitios 76 D 4
35420 Los Tilos 76 B 4
35308 Lugarejos 75 B 3

35340 Madrelagua 76 B 4
35212 Marpequena 76 C 6
35229 Marzagan 76 B 5
35100 Maspalomas
        76 E 4
35107 Matorral 76 D 5
35338 Miraflor 76 B 4/5
35140 Mogán 75 D 3
35106 Montaña de Ladata
        75 E 4
35310 Monte Lentiscal
        76 B 5
35106 Monteleón 75 D 4

35330 Ojaro 76 B 4

35120 Parchel 75 E 3
35457 Paso Maria de Los
        Santos 75 B 4
35129 Patalavaca 75 E 3
35215 Piletilla 76 C 5
35309 Pino Santo 76 B 5
35106 Playa de Maspalomas
        76 E 4
35214 Playa de Melenara
        76 C 6
35214 Playa de Salinetas
        76 C 6
35478 Playa de Tasarte
        75 D 2
35214 Playa del Hombre
        76 C 6
35100 Playa del Inglés
        76 E 4
35220 Polígono de Jinámar
        76 B 5
35119 Poligori Industrial
        del Arinaga
        76 D 5
35119 Pozo Izquierdo
        76 D 5
35479 Puerto de la Aldea
        75 C 2
35469 Puerto de la Caleta
        75 A 3
35489 Puerto de las Nieves
        75 B 3
35138 Puerto de Mogán
        75 D 3
35469 Puerto de Sardina
        75 A 3
35106 Puerto Deportivo de
        Pasito Blanco
        75 E 4
35460 Puerto Nuevo 75 A 4
35130 Puerto Rico 75 E 3

35216 Rincón 76 C 5
35280 Risco Blanco
        76 C 4

35107 San Agustín
        76 E 4/5
35413 San Andrés 76 A 4
35421 San Bartolomé de
        Fontanales
        75 B 4
35290 San Bartolomé de
        Tirajana 76 C 4
35016 San Cristóbal 76 B 5
35413 San Felipe 76 A 4

35194 San Francisco de
        Paula 76 B 5
35338 San Isidro 75 A 3
35015 San José/Las Palmas
        de Gran Canaria
        76 B 5
35307 San José/Santa
        Brigida 76 B 5
35196 San Lorenzo 76 B 5
35489 San Pedro 75 B 3
35300 Santa Brigida
        76 B 5
35280 Santa Lucía 76 C 4/5
35440 Santa María de Guía
        de Gran Canaria
        75 A 4
35411 Santidad 76 B 5
35110 Sardina/Aldea Blanca
        76 D 5
35469 Sardina/Gáldar 75 A 3
35468 Saucillo 75 B 4
35012 Schamán 76 B 5
35193 Siete Puertas
        76 B 5
35106 Sonnenland 76 E 4
35128 Soria 75 C 3
35280 Sorrueda 76 D 4/5
35458 Suerte 76 B 5

35149 Tabaibales 75 D 3
35017 Tafira Alta 76 B 5
35194 Tafira Baja 76 B 5
35197 Tamaraceite
        76 B 5
35140 Tanigue 75 D 3
35478 Tasarte 75 C 3
35478 Tasártico 75 C 2
35138 Taurito 75 D 3
35360 Tejeda 75 C 4
35200 Telde 76 C 5
35270 Temisas 76 C 5
35430 Tenoya 76 B 5
35216 Tenteniguada
        76 C 5
35330 Teror 76 B 4
35478 Tocodomán
        75 C 3
35432 Trapiche 76 A 4
35422 Trujillo 76 B 4

35008 Urbanización El
        Cebadal 76 B 5
35107 Urbanización Playa del
        Aguila 76 E 5
35139 Urbanización del Cura
        75 D 3
35328 Utiaca 76 B 4

35200 Valle de Los Nueve
        76 C 5
35218 Valle de San Roque
        76 C 5
35340 Valleseco 76 B 4
35349 Valsendero 76 B 4
35217 Valsequillo de Gran
        Canaria 76 C 5
35110 Vecindario 76 D 5
35328 Vega de San Mateo
        76 C 5
35001 Vegueta 76 B 5
35149 Veneguéra 75 D 2
35457 Verdejo 75 B 4
35412 Visvique 76 B 5

EL HIERRO · LA GOMERA

38892 Acardece 81 B 1
38830 Agulo 81 A 2
38812 Alajeró 81 B 2
38812 Almácigos 81 B 2
38852 Alojera 81 A 1
38800 Aluce 81 B 3
38812 Antonocojo 81 B/C 2
38850 Arguamul 81 A 2

125

I N D E X · O R T S R E G I S T E R · I N D I C E · Í N D I
P L A A T S N A M E N R E G I S T E R · R E J S T Ř Í K   M Í S

E

38860 Arguayoda 81 B 2
38892 Arure 81 B 1
38813 Ayamosna 81 B 3

38849 Banda de las Rosas
    81 A 2
38811 Barranco de
    Santiago 81 B 2
38811 Benchijigua 81 B 2
38916 Betenama 81 E 3

38910 Caleta 81 E 3
38813 Casas Blancas
    81 B 3
38813 Contrera 81 B 3
38852 Cubaba 81 A 1
38800 Cuevas Blancas
    81 B 3

38891 Chejelipes 81 B 3
38850 Chigueré 81 A 2
38869 Chipude 81 B 2

38900 Echedo 81 D 3
38891 El Atajo 81 B 3
38813 El Cabrito 81 B 3
38849 El Carmen 81 A 2
38890 El Cedro 81 B 2
38860 El Drago 81 B 2
38829 El Estanquillo
    81 A 2
38879 El Guro 81 B 1
38879 El Hornillo 81 B 1
38811 El Joradillo 81 C 3
38800 El Molinito 81 B 3
38829 El Palmar 81 A 3
38914 El Pinar 81 F 3
38800 Encherada 81 B 3
38852 Epina 81 A 2
38916 Erese 81 E 3

38911 Frontera 81 E 2

38869 Gerián 81 B 1
38916 Guarazoca 81 E 3
38911 Guinea 81 E 2

38820 Hermigua 81 A 2
38916 Hoyo del Barrio
    81 E 3

38869 Igualero 81 B 2
38812 Imada 81 B 2
38915 Isora 81 E 3

38869 Jagüe 81 B 2
38800 Jaragán 81 B 3
38916 Jarales 81 E 3
38813 Jerdune 81 B 2

38870 La Calera 81 B 1
38812 La Cantera 81 C 2
38915 La Cuesta 81 E 3
38869 La Dama 81 B 2
38869 La Debesa 81 B 2
38891 La Laja 81 B 2
38890 La Palmita 81 A 2
38891 La Playa 81 A 2
38849 La Quilla 81 A 2
38869 La Rajita 81 B 2
38915 La Restinga 81 F 3
38915 La Torre 81 E 3
38879 La Vizcaina 81 B 1
38811 Laguna de Santiago
    81 C 2
38829 Las Casas 81 A 2
38914 Las Casas 81 F 3
38869 Las Hayas 81 B 2
38916 Las Montañetas
    81 E 3
38829 Las Nuevitas
    81 A 2/3
38911 Las Puntas 81 E 3
38890 Las Rosas 81 A 2
38915 Las Rosas 81 E 3

38811 Las Toscas 81 B 2
38913 Las Toscas 81 E 2
38811 Lo del Gato 81 B 2
38879 Lomo del Balo
    81 B 1
38890 Los Aceviños
    81 A 2
38879 Los Granados
    81 B 1
38913 Los Llanilos 81 E 2
38915 Los Llanos 81 E 3
38911 Los Mocanes
    81 E 2

38829 Llano Campos
    81 A 3

38849 Macayo 81 A 2
38890 Meriga 81 A 2
38916 Mocanal 81 D 3

38811 Pastrana 81 B 2
38869 Pavón 81 B 2
38870 Playa de la Calera
    81 B 1
38811 Playa de Santiago
    81 C 2
38916 Pozo de las
    Calcosas 81 D 3
38912 Pozo de Sabinosa
    81 E 2
38910 Pozo de la Estaca
    81 E 3

38812 Quise 81 B 2

38890 Rosa de las Piedras
    81 A 2

38912 Sabinosa 81 E 2
38915 San Andrés
    81 E 3
38891 San Antonio y Pilar
    81 B 3
38869 San Sebastián
    81 B 2
38800 San Sebastián de la
    Gomera 81 B 3
38813 Seima 81 B 3

38852 Taguluche/Arure
    81 B 1
38829 Taguluche/Hermigua
    81 A 3
38914 Taibique 81 F 3
38910 Tamaduste 81 D 3
38813 Targa 81 B 2
38850 Tazo 81 A 1
38811 Tecina 81 C 2/3
38811 Tejiade 81 B 2
38910 Temijiraque 81 E 3
38913 Tigaday 81 E 2
38915 Tiñor 81 E 3
38869 Topogache 81 B 2

38891 Valle Abajo 81 A 2
38870 Valle Gran Rey
    81 B 1
38840 Vallehermoso 81 A 2
38900 Valverde 81 E 3
38811 Vegalpala 81 B 2
38870 Vueltas 81 B 1

38811 Zarcita 81 B 2

LANZAROTE

35540 Alegranza 79 A 3
35550 Argana Alta 79 D 3
35550 Argana Baja 79 D 3
35550 Arrecife 79 D 3
35542 Arrieta 79 C 3/4
35570 Atlante del Sol
    79 E 1

35558 Bajamer 79 C 3

35540 Caleta del Sebo
    79 B 3
35562 Casas de La Florida
    79 D 2
35542 Casas de las
    Escamas 79 C 4
35541 Casas la Breña
    79 C 4
35560 Caserío de Teneza
    79 C 2
35543 Charco del Palo
    79 C 4
35572 Conil 79 D 2
35570 Cortijo de la Punta
    79 E 1

35570 El Berrugo 79 E 1
35540 El Cortijo 79 A 3
35570 El Cortijo de la
    Mareta 79 E 1
35560 El Cuchillo 79 C 2
35570 El Golfo 79 D 1
35572 El Guardia de Abajo
    79 D 2
35562 El Islote 79 D 2
35560 El Melián 79 C 2
35571 El Mesón 79 D 2
35539 El Mojón 79 C 3
35570 El Papagayo
    79 E 1
35572 El Rincón 79 D 2

35570 Femés 79 E 2

35509 Grandos 79 D 3
35544 Guatiza 79 C 3
35560 Guigan 79 D 2
35559 Güime 79 D 3
35541 Guinate 79 C 3

35520 Haría 79 C 3

05570 Islote de la Vega
    79 D 1

35570 Juán Perdomo
    79 D 1

35571 La Asomada
    79 D 2
35558 La Caldera 79 C 2
35558 La Caleta de Famara
    79 C 4
35560 La Costa 79 C 2
35570 La Degollada
    79 D/E 1
35572 La Degollada
    79 D 2
35570 La Hoya 79 D 1
35560 La Santa 79 C 2
35560 La Vegueta 79 D 2
35571 La Vegueta 79 D 2
35539 Laderas de
    Teneüime
    79 C 3
35570 Las Breñas 79 E 1
35570 Las Casitas
    79 D/E 2
35558 Las Laderas
    79 C 3
35541 Las Rositas 79 C 3
35541 Las Tabaibitas
    79 D 3
35518 Los Mojones
    79 D/E 2
35541 Los Molinos 79 C 3
35570 Los Morilles 79 D 1
35519 Los Porcillos
    79 D 2
35539 Los Valles 79 C 3

35571 Mácher 79 D 2
35541 Máguez 79 C 3

35570 Maisón 79 E 1
35543 Mala 79 C 3
35560 Mancha Blanca
    79 D 2
35572 Masdache 79 D 2
35572 Matechuelos
    79 D 2
35570 Montaña Baja
    79 E 1
35559 Montaña–Blanca
    79 D 2
35562 Mozaga 79 D 3
35558 Muñique 79 C 2

35509 Nazaret 79 D 3

35541 Órzola 79 B 4

35540 Pedro Barba 79 B 3
35570 Playa Blanca
    79 E 1
35509 Playa Honda 79 D 3
35570 Playa Quemada
    79 E 2
35509 Playa del Cable
    79 D 3
35570 Puerto Calero
    79 E 2
35510 Puerto del Carmen
    79 E 2
35542 Punta de Mujeres
    79 C 4

35550 San Bartolomé
    79 D 3
35560 Santa Sport
    79 C 2
35558 Sóo 79 C 2

35542 Tabayesco 79 C 3
35509 Tahíche 79 D 3
35560 Tajaste 79 D 2
35561 Tao 79 D 2
35572 Tegoyo 79 D 2
35530 Teguise 79 D 3
35539 Teseguite 79 D 3
35558 Tiagua 79 D 2
35572 Tias 79 D 2
35560 Tinajo 79 C 2
35560 Tinguatón
    79 D 2

35570 Uga 79 D 2
35544 Urbanización Anavc
    79 C 4
35509 Urbanización Costa
    Teguise 79 D 3
35558 Urbanización Famara
    79 C 3
35509 Urbanización Las
    Cabreras 79 D 3
35544 Urbanización
    Los Cocoteros
    79 C 4
35509 Urbanización Oasis de
    Nazaret 79 D 3
35558 Urbanización Vista
    Gracioasa 79 C 3

35572 Vegas de Tegoyo
    79 D 2

35570 Yaiza 79 D 1
35541 Yé 79 C 3
35560 Yuco 79 D 2

LA PALMA

38767 Argual 74 C 2

38726 Barlovento
    74 A 3
38758 Barrial 74 C 2
38711 Beltain 74 C 3

38729 Bermudez 74 B 3
38739 Brejilla 74 C 3

38738 Callejones 74 D 3
38788 Casas de Fuente
    Grande 74 A/B 1
38437 Casas del Jaral
    74 A 2
38760 Celta 74 C 2
38769 Charco Verde
    74 D 2
38788 Cueva de Agua
    74 A 1

38788 Don Pedro 74 A 2

38738 El Calvario 74 D 3
38788 El Castillo 74 A/B 1
38714 El Cercado 74 B 3
38749 El Charco 74 D 2
38712 El Fuerte 74 C 3
38714 El Granel 74 B 3
38788 El Mudo 74 A 2
38489 El Palmar 74 A 2
38750 El Paso 74 C 2
38789 El Pinar 74 B 2
38769 El Remo 74 D 2
38728 El Tablado 74 A 2

38728 Franceses 74 A 2

38727 Gallegos 74 A 3

38729 Hoyagrande 74 A 3

38780 Jesus a la Costa
    74 B 1/2
38788 Juan Adalio 74 A 2

38760 La Caldera 74 C 2
38713 La Cuesta 74 C 3
38714 La Galga 74 B 3
38712 La Laguna 74 C 2
38712 La Montaña 74 C 3
38739 La Rosa 74 C 3
38738 La Sabina 74 D 3
38737 La Tosca 74 A 3
38727 Las Cabezadas
    74 C 2
38749 Las Caletas 74 F 3
38768 Las Hoyas 74 D 2
38749 Las Indias 74 F 2
38759 Las Manchas
    74 D 2
38713 Las Nieves 74 C 3
38726 Las Paredes
    74 A 3
38788 Las Tricias 74 B 1
38712 Ledas de Abajo
    74 C 3
38788 Lomada Grande
    74 A 1
38738 Lomo Oscuro 74 D 3
38712 Los Cancajos
    74 C 3
38729 Los Galguitos
    74 B 3
38760 Los Llanos de
    Aridane 74 C 2
38738 Los Picachos
    74 D 3
38749 Los Quemados
    74 F 2
38788 Los Sables 74 A 2
38729 Los Sauces
    74 A 3
38788 Llano Negra
    74 A 2

38738 Malpaises 74 D 3
38730 Mazo 74 D 3
38700 Mirca 74 B/C 3
38739 Monte 74 C 3
38738 Monte de Luna
    74 D 3

Puerto de Tazacorte

LA PALMA · TENERIFE ·

Soldeu

38779 Puerto de Tazacorte
    74 C 1
38729 Puerto Espindola
    74 A 3
38769 Puerto Naos
    74 D 2
38789 Puntagorda 74 B 1
38715 Puntallana 74 B 3

38729 Ramirez 74 A 3
38714 Rehoya 74 B 4
38728 Roque Faro 74 A 2

38729 San Andrés 74 A 3
38712 San José de Breña
    Baja 74 C 3
38759 San Nicolas de
    Abajo 74 D 2
38710 San Pedro de Breña
    Alta 74 C 3
38700 Santa Cruz de la
    Palma 74 C 3
38715 Santa Lucia 74 B 3
38437 Santo Domingo de
    Garafía 74 A 2
38759 Santuario de Fatima
    74 D 2

38780 Tabladito 74 B 1
38759 Tacande 74 C 2
38758 Tacande de Arriba
    74 C 2
38769 Tajuya 74 C 2
38729 Tanque 74 A 3
38770 Tazacorte 74 C 2
38715 Tenagua 74 B 3
38738 Tigalate 74 D 3
38738 Tiguerorte
    74 D 3
38780 Tijarafe 74 B 1
38789 Tinizara 74 B 1
38769 Todoque 74 C 2
38727 Topaciegas
    74 A 3
38767 Triana 74 C 2

TENERIFE

38588 Abades 78 D 5
38687 Abama 77 D 2
38688 Acojeja 77 D 2
38670 Adeje 77 D 3
38139 Afur 78 A 6
38355 Agua Garcia
    78 B 5
38310 Aguamansa 78 C 4
38591 Aguerche 78 C 5
38686 Alcalá 77 D 2
38628 Aldea Blanca del
    Llano 77 E 3
38129 Almáciga 78 A 6
38550 Arafo 78 C 5
38540 Araya 78 B/C 5
38612 Arenas del Mar
    77 E 4
38689 Arguayo 77 C 2
38260 Arico 78 D 4
38589 Arico Viejo 78 D 4
38688 Aripe 77 D 2
38678 Armeñime 77 D 2
38640 Arona 77 D 3

38250 Bajamar 78 A 5
38108 Barranco Grande
    78 B 5
38510 Barranco Hondo
    78 B 5
38294 Batán de Abajo
    78 A 4
38294 Batán de Arriba
    78 A 6
38129 Benijo 78 A 6
38313 Benijos 77 C 4
38437 Buen Paso 77 B 3

38480 Buenavista del
    Norte 77 B 2
38626 Buzanada 77 E 3

38626 Cabo Blanco
    77 E 3
38588 Callao del Rio
    78 D/E 4
38588 Callao del Rio
    78 E 4
38678 Callao Salvaje
    78 D 5
38530 Candelaria 78 C 5
38270 Casa de Carta
    78 A 5
38611 Casas de las
    Montañas 78 E 4
38617 Castro 77 E 4
38440 Cerro Gordo
    77 B/C 3
38630 Costa del Silencio
    77 E 3
38489 Cruz de Gilda
    77 C 2
38570 Cruz del Roque
    78 D 5
38413 Cruz Santa 77 B 4
38438 Cueva del Viento
    77 C 3
38489 Cuevas de Palmas
    77 C 2

38627 Chajaña 78 D 4
38129 Chamorga 78 A 6
38627 Chayofa 77 E 3
38688 Chiguergue 77 D 2
38594 Chimiche 78 D 4/5
38689 Chío 77 C 2
38688 Chirche 77 D 2
38617 Chuchurumbaohe
    77 E 4

38438 El Amparo 77 C 3
38310 El Bebedero
    78 B 4
38310 El Camino de
    Chasna 78 B/C 4
38591 El Escobonal
    78 C 5
38639 El Fraile 77 E 3
38458 El Guincho 77 B 3
38611 El Guirre 78 E 4
38688 El Jaral 77 D 2
38612 El Médano 77 E 4
38297 El Ortigal 78 B 5
38489 El Palmar 77 C 2
38297 El Portezuelo
    78 A 5
38629 El Portillo 77 C 4
38412 El Puerto de la
    Rambla 77 B 4
38593 El Río 78 D 4
38617 El Salto 77 D 4
38360 El Sauzal 78 B 5
38509 El Socorro 78 C 5
38728 El Tablado 78 C 5
38108 El Tablero 78 B 5
38435 El Tanque 77 B/C 2
38417 El Toscal 77 B 4
38435 Erjos 77 C 2
38614 Escalona 77 D 3

38670 Fañabé 77 D 3
38570 Fasnia 78 C 5
38629 Frontón de San
    Miguel 77 D 3

38450 Garachico 77 B 2
38459 Genovés 77 B/C 3
38600 Granadilla de Abona
    77 D 4
38330 Guamasa 78 B 5
38627 Guaza 77 E 3
38680 Guía de Isora
    77 D 2

38500 Güimar 78 C 5

38413 Hoya de Farras
    77 C 4

38430 Icod de los Vinos
    77 B 3
38414 Icod el Alto 77 B 3
38615 Ifonche 77 D 3
38520 Igueste de
    Candelarias
    78 B 5
38140 Igueste de San
    Andrés 78 A 6/7

38588 Jardín del Atlántico
    78 D 4

38679 La Caleta 77 D 2
38460 La Cáleta 77 B 2
38600 La Cantera 77 D 4
38340 La Caridad 78 B 5
38589 La Cisnera 78 D 4
38479 La Costa 77 B 2
38437 La Costa 77 B 3
38008 La Cuesta 78 B 6
38589 La Degollada 78 D 4
38290 La Esperanza
    78 B 5
38311 La Florida 78 B 4
38627 La Florida 78 D 4
38440 La Guancha 77 B 3
38509 La Hidalga 78 C 5
38588 La Jaca 78 D 4
38588 La Listada 78 D 4/5
38389 La Mantánza de
    Acentejo 78 B 5
38639 La Mareta 77 E 4
38560 La Medida 78 C 5
38459 La Montañeta
    77 C 2
38300 La Orotava 78 B 4
38410 La Rambla 77 B 3
38649 La Sabinita 78 D 4
38435 La Tierra del Trigo
    77 C 2
38439 La Vega 77 C 3
38389 La Victoria de
    Acentejo 78 B 4
38579 La Zarza 78 C 4
38400 Las Arenas 77 B 4
38520 Las Caletillas
    78 B 5
38740 Las Canarios
    (Fuencaliente)
    74 F 2
38293 Las Canteras 78 A 5
38629 Las Cañadas del
    Teide 77 C 4
38294 Las Carboneras
    78 A 6
38540 Las Cuevecitas
    78 C 5
38570 Las Eras 78 D 5
38685 Las Fuentes 77 D 3
38631 Las Galletas 77 E 3
38415 Las Llanadas
    77 C 4
38689 Las Manchas
    77 C 2
38293 Las Mercedes
    78 A 6
38677 Las Moraditas
    77 D 3
38617 Las Palomas
    77 D 4
38489 Las Portelas
    77 C 2
38290 Las Rosas/La
    Esperanza 78 B 5
38413 Las Rosas/La Guancha
    77 B 3
38594 Las Vegas 77 D 4
38290 Lomo Pelado
    78 B 5

38129 Lomo de Las Bodegas
    78 A 6
38590 Lomao de Mena
    78 C 5
38639 Los Abrigos 77 E 4
38291 Los Baldíos 78 B 5
38616 Los Blanquitos
    77 D 4
38489 Los Carrizales
    77 C 2
38650 Los Cristianos
    77 E 3
38589 Los Gavilanes
    78 D 4
38683 Los Gigantes
    77 C 2
38410 Los Realejos
    77 B 4
38470 Los Silos 77 B/C 2

38291 Llano el Moro
    78 B 5

38509 Malpais 78 C 5
38677 Marazul 77 D 2
38180 María Jiménez 78 A 6
38489 Masca 77 C 2
38358 Mesa del Mar
    78 A 5
38660 Miraverde 77 E 3

38560 Pájara 78 C 5
38627 Palm-Mar 77 E 3
38415 Palo Blanco
    77 B/C 4
38292 Pedro Alvarez
    78 A 5
38310 Pinolerís 78 B 4
38650 Playa de las
    Américas 77 E 3
38678 Playa Paraiso
    77 D 2
38588 Porís de Abona
    78 D 5
38435 Puerto de Erjos
    77 C 2
38500 Puerto de Güimar
    78 C 5
38400 Puerto de la Cruz
    77 B 4
38683 Puerto de Santiago
    77 C 2
38400 Punta Brava
    77 B 4
38240 Punta del Hidalgo
    78 A 5

38109 Radazul 78 B 5
38001 Ramonal 78 B 5
38359 Ravelo 78 B 5
38678 Ricasa 77 D 2
38435 Ruigómez 77 C 2

38579 Sabina Alta
    78 D 4/5
38649 Sabinita 77 E 3
38120 San Andrés 78 A 6
38296 San Bartolomé de
    Geneto 78 B 5
38470 San Bernardo
    77 B 2
38200 San Cristóbal de La
    Laguna 78 B 5/6
38208 San Diego 78 B 5
38660 San Eugenio
    77 E 3
38611 San Isidro 77 E 4
38435 San José de los Llanos
38459 San Juán del Raparo
    77 C 2
38687 San Juán 77 D 2
38420 San Juán de la Rambla
    77 B 3

38430 San Marcos 77 B 3
38620 San Miguel 77 D 3
38588 San Miguel de Tajao
    78 D 4
38434 Santa Barbara 77 B 3
38070 Santa Cruz de Tenerife
    78 B 5
38109 Santa Maria del Mar
    78 B 5
38390 Santa Ursula 78 B 4
38436 Santiago del Teide
    77 C 2
38108 Sobradillo 78 B 5

38190 Tabaiba Alta el
    Rosario 78 B 5
38294 Taborno 78 A 6
38108 Taco 78 B 5/6
38350 Tacoronte 78 B 5
38130 Taganana 78 A 6
38628 Tamaide 77 E 3
38684 Tamaimo 77 C 2
38677 Taucho 77 D 3
38280 Tegueste 78 A 5
38260 Tejina 78 A 5
38685 Tejina de Isora 77 D 2
38631 Ten-Bel 77 E 3
38489 Teno Alto 77 C 2
38489 Teno Bajo 77 C 1
38677 Tijoco de Abajo
    77 D 2
38677 Tijoco de Arriba
    77 D 3
38660 Torviscas 77 E 3
38615 Trevejos 77 D 3
38649 Tunez 77 D 3

38180 Valle Brosque
    78 A 6
38180 Valle Crispín 78 A 6
38270 Valle Guerra 78 A 5
38436 Valle de Arriba 77 C 2
38626 Valle de San Lorenzo
    77 E 3
38649 Vento 77 D 3
38680 Vera de Erque
    77 D 3
38613 Vilaflor 77 D 3
38398 Vista Paraíso
    78 B 4

AND

AD500 Andorra la Vella
    12 D 23
AD100 Canillo 12 D 23
AD300 El Serrat 12 D 23
AD200 Encamp 12 D 23
AD400 La Messana 12 D 23
AD700 Les Escaldes
    12 D 23
AD300 Llorts 12 D 23
AD300 Ordino 12 D 23
AD400 Pal 12 D 22
AD100 San Joan 12 D 23
AD600 Sant Juliá de Loria
    12 E 22
AD100 Soldeu 12 D 23

PORTUGAL · PORTUGAL · PORTUGALLO
PORTUGAL · PORTUGAL
PORTUGAL · PORTUGAL
PORTUGALSKO · PORTUGALSKO · PORTUGALIA

1:400 000

0 5 10 20 30 40 km

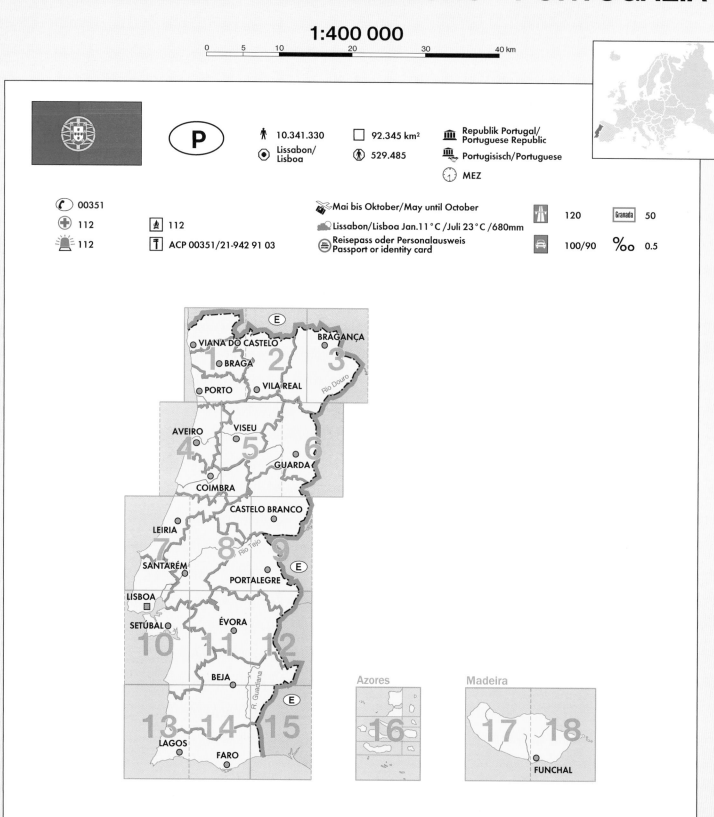

P

👤 10.341.330 ⬚ 92.345 km² 🏛 Republik Portugal/ Portuguese Republic

⊙ Lissabon/ Lisboa 👥 529.485 🏛 Portugisisch/Portuguese

🕐 MEZ

☎ 00351

✚ 112 🔥 112

🚨 112 ⓣ ACP 00351/21-942 91 03

✈ Mai bis Oktober/May until October

🌡 Lissabon/Lisboa Jan.11°C /Juli 23°C /680mm

🛂 Reisepass oder Personalausweis Passport or identity card

🛣 120 Granada 50

🚗 100/90 ‰ 0.5

E

VIANA DO CASTELO BRAGANÇA
1 BRAGA 2 3
PORTO VILA REAL Rio Douro

AVEIRO VISEU
4 5 6
GUARDA
COIMBRA

CASTELO BRANCO
LEIRIA
7 8 Rio Tejo 9
SANTARÉM PORTALEGRE E

LISBOA
SETÚBAL ÉVORA
10 11 12
BEJA R. Guadiana
E

13 14 15
LAGOS FARO

Azores
16

Madeira
17 18
FUNCHAL

freytag & berndt
www.freytagberndt.com
© FREYTAG-BERNDT u. ARTARIA KG, 1230 VIENNA, AUSTRIA, EUROPE

Legend Legende Legenda Leyenda Legenda Legende
Signaturforklaring Vysvětlivky Vysvetlivky Legenda

Motorway; Projected motorway
Autobahn; Autobahn geplant
Autostrada; Autostrada in progetto
Autopista; Autopista en proyecto
Auto estrada; Auto-estrada em projecto
Autosnelweg; Autosnelweg in ontwerp
Motorvej; Motorvej projekteret
Dálnice; Plánovaná dálnice
Diaľnica; Plánovaná diaľnica
Autostrady; Autostrady projektowane

Seat of the federal government; Provincial capital
Bundeshauptstadt; Landeshauptstadt
Capitale federale; Città-capoluogo
Capital federal; Capital de provincia
Capital; Capital de distrito
Hoofdstad; Provinciehoofdstad
Hovedstad; Administrationssæde
Hlavní město; Sídlo kraje
Hlavné mesto štátu; Krajské mesto
Stolice państw; Miasta wojewódzkie

LISBOA

FARO

Filling station; Service area - with overnight accomodation
Tankstelle; Autobahnraststation - mit Übernachtung
Distributore di benzina, Aera di servizio con motel
Gasolinera; Área de servicio - motel
Posto de gasolina; Área de serviço - hotel
Tankstation; Wegrestaurant met overnachting
Bensinstation; Motorvejsrestauration med hotel
Čerpací stanice; Dálniční odpočivadlo - s možností přenocování
Čerpacia stanica; Areál autoslužieb s možnosťou prenocovania
Stacja benzynowa; Miejsca obsługi podróżnych z noclegiem

Vendas Novas

Main - railway line; Subsidiary railway, Rack; Cable railway
Hauptbahn; Nebenbahn, Zahnradbahn; Seilschwebebahn
Linea ferrovia principale; Linea ferrovia secondaria; Ferrovia a cremagliera; Funivia
Linea férrea principal; - secundaria; Linea de cremallera; Funicular
Ferrovia principal; Ferrovia secundária; Elevador de cremalheira; Teleférico
Spoor; Zijspoor; Tandradspoor; Kabelbaan
Jernbane, hovedbane, sidebane; Tandhjulsbane; Tovbane
Hlavní železniční trať; Vedlejší železniční trať; Ozubená dráha; Lanovka
Hlavná železnica; Vedľajšia železnica; Ozubnicová železnica; visutá lanová dráha
Koleje główne; Koleje drugorzędne; Koleje zębate; Koleje linowe

Motorway under construction with scheduled opening date
Autobahn in Bau mit Fertigstellungstermin
Autostrada in costruzione con data di apertura
Autopista en construcción (fecha de apertura)
Auto-estrada em construção com data de inauguração
Autosnelweg in aanleg (datum openstelling bekend)
Motorvej under opførsel med datum for indvielse
Dálnice ve stavbě s termínem dokončení
Rozostavaná diaľnica s termínom dokončenia
Autostrady w budowie z terminem otwarcia

2020

Car - ferry; Passenger - ferry
Autofähre; Personenfähre
Traghetto per il automobile; Traghetto per passeggeri
Transbordador para coches;Transbordador para pasajeros
Ferry-boat; Barco de passageiros
Autoveerboot; Personenveerboot
Bilfærge; Personfærge
Trajekt pro automobily; Převoz
Autokompa; Kompa
Promy samochodowe; Promy osobowe

Motorway with interchange
Autobahn mit Anschlussstelle
Autostrada con raccordo
Autopista con conexión
Auto-estrada com ligação
Autosnelweg, aansluitingen volledig
Motorvej med komplet tilkørsel
Dálnice s nájezdem
Diaľnica s nájazdom
Autostrady z węzłami

Alcains

Military reservation; Nature reserve
Truppenübungsplatz; Naturschutzgebiet
Campo di addestramento militare; Area naturale protetta
Campo de maniobras militares; Reserva natural
Área exercicio militar; Reserva ecológica
Militair oefetenterrein; Natuurreservaat
Spærrat militærisk område; Nationalpark
Vojenské cvičiště; Přírodní rezervace
Vojenský cvičný priestor; Prírodná rezervácia
Poligon wojskowy; Rezerwat przyrody

Dual carriageway; Primary route
Fernverkehrsstraße, 4 - spurig; Fernverkehrsstraße
Strada di grande comunicazione a quattro corsie; Strada di grande comunicazione
Autovia de 4 carriles; Carretera nacional
Itnerário principal com 4 faixas; Estrada nacional
Autoweg, 4 rijstroken; Autoweg
Mototrfikvej med 4 baner; Fjemtrafikvej
Dálková silnice, čtyřproudová; Dálková silnice
Diaľková cesta štvorpruhová; Diaľková cesta
Drogi dwujezdniowe; Drogi główne

National boundary; Provincial boundary
Staatsgrenze; Landesgrenze
Confine di Stato; Confine regionale
Frontera nacional; Límite de provincia
Fronteira; Limite de província
Staatsgrens; Provinciegrens
Statsgrænse; Amtsgraense
Státní hranice; Krajská hranice
Štátna hranica; Hranica kraja
Granice państw; Granice województw

Main road; Secondary road
Hauptstraße; Nebenstraße
Strada principale; Strada secondaria
Carretera principal; Carretera secundaria
Estrada principal; Estrada secundária
Belangrijke verkeersader; Secundaire weg
Vigtig hovedvej; Hovedvej
Hlavní silnice; Vedlejší silnice
Hlavná cesta; Vedľajšia cesta
Drogi drugorzędne; Drogi lokalne

International airport; Airport
Internationaler Flughafen; Flugplatz
Aeroporto internazionale; Aeroporto
Aeropuerto Internacional; Aeropuerto
Aeroporto internacional; Aeroporto
Internationale vliegveld; Vliegveld
Intern. Lufthavn; Lufthavn
Mezinárodní letiště; Letiště
Medzinárodné letisko; Lisko
Porty lotnicze międzynarodowe; Lotniska

Roads under construction; Scenic route
Straßen in Bau; Landschaftlich besonders schöne Strecke
Strade in costruzione; Tratto di paesaggio particolarmente bello
Calles en construcción; Ruta panorámica
Estrada em construção; Caminho muito pitoresco
Straten in aanleg; Schilderachting traject
Vej under opførseltraten; Landskabelig smuk vejstrækning
Silnice ve stavbě; Trasa vedoucí obzvlášť krásnou krajinou
Cesty vo výstavbe; Zvlášť pekná prírodná cesta
Drogi w budowie; Drogi piekne widokowo

Monastery, church; Manor-house, castle; Ruin; Telecommunications tower
Kloster, Kirche; Schloss, Burg; Ruine; Sender
Convento, chiesa; Castello, fortezza; Rovine; Stazione transmittente
Monasterio, iglesia; Mansión, fortaleza ; Ruinas;Torre de comunicaciones
Convento, igreja; Castelo, fortaleza; Ruinas; Retransmissor
Klooster, kerk; Kasteel, burcht; Ruïne; Zender
Kloster, kirke; Slot; Borgruin; Vysílač
Klášter, kostel; Zámek, hrad; Zřícenina; Vysílač
Kláštor, kostol; Zámok, hrad; Ruiny; Vysielač
Klasztory, kościoły; Zamki; Ruiny; Maszty nadawcze

Road closed during the cold season (Primary routes class "A" & "B"roads)
Wintersperre (auf Fern - und Hauptstraßen)
Chiusura invernale (di strade di grande comunicazione e principali)
Carretera cerrada en invierno (carretera nacional y principal)
Impedimento de inverno (estrada nacional e principal)
In de winter afgesloten (auto- en hoofdwegen)
Spærret om vinteren (fjemtrafikvej, hovedvej)
Zimní uzavírka (na dálkových a hlavních silnicích)
Zimné uzávery (na diaľkových a hlavných cestách)
Drogi zamknięte zimą (główne i drugorzędne)

XII-III

Place of particular interest; Monument; Look - out tower
Besonders sehenswertes Objekt; Denkmal; Aussichtswarte
Località di grande interesse; Monumento; Torre panoramica
Lugar de interés; Monumento; Mirador
Local de interesse especial; Monumento; Vista panorâmica
Bijzondere bezienswaardigheden; Gedenkteken; Uitzichttoren
Seværdighed; Mindesmærke; Udsigtstårn
Obzvlášť zajímavý objekt; Pomník; Vyhlídkové místo
Mimoriadne pozoruhodný objekt; Pamätník; Vyhliadková veža
Miejsca warte zwiedzenia; Pomniki; Wieże widokowe

Toll road; Camino de Santiago; Gradient; Mountain pass
Mautstraße; Jakobsweg; Steigungen; Pass
Strada a pedaggio; Cammino di San Giacomo, Pendenze; Passo di montagna
Carretera de peaje; Camino de Santiago, Pendiente; Puerto de montaña
Estrada com portagem; Caminho do Santiago; Inclinação; Passo de montana
Tolweg; Jacobsweg; Stijging; Bergpas
Toldvej; Jakobvej; Stigning; Bjergpas
Silnice s poplatkem; Svatojakubská cesta, Stoupání; Průsmyk
Cesta s mýtnym poplatkom; Cesta sv. Jakuba; Stúpania, Priesmyk
Drogi płatne; Droga św. Jakuba; Strome podjazdy; Przełęcz

Camino
de Santiago

15%-20%
10%-15%   30%

Antique sites; Cave; Hotel, inn, mountain cabin
Antike Ruinenstätte; Höhle; Hotel, Gasthof, Schutzhütte
Luoghi con rovine; Grotta; Albergo, trattoria, rifugio
Yacimiento arqueológico; Cueva; Hotel, albergue, refugio
Sitio arqueológico; Gruta; Hotel, albergue, pousada
Antieke ruïne; Grot; Hotel, gasthuis, schuilhut
Ruiner, oldtidsminde; Hule; Hotel, krog bjerghytte
Antické zříceniny; Jeskyně (přístupná veřejnosti); Hotel, hostinec, horská chata
Antické zrúcaniny; Sprístupnená jaskyňa; Hotel, penzión, horská chata
Ruiny antyczne; Jaskinie; Hotele, zajazdy, schroniska górskie

Distances in kilometres
Entfernungen in km
Distanze in km
Distancias en km
Distância em quilómetros (km)
Afstanden in km
Afstand i km
Vzdálenosti v km
Vzdialenosti v km
Odległości w km

8 4   4

4 4
8

Marina; Lighthouse; Camping site; Spa; Scenic viewpoint; Golf-course
Marina; Leuchtturm; Campingplatz; Heilbad; Schöner Ausblick; Golfplatz
Marina; Faro; Campeggio; Località termale; Vista panoramica; Campo da golf
Puerto deportivo; Faros; Camping; Estación termal; Vista panorámica; Campo de golfe
Marina, Farol; Parque de campismo; Termas; Vista panorámica; Campo de golfe
Jachthaven; Vuurtoren; Kampeerterrein; Kuurbad; Uitzichtpunt panorama; Golfterrein
Lystbådehavn; Fyrtårn; Campingplads; Kurbad; Udsigtspunkt; Golfbane
Přístav; Maják; Kemping; Lázně; Krásný výhled; Golfové hřiště
Prístav; Maják; Kemping; Kúpele; Pekný výhľad; Golfové ihrisko
Porty jachtowe; Latarnia morska; Campingi; Uzdrowiska; Punkty widokowe; Pola golfowe

Motorway; European route; Road numbers
Autobahn; Europastraße; Straßennummern
Autostrada; Strada europea; Numerazione delle strade
Autopista; Carretera europea; Número de la carretera
Autostrada; Strada europea; Identificação da estrada
Autosnelweg; Europese weg; Wegnummers
Motorvej; Europavej; Vejnummer
Dálnice; Evropská silnice; Číslo silnice
Diaľnica; Európska cesta; Číslo cesty
Numery autostrad; Dróg miedzynarodowych; Dróg krajowich

A7 E15
IP 6 324
A-490 N230

Summit; Height; World Heritage
Gipfel; Höhe; Weltkulturerbe
Vertice; Altezza; Patrimoni dell'umanilà
Cumbre; Altura; Patrimonio de la Humanidad
Cúpula; Altura; Património Mundial
Top; Hoogte; Wereldergoed
Topmøde; Højde; Verdensarvsliste
Vrcholek; Výška; Seznam světového dědictví
Vrchol; Výška; Lokalita svetového dedičstva
Jczczyt; Wysokość; Obiekty z listy dziedzictwa UNESCO

Estrela
Torre
1993

1:400 000

0   5   10   20   30 km

Azores

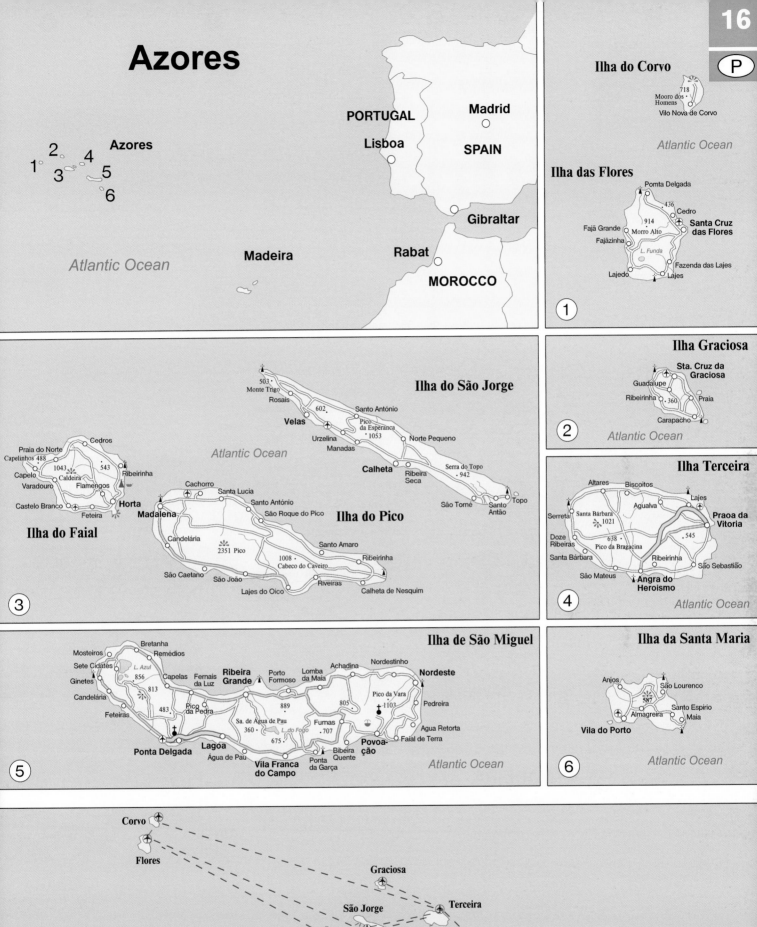

PORTUGAL
Madrid
Lisboa
SPAIN

Gibraltar

Rabat

MOROCCO

Madeira

Atlantic Ocean

Azores

1 2 4
3 5
6

Ilha do Corvo

Mooro dos Homens 718
Vilo Nova de Corvo

Atlantic Ocean

Ilha das Flores

Pomta Delgada
436
Cedro
Fajã Grande
914
Morro Alto
Santa Cruz das Flores
Fajãzinha
L. Funda
Lajedo
Fazenda das Lajes
Lajes

①

Ilha do São Jorge

503 Monte Trigo
Rosais
602
Velas
Santo António
Pico da Esperança 1053
Urzelina
Manadas
Norte Pequeno
Calheta
Ribeira Seca
Serra do Topo 942
São Torné
Santo Antão
Topo

Atlantic Ocean

Praia do Norte
Cedros
Capelinhos 488
1043 543
Capelo
Caldeira
Ribeirinha
Varadouro
Flamengos
Castelo Branco
Horta
Feteira

Ilha do Faial

Cachorro
Santa Lucia
Santo António
São Roque do Pico
Madalena
Candelária
2351 Pico
Santo Amaro
1008 Cabeco do Caveiro
Ribeirinha
São Caetano
São João
Riveiras
Lajes do Oico
Calheta de Nesquim

Ilha do Pico

③

Ilha Graciosa

Sta. Cruz da Graciosa
Guadalupe
Ribeirinha 360
Praia
Carapacho

Atlantic Ocean

②

Ilha Terceira

Altares
Biscoitos
Serreta
Santa Bárbara 1021
Agualva
Lajes
Doze Ribeiras
638 Pico da Bragacina
545
Praoa da Vitoria
Santa Bárbara
Ribeirinha
São Sebastião
São Mateus
Angra do Heroismo

Atlantic Ocean

④

Ilha de São Miguel

Mosteiros
Bretanha
Remédios
Sete Cidátes
L. Azul
856
Ginetes
Capelas
Fernais da Luz
Ribeira Grande
Porto Formoso
Lomba da Maia
Achadina
Nordestinho
Nordeste
Candelária
813
Feteiras
483
Pico da Pedra
889
805
Pico da Vara
1103
Pedreira
Sa. de Água de Pau
360
675
Furnas 707
Agua Retorta
L. do Fogo
Faial de Terra
Ponta Delgada
Lagóa
Água de Pau
Bibeira Quente
Povoa-ção
Vila Franca do Campo
Ponta da Garça

Atlantic Ocean

⑤

Ilha da Santa Maria

Anjos
São Lourenco
587
Santo Espírio
Almagreira
Maia
Vila do Porto

Atlantic Ocean

⑥

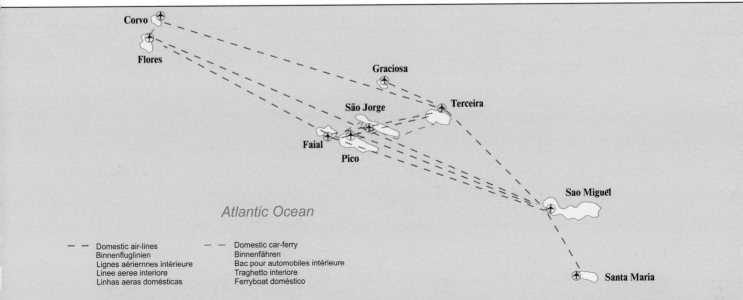

Corvo

Flores

Graciosa

São Jorge
Terceira

Faial
Pico

Sao Miguel

Atlantic Ocean

Santa Maria

– – Domestic air-lines
Binnenfluglinien
Lignes aériernnes intérieure
Linee aeree interiore
Linhas aeras domésticas

– – Domestic car-ferry
Binnenfähren
Bac pour automobiles intérieur
Traghetto interiore
Ferryboat doméstico

P

④ ⑤ ⑥ ⑦

Ilhéu de Fora

Baixa do Meio

Focinho do Forte

Ilhéu da Fonte de Areia
Enseada do Gilherme
Porto das Eiras
Estação Loran
Pires
Lombo Celado
Ilhéu das Cenouras
Furnas das Amasiadas

Rocha do Gasparão
Serra
de Dentro
Faja Grande
Pontinha
Parede da Mão Esquerda **A**

Porto da Fonte da Rib.
Camacha
Ponta de S. Miguel

Mornos ou Covinhas
161
Pico do
Castelo
Serra
del Fora
Calhau
Ponta dos Ferreiros

Ponta do Varadouro
Corgas
Porto dos Frades

Urnal Pequeno
Linhares
Dragonal
233
Prainha

Campo
de Cima
Tanquer
3,5
Port de
Abrigo
Boqueirão de Cima

Marinhas Passada
S. Sebastião
Rocha Quebrada
PORTO SANTO
19
Escadinha

Ponta da Bebeira
(Vila Baleira)
Ilhéu de Cima **B**

Ponta de Canaveira
Pico de
Ana Ferreira
Campo
de Baixo

Ilhéu de Ferro
Lajes
Espigão
283

Ribeiros
235
Pontã

Ponta da Cabra
111

Ponta do Gabriel

Furminhas
Ponta da Cahlheta

Boqueirão de Baixo

Farilhão Pequeno
Prainha

Moledo Ruivo
Ponta do Inferno
170
Portinho

Ponta da Isabel
Ilhéu de Baixo ou da Cal

Ponta do Patacho

Ponta do Ilhéu

Ponta de S. Jorge

Arco de
S. Jorge
Pedra Funda
Achada
Grande

41
507
São Jorge

825
Rainha

Arco de
S. Jorge
Reibeira
Funda
478
SANTANA
VE 1
Fajã
S. Jorge
Ilha
Pico de Catarina Pires
Fajã do
Penedo
Ponta do Clérigo

1492
Faial

pitadas
878
Garajoa
638
Penha
da Galé

Achada do Roque
Corujeira
de C.
Penha de Águia

Caldeirão do Inferno
Pico das Pedras
1270
Lombo
de Galego
590
Porto da Cruz **C**

1862
Chiquieiros
da Queimada
ER-103
Espigão Amarelo

Pico Ruivo de Santana
1416
Cruzinhas
**São Roque
do Faial**
11
Larano
Pico da Coroa
738
Ponta do
Bode
Ilhéu de
Garajós
Ponta do
Rosto
Pedra
Furada

Pico do Furão
1847
Fajã do
Cedro Gordo
Achado do
Pau Bastião
Pedreiro
792
Majata
Funduras
518
Pico das Roçadas
379
Estreito

Riba da Melaita
Folhadal
Ponta de São
Lourenço
Ponta do
Buraco
Ilhéu de Agostinho

Pico do Arieiro
1818
Riebeiro Frio
Riba Primeira
Fajã dos
Rotos
Castanho
589
Caniçal
VR 1
Rochinha

Achada
Cedro
1720
Cabeço da Lenha
1476
Ribeira do
Machico
Ribeira Seca
ER-109
Pedra do Pássaro
Pedra
das Gaivotas
Ilhéu do Farol

Pico do Furão
1759
ER-102
Landeiros
9
VE 1
Pedra da Eira
Porto de
Santa Maria
90
Cais

VE 6
ER-202
8
**Santo
António**
ER-239

Chão dos Balcões
1481
Paso de
Poiso
Pico dos Porcos
956
João Ferino
ER-207
MACHICO **D**

Esteios
1344
Ribeiro João
Goncalves
Pont Queimada

ER-107
17
Curral Velho
Água de Pena

Pico Alto
1129
12
ER-203
Águas Mansas
11
Santa Catarina

ER-103
ER-102
763
Eiroses
Palmeira
VR 1
SANTA CRUZ

Monte
944
Infante
Vale
Paraiso
São Pedro

traito da
nara de
os
S. Roque
Camacha
São João

Santo António
ER-102
Gaula

VR 1
ER-205
Porto Novo

São Gonçalo
VE 5
14
ER-204
Caniço

São Martinho
Ponta da Atalaia
Ponta dos Reis Magos

Ponta Gorda
FUNCHAL
Ponta do Garajau
Ponta da Oliveira **E**

④ ⑤ ⑥ ⑦

A dos Cunhados ⓟ **Antuzede**

A

2560 A dos Cunhados 7 G 3
2500 A dos Francos 7 G 3
2510 A dos Negros 7 G 3
5000 Abaças 2 C 6
4750 Abade de Neiva 1 B 4
4860 Abadim 1 B 6
5370 Abambres 2 B 7
4950 Abedim 1 B 4
7540 Abela 11 J 4
3100 Abiul 8 F 4
4600 Aboadela 1 C 6
6120 Aboboreira 8 F 5
4730 Aboim da Nóbrega 1 B 5
4970 Aboim das Choças 1 B 5
4600 Aboim/Borba de Godim 1 C 5
4820 Aboim/Cabeceiras de Basto 1 B 5
4750 Aborim 1 B 4
2025 Abrã 7 G 4
4560 Abragao 1 C 5
2200 Abrantes 8 G 5
3500 Abraveses 5 D 6
5370 Abreiro 2 C 7
2580 Abrigada 7 G 3
6005 Abrunhal 9 F 7
3140 Abrunheira 4 E 4
3530 Abrunhosa-a-Velha 5 D 6
2640 Achada 10 H 3
2000 Achete 7 G 4
5160 Açoreira 6 C 7
6300 Adão 6 E 7
4710 Adaúfe 1 B 5
4960 A-da-Velha 1 A 5
6355 Ade 6 D 8
5160 Adeganha 2 C 7
7830 A-do-Pinto 15 K 7
5120 Adorigo 2 C 6
3750 A-dos-Ferreiros 4 D 5
5000 Adoufe 2 C 6
4970 Adrao 1 B 5
4900 Afife 1 B 4
5450 Afonsim 2 B 6
3750 Agadão 4 D 5
4615 Agilde 1 C 5
2100 Agolada de Cima 11 G 4
5350 Agrobom 3 C 8
5335 Agrochao 3 B 7
7920 Água de Peixes 11 J 6
4825 Água Longa 1 C 5
5430 Água Revés e Crastro 2 B 7
3750 Aguada de Baixo 4 D 5
3750 Aguada de Cima 4 D 5
2735 Agualva-Cacém 10 H 3
6090 Águas 6 E 7
2240 Águas Belas/ Freixianda 8 F 5
6320 Águas Belas/ Sabugal 6 E 7
3560 Águas Boas 5 D 6
2965 Águas de Moura 10 H 4
8800 Águas dos Fusos 14 L 6
5400 Águas Frias/Chaves 2 B 7
8100 Águas Frias/S. Bartolomeu de Messines 14 L 5

4425 Aguas Santas 1 C 4
5210 Águas Vivas 3 C 9
4495 Aguçadoura 1 C 4
3260 Aguda 8 F 5
3750 Águeda 4 D 5
4970 Aguia 1 B 5
7090 Aguiar 11 J 6
3570 Aguiar da Beira 5 D 6
5385 Aguieiras 2 B 7
4870 Agunchos 2 C 6
5340 Ala 3 B 7
7300 Alagoa 9 G 6
7750 Alamo 14 K 6
7250 Alandroal 12 H 7
6300 Albardo 6 D 7
7580 Albergaria 11 J 4
3850 Albergaria-a-Nova 4 D 5
3850 Albergaria-a-Velha 4 D 5
3100 Albergaria dos Doze 8 F 4
7800 Albernoa 14 K 6
8200 Albufeira 14 L 5
2490 Alburitel 8 F 4
2645 Alcabideche 10 H 3
7580 Alcácer do Sal 11 J 4
7090 Alcáçovas 11 J 5
3530 Alcafache 5 D 6
6060 Alcafozes 9 F 7
6230 Alcaide 5 E 7
6005 Alcains 9 F 7
2025 Alcanede 7 G 4
2380 Alcanena 7 G 4
2000 Alcanhões 7 G 4
8365 Alcantarilha 14 L 5
2230 Alcaravela 8 F 5
8970 Alcaria Alta 14 L 6
8800 Alcaria Fria 14 L 6
7750 Alcaria Longa 14 K 6
7750 Alcaria Ruiva 14 K 6
8200 Alcaria/Boliqueime 14 L 5
8950 Alcaria/Castro Marim 15 L 7
6230 Alcaria/Fundão 5 E 6
2480 Alcaria/Port de Mós 7 F 4
7960 Alcaria/Vidigueira 11 J 6
8950 Alcarias 15 L 6
2460 Alcobaça 7 F 4
2040 Alcobertas 7 G 4
2890 Alcochete 10 H 4
2065 Alcoentre 7 G 4
3670 Alcofra 5 D 5
6230 Alcongosta 5 E 7
2350 Alcorochel 8 G 4
7480 Alcôrrego 11 G 6
8970 Alcoutim 15 L 7
3260 Aldeia da Cruz 8 F 5
7430 Aldeia da Mata 8 G 6
6230 Aldeia da Mata da Rainho 5 E 7
6320 Aldeia da Ponte 6 E 8
2025 Aldeia da Ribeira/ Alcanede 7 G 4
6100 Aldeia da Ribeira/ Sertã 8 F 5
6320 Aldeia da Ribeira/ Vilar Maior 6 E 8
8100 Aldeia da Tor 14 L 5
7200 Aldeia da Venda 12 H 7
7670 Aldeia das Amoreiras 14 K 5
3400 Aldeia das Dez 5 E 6

2925 Aldeia de Irmão 10 H 3
6230 Aldeia de Joanes 5 E 6
6090 Aldeia de João Pires 9 E 7
3620 Aldeia de Nacomba 5 D 6
6060 Aldeia de Santa Margarida 9 E 7
6320 Aldeia de Santo António 6 E 7
6225 Aldeia de São Francisco de Assis 5 E 6
6355 Aldeia de São Sebastião 6 D 8
6320 Aldeia do Bispo/ Alfaiates 6 E 8
6300 Aldeia do Bispo/ Belmonte 6 E 7
6090 Aldeia do Bispo/ Penamacor 6 E 7
6200 Aldeia do Carvalho 5 E 7
7770 Aldeia do Corvo 14 K 6
2200 Aldeia do Mato 8 F 5
3100 Aldeia do Rio 8 F 4
7900 Aldeia do Ronquenho 14 K 5
6200 Aldeia do Souto 5 E 7
7600 Aldeia dos Delbas 14 K 5
7700 Aldeia dos Fernandes 14 K 5
7670 Aldeia dos Grandaços 14 K 5
7700 Aldeia dos Neves 14 K 5
2580 Aldeia Galega da Merceana 7 G 3
7830 Aldeia Nova de São Bento 15 K 7
6230 Aldeia Nova do Cabo 5 E 6
5210 Aldeia Nova/Pena Branca 3 B 9
6350 Aldeia Nova/Pinhel 6 D 8
6420 Aldeia Nova/ Trancoso 5 D 7
7480 Aldeia Velha 8 G 5
6300 Aldeia Viçosa 6 D 7
7960 Aldeias/Gouveia 11 J 6
5110 Aldeias/Lamego 5 C 6
6290 Aldeias/Pedrógão 5 E 6
4905 Aldreu 1 B 4
7300 Alegrete 9 G 7
4900 Além do Rio 1 B 4
2580 Alenquer 7 G 3
5300 Alfaiao 3 B 8
6320 Alfaiates 6 E 8
8670 Alfambra 13 L 4
5350 Alfândega da Fé 3 C 8
5450 Alfarela de Jales 2 C 6
3130 Alfarelos 4 E 4
2970 Alfarim 10 J 3
2460 Alfeizerão 7 F 3
4445 Alfena 1 C 4
8550 Alferce 13 L 5
2200 Alferrarede 8 G 5
6030 Alfrivida 9 F 6
7900 Alfundão 11 J 5
3350 Algaça 4 E 5
7595 Algalé 11 J 5
5445 Algeriz 2 B 7
2950 Algeruz 10 H 4

7750 Algodor 14 K 6
6370 Algodres/Fornos de Algodres 5 D 6
6440 Algodres/Villa Nova de Foz Côa 6 D 7
5230 Algoso 3 C 8
8365 Algoz 14 L 5
2550 Alguber 7 G 3
2705 Algueirão-Mem Martins 10 H 3
3080 Alhadas 4 E 4
3650 Alhais 5 D 6
2600 Alhandra 10 H 3
4750 Alheira 1 B 4
4690 Alhões 5 D 5
2860 Alhos Vedros 10 H 3
5070 Alijó 2 C 7
8670 Aljezur 13 L 4
2460 Aljubarrota 7 F 4
7600 Aljustrel 14 K 5
3450 Almaça 4 E 5
6000 Almaceda 9 E 6
2800 Almada 10 H 3
3100 Almagreira 8 F 4
3040 Almalaguês 4 E 5
8135 Almancil 14 L 5
2715 Almargem do Bispo 10 H 3
8150 Almargens 14 L 6
6100 Almegue 8 F 5
6350 Almeida 6 D 8
2080 Almeirim 7 G 4
5150 Almendra 6 C 7
7700 Almodôvar 14 K 5
6440 Almofala/Castelo Rodrigo 6 D 8
3600 Almofala/Pendilhe 5 D 6
7630 Almograve 13 K 4
3250 Almoster/Abiul 8 F 5
2000 Almoster/Santarém 7 G 4
6050 Alpalhão 9 G 6
6230 Alpedrinha 5 E 7
2460 Alpedriz 7 F 4
4575 Alpendurada e Matos 5 C 5
2090 Alpiarça 8 G 4
8150 Alportel 14 L 6
3080 Alqueidão 4 E 4
2480 Alqueidão da Serra 7 F 4
3850 Alquerubim 4 D 5
7220 Alqueva 12 J 6
8100 Alte 14 L 5
7440 Alter do Chão 9 G 6
2040 Alto da Serra 7 G 4
8900 Altura 15 L 6
5460 Alturas do Barroso 2 B 6
3600 Alva 5 D 6
5030 Alvacoes do Corgo 2 C 6
4870 Alvadia 2 C 6
2480 Alvados 7 F 4
6030 Alvaiade 9 F 6
3250 Alvaiázere 8 F 5
7565 Alvalade 14 K 5
4905 Alvaraes 1 B 4
4960 Alvaredo 1 A 5
4795 Alvarelho/Santo Tirso 1 C 4
5430 Alvarelhos/Chaves 2 B 7
4540 Alvarenga 5 D 5
3330 Alvares/Castanheira de Pera 8 E 5
7750 Alvares/Mértola 14 K 6
6160 Álvaro 8 F 6
2205 Alvega 8 G 5
6300 Alvendre 6 D 7
6400 Alverca da Beira 6 D 7
2615 Alverca do Ribatejo 10 H 3

7750 Alves 15 K 6
2305 Alviobeira 8 F 5
6040 Alvisquer 8 F 6
4860 Alvite/Cabeceiras de Basto 1 C 5
3620 Alvite/Moimenta da Beira 5 D 6
7920 Alvito 11 J 6
6150 Alvito da Beira 8 F 6
6270 Alvoco da Serra 5 E 6
3400 Alvoco das Várzeas 5 E 6
8500 Alvor 13 L 4
3240 Alvorge 8 F 5
2500 Alvorninha 7 G 3
2721 Amadora 10 H 3
4600 Amarante 1 C 5
7885 Amareleja 12 J 7
4720 Amares 1 B 5
3040 Ameal 4 E 4
5140 Amedo 2 C 7
8100 Ameixial 14 L 6
6120 Amêndoa 8 F 5
8100 Amendoeira/Loulé 14 L 6
5340 Amendoeira/Macedo de Cavaleiros 3 B 8
7750 Amendoeira/Mértola 14 K 6
2025 Amiães de Baixo 7 G 4
2025 Amiães de Cima 7 G 4
6040 Amieira Cova 8 G 6
6050 Amieira do Tejo 8 F 6
6160 Amieira/Pedrogão Grande 8 F 6
7220 Amieira/Portel 12 J 6
5070 Amieiro 2 C 7
3330 Amiosinho 8 E 5
3330 Amioso 8 E 5
4900 Amonde 1 B 4
2400 Amor 7 F 4
2845 Amora 10 H 3
3780 Amoreira da Gândara 4 E 4
2200 Amoreira/Abrantes 8 G 5
6355 Amoreira/Guarda 6 D 7
2510 Amoreira/Óbidos 7 G 3
8800 Amoreira/Vaqueiros 14 L 6
7670 Amoreiras 14 K 5
4495 Amorim 1 C 4
4900 Amorosa 1 B 4
3780 Anadia 4 E 5
3060 Ança 4 E 4
2480 Andam 7 F 4
5000 Andraes 2 C 6
2230 Andreus 8 F 5
5425 Anelhe 2 B 6
3850 Angeja 4 D 4
5230 Angueira 3 B 9
4900 Anha 1 B 4
4950 Anhoes 1 B 5
4850 Anjos 1 B 5
3150 Anobra 4 E 4
4660 Anreade 5 C 6
3240 Ansião 8 F 5
6350 Ansul 6 D 8
4500 Anta 4 C 4
3040 Antanhol 4 E 5
4740 Antas/Castelo do Neiva 1 B 4
3550 Antas/Fornos de Algodres 5 D 6
3630 Antas/Moimenta da Beira 5 D 7
5470 Antigo de Sarraquinhos 2 B 6
3000 Antuzede 4 E 5

Apúlia ⓟ **Cabeço** Ⓟ

4740 Apúlia 1 C 4
3885 Arada 4 D 4
3800 Aradas 4 D 4
6090 Aranhas 6 E 7
4930 Arao 1 A 4
3140 Arazede 4 E 4
3475 Arca 5 D 5
5340 Arcas/Torre de Dona
    Chama 2 B 7
3600 Arcas/Villa Cova á
    Coelheira 5 D 6
4860 Arco de Baúlhe
    1 C 6
4970 Arcos de Valdevez
    1 B 5
5470 Arcos/Chaves
    2 B 6
7100 Arcos/Estremoz
    12 H 6
5120 Arcos/Moimenta da
    Beira 5 C 6
5425 Arcossó 2 B 6
3680 Arcozelo das Maias
    4 D 5
4750 Arcozelo/Barcelos
    1 B 4
6290 Arcozelo/Gouveia
    5 D 6
4405 Arcozelo/Ponte de
    Lima 4 C 4
4900 Arcozelo/Valadares
    1 B 4
3620 Arcozelos 5 D 6
5460 Ardaos 2 B 6
3260 Arega 8 F 5
4740 Areia 1 C 4
2205 Areia de Baixo
    8 G 5
2240 Areias 8 F 5
4755 Areias de Vilar
    1 B 4
2510 Arelho 7 G 3
4900 Areosa 1 B 4
6050 Arez 8 G 6
4910 Arga de Baixo
    1 B 4
4910 Arga de São Joao
    1 B 4
3300 Arganil 5 E 5
5400 Argemil 2 B 7
4505 Argoncilhe 4 C 4
5230 Argozelo 3 B 8
5110 Aricera 5 C 6
3620 Ariz 5 D 6
8365 Armação de Pêra
    14 L 5
5110 Armamar 5 C 6
4820 Armil 1 C 5
3640 Arnas 5 D 7
6050 Arneiro 9 F 6
4890 Arnoia 1 C 5
3730 Arões 4 D 5
4820 Aroes (São Romao)
    1 C 5
4800 Arosa 1 B 5
4540 Arouca 5 D 5
2410 Arrabal 7 F 4
6060 Arraial da Poupa
    9 F 7
7040 Arraiolos 11 H 6
3100 Arrancada 8 F 4
2630 Arranhó 10 H 3
2840 Arrentela 10 H 3
2140 Arrepiado 8 G 5
3350 Arrifana/Coimbra
    4 E 5
6300 Arrifana/Guarda
    6 D 7
3700 Arrifana/Saõ João
    da Madeira
    4 D 5
6320 Arrifana/Vilar Maior
    6 D 8
7340 Arronches 9 G 7
2040 Arrouquelas 7 G 4
2040 Arruda dos Pisões
    7 G 4
2630 Arruda dos Vinhos
    10 H 3

4480 Árvore 1 C 4
3100 Asanha da Paz
    7 F 4
3040 Assafarge 4 E 5
2705 Assafora 10 H 3
5360 Assares 2 C 7
2305 Asseiceira 8 F 5
2560 Assenta 7 G 3
2350 Assentiz/Ourem
    8 F 4
2040 Assentiz/Rio Maior
    7 G 4
7450 Assumar 9 G 7
6230 Atalaia do Campo
    9 E 7
6030 Atalaia/Castelo
    Branco 9 F 6
2260 Atalaia/
    Entroncamento
    8 G 5
6040 Atalaia/Nisa 8 G 6
6400 Atalaia/Pinhel
    6 D 7
4880 Atei 2 C 6
5225 Atenor 3 C 9
2490 Atouguia 8 F 4
2525 Atouguia da Baleia
    7 G 3
3860 Avanca 4 D 4
5370 Avantos 2 B 7
2240 Ave Casta 8 F 5
2050 Aveiras de Baixo
    7 G 4
2050 Aveiras de Cima
    7 G 4
3800 Aveiro 4 D 4
5230 Avelanoso 3 B 9
3240 Avelar 8 F 5
6300 Avelãs da Ribeira
    6 D 7
3780 Avelãs de Caminho
    4 E 5
3780 Avelãs de Cima
    4 E 5
4700 Aveleda/Braga 1 B 5
5300 Aveleda/Bragança
    3 B 8
5400 Aveledas 2 B 7
6430 Aveloso 6 D 7
4495 A-Ver-o-Mar 1 C 4
5370 Avidagos 2 C 7
4430 Avintes 1 C 4
7480 Avis 8 G 6
3400 Avô 5 E 6
5100 Avoes 5 C 6
2050 Azambuja 7 G 4
7000 Azarujinha 11 H 6
7450 Azeiteiros 12 G 7
2705 Azenhas do Mar
    10 H 3
3420 Ázere 5 E 5
2100 Azervadinha 11 H 5
4910 Azevedo 1 B 4
6400 Azevo 6 D 7
4980 Azias 1 B 5
2150 Azinhaga 8 G 4
8950 Azinhal/Castro
    Marim 15 L 7
7750 Azinhal/Mértola
    14 K 6
6350 Azinhal/Pinhel
    6 D 8
2040 Azinheira 7 G 4
7570 Azinheira dos Barros
    11 J 5
5200 Azinhoso 3 C 8
2970 Azóia 10 J 3
2400 Azoia 7 F 4
2000 Azóia de Baixo
    7 G 4
2665 Azueira 7 G 3

B

5300 Baçal 3 B 8
6320 Badamalos 6 E 8
5340 Bagueixe 3 B 8
4640 Baiao 1 C 5
4640 Baiao (Santa
    Leocádia) 1 C 5

3660 Baiões 5 D 5
6150 Bairrada 8 F 6
7000 Bairro dos Canaviais
    11 H 6
2496 Bairro/Assentiz
    8 F 4
2580 Bairro/Olhalvo
    7 G 3
4770 Bairro/Santo Tirso
    1 C 5
4570 Balazar 1 C 4
7200 Baldio 12 J 7
3620 Baldos 5 D 6
2520 Baleal 7 G 3
7800 Baleizão 11 J 6
4905 Balugaes 1 B 4
8970 Balurcos 15 L 6
6360 Baraçal/Celorico da
    Beira 5 D 7
6320 Baraçal/Sabugal
    6 E 7
6300 Baracão 6 D 7
8600 Barão de São João
    13 L 4
8650 Barão de São Miguel
    13 L 4
7350 Barbacena 12 H 7
6000 Barbaido 9 F 6
6440 Barca da Alva
    6 C 8
4740 Barca do Lago
    1 B 4
5370 Barcel 2 C 7
4755 Barcelinhos 1 B 4
4750 Barcelos 1 B 4
6215 Barco 5 E 6
5120 Barcos 5 C 6
3050 Barcouço 4 E 5
6230 Barocca 5 E 6
6225 Barocca Grande
    5 E 6
2400 Barosa 7 F 4
4740 Barqueiros/Fonte
    Boa 1 C 4
5040 Barqueiros/Mesao
    Frio 2 C 6
2410 Barracão 7 F 4
8970 Barrada/Martim
    Longo 14 L 6
2205 Barrada/Rossio ao
    Sul de Tejo
    8 G 5
7580 Barrancão 11 H 5
8150 Barranco do Velho
    14 L 6
7230 Barrancos 12 J 8
2400 Barreira/Maceira
    7 F 4
6430 Barreira/Trancoso
    6 D 7
2205 Barreiras 8 G 5
2830 Barreiro 10 H 3
3465 Barreiro de
    Besteiros 5 D 5
2400 Barreiros/Marrazes
    7 F 4
3500 Barreiros/Sátão
    5 D 6
5450 Barrela 2 C 6
2640 Barril 7 G 3
3305 Barril de Alva 5 E 6
2460 Bárrio/Nazaré 7 F 3
4990 Bárrio/Ponte de
    Lima 1 B 4
4660 Barrô/Mesao Frio
    2 C 6
3750 Barrô/Oiã 4 D 5
2130 Barrosa 10 H 4
4620 Barrosas(Santa
    Eulália) 1 C 5
7580 Barrosinha 11 J 5
7570 Bartolomeu 11 J 5
4860 Basto (São
    Clemente) 1 C 6
2440 Batalha 7 F 4
2300 Beberriqueira 8 F 5
5460 Beça 2 B 6
2240 Beco 8 F 5
3860 Beduído 4 D 4

3430 Beijós 5 D 6
7330 Beirã 9 G 7
5140 Beira Grande 2 C 7
7800 Beja 11 J 6
3750 Belazaima do Chão
    4 D 5
3150 Belide 4 E 4
6250 Belmonte 5 E 7
6040 Belver/Mação
    8 G 6
5140 Belver/Vila Flor
    2 C 7
5200 Bemposta/
    Mogadouro
    3 C 8
6090 Bemposta/
    Penamacor
    9 E 7
2205 Bemposta/Tramagal
    8 G 5
8375 Benaciate 14 L 5
8100 Benafim 14 L 5
2130 Benavente 10 H 4
7480 Benavila 8 G 6
7160 Bencatel 12 H 7
6320 Bendada 6 E 7
2475 Benedita 7 G 4
1500 Benefica 10 H 3
6300 Benespera 6 E 7
3305 Benfeita 5 E 6
2080 Benfica do Ribatejo
    7 G 4
5360 Benlhevai 2 C 7
6090 Benquerença 6 E 7
6000 Benquerenças
    9 F 6
8600 Bensafrim 13 L 4
7800 Beringel 11 J 6
3500 Bertelhe 5 D 6
3630 Beselga 5 D 7
8100 Besteiros/Loulé
    14 L 6
7300 Besteiros/Portalegre
    9 G 7
5140 Besteiros/Torre de
    Moncorvo 2 C 7
2305 Bezelga 8 F 5
7750 Bicada 14 K 6
2205 Bicas 8 G 5
4940 Bico 1 B 4
7630 Bicos 13 K 5
5100 Bigorne 5 C 6
4880 Bilhó 2 C 6
6320 Bismula 6 E 8
3510 Boa Aldeia 5 D 5
6110 Boa Farinha 8 F 5
3080 Boa Viagem 4 E 4
2410 Boa Vista 7 F 4
4990 Boalhosa 1 B 5
7050 Boavista 11 H 5
7540 Boavista do Paiol
    13 K 4
7630 Boavista dos
    Pinheiros
    13 K 4
5400 Bobadela/Chaves
    2 B 7
3405 Bobadela/Oliveira do
    Hospital 5 E 6
5460 Bobadela/Sapelos
    2 B 6
3510 Bodiosa 5 D 6
4575 Boelhe 1 C 5
6400 Bogalhal 6 D 7
6185 Bogas de Baixo
    8 E 6
6230 Bogas de Cima
    9 E 6
6230 Bogas do Meio
    9 E 6
3780 Boialvo 4 D 5
2040 Boiças 7 G 4
4930 Boivao 1 A 4
2496 Boleiros 7 F 4
3060 Bolho 4 E 4
2525 Bolhos 7 G 3
8100 Boliqueime 14 L 5
2540 Bombarral 7 G 3
7150 Borba 12 H 7

4890 Borba da Montanha
    1 C 5
4615 Borba de Godim
    1 C 5
5000 Borbela 2 C 6
8670 Bordeira 13 L 4
3330 Bordeiro 5 E 5
5340 Bornes 3 C 7
5450 Bornes de Aguiar
    2 B 6
5470 Borralha 1 B 6
3465 Borralhal 5 E 5
4600 Bostelo 1 C 6
3020 Botão 4 E 5
5460 Boticas 2 B 6
5385 Bouça 2 B 7
6400 Bouça Cova 6 D 7
5430 Boucoaes 2 B 7
4485 Bougado 1 C 4
4720 Bouro 1 B 5
6230 Boxinos 5 E 6
3330 Braçal 5 E 5
7555 Bracial 13 K 4
4700 Braga 1 B 5
5450 Bragado 2 B 6
5300 Bragança 3 B 8
3850 Branca 4 D 5
4980 Bravaes 1 B 5
7830 Brinches 12 J 6
5340 Brinço 2 B 7
4800 Briteiros(Santo
    Estevao) 1 B 5
4890 Britelo/Celorico de
    Basto 1 C 6
4980 Britelo/Ponte da
    Barca 1 B 5
5100 Britiande 5 C 6
4800 Brito 1 C 5
7490 Brotas 11 H 5
5200 Bruçó 3 C 8
4840 Brufe 1 B 5
5140 Brunheda 2 C 7
7570 Brunheira 11 J 5
7645 Brunheiras 13 K 4
3130 Brunhós 4 E 4
5200 Brunhoso 3 C 8
5200 Brunhozinho 3 C 8
3080 Buarcos 4 E 4
2670 Bucelas 10 H 3
4860 Bucos 1 B 5
8650 Budens 13 L 4
3870 Bunheiro 4 D 4
3140 Bunhosa 4 E 4
5340 Burga 2 C 7
4540 Burgo 4 D 5
5400 Bustelo/Chaves
    2 B 7
4690 Bustelo/Nespereira
    5 C 5
3770 Bustos 4 E 4

C

3620 Cabaços/Moimenta
    da Beira 5 C 6
4990 Cabaços/Ponte de
    Lima 1 B 4
4970 Cabana Maior
    1 B 5
8800 Cabanas 14 L 6
2580 Cabanas de Torres
    7 G 3
3430 Cabanas de Viriato
    5 E 6
5370 Cabanelas 2 B 7
5450 Cabanes 2 B 6
6270 Cabeça 5 E 6
5160 Cabeça Boa 2 C 7
2480 Cabeça das Pombas
    7 G 4
7200 Cabeça de Carneiro
    12 H 7
7800 Cabeça Gorda
    14 K 6
4575 Cabeça Santa
    1 C 5
7490 Cabeço 11 H 5
4860 Cabeceiras de Basto
    1 B 6
3070 Cabeço 4 E 4

2230 Cabeço das Mós
　　　8 F 5
7460 Cabeço de Vide
　　　9 G 6
6000 Cabeço do Infante
　　　9 F 6
6110 Cabeço do Poço
　　　8 F 5
6060 Cabeço Monteiro
　　　9 F 7
6100 Cabeçudo　8 F 5
4900 Cabodelo　1 B 4
2040 Cabos　7 G 4
4990 Cabraçao　1 B 4
3330 Cabreira　5 E 5
4970 Cabreiro　1 B 5
4540 Cabreiros　5 D 5
7050 Cabrela　11 H 5
3600 Cabril/Nespereira
　　　5 D 5
3320 Cabril/Vidual　5 E 6
5470 Cabril/Viera do
　　　Minho　1 B 5
5230 Caçarhelos　3 B 9
4890 Caçarilhe　1 C 5
8800 Cachopo　14 L 6
3800 Cacia　4 D 4
2580 Cadafais　7 G 3
6040 Cadafaz/Pego　8 G 6
3330 Cadafaz/Vilarinho
　　　5 E 5
2550 Cadaval　7 G 3
3060 Cadima　4 E 4
6000 Cafede　9 F 6
7300 Caia　9 G 7
7350 Caia e São Pedro
　　　12 H 7
7700 Caiada　14 K 6
4624 Caíde de Rei　1 C 5
7350 Calçadinha　12 H 7
3570 Caldas da Cavaca
　　　5 D 6
3525 Caldas da Felgueira
　　　5 E 6
2500 Caldas da Rainha
　　　7 G 3
4660 Caldas de Aregos
　　　5 C 5
6260 Caldas de
　　　Manteigas　5 E 6
8550 Caldas de
　　　Monchique
　　　13 L 4
3430 Caldas de São
　　　Gemil　5 D 6
4840 Caldas do Geres
　　　1 B 5
3510 Calde　5 D 6
4800 Caldelas/Guimaraes
　　　1 C 5
4720 Caldelas/Vila Verde
　　　1 B 5
4760 Calendário　1 C 4
2615 Calhandriz　10 H 3
4990 Calheiros　1 B 4
3840 Calvão/Bustos
　　　4 E 4
5400 Calvao/Chaves
　　　2 B 6
2480 Calvaria de Cima
　　　7 F 4
5300 Calvelhe　3 B 8
4830 Calvos　1 B 5
3670 Cambarinho　5 D 5
6185 Cambas　8 E 6
5470 Cambeses do Rio
　　　2 B 6
3670 Cambra　5 D 5
5100 Cambres　2 C 6
4910 Caminha　1 B 4
4880 Campanhó　2 C 6
5000 Campea　2 C 6
3260 Campelo　8 E 5
2565 Campelos　7 G 3
3670 Campia　5 D 5
7200 Campinho　12 J 7
3500 Campo　5 D 6
5230 Campo de Víboras
　　　3 B 8

4840 Campo do Geres
　　　1 B 5
7370 Campo Maior
　　　12 G 7
7630 Campo Redondo
　　　13 K 4
4830 Campos/Braga
　　　1 B 5
5460 Campos/Chaves
　　　2 B 6
4920 Campos/Valença
　　　1 B 4
4850 Campos/Viera do
　　　Minho　1 B 5
4600 Canadelo　1 C 6
3460 Canas de Santa
　　　Maria　5 D 5
3525 Canas de Senhorim
　　　5 D 6
5430 Canaveses　2 B 7
3200 Candal　4 E 5
5335 Candedo/Bragança
　　　2 B 7
5090 Candedo/Vila Flor
　　　2 C 7
4920 Candemil/Amarante
　　　1 B 4
4600 Candemil/Valença
　　　1 C 6
3420 Candosa　5 E 6
5360 Candoso　2 C 7
4890 Canedo de Basto
　　　1 C 6
5460 Canedo/Chaves
　　　2 B 6
4525 Canedo/Sandim
　　　4 C 5
4540 Canelas/Nespereira
　　　5 D 5
3865 Canelas/Salreu
　　　4 D 4
2985 Canha　11 H 4
7900 Canhestros　11 J 5
4850 Caniçada　1 B 5
3060 Caniceira　4 E 4
4400 Canidelo　1 C 4
7470 Cano　11 H 6
3060 Cantanhede　4 E 4
4850 Cantelaes　1 B 5
2425 Canto　7 F 4
4905 Capareiros　1 B 4
3465 Caparrosa　5 D 5
4575 Capela/Lagares
　　　1 C 5
6120 Capela/Mação
　　　8 F 6
7250 Capelins　12 H 7
5450 Capeludos　2 B 6
6230 Capinha　5 E 7
3475 Caramulo　5 D 5
2410 Caranguejeira
　　　7 F 4
4750 Carapeços　1 B 4
3070 Carapelhos　4 E 4
3420 Carapinha　5 E 5
3140 Carapinheira　4 E 4
3570 Carapito　5 D 7
5370 Caravelas　2 C 7
5230 Carção　3 B 8
5160 Cardanha　2 C 7
6120 Cardigos　8 F 5
6160 Cardosa　9 F 6
4900 Careço　1 B 4
6250 Caria/Covilhã　5 E 7
3620 Caria/Moimenta da
　　　Beira　5 D 6
7200 Caridade　12 J 6
5070 Carlao　2 C 7
2565 Carmões　7 G 3
2795 Carnaxide　10 H 3
4600 Carneiro　1 B 4
6420 Carnicães　6 D 7
3100 Carnide　7 F 4
2580 Carnota　5 D 5
3050 Carquejo　4 E 5
4660 Cárquere　5 C 6
5300 Carragosa　3 B 8
6270 Carragozela　5 E 6
4970 Carralcova　1 B 5

5340 Carrapatas　3 B 8
8670 Carrapateira　13 L 4
6360 Carrapichana　5 D 7
6120 Carrascal　8 F 6
2565 Carrasqueira　7 G 3
5140 Carrazeda de
　　　Ansiaes　2 C 7
5300 Carrazedo　3 B 8
5445 Carrazedo de
　　　Montenegro
　　　2 B 7
3640 Carregal　5 D 6
3430 Carregal do Sal
　　　5 E 5
3720 Carregosa　4 D 5
2140 Carregueira　8 G 5
2305 Carregueiros　8 F 5
4775 Carreira　1 C 4
7300 Carreiras　9 G 7
6060 Carriçal　9 F 7
3100 Carriço　7 F 4
7750 Carros　14 K 6
2070 Cartaxo　7 G 4
5090 Carva　2 C 6
5370 Carvalhais/
　　　Mirandela　2 B 7
3080 Carvalhais/Paião
　　　4 E 4
3660 Carvalhais/São
　　　Pedro do Sul
　　　5 D 5
2500 Carvalhal Benfeito
　　　7 G 3
3670 Carvalhal de
　　　Vermilhas　5 D 5
6300 Carvalhal Meão
　　　6 E 7
3525 Carvalhal Redondo
　　　5 D 6
7570 Carvalhal/Alcácer do
　　　Sal　10 J 4
4755 Carvalhal/Barcelos
　　　1 B 4
2540 Carvalhal/Bombarral
　　　7 G 3
3600 Carvalhal/Castro
　　　Daire　5 D 6
6400 Carvalhal/Guarda
　　　6 D 7
6100 Carvalhal/Pedrogão
　　　Grande　8 F 5
7300 Carvalhal/Portalegre
　　　9 G 7
2230 Carvalhal/Sardoal
　　　8 F 5
5460 Carvalhelos　2 B 6
5360 Carvalho de Egas
　　　2 C 7
4890 Carvalho/Celorico de
　　　Basto　1 C 5
3360 Carvalho/Pampilhosa
　　　4 E 5
3600 Carvalhosa　5 D 6
5090 Carvas　2 C 7
5350 Carviçais　3 C 8
2425 Carvide　7 F 4
2565 Carvoeira/Aldeia
　　　Galega da
　　　Mercrana　7 G 3
2655 Carvoeira/Ericeira
　　　10 H 3
8400 Carvoeiro/Lagoa
　　　13 L 5
6120 Carvoeiro/Mação
　　　8 F 6
7050 Casa Branca/
　　　Alcácer do Sal
　　　11 H 5
7580 Casa Branca/
　　　Alcáçovas
　　　11 J 5
7470 Casa Branca/
　　　Vimieiro　11 H 6
7555 Casa Nova　13 K 4
2200 Casais de Revelhos
　　　8 F 5
8550 Casais/Monchique
　　　13 L 4
2305 Casais/Tomar　8 F 5

3050 Casal Comba　4 E 5
6300 Casal de Cinza
　　　6 D 7
3200 Casal de Ermo　4 E 5
5085 Casal de Loivos
　　　2 C 6
2435 Casal dos Bernardos
　　　8 F 4
2425 Casal Novo　7 F 4
6370 Casal Vasco　5 D 6
2090 Casalinho　8 G 4
2750 Cascais　10 H 3
7580 Casebres　11 H 5
6225 Casegas　5 E 6
7780 Casével/Castro
　　　Verde　14 K 5
2000 Casével/
　　　Entroncamento
　　　8 G 4
3640 Castainço　5 D 7
3280 Castanheira de Pêra
　　　8 E 5
2600 Castanheira do
　　　Ribatejo　7 G 4
3750 Castanheira do
　　　Vogua　4 D 5
6300 Castanheira/Guarda
　　　6 D 7
5200 Castanheira/
　　　Mogadouro
　　　3 C 8
6420 Castanheira/
　　　Trancoso　5 D 7
5470 Castanheira/
　　　Travassos　2 B 6
3080 Castanheiro　4 E 4
5130 Castanheiro do Sul
　　　5 C 6
5070 Castedo/Alijó　2 C 7
5160 Castedo/Torre de
　　　Moncorvo
　　　2 C 7
6430 Casteição　6 D 7
5400 Castelaos/Chaves
　　　2 B 6
5340 Castelaos/Macedo
　　　de Cavaleiros
　　　3 B 8
6320 Casteleiro　6 E 7
6230 Castelejo　5 E 6
3100 Castelhanas　7 F 4
8970 Castelhanos　14 L 6
6355 Castelo Bom　6 D 8
6000 Castelo Branco/
　　　Escalos de Baixo
　　　9 F 7
5200 Castelo Branco/
　　　Mogadouro
　　　3 C 8
4550 Castelo de Paiva
　　　4 C 5
3550 Castelo de Penalva
　　　5 D 6
7320 Castelo de Vide
　　　9 G 7
4900 Castelo do Neiva
　　　1 B 4
5150 Castelo Melhor
　　　6 C 7
6355 Castelo Mendo
　　　6 D 8
6230 Castelo Novo　9 E 7
6440 Castelo Rodrigo
　　　6 D 8
6100 Castelo/Cernache do
　　　Bom Jardim
　　　8 F 5
6120 Castelo/Mação
　　　8 F 6
3620 Castelo/Moimenta da
　　　Beira　5 C 6
3660 Castelo/São Pedro
　　　do Sul　5 D 5
3465 Castelões
　　　5 D 5
5300 Castrelos　3 B 8
3600 Castro Daire　5 D 6
5300 Castro de Avelas
　　　3 B 8

4960 Castro Laboreiro
　　　1 A 5
8950 Castro Marim
　　　15 L 7
5340 Castro Roupal
　　　3 B 8
7780 Castro Verde
　　　14 K 5
5200 Castro Vicente
　　　3 C 8
6290 Cativelos　5 D 6
6160 Cava　8 F 5
6300 Cavadoude　6 D 7
7630 Cavaleiro　13 K 4
3500 Cavernães　5 D 6
4860 Caves　2 B 6
2435 Caxarias　8 F 4
6000 Cebolais de Cima
　　　9 F 6
5370 Cedaes　2 C 7
5155 Cedovim　6 C 7
3740 Cedrim　4 D 5
6060 Cegonhas Novas
　　　9 F 7
3040 Ceira　4 E 5
4950 Ceivaes　1 A 5
2460 Cela Velha　7 F 3
2460 Cela/Alcobaça
　　　7 F 3
5320 Celas　3 B 8
3300 Celavisa　5 E 5
4850 Celeirô　1 B 5
4700 Celeirós　1 B 5
5060 Celeiros　2 C 6
6360 Celorico da Beira
　　　5 D 7
4890 Celorico de Basto
　　　1 C 6
3730 Cepelos　4 D 5
3500 Cepões　5 D 6
3300 Cepos　5 E 6
2435 Cercal　7 F 4
2550 Cercal/Alcoentre
　　　7 G 3
7555 Cercal/São Luis
　　　13 K 4
3130 Cercal/Soure　4 E 4
5210 Cercio　3 C 9
4930 Cerdal　1 B 4
5460 Cerdeda　2 B 6
3305 Cerdeira/Arganil
　　　5 E 6
6320 Cerdeira/Vilar Maior
　　　6 D 7
3330 Cerdeira/Vilarinho
　　　5 E 5
4850 Cerdeirinhas　1 B 5
5350 Cerejais　3 C 8
6400 Cerejo　6 D 7
3040 Cernache　4 E 5
6100 Cernache do Bom
　　　Jardim　8 F 5
8100 Cerro/Alte　14 L 5
8100 Cerro/Loulé　14 L 5
4870 Cerva　2 C 6
4730 Cervaes　1 B 4
5470 Cervos　2 B 6
5470 Cha/Travassos
　　　2 B 6
5070 Cha/Vila Real　2 C 7
4860 Chacim/Cabeceiras
　　　de Basto　1 B 6
5340 Chacim/Macedo de
　　　Cavaleiros　3 C 8
4840 Chamoim　1 B 5
2140 Chamusca　8 G 5
7440 Chança　8 G 6
7440 Chancelaria/Crato
　　　8 G 6
2350 Chancelaria/Torres
　　　Novas　8 F 4
2500 Chão da Parada
　　　7 G 3
6050 Chão da Velha
　　　8 F 6
6120 Chão de Codes
　　　8 F 5
3240 Chão de Couce
　　　8 F 5

Chão de Lopes Grande ⓟ **Ferreira/Macedo de Cavaleiros** Ⓟ

6120 Chão de Lopes Grande 8 F 5
2240 Chãos/Casais 8 F 5
2565 Chãos/Ventosa 7 G 3
7555 Charnequinha 13 K 4
5150 Chãs 6 D 7
3530 Chãs de Tavares 5 D 6
5120 Chavães 5 C 6
6120 Chaveira 8 F 6
6350 Chavelhas 6 D 8
5400 Chaves 2 B 7
6400 Cheiras 6 D 7
2640 Cheleiros 10 H 3
4755 Chorente 1 C 4
2140 Chouto 8 G 5
7050 Ciborro 11 H 5
5210 Cicouro 3 B 9
4980 Cidadelhe/Arcos de Valdevez 1 B 5
6400 Cidadelhe/Pinhel 6 D 7
7160 Ciladas 12 H 7
5110 Cimbres 5 C 6
6440 Cinco Vilas 6 D 8
4690 Cinfães 5 C 5
5320 Cisterna 2 B 7
8970 Clarines 14 L 6
5370 Cobro 2 C 7
5140 Codeçais 2 C 7
4890 Codeçoso/Borba de Godim 1 C 5
5470 Codeçoso/Travassos 2 B 6
6300 Codesseiro 6 D 7
5460 Codessoso 2 B 6
5300 Coelhoso 3 B 8
3280 Coentral 8 E 5
6420 Cogula 6 D 7
3000 Coimbra 4 E 5
2425 Coimbrão 7 F 4
8970 Coito 14 L 6
3305 Coja 5 D 6
2985 Colar de Perdizes 10 H 4
2705 Colares 10 H 3
3330 Colmeal 5 E 5
6250 Colmeal da Torre 5 E 7
2410 Colmeias 7 F 4
7630 Colos 14 K 5
6040 Comenda 8 G 6
7580 Comporia 10 J 4
2205 Concavada 8 G 5
7670 Conceição/Aljustrel 14 K 5
8000 Conceição/Faro 14 L 6
8800 Conceição/Tavira 14 L 6
3150 Condeixa-a-Nova 4 E 5
3150 Condeixa-a-Velha 4 E 5
6150 Conqueiros 8 F 6
2250 Constância 8 G 5
5210 Constantim/Especiosa 3 B 9
5000 Constantim/Mateus 2 C 6
3530 Contensas de Baixo 5 D 6
5470 Contim 2 B 6
3060 Cordinhã 4 E 4
6150 Corgas 8 F 6
6430 Coriscada 6 D 7
4920 Cornes 1 B 4
4795 Coronado 1 C 4
2040 Correias 7 G 4
2855 Corroios 10 H 3
8950 Corte do Cago 15 L 6
7750 Corte do Pinto 15 K 7
7700 Corte Figueira 14 L 5

7750 Corte Gafo de Baixo 14 K 6
7750 Corte Gafo de Cima 14 K 6
8100 Corte João Marques 14 L 6
7750 Corte Pequena 14 K 6
8970 Corte Serranos 14 L 6
7750 Corte Sines 14 K 6
8970 Corte Tabeliáo 15 L 6
7600 Corte Vicente Anes 14 K 5
7700 Corte Zorrinha 14 K 5
3885 Cortegaça/Esmoriz 4 D 4
3450 Cortegaça/Mortágua 4 E 5
8100 Cortelha 14 L 6
8950 Cortelha 14 L 6
7960 Cortes de Baixo 11 J 6
6215 Cortes do Meio 5 E 6
8970 Cortes Pereiras 15 L 6
2410 Cortes/Leiria 7 F 4
3330 Cortes/Pedrogão Grande 8 F 5
3570 Cortiçada 5 D 6
7050 Cortiçadas do Lavre 11 H 5
6360 Cortiço da Serra 5 D 7
5340 Cortiços 3 B 7
2100 Coruche/Benavente 11 H 4
3570 Coruche/Sátão 5 D 6
2425 Corucho 7 F 4
5340 Corujas 3 B 8
3070 Corujeiras 4 E 4
2970 Corva 10 J 3
7200 Corval 12 J 7
2825 Costa da Caparica 10 H 3
3080 Costa de Lavos 4 E 4
7500 Costa de Santo António 10 J 4
3500 Cota 5 D 6
6420 Cótimos 6 D 7
2500 Coto 7 G 3
2100 Couço 11 H 5
4940 Coura 1 B 4
4960 Cousso 1 A 5
4780 Couto 1 C 5
3510 Couto de Cima 5 D 5
3740 Couto de Esteves 4 D 5
6100 Couxaria 8 F 5
3100 Covão da Silva 8 F 4
2380 Covão do Feto 7 G 4
3840 Covão do Lobo 4 E 4
5460 Covas do Barroso 2 B 6
5060 Covas do Douro 2 C 6
3660 Covas do Rio 5 D 5
3420 Covas/Oliveira do Hospital 5 E 6
4920 Covas/Valença 1 B 4
5470 Covelaes 2 B 6
4830 Covelas 1 B 5
5050 Covelinhas 2 C 6
5470 Covelo do Geres 1 B 6
4515 Covelo/Gondomar 1 C 5
3420 Covelo/Tábula 5 E 5

4840 Covide 1 B 5
6200 Covilhã 5 E 6
3060 Covões 4 E 4
2460 Coz 7 F 4
7430 Crato 9 G 6
4415 Crestuma 4 C 4
4755 Cristelo 1 C 4
2480 Cruz da Légua 7 F 4
2985 Cruzamento de Pegões 11 H 4
7940 Cuba 11 J 6
4960 Cubalhao 1 A 5
3600 Cujó 5 D 6
7200 Cumeada/Reguengos de Monsaraz 12 J 6
6100 Cumeada/Sertã 8 F 5
3230 Cumeeira 8 F 5
5030 Cumieira 2 C 6
3530 Cunha Baixa 5 D 6
4940 Cunha/Arcos de Valdevez 1 B 4
3640 Cunha/Trancoso 5 D 7
4860 Cunhas 2 B 6
7440 Cunheira 8 G 6
5400 Curalha 2 B 7
5335 Curopos 2 B 7
5460 Curros/Chaves 2 B 6
5445 Curros/Valpaços 2 B 7
4740 Curvos 1 B 4

D

5400 Dadim 2 B 7
3460 Dardavaz 5 E 5
4900 Darque 1 B 4
3560 Decermilo 5 D 6
3130 Degrácias 8 E 4
5300 Deilao 3 B 8
4905 Deocriste 1 B 4
5120 Desejosa 5 C 6
3680 Destriz 4 D 5
5320 Dine 3 B 8
7700 Dogueno 14 L 6
2565 Dois Portos 7 G 3
6040 Domingos da Vinha 8 F 6
6200 Dominguizo 5 E 6
5300 Donai 3 B 8
6230 Donas 5 E 7
5470 Donoes 2 B 6
3320 Dornelas do Zêzere 5 E 6
5460 Dornelas/Covas do Barroso 2 B 6
3740 Dornelas/Palmaz 4 D 5
3570 Dornelas/Sátão 5 D 6
4720 Dornelas/Vila Verde 1 B 5
2240 Dornes 8 F 5
5210 Duas Igrejas 3 C 9
4700 Dume 1 B 5
4905 Durraes 1 B 4

E

5320 Edral 2 B 7
5320 Edrosa 3 B 8
5340 Edroso 3 B 8
3150 Ega 4 E 4
4740 Eira de Ana 1 B 4
3570 Eirado 5 D 7
3020 Eiras 4 E 5
5320 Eiras Maiores 3 B 8
7750 Eirinha 14 K 6
3800 Eixo 4 D 4
7350 Elvas 12 H 7
2640 Encarnação 7 G 3
7780 Entradas 14 K 5
4980 Entre Ambos-os-Rios 1 B 5
4575 Entre-os-Rios 4 C 5
2330 Entroncamento 8 G 5

6120 Envendos 8 F 6
6230 Enxabarda 5 E 6
2665 Enxara do Bispo 7 H 3
6215 Erada 5 E 6
2070 Ereira 7 G 4
2655 Ericeira 10 H 3
4970 Ermelo/Ponte da Barca 1 B 5
4880 Ermelo/Vila Real 2 C 6
3070 Ermida/Mira 4 E 4
4980 Ermida/Ponte de Barca 1 B 5
6100 Ermida/Sertã 8 F 6
3460 Ermida/Tondela 5 D 5
7565 Ermidas 11 K 5
7540 Ermidas Sado 11 J 5
2100 Erra 11 H 5
6400 Ervas Tenras 6 D 7
7480 Ervedal/Avis 11 G 6
3405 Ervedal/Carregal do Sal 5 E 6
5400 Ervededo 2 B 6
2425 Ervedeira/Monte Redondo 7 F 4
7400 Ervedeira/Ponte de Sor 8 G 5
5130 Ervedosa do Douro 2 C 7
5320 Ervedosa/Torre de Dona Chama 2 B 7
6400 Ervedosa/Trancoso 6 D 7
7600 Ervidel 14 K 5
5430 Ervoes 2 B 7
6440 Escalhão 6 D 8
6005 Escalos de Baixo 9 F 7
6005 Escalos de Cima 9 F 7
3270 Escalos do Meio 8 F 5
6230 Escarigo/Benquerença 6 E 7
6440 Escarigo/Pinhel 6 D 8
4540 Escariz 4 D 5
2125 Escaroupim 7 G 4
4700 Escudeiros 1 C 5
3640 Escurquela 5 C 6
7320 Escusa 9 G 7
6160 Esfrega 8 F 6
3885 Esmoriz 4 D 4
5340 Espadanedo 3 B 8
8100 Espargal 14 L 5
3420 Espariz 5 E 5
5210 Especiosa 3 B 9
7340 Esperança 9 G 7
8600 Espiche 13 L 4
3230 Espinhal 8 E 5
2065 Espinheira 7 G 4
3750 Espinhel 4 D 5
4500 Espinho/Anta 4 C 4
3450 Espinho/Nelas 4 E 5
3530 Espinho/Vila Nova de Monsarros 5 D 6
5300 Espinhosela 3 B 8
5335 Espinhoso 2 B 7
7750 Espírito Santo 14 K 6
2435 Espite 8 F 4
4540 Espiunca 5 D 5
4700 Esporoes 1 B 5
4740 Esposende 1 B 4
7750 Espragosa 14 K 6
7780 Estação de Ourique 14 K 5
3860 Estarreja 4 D 4
4710 Este 1 B 5
4570 Estela 1 C 4
3600 Ester 5 D 5
5180 Estevais 3 C 8

8135 Esteval 14 L 6
8000 Estói 14 L 6
8400 Estômbar 13 L 5
4900 Estoraos 1 B 4
2765 Estoril 10 H 3
8800 Estorninhos 14 L 6
5050 Estrada 2 C 6
6160 Estreito 8 F 6
7885 Estrela 12 J 7
7100 Estremoz 12 H 6
5350 Eucisia 3 C 7
7000 Évora 11 H 6
2460 Évora de Alcobaça 7 F 4
7100 Évora Monte 12 H 6
4970 Extremo 1 B 5

F

4990 Facha 1 B 4
2460 Facho 7 F 3
4820 Fafe 1 C 5
4860 Faia 1 C 6
3510 Fail 5 D 6
5300 Failde 3 B 8
5400 Faioes 2 B 7
3320 Fajão 5 E 6
3700 Fajões 4 D 5
7200 Falcoeiras 12 J 6
2460 Famalicão/Cela 7 F 3
6300 Famalicão/Manteigas 5 E 7
2450 Fanhais 7 F 4
2670 Fanhões 10 H 3
4510 Fânzeres 1 C 4
4740 Fao 1 B 4
3510 Farminhão 5 D 5
8000 Faro 14 L 6
7940 Faro do Alentejo 11 J 6
3670 Fataunços 5 D 5
6230 Fatela 5 E 7
2495 Fátima 7 F 4
5070 Favaios 2 C 7
7400 Fazenda 3 B 6
2100 Fazendas das Figueiras 11 H 4
2080 Fazendas de Almeirim 8 G 4
3060 Febres 4 E 4
4520 Feira 4 D 4
8800 Feiteira 14 L 6
4750 Feitos 1 B 4
5350 Felgar 3 C 8
3730 Felgueira 4 D 5
5350 Felgueiras/Mogadouro 3 C 8
4660 Felgueiras/Resende 5 C 6
4610 Felgueiras/Torre de Moncorvo 1 C 5
5160 Felgueiras/Torrados 2 C 7
3865 Fermelã 4 D 4
3750 Fermentelos 4 D 4
4890 Fermil 1 C 6
8970 Fernandilho 14 L 6
2865 Fernão Ferro 10 H 3
6300 Fernão Joanes 5 E 7
5350 Ferradosa 3 C 8
8400 Ferragudo 13 L 4
5470 Ferral 1 B 6
2230 Ferraria 8 F 5
3560 Ferreira de Aves 5 D 6
7900 Ferreira do Alentejo 11 J 5
2240 Ferreira do Zêzere 8 F 5
4940 Ferreira/Arcos de Valdevez 1 B 5
4590 Ferreira/Lordelo 1 C 5
5340 Ferreira/Macedo de Cavaleiros 3 B 8

Ferreira-a-Nova · P · **Lajeosa/Alfaiates**

3080 Ferreira-a-Nova 4 E 4
8200 Ferreiras 14 L 5
3640 Ferreirim/Moimenta da Beira 5 D 7
5100 Ferreirim/Tarouca 5 C 6
4720 Ferreiros 1 B 5
3460 Ferreiros do Dão 5 E 5
2520 Ferrel 7 G 3
6200 Ferro 5 E 7
5470 Fervidelas 2 B 6
5470 Fiaes do Rio 2 B 6
5460 Fiaes do Tâmega 2 B 6
5430 Fiaes/Chaves 2 B 7
4505 Fiães/Espinho 4 D 4
4960 Fiaes/Melgaço 1 A 5
6420 Fiães/Trancoso 5 D 7
3430 Fiais da Telha 5 E 6
3405 Fiais do Beira 5 E 6
3460 Fial 5 D 5
3080 Figueira da Foz 4 E 4
6440 Figueira de Castelo Rodrigo 6 D 8
3360 Figueira de Lorvão 4 E 5
7900 Figueira dos Cavaleiros 11 J 5
7480 Figueira e Barros 8 G 6
5100 Figueira/Lamego 5 C 6
5200 Figueira/Mogadouro 3 C 8
6150 Figueira/Sertã 8 F 6
7565 Figueiras 14 K 5
6100 Figueiredo 8 F 6
3670 Figueiredo das Donas 5 D 5
3660 Figueiredo de Alva 5 D 6
7780 Figueirinha 14 K 6
3260 Figueiró da Granja 5 D 7
6290 Figueiró da Serra 5 D 7
3130 Figueiró do Campo 4 E 4
3260 Figueiró dos Vinhos 8 F 5
5090 Fiolhoso 2 C 6
7430 Flor da Rosa 9 G 6
6320 Foios 6 E 8
5110 Folgosa 2 C 6
6290 Folgosinho 5 D 6
4635 Folhada 1 C 5
5000 Folhadela 2 C 6
6270 Folhadosa 5 E 6
3300 Folques 5 E 5
7570 Fontainhas 10 J 4
3640 Fonte Arcada 5 D 6
4740 Fonte Boa/Barcelos 1 B 4
7630 Fonte Boa/Odemira 13 K 4
2825 Fonte da Telha 10 H 3
5210 Fonte de Aldeia 3 C 9
3330 Fonte Limpa 8 E 5
6000 Fonte Longa/Castelo Branco 9 F 6
6430 Fonte Longa/Vila Flor 6 C 7
5140 Fonte Longa/Vila Nova de Foz Côa 2 C 7
5050 Fontelas 2 C 6
5030 Fontes 2 C 6
8365 Fontes da Matosa 14 L 5
7630 Fontinha 13 K 4

4930 Fontoura 1 B 4
6320 Forcalhos 6 E 8
4740 Forjaes 1 B 4
3560 Forles 5 D 6
2435 Formigais 8 F 5
4485 Fornelo 1 C 4
4820 Fornelos/Fafe 1 C 5
4690 Fornelos/Nespereira 5 C 5
4990 Fornelos/Ponte de Lima 1 B 4
3570 Forninhos 5 D 6
6360 Forno Telheiro 5 D 7
5180 Fornos 3 C 8
6370 Fornos de Algodres 5 D 6
5430 Fornos do Pinhal 2 B 7
7050 Foros da Adúa 11 H 5
7540 Foros da Caiada 13 K 4
2100 Foros da Fonte de Pau 11 H 5
7170 Foros da Fonte Seca 12 H 6
2100 Foros da Salgueirinha 11 H 4
2120 Foros de Salvaterra 10 G 4
7050 Foros de Vale de Figueira 11 H 5
7425 Foros do Arrão 8 G 5
2100 Foros do Biscainho 10 H 4
7050 Foros do Cortiço 11 H 5
7170 Foros do Freixo 12 H 6
7425 Foros do Mocho 8 G 5
7300 Fortios 9 G 7
2080 Foz 8 G 5
3260 Foz de Alge 8 F 5
3200 Foz de Arouce 4 E 5
2500 Foz do Arelho 7 G 3
8550 Foz do Arroio 13 L 4
6030 Foz do Cobrão 8 F 6
4515 Foz do Sousa 4 C 5
6185 Foz Giraldo 9 E 6
5130 Foz Tua 2 C 7
4760 Fradelos 1 C 4
5385 Fradizela 2 B 7
3500 Fragosela 5 D 6
4905 Fragoso 1 B 4
2040 Fráguas/Rio Maior 7 G 4
3650 Fráguas/Vila Nova 5 D 6
4700 Fraiao 1 B 5
5300 França 3 B 8
5370 Franco 2 C 7
6030 Fratel 8 F 6
4595 Frazao 1 C 5
4594 Freamunde 1 C 5
5370 Frechas 2 C 7
4600 Fregim 1 C 5
6355 Freineda 6 D 8
2565 Freiria/Azueira 7 G 3
5450 Freiria/Vila Real 2 C 6
4820 Freitas 1 B 5
6440 Freixeda do Torrão 6 D 7
5450 Freixeda/Chaves 2 B 6
5370 Freixeda/Mirandela 2 C 7
6000 Freixial do Campo 9 F 6

2435 Freixianda 8 F 5
5300 Freixiedo 3 B 8
4900 Freixieiro de Soutelo 1 B 4
5360 Freixiel 2 C 7
3530 Freixiosa/Mangualde 5 D 6
5210 Freixiosa/Miranda do Douro 3 C 9
4600 Freixo de Baixo 1 C 5
5180 Freixo de Espada -à- Cinta 6 C 8
5155 Freixo do Numão 6 C 7
6355 Freixo/Guarda 6 D 7
3450 Freixo/Mortágua 5 E 5
4990 Freixo/Vila Verde 1 B 4
4640 Frende 1 C 6
5320 Fresulfe 3 B 8
4600 Fridao 1 C 5
4930 Friestas 1 A 4
5430 Frioes 2 B 7
3360 Friumes 4 E 5
7460 Fronteira 12 G 6
6110 Fundada 8 F 5
6230 Fundão 5 E 7
2350 Fungalvaz 8 F 5
3150 Furadouro/ Condeixa-a- Velha 4 E 5
3880 Furadouro/Ovar 4 D 4
8950 Furnazinhas 14 L 6
6120 Furtado 8 F 6
8700 Fuzeta 14 L 6

G

4950 Gadrachao 1 B 4
2510 Gaeiras 7 G 3
3840 Gafanha da Boa Hora 4 D 4
3830 Gafanha da Encarnação 4 D 4
3830 Gafanha da Nazaré 4 D 4
3830 Gafanha da Vagueira 4 D 4
3830 Gafanha do Carmo 4 D 4
7040 Gafanhoeira 11 H 5
7430 Gáfete 9 G 6
6300 Gagos 6 D 7
6250 Gaia 5 E 7
3080 Gala 4 E 4
5050 Galafura 2 C 6
7240 Galeana 12 J 7
7400 Galveias 8 G 6
4755 Gamil 1 B 4
2025 Gançaria 7 G 4
4890 Gandarela 1 C 5
4990 Gandra/Ponte de Lima 1 B 4
4930 Gandra/Valença 1 A 4
4585 Gandra/Valongo 1 C 5
4930 Ganfei 1 A 4
6030 Gardete 8 F 6
4830 Garfe 1 B 5
7670 Garvão 14 K 5
3140 Gatões 4 E 4
6040 Gavião/Pego 8 G 6
4760 Gaviao/Vila Nova de Familicão 1 C 4
4970 Gavieira 1 B 5
5350 Gebelim 3 C 8
4475 Gemunde 1 C 4
5210 Genísio 3 B 9
2525 Geraldes 7 G 3
4905 Geraz do Lima 1 B 4
4980 Germil 1 B 5
4640 Gestaçô 1 C 6
3130 Gesteira 4 E 4

5320 Gestosa 2 B 7
3280 Gestosa Cimeira 8 E 5
3660 Gestoso 4 D 5
6150 Giesteiras Cimeiras 8 F 6
6225 Giesteria 5 E 6
8100 Gilvrazino 14 L 5
5300 Gimonde 3 B 8
8970 Giões 14 L 6
7780 Giraldos 14 K 5
7100 Glória 12 H 6
2125 Glória do Ribatejo 7 G 4
4720 Goaes 1 B 5
4730 Godinhanços 1 B 5
3330 Góis 5 E 5
2150 Golegã 8 G 5
5370 Golfeiras 2 C 7
7700 Gomes Aires 14 K 5
4800 Gonça 1 B 5
6300 Gonçalo 5 E 7
6300 Gonçalo Bocas 6 D 7
4810 Gondar/Amarante 1 C 5
4600 Gondar/Joane 1 C 5
4920 Gondarém 1 B 4
4930 Gondelim 1 B 4
2490 Gondemaria 8 F 4
5300 Gondesende 3 B 8
4860 Gondiaes 2 B 6
4420 Gondomar 1 C 4
4930 Gondomil 1 A 4
4970 Gondoriz 1 B 5
4820 Gontim 1 B 5
2080 Gorjão 8 G 5
3600 Gosende 5 C 6
5300 Gostei 3 B 8
5450 Gouvaes de Serra 2 C 6
6400 Gouveia/Guarda 6 D 7
6290 Gouveia/Seia 5 E 6
5350 Gouveia/Vila Flor 3 C 8
5060 Gouvinhas 2 C 6
4640 Gove 1 C 5
3270 Graça 8 F 5
2665 Gradil 7 H 3
3570 Gradiz 5 D 6
5470 Gralhas 2 B 6
4690 Gralheira 5 C 6
5470 Gralhós/Chaves 2 B 6
6340 Gralhós/Macedo de Cavaleiros 3 B 8
3400 Gramaça 5 E 6
7570 Grândola 11 J 4
2125 Granho Novo 10 G 4
3130 Granja do Ulmeiro 4 E 4
3610 Granja Nova 5 C 6
7240 Granja/Amareleja 12 J 7
5225 Granja/Miranda do Douro 3 B 9
3630 Granja/Moimenta da Beira 5 C 7
7050 Granja/Vendas Novas 11 H 4
5070 Granja/Vila Real 2 C 7
3640 Granjal 5 D 6
4415 Grijó 4 C 4
5300 Grijó de Parada 3 B 8
3230 Grocinas 8 F 5
4980 Grovelas 1 B 5
5300 Guadramil 3 B 8
6300 Guarda 6 D 7
6300 Guarda-Gare 6 D 7
3475 Guardão 5 D 5
7700 Guedelhas 14 L 6
7780 Guerreiro 14 K 6
8970 Guerreiros do Rio 15 L 7

8200 Guia/Albufeira 14 L 5
3100 Guia/Monte Redondo 7 F 4
5000 Guiaes 2 C 6
3640 Guilheiro 5 D 7
4810 Guimaraes 1 C 5

H

5155 Horta 6 C 7
5160 Horta da Vilariça 2 C 7
7250 Hortinhas 12 H 7

I

6060 Idanha-a-Nova 9 F 7
6060 Idanha-a-Velha 9 F 7
5210 Ifanes 3 B 9
2640 Igreja Nova 10 H 3
2240 Igreja Nova do Sobral 8 F 5
7040 Igrejinha 11 H 6
3830 Ílhavo 4 D 4
4810 Infantas 1 C 5
6250 Inguias 6 E 7
4940 Insalde 1 B 4
6160 Isna 8 F 6
5300 Izeda 3 B 8

J

4600 Jacente 1 C 5
3320 Janeiro de Baixo 8 E 6
6185 Janeiro de Cima 8 E 6
6300 Jarmelo 6 D 7
8150 Javali 14 L 6
4770 Joane 1 C 5
6300 João Antão 6 E 7
7750 João Serra 14 K 6
4970 Jolda 1 B 5
5090 Jou 2 C 7
4510 Jovim 1 C 4
4610 Jugueiros 1 C 5
6350 Junça 6 D 8
6370 Juncais 5 D 6
6000 Juncal do Campo 9 F 6
6030 Juncal/Mação 8 F 6
2480 Juncal/Pedreiras 7 F 4
7600 Jungeiros 14 K 5
8950 Junqueira/Ayamonte 15 L 7
3730 Junqueira/Castelões 4 D 5
5160 Junqueira/Vila Flor 2 C 7
7250 Juromenha 12 H 7
5000 Justes 2 C 6

L

8970 Laborato 14 L 6
4485 Labruge 1 C 4
4990 Labrujó 1 B 4
5000 Ladares 2 C 6
6030 Ladeira 8 F 6
6060 Ladoeiro 9 F 7
4560 Lagares/Gondomar 1 C 5
3405 Lagares/Oliveira do Hospital 5 E 6
6290 Lagarinhos 5 E 6
3240 Lagarteira 8 F 5
6360 Lageosa do Mondego 5 D 7
5340 Lagoa/Mogadouro 3 C 8
8400 Lagoa/Silves 13 L 5
5180 Lagoaça 3 C 8
8600 Lagos 13 L 4
3405 Lagos da Beira 5 E 6
4730 Laje 1 B 5
6320 Lajeosa/Alfaiates 6 E 8

Lajeosa/Tondela ⓟ

3460 Lajeosa/Tondela 5 D 6
6270 Lajes/Gouveia 5 E 6
8800 Lajes/Santa Catarina da Fonte Bispo 14 L 6
5100 Lalim 5 C 6
4750 Lama 1 B 4
5470 Lama Cha 2 B 6
5400 Lama de Arcos 2 B 7
5340 Lamalonga 2 B 7
5000 Lamares 2 C 6
2350 Lamarosa 8 F 5
3560 Lamas de Ferreira 5 D 6
4960 Lamas de Mouro 1 A 5
5000 Lamas de Olo 2 C 6
5370 Lamas de Orelhao 2 C 7
5340 Lamas de Podence 3 B 8
2550 Lamas/Cadaval 7 G 3
3220 Lamas/Miranda do Corvo 4 E 5
3600 Lamas/Vila Cova á Coelheira 5 D 6
5470 Lamas/Vila da Ponte 2 B 6
6400 Lamegal 6 D 7
5100 Lamego 5 C 6
4820 Lameira 1 C 5
6400 Lameiras 6 D 7
3640 Lamosa 5 D 6
5340 Lançao 3 B 8
2500 Landal 7 G 3
5320 Landedo 3 B 7
3660 Landeira/Arões 5 D 5
2965 Landeira/Marateca 10 H 4
4910 Lanhelas 1 B 4
4900 Lanheses 1 B 4
3525 Lapa do Lobo 5 E 6
2070 Lapa/Aveiras de Cima 7 G 4
3640 Lapa/Vila Nova de Paiva 5 D 6
2350 Lapas 8 G 4
3020 Larçã 4 E 5
6005 Lardosa 9 F 7
3080 Lares 4 E 4
5160 Larinho 2 C 7
4570 Laundos 1 C 4
6230 Lavacolhos 5 E 6
5140 Lavandeira 2 C 7
3350 Lavegadas 4 E 5
3080 Lavos 4 E 4
4455 Lavra 1 C 4
5460 Lavradas 2 B 6
2835 Lavradio 10 H 3
7050 Lavre 11 H 5
5100 Lazarim 5 C 6
5430 Lebuçao 2 B 7
4450 Leça da Palmeira 1 C 4
4465 Leça do Bailio 1 C 4
3660 Leirados 5 D 5
2400 Leiria 7 F 4
3070 Leitões 4 E 4
6000 Lentiscais/Castelo Branco 9 F 7
8200 Lentiscais/Paderne 14 L 5
3620 Leomil/Moimenta da Beira 5 D 6
6350 Leomil/Nave de Haver 6 D 8
5180 Ligares 6 C 8
4750 Lijó 1 B 4
5340 Limaos 3 B 8
4870 Limoes 2 C 6
4980 Lindoso 1 B 5
2305 Linhaceira 8 F 5
6360 Linhares/Guarda 5 D 7

5140 Linhares/Torre de Moncorvo 2 C 7
1000 Lisboa 10 H 3
8800 Livramento 14 L 6
4610 Lixa 1 C 5
3460 Lobão da Beira 5 D 5
3530 Lobelhe de Mato 5 D 6
5360 Lodoes 2 C 7
4920 Loivo 1 B 4
5425 Loivos 2 B 6
4640 Loivos do Monte 1 C 6
6320 Lomba 6 E 7
7780 Lombador 14 K 6
7750 Lombardos 14 K 6
5340 Lombo 3 C 8
3840 Lombomeão 4 D 4
7400 Longo Mel 8 G 6
4800 Longos 1 B 5
4950 Longos Vales 1 A 5
5120 Longra 5 C 6
6430 Longroiva 6 D 7
4815 Lordelo/Caldas de Vizela 1 C 5
4580 Lordelo/Paredes 1 C 5
3510 Lordosa 5 D 6
6270 Loriga 5 E 6
3360 Lorvão 4 E 5
8100 Loulé 14 L 5
4525 Louredo/Lourosa 4 D 5
4850 Louredo/Viera do Minho 1 B 5
5030 Louredo/Vila Real 2 C 6
3500 Loureiro de Silgueiros 5 D 6
3720 Loureiro/Avanca 4 D 4
5050 Loureiro/Peso da Régua 2 C 6
2670 Loures 10 H 3
3100 Louriçal 7 E 4
6005 Louriçal do Campo 9 E 6
2530 Lourinhã 7 G 3
4760 Louro 1 C 4
4535 Lourosa/Fieãs 4 D 4
3400 Lourosa/Oliveira do Hospital 5 E 6
3200 Lousã 4 E 5
2670 Lousa/Almargem do Bispo 10 H 3
6005 Lousa/Escalos de Cima 9 F 7
5160 Lousa/Torre de Moncorvo 2 C 7
6110 Lousa/Vila de Rei 8 F 5
4620 Lousada 1 C 5
4624 Lousada/Freamunde 1 C 5
4920 Lovelhe 1 B 4
8135 Ludo 14 L 6
4600 Lufrei 1 C 5
3550 Lusinde 5 D 6
3050 Luso 4 E 5
4620 Lustosa 1 C 5
8600 Luz/Lagos 13 L 4
8800 Luz/Moncarapacho 14 L 6
7240 Luz/Murão 12 J 7
7665 Luzianes 13 K 5

M

6250 Maçaínhas 6 E 7
6300 Maçainhas de Baixo 5 D 7
6360 Maçal do Chão 6 D 7
6120 Mação 8 F 6
3250 Maçãs de Caminho 8 F 5

3250 Maçãs de Dona Maria 8 F 5
3885 Maceda 4 D 4
5340 Macedo de Cavaleiros 3 B 8
5300 Macedo do Mato 3 B 8
5200 Macedo do Peso 3 C 8
6370 Maceira/Celorico da Beira 5 D 7
2405 Maceira/Leiria 7 F 4
7860 Machados/Moura 12 J 7
8150 Machados/São Brás de Alportel 14 L 6
3320 Machio 8 E 5
3750 Macieira de Alcoba 4 D 5
3730 Macieira/Castelões 5 D 5
3660 Macieira/Castro Daire 4 D 5
4755 Macieria de Rates 1 C 4
3640 Macieria/Moimenta da Beira 5 D 7
3750 Maçinhata do Vouga 4 D 5
5350 Maçores 6 C 8
2305 Madalena 8 F 5
4400 Madalena/Vila Nova de Gaia 1 C 4
6160 Madeira 8 F 5
2640 Mafra 10 H 3
2705 Magoito 10 H 3
5100 Magueija 5 C 6
4860 Magusteiro 2 B 6
4470 Maia 1 C 4
3080 Maiorca 4 E 4
2460 Maiorga 7 F 4
5400 Mairos 2 B 7
6320 Malcata 6 E 7
6355 Malhada Sorda 6 D 8
3600 Malhada/Vila Cova ã Coelheira 5 D 6
6110 Malhada/Vila de Rei 8 F 5
5210 Malhadas 3 B 9
7645 Malhadinhas 13 K 4
2380 Malhou 7 G 4
6350 Malpartida 6 D 8
7555 Malpensado 13 K 4
6000 Malpica do Tejo 9 F 7
6400 Malta 6 D 7
2755 Malveira/Alcabideche 10 H 3
2665 Malveira/Mafra 10 H 3
3770 Mamarrosa 4 E 4
4605 Mancelos 1 C 5
7600 Mancoca 14 K 5
3530 Mangualde 5 D 6
3660 Manhouce 5 D 5
6400 Manigoto 6 D 7
2065 Manique do Intendente 7 G 4
4540 Mansores 4 D 5
8900 Manta Rota 15 L 6
6260 Manteigas 5 E 6
7750 Manuel Galo 14 K 6
4740 Mar 1 B 4
7480 Maranhão 11 G 6
2965 Marateca 10 H 4
8000 Marchil 14 L 6
7340 Marco 9 G 7
4630 Marco de Canavezes 1 C 5
3550 Mareco 5 D 6

7830 Margalejas 15 J 6
6040 Margem 8 G 6
8670 Maria Vinagre 13 L 4
6430 Marialva 6 D 7
3080 Marinha das Ondas 7 E 4
2430 Marinha Grande 7 F 4
2125 Marinhais 7 G 4
4740 Marinhas 1 B 4
7960 Marmelar 12 J 6
2040 Marmeleira/Azóia de Baixo 7 G 4
3450 Marmeleira/Mortagua 4 E 5
6300 Marmeleiro/Guarda 6 E 7
6100 Marmeleiro/Sertã 8 F 5
8550 Marmelete 13 L 4
5370 Marmelos 2 C 7
7630 Maroufenha 13 K 4
4730 Marrancos 1 B 4
2400 Marrazes 7 F 4
2530 Marteleira 7 G 3
6230 Martianas 9 E 7
4755 Martim 1 B 4
6000 Martim Branco 9 F 6
8970 Martim Longo 14 L 6
2200 Martinchel 8 F 5
2445 Martingança 7 F 4
7330 Marvão 9 G 7
3260 Marvila 8 F 5
5140 Marzagao 2 C 7
5370 Mascarenhas 2 B 7
6440 Mata de Lobos 6 D 8
3100 Mata Mourisca 7 F 4
7040 Mata/Arraiolos 11 H 5
2350 Mata/Chancelaria 8 F 4
6005 Mata/Escalos de Baixo 9 F 7
2565 Matacães 7 G 3
6370 Matança 5 D 6
3080 Matas 7 E 4
5230 Matela 3 B 8
5000 Mateus 2 C 6
4990 Mato 1 B 4
2150 Mato de Miranda 8 G 4
4451 Matosinhos 1 C 4
6000 Maxiais/Castelo Branco 8 F 6
6150 Maxiais/Sertã 9 F 6
6135 Maxial/Fundão 9 E 6
2565 Maxial/Ramalhal 7 G 3
6100 Maxial/Sertã 8 F 5
6120 Maxieira 8 F 6
4900 Mazarefes 1 B 4
4950 Mazedo 1 A 5
5100 Mazes 5 C 6
5180 Mazouco 6 C 8
4900 Meadela 1 B 4
3050 Mealhada 4 E 5
3320 Meãs 5 E 6
3140 Meãs do Campo 4 E 4
2580 Meca 7 G 3
6430 Meda 6 D 7
3420 Meda de Mouros 5 E 5
4515 Medas 4 C 5
6060 Medelim 9 E 7
5030 Medroes 2 C 6
6090 Meimão 6 E 7
6090 Meimoa 6 E 7
4620 Meinedo 1 C 5
5200 Meirinhos 3 C 8
5300 Meixedo/Bragança 3 B 8
4900 Meixedo/Ponte de Lima 1 B 4

Moimenta da Beira ⓟ

5470 Meixedo/Travassos 2 B 6
5470 Meixide 2 B 6
4595 Meixomil 1 C 5
5340 Meles 2 B 7
4960 Melgaço 1 A 5
5320 Melhe 3 B 8
7570 Melides 10 J 4
6290 Melo 5 D 6
4515 Melres 4 C 5
6110 Melriça 8 F 5
2410 Memória 8 F 4
2480 Mendiga 7 G 4
7750 Mértola 14 K 6
4950 Merufe 1 A 5
4810 Mesao Frio/Guimaraes 1 C 5
5040 Mesao Frio/Lamego 2 C 6
6150 Mesão Frio/Mação 8 F 6
4640 Mesquinhata 1 C 5
7750 Mesquita 15 K 6
6360 Mesquitela/Fornos de Algodres 5 D 7
3530 Mesquitela/Mangualde 5 D 6
6355 Mesquitela/Nave de Haver 6 D 8
7600 Messejana 14 K 5
8500 Mexilhoeira Grande 13 L 4
4970 Mezio/Arcos de Valdevez 1 B 5
3600 Mezio/Tarouca 5 D 6
3420 Midões 5 E 6
2400 Milagres 7 F 4
5370 Milhais 2 C 7
5300 Milhao 3 B 8
7665 Milharadas 13 K 4
2665 Milharado 10 H 3
4755 Milhazes 1 C 4
6110 Milreu 8 F 5
7800 Mina da Juliana 14 K 5
7750 Mina de São Domingos 15 K 7
7250 Mina do Bugalho 12 H 7
7570 Minas da Caveira 11 J 5
4840 Minas dos Carris 1 B 5
2395 Minde 7 F 4
4485 Mindelo 1 C 4
6360 Minhocal 5 D 7
8365 Miões 14 L 5
3560 Mioma 5 D 6
3070 Mira 4 E 4
2485 Mira d`Aire 7 F 4
3130 Mira Olhos 4 E 4
5370 Miradeses 2 B 7
2530 Miragaia 7 G 3
4970 Miranda 1 B 4
3220 Miranda do Corvo 4 E 5
5210 Miranda do Mouro 3 B 9
5370 Mirandela 2 C 7
3360 Miro 4 E 5
6355 Miuzela 6 D 7
4540 Mizarela 4 D 5
2000 Moçarria 7 G 4
4485 Modivas 1 C 4
3600 Mões 5 D 6
5320 Mofreita 3 B 8
5200 Mogadouro 3 C 8
5140 Mogo de Malta 2 C 7
5320 Moimenta 3 B 8
3620 Moimenta da Beira 5 D 6

6290 Moimenta da Serra 5 E 6
3530 Moimenta de Maceira Dão 5 D 6
6420 Moimentinha 6 D 7
7080 Moinhola 11 H 4
2425 Moita da Roda 7 F 4
3420 Moita da Serra 5 E 6
2530 Moita dos Ferreiros 7 G 3
3780 Moita/Anadia 4 E 5
2445 Moita/Maceira 7 F 4
2860 Moita/Pinhal Novo 10 H 4
6150 Moitas 8 F 6
2380 Moitas Venda 7 G 4
7665 Moitinhas 13 L 4
7425 Moitinhas Novas 8 G 5
4890 Molares 1 C 6
4540 Moldes 5 D 5
3600 Moledo/Vila Cova á Coelheira 5 D 6
4910 Moledo/Vila Praia de Âncora 1 B 4
3460 Molelos 5 D 5
2460 Molianos 7 F 4
7800 Mombeja 11 J 5
4950 Monção 1 A 5
8700 Moncarapacho 14 L 6
8550 Monchique 13 L 4
3610 Mondim da Beira 5 C 6
4880 Mondim de Basto 1 C 6
5090 Monfebres 2 C 7
7450 Monforte 12 G 7
6005 Monforte da Beira 9 F 7
6060 Monfortinho 9 E 8
3320 Moninho 8 E 6
2380 Monsanto/Alcanena 7 G 4
6060 Monsanto/Idanha-a-Nova 9 E 7
7200 Monsaraz 12 J 7
4830 Monsul 1 B 5
5470 Montalegre 2 B 6
6050 Montalvão 9 F 6
7425 Montargil 8 G 5
4900 Montaria 1 B 4
4820 Monte 1 B 5
8375 Monte Alto 14 L 5
7830 Monte Branco 12 J 7
6050 Monte Claro 8 F 6
4825 Monte Córdova 1 C 5
8100 Monte da Charneca 14 L 5
7430 Monte da Pedra 8 G 6
7000 Monte das Flores 11 H 6
8950 Monte de Baixo Grande 14 L 6
6000 Monte de Goula 9 F 6
7220 Monte do Trigo 11 J 6
7750 Monte dos Corvos 14 K 6
7600 Monte dos Poços 14 K 5
7780 Monte dos Viseus 14 K 6
7750 Monte Fernandes 14 K 6
6030 Monte Fidalgo 9 F 6
6000 Monte Gordo/Sertã 9 F 6
8901 Monte Gordo/Vila Real de Santo António 15 L 7

8150 Monte Grande 14 L 6
6300 Monte Margarida 6 E 7
7750 Monte Moreanes 15 K 6
7830 Monte Nova de Ferradura 15 K 7
6355 Monte Perobolço 6 D 8
2425 Monte Real 7 F 4
2565 Monte Redondo/ Torres Vedras 7 G 3
2425 Monte Redondo/ Vieira de Leiria 7 F 4
7170 Monte Virgem 12 H 6
4900 Montedor 1 B 4
3600 Monteiras 5 D 6
5450 Monteiros/Bragado 2 B 6
6300 Monteiros/Guarda 6 D 7
2715 Montelavar 10 H 3
7050 Montemor-o-Novo 11 H 5
3140 Montemor-o-Velho 4 E 4
6300 Montes 6 D 7
6150 Montes da Senhora 8 F 6
7250 Montes Juntos 12 H 7
8100 Montes Novos 14 L 6
7580 Montevil 10 J 4
5300 Montezinho 3 B 8
2870 Montijo 10 H 4
7200 Montoito 12 H 6
5320 Montouto 3 B 8
7490 Mora/Couço 11 H 5
5230 Mora/Mogadouro 3 C 8
5340 Morais 3 C 8
4815 Moreira de Cónegos 1 C 5
6420 Moreira de Rei 6 D 7
4890 Moreira do Castelo 1 C 5
4820 Moreira do Rei 1 C 5
4950 Moreira/Monção 1 A 5
4470 Moreira/Perafita 1 C 4
5400 Moreiras 2 B 7
7340 Moreiros 9 G 7
5470 Morgade 2 B 6
3450 Mortágua 4 E 5
7570 Mortaisinhos 10 J 4
5300 Mós/Bragança 3 B 8
3600 Mós/Castro Daire 5 D 5
5320 Mós/Torre de Dona Chama 3 B 8
5350 Mós/Torre de Moncorvo 3 C 8
5155 Mós/Vila Nova de Foz Côa 6 C 7
3600 Mosteirô 5 D 6
3460 Mosteiro de Fráguas 5 D 5
7750 Mosteiro/Mértola 14 K 6
6160 Mosteiro/Oleiros 8 F 6
3270 Mosteiro/Pedrogão Grande 8 F 5
6100 Mosteiro/Sertã 8 F 5
7340 Mosteiros 9 G 7
7200 Motrinos 12 J 7
7860 Moura 12 J 7
3305 Moura da Serra 5 E 6

3600 Moura Morta 5 D 6
7240 Mourão 12 J 7
3460 Mouraz 5 E 5
4755 Moure/Barcelos 1 B 4
4730 Moure/Vila Verde 1 B 5
6005 Mourelo 9 E 6
5470 Mourilhe 2 B 6
2910 Mourisca 10 H 4
2200 Mouriscas 8 F 5
4580 Mouriz 1 C 5
3420 Mouronho 5 E 5
3750 Moutedo 4 D 5
3500 Mozelos 5 D 6
7540 Muda 13 K 4
2125 Muge 7 G 4
3500 Mundão 5 D 6
5090 Murça/Mirandela 2 C 7
5155 Murça/Vila Nova de Foz Côa 6 C 7
5340 Murçós 3 B 8
5385 Múrias 2 B 7
4795 Muro 1 C 4
2080 Murta 8 G 5
3060 Murtede 4 E 4
3870 Murtosa 4 D 4
5155 Muxagata 6 C 7

N

6290 Nabais 5 D 6
5360 Nabo 2 C 7
2500 Nadadouro 7 G 3
3620 Nagosa 5 C 6
5130 Nagozelo do Douro 2 C 7
7750 Namorados 14 K 6
3460 Nandufe 5 D 5
5370 Navalho 2 C 7
6320 Nave 6 E 8
6355 Nave de Haver 6 D 8
6440 Nave Redonda/ Lumbrales 6 D 8
7665 Nave Redonda/ Monchique 13 L 5
6350 Naves 6 D 8
2450 Nazaré 7 F 3
5470 Negroes 2 B 6
4900 Neiva 1 B 4
3520 Nelas 5 D 6
6100 Nesperal 8 F 5
4690 Nespereira/Cinfães 5 C 5
6290 Nespereira/Gouveia 5 D 6
7700 Neves da Graça 14 K 6
4730 Nevogilde 1 B 5
6000 Ninho do Açor 9 F 6
6050 Nisa 9 F 6
5400 Nogueira da Montanha 2 B 7
3400 Nogueira do Cravo 5 E 6
5300 Nogueira/Bragança 3 B 8
3500 Nogueira/Sátão 5 D 6
5000 Nogueira/Vila Real 2 C 6
8300 Norinha 14 L 5
7000 Nossa Senhora da Boa Fé 11 H 5
7000 Nossa Senhora da Graça do Divor 11 H 6
7370 Nossa Senhora da Graça dos Degolados 12 G 7
7000 Nossa Senhora da Torega 11 H 5
7800 Nossa Senhora das Neves 11 J 6
7000 Nossa Senhora de Machede 11 H 6

5090 Noura 2 C 7
5430 Nozelos/Chaves 2 B 7
5160 Nozelos/Vila Flor 2 C 7
5155 Numão 6 C 7
5320 Nunes 3 B 8

O

2510 Óbidos 7 G 3
8670 Odeceixe 13 L 4
8950 Odeleite 15 L 7
8300 Odelouca 13 L 5
7630 Odemira 13 K 4
8600 Odiáxere 13 L 4
2675 Odivelas/Amadora 10 H 3
7900 Odivelas/Ferreira do Alentejo 11 J 5
2780 Oeiras 10 H 3
4740 Ofir 1 B 4
3770 Oiã 4 D 4
2300 Olalhas 8 F 5
5130 Olas 6 C 7
4575 Oldroes 1 C 5
6060 Oledo 9 F 7
6160 Oleiros 8 F 6
2580 Olhalvo 7 G 3
8700 Olhão 14 L 6
7900 Olhas 11 J 5
2510 Olho Marinho 7 G 3
2435 Olival/Ourem 8 F 4
4415 Olival/Perozinho 4 C 4
3660 Oliveira 5 D 5
3720 Oliveira de Azeméis 4 D 5
3500 Oliveira de Barreiros 5 D 6
3680 Oliveira de Frades 5 D 5
3770 Oliveira do Bairro 4 D 5
3430 Oliveira do Conde 5 E 6
4690 Oliveira do Douro 5 C 5
3400 Oliveira do Hospital 5 E 6
3360 Oliveira do Mondego 4 E 5
3810 Oliveirinha 4 D 4
5340 Olmos 3 C 8
7860 Orada/Orbacém 12 J 6
7150 Orada/Pedrógão 12 H 7
4910 Orbacém 1 B 4
6230 Orca 9 E 7
7220 Oriola 11 J 6
4730 Oriz 1 B 5
6200 Orjais 5 E 7
6120 Ortiga 8 G 5
2425 Ortigosa 7 F 4
6185 Orvalho 8 E 6
2580 Ota 7 G 4
3840 Ouca 4 D 4
5400 Oucidres 2 B 7
7370 Ouguela 9 G 7
5425 Oura 2 B 6
2490 Ourem 8 F 4
3060 Ourentã 4 E 4
7670 Ourique 14 K 5
6230 Ourondo 5 E 6
5320 Ousilhao 3 B 8
2900 Outão 10 J 4
2565 Outeiro da Cabeça 7 G 3
6430 Outeiro de Gats 6 D 7
5400 Outeiro Seco 2 B 7
5300 Outeiro/Bragança 3 B 8
3660 Outeiro/Castro Daire 5 D 6
5470 Outeiro/Travassos 2 B 6
4900 Outeiro/Viana do Castelo 1 B 4

2040 Outeiro da Cortiçada 7 G 4
3060 Outil 4 E 4
5100 Ovadas 5 C 6
3880 Ovar 4 D 4
3440 Óvoa 5 E 5

P

5200 Paçô 3 C 8
5120 Paço 5 C 6
2780 Paço de Acros 10 H 3
4560 Paço de Sousa 1 C 5
5300 Paçó/Bragança 3 B 8
5320 Paçó/Vilarinho 3 B 8
6290 Paços da Serra 5 E 6
4590 Paços de Ferreira 1 C 5
4625 Paços de Gaiolo 5 C 5
3670 Paços de Vilharigues 5 D 5
8200 Paderne/Algoz 14 L 5
4960 Paderne/Melgaço 1 A 5
4700 Padim da Graça 1 B 5
4940 Padornelo 1 B 4
5470 Padornelos 2 B 6
6150 Padrão 8 F 6
5445 Padrela 2 B 7
5470 Padroso 2 B 6
5385 Pádua Freixo 2 B 7
6430 Pai Penela 6 D 7
5370 Pai Torto 2 B 7
6000 Paiágua 9 F 6
2305 Paialvo 8 F 5
3080 Paião 4 E 4
2550 Painho 7 G 3
4860 Painzela 1 B 5
2240 Paio Mendes 8 F 5
6400 Pala/Pinhel 6 D 7
3450 Pala/Sobral 4 E 5
5210 Palaçoulo 3 C 9
3770 Palhaça 4 D 4
6100 Palhais/Sertã 8 F 5
6420 Palhais/Trancoso 5 D 7
8800 Palheirinhos 14 L 6
3080 Palheiros de Quiaios 4 E 4
5090 Palheiros/Mirandela 2 C 7
7670 Palheiros/Ourique 14 K 5
7580 Palma 11 J 4
3720 Palmaz 4 D 5
4905 Palme 1 B 4
4700 Palmeira 1 B 5
8670 Palmeirinha 13 L 4
2950 Palmela 10 H 4
6000 Palvarinho 9 F 6
3050 Pampilhosa 4 E 5
3320 Pampilhosa da Serra 8 E 6
7900 Panasqueira/ Ferreira do Alentejo 11 J 5
6225 Panasqueira/Fundão 5 E 6
7670 Panoias 14 K 5
6300 Panoias de Cima 6 D 7
4750 Panque 1 B 4
3430 Papízios 5 E 5
4850 Parada de Bouro 1 B 5
5000 Parada de Cunhos 2 C 6
3600 Parada de Ester 5 D 5
4730 Parada de Gatim 1 B 4
3460 Parada de Gonta 5 D 6

Parada de Monteiros (P) **Praia de Paramos** P

5450 Parada de Monteiros 2 B 6
5060 Parada de Pinhao 2 C 6
4960 Parada do Monte 1 A 5
5300 Parada/Bragança 3 B 8
3430 Parada/Carregal do Sal 5 E 5
6355 Parada/Guarda 6 D 7
5350 Parada/Mogadouro 3 C 8
4880 Paradança 1 C 6
5060 Paradela de Guiaes 2 C 6
3740 Paradela/Albergaria-a-Velha 4 D 5
4970 Paradela/Arcos de Valdevez 1 B 5
5400 Paradela/Chavez 2 B 7
5210 Paradela/Miranda do Douro 3 B 9
5470 Paradela/Mogadouro 2 B 6
5120 Paradela/Tarouca 5 C 6
5200 Paradela/Travassos 3 C 8
5300 Paradinha Velha 3 B 8
5340 Paradinha/Macedo de Cavaleiros 3 C 8
3620 Paradinha/Tarouca 5 C 6
5300 Paradinho Nova 3 B 8
4550 Paraiso 4 C 5
5140 Parambos 2 C 7
5300 Parâmio 3 B 8
4500 Paramos 4 D 4
3465 Paranho 5 D 5
6270 Paranhos 5 E 6
2400 Parceiros 7 F 4
3250 Parcerias 8 F 5
7160 Pardais 12 H 7
4880 Pardelhas 2 C 6
3860 Pardilhó 4 D 4
2775 Parede 10 H 3
5130 Paredes da Breira 5 C 7
4940 Paredes de Coura 1 B 4
4630 Paredes de Viadores 1 C 5
5300 Paredes/Bragança 3 B 8
4580 Paredes/Penafiel 1 C 5
8150 Parizes 14 L 6
2140 Parreira 8 G 5
6005 Partida 9 E 6
2430 Passagem 7 F 4
4860 Passos/Cabeceiras de Basto 1 C 5
5370 Passos/Mirandela 2 C 7
3460 Passos/Mosteiro da Fráguas 5 D 6
5400 Pastoria 2 B 6
8200 Patã de Baixo 14 L 5
2445 Pataias 7 F 4
6215 Paul 5 E 6
2200 Paúl 8 F 5
4660 Paus 5 C 6
7490 Pavia 11 H 5
6000 Pé da Serra 9 F 6
8700 Pechão 14 L 6
4550 Pedorido 4 C 5
4900 Pedra Alta 1 B 4
4755 Pedra Furada 1 C 4
4820 Pedraido 1 B 5
8650 Pedralva 13 L 4
5470 Pedrario 2 B 6

7600 Pedras Brancas 14 K 5
5450 Pedras Salgadas 2 B 6
2480 Pedreiras 7 F 4
3270 Pedrógão Grande 8 F 5
6100 Pedrógão Pequeno 8 F 5
7960 Pedrógão/Beja 12 J 6
6090 Pedrógão/Peamacor 9 E 7
2350 Pedrógão/Torres Novas 8 F 4
7050 Pedrógão/Vendas Novas 11 H 5
2425 Pedrógão/Vieira de Leiria 7 F 4
6300 Pega 6 E 7
5070 Pegarinhos 2 C 7
2205 Pego 8 G 5
2985 Pegões-Estação 11 H 4
6060 Peireial 9 F 7
3100 Pelariga 8 F 4
3250 Pelmá 8 F 5
8100 Pena 14 L 5
5210 Pena Branca 3 B 9
6320 Pena Lobe 6 E 7
5200 Pena Róia 3 C 8
3570 Pena Verde 5 D 7
5090 Penabeice 5 C 7
3360 Penacova 4 E 5
4560 Penafiel 1 C 5
3400 Penalva de Alva 5 E 6
3550 Penalva do Castelo 5 D 6
6090 Penamacor 6 E 7
3650 Pendilhe 5 D 6
6300 Penedo da Sé 6 E 7
7800 Penedo Gordo 14 K 6
3640 Penedono 5 D 7
3230 Penela 8 E 5
3630 Penela da Beira 5 C 7
6440 Penha de Aguia 6 D 7
6060 Penha Garcia 9 E 7
6200 Penhas da Saúde 5 E 6
5320 Penhas Juntas 3 B 7
6120 Penhascoso 8 F 5
2520 Peniche 7 G 3
7750 Penilhos 14 K 6
5450 Pensalvos 2 B 6
4960 Penso/Melgaço 1 A 5
3640 Penso/Moimento da Beira 5 D 6
5100 Penude 5 C 6
8365 Pêra 14 L 5
6300 Pêra do Moço 6 D 7
6200 Peraboa 6 E 7
4455 Perafita 1 C 4
5090 Perafita 2 C 6
6030 Perais 9 F 6
2550 Peral/Cadaval 7 G 3
6150 Peral/Vila de Rei 8 F 6
6030 Perdigão 8 F 6
5340 Peredo 3 C 8
5200 Peredo da Bemposta 3 C 8
5160 Peredo dos Castelhanos 6 C 7
3140 Pereira/Ameal 4 E 4
8500 Pereira/Mexilhoeira Grande 13 L 4
5370 Pereira/Mirandela 2 C 7
5470 Pereira/Venda Nova 2 B 6

7665 Pereiras 14 L 5
2580 Pereiro de Palhacana 7 G 3
8970 Pereiro/Alcoutim 14 L 6
2240 Pereiro/Freixianda 8 F 5
6120 Pereiro/Mação 8 F 5
5120 Pereiro/Moimenta da Beira 5 C 7
6400 Pereiro/Pinhel 6 D 7
8700 Pereiro/São Brás de Alportel 14 L 6
5140 Pereiros 2 C 7
4750 Perelhal 1 B 4
6150 Pergulho Cimeiro 8 F 6
8375 Perna Seca 14 L 5
2000 Pernes 7 G 4
2550 Pêro Moniz 7 G 3
8670 Pero Negro 13 L 4
2715 Pêro Pinheiro 10 H 3
6300 Pêro Soares 5 D 7
6230 Pêro Viseu 5 E 7
7900 Peroguarda 11 J 5
4415 Perozinho 4 C 4
4900 Perre 1 B 4
7330 Perreiro 9 G 7
5050 Peso da Régua 2 C 6
6200 Peso/Covilhã 5 E 6
5200 Peso/Mogadoura 3 C 8
7960 Peso/Pedrógão 11 J 6
3320 Pessegueiro 8 E 5
3740 Pessegueiro do Vouga 4 D 5
5300 Petisqueira 3 B 8
6350 Peva/Nave de Haver 6 D 8
3620 Peva/Vila Nova da Paiva 5 D 6
2240 Pias/Freixianda 8 F 5
4950 Pias/Monção 1 A 4
7830 Pias/Vale de Vargo 15 J 7
7670 Piçarras 14 K 5
4730 Pico de Regalados 1 B 5
7750 Picoitos 15 K 6
5210 Picote 3 C 9
2430 Pilado 7 F 4
3660 Pindelo dos Milagres 5 D 6
3550 Pindo 5 D 6
5300 Pinela 3 B 8
5230 Pinelo 3 B 8
5140 Pinhal do Norte 2 C 7
6270 Pinhanços 5 E 6
5085 Pinhao 2 C 6
3720 Pinheiro da Bemposta 4 D 5
3420 Pinheiro de Coja 5 E 6
2140 Pinheiro Grande 8 G 5
5320 Pinheiro Novo 2 B 7
2910 Pinheiro/Alcácer do Sal 10 J 4
4830 Pinheiro/Braga 1 B 5
4575 Pinheiro/Cabeça Santa 1 C 5
3600 Pinheiro/Castro Daire 5 D 6
3680 Pinheiro/Oliveira de Frades 5 D 5
3570 Pinheiro/Vila Nova de Paiva 5 D 7
6400 Pinhel 6 D 7
5460 Pinho/Chaves 2 B 6
3660 Pinho/São Pedro do Sul 5 D 5
6400 Pínzio 6 D 7

3305 Piódão 5 E 6
3050 Pisão/Arazede 4 E 5
7300 Pisão/Portalegre 9 G 6
5470 Pitoes das Júnias 2 B 6
3060 Pocariça 4 E 4
2965 Poceirão 10 H 4
3070 Poço da Cruz 4 E 4
6430 Poço do Canto 6 C 7
6355 Poço Velho 6 D 8
5340 Podence 3 B 8
3230 Podentes 4 E 5
5100 Poiares/Peso da Régua 2 C 6
5180 Poiares/Torre de Moncorvo 6 C 8
6000 Pomar 8 F 6
6400 Pomares/Guarda 6 D 7
3305 Pomares/Oliveira do Hospital 5 E 6
7340 Pombal/Arronches 9 G 7
5350 Pombal/Mogadouro 3 C 7
3100 Pombal/Pelariga 8 F 4
5140 Pombal/Vila Flor 2 C 7
3130 Pombalinho/Redinha 8 E 5
2150 Pombalinho/São Vicente do Paul 8 G 4
5300 Pombares 3 B 8
2240 Pombeira 8 F 5
3300 Pombeiras 5 E 5
3300 Pombeiro da Beira 5 E 5
5470 Pondras 2 B 6
4730 Ponte 1 B 5
4980 Ponte da Barca 1 B 5
3640 Ponte de Abade 5 D 7
4990 Ponte de Lima 1 B 4
7400 Ponte de Sor 8 G 5
3840 Ponte de Vagos 4 E 4
2560 Ponte do Rol 7 G 3
4600 Ponte Nova 1 C 5
2070 Pontével 7 G 4
5070 Pópulo 2 C 6
8400 Porches 14 L 5
5200 Porrais 3 C 8
7300 Portalegre 9 G 7
7220 Portel 11 J 6
4870 Portela de Santa Eulália 2 B 6
4730 Portela de Vade 1 B 5
3140 Portela/Ança 4 E 4
4970 Portela/Arcos de Valdevez 1 B 5
8800 Portela/Lajes 14 L 6
4950 Portela/Monçao 1 B 5
6110 Portela/Vila de Rei 8 F 5
5000 Portela/Vila Real 2 C 6
8600 Portelas 13 L 4
5300 Portelo 3 B 8
8500 Portimão 13 L 4
4000 Porto 1 C 4
2135 Porto Alto 10 H 4
7520 Porto Covo da Bandeira 13 K 4
3320 Porto da Balça 5 E 6
6300 Porto da Carne 6 D 7
7330 Porto da Espada 9 G 7
7630 Porto das Barcas 13 K 4

8500 Porto de Lagos 13 L 4
2480 Porto de Mós 7 F 4
2070 Porto de Muge 7 G 4
6355 Porto de Ovelha 6 D 8
2460 Porto do Carro 7 F 4
3320 Portolo do Fojo 8 F 5
4960 Portos 1 A 5
3060 Portunhos 4 E 4
4900 Portuzelo 1 B 4
5430 Possacos 2 B 7
7350 Posto Fiscal do Caia 12 H 7
6300 Pousada 6 D 7
3100 Pousadras Vedras 8 F 4
3240 Pousaflores 8 F 5
6320 Pousafoles do Bispo 6 D 7
6400 Póvoa d`El-Rei 6 D 7
3060 Póvoa da Lomba 4 E 4
5425 Póvoa de Agrações 2 B 6
6230 Póvoa de Atalaia 9 E 7
3530 Póvoa de Cervães 5 D 6
4830 Póvoa de Lanhoso 1 B 5
3420 Póvoa de Midões 5 E 6
2560 Póvoa de Penafirme 7 G 3
3630 Póvoa de Penela 5 C 7
6000 Póvoa de Rio de Moinhos 9 F 6
2625 Póvoa de Santa Iria 10 H 3
2000 Póvoa de Santarém 7 G 4
4490 Póvoa de Varzim 1 C 4
6420 Póvoa do Concelho 6 D 7
7320 Póvoa e Meadas 9 F 6
7860 Póvoa/Oliva de la Frontera 12 J 7
5210 Póvoa/Pena Branca 3 B 9
3650 Póvoa/Pendilhe 5 D 6
3500 Povolide 5 D 6
5225 Prado Gatao 3 C 9
4730 Prado(Santa Maria) 1 B 5
6360 Prados/Guarda 5 D 7
6400 Prados/Pinhel 6 D 7
2550 Pragança 7 G 3
4405 Praia da Aguda 4 C 4
2530 Praia da Areia Branca 7 G 3
3830 Praia da Barra 4 D 4
2900 Praia da Comenda 10 H 4
4405 Praia da Granja 4 C 4
3060 Praia da Tocha 4 E 4
2705 Praia das Maças 10 H 3
2925 Praia de Alpertuche 10 J 4
3885 Praia de Cortegaça 4 D 4
3885 Praia de Esmoriz 4 D 4
3070 Praia de Mira 4 E 4
4500 Praia de Paramos 4 D 4

P

Praia de Tróia   P   **Santa Luzia/Tavira**

7580 Praia de Tróia 10 J 4
2430 Praia de Viera 7 F 4
2755 Praia do Guincho 10 H 3
2260 Praia do Ribatejo 8 G 5
7450 Prazeres 12 H 7
4800 Prazins(Santa Fulemia) 1 C 5
3130 Presa 4 E 4
3750 Préstimo 4 D 5
6150 Proença-a-Nova 8 F 6
6060 Proença-a-Velha 9 E 7
4970 Proselo 1 B 5
6430 Prova 6 D 7
5060 Provesende 2 C 6
3250 Pussos 8 F 5

Q
5320 Quadra 3 B 7
6320 Quadrasais 6 E 8
8125 Quarteira 14 L 5
8700 Quatrim do Sul 14 L 6
2065 Quebradas 7 G 4
4990 Queijada 1 B 4
4820 Queimadela 1 B 5
3670 Queirã 5 D 5
3650 Queiriga 5 D 6
6370 Queiriz 5 D 7
8700 Quelfes 14 L 6
2746 Queluz 10 H 3
8100 Querença 14 L 6
3080 Quiaios 4 E 4
5450 Quinta 2 C 6
6440 Quintã de Pero Martins 6 D 7
2950 Quinta do Anjo 10 H 4
7540 Quinta do Corona 14 K 5
5300 Quintanilha 3 B 8
3810 Quintãs 4 D 4
2040 Quintas 7 G 4
3870 Quintas do Norte 4 D 4
3530 Quintela de Azurara 5 D 6
5300 Quintela de Lampaças 3 B 8
7800 Quintos 14 K 6
5320 Quirás 2 B 7

R
7300 Rabaça 9 G 7
3230 Rabaçal/Soure 8 E 5
6430 Rabaçal/Trancoso 6 D 7
6150 Rabacinas 8 F 6
5300 Rabal 3 B 8
4590 Raimonda 1 C 5
4550 Raiva 4 C 5
5450 Raiz do Monte 2 C 6
3100 Ramalhais de Cima 8 F 4
2565 Ramalhal 7 G 3
6430 Ranhados/Vila Nova de Foz Côa 6 D 7
3500 Ranhados/Viseu 5 D 6
2080 Raposa 8 G 4
8650 Raposeira 13 L 4
6320 Rapoula do Côa 6 E 7
3560 Rãs 5 D 6
4570 Rates 1 C 4
6360 Ratoeira 5 D 7
4600 Real 1 C 5
4550 Real/Castelo de Paiva 4 C 5
3550 Real/Mangualde 5 D 6
6420 Reboleiro 5 D 7
6320 Rebolosa 6 E 8

5300 Rebordaos 3 B 8
4600 Rebordelo/Celorico de Basto 1 C 6
5335 Rebordelo/Chaves 2 B 7
5300 Rebordinhos 3 B 8
4990 Rebordoes/Ponte de Lima 1 B 4
4795 Rebordoes/Santo Tirso 1 C 5
5425 Rebordondo 2 B 6
4920 Reboreda 1 B 4
4585 Recarei 1 C 5
3100 Redinha 8 E 4
5400 Redondelo 2 B 6
7170 Redondo 12 H 6
5300 Reféga 3 B 8
4990 Refoios do Lima 1 B 4
4820 Regadas 1 C 5
4820 Rego 1 C 5
3250 Rego da Murta 8 F 5
2400 Regueira de Pontes 7 F 4
7050 Reguengo 11 H 5
2440 Reguengo do Fetal 7 F 4
2530 Reguengo Grande 7 G 3
7200 Reguengos de Monsaraz 12 J 6
6440 Reigada 6 D 8
3680 Reigoso 4 D 5
7630 Relíquias 14 K 5
6150 Relva da Louça 8 F 6
3300 Relvas 5 E 6
4755 Remlhe 1 C 4
5200 Remondes 3 C 8
6320 Rendo 6 E 7
4990 Rendufe/Arcos de Valdevez 1 B 4
4720 Rendufe/Vila Verde 1 B 4
4830 Rendufinho 1 B 5
4585 Repordosa 1 C 5
3800 Requeixo 4 D 4
3600 Reriz 5 D 6
4660 Resende 5 C 6
6000 Retaxo 9 F 6
7370 Retiro 12 H 7
5450 Revel 2 C 6
2350 Riachos 8 G 4
4910 Riba de Âncora 1 B 4
4765 Riba de Ave 1 C 5
4950 Riba de Mouro 1 A 5
4640 Ribadouro 5 C 5
3510 Ribafeita 5 D 6
5140 Ribalonga/Torre de Moncorvo 2 C 7
5070 Ribalonga/Vila Real 2 C 6
2530 Ribamar/Lourinhã 7 G 3
2640 Ribamar/Santo Isidoro 7 G 3
6290 Ribamondego 5 D 6
4890 Ribas 1 C 5
3850 Ribeira de Fráguas 4 D 5
7300 Ribeira de Nisa 9 G 7
4870 Ribeira de Pena 2 B 6
7630 Ribeira do Seissal 13 K 4
6300 Ribeira dos Carinhos 6 D 7
3880 Ribeira/Ovar 4 D 4
4990 Ribeira/Ponte de Lima 1 B 4
4840 Ribeira/Vila Verde 1 B 5
3680 Ribeiradio 4 D 5
4764 Ribeirão 1 C 4
5360 Ribeirinha 2 C 7
4820 Ribeiros 1 C 5

3600 Ribolhos 5 D 6
4845 Rio Caldo 1 B 5
2435 Rio de Couros 8 F 5
5320 Rio de Fornos 3 B 7
3500 Rio de Loba 5 D 6
6420 Rio de Mel 5 D 7
2200 Rio de Moinhos/ Abrantes 8 G 5
7600 Rio de Moinhos/ Aljustrel 14 K 5
7150 Rio de Moinhos/ Estremoz 12 H 6
3560 Rio de Moinhos/ Sátão 5 D 6
7595 Rio de Moinhos/ Torrão 11 J 5
4575 Rio de Moinhos/Vila Boa do Bispo 1 C 5
2635 Rio de Mouro 10 H 3
5300 Rio de Onor 3 B 8
4860 Rio Douro 1 B 6
5300 Río Frío 3 B 8
4970 Rio Frio/Arcos de Valdevez 1 B 5
2040 Rio Maior 7 G 4
4480 Rio Mau/Póvoa de Varzim 1 C 4
4730 Rio Mau/Vila Verde 1 B 4
3450 Rio Milheiro 5 E 5
4435 Rio Tinto 1 C 4
6290 Rio Torto/Gouveia 5 D 6
5430 Rio Torto/Valpaços 2 B 7
3220 Rio Vide 4 E 5
3640 Riodades 5 C 6
5060 Roalde 2 C 6
6300 Rocamondo 6 D 7
3740 Rocas do Vouga 4 D 5
2550 Rochaforte 7 G 3
6000 Rochas de Baixo 9 F 6
6300 Rochoso 6 D 7
3330 Roda Fundeira 8 E 5
4960 Rodeiro 1 A 5
8670 Rogil 13 L 4
5360 Róios 2 C 7
7780 Rolão 14 K 6
2540 Roliça 7 G 3
4940 Romarigaes 1 B 4
3560 Romãs 5 D 6
2000 Romeira 7 G 4
5370 Romeu 2 B 7
7540 Roncão 10 J 4
7750 Ronçao 14 L 6
4800 Ronfe 1 C 5
4795 Roriz 1 C 5
4750 Roriz/Barcelos 1 B 4
3550 Roriz/Sátão 5 D 6
7250 Rosário/Alandroal 12 H 7
7700 Rosário/Ourique 14 K 5
6060 Rosmaninhal 9 F 7
3600 Rossão 5 D 6
4540 Rossas/Burgo 4 D 5
4850 Rossas/Viera do Minho 1 B 5
2205 Rossio ao Sul do Tejo 8 G 5
3620 Rua 5 D 6
4940 Rubiaes 1 B 4
4850 Ruivaes 1 B 5
4980 Ruivos 1 B 5
6320 Ruivós 6 E 8
2565 Runa 7 G 3
6320 Ruvina 6 E 7

S
4950 Sá/Melgço 1 A 5
5430 Sá/Valpaços 2 B 7

2305 Sabacheira 8 F 5
7665 Sabóia 13 L 5
5060 Sabrosa 2 C 6
5450 Sabroso 2 B 6
6320 Sabugal 6 E 7
3460 Sabugosa 5 D 5
7040 Sabugueiro/Arraiolos 11 H 5
6270 Sabugueiro/Seia 5 E 6
2685 Sacavém 10 H 3
7875 Safara 12 J 7
6400 Safurdão 6 D 7
4950 Sago 1 A 5
8650 Sagres 13 L 4
4850 Salamonde 1 B 5
6050 Salavessa 9 F 6
5200 Saldanha 3 C 8
5350 Saldonha 3 C 8
6360 Salgueirais 5 D 7
6400 Salgueiral 6 D 7
6000 Salgueiro do Campo 9 F 6
6230 Salgueiro/Capinha 5 E 7
2540 Salgueiro/Carvalhal 7 G 3
5200 Salgueiro/ Mogadouro 3 C 8
3840 Salgueiro/Vagos 4 D 4
8100 Salir 14 L 5
2500 Salir de Matos 7 G 3
2500 Salir do Porto 7 G 3
3865 Salreu 4 D 4
5300 Salsas 3 B 8
5340 Salselas 3 B 8
5470 Salto 2 B 6
7800 Salvada 14 K 6
4600 Salvador do Monte 1 C 5
2080 Salvador/Fazendas de Almeirim 8 G 5
6090 Salvador/Penamacor 9 E 7
2120 Salvaterra de Magos 7 G 4
4950 Salvaterra de Miño 1 A 5
6060 Salvaterra do Extremo 9 F 8
3610 Salzedas 5 C 6
5400 Samaiôis 2 B 7
5350 Sambade 3 C 8
6270 Sameice 5 E 6
6260 Sameiro 5 E 7
5300 Samil 3 B 8
5100 Samodaes 2 C 6
5360 Samoes 2 C 7
2135 Samora Correia 10 H 4
2890 Samouco 10 H 3
5200 Sampaio/Mogadouro 3 C 8
2970 Sampaio/Sesimbra 10 J 3
5360 Sampaio/Vila Flor 2 C 7
4980 Sampriz 1 B 5
3130 Samuel 4 E 4
4800 Sande/Braga 1 B 5
4625 Sande/Vila Boa do Bispo 1 C 5
4415 Sandim 4 C 4
6270 Sandomil 5 E 6
4595 Sanfins de Ferreira 1 C 5
5070 Sanfins do Douro 2 C 6
5400 Sanfins/Chaves 2 B 7
5430 Sanfins/Valpaços 2 B 7
3780 Sangalhos 4 E 5
5000 Sanguinhedo 2 C 6
5200 Sanhoane 3 C 8

5400 Sanjurge 2 B 6
8000 Santa Bárbara de Nexe 14 L 6
7780 Santa Bárbara de Padrões 14 K 6
2530 Santa Bárbara/ Lourinhã 7 G 3
7665 Santa Bárbara/ SãoTeotónio 13 L 4
3650 Santa Bárbara/Sátão 5 D 6
8800 Santa Catarina da Fonte do Bispo 14 L 6
2495 Santa Catarina da Serra 7 F 4
7580 Santa Catarina/ Alcácer 11 J 5
2500 Santa Catarina/ Benedita 7 G 3
2305 Santa Cita 8 F 5
7700 Santa Clara-a-Nova 14 L 5
7665 Santa Clara-a-Velha 13 K 5
7800 Santa Clara do Louredo 14 K 6
3440 Santa Comba Dão 5 E 5
5300 Santa Comba de Rossas 3 B 8
5360 Santa Comba de Vilariça 2 C 7
6270 Santa Comba/ Gouveia 5 E 6
4990 Santa Comba/Ponte de Lima 1 B 4
5150 Santa Comba/Vila Nova de Foz Côa 6 D 7
5340 Santa Combinha 3 B 8
3660 Santa Cruz da Trapa 5 D 5
4640 Santa Cruz do Douro 1 C 5
4990 Santa Cruz do Lima 1 B 5
7700 Santa Cruz/ Almodôvar 14 L 6
5320 Santa Cruz/ Bragança 3 B 8
7540 Santa Cruz/Santo André 10 J 4
2560 Santa Cruz/Silveira 7 G 3
2410 Santa Eufémia/Leiria 7 F 4
6400 Santa Eufémia/ Trancoso 6 D 7
5070 Santa Eugénia 2 C 7
2665 Santa Eulália/ Almargem do Bispo 10 H 3
7350 Santa Eulália/ Campo Maior 12 G 7
6270 Santa Eulália/Seia 5 E 6
7830 Santa Iria 15 K 6
2695 Santa Iria de Azóia 10 H 3
7040 Santa Justa/ Arraiolos 11 H 6
2100 Santa Justa/Couço 11 G 5
8970 Santa Justa/Martim Longo 14 L 6
5400 Santa Leocadia 2 B 7
5120 Santa Leocádia 5 C 6
7670 Santa Luzia/São Luis 14 K 5
8800 Santa Luzia/Tavira 14 L 6

Santa Luzia/Viana do Castelo ⓟ **Senhora da Peneda** Ⓟ

4900 Santa Luzia/Viana do Castelo 1 B 4
7570 Santa Margarida da Serra 10 J 4
7570 Santa Margarida do Sádão 11 J 5
5445 Santa Maria de Emeres 2 B 7
4550 Santa Maria de Sardoura 4 C 5
4640 Santa Marinha do Zezere 1 C 6
4870 Santa Marinha/Cabeceiras de Basto 2 B 6
4950 Santa Marinha/Monçao 1 A 5
6270 Santa Marinha/Seia 5 E 6
8970 Santa Marta 15 L 6
5450 Santa Marta da Montanha 2 B 6
5030 Santa Marta de Penaguiao 2 C 6
7580 Santa Susana/Alcácer do Sal 11 J 5
7000 Santa Susana/Èvora 12 H 6
5430 Santa Valha 2 B 7
7800 Santa Vitória 14 K 5
7100 Santa Vitória do Ameixial 12 H 6
5320 Santahla 2 B 7
6300 Santana da Azinha 6 E 7
7670 Santana da Serra 14 K 5
7750 Santana de Cambas 15 K 6
3080 Santana/Alhadas 4 E 4
2970 Santana/Sesimbra 10 J 3
7220 Santana/Vidigueira 11 J 6
3520 Santar 5 D 6
2000 Santarém 7 G 4
3240 Santiago da Guarda 8 F 5
3465 Santiago de Besteiros 5 D 5
3530 Santiago de Cassurrães 5 D 6
3100 Santiago de Litém 8 F 4
2230 Santiago de Montalerge 8 F 5
7540 Santiago do Cacém 10 J 4
7050 Santiago do Escoural 11 H 5
2630 Santiago dos Velhos 10 H 3
7200 Santiago Maior 12 H 7
5110 Santiago/Lamego 5 C 6
5200 Santiago/Mogadouro 3 C 8
6270 Santiago/Seia 5 E 6
7450 Santo Aleixo 12 H 7
7875 Santo Aleixo da Restauração 12 J 7
4870 Santo Alexio de Além Tâmega 2 B 6
7875 Santo Amador 12 J 7
7470 Santo Amaro 12 H 6
6000 Santo André das Tojeiras 9 F 6
2830 Santo André/Barreiro 10 H 3

5470 Santo André/Chaves 2 B 6
7500 Santo André/Santiago do Cácem 10 J 4
7330 Santo António das Areias 9 G 7
5400 Santo António de Monforte 2 B 7
2665 Santo Estêvão das Galés 10 H 3
5400 Santo Estêvão/Chaves 2 B 7
6320 Santo Estêvão/Sabugal 6 E 7
2130 Santo Estêvão/Samora Correira 10 H 4
8800 Santo Estêvao/Tavira 14 L 6
7350 Santo Ildefonso 12 H 7
2640 Santo Isidoro 7 H 3
2985 Santo Isidro de Pegões 10 H 4
2590 Santo Quintino 7 G 3
4780 Santo Tirso 1 C 5
3140 Santo Varão 4 E 4
6120 Santos 8 F 6
3500 Santos Evos 5 D 6
5230 Santulhao 3 B 8
7700 São Barnabé 14 L 5
6040 São Bartolomeu 8 G 6
7540 São Bartolomeu da Serra 10 J 4
8375 São Bartolomeu de Messines 14 L 5
7750 São Bartolomeu de Via Glória 14 K 6
7220 São Bartolomeu do Outeiro 11 J 6
2530 São Bartolomeu dos Galegos 7 G 3
4940 São Bento da Porta 1 B 4
7100 São Bento de Ana Loura 12 H 7
7100 São Bento do Ameixial 12 H 6
7100 São Bento do Cortiço 12 H 6
7830 São Brás 14 K 6
8150 São Brás de Alportel 14 L 6
7800 São Brissos/Beja 11 J 6
7050 São Brissos/Èvora 11 H 5
3510 São Cipriano 5 D 6
7050 São Cristóvão 11 J 5
7540 São Domingos 13 K 4
2205 São Facundo 8 G 5
4405 São Felix da Marinha 4 C 4
7540 São Francisco da Serra 10 J 4
7050 São Geraldo 11 H 5
7040 São Gregório 11 H 6
3800 São Jacinto 4 D 4
5230 São Joanico 3 B 9
3600 São Joaninho/Pendilhe 5 D 6
3440 São Joaninho/Santa Comba Dão 5 E 5
3420 São João da Boa Vista 5 E 5
5445 São Joao da Corveira 2 B 7
3700 São João da Madeira 4 D 5

5130 São Joao da Pesqueira 2 C 7
2040 São João da Ribeira 7 G 4
3680 São João da Serra 4 D 5
2695 São João da Talha 10 H 3
2705 São João das Lampas 10 H 3
3440 São João de Areias 5 E 5
5100 São João de Fontoura 5 C 6
3850 São João de Loure 4 D 4
3500 São João de Lourosa 5 D 6
7600 São João de Negrilhos 14 K 5
3610 São João de Tarouca 5 D 6
4520 São João de Ver 4 D 4
3020 São João do Campo 4 E 4
3475 São João do Monte/Guardão 4 D 5
3520 São João do Monte/Nelas 5 D 6
6110 São João do Peso 8 F 5
7750 São João dos Caldeireiros 14 K 6
2600 São João dos Montes 10 H 3
5320 São Jomil 2 B 7
4970 São Jorge 1 B 5
6225 São Jorge da Beira 5 E 6
2100 São José da Lamarosa 8 G 5
6120 São José das Matas 8 F 6
7300 São Julião 9 G 7
5400 São Julião de Montenegro 2 B 7
5300 São Julião de Palácios 3 B 8
7100 São Lourenço de Mamporcão 12 H 6
5060 São Lourenço de Ribapinhao 2 C 6
3780 São Lourenço do Bairro 4 E 5
7630 São Luís 13 K 4
2495 São Mamede 7 F 4
5070 São Mamede de Ribatua 2 C 7
7570 São Mamede do Sádão 11 J 5
7000 São Manços 11 J 6
7780 São Marcos da Ataboeira 14 K 6
7200 São Marcos do Campo 12 J 6
8375 São Marcos sa Serra 14 L 5
5300 São Martín del Pedroso 3 B 8
3300 São Martinho da Cortiça 5 E 5
3720 São Martinho da Gândara 4 D 4
7670 São Martinho das Amoreiras 14 K 5
5110 São Martinho das Chãs 5 C 6
5210 São Martinho de Angueira 3 B 9
5060 São Martinho de Antas 2 C 6

4660 São Martinho de Mouros 5 C 6
5200 São Martinho do Peso 3 C 8
2460 São Martinho do Porto 7 F 3
7800 São Matias 11 J 6
6060 São Miguel de Acha 9 E 7
7000 São Miguel de Machede 11 H 6
3350 São Miguel de Poiares 4 E 5
3560 São Miguel de Vila Boa 5 D 6
4540 São Miguel do Mato 4 D 5
3460 São Miguel do Outeiro 5 D 5
7750 São Miguel do Pinheiro 14 K 6
2205 São Miguel do Rio Torto 8 G 5
6290 São Paio 5 D 6
3360 São Paio da Farinha Podre 5 E 5
3000 São Paulo de Frades 4 E 5
5470 São Pedro 2 B 6
2560 São Pedro da Cadeira 7 G 3
4510 São Pedro da Cova 1 C 4
4930 São Pedro da Torre 1 B 4
5400 São Pedro de Agostém 2 B 7
3360 São Pedro de Alva 5 E 5
3720 São Pedro de Casteloes 4 D 5
2430 São Pedro de Muel 7 F 3
6350 São Pedro de Rio Seco 6 D 8
5300 São Pedro de Serracenos 3 B 8
7750 São Pedro de Solis 14 L 6
5370 São Pedro de Vale do Conde 2 C 7
5430 São Pedro de Veiga de Lila 2 C 7
6150 São Pedro do Esteval 8 F 6
3660 São Pedro do Sul 5 D 5
5385 São Pedro Velho 2 B 7
6270 São Romão 5 E 6
7595 São Romão do Sado 11 J 5
5370 São Salvador 2 C 7
7330 São Salvador da Aramenha 9 G 7
7460 São Saturnino 12 G 6
7000 São Sebastião da Giesteira 11 H 5
7750 São Sebastião dos Carros 14 K 6
3020 São Silvestre 4 E 4
6050 São Simão 9 F 6
3100 São Simão de Litém 8 F 4
7630 São Teotónio 13 K 4
5000 São Tomé do Castelo 2 C 6
2100 São Torcato/Coruche 11 H 4
4800 São Torcato/Guimaraes 1 C 5
5400 São Vicente 2 B 7
6005 São Vicente da Beira 9 E 6
3680 São Vicente de Lafões 5 D 5

3880 São Vicente de Pererira Juzã 4 D 4
2000 São Vicente do Paul 7 G 4
7350 São Vicente e Ventosa 12 H 7
4920 Sapardos 1 B 4
2590 Sapataria 10 H 3
5460 Sapelos 2 B 6
5460 Sapiaos 2 B 6
7750 Sapos 14 K 6
6160 Sardeiras da Baixo 8 F 6
2230 Sardoal 8 F 5
2860 Sarilhos Grande 10 H 4
8100 Sarnadas 14 L 5
6030 Sarnadas de Ródão 9 F 6
3300 Sarnadela 5 E 5
6160 Sarnandas de Baixo 8 F 6
6160 Sarnandas de São Simão 8 F 6
5470 Sarraquinhos 2 B 6
6000 Sarzedas 9 F 6
3240 Sarzedela 8 F 5
3300 Sarzedo/Arganil 5 E 5
6200 Sarzedo/Covilhã 5 E 7
3620 Sarzedo/Moimenta da Beira 5 C 6
3560 Sátão 5 D 6
6270 Sazes da Beira 5 E 6
3360 Sazes do Lorvão 4 E 5
5400 Seara Velha 2 B 6
5155 Sebadelhe 6 C 7
6420 Sebadelhe da Serra 5 D 7
3300 Secarias 5 E 5
7440 Seda 8 G 6
5050 Sedielos 2 C 6
3620 Segões 5 D 6
6060 Segura 9 F 8
6270 Seia 5 E 6
2435 Seiça 8 F 4
4820 Seidoes 1 C 5
4870 Seirós 2 B 6
5320 Seixas/Quadra 2 B 7
5155 Seixas/Vila Nova de Foz Côa 6 C 7
4910 Seixas/Vila Praia de Áncora 1 B 4
3070 Seixo 4 E 4
3405 Seixo da Beira 5 E 6
5140 Seixo de Ansiaes 2 C 7
5360 Seixo de Manhoses 2 C 7
6320 Seixo do Côa 6 E 7
8550 Selão Branco 13 L 4
5425 Selhariz 2 B 7
4810 Selho (São Jorge) 1 C 5
7960 Selmes 11 J 6
5140 Selores 2 C 7
7700 Semblana 14 K 6
3220 Semide 4 E 5
2140 Semideiro 8 G 5
5300 Sendas 3 B 8
5350 Sendim da Serra 3 C 8
5210 Sendim/Miranda do Douro 3 C 9
5470 Sendim/Travassos 2 B 6
6060 Senhora da Graça 9 F 7
7700 Senhora da Graça de Padrões 14 K 6
4970 Senhora da Peneda 1 B 5

3520 Senhorim 5 D 6
6355 Senouras 6 D 8
3060 Sepins 4 E 5
7630 Septalinho 13 K 4
5160 Sequeiros 6 C 7
5230 Serapicos/Angueira
 3 B 9
5300 Serapicos/Macedo
 de Cavaleiros
 3 B 8
5430 Serapicos/Valpaços
 2 B 7
4990 Serdedelo 1 B 4
3640 Sernancelhe 5 D 7
4595 Seroa 1 C 5
7830 Serpa 15 K 6
3200 Serpins 4 E 5
2300 Serra 8 F 5
2525 Serra d`el-Rei 7 G 3
2380 Serra de Santo
 António 7 F 4
2500 Serra do Bouro 7 G 3
2970 Serra do Cabo
 10 J 3
2460 Serra dos Mangues
 7 F 3
6030 Serrasqueira 9 F 6
2480 Serro Ventoso 7 F 4
6100 Sertã 8 F 5
4830 Serzedelo 1 B 5
2970 Sesimbra 10 J 3
8200 Sesmarias 14 L 5
7780 Sete 14 K 6
2900 Setúbal 10 H 4
5030 Sever 2 C 6
3740 Sever do Vouga
 4 D 5
5445 Sevivas 2 B 7
5470 Sezelhe 2 B 6
5340 Sezulfe 3 B 7
3550 Sezures 5 D 6
5225 Silva 3 B 9
3740 Silva Escura 4 D 5
4500 Silvade 4 D 4
6230 Silvares 5 E 6
4820 Silvares (São
 Martinho) 1 C 5
2560 Silveira 7 G 3
4775 Silveiros 1 C 4
8300 Silves 14 L 5
3330 Simantorta 5 E 5
3420 Sinde 5 E 5
7520 Sines 13 K 4
2710 Sintra 10 H 3
4970 Sistelo 1 B 5
8100 Sítio das Eguas
 14 L 5
4970 Soajo 1 B 5
4630 Soalhaes 1 C 5
6230 Soalheira 9 E 7
6060 Soalheiras 9 F 7
4440 Sobrado 1 C 5
6000 Sobrainho da
 Ribeira 8 F 6
6150 Sobrainho dos Gaios
 8 F 6
2640 Sobral da Abelheira
 7 H 3
7875 Sobral da Adiça
 15 J 7
2510 Sobral da Lagoa
 7 G 3
6300 Sobral da Serra
 6 D 7
6225 Sobral de Casegas
 5 E 6
2590 Sobral de Monte
 Agraço 7 G 3
6000 Sobral do Campo
 9 F 6
6370 Sobral Pichorro
 5 D 7
3320 Sobral Valado 8 E 6
3450 Sobral/Montagua
 4 E 5
6160 Sobral/Pedrogão
 Grande 8 F 5
6150 Sobreira Formosa
 8 F 6

4585 Sobreira/Gondomar
 1 C 5
2480 Sobreira/Minde
 7 F 4
5320 Sobreiro de Baixo
 3 B 7
5320 Sobreiro de Cima
 2 B 7
3850 Sobreiro/Albergaria-
 a-Velha 4 D 4
2640 Sobreiro/Ericeira
 10 H 3
7630 Sobreiro/São
 Teotónio 13 K 4
4700 Sobreposta 1 B 5
4580 Sobrosa 1 C 5
5350 Soeima 3 C 8
5320 Soeira 3 B 8
7555 Sol Posto 13 K 4
5470 Solveira 2 B 6
7555 Sonega 13 K 4
5430 Sonim 2 B 7
4920 Sopo 1 B 4
6320 Sortelha 6 E 7
5340 Sortes 3 B 8
3840 Sosa 4 D 4
8970 Soudes 14 L 6
3130 Soure 4 E 4
6400 Souro Pires 6 D 7
7470 Sousel 12 H 6
3020 Souselas 4 E 5
4690 Souselo 5 C 5
5450 Soutelinho 2 C 6
5400 Soutelinho da Raia
 2 B 6
5450 Soutelo de Aguiar
 2 C 6
5130 Soutelo do Douro
 2 C 7
5340 Soutelo Mourisco
 3 C 8
5300 Soutelo/Bragança
 3 B 8
5400 Soutelo/Chaves
 2 B 6
5200 Soutelo/Mogadouro
 3 C 8
4730 Soutelo/Vila Verde
 1 B 5
5385 Soutihla 2 B 7
2425 Souto da
 Carpalhosa
 7 F 4
6230 Souto da Casa
 5 E 6
5160 Souto da Velha
 3 C 8
3570 Souto de Aguiar da
 Beira 5 D 6
6420 Souto Maior/
 Trancoso 6 D 7
5060 Souto Maior/Vila
 Real 2 C 6
2230 Souto/Abrantes
 8 F 5
6320 Souto/Alfaiates
 6 E 8
4970 Souto/Ponte de
 Barca 1 B 5
3630 Souto/Vila Nova de
 Foz Côa 5 C 7
3620 Soutosa 5 D 6
5370 Succaes 2 C 7
3660 Sul 5 D 5
7400 Sume 8 G 6

T

6000 Taberna Seca
 9 F 6
3420 Tábua 5 E 5
5120 Tabuaço 5 C 6
4810 Tabuadelo 1 C 5
4635 Tabuado 1 C 5
4700 Tadim 1 B 5
4930 Taiao 1 B 4
2985 Taipadas 10 H 4
4800 Taipas 1 C 5
3740 Talhadas 4 D 5
5340 Talhas 3 C 8

5340 Talhinhas 3 B 8
7570 Tanganhal 11 J 4
4950 Tangil 1 A 5
3130 Tapéus 8 E 4
3610 Tarouca 5 C 6
4690 Tarouquela 5 C 5
3080 Tavarede 4 E 4
3040 Taveiro 4 E 4
6030 Tavila 9 F 6
8800 Tavira 14 L 6
5120 Távora/Lamego
 5 C 6
4970 Távora/Ponte de
 Barca 1 B 5
5445 Tazem 2 B 7
4700 Tebosa 1 C 5
2040 Teira 7 G 4
6285 Teixeira/Covilhã
 5 E 6
4640 Teixeira/Mesao Frio
 2 C 6
5225 Teixeira/Mogadouro
 3 C 8
3300 Teixeira/Oliveira do
 Hospital 5 E 6
3610 Teixelo 5 D 6
6200 Teixoso 5 E 7
3850 Telhadela 4 D 5
6230 Telhado 5 E 6
7200 Telheiro 12 J 7
5450 Teloes 2 C 6
4690 Tendais 5 C 5
3140 Tentúgal 4 E 4
7250 Terena 12 H 7
3530 Termas 5 D 6
6060 Termas de
 Monfortinho
 9 F 8
4840 Terras do Bouro
 1 B 5
6320 Terreiro das Bruxas
 6 E 7
6420 Terrenho 5 D 7
5300 Terroso 3 B 8
7350 Terrugem/Elvas
 12 H 7
2705 Terrugem/Sintra
 10 H 3
6000 Tinalhas 9 F 6
5430 Tinhela 2 B 7
5450 Tinhela de Baixo
 2 B 6
5200 Tó 3 C 8
3060 Tocha 4 E 4
7050 Tojal 11 H 5
2530 Toledo 7 G 3
7430 Tolosa 8 G 6
2300 Tomar 8 F 5
3460 Tonda 5 E 5
3460 Tondela 5 D 5
5000 Torgueda 2 C 6
2500 Tornada 7 G 3
4650 Torrados 1 C 5
3880 Torrão Lameiro
 4 D 4
7595 Torrão/Alcácer do
 Sal 11 J 5
4675 Torrão/Alpendurada
 e Matos 4 C 5
7400 Torre das Vargens
 8 G 6
7000 Torre de Coelheiros
 11 J 6
5385 Torre de Dona
 Chama 2 B 7
5160 Torre de Moncorvo
 2 C 7
5060 Torre de Pinhao
 2 C 6
3240 Torre de Vale de
 Todos 8 F 5
5400 Torre do Couto 2 B 7
6420 Torre do Terrenho
 5 D 7
7600 Torre Vã 14 K 5
7580 Torre/Carvalhal
 10 J 4
6060 Torre/Idanha-a-Nova
 9 F 8

4900 Torre/Meadela 1 B 4
6320 Torre/Sabugal 6 E 7
3510 Torredeita 5 D 5
3870 Torreira 4 D 4
6420 Torres 6 D 7
3000 Torres do Mondego
 4 E 5
2350 Torres Novas 8 G 4
2560 Torres Vedras 7 G 3
7570 Torroal 10 J 4
3300 Torrozelas 5 E 6
6270 Torrozelo 5 E 6
6200 Tortosendo 5 E 6
5155 Touça 6 C 7
4480 Touguinha 1 C 4
6060 Toulões 9 F 7
6270 Tourais 5 E 6
5470 Tourém 2 B 6
3465 Tourigo 5 E 5
7630 Touril 13 K 4
3650 Touro 5 D 6
4635 Toutosa 1 C 5
4980 Touvedo (São
 Lourenço)
 1 B 5
2825 Trafaria 10 H 3
2205 Tramagal 8 G 5
6420 Trancoso 5 D 7
4605 Travanca 1 C 5
3405 Travanca de Lagos
 5 E 6
3530 Travanca de Tavares
 5 D 6
3360 Travanca do
 Mondego 5 E 5
5320 Travanca/Bragança
 3 B 8
5200 Travanca/
 Mogadouro
 3 C 8
3720 Travanca/Palmaz
 4 D 5
5400 Travancas 2 B 7
3750 Travassô 4 D 4
4820 Travassós 1 C 5
4830 Travassos/Braga
 1 B 5
5470 Travassos/Morgade
 2 B 6
3440 Treixedo 5 E 5
2025 Tremes 7 G 4
5450 Tresminas 2 C 6
4640 Tresouras 1 C 6
5130 Trevões 5 C 7
3450 Trezói 4 E 5
7800 Trigaches 11 J 6
6285 Trigais 5 E 6
7800 Trindade/Aljustrel
 14 K 6
5360 Trindade/Vila Flor
 2 C 7
6300 Trinta 5 D 7
6100 Trisio 8 F 5
4795 Trofa 1 C 4
3750 Trofa 4 D 5
5400 Tronco 2 B 7
4950 Troporiz 1 A 4
3770 Troviscal/Bustos
 4 E 4
6100 Troviscal/Sertã
 8 F 5
4950 Troviscoso 1 A 5
2430 Trutas/Marinha
 Grande 7 F 4
6110 Trutas/Vila de Rei
 8 F 5
5320 Tuizelo 2 B 7
8365 Tunes (Gare) 14 L 5
2565 Turcifal 7 G 3
2460 Turquel 7 G 4

U

2140 Ulme 8 G 5
8800 Umbria 14 L 6
6215 Unhais da Serra
 5 E 6
3320 Unhais-o-Velha
 5 E 6
2685 Unhos 10 H 3

2435 Urqueira 8 F 4
7300 Urra 9 G 7
5200 Urrós 3 C 9
5160 Urros 6 C 7
5230 Uva 3 C 8

V

3050 Vacariça 4 E 5
3840 Vagos 4 D 4
7450 Vaiamonte 9 G 6
4485 Vairao 1 C 4
2070 Valada 7 G 4
3660 Valadares/Oliveira
 de Frades 5 D 5
4400 Valadares/Vila Nova
 de Gaia 1 C 4
2450 Valado dos Frades
 7 F 3
6000 Valbom/Alcains
 9 F 6
6400 Valbom/Pinhel 6 D 7
5100 Valdigem 2 C 6
4730 Valdreu 1 B 5
5340 Valdrez 3 B 8
6420 Valdujo 6 D 7
4970 Vale 1 B 5
2395 Vale Alto 7 F 4
7630 Vale Beijinha 13 K 4
5340 Vale Benfeito 3 C 8
2540 Vale Covo 7 G 3
5200 Vale da Madre
 3 C 8
3780 Vale da Mó 4 E 5
6150 Vale da Mua 8 F 6
2070 Vale da Pinta 7 G 4
5340 Vale da Porca 3 B 8
8100 Vale da Rosa
 14 L 6
7460 Vale da Seda 8 G 6
6090 Vale da Senhora da
 Póvoa 6 E 7
6005 Vale da Torre 9 E 7
6150 Vale da Ursa 8 F 6
6040 Vale da Vinha 8 G 6
6320 Vale das Éguas
 6 E 7
5335 Vale das Fontes
 2 B 7
2205 Vale das Mós 8 G 5
7400 Vale de Açor 8 G 6
7750 Vale de Açor de
 Cima 14 K 6
6440 Vale de Afonsinho
 6 D 7
7600 Vale de Água/
 Aljustrel 14 K 5
7540 Vale de Água/São
 Domingo 13 K 4
5210 Vale de Águia
 3 B 9
5230 Vale de Algoso
 3 C 8
5400 Vale de Anta 2 B 6
5370 Vale de Asnes 2 C 7
6360 Vale de Azares
 5 D 7
3730 Vale de Cambra
 4 D 5
2140 Vale de Cavalos
 8 G 4
6350 Vale de Coelha
 6 D 8
6320 Vale de Espinho
 6 E 8
6300 Vale de Estrela
 6 D 7
7630 Vale de Ferro
 13 K 4
2000 Vale de Figueira/
 Achete 8 G 4
5130 Vale de Figueira/Vila
 Nova de Foz
 Côa 6 C 7
5230 Vale de Frades
 3 B 9
5385 Vale de Gouvinhas
 2 B 7
7580 Vale de Guizo
 11 J 5

Vale de Ílhavo ⓟ   Vilarinho dos Freires ⓟ

3830 Vale de Ílhavo 4 D 4
5335 Vale de Janeiro
       2 B 7
6400 Vale de Madeira
       6 D 7
5085 Vale de Mendiz
       2 C 6
5210 Vale de Mira 3 C 9
7000 Vale de Moura
       11 H 6
6350 Vale de Mula 6 D 8
2445 Vale de Paredes
       7 F 3
2070 Vale de Pedra 7 G 4
6230 Vale de Prazeres
       5 E 7
3450 Vale de Remígio
       4 E 5
7800 Vale de Rocins
       14 K 6
5370 Vale de Salgueiro
       2 B 7
2000 Vale de Santarém
       7 G 4
7630 Vale de Santiago
       14 K 5
5385 Vale de Telhas
       2 B 7
5360 Vale de Torno 2 C 7
7830 Vale de Vargo
       15 K 7
7425 Vale de Vilão 8 G 5
7565 Vale de Zebro
       14 K 5
7400 Vale do Arco 8 G 6
6030 Vale do Homem
       9 F 6
8100 Vale do Judeu
       14 L 5
8135 Vale do Lobo 14 L 5
2050 Vale do Paraíso
       7 G 4
6100 Vale do Pereiro
       8 F 5
7430 Vale do Peso 9 G 6
7750 Vale do Poco 15 K 6
5200 Vale do Porco 3 C 8
6420 Vale do Seixo 6 D 7
6060 Vale Feitoso 9 E 8
8375 Vale Figueira 14 L 5
6200 Vale Formoso 5 E 7
5360 Vale Frechoso 2 C 7
7555 Vale Manhãs 13 K 4
5300 Vale Nogueira 3 B 8
5350 Vale Pereiro 3 C 8
5370 Vale Verde/
       Mirandela 2 C 7
6350 Vale Verde/Pinhel
       6 D 8
7565 Vale Vinagre 14 K 5
3880 Válega 4 D 4
4930 Valença 1 A 4
5120 Valença do Douro
       2 C 6
7830 Vales Mortos 15 K 7
8670 Vales/Aljezur 13 L 4
6150 Vales/Castelo
       Branco 8 F 6
7630 Vales/Cercal 13 K 4
5430 Vales/Mirandela
       2 C 7
8800 Vales/Santa
       Catarina 14 L 6
5350 Vales/Vila Flor
       3 C 8
6270 Valezim 5 E 6
2230 Valhascos 8 F 5
6300 Valhelhas 5 E 7
5090 Valongo de Milhais
       2 C 7
3750 Valongo do Vouga
       4 D 5
5130 Valongo dos Azeites
       5 C 7
7480 Valongo/Alter do
       Chão 8 G 6
4440 Valongo/Tio Tinto
       1 C 4
5450 Valoura 2 B 6

5430 Valpaços 2 B 7
2480 Valverde/Alcobertas
       7 G 4
6230 Valverde/Fundão
       5 E 7
5200 Valverde/Mogadouro
       3 C 8
3570 Valverde/Trancoso
       5 D 6
5350 Valverde/Vila Flor
       3 C 8
8970 Vaqueiros 14 L 6
5300 Varge 3 B 8
7300 Vargem 9 G 7
5200 Variz 3 C 8
4820 Várzea Cova 1 B 5
4635 Várzea da Ovelha
       1 C 5
3610 Várzea da Serra
       5 D 6
5100 Várzea de Abrunhais
       5 C 6
5130 Várzea de Trevões
       5 C 7
6100 Várzea dos
       Cavaleiros 8 F 5
4970 Várzea/Arcos de
       Valdevez 1 B 5
2000 Várzea/Azóia de
       Baixo 7 G 4
4610 Várzea/Felgueiras
       1 C 5
3660 Várzea/São Pedro
       do Sul 5 D 5
4940 Vascoes 1 B 4
3670 Vasconha da Serra
       5 D 5
6400 Vascoveiro 6 D 7
5430 Vassal 2 B 7
2510 Vau 7 G 3
5430 Veiga de Lila 2 B 7
7100 Veiros 12 H 6
6300 Vela 6 E 7
6050 Velada 9 F 6
6360 Velosa 6 D 7
4910 Venade 1 B 4
6420 Venda do Cepo
       5 D 7
5470 Venda Nova/
       Borralha 2 B 6
2305 Venda Nova/Casais
       8 F 5
6120 Venda Nova/Mação
       8 F 6
7080 Vendas Novas
       11 H 5
7200 Vendinha 12 J 6
3050 Ventosa do Bairro
       4 E 5
2580 Ventosa/Abrigada
       7 G 3
4850 Ventosa/Braga
       1 B 5
3670 Ventosa/Oliveira de
       Frades 5 D 5
2565 Ventosa/Torres
       Vedras 7 G 3
5200 Ventozelo 3 C 8
7220 Vera Cruz 11 J 6
6200 Verdelhos 5 E 7
7540 Vergeira 13 K 4
2550 Vermelha 7 G 3
8100 Vermelhos 14 L 5
6440 Vermiosa 6 D 8
3100 Vermoil 8 F 4
4770 Vermoim 1 C 5
3140 Verride 4 E 4
2460 Vestiaria 7 F 4
5470 Viade de Baixo 2 B 6
2625 Vialonga 10 H 3
7090 Viana do Alentejo
       11 J 5
4900 Viana do Castelo
       1 B 4
4640 Viariz 1 C 6
4775 Viatodos 1 C 4
5425 Vidago 2 B 6
2500 Vidais 7 G 3
6285 Vide 5 E 6

6360 Vide entre Vindas
       5 D 7
6300 Videmonte 5 D 7
6160 Vidigal/Castelo
       Branco 8 F 6
7080 Vidigal/Vendas
       Novas 11 H 5
7960 Vidigueira 11 J 6
3320 Vidual 5 E 6
5200 Viduedo 3 C 8
2430 Vieira de Leiria
       7 F 4
3100 Vieirinhos 7 F 4
4850 Viera do Minho
       1 B 5
7940 Vila Alva 11 J 6
7800 Vila Azeda 14 J 6
6320 Vila Boa 6 E 7
5320 Vila Boa de Ousilhao
       3 B 8
4635 Vila Boa de Quires
       1 C 5
4625 Vila Boa do Bispo
       1 C 5
6360 Vila Boa do
       Mondego 5 D 7
7350 Vila Boim 12 H 7
4980 Vila Cha (São Joao
       Baptista) 1 B 5
5210 Vila Cha de Braciosa
       3 C 9
2070 Vila Chã de Ourique
       7 G 4
3500 Vila Chã de Sá
       5 D 6
3720 Vila Chã de São
       Roque 4 D 5
3510 Vila Chã do Monte
       5 D 5
3100 Vila Chã/Abiul 8 F 4
6370 Vila Chã/Celorici da
       Beira 5 D 7
5070 Vila Cha/Cha 2 C 7
4740 Vila Cha/Esposende
       1 B 4
4485 Vila Cha/Labruge
       1 C 4
4600 Vila Chao de Marao
       1 C 5
6290 Vila Cortês da Serra
       5 D 6
5000 Vila Cova 2 C 6
3650 Vila Cova á
       Coelheira 5 D 6
6270 Vila Cova á Colheira
       5 E 6
3305 Vila Cova de Alva
       5 E 6
3550 Vila Cova do Covelo
       5 D 6
3640 Vila da Ponte/
       Moimenta da
       Beira 5 D 6
5470 Vila da Ponte/
       Travassos 2 B 6
3130 Vila da Rainha
       4 E 4
5200 Vila de Ala 3 C 8
3720 Vila de Cucujães
       4 D 5
7960 Vila de Frades
       11 J 6
4905 Vila de Punhe 1 B 4
6110 Vila de Rei 8 F 5
8650 Vila do Bispo 13 L 4
4480 Vila do Conde 1 C 4
6320 Vila do Touro 6 E 7
3270 Vila Facaia 8 F 5
7350 Vila Fernando/Elvas
       12 H 7
6300 Vila Fernando/
       Guarda 6 E 7
5360 Vila Flor 2 C 7
4970 Vila Fonche 1 B 5
3405 Vila Franca 5 E 6
6290 Vila Franca da Serra
       5 D 6
6420 Vila Franca das
       Naves 6 D 7

2600 Vila Franca de Xira
       10 H 4
2665 Vila Franca do
       Rosário 10 H 3
2925 Vila Fresca de
       Azeitão 10 H 4
6300 Vila Garcia 6 D 7
3560 Vila Longa 5 D 6
3660 Vila Maior 5 D 5
5040 Vila Marim/Mesao
       Frio 2 C 6
5000 Vila Marim/Vila Real
       2 C 6
2380 Vila Moreira 7 G 4
2925 Vila Nogueira de
       Azeitão 10 H 3
3140 Vila Nova da Barca
       4 E 4
7920 Vila Nova da
       Baronia 11 J 5
2260 Vila Nova da
       Barquinha 8 G 5
2050 Vila Nova da Rainha
       7 G 4
3130 Vila Nova de Anços
       4 E 4
8900 Vila Nova de Cacela
       15 L 6
4920 Vila Nova de
       Cerveira 1 B 4
4760 Vila Nova de
       Famalicão 1 C 4
5150 Vila Nova de Foz
       Côa 6 C 7
4400 Vila Nova de Gaia
       1 C 4
7645 Vila Nova de
       Milfontes 13 K 4
3780 Vila Nova de
       Monsarros 4 E 5
3420 Vila Nova de
       Oliveirinha 5 E 6
3650 Vila Nova de Paiva
       5 D 6
3350 Vila Nova de Poiares
       4 E 5
7500 Vila Nova de Santo
       André 10 J 4
2065 Vila Nova de São
       Pedro 7 G 4
6290 Vila Nova de Tazem
       5 D 6
3330 Vila Nova do Ceira
       5 E 5
3220 Vila Nova/Miranda
       do Corvo 8 E 5
2300 Vila Nova/Tomar
       8 F 5
4860 Vila Nune 1 C 6
5460 Vila Pequena 2 B 6
3440 Vila Pouca 5 E 5
5450 Vila Pouca de Aguiar
       2 B 6
4910 Vila Praia de Âncora
       1 B 4
5000 Vila Real 2 C 6
8900 Vila Real de Santo
       António 15 L 7
7940 Vila Ruiva/Alvito
       11 J 6
6370 Vila Ruiva/Fornos de
       Algodres 5 D 6
3520 Vila Ruiva/Nelas
       5 D 6
3150 Vila Seca/
       Almalaguês
       4 E 5
4755 Vila Seca/Fonte Boa
       1 B 4
5110 Vila Seca/Peso da
       Régua 5 C 6
6030 Vila Velha de Ródão
       9 F 6
5400 Vila Verde da Raia
       2 B 7
7830 Vila Verde de
       Ficalho 15 K 7
2580 Vila Verde dos
       Francos 7 G 3

4730 Vila Verde/Braga
       1 B 5
5320 Vila Verde/Bragança
       3 B 8
3080 Vila Verde/Figueira
       4 E 4
5370 Vila Verde/Mirandela
       2 C 7
5070 Vila Verde/Vila Real
       2 C 6
7160 Vila Viçosa 12 H 7
8125 Vilamoura 14 L 5
6185 Vilar Barroco 8 F 6
5350 Vilar Chao/
       Mogadouro
       3 C 8
4850 Vilar Chao/Viera do
       Minho 1 B 5
6440 Vilar de Amargo
       6 D 7
4860 Vilar de Cunhas
       2 B 6
4880 Vilar de Ferreiros
       2 C 6
5370 Vilar de Ledra 2 B 7
5320 Vilar de Lomba
       2 B 7
5070 Vilar de Maçada
       2 C 6
4910 Vilar de Mouros
       1 B 4
4900 Vilar de Murteda
       1 B 4
5400 Vilar de Nantes
       2 B 7
5320 Vilar de Ossos 3 B 7
5470 Vilar de Perdizes
       2 B 6
5320 Vilar de Peregrinos
       3 B 7
5200 Vilar de Rei 3 C 8
5340 Vilar do Monte 3 B 8
6110 Vilar do Ruivo 8 F 5
6355 Vilar Formoso 6 D 8
6320 Vilar Maior 6 E 8
5320 Vilar Seco de Lomba
       2 B 7
5230 Vilar Seco/Miranda
       do Douro 3 B 9
3520 Vilar Seco/Nelas
       5 D 6
6440 Vilar Torpim 6 D 8
5460 Vilar/Chaves 2 B 6
3620 Vilar/Moimenta da
       Beira 5 D 6
4840 Vilar/Vila Verde
       1 B 5
5430 Vilarandelo 2 B 7
5400 Vilarelho da Raia
       2 B 7
5350 Vilarelhos 2 C 7
5350 Vilares de Vilariça
       2 C 7
6420 Vilares/Trancoso
       6 D 7
5090 Vilares/Vila Real
       2 C 6
5140 Vilarinho da
       Castanheira
       2 C 7
5360 Vilarinho das
       Azenhas 2 C 7
5425 Vilarinho das
       Paranheiras
       2 B 6
5340 Vilarinho de
       Agrochao 2 B 7
5085 Vilarinho de Cotas
       2 C 6
5000 Vilarinho de
       Samarda 2 C 6
5060 Vilarinho de São
       Romao 2 C 6
3780 Vilarinho do Bairro
       4 E 4
5340 Vilarinho do Monte
       2 B 7
5050 Vilarinho dos Freires
       2 C 6

Vilarinho dos Galegos   (P) · **MADEIRA**   **Zóio**

5200 Vilarinho dos
    Galegos   3 C 8
5460 Vilarinho Seco   2 B 6
3660 Vilarinho/Aroês
    5 D 5
5300 Vilarinho/Bragança
    3 B 8
3200 Vilarinho/Lousã
    4 E 5
5470 Vilarinho/Travassos
    2 B 6
4730 Vilarinho/Vila Verde
    1 B 5
5130 Vilarouco   5 C 7
5425 Vilas Boas/Chaves
    2 B 6
5360 Vilas Boas/Vila Flor
    2 C 7
6030 Vilas Ruivas   9 F 6
5400 Vilela do Tamega
    2 B 6
4970 Vilela Seca   1 B 5
5400 Vilela Seca   2 B 7
5450 Vilela/Bragado
    2 B 6
5060 Vilela/Mateus   2 C 6
2530 Vimeiro/A dos
    Cunhados   7 G 3
2460 Vimeiro/Santa
    Catarina   7 G 3
7040 Vimieiro/Estremoz
    11 H 6
3440 Vimiero/Santa
    Comba Dão   5 E 5
5230 Vimioso   3 B 8
5320 Vinhais   3 B 8
5340 Vinhas   3 B 8
6290 Vinhó   5 E 6
5050 Vinhós   2 C 6
3500 Viseu   5 D 6
3830 Vista Alegre   4 D 4
4990 Vitorino das Donas
    1 B 4
7700 Viuvas   14 K 6
5460 Viveiro   2 B 6
4815 Vizela   1 C 5
3670 Vouzela   5 D 5
5450 Vreia de Bornes
    2 B 6
5450 Vreia de Jales   2 C 6

Z
2970 Zambujal de Cima
    10 J 3
3150 Zambujal/Condeixa-
    a-Velha   4 E 5
2965 Zambujal/Marateca
    10 H 4
8970 Zambujal/Vaqueiros
    14 L 6
7630 Zambujeira do Mar
    13 K 4
7630 Zambujeiras   13 K 4
5200 Zava   3 C 8
8650 Zavial   13 L 4
5370 Zebras   2 C 7
6060 Zebreira   9 F 7
5140 Zedes   2 C 7
2350 Zibreira   8 G 4
5300 Zóio   3 B 8

MADEIRA
9325 Achada   17 D 4
9240 Achada da Madeira
    17 C 4
9360 Achada e Levada do
    Poiso   17 D 3
9230 Achada Grande
    18 B 5
9270 Achadas da Cruz
    17 B 2
9240 Achado do Loural
    17 C 3
9230 Achado do Pau
    Bastiän   18 C 5
9200 Água de Pena
    18 D 6
9100 Águas Mansas
    18 D 5
9385 Amparo   17 C 1
9360 Anjos   17 D 3
9370 Arco da Calheta
    17 D2
9230 Arco de S. Jorge
    18 B 4

9240 Boaventura   17 B 4

9385 Cabo   17 B 1
9370 Calheta   17 D 2
9135 Camacha/Funchal
    18 D 5
9400 Camacha/Porto
    Santo   18 A 7
9300 Cãmara de Lobos
    17 D 4
9350 Campanário   17 D 3
9400 Campo de Baixo
    18 B 7
9400 Campo de Cima
    18 B 6
9400 Campo de Cima
    18 B 6
9360 Canhas   17 D 3
9200 Caniçal   18 C 6
9125 Caniço   18 D 5
9325 Choro   17 D 4
9230 Corujeira de Caixo
    18 C 5
9230 Cruzinhas   18 C 5
9000 Curral das Freiras
    17 D 4
9100 Curral Velho   18 D 5

9400 Dragonal   18 A 7

9350 Espigão   17 D 3
9400 Estação Loran
    18 A 7
9325 Estraito da Camara
    de Lobos
    18 D 4
9370 Estreito da Calhéta
    17 C 2

9230 Faial   18 C 5
9000 Fajã Escura
    17 C 4
9240 Fajã Grande   18 C 4
9370 Fajã da Ovelha
    17 C 1
9270 Fajã das Contrairas
    17 B 2
9230 Fajã do Cedro Gordo
    18 C 5
9240 Fajã do Penedo
    18 C 4
9000 Fajã dos Cardos
    17 C 4
9200 Fajã dos Rotos
    18 C 6
9350 Fajã dos Vinháticos
    17 C 3
9225 Folhadal   18 C 5
9350 Fontes   17 D 4
9300 Fonthainhas
    17 D 4
9350 Fumas   17 D 3
9000 Funchal   18 D5

9100 Gaula   18 D 6
9240 Ginjas   17 C 3

9230 Ilha   18 C 5

9370 Jardim do Mar
    17 C 2
9100 João Ferino
    18 D 5

9240 Lahco   17 C 3
9350 Laje   17 D 3
9240 Lameiros   17 C 3
9200 Landeiros   18 C 6
9225 Larano   18 C 6
9270 Levada Grande
    17 B 2
9360 Lombada   17 D 3
9385 Lombada Velha
    17 B 1
9370 Lombada dos
    Marinheiros
    17 C 1
9350 Lombo Furado
    17 D 4
9230 Lombo de Galego
    18 C 5
9370 Lombo do Doutor
    17 D 2
9370 Lombo do Salão
    17 C 2
9200 Machico   18 D 6
9360 Madalena do Mar
    17 D 2
9225 Majata   18 C 5
9370 Maloeira   17 C 2
9350 Meia Légua
    17 D 3
9050 Monte   18 D 5

9100 Palmeira   18 D 5
9240 Passo   17 C 3
9370 Paul do Mar
    17 C 1/2
9385 Pedregal   17 B 1
9230 Penha da Galé
    18 C 5
9000 Pico do Furão
    18 C 4
9400 Ponta   18 B 6
9240 Ponta Delgada
    17 B 4
9385 Ponta do Pargo
    17 C 1
9360 Ponta do Sol   17 D 3
9400 Port de Abrigo
    18 A 7
9270 Porto Moniz
    17 B 2
9400 Porto Santo (Vila
    Baleira)   18 B 7
9225 Porto da Cruz
    18 C 5
9370 Prazeres   17 C 2

9300 Quinta Grande
    (Igreja)   17 D 4

9370 Rabaçal   17 C 2
9370 Raposeira do
    Lugarinho
    17 C 2
9370 Raposeira do
    Serrado   17 C 2
9370 Referta   17 C 2
9230 Reibeira Funda
    18 B 4
9270 Reibeira da Janela
    17 B 2
9350 Ribeira Brava
    17 D 3
9270 Ribeira Funda
    17 B 2
9240 Ribeira Grande
    17 C 3/4
9200 Ribeira Seca   18 C 6
9350 Ribeira da Tábua
    17 D 3

9200 Ribeira de Machico
    18 C 5
9100 Ribeiro João
    Goncalves
    18 D 5
9230 Riebeiro Frio
    18 C 5
9200 Rochinha   18 C 6
9240 Rosário   17 C 3

9100 Santa Catarina
    18 D 6
9100 Santa Cruz   18 D 6
9230 Santana   18 C 5
9000 Santo António
    18 D 4
9200 Santo António da
    Serra   18 D 5
9000 São Gonçalo
    18 D 5
9100 São João   18 D 6
9230 São Jorge   18 B 5
9000 São Martinho
    18 D 4
9100 São Pedro   18 D 6
9000 São Roque   18 D 4
9230 São Roque do Faial
    18 C 5
9240 São Vicente   17 C 3
9000 Seara Velha
    17 D 4
9270 Seixal   17 B 3
9350 Serra de Água
    17 C/D 3
9400 Serra de Dentro
    18 A 7
9400 Serre del Fora
    18 A 7

9350 Tábua   17 D 3
9240 Tanque   17 B 4
9400 Tanquer   18 A 7
9350 Terreiro   17 D 4

9135 Vale Paraisa
    18 D 5
9240 Vargem   17 C 3

CITY MAPS · STADTPLÄNE · PIANTE DI CITTÀ · PLANOS DE LA CIUDAD · PLANTA DA CIDADE · PLATTEGRONDEN · BYKORT · PLÁNY MĚST · PLÁNY MIEST · PLANY MIASTA

Legend · Legende ·Legenda · Leyenda · Legenda

Legende · Signaturforklaring · Vysvětlivky · Vysvetlivky · Legenda 2

3

Barcelona 4

Bilbao 5

Granada .... 6 – 7

Lisboa 8

Porto .... 9 – 11

Madrid 12

Santiago de Compostella 13

Sevilla 14

Valencia ....

Street index · Straßenverzeichnis · Indice stradale · Callejero ·

Índice das estradas · Straatnamenregister · Gadefortegnelse ·

Rejstřík ulic · Register názvov ulíc a námestí · Skorowidz ulic.. 15 – 24

KEY PLAN · BLATTÜBERSICHT · TAVOLA RIASSUNTIVA DELLE PAGINE · VISTA DE LA PÁGINA · VISTA GERAL DAS PÁGINAS · BLADOVERZICHT · KORTBLADSOVERSIGT · KLAD LISTŮ · PREHĽAD KLADU LISTOV · SKOROWIDZ ARKUSZY

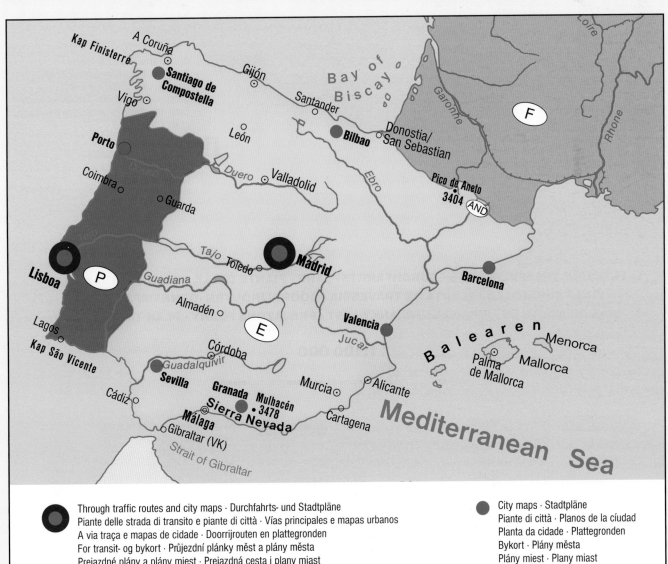

Through traffic routes and city maps · Durchfahrts- und Stadtpläne
Piante delle strada di transito e piante di città · Vías principales e mapas urbanos
A via traça e mapas de cidade · Doorrijrouten en plattegronden
For transit- og bykort · Průjezdní plánky měst a plány města
Prejazdné plány a plány miest · Prejazdná cesta i plany miast

City maps · Stadtpläne
Piante di città · Planos de la cíudad
Planta da cidade · Plattegronden
Bykort · Plány města
Plány miest · Plany miast

CITY MAPS · STADTPLÄNE · PIANTE DI CITTÀ · PLANOS DE LA CIUDAD · PLANTA DA CIDADE
PLATTEGRONDEN · BYKORT · PLÁNY MĚST · PLÁNY MIEST · PLANY MIASTA

1:15 000

0   100   200   300   400   500   600   700   800   900   1000 m

Public building (selection) · Öffentliche Gebäude (Auswahl)
Edificio pubblico (selezione) · Edificio público (selección)
Edifícios públicos (selecção) · Openbare gebouwen (keuze)
Offentlig bygning (udvalg) · Veřejná budova (výběr)
Verejné budovy (výběr) · Budynki użyteczności publicznej (wybór)

Motorway · Autobahn
Autostrada · Autopista
Auto-estrada · Autosnelweg
Motorvej · Dálnice
Diaľnica · Autostrady

Church, chapel · Kirche, Kapelle
Chiesa, cappela · Iglesia, capilla
Igreja, capela · Kerk, kapel
Kirke, kapel · Kostel, kaple
Kostol, kaplnka · Kościół, kaplice

Through road · Durchfahrtsstraße
Strada di transito · Travesía
Estrada para o trânsito local · Doorrijstraat
Gennemfartsvej · Průjezdní silnice
Prejazdná cesta · Ulice przelołowe

Cemetery · Friedhof
Cimitero · Cementario
Cemitério · Begraafplatz
Kirkegård · Hřbitov
Cintorín · Cmentarze

Athletic grounds · Sportplatz
Campo sportivo · Campo de deportes
Campo de desportos · Sportterrein
Sportplads · Hřiště
Športové ihrisko · Tereny sportowe

Pedestrian precinct · Fußgängerzone
Zona pedonale · Calle peatonal
Zona pedonal · Voetgangerszone
Gågade · Pěší zóna
Pešia zóna · Ulice tylko dla pieszych

Police · Polizei
Policia · Policía
Polícia · Politie
Politi · Policie
Polícia · Policja

Estación

Railway · Eisenbahn
Ferrovia · Ferrocarril
Caminho-de-ferro · Spoor
Jernbane · Železnice
Železnica · Koleje

Built-up area · Verbaute Fläche
Superficie edificabile · Zona edificada
área edificada · Bebygget areal
Bebouwde oppervlakte · Zastavěné plochy
Zastavaná plocha · Powierzchnia zabudowana

Underground · U-Bahn
Métro · Metropolitana
Metropolitano · Metro
Metro · Metro
Metro · Metro

Information · Information
Informazioni · Información
Informação · Informatie
Information · Informace
Informácie · Informacja

THROUGH TRAFFIC ROUTES · DURCHFAHRTSPLÄNE · PIANTE DELLE STRADA DI TRANSITO ·
VÍAS PRINCIPALES · PLANTA DE TRAVESSIA · DOORRIJROUTEN ·GENNEMFARTSVEJ ·
VÍAS PRINCIPALES · PRÙJEZDNÍ PLÁNKY MÌST · PREJAZDNÉ PLÁNY · PLAN TRANZYTOWY

1:100 000

0   1   2   3   4   5   6   7 km

Motorway · Autobahn
Autoroute · Autostrada
Auto-estrada · Autosnelweg
Motorvej · Dálnice
Diaľnica · Autostrady

Dual carriageway · Schnellstraße
Superstrada · Autovía
Via rápida · Snelweg
Hurtigvej · Rychlostní silnice
Rýchlostná cesta · Drogi ekspresowe

Secondary through road · Durchfahrtsstraße
Strada di transito · Travesía
Estrada para o trânsito local · Doorrijstraat
Gennemfartsvej · Průjezdní silnice
Prejazdná cesta · Ulice przelołowe

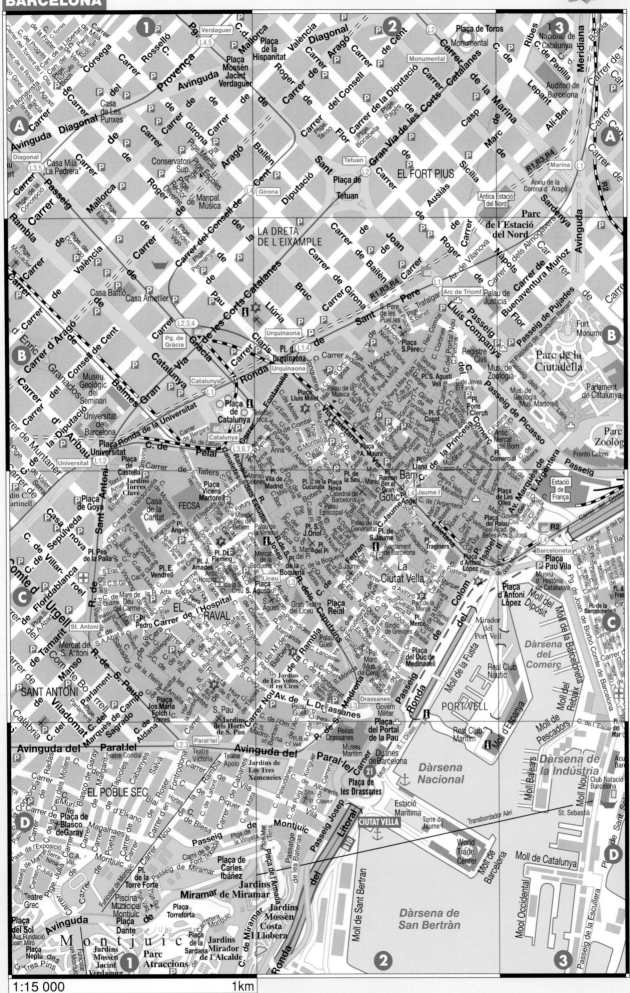

1:15 000   1km

GRANADA

1:15 000   1km

RIO

Tejo

Sacavém

Camarate

Portela
Moscavide

Doca dos Olivais
Feira International

Porto da Praia

Samouco

Quinta da Póvoa

○Montijo
Air Base

Aeromar

Esteiro Furado

Rosário Galo

Barra-a-Barra
Baixa da Banheira
Lavradio

Ponta da Pasadeira

BARREIRO

Prior
Velho

Olival Basto

Olivais
Av. de Berlim

Av. Marechal Gomes da Costa
Dom Henrique
R. da Cintura
do Porto
Av. Infante

Chelas

Madre de Deus

Museu de Azulejos

Castelo de São Jorge
Alfama Sé
Patriarcal

Póvoa de
Santo Adrião

Aeroporto
de Lisboa

Ameixoeira

Av. Marechal Craveiro Lopes
Av. do Brasil

Olivais Sul

Av. Almirante Reis
R. Morais Soares

LISBOA

Cacilhas

**Cova da
Piedade**

Arroja

Av. Padre Cruz

EIXO Norte-Sul

Alvalade

Museu Calouste
Gulbenkian

Arco-Cego
A. de Aguiar

R. P. de Melo
Parque de
Eduardo VII

Av. António A. de Aguiar

Av. da Liberdade

Jardim
Botânico

Av. Ribeira das Naus

Almada

Christo Rei

Pragal

ODIVELAS

Lumiar

Carnide

Pontinha

Jardim
Zoologic

Matos

Estádio
da Luz

São Sebastião

R. Joaquim
de Aguiar
R. Dom
João

Basílica da
Estrela

Av. Inf. Santo

Museu de
Arte Antiga

Av. da India

Av. de Ceuta

Av. da Ponte
Ponte 25 de Abril

ALMADA

Ramada

Famões

Paiã

Benfica

Av. Gen. Norton de
Estrada de Benfica

Parque
Florestal

Parque de
Monsanto

MONSANTO

Caramao

Belém

Banática

Caparica

Presa

A-da-Beja

Idanha

Belas

Massama

AGUALVA-CACÉM

AMADORA

Rua Elias Garcia

Damaia

Buraca

QUELUZ

Palácio Nacional

Tercena

Barcarena

Queluz
de Baixo

Carnaxide

Outorela

Linda-a-Velha

Algés

MIRAFLORES

Dafundo

Av. das
Descobertas
Av. Dom
Vasco da Gama
Av. Marginal

Torre de Belém

Mosteiro dos
Jerónimos

Porto Brandão

Murfacem

Corvina

Torre

Trafaria

_Cova do
Vapor_

Praia de Mata

Quinta de Santo António

Quebrada

Queijas

Caxias

EST. NAC

1km

1:100 000

LISBOA

1:15 000   1km

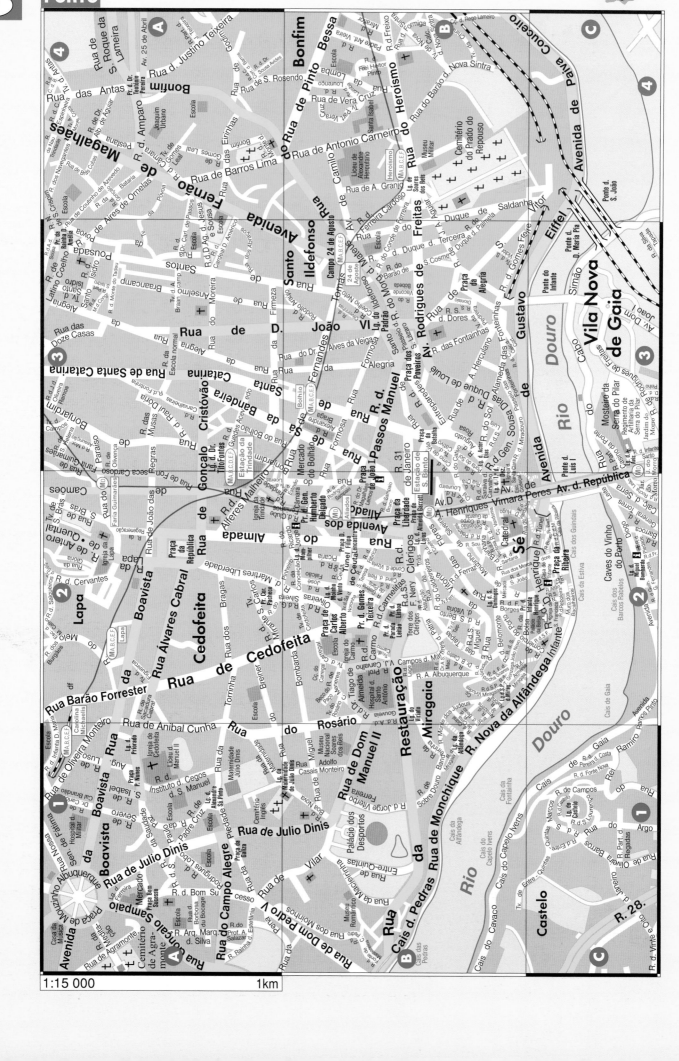

1:15 000   1km

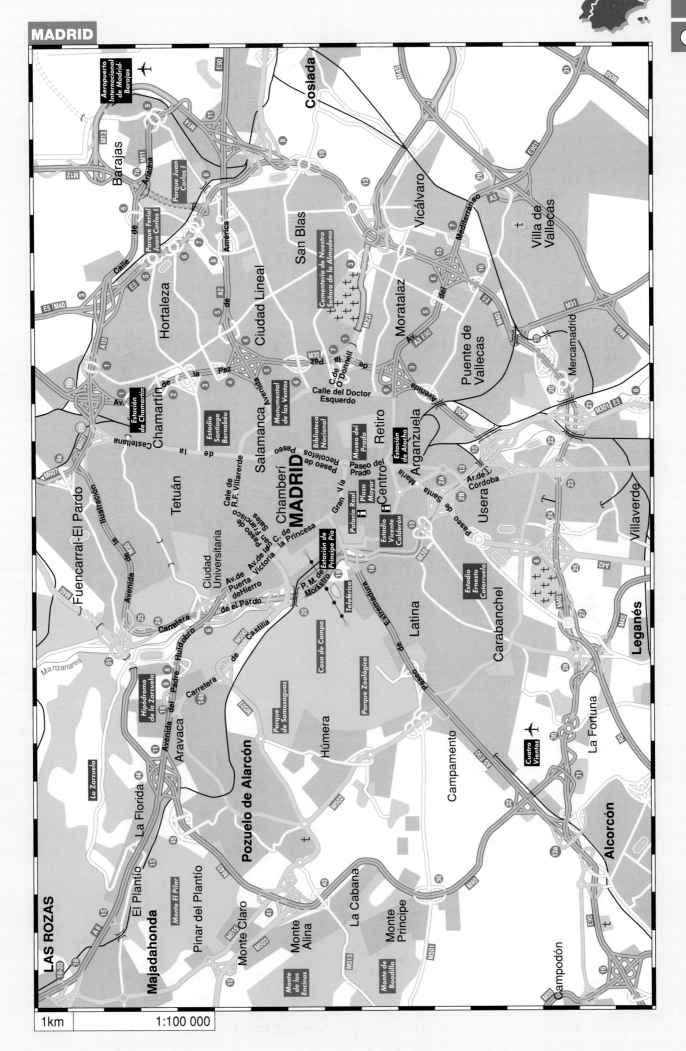

MADRID

Aeropuerto Internacional de Madrid-Barajas

Barajas

Coslada

Parque Ferial Juan Carlos I

Parque Juan Carlos I

San Blas

Vicálvaro

Villa de Vallecas

Hortaleza

Ciudad Lineal

Cementerio de Nuestra Señora de la Almudena

Moratalaz

Mercamadrid

M30

C. de O'Donell

Calle del Doctor Esquerdo

Puente de Vallecas

Estación de Chamartín

Av.

Chamartín

de la Castellana

Estadio Santiago Bernabéu

Monumental de las Ventas

Biblioteca Nacional

Museo del Prado

Retiro

Estación de Atocha

Arganzuela

Fuencarral-El Pardo

Tetuán

Cale de R.F.Villaverde

Paseo de San Francisco

Chamberí

MADRID

Paseo de Recoletos

Centro

Ar.de Córdoba

Usera

Villaverde

Ilustración

Ciudad Universitaria

Av. de la C. de la Princesa

Victoria

Gran Vía

Paseo del Prado

Paseo de Santa María

Palacio Real

Plaza Mayor

Puerta deHierro

de el Pardo

Estación de Príncipe Pío

Estadio Vicente Calderón

Estadio Ernesto Colorruelo

Manzanares

Hipódromo de la Zarzuela

P. M. de Monistro

Teleférico

Casa de Campo

Latina

Carabanchel

Leganés

La Zarzuela

Carretera

del Padre

Huidobro

de Castilla

Parque Zoológico

Campamento

La Fortuna

Aravaca

Parque de Somosaguas

Húmera

Cuatro Vientos

La Florida

El Plantío

Pozuelo de Alarcón

Monte El Pilar

LAS ROZAS

Majadahonda

Pinar del Plantío

Monte Claro

Monte Alina

La Cabana

Monte Principe

Alcorcón

Campodón

Monte de las Encinas

Monte de Boadilla

1km   1:100 000

1:15 000   1km

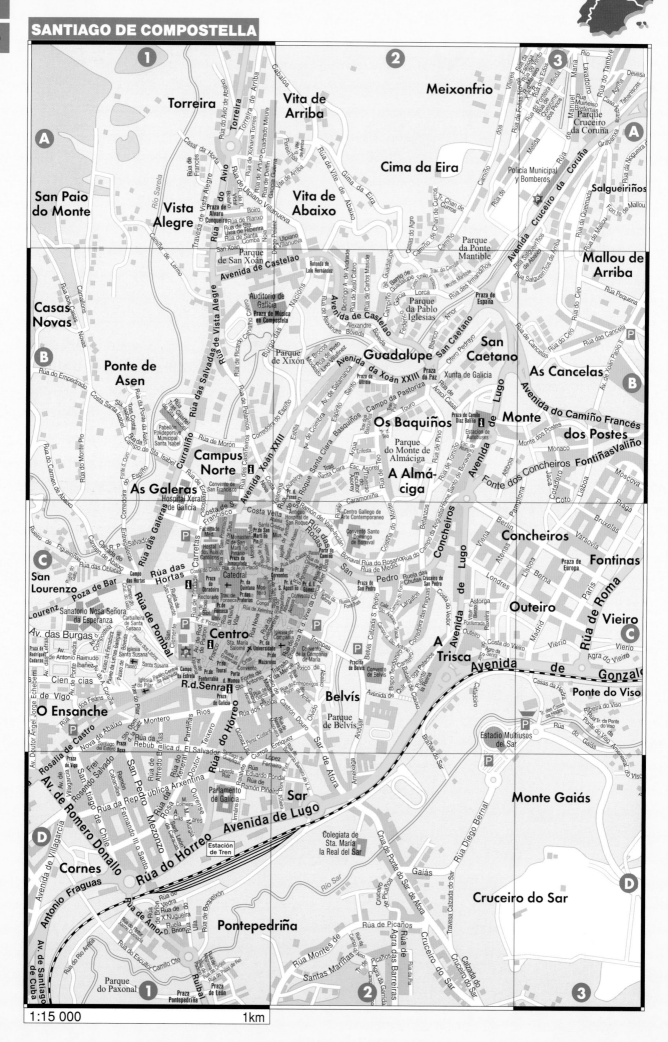

1:15 000   1km

SEVILLA

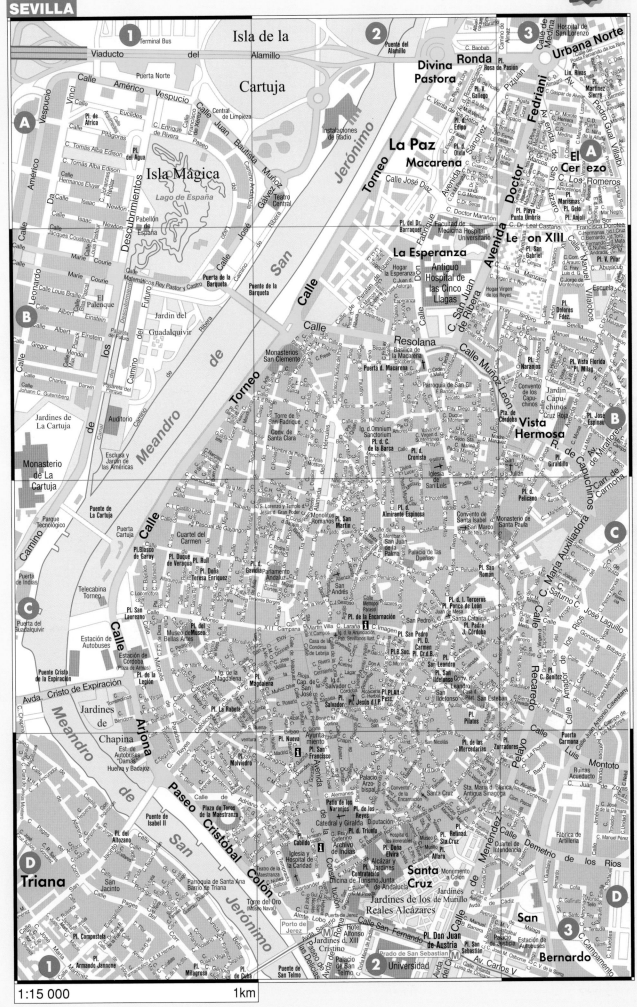

Isla de la
Cartuja

Terminal Bus

Viaducto   del   Alamillo

Puente del
Alamillo

Divina
Pastora

Ronda

Urbana Norte

Hospital de
San Lorenzo

Puerta Norte

Calle   Américo   Vespucio

Central
de Limpieza

La Paz
Macerena

Fedriani

El
Cerezo

Calle José Díaz

Isla Mágica

Lago de España

Instalaciones
de Radio

Teatro
Central

Leon XIII

La Esperanza

Pabellón
de España

Facultad de
Medicina Hospital
Universitario

Antiguo
Hospital de
las Cinco
Llagas

Puerta de la
Barqueta

Puente de
la Barqueta

Jardin del
Guadalquivir

Pasarela del
Futuro

Resolana

Basilica de
la Macarena

Vista
Hermosa

Jardines de
La Cartuja

Auditorio

Monasterio
San Clemente

Torneo

Parroquia de San Gil

Convento
de los
Capu-
chinos

Monasterio
de La
Cartuja

Esclusa y Jardín de
las Américas

Torre de
San Fadrique
Conv. de
Santa Clara

Iglesia
de
San Luis

Convento de
Santa Paula

Parque
Tecnológico

Puente de
La Cartuja

Puerta
Cartuja

Cuartel del
Carmen

Monolitos
Romanos

Pl. San
Martin

Palacio de las
Dueñas

Monasterio
de Santa Paula

Puerta
de Indias

Telecabina
Torneo

Pl. Blasco
de Garay
Pl. Duque
de Veragua   Pl. Rull

Pl. Doña
Teresa Enríquez

Gavidia
Parlamento
Andaluz

San Juan
de la
Palma

Pl. San
Román

Puerta del
Guadalquivir

Pl. San
Laureano

Estación de
Autobuses

Pl. de la Encarnación

Estación de
Córdoba
(Plaza de Armas)

Pl. del
Museo
Bellas Artes

Pl. de la
Legión

Campana

Puente Cristo
de la Expiración

Pl. Nueva
Ayunta-
miento

Pl. San
Francisco

Puerta
Carmona

Avda.   Cristo de Expiración

Jardines
de
Chapina

Est. de
Autobuses
"Damas"
Huelva y Badajoz

Pl. La Rabeta

Pl. Jesús
Salvador

Pl.
Pilatos

Ruinas
Acueducto

Pl. del
Altozano

Puente de
Isabel II

Plaza de Toros
de la Maestranza

Patio de
los
Naranjos

Catedral y Giralda

Santa Cruz

Triana

Teatro de
la Maestranza

Iglesia y
Hospital
de la Caridad

Archivo
de Indias

Alcázar y
Jardines

Reales Alcázares

San

Parroquia de Santa Ana
Barrio de Triana

Torre del Oro
(Museo Naval)

Jardines de los de Murillo

Santa
Cruz

Bernardo

Pl. Compostela

Porto de
Jerez

Hotel
Alfonso
XIII

Pl. Don Juan
de Austria

Estación de
Autobuses

Pl.
Armando Jannone

Pl.
Milagrosa

Palacio
de San
Telmo

Jardines d.
Cristino

Universidad

Puente de
San Telmo

Prado de San Sebastián

1:15 000   1km

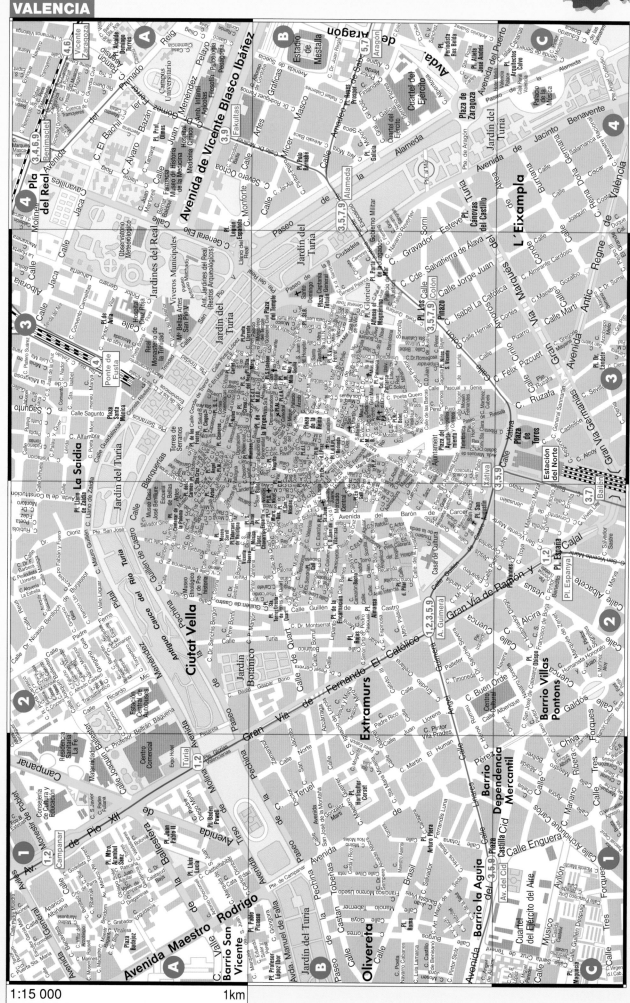

1:15 000   1km

STREET INDEX · STRASSENVERZEICHNIS · INDICE STRADALE · CALLEJERO · INDICE DAS ESTRADAS ·
STRAATNAMENREGISTER · GADEFORTEGNELSE · REJSTŘÍK ULIC · REGISTER NÁZVOV ULÍC A NÁMESTÍ · SKOROWIDZ ULIC

15

E

This street index only includes streets and squares that are shown on the map.
In diesem Straßenverzeichnis scheinen ausschließlich jene Straßen, Gassen, Wege und Plätze auf, die im Kartenteil dargestellt werden.
In questo indice compaiono esclusivamente strade, vie, vicoli e piazze rappresentate nelle carte
En este índice de calles aparecen exclusivamente calles, callejones, caminos y plazas que estén representadas en el mapa parcial.
Neste índice das estradas só aparecem as ruas, vielas, caminhos e praças, que estão representados na mapa.
In dit straatnamenregister staan alleen maar straten, steegjes, paden en pleinen die ook op de plattegrond te zien zijn.
Denne gadefortegnelse omfatter udelukkende de gader, stræder, veje og pladser, der vises i kortdelen.
V tomto rejstříku jsou uvedeny pouze ty ulice, uličky, cesty a náměstí, které se objevují na mapě.
V registri názvov ulíc sú uvedené len tie ulice a námestia, ktoré sa nachádzajú v mapovej časti.
W niniejszym wykazie ulic ujęte są wyłącznie te ulice, uliczki, drogi i place, które przedstawione zostały w części zawierającej mapę.

3

Barcelona

A
Abaixadors, Carrer C 2
Abdó Terradas, Carrer de A 1
Aglà, Carrer d' C 2
Agullers, Carrer dels C 2
Agusti Duran i Sant Pere, Carrer de C 1
Albareda, Carrer de D 2
Aldana, Carrer de C/D 1
Ali-Bei, Carrer de A 2/3, B 2
Allaola, Carrer de l' B 2
Almogàvers, Carrer de A 3, B 2/3
Amadeu Vives, Carrer d' B 2
Amargós, Carrer d' B 2
Ample, Carrer C 2
Àngels, Plaç a de l' C 2
Àngels, Carrer d' C 1
Àngels, Plaç a dels C 1
Antic de Sant Joan, Carrer B/C 3
Antic Valencia, Cami D 1
Antoni López, Plaç a d' C 2
Antoni López, Plaç a d' C 2
Antoni Maura, Plaç a B 2
Aragó, Carrer de A 1/2, B 1
Arai, Carrer de n' C 2
Arc de Sant Agusti, Carrer de l' C 2
Arc de Sant Pau, Carrer de l' C 1
Arc del Teatre, Carrer de l' C/D 2
Arcs, Carrer dels B/C 2
Argenter, Carrer d' B 2
Argenteria, Carrer de l' C 2
Aribau, Carrer d' B 1
Armada, Plaç a de l' D 2
Arolas, Carrer de l' C 2
Assaonadors, Carrer dels B 2
Aurora, Carrer de l' C 1
Ausiàs Marc, Carrer de A 2/3, B 2
Avinguda Diagonal A 1/2
Avinyó, Carrer d' C 2

B
Bailèn, Carrer de A 1/2, B 2
Balmes, Carrer de B 1
Banca, Ptge. C 2
Banys Nous, Carrer dels C 2
Banys Vells, Carrer dels C 2
Banys, Ptge. C 2
Barceloneta, Plaç a de la C 3
Basea, Carrer C 2
Baterias, Passatge de les D 2
Beates, Carrer B 2
Bergara, Carrer B 1
Bertrellans, Carrer de B 2
Bisbe, Carrer del C 2
Bisbe Laguarda, Carrer de C 1
Blai, Carrer de D 1
Blanqueria, Carrer B 2
Blasco de Garay, Carrer de D 1
Blasco de Garay, Plaç a de D 1
Blesa, Carrer de D 1
Bocabella, Ptge. A 2
Bolivia, Carrer de A 3
Boltres, Carrer d'en C 2
Bonsuccés, Carrer del C 1
Boquer, Carrer B 2
Boqueria, Carrer de la C 2
Boqueria, Plaç a de la C 2
Bòria, Carrer C 2
Born, Passeig C 2
Bot, Carrer del C 1
Boters, Carrer de C 2
Bou de Sant Pere, Carrer de B 2
Bruc, Carrer del A 1, B 1/2
Buenaventura Muñoz, Carrer de B 3

C
Cabanes, Carrer de D 1
Cabres, Carrer C 1/2
Cacador, Carrer C 2
Cadena, Carrer de la C 1
Cadena, Passatge de la C 3
Camprodon, Carrer de A 1
Camps Elisis, Ptge. A/B 1
Can Sitiar, Carrer C 1
Canaletes, Rambla B/C 1
Canuda, Carrer de B/C 2
Canvis Nous, Carrer dels C 2
Canvis Vells, Carrer dels C 2
Capellans, Carrer dels C 1
Caputxins, Rambla dels C 2
Carabassa, Carrer de C 2
Carbonell, Carrer de C 3
Carders, Carrer dels B 2
Cariteo, Carrer de D 1
Carles Ibáñez, Plaç a de C 3
Carles, Passeig de A 2/3, B 3
Carme, Carrer del C 1
Carrera, Carrer de D 2
Carretes, Carrer de les C 1
Casanova, Carrer de C 1
Casp, Carrer de A 2/3, B 1/2
Castella, Plaç a de B/C 1
Catalunya, Plaç a de B 1
Catalunya, Rambla de A/B 1
Catedral, Avinguda de la B 2
Cendra, Carrer de C 1
Cera, Carrer de la C 1
Cervelló, Carrer C 2
Cid, Carrer del C/D 2
Cinturó del Litoral D 2
Cirera, Carrer C 2
Còdols, Carrer de C 2
Colom, Passeig de C 2
Colomines, Carrer B 2
Coloms, Ptge. de C 1/2
Comerç, Carrer del B 2/3
Comercial, Carrer B 3
Comercial, Plaç a de B 2
Comtal, Carrer de B 2
Comtes, Carrer C 2
Concepció, Ptge. de la A 1
Consell de Cent, Carrer del A 1/2, B 1
Consolat del Mar, Carrer del C 2
Copons, Carrer de B 2
Corders, Carrer B 2
Córsega, Carrer de A 1
Cortines, Carrer de B 2
Credit, Ptge. del C 2
Cremat Gran, Carrer del B 2
Creu dels Mollers, Carrer de la D 1
Cucurulla, Carrer de B/C 2
Cucurulla, Plaç a de la C 2

D
Dante, Plaç a D 1
Desert, Ptge. del D 1
Diputació, Carrer de la A 1/2, B/C 1
Doctor Fleming, Plaç a C 1
Doctor Joaquim Dou, Carrer del C 1
Domingo, Ptge. de B 1
Dubte, Carrer de C 1
Duc de la Victòria, Carrer del, Carrer del C 2
Duc de Medinaceli, Plaç a del C 2
Duran i Bas, Carrer de B 2

E
Egipciaques, Carrer de les C 1
Elcano, Carrer d' D 1
Elisabeths, Carrer d' C 1
Elisabeths, Ptge. d' C 1
Emili Venderell, Plaç a d' C 1
Enric Granados, Carrer d' B 1
Erasme de Janer, Carrer d' C 1
Escoles, Ptge. A 1
Escudellers Blancs, Carrer dels C 2
Escudellers, Carrer dels C 2
Escudellers, Ptge. dels C 2
Escuder, Carrer d' B 2
Escullera, Passeig de la C 3
Espalter, Carrer d' C 1
Esparteria, Carrer C 2/3
Est, Carrer de l' C 2
Estruc, Carrer d' B 2
Estudis, Rambla dels C 1/2
Exposició, Passeig de D 1

F
Ferlandina, Carrer de C 1
Ferran, Carrer de C 2
Flassaders, Carrer dels B 2
Floridablanca, Carrer de C 1
Floristes de la Rambla, Carrer C 1
Flors, Carrer de les C/D 1
Fonollar, Carrer de B 2
Fontanella, Carrer B 1/2
Fontrodona, Carrer d'en D 1
Font-Trobada, Cami de la D 1
Francesc Cambó, Avinguda de, B 2
Francesc d'Aranda, Carrer de B 3
Fraternitat, Carrer de la A 1
Freixures, Carrer de les B 2
Fusina, Carrer B 2/3
Fusteria, Carrer de la C 2

G
Gegants, Carrer C 2
General Alvarez de Castro, Carrer del C 2
General Castaños, Carrer del C 3
Gignàs, Carrer C 2
Ginjol, Carrer C 2
Giralt, Carrer de B 2
Giriti, Carrer C 2
Girona, Carrer de A 1/2, B 2
Gombau, Carrer B 2
Goya, Plaç a de C 1
Gràcia, Passeig de A/B 1
Gran Via de les Corts Catalanes, Avinguda de la B/C 1, A/B 2
Gravina, Carrer de B 1
Groc, Carrer de C 2
Guiter, Carrer de C 1
Gurugú, Passatge del D 1
Gutemberg, Carrer de C 2

H
Hispanitat, Plaç a de la A 2
Hort de la Bomba, Carrer de l' C 1
Hort de Sant Pau, Carrer de l' C 1
Hortes, Carrer de D 1
Hospital, Carrer de l' C 1
Hospital, Ptge. de l' C 1

I
Indústria, Ptge. B 2
Isabel II, Passeig de C 2

J
Jaume Giralt, Carrer de B 2
Jaume i Fabra, Carrer de D 1
Jaume I, Carrer de C 2
Joachim Renart, Passeig de B 3

Joan Amades, Plaç a C 1
Joaquim Pou, Carrer de B 2
Joaquin Costa, Carrer C 1
Jonqueres, Carrer de les B 2
Josep Anselm Clavé, Carrer de C 2
Josep Carner, Passeig D 2
Josep Maria Folch i Torres, Plaç a de C 1
Jovellanos, Carrer de B/C 1
Julià Portet, Carrer de C 2
Julià, Carrer de D 1
Julià, Ptge. de D 1
Junta de Comerc, Carrer C 1/2

L
Lafont, Carrer de D 1
Laietana, via B/C 2
Lallum, Avinguda de B 1
Lancaster, Carrer de C 1
Lepant, Carrer de A 2/3
Les Drassanes, av. de C 2
Libertat, Carrer de la A 1
Llana, Plaç a de la B/C 2
Llàstics, Carrer de B 2
Llauder, Carrer C 2/3
Lleialtat, Carrer de la A 1
Lleó, Carrer de C 1
Lleona, Carrer C 2
Llibreteria, Carrer C 2
Lluis Companys, Passeig B 2/3
Lluis Cutchet, Passatge de C 1
Lluis el Piadós, Carrer de B 2
Lluis Millet, Plaç a de B 2
Lluna, Carrer de la C 1
Lope Braille, Carrer del C 1

M
Magalhaes, Carrer de D 1
Magarola, Carrer de C 2
Magatzems, Carrer de B 2
Magdalenes, Carrer de B 2
Malciunat, Carrer C 2/3
Mallorca, Carrer de A 1/2, B 1
Malnom, Carrer de C 1
Manresa, Carrer de B 2
Manso, Carrer de C 1
Mar i Terra, Ptge. D 2
Mar, Carrer del C 3
Mar, ronda del C 2/3, D 2
Mare de Déu del Pilar, Carrer de la B 2
Margarit, Carrer de D 1
Mariners, Carrer dels C 3
Marquès de Barberà, Carrer del C 2
Marquès de Campo Sagrado, carre del C/D 1
Marquès de L'Argentera, Avinguda del B/C 3
Marquesa, Carrer de la C 3
Marquet, Carrer d' C 2
Martras, Passeig de D 1
Massanet, Carrer de B 2
Mata, Carrer de D 1
Mediterrània, Carrer de C 3
Méndez Núñez, Carrer de B 2
Méndez Vigo, Ptge. A 2
Mercader, Ptge. B 1
Mercaders, Ptge. de B 2
Mercat, Ptge. C 1
Mercè, Carrer de la C 2
Mercè, Plaç a de la C 2
Meridiana, Avinguda A/B 3
Metges, Carrer de B 2
Mil Vuit-Cents, Ptge. de C 1

Milà, Carrer de A 1
Mirallers, Carrer dels C 2
Miramar, Avinguda de D 1
Miramar, Carrer de D 1/2
Miramar, Passeig de D 1
Moles, Carrer de B 2
Mònec, Carrer del B 2
Monjo, Carrer de C 3
Montalegre, Carrer de C 1
Montcada, Carrer C 2
Montjuïc del Carme, Carrer dels C 1
Montjuïc, Carrer de D 1
Montjuïc, carretera de D 1
Montjuïc, Passeig de D 1/2
Montserrat, Carrer de C 1
Montsió, Carrer de B 2
Mosques, Carrer B/C 2
Mossèn Jacint Verdaguer, Plaç a A 1
Murillo, Carrer de D 1

N
Nacional, Passeig C 3
Nàpols, Carrer de A 2, B 2/3
Neptù, Plaç a D 1
Notariat, Carrer del C 1
Nou de Dulce, Carrer C 1
Nou de la Rambla, Carrer C/D 1/2
Nou de Sant Francesc, Carrer C 2
Nova, Plaç a C 2

O
Obradors, Carrer C 2
Ocata, Carrer d' C 3
Olles, Plaç a de les C 2
Om, Carrer, de l' C/D 2
Ortigosa, Carrer d' B 2

P
Padilla, Carrer de A 3
Pagès, Ptge. A 2
Palau, Carrer C 2
Palau, Plaç a del C 2/3
Paludàries, Carrer de D 2
Palla, Carrer de la C 2
Palma Sant Just, Carrer C 2
Palma, Carrer D 1
Paloma, Carrer de la C 1
Paradis, Carrer de C 2
Paral-lel, Avinguda del D 1/2
Parc, Carrer del C 2
Pare Gallifa, Carrer del B/C 2
Parlament, Carrer del C/D 1
Parlament, Ptge. C 1
Pasedes, Carrer de C/D 2
Patriarca, Ptge. B 2
Pau Claris, Carrer de A 1, B 1/2
Pau Vila, Plaç a C 3
Pau, Passatge la C 2
Pedró, Plaç a del C 1
Pelai, Carrer de B 1
Penedides, Carrer de les C 2
Peracamps, Carrer de C/D 2
Perill, Carrer de D 1
Permanyer, Ptge. B 1
Perot Lolladre, Carrer de C 2
Pes de la Palla, Plaç a del C 1
Pescadors, Carrer dels C 3
Petons, Carrer dels B 2
Petritxol, Carrer del C 2
Petxina, Carrer d' C 2
Peu de la Creu, Carrer de C 1
Pi, Carrer del C 2
Pi, Plaç a del C 2
Picalquers, Carrer de C 1
Picasso, Passeig de B 2/3
Pietat, Carrer de la C 2
Pintor Fortuny, Carrer del C 1
Piquer, Carrer de D 1
Pizarro, Carrer de C 3

Pla, Ptge. A 1
Plata, Carrer C 2
Poeta Cabanyes, Carrer de D 1
Pons i Clerch, Plaç a de B 2
Porta Ferrissa, Carrer de C 2
Portal de l'Àngel, Avinguda del B 2
Portal de la Pau, Plaç a C/D 2
Portal Nou, Carrer de B 2
Princep de Viana, Carrer del C 1
Princesa, Carrer de la B/C 2
Progrès, Carrer del A 1
Provenç a, Carrer de A/B 1
Puig i Xoriguer, Carrer de D 2
Pujades, Passeig de B 3

Q
Quintana, Carrer de la C 2

R
Radas, Carrer de D 1
Ramelleres, Carrer de les C 1
Ramon Amadeu, pita de B 1/2
Ramon Berenguer el Gran, Plaç a de C 2
Ramon Berenguer el Vell, Carrer de B 2
Ramon Mas, Carrer de B 2
Rauric, Carrer d'en C 2
Rec Comtal, Carrer del B 2
Rec, Carrer del B 2
Rector Bruguera, Carrer B 2
Rector Oliveras, Ptge. C 2
Reina Amàlia, Carrer de la C 1
Reina Cristina, Carrer de la C 2/3
Relal, Plaç a C 2
Requesens, Carrer de C 1
Ribera, Carrer de B 2
Ribes, Carrer de A 2/3, B 2
Riera Alta, Carrer de la C 1
Riera Baixa, Carrer de la C 1
Riereta, Carrer C 1
Ripoll, Carrer de B 2
Rivadeneyra, Carrer de B 1/2
Robador, Carrer d'en C 1/2
Roca, Carrer C 2
Roger de Flor, Carrer de A 1/2, B 2/3
Roger de Llúria, Carrer de A 1, B 1/2
Roig, Carrer de C 1
Romulo Boch, Passatge de A 1
Rosa, Carrer C 2
Roser, Carrer de la C 2
Rosselló, Carrer del A 1
Rull, Carrer d'en C 2

S
Sabateret, Carrer B 2
Sagristans, Carrer dels B 2
Sal, Carrer de C 3
Salvà, Carrer de D 1
Salvador, Carrer del C 1
San Llàtzer, Carrer de A 1
Sant Agusti Vell, Plaç a de B 2
Sant Agusti, Plaç a de A 1
Sant Agusti, Plaç a de C 1/2
Sant Antoni Abad, Ptge. C 1
Sant Antoni Abat, Carrer de C 1
Sant Antoni de Pàdua, Carrer de C 1
Sant Antoni, ronda de C 1
Sant Bartomeu, Carrer C 1

Sant Benet, Ptge. B 2
Sant Bernat, Ptge. de C 1
Sant Bertran, Carrer de D 2
Sant Bonaventura, Carreró de B/C 2
Sant Climent, Carrer de C 1
Sant Cristófol, arc de B 2
Sant Cugat, Plaç a de B 2
Sant Domènec del Call, Carrer de C 2
Sant Erasme, Carrer de C 1
Sant Gil, Carrer de C 1
Sant Honorat, Carrer de C 2
Sant Jaume, Plaç a de C 2
Sant Jeromi, Carrer de C 1
Sant Joan, Passeig de A 1/2, B 2
Sant Josep Oriol, Carrer de C 1
Sant Josep Oriol, Plaç a de C 2
Sant Josep, Rambla de C 1
Sant Marti, Carrer de C 1
Sant Oleguer, Carrer de C 1
Sant Pacià, Carrer de C 1
Sant Pau, Carrer C 1/2, D 1
Sant Pau, ronda de C/D 1
Sant Pere Més Alt, Carrer de B 2
Sant Pere Més Baix, Carrer de B 2
Sant Pere Mitjà, Carrer de B 2
Sant Pere, Plaç a B 2
Sant Pere, ronda de B 1/2
Sant Rafael, Carrer de C 1
Sant Ramon, arc de C 2
Sant Ramon, Carrer de C 2
Santa Anna, Carrer de B/C 1/2
Santa Elena, Carrer de A 1
Santa Eulàlia, Carrer A 1
Santa Madrona, Carrer D 1/2
Santa Madrona, portal de C/D 2
Santa Margarida, Carrer de C 2
Santa Mónica, Carrer de A 1
Santa Tecla, Carrer de A 1
Sardana, Plaç a de la D 1
Sardenya, Carrer de A 2/3, B 3
Seca, Carrer B/C 2
Sepúlveda, Carrer de C 1
Sèquia, Carrer de B 2
Serra, Carrer de la C 2
Serrahima, Passatge de D 1
Seu, plaç de la C 2
Sicilia, Carrer de A 2
Sidé, Carrer del B 2
Sils, Carrer de C 2
Simó Oller, Carrer de C 2
Siracusa, Carrer de A 1
Sol, Plaç a del D 1
Sombrerers, Carrer C 2
Sota Muralla, pas de C 2/3
Sots-tinent Navarro, Carrer del C 2

T
Tallers, Carrer de B/C 1
Tamarit, Carrer de C 1
Tantarantana, Carrer B 2
Tàpies, Carrer de C 1/2
Tapioles, Carrer de D 1
Tarròs, Carrer de la B 2
Tasso, Ptge. A 2
Tetuan, Plaç a de A 2
Tigre, Carrer de la C 1

Til. Lers, Passeig dels B 3
Tordera, Carrer de A 1
Toros, Plaç a de A 2/3
Torre Forte, Plaç a de la D 1
Torreforta, Plaç a D 1
Torrent de l'Olla, Carrer del A 1
Torres i Amat, Carrer de C 1
Torres, Carrer de A 1
Trafalgar, Carrer de B 2
Tragi, Carrer B 2
Traginers, Plaç a dels C 2
Tres Pins, Carrer dels D 1

U
Universitat, Plaç a B 1
Universitat, ronda de la B 1

V
València, Carrer de A 1/2, B 1
Valeri Serra, Ptge. de B/C 1
Valldonzella, Carrer de C 1
Valquiria, Passatge de la D 1
Venus, Carrer de D 1
Verdaguer i Callis, Carrer de B 2
Vermel, Carrer B 2
Vicens Martorell, Plaç a C 1
Vico, Carrer de C 2
Victòria, Carrer de la B 2
Vila de Madrid, Plaç a de la C 2
Vila i Vilà, Carrer de D 1/2
Viladecols, baixada C 2
Viladomat, Carrer de C/D 1
Vilanova, av. de A/B 2
Villarroel, Carrer de C 1
Vinyeta, Ptge. de la D 1/2
Virreina, Ptge. de la C 1
Vistalegre, Carrer de C 1

X
Xulcá, Carrer de C 1

Bilbao

4

A
A. Uribarri, Tr. A 4
Abando (en Construcción), Avenida de A 2/3
Acehal, C. A/B 3
Aguirre, C. B 4
Aita Donosti, Plaza B 2
Alcalde Uhagón, C. B 2
Aldana, Cº. C 2
Almirantes Oquendo, C. A 4
Altamira B 1
Alto Somosierra, Pl. C 3
Altube, Calle C 2
Altube, Part. C 2
Amadeo Deprit, Calle B4
Ametzola, Pl. B 2
Amistad, C. B 3
Amparo, Calle B 3
Andrés Eliseo Mañaricúa, Calle (C.) C 3
Andrés Isasi, Calle C 2/3
Ángela (Á.) Figuera, Calle B/C 3
Anselma de Salces, C. A 3
Antonio Gaztañeta, C. B/C 2
Araba, Calle A 1/2
Aralar, C. A 4
Arane, Calle C 3
Araneko, Calle A 1/2
Araneko, Camino a 1
Arbieto, C. B 3
Arbolagane, C. A 1
Arbolantxa, C. A 3
Arechaga, C. b 3
Arechavaleta, C. B 2
Arenal, Muelle del B 4
Arenal, Paseo B 4
Arenal, Puente B 3
Arnotegui, Calle B 3
Arriaga, Plaza B 3
Arriquibar, Plaza B 3
Artasamina, Calle A 3
Artekale, Calle B 4
Askao, C. B 4
Askatasuna, Avenida (Av.) C 3/4
Astarloa, Calle B 3
Atxuri, Calle B/C 4
Auntzetxeta, Calle B/C 1
Aureliano Valle, C. B 2
Autonomía, Calle B 2/3
Ávila, C. B 2
Ayala, C. B 3
Ayunt., Puente A 3
B
B. Urib., Tr. A 4
B. Aldamar, C. A/B 3
Bailén, Calle B 3
Bakio, C. A 4
Banco Bilbao, C. B 4
Banco d.España, C. B 4
Barraincúa, C. A 3
Barrenkale Barrena, C. B 3
Barrenkale, C. B 3/4
Basurto B 1
Basurto a Kastrejana, Carretera B 1/2
Batalla de Lepanto, C. B 4
Batalla de Padura, C. C 3
Begoñazpi, C. B 4
Belostikale, C. B 4
Benidorm, Calle A 1
Benito Alberdi, C. C 2
Bentzarra, Calle B 1
Berástegui, C. B 3
Bergara, Av. C 3
Bertendona, C. B 3
Biarritz, C. C 2
Bidebarrieta, C. B 3/4
Bilbao La Vieja, C. B 4
Biribila, Plaza B 3
Bombero Echániz, Plaza B 2
Bosque, Cº. B 4
Bruño Mauric. Zabala, Calle B/C 3
Buenos Aires, C. B 3
Burgos, Calle A 1/2
C
C. Uribarri, Tr. A 4
Calixto Díez, C. B 2
Calixto Leguina, C. A 4
Calzadas de Mallona B 4
Camilo Villabaso, Calle C 2
Campo de Volantín, Paseo A 3
Campuzano, Plaza B 2
Caños, Paseo C 4
Cantábrico, Autovía del B 1-C 2
Cantalojas, C. B 3
Cantarranas, C. B/C 4
Cantera, C. B 3
Cantera, Pl. B 3
Capuchinos de Basurto, Cº. B 1
Capuchinos Deusto, C. A 1/2
Carmelo Gil, C. B 2
Carmelo, Calle del B 4
Carnicería Vieja, C. B 4
Caserío Larrazabal A 4
Castaños, Calle A 3
Celso Negeruela, C. A 3
Cinturería, C. B 4
Ciudad Jardín A 3
Ciudad Jardín, Tr. A 3/4
Ciudadela, Calle C 2
Colón de Larreategui, Calle A 2, A/B 3
Concepción, C. B 3
Concepción, Tr. B 3
Conde Arteche, Alameda A 2
Conde Mirasol, C. B 3
Corazón de María, Pl. B 3
Correo, Calle B 4
Cosme Echevarrieta, C. A 3
Costa, Pa. B 3
Cristo, Calle A 4
Cuesta Olabeaga B 1
Cueva de Arenaza, C. A 1
D
D. Entrecanales, C. C 2
Deusto, Puente A 2
Dieciséis de Agosto, Tr. B 4
Diputación, C. B 3
Dique, C. B 1
Doctor Areilza, Alameda B 2
Don Diego López de Haro, Gran Vía B 2/3
Donostia San Sebastián, Calle C 3
Dos d. Mayo, Calle B 3
Dr. Espinosa Orive, Calle C 3
Dr. F. Landín,C. B 2
Dr. Fleming, Pl. B 3
Dr. Alberca, C. A 4
Dr. Díaz Emparanza, C. C 2
E
Echevarría, C. B 3/4
Eduardo Victoria de Lecea, Avenida A 2
Egaña, Calle B 2/3
Egileor, C. A 1
Elcano, Calle A 2/3, B 3
Elexabarri, Cº. C 2
Elizalde, Calle B 4
Emilio Olabarrieta, Plaza A 1
Emilio Arrieta, C. C 2/3
Enderika, C. A 3
Enécuri, Avenida A 1
Enekuri, Etorbidea (Etorb.) A 1
Enrique Eguren, C. B 2
Ensanche, Plaza B 3
Entrambasaguas, Estrada B 1
Epalza, Calle A 3
Ercilla, Calle A 3, B 2/3
Erdikoetxe, C. A 1
Ernesto Erkoreka, Plaza A 3/4
Errekakoetxe, C. B 3
Errekaldeberri, C. C 2
Eskurtze, Calle C 2/3
Esperanza, C. B 4
Espinosa, Travesía A/B 1
Estación de Basurto, Calle B 1/2, C 2
Estufa, C. B 4
Etxezuri, Camino A 1
Euskalduna, C. B 3
Euskalduna, Puente A 2
F
Federico Moyúa, Plaza B 3
Felipe Serrate, C. B 2
Fernández del Campo, Calle B 2/3
Ferrocarril, Avenida B 2
Fika ,Calle B/C 4
Fontecha y Salazar, C. A 3
Francisco Maciá, C. A 2
Fuente, Callejón A 1
Fueros, C. B 4
Funicular, Pl. A 3
G
García Salazar, Calle B 3
Gardoqui, C. B 3
General Latorre, Plaza B 2
General Castillo. C. B 3
General Concha, Calle B 3
General Eguía, Calle B 2
General Eraso, Calle A 1
General Salazar, Calle B 2
Gimnasio, C. B 3
Gipuzkoa, Calle A 1/2
Gorbeia, C. A 2
Gord., Tr. C 2
Gordóniz, Calle B/C 2
Gorliz, C. A 4
Gotia, C. Par. B 3
Goya, C. C 2
Gregorio de la Revilla, Calle B 2
Guardia Bernar Alonso, C. A 3/4
Guardia Civil, Pl. B 2
Guiña, Estrada C 3
Gurtubay, C. B 1
H
Heliodoro de la Torre, C. A 2
Henao Calle Henao, Calle A 2/3
Hermanos Aguirre, C. A 2
Hernani, Calle B 3
Heros, Calle A 3
Huertas de la Villa, Calle A 3
Hurtado de Amézaga, Calle B 3
I
Ibáñez de Bilbao, Calle A/B 3
Ibarrekolanda, Camino A 1
Idigoras (I.) Acebal, C. A/B 3
Indautxu B 2
Indautxu, Plaza B 2
Iparraguirre, Calle A 3, B 2/3
Irala, Calle B/C 3
Irala, Travesía C 3
Iruña, Calle A 1
Isleta, C. A 3
Iturribarría, C. B 1/2
Iturribide, Calle B 4
Iturribide, Particular B 4
Iturriondo, Plaza A 4
Iturriza, C. B 3
J
J. Anselmo Clavé, Paseo A/B 2
J. Bolívar, C. B 4
J.Intsausti „Uzturre", Pl. A 3
Jado, Plaza A/B 3
Jaén, Calle C 2
Jardín Txikerra, C. C 2
Jardines, C. B 3/4
Jardines Gernika C 3/4
Jaro (J.) de Arana , Pl. C 3
Jon de Arróspide, Calle A 1/2
José Olabarria, C. B 2
José M. Olabarri, C. B 3
José María Escuza, C. B 2
Juan A. Zunzunegui, Av. B 2
Juan Carlos de Gortázar, Calle (C.) C 3/4
Juan Viar, C. C 4
Juan de Urbieta, C. A 1
Juan de Ajuriaguerra, Calle A 2/3
Juan de Garay, Calle B/C 3
Juan (J.) de Gardeazabal, C. C 4
Julián Zugazagoitia, Calle C 3/4
Julio Lazúrtegui, Plaza A 1
Julio Urquijo, C. A 1
Junquera, Cº. A/B 1
K
Kirikiño, Avenida B/C 3
Kobeta, Camino B 1
Kurutza, Cº. C 2
L
La Encarnación, C. B/C 4
La Ribera, Pte. B 3
La Casilla, Plaza B 2
La Cruz, C. B 4
La Encarnación, Plaza B 4
La Merced, Muelle B 3
La Popular A 4
La Ribera B 1
La Ribera Arenal, C. B 3/4
La Ribera, Calle B 3/4
La Salve, Calle A 3
La Salve, Plaza A 3
Labayru, Calle B 2
Laburdi, Av. B 3
Laguna, C. B 3
Lamana, C. B 3
Landeta, Camino A 4
Larrako Torre, C. A 1
Ledesma, Calle B 3
Lehendakari Aguirre, Avenida A 1/2
Lersundi, Calle A 3
Lezeaga, Calle B 1
Licenciado Poza, Calle B 2/3
Logroño, C. A 1/2
Lotería, C. B 4
Luis Iruarrizaga, C. B 3
Luis Briñas, Calle B 2
Luis de Castresana, Calle (C.) C 3/4
Luis Power, Calle A 2
Lutxana, C. B 3
Luzarra, Calle A 1/2
M
Machín, C. B 3
Madariaga, Avenida A 1/2
Maestro (M.) Iciar, C. B 4
Maestro (M.) Mendiri, C. B 4
Mala, Estrada B/C 2
Mallona, Travesía B 4
Mandobide, C. A 3
Manuel Allende, C. B 2
Mar Mediterráneo, C. A 1
Marcelino (M.) Oreja, C. B 2
María Muñoz, C. B 4
María Díaz de Haro, Calle B 2
Marina, C. A 3
Marqués d. Puerto, C. B 3
Martín (M.) Agüero, C. B 3
Marzana, C. B 3/4
Marzana, Muelle B 3/4
Masustegi, Estrada B/C 1
Matiko, Calle A 3/4
Maurice Ravel, Avenida A 3/4
Máximo Aguirre, Calle A/B 2
Mazarredo, Alameda A 2/3, B 3
Mazustegi, C. B 4
Medina de Pomar, C. C 3
Mena, Calle B 3
Menéndez Pelayo, C. B/C 4
Menéndez (M.) Pelayo, C. C 4
Merced, C. B 3
Merced, Puente B 3
Miguel Unamuno, Pl. B 4
Mina San Luis, Calle B/C 3/4
Miraflores, Avenida C 4
Miribilla, C. B 3
Monasterio, C. C 3
Moncada, C. C 2
Monte Ganekogorta, C. A 1
Monte Jata, C. A 1
Monte Arno, Calle A 4
Monte (M.) Oiz, C. A 4
Monte (M.) Izaro, C. A 4
Montevideo, Avenida B 1
Moraza, Pl. A 3
Morgan Ribera de Botica, Calle A 1/2
Muelle de Urazurrutia C 4
Muelle de Uribitarte A 3
Muelle del Arenal A/B 4
Muelle Olabeaga B 1
Múgica y Butrón, C. A 3
Muros de San Pedro A 3
Museo, Plaza A 2
Músico Guridi, Plaza A 4
Músico Sarasate, C. A 1
N
Naja, Calle B 3
Navarra, C. B 3
Nerbioi, C. A 3
Nicolás Alcorta, C. B 3
Novia de Salcedo, C. B/C 2
Nuestra Señora Monserrat, C. C 3
Nueva, C. B 3
Nueva, Pl. B 4
O
Obispo Orueta, C. A 3
Olabeaga B 1
Olabeaga R., C. A 1
Olano, Calle B 3
Olite-Elibarri, C. B 2
Oll. Altas, C. C 4
Oll. Bajas, C. C 4
Ollerías Altas, Tr. C 4
Ollerías Bajas, Tr. C 4
P
P. Zubidurre, C. B 2
Pa. Esnarrizaga, C. A 4
Pablo Alzola, Calle B/C 2
Pablo Picasso, Calle B 3
Padre Lojendio, C. B 3
Padre Larramendi, C. C 2
Padre (P.) Remig (R.) Vilariño, C. B 4
Párroco Ugaz, Trv. B 4
Particular Norte, C. B 3
Particular Olagorta, Calle A 1
Particular Sagarduy, C. A/B 1
Pastor Buen, C. A 4
Pedro Basterrechea, Plaza B 3
Pedro Eguillor, Pl. B 3
Pedro M. Artola, C. B 3
Pedro (P.) Ibarretxe (I.), C. B 3
Pelota, C. B 3
Pérez Galdós, Calle B 1/2
Perro, C. B 3/4
Pintor Etxenagusia, C. A 1
Pintor Lecuona, Av. B 2
Pintores Arrúe, C. A 1
Pío Baroja, Pl. A 3
Plácido Careaga, Plaza A 1
Plaza Celso Negeruela A 3
Plaza Venezuela B 3
Plentzia, C. A 4
Poeta Blas de Otero, Calle A 1/2
Polvorín, Calle B 4
Portal (P.) de Zamudio (Zam.), C. A 4
Portugalete, Trv. A 3
Prim, Calle B 4
Princ. (Príncipe) de Virana, C. A 3
Príncipe, C. B 3
Príncipes de España, Puente A 3
Prolongación Goya, C. C 2
Puerto de la Paz, Avda. A 2
Q
Quintana, Calle A 4
R
Rafael Sánchez Mazas, Paseo A 2
Rafaela Ybarra, Calle A 2
Ramón y Cajal, Avenida A 1/2
Ramon (R.) y Cajal (Ca.), Trv. A 2
Rapas Uribitarte, C. A 3
Recalde a Larrasquitu, Carretera C 2
Recalde, Alameda A/B 3
Recalde, Pl. C 2
Resurrección M. Azcue, C. B/C 4
Reyes Católicos, C. C 3
Ribera de Deusto A/B 1
Ribera de Deusto Vieja A 1/2
Ribera de Zorrotzaurre A/B 1
Ricardo Arregui, Calle A 3/4
Ripa, C. B 3
Rodríguez Arias, Calle B 2/3
Roncesv., C. A 4
Ronda, Calle B 4
Rvdo. Hermano Lasalle, Pl. C 4
S
S. Juan., Pl. B 4
S. Valentín de Berriochoa, C. A 4
Sabino Arana, Avenida B 2
Sagrada Familia, C. A 1
Sagrado Corazón, Plaza A/B 2
Salou, C. C 2
San Esteban, C. B/C 4
San Felicísimo, Camino A/B 1
San Felicísimo, Plaza A 1
San Francisco de Asís, C. B 3
San Francisco Javier, Plaza B 2
San Francisquito, C. C 4
San José, Plaza A 3
San Agustín, Estrada A 3/4
San Antón, Puente B 4
San Francisco, Calle B 3
San Mamés B 2
San Mamés, Alameda B 2/3
San Nicolás de Olabeaga, C. B 1
San Pedro de Deusto A 1
San Pedro, Plaza A 2
San Pío X, Plaza A 2
San Roque, C. A 3
San Vicente, C. A/B 3
San Vicente, Pl. A 3
Sancho Azpeitia, C. A 2
Santa Ana B 1
Santa María, C. B 3
Santa (S.) Mónica, C. B 4
Santander, C. A 1/2
Santiago B 1
Santiago, C. B 3/4
Santiago, Pl. B 4
Santiago de Compostela, Calle C 3
Santurtzi, C. A 4
Santutxu, Calle B/C 4
Sarrikoalde, Plaza A 1
Sendeja, C. A/B 4
Severo Unzúe, Calle C 2
Simón Bolívar, C. B 2
Solokoetxe, Calle B 4
Solokoetxe, Es. B 4
Sombrerería, C. B 4
Somera, Calle B 4
Sorkunde, C. B 4
Subida Buenavista, C. A 2
T
T. Constantino, C. B 3
Telesf. Aranzadi, C. B 3
Tellagorri, C. B 2
Tendería, C. B 4
Tiboli, Calle A 3
Tiboli, Travesía A 3
Tolosa, Calle C 2
Toros Vista Alegre, Pl. de B 2
Torre (T.), C. B 4
Torres Quevedo, Plaza B 1/2
Trauko, Calle A 4
Trauko, Tr. A 4
Tres Pilares, Pl. B 3/4
Tristán (Tr.) Leguizamón, C. A 3
Troka, Camino B 1
Tutulu, Calle A 4
Txakoli, C. A 1
U
Ugalde Par. B 3
Universidades, Avenida A 2/3
Urazurrutia, Calle B/C 4
Urazurrutia, Muelle de C 4
Uribarri, C. A 4
Uribitarte, Calle A 3
Uribitarte, Travesía A/B 3
Urizar, Plaza C 3
Urkiola, C. B/C 2
Urquijo, Alameda B 2/3
Urrutia, C. B 2
Uturralde, C. B 4
V
Venezuela, Plaza B 3
Ventas, Estrada B 1
Ventosa, Camino B 1/2
Vía Vieja de Lezama, Camino A 3/4, B 4
Víctor, C. B 4
Villarías, C. B 3
Virgen de Begoña, Calle B 4
Vista Alegre, C. B 3
Vitoria (V.) Gasteiz, Calle (C.) B 3
Viuda de Epalza, C. B 4
X
Xenpelar, C. C 3
Z
Zabala, Traversía C 3
Zabalbide, Calle de B 4
Zabálburu, Plaza B 3
Zankoeta, Calle B 2
Zarandoa, Avenida de A 1
Zuberoa, Avenida B/C 3
Zubizuri A 3
Zugastinovia, C. B 2
Zumaia, Calle A 4
Zumalacarregui, Avenida A/B 4
Zumárraga, C. B 4
Zumárraga, Calle B 4
Zumárraga, Plaza B 4
Zurbaran, Camino A/B 4
Zurbaran, Pa. A 4

Granada

5

A
A. Castro (C.), C. B/C 2
Abad, Plta. del B 2
Abarqueros, Cta. B 2
Abeja, C. A 2
Abén Humeya, C. C 2
Abenamar (Abenam.), C. B 2
Abencerrajes , Camino de los D 2/3
Abogado, Callejuela d. C 3
Abu Ishac, C. C 2
Abu Said, C. C/D 2
Aceituno, Cuesta A 2/3
Acequia Gorda (G.), Cjón. C 2
Acequia, Plta. C 3
Acosta (A.) Inglot, C. A 1
Adelfa, C. D 1/2
Adelfas, Paseo de las B 3
Afán Ribera, C. C 2
África, C. D 2
Agua, C. A/B 2
Agua, Calle A 1/2
Aguado, C. C 2
Águila, C. C 1/2
Aguirre (A.), C. B 2
Agustín Lara, Calle D 2
Agustina de Aragón, C. C 1/2
Aire Alta, C. B 2
Aire, C. B 2
Aixa, Cuesta C 2
Alamillos, C. B/C 2
Álamos des Marqués, C. (Á. d. M., C.) B 2
Alamos (A.) des Marques (M.), Plta. B 2
Albahaca, C. D 1
Albeida, Plta. B 3
Albert Einstein, Pl. B 1
Alberzana, Cjón. de la A 2
Albuñol, C. D 1/2
Alcaicería (Alcaic.), C. B 2
Alcalá de Henares, C. D 3
Alcantarilla (Alcant.), Cjón. C 2
Alcazaba, Muralla de la B 2
Alcázar del Genil, C. D 2
Alhacaba, Cuesta de B 2
Alhama d. Granada, C. D 1/2
Alhamar , Calle C 1/2
Alhóndiga, C. B/C 2
Aliatar, Pl.de B 2
Aljibe Polo, Pl. B 2
Aljibe d. l. Vieja (V.), C. A/B 2, A 3
Aljibe d. l. Gitana, C. B 2
Aljibe (A.) de Trillo (T.), C B 2
Aljibe (A.) de Trillo (T.), Cj. B 2
Aljibe (A.) de Trillo (T.), Cta. B 2
Aljibe (A.) des Gato, C. B 2
Almanzora Alta (A.), C. B 2
Almanzora Baja, C. B 2
Almendros, C. A 3
Almenillas, C. B 1
Almés (A.), C. B 2
Almes, Pl. B 2
Alminares del Genil, C. C 2
Almirante (A.) Sebura, C. A 1
Almirante (Alm.), Plta. B 2
Almirante, C. B 2
Almirec., C. B 2
Almona Boquerón, C. B 2
Almona del Campillo, C. (A.Camp., C.) C 2
Almona San Juan Dios, C. B 1
Almona (Al.) Vieja, C. B 1
Almona, C. B 2
Almona, Plta. B 2
Alonso Cano, C. B 1
Alpargateros Alto, C. A 2
Alpargateros (Alp.) Bajo, C. A 2
Alpargateros, C. A 2
Alpargateros, Pl. A/B 2
Alpujarra (A.), C. C 1
Alta Bco. A. C 3
Alta de Cartuja, C. A 2
Álvaro (Á.) de Bazán, C. B 2
Álvaro Aparicio, C. A 2
América, Avenida de D 3
Ampola, C. D 2
Ancha d. l. Virgen, C. C 2
Ancha de Capuchinos, Avenida de A 1/2
Ancha de Gracia, C. C 1
Ancha, C. C 2
Andaluces, Avenida A 1
Andrea Navagiero, C. D 2
Andrés, C. C/D 2
Andrés, Calle D 2
Ángel Barrios, C. C 1
Ángel Ganivet, C. C 2
Ángel, C. C 1/2
Ángel, Cjón. del C/D 2
Ángel, Pl. del D 2
Ángulo, C. B 1
Antequeruela Alta, C. C 3
Antequeruela Baja, C. C 3
Antonino, Cjón. C 1
Antonio Dalmases, C. C 2
Arabial, Calle B/C 1
Arabial, Pje. D 2
Arandas, C. B 2
Arco (Arc.) de las Cucharas (Cuch.), C. B 2
Areas, Cjón C 2
Arenal, C. A 1
Arenales, C. D 3
Arjona, Cjón. B/C 2
Arquitecto Torres Baldas, C. D 2
Arriola, C. B 1/2
Arteaga, C. B 2
Asturias (Ast.), C. D 2
Atarazana (Ataraz.) Vieja, C. B 2
Atarazana, C. B 2
Aureola (Aur.), C. D 2
Ave María, C. C 2/3
Aviador Dávila, C. D 2/3
Ávila Segovia, C. B 1
Aydanamar, Cjón. de A 2
Azacayas, C. B 2
Azacayuela de San Pedro, C. (Azac. S. P., C.) B 2
Azhuma, C. C 2
Azor, C. A 1
Azorín, C. C 1
B
B., C. B 2
Babolé (B.), C. B 2
Bachiller (B.) Sansón, C. D 3
Bailén, C. D 2
Baja de San (S.) Ildefonso (Ildef.) C. A 2
Baja Cárcel, C. B 2
Bajo de Huétor-Vega, Camino D 3
Baleares, C. D 2
Ballesteros (Ballest.)., C. B/C 2
Banderas (Band.), C. D 2
Bañuelo (Bañ.), C. B 2
Barcelona, Avenida de D 1/2
Barranco de Los Naranjos A 3
Barranco (Bco.) de Tello B 2
Barranco, C. C 3
Basilios, Paseo de los C 2/3
Bco. del Abogado C 3
Beaterio (B.) Santísimo (S.), C. B 2
Beethoven, C. D 1
Belén, C. C 2/3
Beltenebros (Bel.), C. D 3
Benalúa (B.), C. B 2
Benalúa, Plta. B 2
Bernarda Alba, Calle D 2
Berrocal (Berr.), Plta. B 2
Beteta, Cuesta de la B 2
Bibataubín, Pl. C 2
Bib-Rambla, Pl. B 2
Bidasoa, C. A 2
Blanca, C. C 1
Blanqueo Nuevo, C. A 2
Blanqueo Viejo, C. A 2
Blanqueo (B.) Viejo (V.), C. C 2/3
Blas Infante, C. D 2
Blasco Reta, C. A 1
Boabdil (Boab.), C. B 2
Bocanegra, C. B 2
Boli, Cjón. B 3
Bolonia, C. D 2
Bomba, Paseo de la C 2/3
Boquerón (Boqu.), C. B 2
Boquerón, Pl. B 2
Boteros (B.), C. B 2
Braj., C. B 3
Bravo, C. B 2
Brujones, C. B 2
Bruselas, C. C 2
Bruselas, C. D 2
Buen (B.) Rostro, C. B 2
Buenos Aires, C. C 1
Buensuceso, Calle B 1/2, C 1
C
C. San Miguel, Pl. B 2
C., Plta. B 2
Caballerizas, C. B 1
Cabras (Cab.), C. B 2
Cádiz, Avenida de D 1/2
Caidero, Cuesta del C 3
Calderería (Cald.)Vieja, C. B 2
Calderería (Calder.) Nueva (N.), C. B 2
Calderón de la Barca, C. C/D 2
Calderón (Cal.), C. D 2
Camino Abencerrajes D 2/3
Camino (Cam.) Peñuelas (Peñ.) D 2
Camp. Bajo C. C 2
Campayas, Cjón. B 2
Campillo, Pl. C 2
Campo Verde, Pl. C 2
Campo d. Príncipe (P.) C 2
Campo Verde (V.), C. C 2
Campos, C. C 1
Campos, Pl. C 2
Canasteros, Acera de B 1
Candil, C. B 3
Candiota, C. B 2
Capellanes (Capel.), C. B 2
Capitán Moreno, C. A/B 2
Capitanía (Cap.), C. B/C 2
Capri, C. D 2
Caracas, C. A 2
Cárcel (C.) Alta, C. B 2
Cardenal Parrado, Calle A 1/2
Cardenal (C.) Cisneros, Pl. A 1
Cardenal (C.) Mendoza, C. B 2
Carlos Pereja, C. B/C 1
Carmen, Pl. C 2
Cármenes de Gadeo, C. A 2
Carnicería (Carn.), C. B 2
Carniceros (Carn.), C. A 2
Carniceros, Pl. A 2
Carretas, Plta. de C 2
Carril de S. Cecilio C 3
Carril, C. A 2
Carro, C. B 2
Cartuja, Paseo de la A 2
Carvajales (Car.), Plta. B 2
Casa (C.) de Paso (P.) B 2
Casas Falange, C. C 3
Cascajal (Cas.), C. B 2
Casillas de Prats, C. C 1
Casino, Acera del C 2
Castañeda, C. C 2
Castillejos (Cast.), Pl. B 2
Castillejos, C. B 2
Cataluña, C. D 2
Cauchiles, Pl. C 2
Cazorla, C. A 2
Cedrán, C. B 2
Cementerio (Cem.), C. B 2

Cenacheros, Camino C 3
Ceniceros, C. B 2
Cerca de Don Gonzalo A/B 3
Cercado Bajo (B.) de Cartuja A 1
Cerro del Caballo, C. D 3
Cervantes, Avenida de C/D 3
Cetti- Meriem, C. B 2
Chapiz, Cuesta del B 2/3
Charca, C. B 2
Charca, Plta. B 2
Chinos, Ctra. B 3
Chinos, Cuesta de los B 3
Chinos, Plta. de B 3
Chirimias (Chir.), C. B 3
Chopo, C. A 3
Churra, Cuesta B 2
Cibeles, C. C 1
Ciego (C.) de Arjona, C. A 1
Ciencia, Avenida de la D 1
Ciprés, C. A 3
Circunvalación, Calle D 2
Cisne, Calle A 1
Ciudad de los Cármeres, Plaza de la A 1
Clavel d. San (S.)José, C. B 2
Clavel (Cl.) de San (S.) Pedro (P.), C. B 2
Clavileño (C.), C. C 3
Cobertizo (Cob.) de Santa (S.) Inés, C. B 2
Cobertizo (Cob.) de Santo (Sto.) Domingo (Dom.), C. B 2
Coca, C. B 2
Cocheras (Coch.) S. Paula, C. B 2
Cocheras (Coch.), C. C 2
Coches, C. C 2
Colcha, C. B 2
Colegio (Col.) Catalino (Cat.), C. B 2
Colegios, C. B 1/2
Colón, Gran Via de B 2
Com. Luis Megias, C. D 1
Comendadoras (Com.) de Santiago (Sant.), C. C 2
Comercio, Pje. C 1
Comino, Pl. B 2
Compás San Jerón., C. B 1
Compositor Ruiz Aznar, C. C 2
Concepción (Conc.), Plta. B 2
Concepción, C. C 2
Concha Espina, C. D 2
Concordia, Plaza C 2
Conde de Cifuentes, C. C 1/2
Conde (C.) d. Tendillas (Tend.), C. B 1
Conde (Con.) Alcala, C. B 2
Conde, C. C 2/3
Conde, Cjón. A 2
Conde, Pl. A 2
Constitución, Avenida de la A/B 1
Consuelo, C. B 2
Contador (Conta.), C. B 2/3
Convalecencia (C.), C. B 2
Cora, Calle la D 1
Cordilleras (Cord.), C. C 2
Corpus (C.) Cristi, C. B 2
Cortijuela, C. c 3
Cristo de Menacelli, C. C 1
Cristo de la Yedra, Calle C 1
Cristo (Cr.) Azucenas, Plta. B 2
Crucero, C. D 2
Cruellas (Cruel.), C. C 2
Cruz de Piedra, Plta. A 2
Cruz Mayo, Pje. A 1
Cruz Verde, Pl. B 2
Cruz d. Piedra, C. B 2
Cruz d. Piedra, C. B 2
Cruz de la Rauda, C. A/B 3
Cruz de Quirós, C. B 2
Cruz (C.) de Arqueros (Arqu.), Plta. B 2
Cruz (Cr.) de Arqueros (Arqu.), C. B 2
Cruz, Pl. A 2
Cuadro de San (S.) Antonio (A.), C. C 1
Cuarto Real de Santo Domingo (Cto. Sto. Dom.), C. C 2
Cubillas (Cub.), C. D 2
Cuchilleros (Cuchill.), Pl. B 2
Cuchilleros, C. B 2
Cue. P., C. B 2
Cuenca, C. B 1
Cuesta del Realejo C 2
Cuestecilla (Cuest.), C. B 2
Cuevas Coloradas, C. B 3
Curatelillo)Cuartel., C. C 2

D

Damasquieros (Damasqu.), C. B/C 2
Dante, C. C 1
Darro, Acera del C 2
Darro, Carrera del B 2/3
Delicias, C. A 2

Descalzas, Pl. B 2
Diego Silos, Pje. B 2
Dilar, Avenida de D 2
Divina (D.) Pastora, Av. B 1
Dom. Lozano, C. A 1/2
Don Bosco, Avenida D 1/2
Don Gonzalo, Cerca de A/B 3
Don (D.) Quijote, C. D 3
Don Simeón, C. B 2
Doña Rosita, C. D 2
Dorotea, C. D 2/3
Dos d. Mayo (M.), C. B 2
Dr. Barraquer, C. A 1
Dr. Enrique (E.) Hernandez (Hdez.), C. A 1
Dr. Felipe (F.) Villalobas (V.), C. A 1
Dr. Fermin (F.) Garrido, C. A 1
Dr. Gómez Román, C. A 1
Dr. Jiménez Diaz, C. A 1
Dr. Jimenez (J.) Garrido (G.), C. A 1
Dr. López Neira, Pl. A 1
Dr. Marin (M.) Lagos, C. C 1/2
Dr. Mesa (M.) Moles, C. A 1
Dr. Royas (R.) Ballesteros (B.), C. A 1
Dr. Victor (V.) Escribano (Esc.), C. A 1
Dr. Adelardo Mora, C. A 1
Dr. Alejandro Otero, C. C/D 1
Dr. Azpitarte, Calle A 1
Dr. Buenaventura, C. C 1
Dr. Castroviejo, C. A 1
Dr. Creus, C. B 2
Dr. Felix Rodriguez de la Fuente, C. B 2
Dr. Fidel (F.) Fernandez (Fern.), C. A 1
Dr. Fleming, C. A 1
Dr. Guirao Gea, Calle A 1
Dr. Jaime Garcia Royo, C. A 1
Dr. López Font, C. C 1
Dr. Marañón, C. A 1
Dr. Muñoz Fernández, C. A 1
Dr. Olóriz, Avenida del A 1
Dr. Pareya (P.) Yébenes, C. A 1
Duende, C. C 2
Dulcinea (D.) d. Toboso, C. C/D 3
Duque de San Pedro de Galatino, Pl. C 3
Duque Galatino, Avda. C 2

E

El Purche d.Laguna, C. B 3
El Castaño, C. D 3
El Castaño, Plta. D 3
El Greco, C. B 2
El Hidalgo, C. C/D 3
El Partal, C. B 3
El Salvador (Salv.), Pl. B 2
Elay (E.) Señán, C. D 2
Elvira, Calle B 2
Emilio (E.) Orozco, Cuest. B 2
Emir, Calle D 1
Emperador Carlos V, Paseo del B 2
Emperatriz Eugenia, Calle B 1
Encarnación (Encarn.), Pl. B 2
Encrucijada (Encr.), C. B 3
Enmedio Alto, Vereda B 3
Enmedio (Enm.) Baja, Ver. B 3
Enrique (Enr.) Gomez (G.) Arbolella (Arbol) C 2
Enriqueta Lozano, C. C 2
Era, C. B 3
Eras de Cristo (E. d. C.), C. A 1
Eras, Altillo de las A 1
Ermita (Erm.), C. B 2
Esc. Silencio, C. B 2
Escoraiza, Cuesta de C 2/3
Escudo (Esc.) d. Carmen, C. B 2
Escuela (Esc.), C. C 2
Escuelas (Esc.), Pl. B 2
Escultor Antonio Martínez Olalla, C. B 2
Escultor Navas Parejo, C. D 2
Escultor (Esc.) López Azalistre, C. C 2
Escutia (Esc.), C. C 2
Esmeralda (Esm.), C. A 2
Espino (Esp.), C. B 2
Espronceda, C. d 2
Esse-H., C. C 2
Estepona, C. C 2
Estrella, C. B 2
Estribo (Estr.), C. B 2
Eudoxia Piriz, Calle C/D 1

F

Fábrica (Fábr.) Vieja (V.), C. B 1
Faisán, Calle A 1
Fajalauza (Fajal.), Cjón. C 2
Fajalauza, C. A 2
Fátima, C. B 2

Fernando de los Rios, Avenida D 1
Flor, Pje. D 2
Florencia, Calle D 2
Fontiveras, Pl. D 2
Fontiveros, C. D 2
Frailes (Fr.) de la Victoria, C. B 3
Franceses, Cjón. B 2
Francisco d. Quevedo, C. C 2
Francisco (F.) Lopéz Jurado, C. D 2
Fray Leopoldo, C. A 1
Fray (Fr.) Hernando (H.) de Talavera (Talav.), C. D 2
Fuente de las Batallas A 2
Fuente del Avellano, Camino B 2
Fuente Nueva, Avenida de la A 1
Fuente Nueva, C. B 1
Fuente (F.) Clara, C. A 2
Fuentes, Pl. C 3
Fuerteventura (Fuer.), C. D 2
Fuerzas Armadas, Av. A 1

G

Gabriel Miró, C. B 1
Galicia (Gal.), C. D 2
Galileo, C. C 1
Gallo, Cjón. B 2
Gallo, Pl. B 2
Garcia (G.) Villatoro, C. C 2
Garcia (Garc.) Morató, C. C 2
Gardenia, C. C/D 1
Garrido, C. A 1
Gato (G.), C. B 2
Gaviota, Calle A 1
General Narváez, C. C 1
Generalife, Paseo del B/C 3
Génova, C. C 1
Gil, Plta. B 2
Gironés, Pl. B/C 2
Gloria, C. B 2
Gloria, Cj. B 2
Glorieta Arabial B/C 1
Gonzalo Gallas, C. B 1
Gonzalo J. Quesada, C. B 2
Goya, C. B 1
Gozo, C. C 2
Grabador D. Robarts, C. B 2
Gracia, C. C 1
Gracia, Pl. de C 1
Gran Capitán, Pl. B 1
Gran Capitán, C. B 1
Granadillo (Gr.), C. B 2
Granados (Gran.), Cta. B 2
Granados, C. C 1
Gregorio Silvestre, C. D 3
Gregorio (G.) Espín, C. B 1
Guadalajara (Guadalaj.), C. D 2
Guadalete, C. A 2
Guadarrama (Guardar.), C. C 2
Guarnón, C. D 3
Guatimocin (Guatim.), C. B 2/3
Guevara Pozo, C. B 1
Guillén (G.) d. Castro, C. C 1
Guinea, C. B 2
Gumiel (G.) San (S.) Pedro, C. B 3
Gumiel (G.) S.José, C. B 2

H

H., C. B 2
Halcón, Calle A 1
Haza Grande, Pl. A 2
Hércules, C. B 2
Hermanos Carazo, C. C 2
Hermosa (H.), C. B 2
Heute, C. C 2
Hileras (Hiler.), C. B 2
Hípica, Pje. D 2
Hnos. Aragón, C. D 2
Honda Realejo, C. C 2
Honda (H.) de San Andrés, C. B 2
Hornillo d. Cartuja , C. A 1/2
Horno Cerezo, C. B 2
Horno de Marina, C. B 2
Horno de Oro, C. B 3
Horno Merced, C. B 2
Horno San (S.) Agustin (Ag.), C. B 2
Horno de Haza, C. B 2
Horno Espadero, C. C 2
Horno (H.) d. Vidrio (Vid.), C. B 2
Horno (H.) de Abad, C. B 1
Horno (H.) Hoyo, C. B 2
Horno (H.) San Matias, C. C 2
Hortensia, C. A 2
Hospicio (Hosp.) Viejo (V.), Pl. A 1
Hospicio, Avenida del A/B 2
Hospital Santa Ana, C. B 2
Hoteles de Belén, C. C 3
Hoya de La Mora, C. D 3
Hoya de San Juan, C. D 3
Huerta Ángeles C 3
Huerto Santo (Sto.) C 3
Huerto (H.) S. Cecilio C 1/2
Huétor-Vega, Carretera de D 3
Humilladero, Plaza C 2

I

Iberia, Calle A 2/3
Iglesia de San Bartolomé (Ig. S. B.) B 2
Imprenta, C. B 2
Infanta Beatriz, C. C 1
Infantas, C. B 2
Infantes (Inf.), Cta. d.
Inmaculda Niña, Pl. D 3
Isaac Albéniz, C. A 1
Isabel La Católica, Pl.
Isla, Cjón. A 2/3
Isleta S. Felipe, C. B 1
Italia, Avenida de D 2

J

Jacinto Benavente, C. B 1
Jalifa A, C. C 3
Jalifa B, C. C 3
Jalifa C, C. C 3
Jalifa, Cjón. C 3
Japón de Daraja, C. D 3
Jaque, Cjón. C 1
Jardin de la Reina, Paseo C/D 1
Jardin (J.) Botanico (Botán.), C. B 1
Jardines, C. B/C 1
Jarrevia (Jarr.), C. C 2
Játiva, C. A 2
Jaudenes (Jaud.), C.
Jaz., C. C 2
Jazmin d. S. P., C. B 2
Jerez, C. C 1
Jesus y Maria, C. C 2
Jilguero, C. A 1
Joaquin (J.) Blume, C. C 1
Joaquin (J.) Costa, C. B 2
José Luis Pérez Pujadas, Calle D 1
José Luis Saenz de Heredia (J. L. S. d. H.), C. D 2
José Maria G. Lopera, C. D 3
José Morell, C. A 1/2
José Recuerda, C. C 1
Joven Marcelo, C. D 2
Juan Cristóbal, C.D 1/2
Juan López, C. C 1
Juan d. I. Cierva, C. C 2
Juan S. Cózar, C. B 1
Juan (J.) de Echevarria (E.), C. D 3
L. Rosales, C. B 1
L. Tablas, C. B 1/2
La Ventanilla, C. B 1
La Caleta A 1
La Cruz, C. C 1/2
La Paz, Calle B 1/2
La Torre, Pje.d. D 2
Labella Dávalos, C. A 1/2
Labor, Pasaje C 1
Larga San Cristobal (Crist.), C. B 2
Larga, Pl. B 2
Las Flores, C. C 1
Las Mercedes, C. C 3
Las Navas, C. C 2
Las Palmas, Paseo de C 3
Las Yeguas, C. C 3
Laur., C. C 2
Laureado L. Muñoz, C. D 2
Laurel Alta del Boquerón (L. A. B.), C. B 2
Lav. Zafra, C. B 2
Lavadero de la Cruz, C. B 1/2
Lavadero de las Tablas, C. B 1
Lavadero Méndez, C. B 2
Lavadero (Lav.) S. Inés, C. B 2
Lavadero (Lavad.) Pl. C 2
Lebrija, Callejón de A 2
León, C. B 2
Lepanto (L.), C. B 2
Libertad, Pl. A/B 2
Libreros (Lib.), C. B 2
Licenciado Vidriera, C. D 3
Limón (Lim.), C. B 2
Linan, Plta. B 2
Lirios, Pje. D 2
Lliberis, C. D 2
Lobos, Pl. B 1
Loja, C. D 2
Lona, Carril de la B 2
Lope de Vega, C. C 1
Los Ayalos, C. D 1
Los Mártires, Paseo de C 3
Los Aljibes, Plaza de B 2/3
Los Frailes, C. C 2
Los Juncos, Calle C/D 1
Los Naranjos, C. B 2
Los Santos, C. B 2
Lucena, C. B 2
Lucia I. Martin, C. B 1
Luis Braille, C. C 1
Luque, Pl. A 2

M

Madre (M.) Rimelque (Riq.), C. B 1
Madre (M.) Teresa, Pl.
Madreselva, C. D 2
Madrid, Avenida de A 1
Maestro Cebrián, C.
Maestro Chueca, C. C 1
Maestro Lecuona, C. C 1/2
Maestro Bretón, C. C 2
Maestro Faus, Calle D 3
Maestro Montero, C. C 1
Maestro Vives, C. C 1/2
Maestro (M.) Alonso, C. C 2
Maestro (M.) José Rodriguez, C. D 3
Málaga, C. B 1/2
Malahá, Calle la D 1
Malvarrosa, C. D 1
Manflor, Pl. A 2
Mano d. Hierro, C. B 1/2
Manuel de Falla, C. C 1
Manuel (M.) Ángeles Ortiz, C. C 2
Manuel (Man.) d. Paso, C. C 2
Maracena, Av. A 1
Marañas., Cta. de B 2
Margarita Xirgú, C. D 2
Maria del Carmen Margarita (Ma. C. Marg.), C. D 3
Maria Auxiliadora, C. D 1
Maria d. l. Miel (M.), Cta. B 2
Maria Luisa de Dios, C. A 1
Mariana Pineda, Pl. C 2
Mariana (M.) Pineda, C. C 2
Mariano de Amo, C. B 1
Marina, C. A 2
Marmolillos de San Lázaro, C. A 1
Marq. Gerona, C. D 2
Marq. d. Falces, C. B 2
Marqués Ensenada, C. B 2
Marqués de Mondéjar, Calle C 1/2
Marquéz de los Vélez, C. C 2
Marquéz Don Gonzalo, Calle C 1
Martin Pérez d. Ayala, C. C 2
Martin Bohórquez, C. C 2
Martinez de la Rosa, C. B 2
Martinez (Mar.) Contreras (Contrer.), Pl. B 2
Martinez, C. C 1
Martos (M.), Pl. C 2
Mataderillo (M.), Cjón. A/B 2
Matadero, Cjón. C 2
Matamoros, Cjón. C 3
Mediterráneo, Avda. del D 1
Melchor Almagro, C. B 1
Méndez Núñez, Calle B 1
Menorca, Pl. B/C 1
Mentidero (Ment.), Cjón. A/B 2
Mentidero (Ment.), Plta. A 2
Merced, C. B 2
Merced, Pl. B 2
Mercedes (Merc.) Bustos, C. C 1
Mesón del Toledano, C. C/D 3
Mesones, C. B 2
Miga, Plta. B 2
Milán, C. D 2
Minas, C. A 1
Minas, C. B 2
Minas, Plta. B 2
Mirador de Rolando, C. A 2
Mirador d. l .Vistillas (Vist.), C. C 3
Mirador de la Sierra, C. D 2
Mirasol, C. C 2
Mirlo, Calle A 1
Misericordia, C. B 1
Molino de la Corteza San Andrés, C. B 2
Molinos Cuesta de C 2/3
Molinos, C. C 2/3
Monachil, C. D 2
Monjas, Cjón. d. l. B 2
Monjas, Cjón. de las D 3
Montalbán, C. B 1
Monte Sedeyo C 3
Monte (M.) de Piedad, B/C 2
Montereina (Mont.), C. B 2
Monteros (Mont.), Cuesta C 2
Montes Claros, C. B 3
Moral Alta, C. C 2
Moral de la Magdalena, C. C 1/2
Moras, C. C 2
Morcillero, Callejón del C 2
Motril, C. D 2
Mozárabe, Calle D 1
Mozart, C. C/D 1
Mulhacén, C. C 2
Murcia, Avenida de A 1/2
Murcia, Carretera de A 1/2
Músico Debussy, C. C 1
Músico Vicente Zarzo, C. C 1
Músico J. Ayala Canto, C. C 2

N

Nápoles, C. D 2
Naranjo (N.), C. C 2
Naranjos, Plta. B 2
Nardos, Pje. D 2
Natalio Rivas, C. B 1/2
Navarra, Calle D 2
Navarrete, C. B 2
Nazaries, C. C 2
Negros, C. B 2
Negros, Pl. B 2
Neptuno, C. A 1
Nevada, C. A 2
Neveros, Camino de los D 3
Nevot, C. C 2/3
Nevot, Plta. B 2
Nicuesa (Nic.), C. C 2
Niño del Royo, Callejón B/C 2/3
Niños (N.) Luchando, C. C 2
No. 1, Plta. D 2
No. 2, Plta. D 2
No. 3, Plta. D 2
No. 4, Plta. D 2
No. 5, Plta. D2
No. 6, Plta. D 2
No. 7, Plta. D 2
No. 8, Plta. D 2
No. 9, Plta. D 2
No. 10, Plta. D 2
No. 11, Plta. D 2
No. 12, Plta. D 2
No. 13, Plta. D 2
No. 14, Plta. D 2
Nogales, Callejón de los C/D 1
Nuestra (Ntra.) Señora (Sra.) de la Salud, C. A 1
Nueva d. Sant., C. B 1/2
Nueva de Cartuja, C. A 1
Nueva de la Virgen, C. A 1
Nueva San Antón, C. C 1/2
Nueva, Pl. B 2
Nueva, Pl. B 2
Nuevo (N.) San Nicolás, Cam. B 2

O

Obispo Hurtado, Calle B/C 1
Obrero C. López, Plta. D 2
Oficios (Ofic.), C. B 2
Oidores, C. B 2
Olivo, C. A 3
Olmo, C. A 2
Omeya, Calle D 1
Orquidea (Orqu.), C. C 2
Ortegas, Pl.de B 2
Óscar Romero, C. D 2

P

Pablo, Avenida de C/D 2
Padre (P.) Ponze (P.) d. Leon, C. C 2
Padre (P.) Suarez, Pl. D 2
Padre (P.) Alcover, C. C 2
Padre (P.) Manjón, Paseo del B 3
Padre (P.) Seco d. Lucena, C. D 2
Pages, C. A 2
Palacios (Pal.), C. C 2
Palencia, Avenida de D 2
Palermo, C. D 2
Palmera, C. A 2
Palmito, C. A 3
Paloma, C. A 1
Pan, C. B 2
Panaderas (Pan.), C. B 2
Panaderos (Panader.), C. B 2
Pañera (P.), C. B 2
Paños (Pañ.), C. B 2
Pardo, C. B 2
Paredón Jesús Penas, C. A 2
Parra Alta de Cartuja, C. A 1/2
Parra de S. Cecilio, C. C 2/3
Parra (P.), C. B 2
Parraga, C. B/C 2
Parrilla, C. C 3
Particular, C. C 2
Pasaje, C. C 1/2
Pasiegas (Pasieg.), Pl. B 2
Pastigo (P.) de Zárate, C. B 2
Pastigo (P.) Velutti (V.), C. B 2
Pavaneras (Pavan.), C. B 2
Pedro Antonio de Alarcón, Calle B/C 1
Pedro Masipe, C. A 2
Peñuelas, Calle D 2
Peñuelas, Plta. A 2
Pérez (P.) Galdós, C. D 2
Pernaleros (P.) Alto (A.), C. B 2
Pernaleros (P.) Bajo (B.), C. B 2
Perodista Ruiz Carnero, C. C 2
Perugia, C. D 2
Pescaderia, C. B 2
Pescado, Cuesta d. C 2
Pianista Pepita Bustamante, Calle D 3
Pianista Rosa Sabater, C. D 3
Pianista (P.) Garcia (G.) Carrillo (Car.), C. B 3
Picón, Carril del B 1
Piedra Santa, C. C 2
Piedra (P.) Santa (S.), Pl. C 2
Pilar (P.) Seco C. B 2
Pinar, C. A 3
Pinchos, Vereda de los A/B 3
Pino, C. B 2/3
Pino, C. C 2
Pintor Velázquez, C. B 1
Pintor Ismael de la Serna, C. D 2
Pintor Manuel Maldonado, Calle C 2
Pintor S. Aedo, C. B 1
Pintor Zuloaga, C. C 1/2
Pintor (P.) Murillo, C. B 2
Pintor (P.) Rodriguez (R.) Acosta, C. B 1
Pintor (P.) López Mezquita, C. B 1
Pio Baroja, C. B 1
Pizarro Cenjor, C. A 1/2
Plata, Cuesta de la D 2
Plegadero Alto (A.), C. B 2
Plegadero Bajo (B.), C. B 2
Poco Trigo, Cjón. A 1
Poeta Eduardo Carranza, C. D 3
Poeta Manuel Benitez Carrasco, Pl. D 2
Poeta Mira de Amescua, C. A 1
Poeta Zorrilla, C. C 2
Poeta Manuel de Góngora, C. C 2
Poeta (P.) César Vallejo, C. D 2/3
Polvorin, Camino de A 3
Porras, Plta. B 2
Porteria (P.) de la Concepcion (Conc.), C. B 2
Portón Baquetas (B.), C. B 2
Postigo (P.) de San (S.) Agustin, C. B 2
Pretorio, Callejón del C/D 2
Primavera, Calle D 2
Principal (Pr.) de San (S.) Bartolomé (Bart.) A 2
Principe (Princ.), C. B 2
Prof. Fontboté, Pl. B 1
Prof. García Gomez, C. C 1
Prof. Sainz C., C. B 1
Prof. T. Díaz, C. B 1
Prof. Agustin Escribano, C. C/D 1
Prof. Motos Guirao, C. B 1
Prof. Tierno Galván, C. C/D 2
Profesor Albareda, C. C 2/3
Profesor Luis Molina Gómez, Calle B/C 1
Profesor Manuel Garzón, Calle D 2
Progreso (Progr.), Cuesta C 2
Prosperidad, C. B/C 1
Puente Brujas C 2
Puente Cabrera B 2
Puente Espinosa B 2
Puente Genil C 2
Puente Rey Chico B 3
Puente Verde C 3
Puente Castañeda C 2
Puente Cristiano, C. C 2
Puente (Pte.) de la Virgen C 2
Puentezuelas, Calle B/C 1/2
Puerta Real de España C 2
Puerta (Pta.) d. Sol, Cjón. C 2
Pulianas, Avenida de A 1
Purchil, C. C 1

Q

Quijada, C. B 2
Quinta Alegre, Pje. D 3

R

Ramirez, Plta. B 2
Real de Cartuja, C. A 2
Real de la Alhambra, C. B 3
Real Sto. Dom., C. C 2
Realejo, Camino del B/C 2, C 3
Realejo, Cuesta del B 2
Realejo, Pl. del C 2
Recogidas, Calle C 1/2
Recogidas, Pje. C 1
Rector Garcia (G.) Duarte, C. B 1
Rector López Argueta, Calle A/B 1
Rector, C. D 2
Regina, Pje. C 2
Reina Mora, C. D 2
Rejas d. I.Virgen, C. C 2
Rejas, C. C 2
Revidero, C. C 2
Rey Chico, Cuesta del B 3
Rey Chico, Plta. B 3
Reyes Católicos, Calle B/C 2
Ribera del Beiro, Calle A 1
Ricardo Arco, C. C 2
Rincón de Asis, C. C 1

Rio (R.) Beiro, Pl. D 3
Rio Bermejales, Plta. D 2
Rio Cacin, C. D 2
Rio (R.) Colomera (C.), C. D 2
Rio (R.) Dauro (Da.), C. D 2
Rio (R.) Fardes (F.), C. D 2
Rio Gualdal., C. D 2
Rio Lecrin, C. D 2
Rio (R.) Monachil (M.), C. D 2
Rio (R.) Zújar (Z.), C. D 2
Rios, Avenida Fernando de los D 1
Risco, Cjón. B 3
Rodrigo d.Campo, Cta.
Roma, C. D 2
Romanilla, Pl. B 2
Ronda, Camino de B/C 1, D 1/2
Ronda, Pje. D 2
Rosal de San Pedro (Ro. S. P.), C. B 2
Rosales, Plta. A 2
Rosario (Ros.) S. Ant., C. C 2
Ruiseñor, C. A 1

S

Sacristia (S.) Risco (Risc.), C. C 2
Sacristia, C. A 2
Sacromonte, Camino del B 3
Sainz (S.) Cantero (Can.), Pje. B 1
Salamanca (Salam.), C. A 1
Salón, Paseo del C 2
Salvador, C. C 2
San Agustin, Pl. B 2
San Antonio, C. C 2
San Bartolomé, Plta. C 2
San Cristobal, Plta. A 2
San Martín, C. B 3
San Pantaleón (Pantal.), Pl. A 1
San Vicente Ferrer, C. B 3
San Agustin (Ag), Cta. B 3
San Agustin, C. B 2
San Agustin, Carril de B 2/3
San Agustin, Vederilla B 3
San Antón Viejo, C. A 2
San Antón, Calle C 2
San Antonio, Camino de A 2
San Antonio, Cuesta de A 2
San Carlos, C. C/D 3
San Cecilio, Cjón. B 2
San Cristóbal, Veredilla de B 2
San Diego, C. C 2
San Gregorio Alto, Calle B 2
San Gregorio, Cta. de B 2
San Ildefonso, Acera de A/B 2
San Isidoro, C. B 1
San Isidro, C. C 2
San Isidro, Pl. de A 1
San Jacinto, C. C 2
San Jaun (J.) Letrán, Pl. A 1
San Jerónimo, C. B 2
San José Baja, C. C 2
San José, C. B 2
San Juan de Dios, Calle B 1
San Juan de los Reyes, Calle B 2/3
San Luis, Calle A 2/3
San Matias, C. C 2
San Miguel Alta, C. B/C 1
San Miguel, A. C A 2/3
San Pedro Mártir, C. C 2
San Pio X, C. D 2
San Sebastián, Paseo de C 2
San (S) Juan d. Letrán, C. A 1
San (S.) Agustin Alto, C. B 2/3
San (S.) Andrés, C. B 2
San (S.) Bartolomé (B.), C. A 2
San (S.) Buenaventura (Buena.), C. B 2
San (S.) Cristóbal, C. A 2
San (S.) Francisco (F.) d. Asis, C. C 2
San (S.) Gregorio (Greg.), Plta. B 2
San (S.) Juan Baja, C. B 2
San (S.) Juan d. l. Cruz, Pl. B 2
San (S.) Luis Alto, Cjón. A 2
San (S.) Miguel (Mig.) Bajo, Pl. A 2
San (S.) Nicolas (N.), C. A 2
San (S.) Nicolas, Cjón. B 2
San (S.) Nicolás, Esp. B 2
San (S.) Nicolás, Pl. B 2
San (S.) Rafael, C. C 2
San (S.) Agustin, C. d. B 2/3
San (S.) José, Plta. B 2
San (S.) Marcos, Cjón. C 2

Sancha, C. M. B 2
Sánchez (Sán.), Pl. B 2
Sanchica, C. D 3
Sancho Panza, C. D 3
Santa Ana, Pl. B 2
Santa Aurelia, C. C 2
Santa Teresa, Pl. C 1
Santa Bárbara, Calle B 1
Santa Clotilde, Calle B 1
Santa Lucia, C. B 2
Santa Teresa, Calle B 1/2
Santa (S.) Catalina (C.), Cjón. C 2
Santa (S.) Catalina (Catal.) Baja (B.), C. C 2
Santa (S.) Inés, Cta. B 2
Santa (S.) Cruz, C. B 1
Santa (S.) Isabel La Real, C. B 2
Santa (Sta.) Candida, C. C 2
Santa (Sta.) Catalina, C. B/C 2
Santa (Sta.) Escolástica, C. B/C 2
Santa (Sta.) Clara, C. D 2
Santa (Sta.) Paula, C. B 2
Santi Espiritu, C. B 2
Santiago González, C. A 1
Santiago, C. C 2
Santillana, Plta. B 2
Santísimo, C. B 2
Santisteban Márquez, C. B 1
Santo Sepulcro, C. D 3
Santo (S.) Cristo, Plta. B/C 2
Santo (S.) Domingo (D.), C. C 2
Santo (Sto.) Domingo (D.) Henares (Hen.), C. B 1
Santo (Sto.) Domingo, Pl. C 2
Santo (Sto.) Domingo, Cjón. C 2
Sarabia, C. C 2
Sederos, C. C 2
Segovia, Calle D 2
Seminario, C. B/C 1
Séneca, C. B 1
Señor, Cjón. C 2
Serrano (Serr.), C. B 2
Severo Ochoa, Calle A/B 1
Sevilla, C. B 1
Sicilia, C. D 2
Sierpe (Si.) Baja, C. C 2
Sierra San (S.) Pedro (P.), C. B 2
Sierra Carretera de C 3
Silleria (Sill.), Plta. B 2
Silleria, C. B 2
Sócrates, Calle B 1
Sol, C. B 1
Sol, Plta. B 2
Sol., C. C 2
Solares, C. C 2/3
Solarillo d. Gracia, C. C 1
Somosierra (Somos.), C. C 2
Sor Cristina Mesa, C. C 2
Sor Cristina de la Cruz de Arteaga, Pl. B 1
Sorozábal, C. C 1
Sos del Rey Católico, C. C 2
Sur, Avenida del A 1

T
Tablas, Calle B 1/2
Taha, Calle la D 1
Tallacarne, Callejón A 2
Tejeiro, C. C 1/2
Tendillas (T.) Santa (S.) Paula (P.), C. B 2
Tenerife, C. D 2
Tiña, C. B 2
Tinajas (T.), C. A 2
Tinajilla D., C. B 2
Tinte, C. B 2
Tirso Molina, C. C 2
Tomasas (Tom.), Cjón. d. B 2
Tomasas, Carril de B 2
Tomillo, C. A 3
Toqueros, Plta. B 3
Toril., C. C 2
Toro, Plta B 2.
Toros, Plaza de A 1
Torre de las Damas, C. D 2
Torre Quebrada, C. D 2
Torre d. I. Pólvora, C. D 3
Torre Pedro de Morales, C. D 2/3
Torres Bermejas, C. B 2
Torres Molina, C. D 2
Tórtola, Calle A 1
Tovar, Plta. B 2
Trabuco, C. B 2
Trajano, Calle B 1
Transv. Peñuelas, C. D 2
Transv., Cjón. C 3
Tres (Tr.) Estrellas, Pl. A 2
Triana Baja, C. B 1
Triana, C. B 1/2
Trinidad (Trin.) Morcillo, C. B 1
Trinidad, C. B 2
Trinidad, Plaza B 2
Triunfo, Acera del A/B 1
Triunfo, Pl. del B 2
Trivino, Plta. B 1/2
Tundidores (Tund.), C. B 2
Turia, C. A 2
Túrin, C. C 1
Turina, C. B 1

U
Universidad (Univ.), Pl. B 2

V
Valentin (V.) Barrecheguren (Barr.), C. B 2
Valenzuela (Valenz.), C. B 3
Valle Inclán, C. B 1
Varela, C. C 2
Vargas, Cjón. C 3
Venecia, C. B 1
Veracruz, C. C 1
Vergeles (Verg.), C. C 2
Verona, C. B 2
Veronica de la Virgen, C. C 2
Verónica de la Magdalena, C. B/C 1, C 2
Victoria Plta. B 3
Victoria, Cjón. B 3
Victoria, Cuesta B 3
Vidrio de San Lázaro, C. A 1
Viejo de Fargue, Camino A 2/3
Viejo (V.), Corr. B 2
Villa Yebra, C. C 3
Villamena (Villam.), Pl. B 2
Violetas, C. D 2
Violón, Paseo del C 1/2
Violón, Paseo del C/D 2
Virgen Blanca, C. C 1
Virgen de Loreto, C. D 2
Virgen del Pilar, C. A 1
Virgen del Rocio, C. D 3
Virgen (V.) de Montserrat, C. C 2, D 2/3
Virgen, Carrera de la C 2
Virgen, Pte. C 2
Vistillas de los Ángeles, C. C 3

Y
Yedra, C. D 1
Yerma, C. D 3
Yeseros, C. A 2
Yesqueros (Yes.), Pl. B 2

Z
Zacatin (Zac.), C. B 2
Zafra (Z.), Concepcion (C.) d. B 2
Zafra, C. B 2
Zafra, Cjón. B 2
Zaida, C. C 1
Zaragozo (Z.), C. C 2
Zenete, Calle B 2
Ziries, C. C 2
Zubia, Camino de la D 2
Zulema, C. A 2

Lisboa

7

A
A.Amaro da Costa, L. D2
A.Andrade, R. B2
Ab. De Peniche, Tv. d. C1
Academia das Ciências, R. da C/D1
A.Cândido, R. A1
A.Cardoso, R. A2
Açores, R. dos A1/2
A.Cout, R. B2
Actor Taborda, R. A1
Actor Tasso, R. B1
Actor Vaie, R. A2
A. de Calv., Cal. C2
Adelas, R. d. C1
A.de Paiva, R. B3
Adro, Tv. do C2
A.Fario, R. A2
Afonso Domingues, R. C3
Água de Flor, Tv. d. C1
Água, R. d. C1
A.Isidoro, R. A2
A.J.Almeida, R. A2
A.J.Ricardo, R. A2
A.J.Vieira, R. B2
A.José de Almeida, Av. A1/2
Alcaide, Tv. do D1
Alecrim, R. do D1
Alegria, Pr. Da C1
Alegria, R. de C1
Alexandre Braga, R. B2
Alexandre Herculano, R. B/C1
Alfândega, R. da D2
Alm., R. d. D1
Almada, Tv. d. D2
Almirante Barroso, R. A/B1
Almirante Reis, Av. A-C2
Alto da Eira, R. do B3
Alves Redol, R. A1
Alves Torgo, R. A2
A.Machado, R. A3
Amaral. Vila B2
A.M.Baptista, R. B2
A.M.Cardoso, R. D1
Amendoeira, R. da C2
A.Monteverde, R. A2
Amoreiras, Tv. das A2
Anchieta, R. D1
Andaluz, Largo do B1
Andaluz, R. do B1
Andrade Corvo, R. B1
Andrade, R. B2
Angelina vidal, R. B/C2
Angola, R. da B2
Angra d. Heroismo, R. B2
Anicelo do Rósario, Pr. B2
Anjos, R. dos B/C2
Ant. Aug. De Aguiar, Av. A/B1
Antero de Quental, R. B/C2
António Enes, R. A1
António Luis Ignácio, R. A3
António Pedro, R. A/B2
Anunciada, Largo da C1
Aparicio, L. B1
A.P.Carrilho, R. A2
A.Pinto, R. A2
Arc., B. d. D1
Arco a Jesus, Tv. do C1
A.Rosa, R. D2
Arroios, R. de A/B2
Arsenal, R. do D1/2
A.Sardinha, Pr. B2
Assunção, R. da D2
Atalaia, R. da D1
Aug.Machado, R. A2
Augusta, R. D2
Aurea, R. D2

B
Bacalhoeiros, R. dos D2
Baixo da Penha, Cam. D. B3
Baixo, R. d. B3
Baldaques, R. dos A2/3
Baptista, R. C2
Barão de Sabrosa, R. A2/3
Barata Salgueiro, R. B/C1
Barb.Benformoso, B. da C2
Barbadinhos, Calç. dos C3
Barrac., R. d. B2
Barroca, R. da D1
B.Costa, R. D1
B. da Costa, R. C3
B.D.Belo,R. d. D1
B.d.Gusmão, R. D2
Beatas, R. das C2/3
Beco da Boavista, R. da D1
Bela Vista, R. da C3
Bempostinha, R. d. B/C2
Bern., B. da B/C2
Bernardin Ribeiro, R. B1
Berta, Vila C3
B.Hora, Tv. da C1
B.Horizonte, R. A3
Bica d.Anjos, Tv. d. C2
Birbantes, B. dos C1/2
B.Lima, R. B1
Boa Hora, L. d. D2
Boavista, R. da D1
Bombarda, R. da C2
Boqueirão de Ferreiros, R. D1
Boqueirão do Duro, R. D1
Borralho, B. B2
Borratém, P. do C2
B.Queir., R. C2
Braamcamp, R. B1
Brasilia, Av. de D1
Broges Grainha, R. B2

C
Cabeço de Bola, Largo de B2
Cabo Verde, R. de B2
Cabral, R. do C3
Cabral, Tv. do D1
Caetanos, R. d. D1
Calado, Trav. Do B2
Calçada da Picheleira, R. A3
Cam. De Ferro, R. d. C3
Cândida, Vila B3
Candoso, Villa A3
Cap.H.Ataide, R. C3
Capitão, R. C2
Cara, Tv. d. C1
Cardal d.S.J., R. do C1
Carl., R. da C1
Carlos Mardel, R. A2
Carmo, L. do D1
Carmo, R. do D2
Carmo, Tv. do D1
Carrascal, Calç. do A3
Carrião, R. do C1
Carv., Tv. d. D1
Carvalho Araújo, R. A2
Carvalho, Vaz de B1
Casal Ribeiro, Av. A1
Cascão, C. do C3
Castelinhos, R. d. B/C2
Castelo Branco Saraiva, R. B3
Castelo, Costa do C/D2
Castilho, R. B/C1
Cavaleiros, R. d. C2
C.Castelo Branco, R. B1
C. da Glória, R. da C1
C. d. Dest., Tv. d. C2
C. de Jes., Tv. d. D1
C. de Oliveira, R. A2
C. de Sousa, R. C1
C. d. Rio, Tv. d. D1
C. d. Santarém, R. d. D2
C.Falcão, R. A2/3
C.Ferr. do Amarai, R. A3
Cegos, R. d. C/D2
Ces. Verde, R. B2
Ch. De Feira, R. d. D2
Chafariz de Dentro, L. d. D3
Chagas, R. das D1
Chile, Pr. do A2
Ciclade da Horta, R. A1/2
Cid de Cardif, R. B2
Cid de Liverpool, R. B2
Cid.Gonç., Tv. d. C2
Cima, R. d. B3
Cinco de Outubro, Av. A1
C.J.Barreiros, R. A2
C.Mardel, R. A2
Colégio, Tv. do C2
Comandante Avintes, Tv. C3
Combro, Calç. d. D1
Comérc., R. do D2
Comércio, P. do D2
Con. D. Monsaraz, R. d. B2
Conceição, R. D2
Concelçao, Tv. da C1
Conda de Redondo, R. B1
Conde d. Pombeiro, L. d. B2
Conde de Valbom, Av. A1
Condes, R. dos C1
Condessa, R. da C/D1
Cons.A. Pedroso, R. C2
Contador-Mor, L. do D2
Conv.d.Encam., L. d. C2
Cor.Lunade Oliveira, R. A3
Cordeiro, R. A1/2
Coronel Eduardo Galhardo, Av. B3
Corpo Santo, L. d. D1
Corpo Santo, R. d. D1
Correeiros, R. dos D2
Corvos, R. d. D3
C.Pestana, R. C2
C.Rib., Pr. B2
C.Ribeiro, R. B2
C.Roby, R. A3
Crucifixo, R. do D2
Cruz d.Anjos, Tv. d. C2
Cruz da Carreira, R. da B1
Curraleira, Qu.d. A3
C.Videira, R. A2

D
Damas, R. d. D2
D.Bar., C. C3
Defensores de Chaves, Av. dos A1
Despacho, Tv. d. B1
D.Est., Tv. de B1
Diário de Noticias, R. C/D1
Dom A. Henriques, Alameda A2
Dom J.C.Câmara, Pr. C1
Dom Luis I., R. D1
Dom Luis, Pr. D1
Dom Pedro IV (Rossio), Pr. C/D2
Dom Pedro V, R. C1
Domasceno Monteiro, R. B/C2
Dona Estefânia, R. de A/B1
Dona Filipa de Vilhena, R. A1
Dona, L. de A1
Doque, R. do C/D1
Dos, Pr. C1
Douradores, R. dos D2
D.Prior Coutinho, R. B1
Dr.A. de Sousa Macedo, Pr. D1
Dr.Alm Amaral, R. B1
Dr.B.A.Gomes, Pr. C3
Dr.L. de Almelda, R. B2/3
Dr.O. Ramos, R. A2
Duque de Ávila, Av. A1
Duque de Cadaval, L. d. C1
Duque de Loulé, Av. B1
Duque de Saldanha, Pr. A1
Duque de Teceira, Pr. D1
Duque d. Palmela, R. B1
Duques de Bragança, R. d. D1

E
E.Araújo, Tv. da B1/2
E.Brazão, R. A2
Eça de Queirós, R. B1
E.Cável, R. A2
E.Costa, R. B3
E.d. Santos, R. B1
E.d. Veiga, R. B2
E.Eduarda, R. A3
Eduardo Coelho, R. C1
Elias Garcia, Av. A1
Emenda, R. da D1
En. Da Gr.Guerra, R. d. B2
Engenheiro Santos Simoẽs, R. A3
Eng.M.Chaves, R. A3
Eng.Vieira da Silva, R. A/B1
Ent. Do Mirante, R. de C3
Env. d.Inglaterra, Tv. D. B1
Esc.Municip., L. d. C2
Escola de Medicina Veterinária, R. B1
Escola do Exército, R. da B2
Escolas Gerals, R. das D2
Es.do Cardal, R. da C1
Estefânia, R. A1/2

F
Fanqueiros, R. dos D2
Farinhas, R. d. C2
F.da Silva, R. A2
F. de Deus, Tv. dos D1
Fé, R. da C1
Félix, Beco B2
Ferr. de Baixo, R. do D1
Ferreira Lapa, R. B1
F.Foreiro, R. B2
Figueira, Pr. Da C2
Filipe Folque, R. A1
F.Lazaro, R. B2
F.Lopes, R. A1
Flores, R. d. D1
Fonte Louro, Az. da A3
Fontes Pereira de Melo, Av. A/B1
Forno d.Maldonado, Tv. d. C2
Forno do Sol, R. d. C2/3
Forno do Tijolo, R. do B2
Forte, C. do C/D3
Forte, Tv. do C2
F.P.Vidal, R. A3
Franc. Sanches, R. A/B2
Francisco Pedro Curado, R. B3
Frei M. do Cenáculo, R. B3
Freiras, Tv. d. C3
Freiras, Tv. das A2
Freiras, Tv. Das A2
F.Ribeiro, R. B2
F.Terenas, R. B2
F.Tomás, R. D1
Funchal, R. do A1/2

G
Gadanho, Vila B3
Garrett, R. D1
Gáveas, R. das D1
G.C. de Quintela, Tv. D1
Gen. Gar. Rosado, R. B1
Gen. J. Padrel, R. C3
Gen. Farinha Beirão, R. B1
General Roçadas, Av. B/C2/3
G. Junqueiro, Av. A2
Glória, Calçada da C1
Glória, R. da C1
Glória, Tv. da C1
Gomes Freire, R. B1/2
Gonçalves Crespo, R. B1
Graça, Cal. da C2
Graça, Caracol da C2
Graça, Largo da C2
Graça, R. da C2
Gr.Lus, R. d. C/D1
Guia, R. d. C2
Guiné, R. de B2

H
Heliodoro Salgado, R. B2
Heróis de Quionga, R. A3
Hor. Seca, R. d. D1
Horta d.Cera, Tv. d. C1
Horta, Tv. da C1
Hospital, Tv. d. C2

I
Ilha d.Principe, R. da B2
Ilha do Faial, Pr. Da A1
Ilha Terceira, R. da A1/2
Ilha, R. da A2
Infante Dom Henrique, Av. D2/3
Inglesinhos, Tv. d. D1
Inst. Bacter., R. d. C1/2
Inst.doV.Mach, R. do D2
Instituto Industrial, R. D1
Int.P.Manique, L. do C2
Ivens, R. D1

J
Jacinta Marto, R. B1/2
Jacinto Nunes, R. A/B 2/3
J.A. das Neves, R. A2/3
J.A.Serrano, R. C2
Jasmim, R. do C1
Jasmim, Tv. do C1
J.Bonifácio, R. B1
J.C.Machado, R. C1
J.Costa, R. A2
J.d.A.Coutinho B3
J.d.Andrade, R. C1
J.d.Meneses, R. A2
J.d.Óbidos, R. C2
J.d.Regras, R. C2
J.d.Tabaco, R. d. D3
Jean Monnet, L. C1
J.Fontana, Pr. B1
J.Maria, R. C2
João Crisóstorno, Av. A1
João de Outeira, R. C2
João do Nascimento Costa, R. A3
João Vaz, Tv. de A1
Joaq., R. C1/2
Jordão, Tv. do C2
José Estevão, R. B2
José Falcão, R. A2
José, Tv. de B2
J.Reg., R. d. C1
Julho, Av. de D1

L
Lagares, R. dos C2
Lagares, Tv. d. C2
Lapa, B. da D3
Larga, Tv. C1
Latino Coelho, R. A1
Lavra, Cal. do C1
Leão, Largo do A2
Leite de Vasconcelo, R. C3
Liberdade, Av. da B/C1
L.Mendonça e Costa, R. A2
L.Monteiro, R. A3
Lóios, L. dos D2
Loreto, R. d. D1
Loureiro, Tv. do C1
L.Pinto Molt., R. B2
L.Simões, R. A2
L.Todi, R. C1
Luciano Cordeiro, R. B1
Luis Bivar, Av. A1
Luz Soriano, R. D1

M
Macau, R. de B2
Machado de Castro, R. C3
Madalena, R. da D2
Mãe, R. d. C1
Maldonado, Tv. do C2
M.A.Martins, R. B2
Manchester, C. de B2
M.Andrade, R. B2
Maria da Fonte, R. B/C2
Maria Luisa, B. da B2
Maria, R. B2
Marq. da Silva, R. B2
Marquês d. Sampaio, Tv. d. D1
Marquês de Pombal, Pr. B1
Marquês de Ponte de Lima, R. do C2
Marquês de Tomar, Av. A1
Martim Moniz, R. C2
M.Bento d. S., R. C1/2
M. de Artilh., R. do D3
M. de Tanc., C. d. D2
M.d.J.Coelho, R. C1
Mercês, Tv. das D1
Met., R. da C1
Mexico, Av. do A2
M.Ferrão, R. B1
M.Gouveia, R. A3
M.Maia, Av. A2
Miguel Bombarda, Av. A1
Mindelo, R. B2
Misericórdia, R. da D1
Mitelo, L. do B/C2
Moçambiq, R. de B2
Moeda, R. da D1
Moinho de Vento, C. do C1
Mónicas, Tv. das C2
Monte, Beco do C2
Monte, Cal. do C2
Monte, C. do C2
Monte, L. do C2
Monte, Tv. do C2
Morais Soares, R. A/B2/3
Mour., R. d. C1
Mour., R. d. C2
M.S.Guedes, R. C2
M. Saldanha, R. D1
M.Sarm., R. B2
M.Vaz, R. C2
Mouz. Da Silveira, R. B/C1
Mouzinho de Albuquer-que, Av. B3
Municipio, Pr. do D2
Museu de Artilharia, L. do D3

N
Nazaré, Tv. do C2
N.d. Dest., R. C2
N.Delg., R. B2/3
N. de S.Francisco, C. D2
N. do Amada, R. D2
Nepomuceno, R. d. D1
Neves Ferreira, R. B2
Newton, R. B2
Notre, R. do D1
Nova d. Trindade, R. D1
Nova de S.Mamede, R. C1
Nova do Loureiro, R. C/D1
Novas Nações, Pr. B2

O
Olarias, L. das C2
Olarias, R. das C2
Olegário Marlarlo, Pr. B2
Oliveira, R. da C/D1
Ollval, Tv. do C3
Outerinho da Amendoeira, L. do C/D3

P
Paço da Rainha, L. B2
Pad., R. d. D2
Padre, R. B1
Paiva Couceiro, Pr. B3
Palma, R. da C2
Palma, Tv. da C2
Palmeira, R. da C1
Palmeira, Tv. da C1
Palmeiras, L. das B1
Palmira, R. B2
Paraiso, R. C3
Paraiso, Tv. d. C3
Pareira, Tv. da C2/3
Parreiras de S. António, Tv. das B1
Particular, R. A2
Particular, R. B3
Pascoal de Melo, R. A/B1/2
Passadiço, R. do B/C1
Passos Manuel, R. B2
Patriacal, C. d. C1
P. de S.Bento, R. d. D1
P.Dias, R. D1
Pedro Nunes, R. A1
Peixinh, B. dos C2
Pena, Tv. d. C2
Penha de França, L. da B2
Penha de França, R. da B/C2
Petingulm, Beco do B2
Pico, R. do A2
Picoas, R. das A1
Pim. D. Ataide, Pto. d. D1
Pina, Av. d. A3
Pinheiro Chagas, R. A1
P.Mitton, R. B2
P.Negras, R. d. D2
Poco d.Cidade, Tv. do D1
Poço dos Mouros, Calç. do A/B2
Poco dos Negros, R. do D1
Poço, C. do B2
Pombeiro, C. d. B2
Ponta Delgada, R. A2
Portas de Santo Antão, R. das C1/2
Portuguesa, Tv. d. D1
Praia da Vitória, Av. A1
Prata, R. da D2
Pretas, R. das C1
Principe Real, Pr. do C1
Prof.C.da Costa, R. B2/3
Prof.M.Fernandes, R. A3
P.S. d.Freitas, R. B2

Q
Quatro de Agosto, R. A3
Queimada, Tv. d. D1
Queiraz, Vila B2
Quinta dos Peixinhos, C. da B3
Quirino da Fonseca, R. A2

R
Rap., Tv. d. C3
R. da Fonseca, R. C1
R.d.Andrade, R. C2
R. da Silva, Tv. A2
R.d.Freitas, L. C2
Rebelo da Silva, R. A2
Rec., Tv. das B1
Reg. dos Anjos, R. B2
Regueta, R. da D2/3
Rem., Tv. d. D1
Remédios, R. dos D3
República, Av. da A1
Ribeira das Naus, Av. da D1/2
Ribeira Nova, Pr. da D1
Rodrigues Sampaio, R. B/C1
Rodrigues, B. C1
Rodrigues, Vila C3
Rogueirão dos Anjos, R. B2
Rosa Araújo, R. C1
Rosa, R. da C/D1
Rosalina, R. C2
Rosário, R. do B2
Rossa Damasceno, R. A2
Ros., Tv. do C1
Rovisco Pais, Av. A2
Rub. Ant. Leitão, R. C1

S
Sabino de Sousa, R. A3
Saco, R. do C2
Sacramento, C. do D1
S.A.d.Capuchos, R. de C1
Salema, Pto. do C2
Salgadeiras, Tv. d. C2
Salitre, R. do C1
Salitre, Tv. do C1
Salvador Correia de Sá, C. D1
Salvador, L. do D2
Salvador, R. do C/D2
San d. Cruz, Tv. C2
Santa Bárbara, L. de B2
Santa Bárbara, R. de B2
Santa Clara, Campo de C3
Santa Engrácia, R. de C3
Santa Luzia, Casal de B1
Santa Maria, R. de B1
Santa Maria, Tv. de B1
Santa Marinha, L. de C2
Santa Marta, R. de B/C1
Santana, C. de C2
S.Antão, Tv. d. C1
S.Ant., C. de B1
Santo André, Cal. de C2
S.Antoinho, L. D1
S.António da Glória, R. de C1
S.António, Tv. de C3
Saõ Bernardino, Tv. De B1
São José, R. de C1
São Julião, R. de D2
São Mamede, R. de D2
São Marçal, R. de C1
São Nicolau, R. de D2
São Paulo, R. de D1
São Sebastião da Pedreira, R. de A/B1
São Tomé, R. de C/D2
Sapadores, R. dos C2/3
Sapateiros, R. d. D2
Saud., R. d. D2
Saúde, Esç. Da C2
Saude, Rua (R.) Sra. C 2
S.Boaventura, R. d. C1
S.Carlos, L. d. D1
S.Catarina, Tv. de D1
S.Cristó., R. d. D2
S.Cruz d.Castelo, L. d. C/D2
S.Cruz d.Castelo, R. d. C/D2
S.Domingos, L. de C2
Sé, Cruz. d. D2
Sé, Lar. da D2
Século, R. do C/D1
Senhora da Glória, R. da C3
Senhora da Graça, Tv. d. C3
Senhora do Monte, R. da C2
Seq., Tv. d. D1
Serpa Pinto, R. D1
S.Est, R. D3
S.Estêvão, L. de D2/3
S.Francisco, Cal. De D2
S.Gens, R. de C2
Sidónio Pais, Av. B1
S.João d. Praça, R. de D2
S.Justa, R. D2
S.Lázaro, B. d. C2
S.Lázaro, R. d. C2
S.Luis da Pena, B. do C2
S.Marinha, R. de C2
S.Martinho, L.d. D2
S.Miguel, R. d. D2
Socied. Farmacêutica, R. da B1
Soi a Chelas, R. do A3
Sol a Santana, R. do C2
Sol, R. do C2/3
Sol, R. do D1
Sousa Martins, R. B1
S.Paulo, Pr. de D1
S.Pedra, R. de D2/3
S.Pedro, Tv. de C1
S.Peixoto, R. A3
Srroios, Largo de A2
S.Saraiva Lima, R.A2/3
S.Sousa, R. d. A3
Stephens, L. dos D1
S.Tomé, R.d.II d. B2
S.Vincente, C. de C/D3
S.Vincente, L. de C2
S.Vincente, R. de C2
S.Vincente, Tv. de C2

T
Taipas, R. das C1
T. d. Trigo, L. d. D2/3
Teix.Pinto, R. B3
Telhal, R. do C1
Telx., R. do C1
Terr., Tv. d. D1
Terreirinho, R. do C2

Terreirinho, Tv. do C2
Terreiro d. Trigo, R. d.
  D2/3
Terros d.Monte, Tv. d.
  C2
Tijoio, C. do C/D3
Tijolo, C. do C1

Tijolo, Pto. do C1
Timor, R. de B2
Tomás Ribeiro, R. A/B1
Torel, Tv. do C1
Triângulo Vermelho, R.
  B2
Trig., Largo dos C2

Trind. Coelho, Pr. D1
Trindade, L. d. D1
Trindade, R. da D1

V
Vale de Santo António,
  R. do C3

Vale, R. do D1
V.Cordon, R. D1
V.d.Jurom., R. d. B2
Verónica, R. da
  C2/3
Vidros, B. dos C3
Vigário, R. d. D3

Vinha, R. da C1
Virgina, R. C2
Viriato, R. A/B1
Visconde de Santarém,
  R. A1/2
Visconde de Valmor, Av.
  A1

Vitória, R. da D2
V.M.Bernardo, R. A/B2
Voz do Operário, R. da
  C2

X
X.C.Rebelo, R. A1

Z
Zagalo, Tv. do C3
Zaire, R. do B2

1 de Dezembro, R.
  C/D1/2
2-A, R. B3

24 de Julho, Avenida
  D 1

10 - 11

Madrid

A
A. Arias, Calle de C5
Abada, Calle de C2
Abades, Calle de D2
Abascal, Calle de José
  A2/3
A. Bello, Calle B/C6
A. Bienvenida, Calle C5
Abreu, Calle de G. B6
Abtao, Calle de, D5
Academica, Calle de l
  C3/4
A. Casero, Calle de
  C5/6
Acedera, Calle de D1
Acuerdo, Calle de B2
Acuña, Calle de Antonio
  B/C4
A. de Aragon, Calle de
  A5
Adelfas, Calle de las D5
A. Díaz Cañabate,
  Calle de D5
Aduana, Calle de la
  C2/3
A. González, Calle de
  B6
A. Grilo, Calle de B2
Aguas, Calle de las D2
Aguila, Calle del D2
Aguilera, Calle de
  Alberto B1/2
Aguinaga, Calle de
  Ramón B6
Agullas, Calle de
  Flosrestán B5/6
Agustin Durán, Calle de
  A5
Ahumada, Calle de
  Marqués A5
Alarcón, Calle de Ruiz
  C/D3
Alberto Aguilera, Calle
  de B1/2
Alberto Bosch, Calle
  D3, C4
Alburquerque, Calle de
  B2/3
Alcade Sáinz de Baranda,
  Calle de C5/6
Alcalá Galiano, Calle de
  B3
Alcalá, Calle de los
  Mártires B1/2
Alcalá, Calle de
  A6, B4-6, C3/4
Alcánatara, Calle de
  Francisco Jancinto
  B1
Alcántara, Calle de
  A/B5
Alfonso XI, Calle de C3
Alfonso XII, Calle de
  C4, D4
Alfonso, Calle de A3
Algeciras, Calle de D1
Almadén, Calle de D3
Almagro, Calle de A/B3
Almeda, Calle de la D3
Almeria, Calle de B6
Almirante, Calle de B3
Alonso Cano, Calle de
  A3
Alonso Heredia, Calle de
  A5
Alonso Martinez, Plaza
  de B3
Alonso, Calle de R.S. C5
Alonso, Calle del
  Maestro B5
Altamirano, Calle de B1
Altimiras, Calle de F.co
  A6
Amaniel, Calle de B2
A. Maura, Calle de
  C3/4
Ambrós, Calle de B6
Américas, Calle de las
  D2
Amorós, Calle de A5
Amparo, Calle del D2/3
Andrés Mellado, Calle
  de A/B1
Andrés Tamayo, Calle de
  A5
Andrés Torrejón, Calle
  de D4
A. Nervo, Calle de D5
Angel Ganivet, Calle de
  D5
Angeles, Cost. de la C2
Anguita, Calle de
  Serrano B3
Aniceto Marinas,
  Calle de B/C1
Antonia Ruiz Soro,
  Calle de A5/6
Antonino Toledano,
  Calle de B5
Antonio Acuña, Calle de
  B/C4
Antonio Pirala, Calle de
  B6
Apodaca, Calle de B3
A. Querol, Calle de D4
Aragon, Calle de A5
Arapiles, Calle de A2
Arco de la Victoria A1
Ardemans, Calle de A5
Areces, Calle Ramón
  D6
Arenal, Calle del C2
Argensola, Calle de B3
Argentina, Paseo de C4
Argumosa, Calle de D3

Arias Montano, Calle de
  D5
Arias, Calle de A. C5
Armeria, Plaza de la C1
Arniches, Calle de
  Carlos D2
Arrando, Calle del
  General A3
Arriasa, Calle de C1
Arrieta, Calle de C2
Arrillaga, Calle Manuel
  Maria D6
Asensio, Calle de Calvo
  A2
Astros, Calle del D5
Astros, Plaza de los D5
Asturias, Calle de P.d.
  B5
A. Terradas, Calle de
  A1/2
Atocha, Calle de C2,
  D3
Atocha, Ronda de D3
Augustin, Calle de S.
  D3
Augusto Figueroa, Calle
  de B/C3
Aunós, Calle de Eduardo
  C5/6
Av. del Mediterráneo
  D5
Av. de Brasilia A6
Av. de Bruselas A6
Av. de Felipe II B5
Av. de la Cuidad de
  Barcelona D3/4
Av. de la Victoria, A1
Av. de los Reyes
  Católicos A1
Av. de los Toreros A5/6
Av. de Méjico C4
Av. de Nazaret D5
Av. de Portugal C1
Av. de Moratalaz D6
Av. del Manzanares D1
Av. del Perú C4
Ave Maria, Calle de D3
Avendaño, Calle D5
Avenida de Menéndez
  de Pelayo, C/D4/5
Ayala, Calle de A4/5
Azcona, Calle de A5

B
Bahamonde, Calle
  deDiego B6
Baja de S. Pablo, Calle
  de la C. B/C2
Bajo de la Virgen de
  Puerto, Paseo de
  C/D1
Balboa, Calle de Núñez
  A/B4
Balién, Calle de C2,
  D1/2
Ballestra, Calle de la
  C2
Barbara Braganza,
  Calle de B3
Barcaiztegui, Calle de
  Sanchéz D5
Barceló, Calle de B3
Barco, Calle del B/C2
Baroja, Calle de Pio
  C/D5
Barquillo, Calle de
  B/C3
Bayona, Calle de A6
B. de Castro, Calle de
  B1
Beatriz de Galindo,
  Calle de D1
Bécquer, Calle de H.nos
  A4
Bejár, Calle de A5
Belén, Calle de B3
Bello, Calle A. B/C6
Belluga, Calle de C.
  A/B6
Benito Gutiérrez,
  Calle de A/B1
Benot, Calle de
  Eduardo C1
Bercial. Calle de D1
B. Garcián, Calle de B2
Bianka de Navarra,
  Calle de B3
Biarritz, Calle de A6
Bienvenida, Calle A. D5
Bisbal, P. la B6
Blanco, Calle de Rufino
  B5/6
Blasco de Garay,
  Calle de A/B2
B.L. Garcia, Calle de
  B2
Bocángel, Calle de B6
Bola, Calle de la C2
Bolivia, P.o de C4
Bonilla, Calle de A5
Bordadores, Calle de
  C2
Bosch, Calle Alberto
  D3, C4
Bosco, Calle de S.J.
  A/B1
Boston, Calle de A5/6
Braganza, Calle de
  Barbara B3
Brasilia, Av. de A6
Bravo Murillo, Calle de
  A2
Bravo, Calle de Juan
  A4/5
Bremen, Calle de A6

Brescia, Calle de A6
Bruselas, Av. de A6
Buen Suceso, Calle del
  B1
Bueno, Calle de Guzmán
  el A1/2, B1

C
Caballero de Gracia,
  Calle del C3
Caballero, Calle de V.
  C5
Cabeza, Calle de la
  D2/3
Cabeza, paseo de Santa
  (Sta.) Maria de (d.)
  la (l.) D 3
Cadarso, Calle de C1
Calatrava, Calle de D2
Callao, Plaza del C2
Callejón de Mercado D1
Calvo Asensio, Calle de
  A2
Calvo, Calle de Rafael
  A3
Camba, Calle de Julio
  A/B6
Campanar, Calle de
  A/B5
Campoamor, Calle de
  B3
Can Menor, P. D5/6
Cañabate, Calle de A.
  Diaz D5
Canalejas, Plaza de C3
Cano, Calle de Alonso
  A3
Cánovas del Castillo,
  Plaza de C3
Caracas, Calle de B3
Cardenal Cisneros,
  Calle de A/B2
Carena, P. D5
Carlos Arniches,
  Calle de D2
Carlos Guillermo F.
  Shaw, Calle de D5
Carlos III, Calle de C2
Carmen, Calle del C2
Carmen, Plaza del C2
Carnero, Calle del D2
Carnoens, Calle de Luis
  D4
Carranza, Calle de B2
Carrera de
  San Francisco D2
Carrera de San Jerónimo
  C2/3
Carrere, Calle de B2
Carretas, Calle de C2
Cartagena, Calle de
  A/B5
Casado del Alisal,
  Calle de C3/4
Casals, Calle de Pablo
  D1
Casarubuelos, Calle de
  A2
Casero, Calle de A.
  C5/6
Casino, Calle del D2
Castaños, Calle de Gen.
  B3
Castelar, Calle de B5/6
Castellana, Paseo de la
  A4, B3/4
Castelló, Calle de A/B4
Castelo, Calle del
  Doctor C4/5
Castilo, Calle de A3
Castro, Calle de B. B5
Católico, Calle de
  Fernando el A1/2
Católicos, de los Reyes
  Av. A1
Cava Alta, Calle de la
  D2
Cava Baja, Calle de la
  D2
Cavanilles, Calle de B5
Cayetano, Calle de S.
  D2
Cayetano, Calle de S.
  D2
Dávila, Calle de Sancho
  B6
Desamparados,
  Cost. de los D3
Descalzas, Plaza las C2
Descargas, Cuesta de
  las D1
Desengaño, Calle del
  C2
Diaz, Calle de F. B6
Diego Bahamonde,
  Calle de B6
Diego de León, Calle de
  A4/5
Divino Pastor, Calle del
  B2
Doce Octubre, Calle del
  C5
Doctor Castelo, Calle del
  C4/5
Doctor Cortezo,
  Calle del C/D2
Doctor Esquerdo,
  Calle del B-D5
Doctor Esquerdo, P. del
  B5
Doctor Fourquet,
  Calle del D3
Doctor G. Ulla, Calle de
  B5
Doctor Laguna, Plaza de
  C5

Cobos de Segovia,
  Calle de D1
Coello, Calle de Claudio
  A-C4
Collegiata, Calle de D2
Colomer, Calle de Luis
  Calvo A6
Colón, Calle de B3
Colón, Plaza de B3
Columbia, Paseo de C4
Columela, Calle de A4/5
Conceial Ben. Martin
  Lozano, Calle del
  D3
Concepción de
  Jerónima, Calle de
  C2
Concepcionistas, Calle
  del. Mártires B5
Conda, del Valle de
  Suchil, Plaza del
  A/B2
Conde de Aranda,
  Calle del C4
Conde de Cartagena,
  Calle del D5
Conde de Casal,
  Plaza del D5
Conde de Elda,
  Calle de A6
Conde de Vilches,
  Calle del A5
Conde de Xiquena,
  Calle de B/C3
Conde del Peñalver,
  Calle de A/B5
Conde Duque, Calle del
  B2
Condes de Torreanaz,
  Calle de los C5/6
Córdoba, Calle de
  Gonzalo A2
Corredera Alta,
  Calle de la B2
Corregidor Diego,
  Calle de D5
Corregidor Rodrigo
  Rodriguez, Calle del
  D6
Cortés, Calle de Donoso
  A1/2
Cortezo, Calle del
  Doctor C/D2
Coslada, Calle de A5
Cost. de la Angeles C2
Cost. de los
  Desamparados D3
Cost. de San Andrés
  D2
Cost. de San Pedro D2
Costa Rica, Plaza de
  C4
Covarrubias, Calle de
  B3
Cruz del Sur, Calle de
  D5
Cruz Verde, Calle de l.
  B2
Cruz, Calle de la C2/3
C.ta de Santo Domingo
  C2
Cuesta de la Vega C1
Cuesta de las Descargas
  D1
Cuesta de San Vicente
  B2, C1/2
Cueva,Calle J. D5
Cuidad de Barcelona,
  Av. de la D3/4
Cuidad de Piasencia,
  Paseo de la C1

D
Daimiel, Calle de D1
Dali, Plaza de Salvador
  B5
D' Almonte, Calle de
  Enrique B/C6
Daoiz, Calle de B2
Daoiz, Calle de C/D4
Dario, G.te Rubén de A3
Dato, Paseo de Eduardo
  A3

Doctor Marañón,
  Plaza del A3
Doctor Thebussen,
  Calle del A6
Dolores Romero,
  Calle de B6
Domingo, Calle de R.
  A5
Don Pedro, Calle de
  D1/2
Don Ramón de la Cruz,
  Calle de A4/5
Donoso Cortés, Calle de
  A1/2
Dorado, P. del C5
Dos de Mayo, Plaza de
  B2
Duque de Alba, Calle de
  D2
Duque de Liria, Calle de
  B2
Duque de Medicaneli,
  Calle de C/D3
Duque de Sesto, Calle
  de B4, B/C5
Duque, Calle de Juan
  D1
Duque, Calle del Conde
  B2
Durán, Calle de Agustin
  A5

E
Echegaray, Calle de C3
Ecija, Calle B1
Ecomienda, Calle de la
  D2
Eduardo Aunós, Calle de
  C5/6
Eduardo Benot, Calle de
  C1
Eduardo Dato, Paseo de
  A3
E. Figueras, Calle de
  C1
Eguilaz, Calle de
  Palafox. A/B3
El Faro A1
El Salvador, P.o de C4
Eloy Gonzalo, Calle de
  A2
Elvira, Calle de B6, C6
Embajadores, Calle de
  D2
Embajadores,
  Glorieta de D2
Emperator Carius V,
  Plaza de D3
Encamación, Calle de
  C2
Enrique d´Almonte,
  Calle de B/C6
Eraso, Calle de A5
Ermitra del Santo, Paseo
  de la A1
Escorial, Calle de B2
Escudo, P. D5
Eslava, Calle de Hilarión
  A1
Espalter, Calle de D3/4
España, Plaza de C1/2
Españoleto, Calle de B3
Esparteros, Calle de
  C2
Espiritu Santo, Calle de
  B2
Esplandiu, Calle de Juan
  C6
Espoz y mina, Calle de
  C2
Esquerdo, Calle del
  Doctor B-D5
Esquerdo, P.del Doctor
  B5
Este, Autovia del D 6
Estrella Polar, Calle de la
  D5/6
Estrella, Calle de la C2
Etreros, Calle de D1
Evaristo S. Miguel,
  Calle del B1

F
Fajardo, Calle de
  Saavedra C/D1
Farmacia, Calle de la
  B3
Fca Moreno, Calle de
  B5
F.co Altimiras, Calle de
  A6
F.co de Rojas. Calle de
  B3
F.co Lastres, Calle de
  B6
F.co Lozano, Calle de
  A1
F.co Ricci, Calle de B2
F. Diaz, Calle B6
Fé, Calle de la D3
Feijioo,Calle de A2
Felipe II, Av. de B5
Felipe V, Calle de C2
Felipe, Calle de C3
Feraz, Calle de A/B1
Fernán González,
  Calle de B/C5
Fernán Núñez, Paseo de
  C/D4
Fernanda, Calle de Luisa
  B1
Fernández de la Hoz,
  Calle de A/B3
Fernando el Católico,
  Calle de A1/2

Fernando el Santo,
  Calle de B3
Fernando VI, Calle de
  B3
Fernandos de los Rios,
  Calle de A1/2
Ferrer del Rio, Calle de
  A5
Ferrer, Calle de San
  Vicente B2
F. Garrido, Calle de A2
Figueras, Calle de E.
  C1
Figueroa, Calle de
  Augusto B/C3
Florestán Aguilar,
  Calle de B5/6
Florida, Paseo de la
  B/C1
F. Moreno Torroba,
  Calle de D5
Formento, Calle de B1
Fortuny, Calle de A/B3
Fósforo, Calle del D1
Francia, Calle de I.P.D.
  D2
Francisco Jancinto
  Alcántara, Calle de
  B1
Francisco Navacerrada,
  Calle A5/6, B5
Francisco Remiro,
  Calle de A5
Francisco Santos,
  Calle de A5/6
Francisco Silvela,
  Calle de A4/5, B5
Francisco, Calle del Rey
  B1
Fucár, Calle de D3
Fuencarral, Calle de
  A2 B2/3 C3
Fuente del Berro,
  Calle de B5
Fuenterrabia, Calle de
  D4
Fuentes, Calle de las
  C2
Fundadores, Calle de los
  B5/6
Fuorquet, Calle del
  Doctor D3
F. Vitoria, Calle de D5

G
G. Abreu, Calle De B6
Galiano, Calle de Alcalá
  B3
Galicia, Plaza de C4
Galileo, Calle de A2
Galindo, Calle de Beatriz
  D1
Gallego, Calle de
  Nicasio B3
Ganivet, Calle de Angel
  D5
Garay, Calle de
  Blasco de A/B2
Garcia de Paredes,
  Calle de A2/3
Garcia, Calle de B.L. B2
Garcián, Calle de B. B2
Garcias Molinas,
  Calle de B2
Garcilaso, Calle de A3
Garrido, Calle de F. A2
Gayarre, Calle de Jul.
  D4
Gaztambide, Calle de
  A1, B1
Gen. Castaños, Calle de
  B3
General Alvarez de
  Castro, Calle de A2
General Arrando,
  Calle del A3
General Campos, Paseo
  del Martinez A3
General Diaz Porlier,
  Calle de A/B5
General Martinez
  Campos, Paseo del
  A3
General Oráa, Calle de
  A4/5
General Pardiñas,
  Calle de A/B4
Genista, Calle de D1
Génova, Calle de B3
Gil Imón, Calle de D1
Gilde Santiváñes, Calle
  C4
Glorieta de Embajadores
  D2
Glorieta de Puerta de
  Toledo C/D2
Gobernador, Calle del
  D3
González, Calle de A.
  B6
González, Calle de
  Fernán B/C5
Gonzalo Córdoba,
  Calle de A2
Gonzalo, Calle de Eloy
  A2/3
Goya, Calle de B3-5
Gran Via de
  San Francisco D1/2
Gran Via B2, C2/3
Granada, Calle de D4
Gravina, Calle de B3
Gregoria, Calle de S. B3
Grilo, Calle de A. B2
G.ta de San Vicente C1

G.te de Rubén Dario
  A3
Guandalupe, Calle N.tra
  S.ta de A5/6
Guatemala, Plaza de
  C4
Gurtubay, Calle de B4
Gutenberg, Calle de D4
Gutiérrez, Calle de
  Benito A/B1
Guzmán el Bueno,
  Calle de A1/2, B1
G.za del Marqués de
  Zafra B6

H
H.nos Bécquer, Calle de
  A4
Hartzbusch, Calle de
  B2
Heredia, Calle de Alonso
  A5
Heredia, Calle de Pedro
  B5/6
Hermenegildo,
  Calle de S. B2
Hermosilla, Calle de
  B4, B5/6
Heros, Calle de Matrín
  de los A1, B1/2
Herradores, Plaza de los
  C2
Hilarión Eslava, Calle de
  A1
Honduras, Plaza de C4
Hortaleza, Calle de
  B3, C3
Hoz, Calle de Fernández
  de la A/B3
Hoz, Calle de Juan de la
  A5
Huertas, Calle de las
  C2/3, D3
Humilladero de la
  Arganzuela, Calle de
  D2

I
I. Mártires Concep-
  cionistas, Calle de
  B5
I. Minas, Calle de B2
I.P.D. Francia, Calle de
  D2
Ibiza, Calle de C5
Ilustration, Calle de la
  C1
Imón, Calle de Gil D1
Imperial, Paseo D1
Independencia,
  Plaza de la C4
Infanta Isabel,
  Paseo de la D3/4
Infantas, Calle de la C3
Iriarte, Calle de A5
Irún, Calle de B/C1
Isaac Peral, Calle de
  A1
Isabel II, Plaza de C2
Iturbe, Calle de B/C5
Izquierdo, Calle de
  Martinez A5/6

J
Jacometrezo, Calle de
  C2
Jardín de San Frederico,
  Calle de B5
Jaúregui, Calle J. D5
J. Cueva, Calle D5
J. de Mena, Calle de
  C3/4
Jenner, Calle de A3
Jericó, Calle de D5
Jernenuño, Calle D1
Jesús Apréndiz, Calle de
  C/D5
Jesús de Valle, Calle de
  B2
Jesús y Maria Lavapié,
  Calle de D2/3
J. Jaúregui, Calle D5
J.C. Mutis, Calle de B6
J.Juan, Calle de B4
J. Marañón, Calle de
  B3
J. Martinez de Velasco,
  Calle de C5
J. Jaúregui, Calle D5
J. Marañón, Calle de
  B3
J. Martinez de Velasco,
  Calle de C5
Joaquin Maria López,
  Calle de A1/2
John Lennon, Paseo de
  C5/6
Jordán, Calle de A2
Jorge Juan, Calle de
  B3-6
José Abascal, Calle de
  A2/3
José Ortega y Casset,
  Calle de A4/5
José Picón, Calle de
  A5
Jover, Calle de Serrano
  B1
J. Quintana, Calle de B2
J. Romero de Torres,
  P.o de D4
J.S. Pescador, Calle de
  D4/5
Juan Alvarez Mendizabal,
  Calle B1

Juan Bravo, Calle de
  A4/5
Juan de Austria, Calle de
  A3
Juan de la Hoz, Calle de
  A5
Juan de Urbieta,
  Calle de D5
Juan Duque, Calle de,
  D1
Juan Esplandiu, Calle de
  C6
Juan, Calle de J. B4
Juan, Calle de Jorge
  B3-6
Juanelo, Calle de D2
Jul. Gayarre, Calle de
  D4
Julio Camba, Calle de
  A/B6
Julio Rey Pastor,
  Calle de D5
J. Valera, Calle de D4

L
Lagasca, Calle de A–
  C4
Laguna, Plaza de Doctor
  C5
Lanuza, Calle de B6
Larra, Calle de B3
Las Descalzas, Plaza
  C2
Las Fuentes, Calle de
  C2
Lastres, Calle de F.co
  B6
Lavapiés, Calle de D2
Lavapiés, Plaza de D3
Lealtad, Plaza de C3
Legatinos, Calle de A2
Lennon, Paseo de John
  C5/6
Leo, Calle de D5
León, Calle de Diego
  A4/5
León, Calle de P. A3
Leon, Calle de R. B2
León, Calle del C3
Lequerica, Calle de
  Mejia B3
Libertad, Calle de la C3
Limón, Calle de B2
Lince, P. D5
Linneo, Calle de D1
Lira, Calle de D5
Liria, Calle de Duque de
  B2
Lisboa, Calle de A1
Lituania, Calle de D6
Lombia, Calle de B5
Londrés, Calle de A5/6
Longoria, Calle de M.G.
  B3
Lope de Rueda, Calle de
  B/C5
Lope de Vega, Calle de
  C3
López de Hoyos,
  Calle de A4
López, Calle de Joaquin
  Maria A1/2
López, Calle de Mateo
  C5
López, Calle de Tomás
  B5
Los Herradores,
  Plaza de C2
Los Olmos, Paseo de
  D2
Lozano, Calle de F.co
  A1
Lozano, Calle del Ben.
  Martin D3
Lozoya, Calle de
  Marqués C5/6
Lozoya, Calle de A2
Luchana, Calle de
  A/B3
Luis Calvo de Colomer,
  Calle de A6
Luis Carnoens, Calle de
  D4
Luis D. Cobeña, Calle
  A5
Luisa Fernanda, Calle de
  B1
Lulio, Calle de Raimundo
  A3
Luna, Calle de la B/C2
L. Villa, Calle de B5

M
Machado, Calle de
  Manuel C/D6
Madera, Calle de la B2
Madrazo, Calle de los
  C3
Maestro Alonso,
  Calle del B6
Maestro Sorozabal,
  Calle de C1
Maestro Villa, Plaza del
  C2
Magallenes, Calle de
  A2
Magdalena, Calle de la
  D2/3
Maiquez, Calle de
  B/C5
Malasaña, Calle de
  Manuela B2
Maldonado, Calle de
  A4/5
Mancebos, Calle de los
  D2

E

P

Manuel Machado, Calle de C/D6
Manuel Maria Arrillaga, Calle D6
Manuela Malasaña, Calle de B2
Manzanares, Av. del D1
Manzanares, Calle de D1
Marañón, Calle de J. B3
Marcenado, Calle de Santa Cruz B1/2
Maria Molina, Calle de A3/4
Maria Teresa, Calle de A5
Marinas, Calle de Aniceto B/C1
Mármoi, Calle de B3
Marqués de Ahumada, Calle del A5
Marqués de Cerralbo, Plaza del B1
Marqués de Cubas, Calle de C3
Marqués de Lozoya, Calle de C5/6
Marqués de Pontejos, Paseo del C4
Marqués de Salamanca, Plaza del B4
Marqués de Santa Ana, Calle del B2
Marqués de Urquijo, Calle del B1
Marqués de Villamagna, Calle de B4
Marqués de Villamejor, Calle de B4
Marqués de Zafra, G.za del B6
Marqués de Zafra, Paseo del B5/6
Marqués del Mondéjar, Calle de B5/6
Marqués del Riscal, Calle del B3
Marti, Calle de B5
Martin de los Heros, Calle de A1, B1/2
Martinez de Izquierdo, Calle de A5/6
Martinez, Plaza de Alonso B3
Mártires Concep-cionistas, Calle de I. B5
Mártires de Alcalá, Calle de los A1/2
Matamala, Calle de Visconde B6
Mateo López, Calle de C5
Maura, Calle de A. C3/4
Mayo, Plaza de Dos de B2
Mayor, Calle C1/2
Mayor, Plaza de C2
Mazarredo, Calle de D1
M. de la Rose, Calle de A4
Medellin, Calle de A3
Mediterráneo, Av. del D5
Mejia Lequerica, Calle de B3
Méjico, Av. de C4
Méjico, Calle de A5
Melancólicos, Paseo de la D1
Meléndez Valdés, Calle de A1/2
Mella, Plaza de Vásquez C3
Mellado, Calle de Andrés A/B1
Mena, Calle de J. de C3 C4
Méndez Núñez, Calle de C3/4

Mendizabal, Calle Juan Alvarez, B1
Menéndez de Pelayo, Avenida de C/4/5, D4, D5
Menorca, Calle de C4/5
Mesón de Paredes, Calle de D2/3
M.G. Longoria, Calle de B3
Miguel Angel, Calle de A3
Miguel Servet, Calle de D2/3
Minas, Calle de I. B2
Mira el Sol, Calle de D2
Modesto Lafuente, Calle de A3
Molina, Calle de Maria A3/4
Molinas, Calle de Garcia B2
Molino de Viento, Calle del A2
Moncloa, Plaza de la A1
Mondéjar, Calle de Marqués B5/6
Moneda, Calle C5
Monserrat, Calle de B3
Montalbán, Calle de C3/4
Monte Esquinza, Calle de A3, B3
Monteleón, Calle de B2
Montera, Calle de la B2
Moratalaz, Av. de D6
Moratin, Calle de D3
Morejón, Calle de A3
Morela, Calle de la D1, D2
Moreno Nieto, Calle de D1
Moreno, Calle de Fca B5
Moret, Paseo de A1
Moreto, Calle de C3, D3
Moyano, Calle de Claudio D3/4
Mozart, Calle de B/C1
M. Silvela, Calle de B3
Muñopedro, Calle de D1
Murcia, Calle de D3
Murillo, Plaza de C3
Mutis, Calle de J.C. B6
Mutis, P.o de Celestino D3
M-30, Túnel C/D 1

N
N.tra S.ta de Guan-dalupe, Calle A5/6
Naciones, Calle de las B5
Narciso Serra, Calle de D4, D5
Navacerada, Calle Francisco A5/6, B5
Navarra, Calle de Bianka de B3
Navéz, Calle de B/C5
Nazaret, Av. de D5
Neguilla,Calle de D1
Nervo, Calle de A. D5
Nicaragua, Plaza de C4
Nicasio Gallego, Calle de B3
Norte, Calle de B2
Noviciado, Calle de B2
Núñez de Arce, Calle de C3
Núñez de Balboa, Calle de A/B4
Núñez, Calle de Méndez C3/4
Núñez, Paseo de Fernán C/D4

O

O´Donnell, Calle de C4-C6
Olavide, Plaza de A3
Olid, Calle de A2
Olivar, Calle de D3
Olmo, Calle del D3
Olmos, Paseo de los D2
Olozaga, Calle de Salustiano C3/4
Orcasitas, Calle A6
Orellana, Calle de B3
Orfila, Calle de B3
Oriente, Plaza de C2
Otero, Calle del A6

P
Pablo Casals, Calle de D1
Padilla, Calle de A4, A/B5
Pajaritos, Calle de los D5
Palafox Eguilaz, Calle de A/B3
Palma, Calle de la B2
Palmas, Calle de las A5
Panamá, Plaza de C4
Paraguay, P.o del C4
Paraiso, Calle de B/C6
Pardiñas, Calle de General A/B4
Paredes, Calle de Garcia A2/3
Parterre, Plaza del C4
Pastor, Calle de Julio Rey D5
P. Can Menor D5/6
P. Carena D5
P.d. Asturias, Calle de B5
P. de Piscis D5
P. del Doctor Esquerdo B5
P. del Dorado C5
Pedro Heredia, Calle de B5/6
Pelayo, Avenida de Menéndez de C/D4/5
Pelayo, Calle de B/C3
Peñascales, Calle de B5/6
Peral, Calle de Isaac A1
Perseo, Calle de D4
Perseo, Plaza de D6
Perú, Av. del C4
Pescador, Calle de J.S. D4/5
P. Escudo D5
Peyre, Calle de B5
Pez Austral, Calle del C/D6
Pez Volador, Calle de C5/6 D5
Pez, Calle del B2
Picón, Calle de José A5
Pilar de Zaragoza, Calle de A5
Pinar, Calle de A4
Pintor Rosales, Paseo del A/B1
Pio Baroja, Calle de C/D5
Pirala, Calle de Antonio B6
Piscis, P. de D5
Pizarra, Calle D1
P. la Bisbal B6
P. León, Calle de A3
P. Lince D5
P.o de Bolivia C4
P.o de Celestino Mutis D3
P.o de El Salvador C4
P.o de J. Romero de Torres D4
P.o de la República de Panamá C4
P.o de S. de Rojas Clemente D3/4

P.o del Paraguay C4
P.o del Salón de Estanque C4
Poeta Esteba Villegas, Calle del D4
Pontejos, Paseo de Marqués de C4
Pontones, Paseo de los D1/2
Ponzano, Calle de A3
Porlier, Calle de General Diaz A/B5
Portugal, Av. de C1
Porvenir, Calle del B5/6
Povedilla, Calle de B5
Pozas, Calle de las B2
Prado, Calle del C3
Prado, Paseo del C/D3
Preciados, Calle de C2
Prim, Calle de C3
Princessa, Calle de A/B1, B2
Principe de Vergara, Calle de A/B4
Principe, Calle del A/B4
Provincia, Plaza de la C2
Puebla, Calle de la C2
Puerta del Sol, Plaza de la C2
Puigc, Calle de B4

Q
Querol, Calle de A. D4
Quesadal, Calle de A3
Quiñones, Calle de C3
Quintana, Calle de J. B2
Quintana, Calle de B1

R
Rafael Calvo, Calle de A3
Raimundo Lulio, Calle de A3
Ramales, Plaza de C2
Ramón Areces, Calle de D6
Ramón de Aguinaga, Calle de B6
R. Bonilla, Calle de A5
R. Domingo, Calle de R. A6
Recoletos, Calle de C3/4
Recoletos, Paseo de C3
Redondilla, Calle de D2
Regalada, Calle de la D5
Reina, Calle de la C3
Remiro, Calle de Francisco A5
República de Cuba, Paseo de la C/D4
República de Panamá, P.ode la C4
Requena, Calle de C2
Rey Francisco, Calle del B1
Rey, Paseo del B/C1
R.G. de Clavijo, Calle de D1
Reyes Magos, Calle de los D5
Reyes, Calle de los D5
Ribera de Curtidores, Calle de la D2
Ricci, Calle de F.co B3
Rio, Calle del Rion C2
Riscal, Calle del Marqués B3
R. Leon, Calle de B2
Robledo, Calle de Romero A/B1
Rodas, Calle de D2
Rodiguez, Calle de Ventura B1/2
Rodriguez, San Pedro, Calle de A1/2
Rojas, Calle de F.co B3

Roma, Calle de A6, B5/6
Romero Robledo, Calle de A/B1
Romero, Calle de Dolores B6
Ronda de Atocha D3
Ronda de Toledo D2
Ronda de Valencia D3
Ronda del Segovia D1/2
Rosaleda, Calle de la B1
Rosales, Paseo del Pintor A/B1
Rosario, Calle del D1
Rose, Calle de M. de la A4
R.S. Alonso, Calle de C5
Rubén Dario, G.te de A3
Ruda, Calle de la D2
Rufino Blanco, Calle de B5/6
Ruiz de Alarcón, Calle de C/D3
Ruiz, Calle de B2
Rulz Perelló, Calle de B5/6
Ruperto Chapi, Paseo de A1
R. Vega, Calle de la A5

S
Saavedra Fajardo, Calle de C/D1
Sacramento, Calle de C2
Sagasta, Calle de B3
Sagunto, Calle de A3
Salamanca, Plaza del Marqués B4
Salas, Calle de A3/4
Salesas, Plaza de B3
Salitre, Calle de D3
Salón de Estanque, P.o del C4
Salud, Calle de la C2
Salustiano Olozaga, Calle de C3/4
Salvador Dali, Plaza de B2
Samaria, Calle de D5
San Andrés, Calle de B2
San Andrés, Cost. de D2
San Bernardo, Calle de A-C2
San Conrado, Calle de D1
San Francisco, Carrera de D2
San Francisco, Gran Via de D1/2
San Francisco, Plaza de D1/2
San Galo, Calle de D1
San Jerónimo, Carrera de C2/3
San Justo, Calle de C2
San Lorenzo, Calle de B3
San Marcos, Calle de C3
San Mateo, Calle de B3
San Mateo, Trav. de B3
San Miguel, Plaza de C2
San Pedro, Calle de Rodriguez A1/2
San Pedro, Cost. de D2
San Quintin, Calle de C2
San Roque, Calle de B/C2
San Rufo, Calle D1
San Vicente Ferrer, Calle de B2

San Vicente, Cuesta de B2, C1/2
San Vicente, G.ta de C1
Sanchéz Barcaiztegui, Calle de D5
Sancho Dávila, Calle de B6
Sandoval, Calle de B2
Sangarcia, Calle D1
Santa Ana, Calle de D2
Santa Bárbara, Plaza de B3
Santa Brigida, Calle de B3
Santa Casilda, Calle de D1/2
Santa Cruz de Marcenado, Calle de B1/2
Santa Engracia, Calle de A3/3
Santa Feliciana, Calle de A3
Santa Inés, Calle de D3
Santa Isabel, Calle de D3
Santa Lucia, Calle de B2
Santa Maria la Real Nieva, Calle de D1
Santa Maria, Calle de D3
Santa Sabina, Calle de D5
Santa Teresa, Calle de B3
Santiago, Calle de C2
Santisima Trinidad, Calle de A3
Santo Domingo, C.ta de C2
Santo Domingo, Plaza de C2
Santocides, Calle de D2
Santos, Calle de Francisco A5/6
S. Augustin, Calle de C3
S. Bernandino, Calle de B2
Segovia, Calle de C1/2, D1
Segovia, Ronda del D1/2
Serra, Calle de Narciso D4/5
Serrano Anguita, Calle de B3
Serrano Jover, Calle de B1
Serrano, Calle de A-C4
Servet, Calle de Miguel D2/3
S. Eugenio, Calle de D3
Sevillia, Calle de C3
S. Gregoria, Calle de B3
Shaw, Calle de Carlos Guillermos F D5
S. Hermenegildo, Calle de B2
Sierra Elvira, Calle de D5
Silva, Calle de C2
Silvela, Calle de Francisco A4/5, B5
Silvela, Calle de M. B3
Sirio, Calle de C/D6
S.J. Bosco, Calle de A/B1
S. Leonardo, Calle de B2
S. Miguel, Calle del Evaristo B1
S. Nicolàs, Calle de C2
Sombrerete, Calle de D2

Soro, Calle de Antonia Ruiz A5/6
Sorozabal, Calle de Maestro C1
S. Rojas Clemente, P.o de D3/4
Suceso, Calle del Buen B1
Suroveste, Autovia del C 1

T
Tabemillas, Calle de D2
Tamayo, Calle de Andrés A5
Terradas, Calle de A. A1/2
Tesoro, Calle del B2
Tetuán, Calle de B2
Thebussen, Calle del Dr. A4
Titulcia, Calle de D5
Toledano, Calle de Antonino B5
Toledo, Calle de C2, D2
Toledo, Glorieta de Puerta de D2
Toledo, Ronda de D2
Tomás López, Calle de B5
Toreros, Av. de los A5/6
Torila, Calle de C2
Toros Monumental de las Ventas, Plaza de A6
Torrecilla del Leal, Calle de D3
Torrejón, Calle de Andrés D4
Torres, P.o de J. Romero de D4
Torroba, Calle de F. Moreno D5
Trafalgar, Calle de A2
Trav. de San Mateo B3
Tres Peces, Calle de los D3
Tribulete, Calle de D2
Tudescos, Calle de los C2
Tutor, Calle de, A/B1 B2

U
Ulla, Calle de Doctor G. B5
Urbieta, Calle de Juan D5
Urquijo, Calle del Marqués de. B1
Uruguay, Paseo de D4/5

V
V. Caballero, Calle de C5
V. Maria, Calle de D5
Valderibas, Calle de D4
Valdés, Calle de Meléndez A1, A2
Valencia, Calle de D3
Valencia, Ronda de D3
Valenzuela, Calle de C3/4
Valera, Calle de J. D4
Vallehermoso, Calle de A/B2
Valores, Calle C5
Valverde, Calle de B3, C2/3
Vaquerias, Calle de las C5
Vásquez de Mella, Plaza de C3
Vedla, Calle de B5
Vega, Calle de R. de la A5
Vega, de la Cuesta C1
Velasco, Calle de J. Martinez C5

Velázquez, Calle de A-C4
Venezuela, Paseo de C4
Ventosa, Calle de la D1
Ventura Rodiguez, Calle de B1/2
Vía, Gran B/C2, C3
Vicálvaro, Calle de C5/6
Victoria, Arco de la A1
Victoria, Av. de la A1
Viento, Calle del Molino de B2
Viera y Clavijo, Calle D5
Villa, Calle de L. B5
Villafranca, Calle de A5/6
Villalar, Calle de C3/4
Villamagna, Calle del Marqués de B4
Villamejor, Calle de Marqués de B4
Villanueva, Calle de B3/4, C4
Villoslada, Calle D 1
Vinateros, Camino (C.) de las D 6
Virgen de la Algeria, Calle de la A6
Virgen de la Paz, Calle de la A6
Virgen de la Pulg, Calle de A6
Virgin de Puerto, Paseo de la C/D1
Viriato, Calle de A2/3
Virtudes, Calle de A3
Visconde de Matamala, Calle de B6
Vitoria, Calle de F. D5
Vizcaya, Calle de D3

W
Walia, Calle de D5

X
Xiquena, Calle de Conde B/C3

Z
Zafra, G.za del Marqués B6
Zorilla, Calle de C3
Zurabano, Calle de A/B3
Zurbarán, Calle de B3
Zurita, Calle de D3

Porto

8

A
Abraços, Rua dos A3/4
Actor Dias, Lg. d. B3
Adolfo Casais Monteiro, Rua B1
Agramonte, Rua de A1
A. Granjo, Rua de B4
Aires de Ornelas, R. de A3/4
Alberto (A.) d. Gouveia, R. d. B1/2
Alegria, Praça da B3
Alegria, Rua da A/B3
Alex (A.) Herculano, Rua de B3
Alexandre Braga, R. d. B3
Alexandre Sá Pinto, Lg. d. A1
Alfândega (Alfân.), R. C2
Alfândega, Lg. Da B1
Alferes Malheiro, R.d. A2/3
Alfonso (A.) de Albuquerque, R. B2
Alfonso (A.) Henriques, Av. D. B2
Aliados, Avenida-dos B2
Almada, Rua-do A/B2
Almeida Garrett, Praça-de B2
Álvares Cabral, Rua A2
Amparo, R. da B2
Anibal Cunha, Rua-de A1/2
Anselmo Braamcamp, Rua-de A3

Anselmo (A.) Braancamp, Tv. d. A3
Antas, Rua-das A4
Antas, Tv.-d. A4
Antero de-Quental, R.-de A2
Antonio-Carneiro, Rua-de B4
Argo, Rua do C1
Armazéns, R.-d. B1/2
Arménia, R. d. B/C2
Arq.-Marques (Marq.) d.-Silva, R. A1
Assunção, R.d. B2
Atafona, R.-d. B2
Augusto (Aug.)-Luso, R.-de A1
Augusto Rosa, R.-d. B2
Aurélia (A.) de Sousa, R. A2
Av. Dom Joao I C3
Avis, Lg.-d. C2/3

B
Bacalheiros, Muro-dos C2
Bainharia, R.-d. B2
Banderinha, R. da B1/2
Barão-d.-Nova-Sintra, Rua-do B4
Barão-de-S. Cosme, R.-do B2
Barão-Forrester, Rua A2
Barroca (Barr.), R. C2
Barroca, R.d. C2
Barros-Lima, Rua-de A4

Batalha, Praça da B3
Bataria, R.-da A4
Beixo, R. C2
Beixo, R. d. C. d. B1/2
Belomonte, R.-d. B2
Boa-Nova, R. d. B1
Boavista, Avenida-da A1
Boavista, Rua-da A1/2
Bolhão, Rua-do A/B3
Bolsa, R. da B/C2
Bom Sucesso, Praça A1
Bom-Sucesso, R.-d. A1
Bonfim, Rua-do A/B4
Bonjardim, Rua-do A/B2/3
Borbosa du-Bocage, Rua-d. A1
Bragas, Rua-dos A2
Brás-Cubas, Rua-de A4
Breiner, Rua-do A/B1/2
Burgães, R.-dos A2

C
Cabo-Simão, Rua-do C3
Caldeireiros, R.-do B2
Câmara-Pestana, R.-d. A4
Camilo, Av.-de B3/4
Camões, Rua-de A1
Campo-24-de-Agosto B3
Campo-Alegre, Rua-do A1
Campos-d.-Mártires-d.-Pátria B2

Campos, R. de C1
Campos, Tv.-d. A3
Candido Cǎnd.)-d.-Reis, R. d. B2
Capelo-Ivens, Cais-do B1
Cardeal-D.-Américo, R.-d. A3/4
Carlos- Alberto, Praça-de B2
Carmelitas, R. d. B2
Carmo, R. d. B2
Carmo, Tv.-d. B2
Carregal, Cç.-Do B2
Carregal, Tv.-d. B2
Carvalheiras, R. d. A3
Casal (C.)-Pedro, R.-d. B1
Casino-da-Ponte, R.-Part. C3
Castelo, Lg. do C1
Castelo, R. d. C1
Cativo, R.-d. B2/3
Cativo, Tv. d. B3
Cavaco, Cais-do B1
C. Corr.-d.-Barros, R. d. A4
Cedofeita, Rua-de A/B2
Cedofeita, Tv.-de B2
Cervantes, R.d. A4
Ceuta, R.-de B2
Ceuta, Túnel de B2
Chã, R.-da B2
China, Tv.-da B2
Cidral (C.) d. Beixo, R. d. B1/2
Cidral de-Cima, R.-d. B1/2

Cima do Muro (C. d. M.), R. d. C2
Cimo-de-Vila, R.-d. B2/3
Clemente (C.)-Meneres, R.-de B2
Clérigos, R.d. B2
Clube Fenianos, R. d. A/B2
Codeçal, Esc. B/C2/3
Coelho-Neto, R.-d. B3
Comércio-do-Porto, R.-do B/C2
Conceição, R.-da A/B2
Conde (C.)-d.-B., R. d. B2
Conde-d.-Vizela, R.-d. B2
Conde-de-Ferreira, R.-do B3/4
Coronel (Cor.) Pacheco, Pr. A2
Corpo da-Guarda, R.-d. B2
Corticeira (C.), R.-d. B3
Corticeira (Cort.), Calç. d. B3
Coutinho-de-Azevedo, Rua-d. A3/4

D
D. Augustinho (Ag.)-d.-Jesus-e-Sou sa, R. d. A3/4
D.-Hugo, Rua-de C2
Diogo-Leite, Avenida C2

Dionisio (D.)-d. Pinho, R. d. C3
D.-João-VI, Rua-de A/B3
Dr. Alberto (Alb.) de Aguiar, R.-de A4
Dr.-Alves-da-Veiga, Rua-do A/B3
Dr. Ant. Sousa Macedo (A. S. Mac.), R.d. B2
Dr.-Barbosa (B.)-Castro, R.-d. B2
Dr.-Carl.-de-Passos, R.-d. A2
Dr.-Carlos Cal-Brandão, R.-de A1
Dr. Magalhães Lemos, R.-do B2
Dr. Sousa-Avides, R.-d. A/B4
Dr.-Teotónio Pereira, Pr.-d. A4
Dr.-Tiago-de Almeida, R. d. B2
Dr.-Tito Fontes, Lg.-d. A3
Dom Manuel II, Rua de B 1
Dom-Pedro-V, Rua-de A/B1
Doze-Casas, Rua-das A3
Duque-de-Loulé, R.-do B3/4
Duque-d.-Palmela, R.-do B3/4
Duque-de-Saldanha, Rua-do B3/4
Duque-d.-Terceira, R.-d. B3

E
Eirinhas, Rua-das A4
Entreparedes, R.-d. B3
Entre-Quintas, R.-d. C1
Entre-Quintas, Rua de B1
Entre–Quintas, Tv.-de B/C1
Escola-normal, R.-da A3
Estevão, R.d. A/B2/3

F
Fábrica, R.-d. B2
Faria-Guimarães, Rua-de A2/3
F.-d. Rocha-Soares, R.-d. B2
Fernandes-Tomás, Rua-de B3
Fernão-de-Magalhães, Avenida A/B3/4
Ferraz (Ferr.), Tv. B2
Ferraz, R. d. B2
Ferreira (F.) Borges, R.-d. B2
Ferreira-Cardoso, R.-d. B3/4
Ferreira, Lg.-d. A1
Figueiroa, Tv.-d. A2
Filipa Lencastre, Praça-d. B2
Firmeza, Rua-da A/B3
Flores, Rua-das B2
Fonseca-Cardoso, Rua-de A2/3
Fontainhas, R.-das B3
Fonte Nova, R. d. B/C1

Fonte-de Massarelos, R.-d. B1
Fonteinhas, Alameda-das B3
Fonteinhas, Passeio-das B/C3
Fontinha, R. d. A3
Formiga, Rua-d. B4
Formosa, Rua B2/3
Franca (Fr.), R. d. C2
Frei-Heitor Pinto, R.-d. B4
Freixo, R. d. B4

G
Gaia, Cais de C1
Galeria de-Paris, R. B2
Galiza, Praça da A1
Gen. Humberto Delgado, Pr.-d. B2
Gen.-Sousa-Dias, R. d. C2
General-Torres, R.-d. C2
Glória, Rua-d. A4
Gomes Leal, Tv.-de A4
Gomes Teixeira, Pr.-d. B2
Gomes-Freire, R.-d. B/C3/4
Gomes-Leal, R.-d. A4
Gonçalo-Cristóvão, Rua-de A2/3
Gonçalo-Sampaio, Rua A1
Gonçalo, R. d. A4
G. Silveira, R. d. A/B2
Guedes-Acevedo, R.-d. A3

Guilherme (Guilh.)
Gomes (G.)
Fernandes, R.-d.
C2
Gustavo-Eiffel,
Avenida-de B/C3

H
Heroismo, Rua-do B4

I
Infanta-D.-Maria, R.-d.
A1/2
Infante-D.-Henrique,
R.-d. C2
Infante Henrique, Pr.-d.
B/C2
Infante Santo, R.-d. C3
Instituto-d.-Cegos
d.-S.-Manuel, R.-d.
A1

J
J.-A.-Aguiar, R.-de
B3/4
João (J.) d. Oliveira
Ramos, R.-d. A3
João-das-Regras,
Rua-de A2/3
João, Praça de B2/3
Jorge-Viterbo Ferreira,
R. d. B1
José -Falcão-, R.-d. B2
J.-Teixeira, R. Part.-d.
A4
Julio-Dinis, Rua-de
A/B1
Justino-Teixeira, Rua-d.
A4

L
Lage, R. d. B2
Lapa, R.-da A2
Latino-Coelho, R.-de
B2
Liberdade, Praça-da
B2
Liceiras, Tv. d. A/B2/3
Lisboa, Pr.-d. B2
Lóios, Lg.-d. B2
Lomba, Rua-da B4
Lomba, Tv.d. B4
Loureiro, R. d. B2
Lourenço, R.-d. B4

M
Macieirinha, Rua-de B1
Mártires-Liberdade,
R.-d. A/B2
Maternidade
de-Júlio-Dinis,
Lg.-Da A/B1
Maternidade, Rua-de
A1
Meditação, R.-da A1
Melo, R.-do A2
Mercadores, Rua-dos
B/C2
Miguel Bombarda, Lg.-d.
A4
Miguel-Bombarda,
Rua-de B1/2
Miradouro, R.-d. B/C3
Miraflor, R.-d. B4
Miragaia, R.-d. B1/2
Mirante, R.-d. A2
Moinho d.-Vento, Lg.-d.
B2
Moinhos, Rua-dos B1

Mompilher, Lg.-d. B2
Monchique, Rua-de B1
Monte (M.)-Cativo,
Esc.-d. A2
Monte-Costa, Tv.-A.
A4
Monte (M.) d. Congrega-
dos (Congr.), R. d.
A3
Monte-d.-Bonfim, R.-d.
A4
Monte-do-Tadeu, R.-d.
B1/2
Moreira (Mor.) As-
sunção, R. d. A3
Moreira, Rua-de A3
Morgado (Morg.)-d.-
Mateus, R.-do B3
Mouzinho-Albuquerque,
Praça-de A1
Mouzinho-da-Silveira,
R.-de B2
Musas, R.-das A3

N
Nau Trindade, R. da
A4
Navegantes, R.-dos A4
Nossa Sen.-de-Fátima,
Rua A1
Nova-da-Alfândega, R.
B/C1/2
Nova (N.) de-S.Crispim,
R. A3/4
Nova-Sintra, Calc.-d.
B4
Nova-Sintra, Tv.-de B4

O
Oliveira Barros, Rua de
B2
Oliveira-Monteiro,
Rua-de A1/2
Oliveiras, R.d. B2
Oliveirinhas, R.-d. B3
Olivença, R.-de A2/3

P
Paço, Beco-do B2
Padrão, Lg.-do B3
Padre-Ant.-Vieira, R.-d.
B4
Padre-Cruz, R. de A1
Paiva Couceiro, Avenida
de B/C4
Parada Leitão, Pr.-d. B2
Paraiso, Rua-d A3/4
Passos-Manuel, R.-d.
B2
Paz, R.-da A1
Pedras, Cais-d. B1
Pedreira, V.-da B3
Pelames, R.-d. B2
Pena (P.) Ventosa, R. d.
B2
Pena, Rua-da A/B1
Pereira d. Costa, R. d.
B1/2
Picaria, R.-d. B2
Piedade, R. d. C2
Piedade, Rua-da A1
Pinheiro, R.-do A/B2
Pinto-Bessa, R.-de
C2/3
P.-Nunes, Praça A1
Porta-do-Sol, R.-da
B2/3

Poveiros, Praça-dos B3
Póvoa, Rua-da A3
Póvoa, Tv.-da A3/4
Priorado, Lg.-d. A1
Prof.-Abel (A.) Salazar,
R. do A1
Prof. V. J.-Carvalho, R.
B2

R
Rainha-D. Amélia, Pr.-Da
A3
Rainha-d.-Estefânia, R.
A1
Ramos Pinto, Avenida
C1/2
Raul-Dória, R.-d. A3
Reboleira, R. d. C2
Regadas, R. Particular
(Part.) d. C1
Regeneração, R.-da A2
Rego-Lameiro, Çç.-d.
B2
Rei Ramiro, Rua do C1
República, Av.-d C2/3
República, Praça da
A2
Restauração, Rua-da
B1/2
Ribeira, Cais-da C2
Ribeira, Rua-da C2
Ricardo Jorge, R.-do
B2
Rocha-Leão, R. d.
C2/3
Rodolfo-Araújo, R.-d.
A/B3
Rodrigues Sampaio,
R.-d. B2

Rodrigues-de-Freitas,
Av. B3/4
Rodrigues-de-Freitas,
R.-de C3
Rodrigues-Lobo, R.-d.
A1
Rosário, Rua-de
A/B1/2
Rosário, Tv.-do B1/2
Rua-Chã, Tv.-d. B2/3

S
Sacadura Cabral, R.-de
A1/2
Sá-da Noronha, Tv. d.
B2
Sá-da-Bandeira, Rua-de
A/B3
Salg., Tv. d. A2
Salgueiros, R.d. A2
Sampaio Bruno, R.-d.
B2
Santa-Catarina, Rua-de
A/B3
Santa (S.)-Isabel, R.-de
A/B3
Santa Isidro, R. Part. A3
Santana, R.-d. B/C2
Santo-Ildefonso, Rua-de
A/B3
Santo-Isidro, R.-d. A3
Santo Isidro, Tv.-d. A3
Santos-Pousada, Rua-de
B2
Saraiva-d. Carvalho, R.
d. B2/3
Saudade, R.-da A1
S. Bento d.-Vitória, R.-d.
B2

Rodrigues-de-Freitas
(cont.)
S. Brás, Rua-de A2
S. Brás, Tv.-de A2
S. Carlos, Tv.-d A2
S. Dionísio, R. B3
S. Domingos, Lg.-d A2
Senhora (S.) d.-Dores,
R. B3
Serra, Calç.-d. C2
Severo, R.-de A1
S. Filipe (F.)-Nery, R. d.
B2
S. Francisco (F.), R. d.
C2
S. Helena, R.-de A3
Silva Tapada, R.-da C3
S. João-Novo, R.-d.
B2
S. João, R.-d. B/C2
S. Lázaro, Passeio-d.
B2
S. Lourenço, R.-d. B2
S. Luis, R. d. B3
S. Marcos, R.-d. C1
S. Miguel, R. d. B2
S. Nicolau (N.), R. C2
Soares dos-Reis, Lg.-de
B4
Sobre-Douro, R.-de B1
Sol, R.-do B3
Sou., R. B2
S. Paulo, R.-d. A1
S. Pedro (P.) d. Miragaia
(Mirag.), Lg.-d. B2
S. Pedro (P.) Miragaia,
R. d. B2
S. Rosendo, Rua-de
A/B4
S. Sebastião, R.-d. B2
S. Teresa, R.-d. B2

S. Vitor, Rua de
B/C3/4
S. Victor, Tv.-d. B3

T
Taip., Tv. d. B2
Taipas, Rua-das B2
T. Coelho, R. d. B2
Terr., Lg. C2
T.-Gonzaga, R. d. B2
Torrinha, Rua-da A1/2
Trás, Rua-de B2
Trindade, R. d. A/B2/3
Túnel, R. d. C2

V
Vandoma, Cç. B2
Vera-Cruz, Rua-de B4
Vera-Cruz, Tv.-Part. B4
Verdades, E. d. B/C2
Vilar, Rua-de A/B1
Vimara-Peres, Av.-de
B/C2
Vinte e Oito d. Janeiro,
R. d. C1
Viriato, Lg.-do B1/2
Virtudes, Cç. B2
Virtudes, R.-d. B2
Visconde Bóbeda, R.-do
B3
Vitória, Rua-da B2

1.º d. Dez., Lg. d.
B2/3
25 de Abril, Avenida (Av.)
A 4
31 de Janeiro, R. B2/3

12

Santiago de Compostela

A
Abaixo, Nova de C 1
A. (Antonio) Casares
D 1
Acibecheria C 1
A. Coruña, Avenida de
D 2
Agra das Barreiras, Rúa
de D 2
Agraria, Casa A 3
Agriña A 3
Agro, Casas do A 2
Alexandre Bóveda A 3
Alexandre Bóveda, Rúa
de B 2
Alfredo Barañas, Rúa de
C/D 1
Algalia de Abaixo C 2
Algalia de Arriba C 2
Aller Ulloa, Rúa de
C 2
Altamira C 2
Altiboia B 2
Alvaro Cunqueiro, Praza
de A 1
Ameas C 2
Ameixaga Andujar
C/D 2
Amor Ruibal, Rúa de
D 1
Antonio, Avenida de
C 1
Antonio (A.) Casares
D 1
Antonio Fraguas,
Avenida de D 1
Anxol Casal, Rúa de
B 2
Arco Placio, Rúa de
C 1
Arriba, Torreira de A 1
Arturo Cuadrado Meure,
Rúa de A 1
Arzúa B 2
Astorga C 2
Atalaia C 1/2
Atenas C 2
Avio de Abaiaixo, Rúa de
A 1
Avio Torreira, Rúa do
A 1

B
Bar, Poza de C 1
Barrio de Guadalupe
B 2
Basquiños B 2
Basquiños, Travesa dos
B 2
Batalla de Clavixo C 2
Belvis C 2
Belvis, Praciña de C 2
Berlin C 2/3
Berna C 2/3
Bernardo Barreiro de V.
V., Rúa de C/D 2
Betanzos C 2
Bispo Teodomiro C 2
Blanco Amor B 2
Boiro A 1
Bonaval C 2
Bóveda, Paseo de
C 1
Brañas do Sar C/D 2
Brion, Rúa de C 1
Brion, Ruela de (d.)
C 1
Brocos B 2
Bruxelas C 3
Burgas, Avenida das
C 1
Burgo das Nacions
B 1/2

C
Cabalos A 2
Caldeireria, Rúa da
C 1/2
Calzada (Calz.) Sto.
(Santo) Antonio
C 2

Calzada do Sar, Travesa
D 2
Calzada S. Pedro C 2
Calz. Sto. Antonio =
Calzada Santo Anto-
nio C 2
Camallons B 1
Camilo Diaz Baliño,
Praza de B 2
Camiño de Lermo
A/B 1
Camiño dos Vilares
A 2
Camiño Francés,
Avenida do B 3
Campo da Angustia, Rúa
de C 2
Campo de Sta. Isabel,
Rúa da B 1
Campo do Amo, Rúa da
D 2
Cancela, Rúa das B 3
Cancelas, Rúa de B 3
Canteiro C 2
Caramoniña, Ruela
B/C 2
Carlos Maside, Rúa de
B 2
Carmen de Abaixo,
Calzada do C 1
Carmen de Abaixo, Rúa
do B/C 1
Carretas C 2
Casal da Horta A 1
Casas da Hedra C 3
Casas da Hedra, Travesa
das C 3
Casas Novas, Rúa dos
B 1
Casas Reais, Rúa das
C 2
Costa Nova B 1
Castelao, Avenida de
B 1/2
Castiñeiros, Rúa des
B 1
Castrón Douro C 2
Catadoiro C 2
Celso Emilio Ferreiro
B 2
Cendal, Travesa do
B 2
Ceo, Rúa de B 3
Cervantes, Praza de
C 2
Chan de Curros, Camiño
de A 2
Chan de Curros, Travesa
A 2
Chufas, Ruela das
C 1
Ciencias, Avenida das
C 1
Coimbra, Avenida de
B 2
Compostela, Avenida de
C 1
Concepción (Concep.)
Arenal C 1
Concheiros C 3
Concheiros, Fonte dos
B 2/3
Conga C 1
Corredoira das Fraguas
C 2
Corredoira do Espiño
C 1
Costa do Cristo C 1
Costa do Vedor C 2
Costa Vella C 1/2
Costiña do Monte C 2
Cotadero B 3
Coto B 3
Cruceira da Coruña,
Avenida di A/B 2/3
Cruceiro de Picaños
D 2
Cruceiro de San Pedro
C 2
Cruceiro do Sar, Calzada
do D 2

Cruz. (Cruzeiro) do Gaio,
Campo do C 1
Cruzeiro (Cruz.) do Gaio,
Campo do C 1
Curraliño B 1
Currós Enriquez C/D
1/2

D
Delfin Gaccia Guerra,
Rúa de A 1
Devesa A 3
Diego Bernal, Rúa D 2
Diego Peláez A 1/2
Domingo A. De
Andreade B 2
Domingo Fontán (Dom.
Font.) D 2
Doutor Angel Jorge
Echeberri, Avenida
C/D 1
Doutor Teixeiro C/D 1

E
Edos, Rúa dos A 3
Eduardo Pondal, Rúa
D 1/2
Empedrado, Rúa do
B 1
Enfesta B 2
Ensinanza, Rúa de
C 1
Entregaleras C 1
Entrepexigos C 2
Entrerrios, Rúa de
B 1/2
Entreruas, Ruela d.
C 1
Esc. Asorey = Escultor
Asorey B 2
Esc. De Aturuxo B 2
Escultor Asorey, Tra-
verso do B 2
Escultor Camino Otero,
Rúa do D 1
Esmoga, Rúa da A 3
España, Praza de B 2
Espirito Santo B 2
Estilla B 2
Estrela, Campo da
C 1
Europa, Praza de C 3

F
Feáns, Rúa dos C 1
Federico Garcia Lorca
B 2
Fernando III o Santo
D 1
Ferradura, Paseo do
C 1
Figueiriñas, Rueiro de
C 1
Figueroa, Avenida de
C 1
Follas Novas, Rúa de
D 1
Fonseca, Praza de
C 1
Fonseca, Travesa de
C 1
Fonteira Infinda, Rúa do
A 3
Fonterrabia, Praza de
C 1
Fontiñas, Ruela das
D 1
Forno, Campo do C 2
Fontiñas B 3
Francés, Rúa de A 1
Franco C 1
Frei Rodendo Salvado
D 1

G
Gaiás D 1
Gaiás, Rúa do C 3
Galeras, Rúa das C 1
Galicia, Praza de C 1
Garcia Blanco (B.), Rúa
de C 1

Garrida, Agra da D 2
Gato, Ruela do C 1
Gima da Eira A 2
Gómez Ulla C/D 1
Gonzalo Torrente
Ballester, Avenida de
C 2/3
Grabanxa A 3
Guadalupe, Camipiño de
B 2

H
Home Santo de Bonaval
B 2
Hórreo, Rúa do C/D 1
Hortas, Campo das
C 1
Hortas, Rúa das C 1

I
Inmaculada, Praza da
C 1
Irmandiños, Rúa des
B 2
Irmáns Raialvite D 1

J
Jaca B 3

L
Lalo Hernández,
Rotonda de B 2
Largatos C 2
Lavandoiro A 3
León, Praza de D 1
Leóns, Paseo dos C 1
Letras, Avenida das
C 1
Letras Galegas, Paseo
da C 1
Lino Villafinez B 2
Lisboa B/C 3
Londres C 2/3
Lopez Ferreiro D 1/2
Loureiros B 2
Lugo, Avenida de
A-C 1/2

M
Madres, Patio de
C 1/2
Madrid C 3
Mallou, Fonte de A 3
Mallou, Rúa de A 3
Mamoa, Porta da C 1
Mantible, Ponte B 2
Manuel (M.) Colmeiro
D 1
Manuel (M.) Murgia
D 1
Manuel Maria, Rúa de
A 3
Mazarelos, Praza de
C 1/2
M. (Manuel) Colmeiro
D 1
Medio, Rúa de C 2
Melida, Rúa de A 2/3
Mercé, Tránsito da C 2
M. (Manuel) Murgía
D 1
Moeda Vella C 1
Mónaco B 3
Mondesto B 2
Monte Pio, Rúa do B 1
Montero Rios C 1
Montes de Santas
Mariñas, Rúa D 2
Morón, Rúa de B 1
Moscova B 3
Muiñeiso Bretemas, Rúa
A 3

N
Negreira, Rúa de D 1
Neira de Mosquera, Rúa
de C 1/2
Nogueira de Mallou, Rúa
da A 3
Noia A 1
Nova, Rúa C 1

O
Oblatas, Rúa das C 1
Obradoiro, Praza do
C 1
Oliveira, Rúa da C 2
Olvido C 2
Ordes, Rúa de D 1
Órfas B 2
Otero Pedrayo B 2
Ourense D 1
Ouro, Fonte de B 1
Outeiro de Sar C 2

P
Padrón, Rúa de D 1
Palas de Rei, Rúa de
D 1
Pamplona B/C 2/3
Paris C 3
Paseo Central da
Alameda C 1
Pastoriza, Campo da
B 2
Past., Trav. = Pastoriza,
Travesa B 2
Paz, Praza da C 2
Pelamios, Rúa des
B 1
Penas, Praza des B 2
Pequena, Rúa B 3
Pereiriñas A 2
Perez Costanti C 1
Pexigo de Abaixo C 2
Pexigo (Pex.) de Arriba,
Rúa do C 2
Pia, Rúa da D 2
Picaños, Rúa do C 2
Picaños, Travese de
D 2
Pilar, Tras do C 1
Piñeiro D 2
Pino, Rúa de B 2
Pinto, Rúa de B 2
Pintor Xaime Quesada,
Rúa do D 1
Pisón, Rúa do C 2
Pitelos, Rúa dos
C 1/2
Pombal, Rúa de C 1
Ponferrada C 2
Ponte de Asén, Rúa da
B 1
Ponte do Viso, Rúa de
C 3
Ponte do Viso, Travesa
da C 3
Pontepedriña, Praza
C 1
Pontevedra, Avenida de
C 1
Porta do Camiño
C 1
Postes, Monte dos B 3
Praga B/C 3
Praterias, Praza das
C 1
Preguntoiro, Rúa do
C 2
Presidente (P.) Salvador,
Rúa (R.) C 1
P. (Presidente) Salvador,
Rúa (R.) C 1
Puente la Reina C 2

Q
Queimada, Rúa da
A 3
Queixume dos Pinos,
Rúa de A 3
Quintana, Praza da
C 1
Quiroga Palacios,
C 1

R
Raimudo Ibañez C 1
Raiña, Rúa da C 1
Ramón Cabanillas
D 1
Ramón del Valle-Inclán

Ramón Piñeiro, Rúa de
D 1/2
Raxeira C 2
República Arxentina,
Rúa da D 1
República de El Salva-
dor, Rúa da C/D 1
Rianxo, Rúa de A 1
Ricardo Carvalho
Calero, Rúa de B 1
Rio Arriba, Rúa do
D 1
Roberto (R.) Vidal
Bolaño, Rua (R.) de
A 1
Rodas, Rúa das C 2
Rod. (Rodrigo) de
Padron, Avenida de
C 1
Rodrigo (Rod.) de
Padron, Avenida de
C 1
Rodriguez Cadarso,
Praza de C 1
Roma, Rúa de C 3
Romero Donallo,
Avenida de C 1
Rosalia de Castro,
Avenida C/D 1
Rosario, Rúa do C 1
Rosa, Rúa da D 1
Roxa, Praza C 1
Roxio, Avenida de C 1
Ruiz, Laverde D 1

S
S. (Santo) Agostiño,
Praza de C 2
S. (Santo) Agostiño, Rúa
de C 2
Salamanca, Avenida de
B 2
Salgueiriños de Abaixo,
Rúa A/B 3
Salgueiriños de Arriba,
Rúa A/B 3
Salvadas, Rúa das B 1
San (S.) Francisco,
Costa de C 1
San Bieito de Anteal-
itares, Rúa de
C 1/2
San Caetano B 2
San Clemente, Ruela de
C 1
San Francisco, Rúa de
C 1
San Maritiño Pinario
(Pin.), Praza de C 1
San Paio do Monte B 1
San Pedro C 2
San Pedro Mezonzo
D 1
San Pedro, Praza de
C 2
San Roque, Rúa de
C 2
San Xoán A 1
Santa Clara B 2
Santa Comba, Rúa de
C 1
Santa Cristina C 1/2
Santa Isabel, Costa
B 1
Santa Susana, Car-
balleira de C 1
Santa Susana, Paseo
C 1
Santiago de Chile D 1
Santiago de Cuba,
Avenida B 1
Santiago de Quayaquil
C/D 1
Santiago del Estero
C/D 1
Sant. León da Caracas
C 2
Santo (Sto.) Antonio,
Campo de C 2

Sar de Alfora C/D 2
Sar de Alfora, Rúa de
Ponte do D 2
Senra, Agro da C 2
Senra, Rúa de A 2
S. (San) Francisco,
Costa de C 1
Sta. Uxia de Riberira,
Rúa de A 1
Sto. (Santo) Antonio,
Campo de C 2
Sto. (Santo) Antonio,
Fonte de C 1
Sto. Domingo (Dom.) de
(d.) la Calz C 1

T
Tabaniscas A 3
Tafona, Ruela da C 2
Tambre, Rúa do A 3
Teo, Rúa de B 2
Teo, Travesa de B 2
Tomiño, Rúa de B 2
Toural, Porta (Pr.) do
C 1
Touro B 2
Tras Costa St. Isabel
B 1
Tras Cuartel de Sta.
Isabel, Rúa B 1
Tras Santa Clara B 2
Trindade, Rúa de C 1
Trisca C 2
Troia, Rúa de C 1
Trompas C 2

U
Ulla, Rúa do D 1
Ulpiano Villanueva A 2
Ulpiano Villanueva, Rúa
de A 1/2
Ultreia, Praza de B 2
Universidade, Praza da
C 1/2

V
Val de Deus C 1
Valiño B 3
Varsovia C 3
Vedra, Rúa de D 1
Vento Mareiro, Rúa de
A 3
Vieiro, Agra da C 2
Vieiro, Costa do C 2/3
Viena C 2
Vierio C 3
Vigo, Praza de C/D 1
Vilar C 1
Villafranca (Villafr.) del
(d.) Bierzo C 2
Villafr. d. Bierzo =
Villafranca del Bierzo
C 2
Villagarcia, Avenida de
C 2
Virxe da Cerca, Rúa d.
C 2
Viso, Ameneiral do
C/D 3
Viso, Ribeira do C 3
Vista Alegre, Rúa de
B 1
Vista Alegre, Travesa de
A 1
Vite de Abaixo, Rúa de
A 2
Vite de Arriba A 2
Vite de Arriba, Travesa
A 2

X
Xasmins B 2
X. C. R., R.d. = Xose
Chao Rego, Rúa de
D 1
Xelmirez, Rúa da C 1
Xeneral Paradiñas, Rúa
do C/D 1
Xerusalèn C 1
Xesú Cabro, Rúa de
B 2

X. (Xoana) Nugueira, Rúa
de D 1
Xoán Paolo II, Avenida
de B 3
Xoana (X.) Nugueira, Rúa
de D 1
Xoán XIII, Avenida da
B 1/2
Xohana Torres, Rúa de
A 1
Xose Chao Rego, Rúa
de (X.C.R., R.d.)
A 3

Sevilla

A

Abad Gordillo, C. del C 1
Abades, Calle de D 2
A. Barrón, Calle D 3
Abreu Bobby D., C. C 1
Abuyacub, C. B 3
Aceituno, C. B/C 3
A. Cerda, C. D 1
Acetres, C. C 2
A. d. Bazán, C. B 1/2
Adelantado, C. B 2
Adriano, Calle de D 1/2
África, Pl. de A 1
Agata, C. A 3
Agua, C. del D 2
Agua, Pl. del A 1
Aguamarina, C. A 3
Aguilar, C. C 1
Aguilas, Calle C 2
Aire, C. D 2
Alamillo, Puente del A 2
Alamillo, Viaducto del A 1/2
Albareda (Albar.), C. C 2
Albaricoque, C. A 2
Albeida, Calle de B 3
Albert Einstein, Calle B 1
Alberto (A.) Lista, C. C 2
Albóndiga, C. de C 2
Albuera, Calle C/D 1
Alcaiceria, C. C 2
Alcalde Isacio Contreras, Calle D 3
Alcánt., C. B/C 3
Alcázares, Calle C 2
Alcores, Pje. D 2
Alcoy, C. C 1/2
Alejo Fernández, Calle D 3
Alemanes, C. D 2
Alfalfa (Alf.), Pl. C 2
Alfalfa, C. C 2
Alfaqueque, C. C 1
Alfareria, Calle de D 1
Alfaro, Pl. D 2
Alfonso XII, Calle C 1/2
Algamitas (Algamit.), C. B 3
Almagro Diego (D.), C. A 3
Almansa, Calle D 1
Almensilla (Alm.), C. B 3
Almez, Camino de A 3
Almirantazgo, C. D 2
Almirante (A.) Apodaca, C. C 2
Almirante (A.) Mazzaredo, C. D 2
Almirante (A.) Ulloa, C. C 1
Almirante (Almir.) Hoyos, C. C 2
Almirante (Almte.) Lobo, C. D 2
Almirante Bonifaz (A. Bonif.), C. C 2
Almirante Espinosa, Pl. d. C 2
Almonaciz, Calle D 3
Almonteños, C. Los A 3
Almudena, C. C 2
Alonso Tello, Calle D 3
Altozano, Pl. del D 1
Álvaez Quintero, Calle C/D 2
Alvarado, C. D 1
Álvarez (A.) Chanca, C. B 3
Amador de los Rios, Calle C 3
Amante Laffón (Am. L.), C. B 3
Amatista (Amat.), C. A 3
Américo Vespucio, Calle A/B 1
Amor de Dios, Calle C 2
Amores, Pje. B 2
Amparo, C. C 2
Andalucia, Camino A 1/2
Andrada, C. B 3
Andreu, C. D 2
Angostillo, C. C 2
Aniceto Sáenz, C. B 2
Anjoli, Pl. A 3
Antillano, C. D 1
Antolinez, C. C 1
Antonia Diaz, C. D 1/2
Antonia Sáenz, C. B 2
Antonio (A.) Pantión, C. B 3
Antonio (A.) Salado, C. C 1
Antonio Susillo, C. B 2
Aponte, C. C 2
Aposentadores (Aposentad.), C. C 2
Archeros (Arch.), C. D 2
Ardilla, C. de la D 1
Arenal, C. D 1
Arequipa, C. A 3
Arfe, C. D 2
Arfián, C. D 1
Argote de Molina, C. D 2
Arguijo, C. C 2
Arias Montano, C. B 2
Arjona, Calle C/D 1
Armando Jannone, Pl. D 1
Armenta (Arm.), Calle D 2/3
Arquímedes, Calle A 1
Arrayán, Calle B 2
Arroyo, Calle del C 3
Arte de la Seda, C. B 2
Atienza, C. C 2
Augusto (Aug.) Plasencia, C. C 2
Aurora, C. D 2
Ave Maria, C. C 2
Avellana, Calle B 3
Averroes, Calle D 3
Azafrán, C. del C 2/3
Aznalfarache (Aznalf.), C. B 3

B

Bacarisas (Bac.), C. D 1
Badajoz, C. C 2
Bailén, Calle de C 1
Bajeles, C. C 1
Bamberg, C. D 2
Baños, Calle de los C 1
Barcelona, C. D 2
Barco, C. C 2
Basilica, C. B 2
B. Casas, C. D 1
Becas, Calle B 2
Belén, C. B 2
Benidorm, C. C 1
Béquer, Calle de B 2
Bermúdez (B.) Plata, C. A 3
Bernardo (B.) Guerra, C. D 1
Bernardo d. Toro, C. B 3
Betis, Calle D 1
Bilbao, C. C/D 2
Blanca (B.) de (d.) los (l.) Rios, C. C 2
Blanca Paloma, C. A 3
Blanquillo, C. B 2
Blas Pascal, Calle B 1
Blasco de Garay, Pl. C 1
Blasco Ibáñez, C. A 3
Bord. R. Ojeda, C. B 2
Borda (B.), C. D 2
Boteros, C. C 2
Brillante, C. A 3
Buen Suceso (B. Suc.), Pl. C 2
Bustos Tavera, Calle C 2
Butrón, C. C 3

C

Cabal, C. C 2
Cabeza del Rey D. Pedro, C. C 2
Cabildo, Pl. D 2
Cabo Noval, C. D 2
Cádiz, Avda. de D 2/3
Calafate, C. D 1
Calatrava, Calle B 2
Calderón (C.) de la Barca, Pl. d. B 2
Caleria, C. C 2
Calle (C.) Baobab A 2
Campamento, Calle D 3
Campana, C. C 2
Campo de los Mártires, Calle C/D3
Campos, C. D 1
Cañal, C. C 2
Canalejas, Calle C 1
Candilejo (C.),C. C 2
Cano y Cueto, Calle D 2
Cantabria, C. C 2
Capitán Vigueras, Calle D 2/3
Capuchinos, R. de B/C 3
Cardenal (Card.) Cervantes, C. C 2
Cardenal Spinola, C. C 1/2
Carlos V, Av. D 2/3
Carlos, Calle C 1/2, D 1
Carmen (C.) Benitez, Pl. C 3
Carmona, Carr. De B/C 3
Carranza (Carr.), C. B 2
Castaños, C. D 1/2
Castelar, C. D 1/2
Castellar, Calle de C 2
Castilla, Calle de D 1
Catalina de Ribera, P. D 2
Cenicero, C. C 2/3
Cepeda, C. C 1
Cereza, C. B 3
Cerrajeria, C. C 2
Cervantes, C. C 2
Céspedes, Calle D 2
Cetina (Cet.), C. B 2
Chapina, C. C 1
Chapineros (Chapin.), C. D 2
Charles Darwin, Calle B 1
Chicarreros (Chicar.), C. D 2
Churruca (Churr.), C. C 2
Cid, Avda. del D 2
Circo, C. D 1
Cisne, C. D 1
Cisneros, C. C 1
Clara de Jesús Montero, C. D 1
Clavellinas (Clav.), C. C 2
Clavijo, C. B 2
Cofia, Calle D 3
Compañia (Comp.), C. C 2
Compostela, Pl. D 1
Conde d.Barajas, C. C 2
Conde Halcón (C. H.), Av. B 3
Conde Cifuentes, Calle D 2
Conde d. Torrejón, C. C 2
Conde de Ibarra, C. D 2
Conde Negro, C. C 3
Constitución, Avenida de la D 2
Conteros, C. D 2
Contratación, Pl. D 2
Contreras (Contr.), C. B 2
Coral, C. A 3
Córdoba, C. C 2
Córdoba, Pta. de B 3
Corinto (Cor.), C. C 3
Corral del Rey, C. C/D 2
Correa (Corr.) d. Arauxo, C. B 3
Cortes, C. Las C 2
Covadonga, C. D 1
Crédito, C. B 2
Cristo de Barios (Cr. d. B.), Pl. C 2
Cristo del Buen (B.) Viaje, C. C 2
Cristo d. Buen Fin, C. B/C 1
Cristo d. Calvario (Calv.), C. C 1
Cristo de Expiración, Avda. C 1
Cristóbal Colón, Paseo D 1/2
Cronista, Pl. d. B 2
Cruces Mariscal, C. D 2
Cruz Roja, Avenida de la B 3
Cuarzo, C. A 2
Cuba, Pl. de D 1
Cuna, Calle de la C 2
Curtidores (Curt.), Pl. D 2
Curtidurias, C. B/C 1

D

Daoiz, C. C 2
Dársena, C. C 1
Deán López (L.) Cepedo (C.), C. C 2
Delicias, Paseo de las D 2
Demetrio de los Rios, Calle D 3
Descalzos, C. C 2
Descubrimientos, Camino de los A-C 1
Diamante, C. A 2/3
Diamela, C. C/D 2
Diaz, C. A 3
Diego (D.) de (d.) Merlo, C.C3
Diego (D.) Puerta, C. A 3
Diego, Calle D 3
Dionisio (Dionis.) Alcalá (A.) Galiano, C. B 3
Divina Pastora, C. B 2
Doctor Fedriani, Avenida A 3, B 2/3
Doctor Marañón, C. A 2
Dolores Fdez., Pl. B 3
Don Pelayo, C. D 2
Don Alonso (A.) El Sabio, C. C 2
Don Fabrique, Calle A/B 2
Don Juan de Austria, Pl. D 2
Don Pedro Niño, C. C 2
Don Remondo, C. D 2
Doña (D.) Carmen, Pl. C 2
Doña Elvira, Pl. D 2
Doña Guiomar (D. Guiom.), C. D 1
Doña (D.) J. R. Puert (Pto.), C. C 1
Doña Teresa Enriquez, Pl. C 1
Doña Maria de Padilla, C. D 2
Doña Maria, Calle de C 2
Doncellas, C. D 2
Dormitorio (Dorm.), C. C 2
Dos de Mayo, C. D 1/2
Dr. Barraquer, Pl. del A/B 2
Dr. Cervi, C. A 2
Dr. D. Rodiño, C. A 2/3
Dr. Jiménez Diaz, C. B 3
Dr. M. Peralta, C. A 2
Dr. Felix R. de la Fuente, C. D 1
Dr. Jaime (J.) Marcos, C. A 3
Dr. Leal Castaño, C. A/B 3
Dr. Morote, C. A 3
Dr. Relimpo, C. C 3
Dr. Royo, C. A 2
Dr. Seras, C. A 2
Dr.Letamendi, C. C 2
Duarte, C. D 1
Dueñas, C. C 2
Duendes, C. D 2
Duque de Montemar, C. B 2
Duque de Veragua, Pl. C 1
Duque Cornejo, Calle B/C 2

E

Edipo, Pl. d. A 2
Eduardo (E.) Cano, C. C 1
El Jobo, C. D 2
Electra, C. A 2
Encarnación, Pl. de la C 2
Enladrillada, C. de la C 2/3
Enrique de Rivera, C. A 1
Ensenada, C. C 2
Escarpín (Esc.), C. C 2
Escoberos, Calle de B 2
Escuderos (Escud.), C. B 2
Escuelas Pias, C. C 2/3
Eslava, C. C 1/2
Esmeralda, C. A 3
Espada, C. D 2
Espartinas (Esp.), C. D 1
Esperanza, C. B 2
Espiritu Santo, C. C 2
Estepona, C. A 3
Estrellita (E.) Castro, C. B 2
Euclides, Calle A 1
Eustaquio (E.) Barrón, Pl. B 2
Evangelista, Calle D 1

F

Fabie, Calle D 1
Fabiola, C. D 2
Faisanes (F.), C. C 2
Fancelli (Fanc.), C. B 2
Farmacéutico E. M. Herrera, C. D 1
Farmacéutico, C. D 1
Farnesio, C. D 2
Faustino Alvarez, Calle de B 2
Fausto, C. A 2
Febo, Calle de D 1
Federico (Fed.) Rubio, C. D 2
Feijoo, C. C 2
Feria, Calle de la B/C 2
Fernán (F.) Sánchez-Tovar (T.), C. B 2
Fernán (F.) Caballero, C. C 1
Fernández (F.) Guadalupe, C. B 3
Fernández (F.) y. González, C. D 2
Fernández de Ardavin F. Ard., C. A 3
Fernando (F.) Álvarez (A.) de Toledo, C. B 3
Fernando d. Mata, C. B 3
Flandes (Flan.), C. C 2
Flecha, C. B 2
Florencia, C. C 3
Florencio Quintero, C. B 3
Flota, C. D 1
F. Mencheta, Calle B 2
Fortaleza, C. D 1
Francisco de Xérez, Calle A 1
Francos, C. de C/D 2
Fray Luis (L.) Sotelo, C. B 2
Fray (F.)Diego (D.) de Deza, C. C 1
Fray Ceferino, C. D 2
Fray Luis de (d.) Granada (G.), C. B 3
Fray Alonso, C. C 3
Fray Diego de Cádiz, C. B 2
Fray Isidoro de Sevilla, Calle B 2/3
Frederico (F.) Sánchez de (d.) Bedolla, C. D 2
Fresa, C. B 2
Froilán de la Serna, C. B 2
Fuente., C. A 3
Futuro, Camino del B 1
Futuro, Pasarela del B 1

G

Galena, C. A 2
Galera, Calle D 1
Galindo, C. C 2
Gallinato, Calle D 3
Gallos, Calle C 3
Gamazo, C. D 2
Gandesa (Gand.), C. D 2
Garci Pérez, C. D 2
Garcia Ramos, C. C 1
Gaspar de Alvear, C. A 3
Gavidia, Pl. d. C 1/2
G. de Rocio, C. A 2/3
Gelo, Pl. A 3
General (Gen.) Moscardó, C. C 2
General Polavieja (Gral. Polav.), C. C 2
General Rios, Calle D 2/3
Genil, C. D 1
Génova, C. D 1
Gerona, Calle C 2
Giraldillo, Pl. B 3
Goles, C. los C 1
González (G.) Meneses, C. A 2
González Cuadrado, C. B/C 2
Gonzalo (G.) Núñez de Sepúlveda (Sepúl.), C. B 3
Gonzalo (G.) Segovia, C. D 1
Gonzalo Bilbao, Calle C 3
Goyeneta, C. C 2
Gracia (G.) F. Palacios, C. D 1
Grana, C. C 2
Granate, C. A 2
Gravina, Calle de C 1
Gregor J. Mendel, Calle B 1
Guadaira, C. D 3
Guadalete, C. B 1
Guadalquivir, Calle B 1/2
Guadalupe, C. C 3
Guadiana, C. B/C 2
Guines (Gui.), C. D 2
Guzmán El B., C. D 2

H

Habana, C. D 2
Harnas, C. D 2
Herbolarios (Herbol.), C. C 2
Hércules, Alameda de B/C 2
Herera el Viejo, C. C 1
Hermanas d. I. Cruz, C. B 3
Hermanos del Rio Rodriguez (Hnos. d. Rio Rdguez.), C. B 3
Hermanos Eluyar, Calle A 1
Hernán (H.) Cortés, C. C 2
Hernand., C. A 3
Hernando (H.) Colón, C. D 2
Herrera Carmona, C. A 3
Hiniesta, C. B 3, C 2
Hitata d. Castillo, C. C 2
Hombre de Piedra, C. B 2
Honderos, C. B 3
Huestes, Calle D 3

I

Imagen, C. C 2
Imperial, Calle C 2
Imperiero (I.) Castillo Lastrucci, C. C 1
Infanta Luisa de Orleans, Calle D 2
Infantes San Blas, C. B/C 2
Inocentes, C. C 2
Inquisición, Cjon. D1
Iris, C. D 1
Irún, Calle D 3
Isaac Newton, Calle A 1
Isla Canela, C. A 3
Itálica, C. C 2

J

Jacinta Martos (Mart.), C. D 1
Jacques Cousteau, Calle A/B 1
Jaira, C. B 2
Jáuregui, C. C 2/3
Javier (Jav.) Lasso (L.) de la Vega, C. C 2
Jerónimo Hernández, C. C 2
Jesus de las Tres Caidas (J. d. Tres C.), C. C 2
Jesús de la Pasión (d. I. P.), Pl. C 2
Jesús de Gran Poder, Calle de C 2
Jesús de la Vera Cruz, C. C 1
Jesús del Gran Poder, Calle B/C 2
Jiménez Aranda, Calle D 3
Jimios Castillejo, C. D 2
Joaquin (J.) Guichot, C. D 2
Joaquin Morales Torres, C. C 3
Joaquin Costa, C. B/C 2
Johann C. Gutemberg, Calle B 1
Johannes Replar, C. A 1
Jorge de Montemayor, C. B 3
José Rodriguez Guerrero (J. R. Guerr.), C. B 3
José (J.) Bermejo, C. A3
José Díaz, Calle A 2
José (J.) Gestoso, C. C 2
José (J.) Maluquer, C. B 3
José (J.) Bengumea, C. D 2
José Cruz Auñón, C. D 1
José de la Cámara, C. D 3
José de Velilla, C. C 2
José Espinau, Pl. B 3
José Luis Luque (J. L. Lu.), C. C 2
José Gálvez, Calle A 1/2, B 1
José Laguillo, C. C 3
José (J.) Izquierdo, C. B 3
José M. Osborne, C. D 2/3
José Maria Martinez, C. D 1
Jovellanos (Jov.), C. C 2
Juan (J.) de Castillo, Calle D 2/3
Juan (J.) de (d.) Oviedo, C. B 2
Juan (J.) M. Rodriguez (Rdguez.) Correa, C. B 3
Juan (J.) Pérez (P.) Montalbán, C. B/C 2
Juan (J.) Robles, C. B 2
Juan de la (J. d. I.) Encina, C. C 2/3
Juan Lugo, C. D 1
Juan Núñez (N.), C. B 3
Juan Antonio Cavestany, Calle C/D 3
Juan Bautista Muñoz, Calle A 1/2
Juan d. Astorga, C. B 2
Juan d. Aviñón, C. D 2
Juan de Vera, C. C 3
Juan de Zoyas, C. D 3
Juan Rabadan, Calle C 1
Julio César, C. C 1
Júpiter, Calle C 3
Justino (J.) de Neve, C. D 2
Justino Matute, C. D 1
Juzgado, Calle C 2/3

L

La Florida, C. D 3
La Maria, C. B 3
La Rabeta, Pl. C 1
Lagar, C. C 2
Lago, Paseo del A/B 1
Lanza, C. C 2
Laraña, C. C 2
Las Carretas (L.Carr.), C. A 3
Legión, Pl. de la C 1
Leiria, Calle de D 1
León XIII, Calle de B 3
León, C. C 3
Leonardo Da Vinci, Calle A/B 1
Leoncillos, C. C 3
Leonor (L.) Dávalos, C. B/C 2
Lepante, C. C 2
Levies, Calle de D 2
Liñán, C. C 1
Linares (Lin.) Rivas, Pl. A 3
Lineros, C. C 2
Liria, Calle B/C 2
Lirio, C. C 2
Llerena, C. de B 3
Locomotora, C. C 1
Lope de Vega, Calle C 3
López (L.) Azme, C. B 3
López Arenas, C. D 1
Louis Braille, Calle B 1
Louis Pasteur, Calle A/B 1
Luca d.Tena, C. D 1
Lucero, C. B 2
Luchana (Luch.), C. C 2
Lucia (L.) de Jesús, C. D 1
Luis (L.) de Vargas, C. C 1
Luis Peraza (L. Per.), C. B 2
Luis Cadarso, C. C 3
Luis Montoto, Calle C/D 3
Lumbreras, Calle de B 2
Luz Arriero, Calle D 1
Lúz, C. C 3

M

Mariano (M.) de Cavia, C. D 2
Maese Rodrigo (M.) Pl. C. D 2
M. de (d.) Dios, C. D 2
Macarena, C. B 2
Macarena, Puerta d. B 2
Macasta, Calle B 2
Madre D. Marquez, C. B 2/3
Madreselva (Mad.), Calle B 3
Madrid, C. D 2
Maestre (M.) Angulo, C. B 3
Maestro (M.) Jiménez, C. D 1
Magallanes, C. D 1
Magdalena, Pl. C 1/2
Málaga, Avenida de D 2/3
Malaquita, C. A 3
Mallol, Passaje C 2/3
Malpartida, C. B 2
Managua (Manag.), C. A 3
Manuel (M.) Cortina, C. C 2
Manuel (M.) Font (F.) de (d.) Anta, C. C 2
Manuel (M.) Rojas (R.) Marcos, C. C/D 2
Manuel (M.) Vázquez (V.) Sagastizábal, C. D 2/3
Manuel Alonso Viceda (M. A. Vic.), C. C 2
Manuel B. Barrera, C. D 2
Manuel Sánchez del (Man. S.) Campo, C. B 3
Manuel Mateos, Calle B 3
Manuel Pérez, C. D 3
Manuel Villalobos, Calle B 3
Manzana, C. de la B 2/3
Mar Negro, C. A 3
Mar Rojo, C. A 3
Maravillas, C. C 2
Marbella, C. A 3
Marco Sancho, C. B/C 2
Marcos d. Cabrera, C. B 2
Maria Auxiliadora, C. C 3
Mariana (M.) Pineda, C. D 2
Marianillo, C. D 1
Marie Courie, Calle B 1
Mariscal, C. D 2
Marismas, Pl. A 3
Mármoles, C. D 2
Marqués (M.) del (d.) Duero, C. C 1
Marqués (M.) de la Mina, C. C 1
Marqués (M.) Esquivel, C. B 2
Marqués d. Lozoya, C. A 3
Marqués de Estella, C. D 3
Marqués de Paradas, Calle C/D 1
Marteles, C. C 3
Martin Villa, C. C 2
Martinez Sierra, Pl. A 3
Martinez Montañés, C. C 1
Mata, C. B 2
Matahacas, C. C 2/3
Matemáticos Rey Pastor y Castro, Calle B 1
Mateo Alemán, C. C 1
Mateos (Mat.), C. C 3
Mateos Gago, Calle D 2
Max Planck, Calle B 1
Mazagón, C. A 3
Medalla (Med.) Milagrosa, C. B 3
Medina, C. B 2
Medina, Calle de A 3
Medinaceli (Med.), C. C 2
Mejias, C. C 2
Mejorada (Mejor.), C. B 2
Méndez Núñez, Calle C/D 2
Mendigorria, C. B 1
Mendoza Rios, C. C 1
Menéndez (M.) Valdés, C. A 3
Menéndez Pelayo, Calle de D 2/3
Meneses (Men.), C. B 3
Menjibar, C. C 2
Mercado (M.), C. B 3
Mercedarias, Pl. de las C 2
Mercedes de Velilla (M. Vell.), C. C 2
Mercurio, C. C 2
Mesón (M.) Moro, C. D 2
Miguel Cid, Calle C 1
Miguel Mañara, C. D 2
Milagrosa (Milag.), Pl. B 3
Milagrosa, Pl. D 1
Miraflores, Av. de B 3
Misericordia, C. C 2
Molino, C. B 2
Molviedro, Pl. D 1
Monasterio (M.) de (d.) Veruela, C. A 2
Monederos (Moned.), C. B 2
Monsalves, Calle C 1
Mora, C. d. la A 2
Morales, C. D 1
Moratin, Calle de C 1/2
Moravia, C. B/C3
Moreno (M.) Lopez, C. C 2
Morera, C. B 2/3
Moreria, C. C 2
Morgado, C. C 2
Morsa, C. B 3
Muñóz (M.) Torrero, C. C 3
Muñoz Leon, Calle B 2/3
Muñoz Olive, C. C 2
Muñoz y Pavón, C. C/D 2
Murillo, C. C 1/2
Museo, Pl. del C 1

N

Naranjo, C. A 2/3
Naranjos, Pl. B 3
Narciso Bonaplata, C. B 1
Navarros, Calle de los C 3
Nebli, C. D 3
Niña de la Alfalfa, C. A 3
Niño Perdido (Perd.), C. C 2
Nueva, Pl. D 2
Núñez d. Balboa, C. D 2

O

O´Donnell, C. C 2
Olivares, C. D 1
Orden d. Malta, C. B 2
Ordreros (O.), C. C 2
Orfila, C. C 2
Orotava, Calle A 3
Ortiz Zúñiga, C. C 2
Osario, C. C 3
Otelo, Pl. d. A 2
Otoño, C. A 3
Otumba, C. C 1/2

P

Pacheco y Núñez del Prado, C. B 2
Padilla, C. C 2
Padre Cañete, C. C 2
Padre J. Córdoba, Pl. C 2
Padre Manjón, C. B 2
Padre Marchena, C. D 1/2
Padre Méndez Casariego, C. C 3
Pages del Corro, Calle D 1
Pajaritos, C. D 2
Palacio Malaver, C. B/C 2
Palma R., C. B 3
Parque, Pasarela del B 1
Parras, Calle B 2
Pascual de Gayangos, Calle C 1
Pastor y Landero, C. D 1
Patio (P.) de Banderas, C. D 2
Patricio (P.) Sáenz, C. B 2
Pavia, C. D 2
Pazos, Cjon. D 3
Pedro (P.) Tafur C. B 2
Pedro (P.) Parias, C. D 2
Pedro del Toro, C. C 1
Pedro Gual Villalbi, Av. A 3
Pedro Miguel, C. B/C 2
Pedro Roldán, C. D 3
Pelay Correa, C. D 1
Pelicano, Pl. d. C 3
Peñaflor, C. D1
Peñuelas, C. C 2
Peratán de Ribera, Calle de B2
Peral, Calle del B 2
Pérez (P.) Galdós, C. C 2
Pérez Garayo, C. B 1
Pérez Galdós, C. C 2
Pérez Hervás, C. C 3
Pescaderia (Pesc.), Pl. C 2
Pescadores (P.), C. C 2
Pilar de Gracia, C. D 1
Pilatos, Pl. C 2
Pimienta (Pim.), C. D 2
Pinto, C. C 3
Pirineos, C. d. I. D 3
Pitágoras, Calle A 1
Pizarro, C. B 1
Placentines, C. D 2
Playa Antilla, C. A 3
Playa de (P.) Chipiona, C. A 3
Playa Matalascañas, C. A 3
Playa Punta Umbria, Pl. A 3
Poeta Fernando de los Rios, Calle del A 3
Polancos, C. de los B 3
Ponce de León, Pl. C 2
Portaceli, C. D 3
Potro, C. C 2
Pozo, C. d. B 2
Previsión, C. B 3
Primavera, Calle A 3
Procurador, C. D 1
P. Sevilla, C. B 1
Puente de la Barqueta, C. B 1
Puente y Pellón, C. C 2
Puerta Carmona, C. D 3
Puerta de Jerez, C. D 2
Puñorostro (Puñor.), C. C 3
Pureza, Calle de la D 1
Purgatorio, Calle B 3

Q

Quevedo, C. C 2
Quijano, Pje. B 2
Quintana (Quint.), C. C 2
Quintana, C. C 1

R

R. González, C. C 1
R. Medina, C. A 3
Rafael (R.) Calvo, Calle C 1
Rafael (R.) Salas González, C. D 1
Rastro, C. D 3
Rayo de Luna, C. A 2
Real, Pta. C 1
Recaredo, Calle C 3
Recreo, C. B 2
Redes, Calle C 1
Refinad., Pl. D 2
Regina, Calle de C 2
Reinosa, C. D 2
Relator, Calle de B 2
Reposo, C. B 2
Requena, C. D 1
Resolana, Calle B 2
Reyes Católicos, C. C/D 1
Reyes, Pl. de los D 2
Ribera, Camino de A 1/2, B 1
Rioja, C. de la C 1/2
Rivero, C. C 2
Rocio, C. D 1
Rocio, Ermita (E.) del (d.) A 3

Rodo, C. D 1/2
Rodrigo Caro, C. D 2
Rodrigo de Triana, Calle D 1
Rodríguez Zapata (R. Zap.), C. D 2
Roelas, C. B 2
Roldana, C. D 2
Roma, Avda. de D 2
Romanticismo, Av. d. A 2
Romeros, C. Los A 3
Rosa de Pasión, Pl. A 2/3
Rosario Vega D 1
Rosario, C. C 2
Rosario, Cta. C 2
Rubens, C. C 2
Ruiseñor, C. D 1
Ruiz (R.) de Gijón, C. B 2
Rull, Pl. C 1

S
Saavedra, C. C 2
Sacra-Familia, C. D 1
Sagasta, C. C 2
Sagunto, C. B 2
Sales (Sal.) y Ferre, C. C 2
Salesianos, C. C 3
Salinas, C. C 3
Salvador, Pl. C 2
San (S.) Andrés, C. C 2
San (S.) Basilio, C. B 2
San (S.) Juan (J.) de (d.) la Palma, C. C 2
San (S.) Juan, C. C 2
San (S.) Julián, C. B 3
San (S.) Primitivo, C. C 3
San Bartolomé (S. B.), C. D 2
San Clemente, C. D 2
San Francisco, Pl. D 2
San Gabriel, Pl. B 3
San Gregorio, C. D 2
San Ildefonso, Pl. C 2
San Juan (S. J.) Bosco, C. d. B 3
San Laureano, Pl. C 1
San Martin, Pl. C 2
San Miguel, C. C 2
San Nicolás, C. D 2
San Román, Pl. C 2
San Sebastián, Pl. D 2
San Bernardo, Barriada D 3
San Diego, C. D 2
San Eloy, Calle C 1/2
San Esteban, Calle C 2/3
San Felipe, C. C 2
San Fernando, Calle D 2
San Francisco (F.) d. Paula, C. C 2
San Hemenegildo, C. B/C3
San Isidoro, C. C 2
San Jacinto, Calle D 1
San Jorge, C. D 1
San José, C. D 2
San Juan de Ávila, C. C 1/2
San Juan de Ribera, C. B 2
San Lázaro, Avenida de A 3
San Leandro, Pl. C 2
San Luis, Calle de B/C 2
San Maestro Quiroga, C. B 3
San Pablo, Calle C 1
San Pedro (P.) Mártir, C. C 1
San Pedro, Pl. C 2
San Roque, C. C 1
San Vicente, Calle de B/C 1
Sánchez (S.) Barcaiztegui, C. C 1
Sánchez Reciente (Sánch R.), C. B 2
Sánchez S. de (d.) Castro, C. C 2
Sánchez Pizjuán, Avenida A 2/3
Sancho Dávila (S. D.), Av. de A 3
Sánchz Perrier, Calle B 2/3
Sanjurjo, Avda. D 2
Santa Ana, Calle de B 1, B/C 2
Santa Clara, Calle de B/C 2
Santa Maria la Blanca, C. D 2
Santander, Calle D 2
Santas Patronas, Calle C/D1
Santiago, Calle C 2/3
Santillana, C. C 2
Santo Rey, C. D 3
Santo Tomás, C. D 2
Sanz y Fores (Fo.) Angeles, C. D 2
Saturno, C. C 3
Sauceda (Sauc.), C. C 1
Segovias, C. D 2
Segui, C. C 2
Segura, C. D 1
Seises, Pje. D 2
Sierpes, Calle C/D 2
Sierra Nevada, C. C 3
Siete (S.) Dolores (D.) de Ntra.Sra., C. C 2
Siete (S.) Revueltas, C. C 2
Socorra, Calle C 2
Sol, Calle del C 2/3
Sollo, C. B 3
Sor Francisca Dorotea, Calle A/B 3
Sor Angela de la Cruz, C. C2
Sorda, C. B 2
Sta. Bárbara, C. C 2
Sta. Cruz, Pl. D 2
Sta. María (M.) Gracia, C. C 2
Sta. Rufina, C. B/C 2
Sta. Lucia, C. C 3
Sta. Marina, C. B 2
Sta. Paula, C. C 2/3
Sta. Teresa (T.), C. D 2
Sta. Teresa, C. D 2
Sta. Vicenta, C. C 1

T
Taf, C. B 2
Talavera, C. B 2
Talgo, C. B 2
Tarifa, C. C 2
Tarin, C. C 2
Temprado, C. D 2
Teniente (Tte.) Vargas (V.) Zúñiga, C. C 1
Teniente Borges, C. C 1/2
Tenorio C. C 3
Tentudia, C. D 3
Teodosio, Calle de B 1/2, C 1
Ter, C. B 2
Terceros, Pl. d. l. C 2
Tetuán, Calle C 2
Tinaja (T.), C. C 2
Tintes, C. C/D 3
Tirso Molina (Mol.), C. C 1
Tomás Alba Edison, C. A 1
Tomás de Ybarra, Calle D 2
Toneleros (Tonel.), C. D 2
Topacio, C. A 3
Torneo, Calle A/B 2, B/C 1
Toros de la Maestranza, Plaza de D 1
Torre de la Higuera, C. A 3
Torreblanca, C. B 2
Torremolinos, C. C 1
Torres, Calle B 2
Torrigiano, C. B 2
Torrijos, C. D 1
Trajano, Calle C 2
Trastámara, C. de C/D 1
Trinidad, Calle C 3
Triunfo, Pl. d. D 2
Trovador, C. D 3
Turmalina, C. A 2/3

U
Ubeda, C. C 3
Unidad, C. D 3
Urbana Norte, Ronda A 2/3
Urquiza, C. de C 3
Urraca (U.) Osorio, C. C 2

V
Valdelagrana, C. A 3
Valderrama (Valder.), C. C 2
Valdés (V.) Leal, C. D 1
Valladares (Vall.), C. D 1
Valladares, C. D 1
Valle, Calle del C 3
Valme, C. D 3
Valvanera, Pje. B 2
Vara (V.) del Rey, C. C 3
Varflora, Calle D 1/2
Vargas (V.) Campos, C. C 2
Vascongadas, C. B 2
V. Deleca, C. D 1
Velarde, Calle D 1
Velázquez, Calle de C 2
Venta de los Gatos, C. A 2
Verano, C. A3
Verde, C. C 2
Verde, C. D 2
Verónica, C. C 3
Vib- Arragel, C. B 2
Vicente (V.) Gallego, Pl. A 2
Victoria, C. D 1
Vida, C. D 2
Vidal, C. D 1
Vidrio, Calle C 2/3, D 2
Viejos, C. C 2
Vila Jamerdana (V. Jamerd.), C. D 2
Villegas, C. C 2
Vinuesa, C. D 2
Virgen (V .) de la Alegría, C. D 2
Virgen (V.) del Mayor (M.) Dolor, C. B 3
Virgen (V.) de la Sierra, C. D 3
Virgen de la Presentación (V. Pres.), C. C 1
Virgen de los Buenos (V. d. l. B.) Libros, C. C 1
Virgen del (V.) Pilar, Pl. B 3
Virgen d. Subterráneo, C. B 2
Virgen d. l. Reyes, C. B 2/3
Virgen de Gracia y Esperanza, C. C 3
Vírgenes, C. C/D 2
Viriato, C. C 2
Vista Hermosa (Vistaherm.), C. B 3
Vista Florida, Pl. B 3
Vulcano, C. B 2

X
Ximénez de Enciso, C. D 2

Y
Yuste, C. B 2

Z
Zafiro, C. A 2/3
Zamora, Pje. D 2/3
Zaragoza, Calle C 1, D 1/2
Zaruen, C. C 1
Zurradores, Pl. D 2/3

Valencia

14

A
Abadia San (A. S.) Martin, C. B 3
Abadia San Nicolás (A. S. Nicol.), C. B 2
Abate, C. B 2/3
Acequia Rascaña, C. A 2
Actor Rivelles, C. B 2
Adresadors, C. B 2
Aire, Senda del A 3
Aladrers (Aladr.), C. B 2
Alameda, Paseo de la B/C 4
Albacete, Calle C 2
Albaida, C. C 1
Albentosa, C. B 4
Alberique, Calle B/C 2
Alboraia, Calle A 3
Alcalde Albors, C. B 1
Alcalde Domingo Torres, Pl. A 4
Alcines, C. A 1
Alcira, C. B/C 2
Alcoy, C. C 3
Alemania, C. A 4
Alfambra, C. A 3
Alfonso de Córdoba, C. A/B 4
Alfonso el Magnánimo, Pl. B 3
Alfons Verdaguer, C. A 1/2
Alfredo Calderón, C. A 2
Alfredo Culla, C. C 1
Alginet, C. B 4
Almansa, Pl. B 2
Almas, C. B 2/3
Almirante (Almir.), C. B 3
Almirante Cardoso, C. C 3
Almirante, C. B 3
Almoina (Al.), Pl. B 3
Almudin, C. A/B 3
Alqueria La Estrella, C. A 2
Alta, C. A 2
Altar S. Vicente (Vic.), C. B 3
Aluders (Alud.), C. B 3
Alvarez (Alva.), C. B 2/3
Álvaro Bazán, C. A 4
Amadeo de Saboya, Calle B 4
Amorosas (A.), C. A 2
Ángel Custodio (Á. Cust.), C. A 3
Ángel de Alcázar, C. B/C 1
Ángel Guimerá, Calle B 1/2
Ángel, Pl. A 3
Angelicot, C. B 2
Angosta Compañía (A. Com.), C. B 3
Antic Regne de València, Avenida C 3/4
Antonio Chocomeli, C. A 1
Antonio Machado, Paseo A 3
Antonio Suárez, C. B/C 4
Aparicio Albiñana, Calle A 1
Aparisi (Ap.) y Guijarro, C. B 3
Aragón, Avda. de B 4
Árbol, Pl. A 2
Archiduque Carlos, Calle B/C 1
Arévalo Baca, C. B 4
Arolas, C. B 2
Arq. Mora, C. B 4
Arquitectos Calvo, Pl. C 4
Artes Gráficas, Calle A/B 4
Art Mayor de la Seda, C. B 1
Arturo Piera, Pl. B 1
Arzobispo (A.), Pl. d. B 3
Arzobispo Fabián y Fuero, C. A 2
Arzobispo Mayoral, C. B 2/3
Arzobispo Melo, C. C 3
Asilo Infancia, C. B 2
Atleta José Andrés, Pl. B 4
Avellanas, C. d. las B 3
Ávila, Pl. de A 3
Ayora, Calle C 1
Ayuntamiento, Plaza del B 3
Azcárraga, Calle B 1/2

B
Badajoz, Plaza A 1
Baden Powell, Pl. A 1
Bailén, C. C 2/3
Bailia, C. A/B 3
Baja, C. A/B 2
Baldoví, C. B 2
Baleares, Av. de las C 4
Ballesteros (Ballest.), C. B 3
Balmes, Calle B 2
Bany dels (B. d.) Pavesos, C. B 3
Bany, C. del B 2
Barcas, Calle de las B 3
Barcelona (Barcelon.), C. B 3
Barchilla (B.), C. B 3
Barón (B.) de Patraix, C. C 1/2
Barón (B.) Herves, C. A/B 3
Barón de Carcer, Avenida del B 2
Barón de San Petrillo, C. A 4
Barón Petres (B. P.), C. B 3
Barrio de Sta. Ana A 4
Batel, C. A 2
Beata Inés, C. C 1
Beata, C. B 2
Beato Gaspar Bono, C. A/B 2
Belén (B.), C. B 2
Belluga, C. B 2
Bellús, C. A 3
Benavites, C. A 1
Beneficiencia, Calle A 2
Benidorm, C. A 1
Benifayó, C. A 1
Bergantín, C. A 2
Bernat Baldoví, C. A 4
Biar, C. A 1
Bisbe, Calle B 3
Bisbesa, C. B 2
Blanes (B.), C. B 2/3
Blanquerias, Calle A 2/3
Bocha, Pl. B 2
Boix, C. A/B 3
Bolonia, C. A 1
Bolsería, C. B 2
Bonaire, C. B 3
Bordadores (Bor.), C. B 3
Bórras (Bórr.), C. A 2/3
Borrull, Calle B 2
Botánico, Calle B 2
Botellas, C. B 2
Brasil, Calle B 1
Bréton de los Herreros (Bret. d. l. Her.), C. B 3
Buen Orden, C. B/C 2
Burgos, Calle B 1
Burguerins (Bu.), C. B 2
Burriana, Calle C 3/4
Busot, C. C 2

C
Caballeros, C. A/B 2/3
Cabillers, C. B 3
Cabrito (Cab.), C. A 2
Cadirers (Cad.), C. B 2/3
Calamocha, C. C 1/2
Calarredes, C. A 2
Calatrava (Cal.), C. B 3
Caldereros (Cald.), C. B 2
Calderón d. l. Barca, C. A 4
Calixto III, Calle B 1/2
Camarón, C. B 2
Cambios (Ca.), C. B 3
Campanar, Avenida de A 1
Cañete, C. B 2
Canoa, C. A 2
Cánovas del Castillo, Pl. B/C 3/4
Cárcel (Cár.) S. Vicente (Vic.), C. B 3
Carda, C. B 2
Cardenal Paya (C. P.), C. B 3
Cardona (C.), C. B 3
Caridad (Car.), C. A 2/3
Carles, C. B 4
Carlos Dinnbier, C. A/B 1
Carmen, Pl. del A 2/3
Carniceros, Calle B 2
Carrasquer (Carras.), C. B 2
Carreras Puchalt, C. A 4
Cartagena, C. B 1
Casa Clemencia, C. A 4
Casilda Castelví, C. C 1
Castan Tobeñas, Calle B 1
Castellón, C. C 3
Castelvins (Cast.), C. B 3
Castielfabib, C. A 1
Castilla, Plaza B/C 1
Castillo de Benisanó, C. B 1
Catadau, C. A/B 1
Catalans (Catal.), C. B 3
Catarroja, C. C 1/2
Cavanilles, Calle A 3/4
Cayuco, C. A 2
Cedaceros (Ceda), C. B 3
Cenia (Cen.), C. B 2/3
Centenar de la Paloma, Pl. A 2
Cerdá y Rico, C. B 1
Cerrajeros (Cerraj.), C. B 3
Cervantes, Calle B/C 2
Chelva, C. C 1
Chile, C. B 4
Chiva, Calle C 1/2
Churat y Sauri, C. C 1
Cid, Avenida del B/C 1
Ciegos, Pl. A 3
Cirilo Amorós, Calle B/C 3/4
Ciscar, Calle C 4
Cisneros, Pl. A 3
Ciudadela, Paseo de la B 3
Cobertizo, C. A 2
Cocinas (Coc.), C. B 3
Colegio del (Col. d.) Patriarca, Pl. B 3
Coll, Pl. B 2
Colom, C. B 2
Colomer, C. B 2
Colón, Calle B/C 3
Compañía (C.), Pl. B 2/3
Comunión (C.) Sa. Juan, Pl. B 2
Concordia (C.), C. A/B 3
Conde Almodóvar (C. Almod.), C. A/B 3
Conde (C.) Buñol, Pl. A/B 2/3
Conde (C.) Carlet, Pl. A 3
Conde (C.) del Real, Pl. A/B 3
Conde (C.) Olocau, C. A/B 3
Conde (Cde.) Salvatierra de Álava, C. B 3
Conde de Altea, Calle C 3/4
Conde de Trenor, Calle A 3
Conde Montornés, C. B 3
Conquista (Con.), C. B 3
Constitución, Avda. de la A 2/3
Convento Carmelitas, C. A 3
Convento (Conv.) S. Francisco, C. B 2/3
Convento (Conv.) Sta. Clara C. B 3
Convento, C. A 3
Convento de la Puridad (C. P.), C. A/B 3
Convento de Jerusalén, C. B/C 2
Corazón de Jesús, C. C 1
Cordellats (Cor.), C. B 2
Corona, C. A 2
Corredores (C.), C. A 2
Correjeria (Corr.), C. B 3
Correo Viejo (C. V.), Pl. B 2/3
Correos, Calle B 3
Cors de la Mare de Deu (C. d. l. M. d. D.), Pl. A/B 3
Cotanda, C. B 3
Covarrubias (C.), C. A 3
Crespin (Cresp.), Pl. B 3
Cronista Carreres, C. B 3
Cronista Jerónimo Zurita (C. J. Z.), C. A/B 3
Cronista Ribelles, C. A 3
Crucero, C. A 2
Cruilles (Cr.), C. A/B 3
Cruz (Cr.) Nueva, C. B 3
Cruz, Pasaje de la B 2
Cuenca de Tramoyeres, C. A 4
Cuenca, Calle B/C 2

D
Damas (D.), C. B 3
Damián Forment (Dam. F.), C. A 3
Denia, C. C 3
Derechos (Der.), C. de los B 3
Devesa Santafe, Pje. C 2
Dr. Beltrán Bigorra, C. A/B 2
Dr. Blay, C. A 1
Dr. Calatayud Baya, C. A 1
Dr. Chiarri, C. A 2
Dr. Collado (C.), Pl. B 3
Dr. Dionisio, C. A 2
Dr. Enrique (E.) López, C. C 1
Dr. F. Barberá, C. A 2
Dr. Gómez Ferrer, C. A 4
Dr. Juan Reglá, C. B 4
Dr. Landete, Pl. C 3
Dr. Moliner, Calle A/B 4
Dr. Montoro, C. A 2
Dr. Montserrat, C. B 2
Dr. Nicasio Benlloch de Burjassot, Calle A 2
Dr. Oloriz, Calle A 2
Dr. Peset Cervera, C. B 2
Dr. Rodríguez Fornos, C. A/B 4
Dr. Romagosa. C. B 3
Dr. Sanchis Bergón, C. A 2
Dr. Sanchis Severa, C. B 2
Dr. Sempere, C. B 1
Dr. Sumsi, C. C 3
Dr. Vicente Zaragoza, C. A 4
Doctor Zamenhof, Calle B 1/2
Don (D.) Juan de Austria, C. B 3
Don (D.) Juan de Vilarrasa, Pl. B 2
Dragaminas, C. A 1
Duato, C. A 3
Duque Calabria (Cal.), C. C 4

E
Edeta (Ed.), C. B 3
Editor (Ed.) Cabrerizo, C. B 2
Editor Manuel (Ed. M.) Aguilar, C. B 2
Eduardo Bosca, C. C 4
Eduardo Soler y Pérez, C. A/B 1
El Bachiller, C. A 4
Embajador Vich, C. B 3
Emperador, C. B 3
En (E.) Blanc, C. B 3
En (E.) Bou, C. B 3
Encarnación, Pl. de la B 2
En Gall, Pl. B/C 2
En Gil, C. B 2
En Gordo, C. B 3
Enguera, Calle C 1
En Llop, C. B 3
En Llopis, C. A 3
En Plom, C. B 2
Enrique Albors, C. C 1
Enrique Gaspar, C. A 2
Enrique Navarro, C. A 4
En (E.) Roda, C. A 3
En Sala (S.), C. B 3
En (E.) Sanz, C. B 2/3
En Sendra, C. B 2
Entenza, C. B 3
Eolo, C. B 4
Ercilla (Erc.), C. B 2/3
Ermita, C. C 2
Ermita (E.), C. A 3
Erudito Orellana, C. B 2
Escalones Lonja (Esc. L.), C. B 2/3
Escolano (Esc.), C. B 2
Escultor Garcia Mas, Calle A 1
España, Pl. C 2
Espartero, C. B/C 2
Esparto, Pl. A/B 2
Espinosa, C. B 2
Esquife, C. A 2
Estrella, C. C 2
E. Vieja (V.), C. B 3
Exarchs, C. B 2

F
Faderio Tomás, C. A 2/3
Falua, C. A 2
Falucho, C. A 2
Fco. B. Esteban, C. A 1
Fco. Llano, C. C 1/2
Félix Pizcueta, C. B/C 3
Fenollosa (Fen.), C. A 2
Fernando El Católico, Gran Via de A/B 1/2
Finlandia, C. B 4
Fleming, C. B 3/4
Flora, C. A 3
Font Rotja, C. C 2
Formoles, C. A 1
Fos, C. A 2
Fraile, C. B 2/3
Francisco Dolz, Calle C 1
Francisco Moreno Usedo, C. B 1
Fresas, C. A 4
Frigola (Fr.), C. A 2/3
Fueros, Pl. de los A 3

G
Gabarra, C. A 2
Gabriel Miró, Calle B 1/2
Galera, C. A 2
Galicia, C. B 4
Galicia, Pl. B 4
Gandia, C. B 2
Garcilaso, C. A 3
Garrigues, C. B 2/3
Gascó, C. A 4
Gascons (G.), C. B 3
Gaudencia, C. A 1
General Avilés, Avenida A 1
General Elio, C. A 3/4
General Palanca, C. B 3
General Sanmartín, C. C 3
General Tovar, C. B 3
Germanias, Gran Via C 3
Gigante (Gig.), C. B 3
Gil Polo (G. P.), C. A 3
Gobernador Viejo, Calle B 3
Godelleta, C. A 1
Góngora, C. B 1
González Martí, C. B 1
Goya, Calle B 1
Grabador Enguidanos, C. A 1
Grabador (Grab.) Selma, C. B 2
Gral. Gil Dolz, C. B 4
Gral. Navarro Sangrán, C. B 3/4
Gral. Prim, C. C 3
Gravador Esteve, C. B 3/4
Gregorio Gea, C. A 1/2
Gregorio Mayans, C. C 3
Guadalaviar, Calle A 3
Guardia Civil, C. A 4
Guillén (G.), C. B 3
Guillén de Castro, C. A/B 2
Guillén Despuig, Calle C 1
Guillén Sorolla, Calle B 2
Guillén, Calle A 2
Gutenberg, C. A 2

H
Harina, C. B 3
Hermanos Vilalonga, C. A 4
Hernán Cortés, Calle B/C 3
Héroe Romeu, C. B 1/2
Hiedra (H.), C. B 2/3
Hierba, C. A/B 3
Historiador Diego, C. B/C 2
Hnos. Rivas, C. B 1
Horno (H.) San Nicolás, Pl. B 3
Horno Hospital, C. B 2
Hornos, Pje. B 3
Horticultor Corset, Pl. B 1
Hospital, Calle del B 2
Huertos, C. A 2
Huesca, C. B 2
Hugo de Moncada, Calle A 3
Humanista Honorato y Juan, C. C 2

I
Ibánez (I.), Pl. B 3
Isabel La Católica, C. B/C 3
Islas Canarias, C. B/C 4
Izquierdo, Pje. B/C 2

J
Jabeque, C. A 2
Jabonera, C. A 3
Jaca, Calle A 3/4
Jacinto Benavente, Avenida de B/C 4
Jai-Ala, C. B 4
Jaime Esteve, C. A 4
Jaime Roig, C. A 4
Jardines (Jard.), C. A 2
Jerónimo Luzatti, C. C 1
Jesús y Maria, C. B 2
Jesús, Calle B/C 2
Joaquín Ballester, Calle A 1/2
Joaquín Costa, Calle C 3/4
Jofrens (Jofr.), C. B 3
Jorge Juan, Calle B/C 3
Jovellanos (Jovel.), C. B 3
Juan Aguilar, C. A 1
Juan Bautista Vives, C. B 1
Juan de Mena, C. B 2
Juan Llorens, Calle B 1/2
Juan Martorell, C. A 4
Juan Menéndez Pelayo, Calle A 4
Juan Pablo II, Pl. A 1
Juan (J.) Plaza, C. A 2
Julio Antonio, C. C 2/3
Juristas (Jur.), C. B 3
Justicia, C. B 3

L
La Cruz (C.), C. A 2/3
La Huerta, C. A 3
La Unión, C. A 3
Landerer, C. A/B 2
Las Calabacas (Caba.), C. B 2/3
Las (L.) Comedias, C. B 3
Las Danzas (L. Danz.), C. B 2
Las (L.) Rejas, C. B 2
Legión Española, Pl. A/B 3/4
Lepanto, Calle B 2
Lérida, Calle A 2/3
Libertad, C. A 3
Libreros (L.), C. B 3
Liñán, C. B 3
Linares, Calle B/C 1
Linterna, C. de la B 3
Liria, Calle A 2
Llano de Zaidia, Pl. A 2
Llano de Zaidia, C. A 2/3
Llimera (Ll.), C. B 3
Lluis Lucía, Pl. A 1
Lonja (Lon.), C. B 2/3
Lope de Vega (L. d. V.), Pl. B 3
Lope de Rueda, Calle B 2
Los (L.) Borja, C. A/B 3
Los Franciscanos (L. Francisc.), C. A 3
Luchente (Luc.), C. B 2
Luis Lamarca, C. B 1
Luis Vives, C. B 3

M
M. Llácer, C. B 2
Macastre, C. A 1
Madre Sacramento, C. A 3
Madrina (M.), C. B 2
Maestre Racional, C. C 4
Maestres, C. d. l. (de los) B 3
Maestro Asensi, C. B 1
Maestro Bagant, C. A 1
Maestro Bellver, Calle C 1
Maestro Clavé, C. B 2/3
Maestro Esteban (E.) Catalá, C. A 4
Maestro Gozalbo, C. C 3
Maestro Guerrero, C. B 1
Maestro Rodrigo, Avenida A/B 1
Maestro Serrano, C. C 3
Maguncia, Pl. C 1
Málaga, Calle A 2
Maldonado, C. B 2
Mallorquins (Mal.), C. B 2
Manises, Pl. A/B 3
Manolo Taberner, Calle B 1
Mantas, C. d. l. B 3
Manuel de Falla, Avda. B 1
Manya, C. A 3
Manzanera, C. A 3
Mar, Calle del B 3
Mare Vella (M. V.), C. A 2/3
María Cristina, Avda. B 3
Mariano Benlliure (M. B.), Pl. B 3
Mariano Ribera, C. C 1
Marines, C. A 1
Marqués Busianos (Marq. Bus.), Pl. B 2
Marqués de Caro, C. A 2
Marqués de Elche, C. C 1
Marqués de San (S.) Juan, C. A/B 1
Marqués de Sotelo, Avda. B/C 3
Marqués de Zenete, C. C 2
Marqués del Turia, Gran Vía B/C 3/4
Marqués (Marq.) d. Dos Aguas, C. B 3
Marqués Mascarell, C. A 4
Marsella (M.), C. B 2
Martí, Calle C 3
Martín El Humano, C. B 1/2
Martín Mengod (M.M.), C. B 3
Martínez Aloy, C. C 2
Martínez Cubels, C. B/C 3
Marva, C. C 2
Matemático Marzal, C. C 2/3
Mauro Guillén, C. A 2
Mco. Padilla (M: Pad.), C. C 3
Médico Vicente (Vte.) Torrent, Av. B 1
Mendoza (Mend.), C. A/B 2/3
Menéndez Pidal, Avenida A 1/2
Mercado, Pl. d. A/B 2
Mesón Morella (M. M.), C. A 2
Micalet, C. B 3
Micer Masco, Calle B 4
Miguel Paredes, C. C 1
Milagro, C. B 3
Milagrosa, C. de la A 3
Minador, C. A 2
Miñana, C. B 3
Miracle de Mocadoret (M. d .M.), C. B 3
Mistral, Calle A 4
Mitro, C. A 2
Mogente, C. B 1
Molinas Sta. Catalina, C. B 3
Molinell, Calle A 3/4
Molino Marquesa, C. A 1
Molino Nou Moles, C. B 1
Monestir de Poblet, Calle A 1
Monforte, C. A/B 3/4
Monjas, C. B 2
Moratin, C. B 3
Morella (Mo.), C. A 2
Moret, C. A 2/3
Moro Zeit, C. B 2
Mosen Fernandes, C. B 3
Mosen Jordi, C. B 1

24

STREET INDEX · STRASSENVERZEICHNIS · INDICE STRADALE · CALLEJERO · ÍNDICE DAS ESTRADAS ·
STRAATNAMENREGISTER · GADEFORTEGNELSE · REJSTŘÍK ULIC · REGISTER NÁZVOV ULÍC A NÁMESTÍ · SKOROWIDZ ULIC

E

Mosen (M.) Milá, Pl. B 3
Mosen Rausell, C. A 1
Mosen Sorell, Pl. A 2
Motonave, C. A 2
Mtro. Arambul Sanz, Pl. A 1
Mtro. Palau, C. B 2
Muñoz Degrain (Degr.), C. B 3
Muñoz Seca, C. B 4
Murillo, C. B 2
Muro (M.) de Sta. Ana, C. A 3
Museo, C. A 2
Música Ayllón, Calle C 1
Músico José Iturbi, C. B 3
Músico López Chavarri, Pl. A/B 2
Músico Magenti, C. A 4
Músico Peydro, C. B 2/3

N
Nador, C. A 3
Na Jordana, Calle A 2
Nápoles (Náp.) y Sicilia, Pl. B 3
Náquera, C. A 2
Narciso Monturiol, C. A 2
Navarra C. B/C 2
Navarro Reverter, C. B 3/4
Navarros (N.), Pl. A 3
Nave, C. de la B 3
Navellos, C. A/B 3
Navío, C. A 2
Negrito, Pl. B 3
Niños S. Vicente, Pl. B 3
Norte, Calle B 1/2
Ntra. Sra. de Gracia, C. B 2
Ntra. Sra. de las Nieves (d. l. N.), C. B 3
Nules, Pl. A 3

O
Obispo Jerón., C. A/B 2/3
Obispo, Pl. C 2
Obispo Soler, C. A 1
Oliag, C. A 4
Olivereta, Calle B 1
Olivo, C. B 3
Ontiyent, C. C 1/2
Orihuela, Calle A 2/3

P
Pablo Picasso, Pl. A/B 1
Padilla, C. B 2
Padre Diego Mirón, Calle A 1
Padre Fullana, C. A 1
Padre Ferris, Calle A 2
Padre Huérfanos, C. A 2/3
Padre Jofre, Calle B/C 2
Padre Muedra, Calle B 3
Padre Rico, C. B 1/2
Palache, C. A 2
Palacio de Justicia (Pal. d. Just.), C. B 3
Palafox (Pal.), C. B 2/3
Palau, C. B 3
Palau y Quer, C. A 2/3
Palleter, Calle B 2
Palomar, C. B 2
Palomino (Palom.), C. A 3
Parra, Cno. de A 1
Pascual y Genís, Calle B 3
Patios (Pat.) d. Frigola, C. B 2
Paz, C. de la B 3
Pechina, Paseo de la A/B 1/2
Pedro III El Grande, C. C 3/4
Pelayo, Calle C 2/3
Pepita, C. A 3
Perdiz (P.), C. A 3
Pere Bonfil, C. A 2
Pérez Bayer, C. B 3
Pérez Estrich, C. B 1/2
Pérez Galdós, Avenida de B/C 1/2
Pérez Puyol, C. B 3
Periodista Azzati, C. B 2/3
Periodista Badia, C. A 4
Periodista Llorente, C. B 2
Periodista Ros Belda, Pl. B 4
Peris Mencheta, C. A 4
Picadero Dos Aguas (P. A.), Pl. B 3
Pilar, Pl. d. B 2
Pinazo, Pl. Los B 3
Pineda (P.), C. A 3
Pintor Benedito, C. C 2
Pintor (P.) Domingo, C. A/B 2

Pintor Fillol (P. F.), C. A 2/3
Pintor Genaro Lahuerta, C. A 3
Pintor López, Calle A 3
Pintor Navarro Llorens, C. C 2
Pintor Pascual Capuz, C. C 1
Pintor Peiro, C. B 4
Pintor Segrelles, C. C 2
Pintor Sorolla, Calle B 3
Pintor Stolz, C. B 1
Pintor Verde, C. B 4
Pintor Vila Prades, C. B 1/2
Pintor Vilar, C. A 3
Pintor Zariñena, C. A/B 2
Pinzón, Calle A/B 2
Pio XII, Avenida de A 1
Pizarro, Calle A 3
Plaza Castilla B/C 1
P. Manjón, C. B 2/3
Poeta Bodria, C. A 3
Poeta Fdez., C. A 2
Poeta Liern, C. B 3
Poeta Llombart (P. Lom.), C. B 2/3
Poeta Llorente, Pl. A/B 3
Poeta Montmeneu, C. A 2/3
Poeta Navarro Cabanes, C. B 1
Poeta Querol, C. B 3
Poeta Quintana, C. B 3
Pollo, C. B 3
Polo Bernabé, Pl. B 4
Popul (Pop.), C. B 2/3
Porchets (P.), Pl. B 3
Porta de la Mar, Pl. B 3
Portal de Valldigna, C. A 2/3
Portillo de (d.) S. Jorge B 3
Pouet S. Vicente (Vic.), C. B 3
Pozo, C. A 2
Preseguer (Pres.), C. B 4
Primado Reig, Avenida del A 4
Prócida (Próc.), C. B 3
Prof. Olmos, Pl. A 4
Profesor Beltrán Báguena, C. A 1/2
Profesor López Ibor, Pl. B 1
Puebla Larga, C. A 4

Puerta Sta. Maria, C. A 1
Puerto, Avenida del B/C 4
Purisima, C. B 3

Q
Quart, Calle de B 2
Quevedo, Calle B 2

R
Rafael Cisternes, C. B 4
Rafol, C. B 2
Raga (Rag.), C. B 2/3
Ramillestes (R.), C. B 2/3
Ramón Gordillo, C. A 4
Ramón Asensio, C. A 4
Ramón Castro, C. C 1/2
Ramón Llin, C. A 2
Ramón y Cajal, Gran Via de B/C 2
Rascaña, C. A 1
Real, Llano del A/B 3
Recaredo, C. B 2
Redención (Red.), C. B 3
Redonda, Pl. B 3
Reina Doña Germana, C. C 4
Reina, Plaza de la B 3
Reloj Viejo (R. Vie.), C. B 3
Repeso (R.), C. B 3
Requena, C. B 2
Reverendo Rafael Tramoyeres, C. A 4
Rex, Pje. B 3
Rey Don Jaime, C. B 2
Reyes Prosper, Pl. B 4
Ribalta (R.), C. B 3
Ribarroja, C. A 1
Ribera, C. B/C 3
Ricardo Mico, Calle A 2
Rio Duero, C. A 4
Ripalda, Calle A 2
Ripalda (Rip.), Pje. B 3
Roca (R.), C. B 2
Rocas, C. A 3
Rodrigo (R.) Bolet, Pl. B 3
Roger de Flor, Calle B 3
Roger de Lauria, Calle B 3
Rojas, Pl. B 2
Roma, Pl. B 1
Rompehielos, C. A 2
Roteros, C. A 2/3
R. Porta Carrasco, C. A 1/2

Ruaya, Calle A 2/3
Rubiols, C. A 2
Ruiz Lihori, C. B 3
Rumbau, C. B 2/3
Russafa, Paseo de B/C 3
Ruzafa, C. C 3
Ruzafa, Pje. C 3

S
Sagasta, C. B 3
Sagrario de Compañía (Sag. d. Com.), C. B 2/3
Sagrario Salvador (Sagr. Salva.), C. A 3
Sagunto, Calle A 3
Salamanca, Calle C 4
Salinas, C. B 2
Salud, C. A 3
Salvador, C. A/B 3
Salvador Sastre, C. C 2
Salvador Ferrandis Luna, C. B 1
Salvador Giner, C. A 2
Samaniego, C. A 3
San (S.) Andrés, C. B 3
San Augustin, Pl. B 2
San (S.) Cristóbal, C. C 2
San (S.) Esteban, Pl. B 3
San (S.) Fernando, C. B 3
San Guillén, C. A 3
San Jacinto, C. B 1/2
San (S.) Javier, C. A 1
San José de Calasanz, C. C 1/2
San José de la Montaña, Avenida B 1/2
San Juan (S. J.), C. B 3
San (S.) Juan de la Cruz, C. A 3
San Lorenzo (S. L.), Pl. A 2
San Nicolas (S. Nicol.), Pl. B 2
San Pablo, C. B 2/3
San Pio V, Calle A 3
San Ramón, C. A 2
San Valero, C. C e
San Vicente (S. Vic.) Ferrer, Pl. B 3
San Vicente Mártir, C. B/C 2/3
Sangre, C. B 3
Sanpedor (S.), C. B 2
Santa Mónica, Plaza A 3
Santa Amalia, C. A 3

Santa Cruz de Tenerife, Calle B/C 1
Sant (S.) Espirit, C. A 4
Santo Cáliz, C. B 3
S. Dionisio, C. A/B 2
Segorve, C. C 3
Senda de Senent, C. C 4
Serrano Flores, C. B 4
Serranos, C. A 3
Severo Ochoa, C. A/B 4
Sevilla, C. C 3
S. Francisco de Borja, C. C 2
S. Ignacio de Loyola, C. B 1/2
Simón Ortiz, C. B 2
S. Jaime (J.) A 3
S. Jaime, Pl. A/B 2
S. Martin, C. B 3
Sociedad Domenech, C. A 4
Sogueros, C. A 2
Soledad (Soled.), C. B 3
Sorni, Calle B 3/4
S. Pedro Pascual C. B 2
St. Bult (B.), Pl. B 3
Sta. Cruz, Pl. A 2/3
Sta. Elena (St. E.), C. A 2/3
Sta. Eulalia (S. Eul.), C. B 3
Sta. Isabel, C. A 3
Sta. Julia, C. B 3
Sta. Margarita (Marg.), Pl. A/B 3
Sta. Maria Micaela, C. A 3
Sta. Rita, C. A 3
Sta. Rosa, C. B 4
Sta. (S.) Irene, C. B 3
Sta. Ursula, Pl. B 2
Sto. Tomás, C. A 3
Subida (Sub.) del Toledano (T.), C. B 3
Submarino, C. A 3
Suecia, Avenida de A/B 4

T
Tabernes de Valldigna, Pl. A 2
Tallada, C. B 3
Tamarit, C. A 4
Tapineria, C. B 3
Tarazona, C. B 2
Tarra, C. A 3

Taula Canvis (T. C.) B 2
Tejedores, C. B 2
Temple, Plaza del B 3
Tenerias (T.), C. A 2/3
Tenor G. Romero, C. A 1
Tertulia, C. B 3
Teruel, C. B 1
Tetuán, Plaza B 3
Timoneda, C. B 2
Tirso de Molina, Avenida A/B 1
Torno del Hospital, C. B 2
Toros, Plaza de C 3
Torpedero, C. A 2
Torres de Quart, Pl. B 2
Torres, C. A 1
Torres, Calle B 1
Tosalet (Tosal.), C. A/B 3
Tossal (T.), Pl. B 2
Totana, Calle B/C 1
Transatlantico, C. A 2
Trànsits (Tràns.), C. B 3
Trenc, C. B 3
Tres Forques, Calle C 1/2
Triador, Calle B 2
Trig, C. A 4
Trinidad, C. A 3
Trinitarios, C. A/B 3
Trinquete de los Caballeros (Trinq. d. l. Cab.), C. B 3
Troya, C. C 2
Tundidores (Tund.), C. B 3
Turia, Calle A/B 2

U
Universidad, C. B 3

V
Vajeros (Caj.), C. B 2
Valdelinares, C. A 1
Valencians (Val.), C. B 2/3
Valeriola, C. B 2
Vall de Crist (V. de Cr.), C. A 3
Valldaura, C. B 3
Valle de la Ballestera. C. A 1
Valle Laguar, C.A 2
Vannes, Pl. C 2
V. de la Salut, C. B 1
V. d. l. Paz, Pl. B 3
Venerable Agnesio, C. C 1
Vera, Camino de A 4

Vergara (V.), C. B 3
Verger, C. B 3
Verónica (V.), C. B 3
Vestuario (Vest.), C. B 3
Vgen. de Campanar, C. A 1
Viana, Calle B 2
Vicente Blasco Ibáñez, Avenida de A 4
Vicente Iborra, Pl. A/B 2
Vicente Maroto, C. C 1
Vicente (V.) Sánchez, C. B 4
Vicente (V.) Ximeno, C. A 2
Victoria (Vic.), C. B 3
Viciana (Vicia.), C. A 3
Vidal (V.), C. B 3
Vieja de la Paja (V. d. l. P.), C. B 2
Vilaragut (Vil.), C. B 3
Villa Muro, C. A 4
Villar del Arzobispo, C. A 1
Villena, C. B 2
Vinalesa, C. A 1
Vinatea (Vina.), C. B 2
Virgen de la Cabeza (d. l. Cab.) C 1
Virgen (V.) Misericordia, C. B 2
Virgen, Pl. de la B 3
Viriato (Vir.), C. A 3
Virués, C. B 3
Visitación, C. B 3
Vives Lierp, C. C 2
V. Lluch, C. B 1
V. Rebollet, C. B 1
Vuelta del Ruiseñor, C. A 3

X
Xàtiva, Calle B/C 2/3
Xàvia, C. A 4
Ximénez (X.) de Sandoval, C. B 3

Z
Zapateros, C. A 3
Zaragoza, Plaza de B 4
Zeluán, C. A 3
Zurradores (Z.), C. B 3

EUROPE · EUROPA · EUROPA
EUROPA · EUROPA · EUROPA
EUROPA · EVROPA · EURÓPA · EUROPA

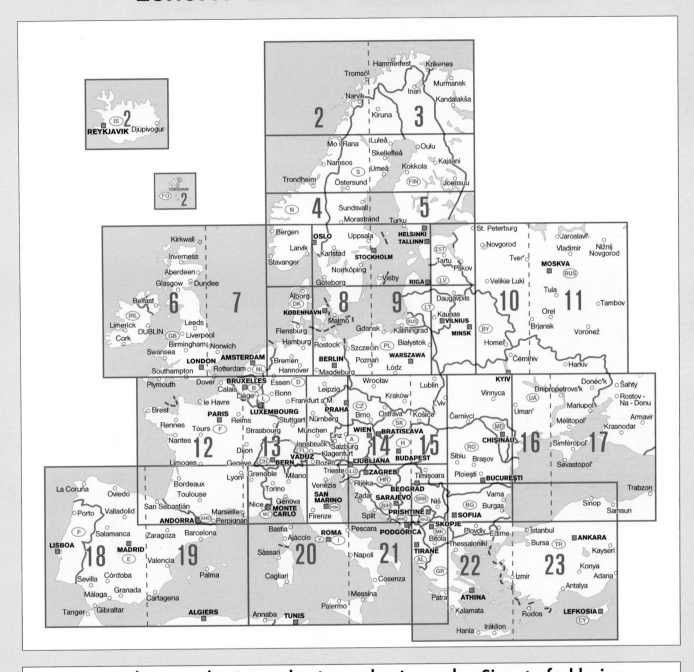

Legend Legende Legenda Leyenda Legenda Signaturforklaring
Legende Vysvětlivky Vysvetlivky Legenda

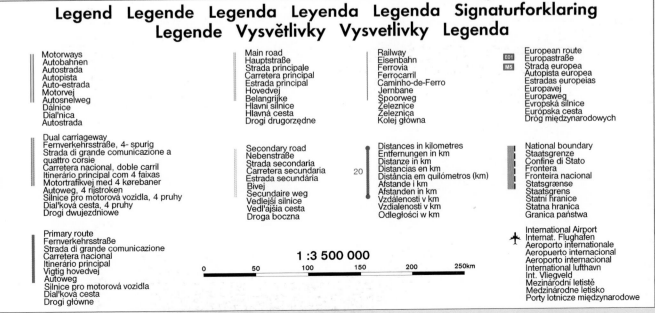

Motorways	Main road
Autobahnen	Hauptstraße
Autostrada	Strada principale
Autopista	Carretera principal
Auto-estrada	Estrada principal
Motorvej	Hovedvej
Autosnelweg	Belangrijke
Dálnice	Hlavní silnice
Dial'nica	Hlavná cesta
Autostrada	Drogi drugorzędne

Railway	European route
Eisenbahn	Europastraße
Ferrovia	Strada europea
Ferrocarril	Autopista europea
Caminho-de-Ferro	Estradas europeias
Jernbane	Europavej
Spoorweg	Europaweg
Železnice	Evropská silnice
Železnica	Európska cesta
Kolej główna	Dróg międzynarodowych

Dual carriageway
Fernverkehrsstraße, 4- spurig
Strada di grande comunicazione a
quattro corsie
Carretera nacional, doble carril
Itinerário principal com 4 faixas
Motortrafikvej med 4 kørebaner
Autoweg, 4 rijstroken
Silnice pro motorová vozidla, 4 pruhy
Dial'ková cesta, 4 pruhy
Drogi dwujezdniowe

Secondary road
Nebenstraße
Strada secondaria
Carretera secundaria
Estrada secundaria
Bivej
Secundaire weg
Vedlejší silnice
Vedl'ajšia cesta
Droga boczna

Distances in kilometres
Entfernungen in km
Distanze in km
Distancias en km
Distância em quilómetros (km)
Afstande i km
Afstanden in km
Vzdálenosti v km
Vzdialenosti v km
Odległości w km

National boundary
Staatsgrenze
Confine di Stato
Frontera
Fronteira nacional
Statsgrænse
Staatsgrens
Statní hranice
Statna hranica
Granica państwa

Primary route
Fernverkehrsstraße
Strada di grande comunicazione
Carretera nacional
Itinerário principal
Vigtig hovedvej
Autoweg
Silnice pro motorová vozidla
Dial'ková cesta
Drogi główne

1 :3 500 000

0   50   100   150   200   250km

International Airport
Internat. Flughafen
Aeroporto internationale
Aeropuerto internacional
Aeroporto internacional
International lufthavn
Int. Vliegveld
Mezinárodni letiště
Medzinárodne letisko
Porty lotnicze międzynarodowe

Ⓐ

Amstetten 14 K 16
Angern 14 K 17
Bad Aussee 14 K 16
Bad Eisenkappel 14 L 16
Bad Gastein 13 L 16
Bad Ischl 13 K 16
Bad Radkersburg 14 L 17
Bad Reichenhall 13 K 16
Baden/Wien 14 K 17
Birkfeld 14 L 17
Bischofshofen 13 L 16
Bludenz 13 L 14
Bregenz 13 L 14
Bruck an der Leitha 14 K 17
Bruck an der Mur 14 L 17
Dornbirn 13 L 14
Drasenhofen 14 K 17
Drosendorf 14 K 17
Eferding 14 K 16
Eibiswald 14 L 17
Eisenerz 14 K 16
Eisenstadt 14 K 17
Engelhartszell 14 K 16
Enns 14 K 16
Erlsbach 13 L 15
Feldkirch 13 L 14
Feldkirchen 14 L 16
Ferlach 14 L 16
Freistadt 14 K 16
Friedberg 14 L 17
Friesach 14 L 16
Gleisdorf 14 L 17
Gmünd/Millstatt 13 L 16
Gmünd/Schrems 14 K 16
Gmunden 14 K 16
Graz 14 L 17
Grein 14 K 16
Gutenstein 14 K 17
Hainburg 14 K 17
Hartberg 14 L 17
Haugsdorf 14 K 17
Heiligenblut 13 L 16
Heiligenkreuz 14 L 17
Hermagor 13 L 16
Hieflau 14 K 16
Hohenau 14 K 17
Hollabrunn 14 K 17
Horn 14 K 17
Imst 13 L 15
Innsbruck 13 L 15
Judenburg 14 L 16
Karlstift 14 K 16
Kirchdorf a. d. Kr. 14 K 16
Klagenfurt 14 L 16
Klosterneuburg 14 K 17
Knittelfeld 14 L 16
Köflach 14 L 17
Königswiesen 14 K 16
Krems 14 K 17
Kremsmünster 14 K 16
Kufstein 13 K 15
Lambach 14 K 16
Landeck 13 L 15
Leibnitz 14 L 17
Leoben 14 L 17
Lienz 13 L 16
Liezen 14 K 16
Lilienfeld 14 K 17
Linz 14 K 16
Lofer 13 K 16
Lunz 14 K 17
Mariazell 14 K 17
Matrei in Osttirol 13 L 16
Mattighofen 13 K 16
Mauterndorf 14 L 16
Mauthausen 14 K 16
Melk 14 K 17
Mistelbach 14 K 17
Mittersill 13 L 15
Mödling 14 K 17
Mondsee 13 K 16
Murau 14 L 16
Mürzzuschlag 14 K 17
Nauders 13 L 15
Neunkirchen/Wiener Neustadt 14 K 17
Nickelsdorf 14 K 17
Ober Pullendorf 14 L 17
Oberdrauburg 13 L 16
Obergurgl 13 L 15
Oberwart 14 L 17
Oetz 13 L 15
Ottenschlag 14 K 17
Pamhagen 14 K 17
Partenen 13 L 15
Radenthein 14 L 16
Radstadt 13 L 16
Reutte 13 L 15

Ried 13 K 16
Rohrbach 14 K 16
Rust 14 K 17
Salzburg 13 K 16
Sankt Anton 13 L 15
Sankt Johann in Tirol 13 K 15
Sankt Pölten 14 K 17
Sankt Veit 14 L 16
Schärding 13 K 16
Scheibbs 14 K 17
Schladming 14 L 16
Schrems 14 K 17
Schwaz 13 L 15
Schwechat 14 K 17
Spielfeld 14 L 17
Spittal an der Drau 13 L 16
Steyr 14 K 16
Stockerau 14 K 17
Straßwalchen 13 K 16
Telfs 13 L 15
Traun 14 K 16
Trieben 14 L 16
Tulln a.d.D. 14 K 17
Velden 14 L 16
Villach 14 L 16
Völkermarkt 14 L 16
Warth 13 L 15
Wels 14 K 16
Weyer 14 K 16
Wien 14 K 17
Wiener Neustadt 14 K 17
Wolfsberg 14 L 16
Wörgl 13 L 15
Zell am See 13 L 16
Zell am Ziller 13 L 15
Zwettl 14 K 17

ⒶⓁ

Berat 21 N 18
Borsh 21 N 18
Burrel 21 N 18
Çorovodë 21 N 19
Durrës 21 N 18
Elbasan 21 N 19
Ersekë 21 N 19
Fier 21 N 18
Fierzë 21 N 19
Fushë Arrëzi 21 N 19
Gramsh 21 N 19
Gjirokastër 21 N 19
Kavajë 21 N 18
Këlcyrë 21 N 19
Korçë 21 N 19
Krujë 21 N 18
Krumë 21 N 19
Kuçovë 21 N 18
Kukës 21 N 19
Leskovik 21 N 19
Lezhë 21 N 18
Librazhd 21 N 19
Lushnjë 21 N 18
Peshkopi 21 N 19
Pëqin 21 N 18
Përmet 21 N 19
Përrenjas 21 N 19
Pogradec 21 N 19
Pukë 21 N 18
Sarandë 21 O 18
Shëngjergj 21 N 19
Shkodër 21 N 18
Tepelenë 21 N 18
Tiranë 21 N 18
Tropojë 21 N 19
Theth 21 N 18
Vlorë 21 N 18

ⒶⓃⒹ

Andorra la Vella 19 M 11

Ⓑ

Aalst 13 J 12
Anderlues 13 J 12
Antwerpen (Anvers) 13 J 12
Arlon 13 K 13
Ath 12 J 12
Bastogne 13 K 13
Bouillon 13 K 13
Brugge (Bruges) 12 J 12
Bruxelles/Brussel 13 J 12
Charleroi 13 J 12
Couvin 13 J 12
De Panne 12 J 12

Dinant 13 J 12
Eekloo 12 J 12
Eupen 13 J 13
Geel 13 J 13
Gembloux 13 J 12
Gent (Gand) 12 J 12
Halle/Bruxelles 13 J 12
Hasselt 13 J 13
Hechtel 13 J 13
Houffalize 13 J 13
Huy 13 J 13
Ieper 13 J 12
Kortrijk 12 J 12
Liège (Luik) 13 J 13
Malmédy 13 J 13
Marche-en-Famenne 13 J 13
Mechelen 13 J 12
Mons 12 J 12
Namur 13 J 12
Oostende 7 J 12
Philippeville 13 J 12
Roeselare 12 J 12
Ronse 12 J 12
Sint Niklaas 13 J 12
Sint Truiden 13 J 13
Tienen 13 J 13
Torhout 12 J 12
Tournai 12 J 12
Turnhout 13 J 12
Verviers 13 J 13
Zeebrugge 7 J 12

ⒷⒼ

Ajtos 22 M 21
Ardino 22 N 21
Asenovgrad 22 N 20
Balčik 22 M 22
Batak 22 N 20
Belene 22 M 21
Belogradčik 22 M 20
Berkovica 22 M 20
Bjala 22 M 21
Bjala Slatina 22 M 20
Blagoevgrad 22 N 20
Botevgrad 22 M 20
Botunec 22 M 20
Burgas 22 M 21
Car Koloman 22 M 21
Carevo 22 N 22
Čepelare 22 N 20
Červen Brjag 22 M 20
Čirpan 22 N 21
Debăr 22 N 21
Devin 22 N 20
Dimitrovgrad/Haskovo 22 N 21
Dobrič 22 M 22
Dolni Lom 22 M 20
Dolno Cerovene 22 M 20
Dospat 22 N 20
Draganovo 22 M 21
Dulovo 22 M 21
Dunavci 22 M 20
Dupnica 22 N 20
Dve Mogili 22 M 21
Elena 22 M 21
Elhovo 22 N 21
Elin Pelin 22 M 20
Etropole 22 M 20
Filipovo 22 N 20
G. Studena 22 M 21
Gabrovo 22 M 21
General Toševo 22 M 22
Gigen 22 M 20
Goce Delčev 22 N 20
Godeč 22 M 20
Harmanli 22 N 21
Haskovo 22 N 21
Hisarja 22 N 20
Isperih 22 M 21
Ivajlovgrad 22 N 21
Jablanica/Botevgrad 22 M 20
Jambol 22 N 21
Kărdžali 22 N 21
Karlovo 22 N 20
Karnobat 22 M 21
Kazanlak 22 M 21
Kesarevo 22 M 21
Kjustendil 22 N 20
Klisura 22 M 20
Kneža 22 M 20
Komunari 22 M 21
Kostenec 22 N 20
Kotel 22 M 21
Kozloduj 22 M 20
Krivodol 22 M 20
Krumovgrad 22 N 21
Kruşari 16 M 22
Kubrat 22 M 21

Kula 22 M 20
Levski 22 M 21
Ljubimec 22 N 21
Lom/Vidin 22 M 20
Loveč 22 M 20
Loznica 22 M 20
Malko Tărnovo 22 N 22
Mezdra 22 M 20
Mihajlovo 22 M 20
Mikre 22 M 21
Montana 22 M 20
Nesebar 22 M 22
Nikopol/Belene 22 M 20
Nova Zagora 22 N 21
Novi Pazar 22 M 21
Obzor 22 M 22
Omurtag 22 M 21
Orjahovo 22 M 20
Panagjurište 22 M 20
Pavlikeni 22 M 21
Pazardžik 22 N 20
Pernik 22 M 20
Peštera 22 N 20
Petrič 22 N 20
Pleven 22 M 20
Plovdiv 22 N 20
Pomorie 22 M 22
Popovo 22 M 21
Primorsko 22 N 22
Provadija 22 M 21
Radnevo 22 N 21
Rakovski 22 N 20
Ravnec 22 M 21
Razgrad 22 M 21
Razlog 22 N 20
Rezovo 22 N 22
Rilski Man. 22 N 20
Rudnik 22 M 22
Ruse 22 M 21
Šabla 23 M 22
Samokov 22 N 20
Sandanski 22 N 20
Silistra 16 M 21
Simeonovgrad 22 N 21
Simitli 22 N 20
Skalica 22 N 21
Sliven 22 M 21
Slivnica 22 M 20
Smjadovo 22 M 21
Smoljan 22 N 20
Sofija 22 M 20
Sozopol 22 N 22
Sredec/Burgas 22 N 21
Sredec/Stara Zagora 22 N 21
Stara Zagora 22 N 21
Šumen 22 M 21
Svilengrad 22 N 21
Svištov 22 M 21
Svoge 22 M 20
Tărgovište 22 M 21
Tervel 22 M 21
Teteven 22 M 20
Todor Ikonomovo 22 M 21
Topolovgrad 22 N 21
Trăn 22 M 20
Trojan 22 M 20
Tutrakan 16 M 21
Tvărdica 22 M 21
Vakarel 22 M 20
Varbica 22 M 21
Varna 22 M 22
Veliko Tărnovo 22 M 21
Velingrad 22 N 20
Vidin 22 M 20
Vraca 22 M 20
Zemen 22 N 20
Zlatica 22 M 20
Zlatni Pjasăci 22 M 22
Zlatograd 22 N 21

ⒷⒾⒽ

Avtovac 21 M 18
Banja Luka 14 M 17
Bihać 14 M 17
Bijeljina 14 M 18
Bileća 21 M 18
Bosanski Petrovac 14 M 17
Brčko 14 M 18
Bugojno 21 M 17
Čapljina 21 M 18
Derventa 14 M 18
Doboj 14 M 18
Donji Vakuf 21 M 17
Drvar 21 M 17
Foča 21 M 18
Glamoč 21 M 17
Goražde 21 M 18
Gradiška 14 L 17

Grude 21 M 17
Hum 21 M 18
Ivanjska 14 M 17
Jablanica/Sarajevo 21 M 18
Jajce 14 M 17
Kalinovik 21 M 18
Kiseljak 21 M 18
Kladanj 21 M 18
Ključ 14 M 17
Kozanska Dubica 14 L 17
Livno 21 M 17
Ljubuški 21 M 18
Maslovare 21 M 18
Medugorje 21 M 18
Miričina 14 M 18
Mostar 21 M 18
Mrkonjić Grad 14 M 17
Neum 21 M 18
Nevesinje 21 M 18
Novi Grad 14 L 17
Pale 21 M 18
Posušje 21 M 17
Prijedor 14 M 17
Prozor 21 M 18
Sanski Most 14 M 17
Sarajevo 21 M 18
Srednje 21 M 18
Široki Brijeg 21 M 18
Teslić 14 M 18
Tomislavgrad 21 M 17
Travnik 21 M 18
Trebinje 21 M 18
Tuzla/Doboj 14 M 18
Vareš 21 M 18
Velika Kladuša 14 L 17
Višegrad 21 M 18
Vlasenica 21 M 18
Zenica 21 M 18
Zvornik 14 M 18
Žepče 14 M 18

ⒷⓎ

Akcjabrski 10 H 22
Asipovičy 10 H 22
Ašmjany 10 H 21
Astyna 9 H 20
Azaryčy 10 H 22
Babrujsk 10 H 22
Baranavičy 10 H 21
Baran' 10 H 23
Barisov 10 H 22
Belomorsk 10 H 21
Berazino 10 H 22
Bešankovičy 10 G 22
Bjahoml' 10 H 22
Bjalyničy 10 H 22
Bjaroza 9 H 20
Bobr 10 H 22
Bobrowniki 9 H 20
Bol. Čučeviči 10 H 21
Braslau 10 G 21
Brěst 9 J 20
Buda-Kašaleva 10 H 23
Bychau 10 H 23
Byciha 10 G 23
Čačersk 10 H 23
Čačevičy 10 H 22
Čareja 10 H 22
Cašniki 10 H 22
Čavusy 10 H 23
Čerykau 10 H 23
Chocimsk 10 H 24
Červen' 10 H 22
Davyd-Haradok 10 J 21
Derečin 9 H 20
Divin 9 J 20
Djaržynsk 10 H 21
Dobruš 10 J 23
Dokšycy 10 H 22
Dousk 10 H 23
Drahičyn 10 J 21
Druja 10 G 21
Dubrovići 10 J 21
Dukora 10 H 22
Dzisna 10 G 22
Dzjatlava 10 H 21
Efsk 10 J 23
Hancavičy 10 H 21
Haradok 10 G 23
Hluša 10 H 22
Hlusk 10 H 22
Hluškavičy 10 J 22
Hlybokae 10 G 22
Homel' 10 J 23
Hojniki 10 J 22
Horki 10 H 23
Hrodna 9 H 20
Hubiči 10 H 23

Indura 9 H 20
Ivacevičy 10 H 21
Ivanava 10 J 21
Ivjanec 10 H 21
Kalinkavyčy 10 J 22
Komarin 10 J 23
Karavacičy 10 J 23
Kascjukovičy 10 H 23
Kazlovičy 10 J 22
Kirausk 10 H 22
Kleck 10 H 21
Kličau 10 H 22
Klimavičy 10 H 23
Kljasčicy 10 G 22
Kljukauka 10 H 23
Knjažycy 10 H 23
Kobryn 9 J 20
Kosava 10 H 21
Krasnapolle 10 H 23
Kryčau 10 H 23
Lel'čycy 10 J 22
Lenin 10 J 21
Lepel' 10 H 22
Lezna 10 G 23
Lida 10 H 21
Ljasnaja 10 J 23
Ljuban'/Salihorsk 10 H 22
Luninec 10 J 21
Mahileu 10 H 23
Malaryta 15 J 20
Malazečna 10 H 21
Mar'ina Horka 10 H 22
Masty 9 H 20
Mazyr 10 J 22
Mery 10 G 22
Mikaševičy 10 J 21
Minsk 10 H 22
Mjadzel' 10 H 21
Monseevščina 10 H 22
Motal' 10 J 21
Mscislau 10 H 23
Naliboki 10 H 21
Naroc' 10 H 21
Navahrudak 10 H 21
Navapolack 10 G 22
Njasviz 10 H 21
Obol' 10 G 22
Orša 10 H 23
Paryčy 10 H 22
Pastavy 10 G 21
Pinsk 10 J 21
Pleščanicy 10 H 22
Polack 10 G 22
Porazava 9 H 20
Prazaroki 10 G 22
Pružany 9 H 20
Radaškovičy 10 H 21
Rahačou 10 J 23
Rečyca 10 J 23
Ružany 9 H 20
Salihorsk 10 H 22
Šarkauščyna 10 G 21
Ščučyn 9 H 20
Semeževo 10 H 21
Sirotina 10 G 22
Šiščyčy 10 H 22
Sjanno 10 H 22
Šklou 10 H 23
Slauharad 10 H 23
Slonim 10 H 21
Sluck 10 H 22
Smaljavičy 10 H 22
Smarhon' 10 H 21
Staraja Belica 10 H 22
Staryja Darohi 10 H 22
Stolin 10 J 21
Stralki 10 G 22
Suraž/Vitebsk 10 G 23
Svetlahorsk 10 H 22
Svir` 10 H 21
Svislač 10 H 22
Talačyn 10 H 22
Tomašovka 15 J 20
Uchvala 10 H 22
Ušačy 10 G 22
Valjar'jany 10 H 21
Valožyn 10 H 21
Varnjany 10 H 21
Vasilevičy 10 J 22
Volkovysk 9 H 20
Vetka 10 H 23
Vicebsk 10 G 23
Vidamlja 9 J 20
Vidzy 10 G 21
Vilejka 10 H 21
Višnevo 10 H 21
Vjatčyn 10 J 22
Vysokae 9 J 20
Žabinka 9 J 20
Zembin 10 H 22
Žitkavičy 10 J 22

Žlobin  BY · CH · CY · CZ · D **Ording** EU

Žlobin 10 H 23
Žodiški 10 H 21
Žodzina 10 H 22

 **CH**

Adelboden 13 L 14
Aigle 13 L 13
Altdorf 13 L 14
Andermatt 13 L 14
Baden/Zürich 13 L 14
Basel 13 K 14
Bellinzona 13 L 14
Bern 13 L 13
Biasca 13 L 14
Biel 13 L 13
Brienz 13 L 14
Brig 13 L 14
Buchs 13 L 14
Burgdorf 13 L 14
Chur 13 L 14
Davos 13 L 14
Delémont 13 L 13
Disentis/Mustér 13 L 14
Flims 13 L 14
Fribourg 13 L 13
Genève 13 L 13
Gletsch 13 L 14
Gstaad 13 L 13
Gümmenen 13 L 13
Interlaken 13 L 14
Konstanz 13 K 14
La Chaux de Fonds 13 L 13
Langenthal 13 L 14
Langnau 13 L 14
Lausanne 13 L 13
Locarno 13 L 14
Lugano 13 L 14
Luzern 13 L 14
Martigny 13 L 13
Montreux 13 L 13
Näfels 13 L 14
Neuchâtel 13 L 13
Olten 13 L 14
Payerne 13 L 13
Porrentruy 13 L 13
Sankt Gallen 13 L 14
Sankt Moritz 13 L 14
Sargans 13 L 14
Schaffhausen 13 K 14
Schwyz 13 L 14
Sion 13 L 13
Solothurn 13 L 14
Splügen 13 L 14
Susch 13 L 15
Thonon-les-Bains 13 L 13
Thun 13 L 14
Vallorbe 13 L 13
Vevey 13 L 13
Wädenswil 13 L 14
Wattwil 13 L 14
Wil 13 L 14
Winterthur 13 L 14
Yverdon 13 L 13
Zermatt 13 L 14
Zug 13 L 14
Zürich 13 L 14

 **CY**

Akrotiri 23 Q 24
Ammochostos (Famagusta) 23 P 24
Episkopi 23 Q 24
Karavostasi 23 P 24
Kouklia 23 Q 24
Kyrenia 23 P 24
Larnaka 23 Q 24
Lefka 23 P 24
Lefkoniko 23 P 24
Lefkosia/Lefkoşa 23 P 24
Lemesos 23 Q 24
Mandria 23 P 24
Morphou 23 P 24
Pafos 23 Q 23
Polis 23 P 23
Rizokarpaso 23 P 24
Salamis 23 P 24
Yialousa 23 P 24

 **CZ**

Aš 13 J 15
Benešov 14 K 16
Beroun 14 K 16

Bor 13 K 16
Brandýs nad Labem- Stará Boleslav 14 J 16
Brno 14 K 17
Bruntál 14 K 17
Břeclav 14 K 17
Čáslav 14 K 16
Černá 14 K 16
Česká Lípa 14 J 16
České Budějovice 14 K 16
Český Brod 14 J 16
Děčín 14 J 16
Dobříš 14 K 16
Doksy 14 J 16
Domažlice 13 K 16
Dvůr Králové 14 J 17
Frýdek-Mistek 14 K 18
Fryšták 14 K 18
Golčův Jenikov 14 K 17
Hartmanice 13 K 16
Havířov 14 K 18
Havlíčkův Brod 14 K 17
Hlinsko 14 K 17
Hodonín 14 K 17
Hradec Králové 14 J 17
Hranice 14 K 18
Cheb 13 J 15
Chomutov 14 J 16
Chrudim 14 K 17
Jáchymov 13 J 16
Jesenik 14 J 17
Jičín 14 J 17
Jihlava 14 K 17
Jindř. Hradec 14 K 17
Kamenice nad Lipou 14 K 17
Kaplice 14 K 16
Karlovy Vary 13 J 16
Karviná 14 K 18
Kladno 14 J 16
Klatovy 13 K 16
Kolín 14 K 17
Královice 13 K 16
Kraslice 13 J 15
Krnov 14 J 18
Kroměříž 14 K 17
Kyjov 14 K 17
Liberec 14 J 17
Litoměřice 14 J 16
Lnáře 14 K 16
Louny 14 J 16
Lubenec 13 J 16
Mariánské Lázně 13 K 16
Mělník 14 J 16
Mladá Boleslav 14 J 16
Mohelnice 14 K 17
Moravské Budějovice 14 K 17
Most 14 J 16
Náchod 14 J 17
Náměšť 14 K 17
Olomouc 14 K 17
Opava 14 K 18
Ostrava 14 K 18
Pardubice 14 J 17
Písek 14 K 16
Plzeň 13 K 16
Poděbrady 14 J 17
Pohořelice 14 K 17
Praha 14 J 16
Prostějov 14 K 17
Přerov 14 K 17
Přeštice 13 K 16
Příbram 14 K 16
Rakovnik 14 J 16
Rokycany 14 K 16
Rychnov nad Kněžnou 14 J 17
Sedlčany 14 K 16
Sokolov 13 J 16
Strakonice 14 K 16
Stříbrná Skalice 14 K 16
Sudoměřice u Bechyně 14 K 16
Svitávka 14 K 17
Svitavy 14 K 17
Šluknov 14 J 16
Šternberk 14 K 17
Šumperk 14 K 17
Tábor 14 K 16
Tanvald 14 J 17
Tavíkovice 14 K 17
Telč 14 K 17
Teplice 14 J 16
Trutnov 14 J 17
Třebíč 14 K 17
Třeboň 14 K 16
Třinec 14 K 18
Uherské Hradiště 14 K 17
Uněšov 13 K 16
Ústí nad Labem 14 J 16
Ústí nad Orlicí 14 K 17
Valašské Meziříči 14 K 18
Varnsdorf 14 J 16
Velké Meziříči 14 K 17

Veltrusy 14 J 16
Veselí nad Lužnicí 14 K 16
Vimperk 14 K 16
Vodňany 14 K 16
Vrchlabí 14 J 17
Vsetín 14 K 18
Vysoké Mýto 14 K 17
Vyškov 14 K 17
Zalužany 14 K 16
Zlín 14 K 18
Znojmo 14 K 17
Žatec 14 J 16
Žďár nad Sázavou 14 K 17

D

Aachen 13 J 13
Aalen 13 K 15
Abensberg 13 K 15
Achern 13 K 14
Adorf 13 J 15
Ahaus 7 J 13
Ahlen 7 J 14
Alfeld 8 J 14
Alsfeld 13 J 14
Altenberg 14 J 16
Altenburg 13 J 15
Altenkirchen/Rostock 8 H 16
Altenkirchen/Siegen 13 J 14
Altenmarkt 13 K 16
Alzey 13 K 14
Amberg 13 K 15
Amelinghausen 8 H 15
Andernach 13 J 14
Angermünde 8 H 16
Anklam 8 H 16
Annaberg-Buchholz 13 J 16
Ansbach 13 K 15
Arnsberg 13 J 14
Arnstadt 13 J 15
Aschaffenburg 13 K 14
Aschersleben 13 J 15
Asendorf 8 H 14
Aue 13 J 16
Auerbach/Nürnberg 13 K 15
Auerbach/Zwickau 13 J 15
Augsburg 13 K 15
Aurich 7 H 13
Bad Bramstedt 8 H 14
Bad Doberan 8 H 15
Bad Düben 13 J 16
Bad Freienwalde 8 H 16
Bad Godesberg 13 J 13
Bad Harzburg 8 J 15
Bad Hersfeld 13 J 14
Bad Homburg 13 J 14
Bad Kreuznach 13 K 14
Bad Langensalza 13 J 15
Bad Lauterberg 13 J 15
Bad Mergentheim 13 K 14
Bad Muskau 13 J 16
Bad Nauheim 13 J 14
Bad Neustadt 13 J 15
Bad Oldesloe 8 H 15
Bad Pyrmont 8 J 14
Bad Salzungen 13 J 15
Bad Segeberg 8 H 15
Bad Tölz 13 K 15
Bad Waldsee 13 K 14
Bad Wildungen 13 J 14
Bad Zwischenahn 7 H 14
Baden-Baden 13 K 14
Bamberg 13 K 15
Barth 8 H 16
Baruth 8 J 16
Bassum 8 H 14
Bautzen 14 J 16
Bayreuth 13 K 15
Bayrisch Eisenstein 13 K 16
Bebra 13 J 14
Beckum 13 J 14
Beelitz 8 J 16
Beeskow 8 J 16
Beilngries 13 K 15
Belzig 8 J 16
Bensheim 13 K 14
Bergen/Hannover 8 H 14
Bergen/Rostock 8 H 16
Berlin 8 J 16
Bernau 8 H 16
Bernburg 13 J 15
Bersenbrück 7 J 14
Biberach 13 K 14
Bielefeld 8 J 14
Bingen 13 K 14
Bitburg 13 K 13
Bitterfeld 13 J 15
Blaubeuren 13 K 14
Böblingen 13 K 14

Bocholt 7 J 13
Bochum 13 J 13
Bohmte 7 J 14
Boizenburg 8 H 15
Bonn 13 J 13
Borkum 7 H 13
Borna 13 J 15
Borshi 13 J 14
Brake 8 H 14
Brandenburg 8 J 16
Braunau am Inn 13 K 16
Braunschweig 8 J 15
Bredstedt 8 H 14
Breitenhees 8 H 15
Bremen 8 H 14
Bremerhaven 8 H 14
Bremervörde 8 H 14
Bretten 13 K 14
Brilon 13 J 14
Bruchsal 13 K 14
Brüel 8 H 15
Brunsbüttel 8 H 14
Burg 8 J 15
Burghausen 13 K 16
Buxtehude 8 H 14
Calmbach 13 K 14
Celle 8 H 15
Cham 13 K 16
Chemnitz 13 J 16
Cloppenburg 7 H 14
Coburg 13 J 15
Cochem 13 J 14
Coesfeld 7 J 13
Coevorden 7 H 13
Cottbus 14 J 16
Crailsheim 13 K 15
Cuxhaven 8 H 14
Dachau 13 K 15
Dannenberg 8 H 15
Darmstadt 13 K 14
Deggendorf 13 K 16
Delmenhorst 8 H 14
Demmin 8 H 16
Dessau 13 J 15
Detmold 8 J 14
Diepholz 7 H 14
Dillenburg 13 J 14
Dillingen 13 K 15
Dingolfing 13 K 15
Dinkelsbühl 13 K 15
Dissen 7 J 14
Döbeln 13 J 16
Dömitz 8 H 15
Donaueschingen 13 K 14
Donauwörth 13 K 15
Dortmund 13 J 14
Dresden 14 J 16
Duderstadt 13 J 15
Duisburg 13 J 13
Düren 13 J 13
Düsseldorf 13 J 13
Ebern 13 J 15
Eberswalde 8 H 16
Ebingen 13 K 14
Eckernförde 8 H 14
Eggenfelden 13 K 16
Ehingen 13 K 14
Eichstätt 13 K 15
Einbeck 8 J 14
Eisenach 13 J 15
Eisenhüttenstadt 8 J 16
Eisfeld 13 J 15
Elmshorn 8 H 14
Elsterwerda 14 J 16
Emden 7 H 13
Emsdetten 7 J 14
Enzlar 13 K 15
Erfurt 13 J 15
Erlangen 13 K 15
Eschwege 13 J 15
Esens 7 H 14
Essen 7 J 13
Esslingen 13 K 14
Euskirchen 13 J 13
Faistenhaar 13 K 15
Feuchtwangen 13 K 15
Finsterwalde 14 J 16
Flensburg 8 H 14
Forchheim 13 K 15
Forst 14 J 16
Frankenberg 13 J 14
Frankfurt a. d. O. 8 J 16
Frankfurt a. M. 13 J 14
Freiberg 13 J 16
Freiburg 13 K 14
Freising 13 K 15
Freital 14 J 16
Freudenstadt 13 K 14
Friedland 8 H 16
Friedrichshafen 13 K 14
Friesack 8 H 16

Fulda 13 J 14
Fürstenau 7 J 14
Fürstenberg 8 H 16
Fürstenfeldbruck 13 K 15
Fürstenwalde 8 J 16
Furth 13 K 16
Füssen 13 K 15
Gaildorf 13 K 14
Gardelegen 8 H 15
Garmisch-Partenkirchen 13 K 15
Geesthacht 8 H 15
Geislingen 13 K 14
Geldern 13 J 13
Gelting 8 H 14
Genthin 8 J 15
Gera 13 J 15
Gießen 13 J 14
Gifhorn 8 J 15
Gnoien 8 H 16
Godelheim 13 J 14
Göhren 8 H 16
Gokels 8 H 14
Goldberg 8 H 15
Göppingen 13 K 14
Görlitz 14 J 16
Goslar 8 J 15
Gotha 13 J 15
Göttingen 13 J 14
Greifswald 8 H 16
Grevesmühlen 8 H 15
Gronau/Enschede 7 J 13
Gronau/Münster 7 J 13
Großenbrode 8 H 15
Guben 14 J 16
Gummersbach 13 J 14
Günzburg 13 K 15
Gunzenhausen 13 K 15
Güstrow 8 H 15
Gütersloh 7 J 14
Haag 13 K 15
Hagen 13 J 14
Hagenow 8 H 15
Hahn 13 J 14
Halle/Leipzig 13 J 15
Halberstadt 8 J 15
Haldensleben 8 J 15
Haltern 7 J 13
Hamburg 8 H 15
Hameln 8 J 14
Hamm 13 J 14
Hammelburg 13 J 14
Hann. Münden 13 J 14
Hannover 8 J 14
Harburg 8 H 15
Harzgerode 13 J 15
Haßfurt 13 J 15
Hechingen 13 K 14
Heide 8 H 14
Heidelberg 13 K 14
Heidenheim 13 K 15
Heilbad Heiligenstadt 13 J 15
Heilbronn 13 K 14
Heldrungen 13 J 15
Helmstedt 8 J 15
Hemau 13 K 15
Herbertingen 13 K 14
Hermeskeil 13 K 13
Herzberg 13 J 16
Hetzerath 13 K 13
Hildesheim 8 J 14
Hof 13 J 15
Hofgeismar 13 J 14
Holzminden 8 J 14
Homburg 13 K 13
Horb 13 K 14
Hoyerswerda 14 J 16
Hünfeld 13 J 14
Husum 8 H 14
Idar-Oberstein 13 K 13
Immenstadt 13 K 15
Ingolstadt 13 K 15
Itzehoe 8 H 14
Jarmen 8 H 16
Jena 13 J 15
Jever 7 H 14
Jüterbog 8 J 16
Kaiserslautern 13 K 14
Kamenz 14 J 16
Karlsruhe 13 K 14
Kassel 13 J 14
Kaufbeuren 13 K 15
Kelheim 13 K 15
Kempten 13 K 15
Kiel 8 H 15
Koblenz 13 J 14
Köln 13 J 13
Korbach 13 J 14
Köthen 13 J 15
Krefeld 13 J 13
Kronach 13 J 15

Krumbach 13 K 15
Kulmbach 13 J 15
Kyritz 8 H 15
Lahr 13 K 14
Landau 13 K 14
Landsberg 13 K 15
Landshut 13 K 15
Lathen 7 H 13
Lauchhammer 14 J 16
Lauenburg 8 H 15
Lechfeld 13 K 15
Leck 8 H 14
Leer 7 H 13
Lehrte 8 J 14
Leipzig 13 J 15
Lemgo 8 J 14
Lengerich 7 J 14
Lichtenfels 13 J 15
Limburg 13 J 14
Lindau 13 K 14
Lingen 7 J 13
Lippstadt 13 J 14
Lobenstein 13 J 15
Lohnsfeld 13 K 14
Lohr 13 K 14
Löningen 7 H 14
Lörrach 13 K 14
Lübbenau 14 J 16
Lübeck 8 H 15
Luckau 14 J 16
Luckenwalde 8 J 16
Ludwigsburg 13 K 14
Ludwigshafen 13 K 14
Ludwigslust 8 H 15
Lüneburg 8 H 15
Lutherstadt Eisleben 13 J 15
Lutherstadt Wittenberg 13 J 16
Magdeburg 8 J 15
Mainburg 13 K 15
Mainz 13 K 14
Mannheim 13 K 14
Marburg 13 J 14
Märkisch Buchholz 8 J 16
Marktredwitz 13 J 15
Mayen 13 J 13
Meiningen 13 J 15
Meißen 14 J 16
Memmingen 13 K 15
Meppen 7 H 13
Merseburg 13 J 15
Merzig 13 K 13
Meschede 13 J 14
Michelstadt 13 K 14
Minden 8 J 14
Mittweida 13 J 16
Mönchen-Gladbach 13 J 13
Morbach 13 K 13
Mosbach 13 K 14
Mühldorf 13 K 16
Müllheim 13 K 14
Münchberg 13 J 15
München 13 K 15
Münster 7 J 14
Munster 8 H 15
Nagold 13 K 14
Nauen 8 H 16
Naumburg 13 J 15
Neubrandenburg 8 H 16
Neumarkt 13 K 15
Neumünster 8 H 14
Neunkirchen/Saarbrücken 13 K 13
Neuruppin 8 H 16
Neuses 13 K 15
Neuss 13 J 13
Neustadt/Freiburg 13 K 14
Neustadt/Gera 13 J 15
Neustadt/Mannheim 13 K 14
Neustadt/Nürnberg 13 K 15
Neustadt/Rostock 8 H 15
Neustrelitz 8 H 16
Niebüll 8 H 14
Nienburg 8 H 14
Norden 7 H 13
Nordenham 8 H 14
Norderney 7 H 13
Nordhausen 13 J 15
Nordhorn 7 J 13
Nördlingen 13 K 15
Northeim 13 J 14
Nürnberg 13 K 15
Oberkirch 13 K 14
Oberstdorf 13 L 15
Oberwesel 13 J 14
Oebisfelde 8 J 15
Offenbach 13 J 14
Offenburg 13 K 14
Oldenburg/Bremen 8 H 14
Oldenburg/Kiel 8 H 15
Oranienburg 8 H 16
Ording 8 H 14

Osnabrück (D)·(DK)·(DZ)·(E) **Cúllar de Baza**

Osnabrück 7 J 14
Osterburg 8 H 15
Osterholz-Scharmbeck 8 H 14
Osterode 13 J 15
Paderborn 13 J 14
Papenburg 7 H 13
Parchim 8 H 15
Pasewalk 8 H 16
Passau 13 K 16
Peine 8 J 15
Perleberg 8 H 15
Pforzheim 13 K 14
Philippsreut 14 K 16
Pinneberg 8 H 14
Pirmasens 13 K 14
Pirna 14 J 16
Plattling 13 K 16
Plau 8 H 15
Plauen 13 J 15
Plön 8 H 15
Potsdam 8 J 16
Prenzlau 8 H 16
Pritzwalk 8 H 15
Prüm 13 J 13
Puttgarden 8 H 15
Rathenow 8 H 15
Ratzeburg 8 H 15
Ravensburg 13 K 14
Recklinghausen 13 J 13
Regen 13 K 16
Regensburg 13 K 15
Reichenbach 13 J 15
Rendsburg 8 H 14
Reuterstadt Stavenhagen
   8 H 16
Reutlingen 13 K 14
Rheine 7 J 14
Ribnitz-Damgarten 8 H 15
Riesa 13 J 16
Röbel 8 H 16
Rochlitz 13 J 16
Rosenheim 13 K 15
Rostock 8 H 15
Rotenburg 8 H 14
Rothenburg ob der Tauber
   13 K 15
Rottweil 13 K 14
Saalfeld 13 J 15
Saarbrücken 13 K 13
Saarburg 13 K 13
Saarlouis 13 K 13
Salzgitter 8 J 15
Salzwedel 8 H 15
Sandau 8 H 15
Sangershausen 13 J 15
Sassnitz 8 H 16
Scherfede 13 J 14
Schleiden 13 J 13
Schleiz 13 J 15
Schleswig 8 H 14
Schlüchtern 13 J 14
Schönebeck 8 J 15
Schrobenhausen 13 K 15
Schwabach 13 K 15
Schwäbisch Gmünd 13 K 14
Schwäbische Hall 13 K 14
Schwandorf 13 K 15
Schwarmstedt 8 H 14
Schwedt 8 H 16
Schweinfurt 13 J 15
Schwenningen 13 K 14
Schwerin 8 H 15
Seebad Heringsdorf 8 H 16
Seelow 8 H 16
Senftenberg 14 J 16
Siegburg 13 J 13
Siegen 13 J 14
Simbach 13 K 16
Singen 13 K 14
Sinzig 13 J 13
Solingen 13 J 13
Soltau 8 H 14
Sömmerda 13 J 15
Sondershausen 13 J 15
Sonneberg 13 J 15
Speyer 13 K 14
Springe 8 J 14
Stade 8 H 14
Stadtkyll 13 J 13
Stallwang 13 K 16
Starnberg 13 K 15
Stendal 8 H 15
Stralsund 8 H 16
Straubing 13 K 16
Strausberg 8 H 16
Stuttgart 13 K 14
Suhl 13 J 15
Sulingen 8 H 14
Sulzbach-Rosenberg 13 K 15
Taufkirchen 13 K 15
Tegernsee 13 K 15

Templin 8 H 16
Teterow 8 H 16
Tirschenreuth 13 K 15
Torgau 13 J 16
Tostedt 8 H 14
Traunstein 13 K 16
Travemünde 8 H 15
Trier 13 K 13
Tübingen 13 K 14
Tuttlingen 13 K 14
Überlingen 13 K 14
Ueckermünde 8 H 16
Uelzen 8 H 15
Ulm 13 K 14
Urfeld 13 K 15
Varel 8 H 14
Vechta 7 H 14
Verden 8 H 14
Villingen 13 K 14
Vilshofen 13 K 16
Waidhs. 13 K 15
Waldbröl 13 J 14
Waldshut 13 K 14
Wallau 13 J 14
Walsrode 8 H 14
Waren 8 H 15
Warendorf 7 J 14
Warnemünde 8 H 15
Warstade 8 H 14
Weiden 13 K 15
Weilheim 13 K 15
Weimar 13 J 15
Weinheim 13 K 14
Weißenburg 13 K 15
Wernberg 13 K 15
Wernigerode 13 J 15
Wertheim 13 K 14
Wesel 7 J 13
Westerland 8 H 14
Westerstede 7 H 14
Wetzlar 13 J 14
Wiedenbrück 7 J 14
Wiesbaden 13 J 14
Wildeshausen 8 H 14
Wilhelmshaven 7 H 14
Wismar 8 H 15
Wittenberge 8 H 15
Wittingen 8 H 15
Wittstock 8 H 16
Woldegk 8 H 16
Wolfach 13 K 14
Wolfsburg 8 J 15
Wolgast 8 H 16
Worms 13 K 14
Wuppertal 13 J 13
Würzburg 13 K 14
Wurzen 13 J 16
Zehdenick 8 H 16
Zeitz 13 J 15
Zella-Mehlis 13 J 15
Zerbst 8 J 15
Zittau 14 J 16
Zollhaus 13 J 14
Zweibrücken 13 K 13
Zwickau 13 J 15

Aabenraa 4 G 14
Aabybro 4 G 14
Aalborg 4 G 14
Aalestrup 4 G 14
Aarhus 8 G 15
Aars 4 G 14
Assens 8 G 14
Bagenkop 8 H 15
Bierget 4 G 14
Bogense 8 G 15
Brande 8 G 14
Esbjerg 8 G 14
Fakse 8 G 15
Fjerritslev 4 G 14
Fredericia 8 G 14
Frederikshavn 4 G 15
Frederikssund 8 G 15
Fåborg 8 G 15
Gedser 8 H 15
Gilleleje 8 G 15
Give 8 G 14
Gram 8 G 14
Grenå 8 G 15
Grindsted 8 G 14
Gylling 8 G 15
Haderslev 8 G 14
Hadsund 8 G 15
Hals 4 G 15
Hanstholm 4 G 14
Helsingør 8 G 16
Herning 8 G 14

Hillerød 8 G 15
Hirtshals 4 F 14
Hjallerup 4 G 15
Hjørring 4 G 14
Hobro 8 G 14
Holbæk 8 G 15
Holstebro 8 G 14
Holsted 8 G 14
Horsens 8 G 14
Hundested 8 G 15
Hurup 8 G 14
Hvide Sande 8 G 14
Juelsminde 8 G 14
Kallinge 8 G 17
Kalundborg 8 G 15
Kerteminde 8 G 15
Kolding 8 G 14
Korsør 8 G 15
Kværndrup 8 G 15
København 8 G 16
Køge 8 G 15
Lakolk 8 G 14
Lemvig 8 G 14
Lohals 8 G 15
Løkken 4 G 14
Maribo 8 H 15
Nakskov 8 H 15
Nexø 8 G 17
Nordborg 8 G 14
Nordskov 8 G 15
Nyborg 8 G 15
Nykøbing/København 8 G 15
Nykøbing/Rostock 8 H 15
Nykøbing Mors 4 G 14
Næstved 8 G 15
Odense 8 G 15
Oksbol 8 G 14
Præstø 8 G 15
Randers 8 G 15
Ribe 8 G 14
Ringkøbing 8 G 14
Ringsted 8 G 15
Roskilde 8 G 15
Rødby 8 H 15
Rødvig 8 G 15
Rønne 8 G 16
Rønnede 8 G 15
Sandvig 8 G 16
Silkeborg 8 G 14
Skagen 4 F 15
Skive 8 G 14
Slagelse 8 G 15
Sonderborg 8 H 14
Spodsberg 8 H 15
Spørring 8 G 15
Stege 8 G 15
Stenbjerg 4 G 14
Struer 8 G 14
Støvring 4 G 14
Svendborg 8 G 15
Sæby 4 G 15
Søllerød 8 G 15
Tarm 8 G 14
Thisted 4 G 14
Thyborøn 4 G 14
Tinglev 8 H 14
Toftlund 8 G 14
Tranebjerg 8 G 15
Tønder 8 H 14
Tørring 8 G 14
Tårnby 8 G 16
Ugerløse 8 G 15
Ulfborg 8 G 14
Varde 8 G 14
Vejle 8 G 14
Viborg 8 G 14
Vordingborg 8 G 15
Ærøskøbing 8 H 15
Ålbæk 4 F 15

DZ

Achaacha 19 P 11
Aïn Abid 20 P 13
Aïn Beïda 20 P 13
Aïn Benian 19 P 12
Aïn Berda 20 P 14
Aïn Defla 19 P 11
Aïn Fakroun 20 P 13
Aïn Kercha 20 P 13
Aïn Kerma 20 P 14
Aïn M'Lila 20 P 13
Aïn Taya 19 P 12
Aïn-El-Hamman 19 P 12
Aïn-el-Türk 18 P 10
Aïn-Yagout 20 P 13
Amizour 19 P 12
Annaba 20 P 14
Arzew 18 P 10

Azazga 19 P 12
Azeffoun 19 P 12
Azzaba 20 P 13
Baali 20 P 13
Béjaïa 19 P 13
Ben M´hidi 20 P 14
Berrahal 20 P 13
Berriche 20 P 13
Bir Chouhada 20 P 13
Blida 19 P 12
Bordj-Ménaiel 19 P 12
Bou Ismall 19 P 12
Bou Kadir 19 P 12
Bouchegouf 20 P 14
Boufarik 19 P 12
Bouzghaia 19 P 11
Chelghoum El Aïd 20 P 13
Chemmora 20 P 13
Cherchell 19 P 11
Chetaibi 20 P 13
Chlef 19 P 11
Chréa 19 P 12
Collo 19 P 13
Constantine 20 P 13
Damous 19 P 11
Dellys 19 P 12
Dréan 20 P 14
El Kala 20 P 14
El Abadia 19 P 11
El Affroun 19 P 12
El Aouinet 20 P 14
El Djezä''ir (Alger) 19 P 12
El Hadjar 20 P 14
El Kseur 19 P 12
El Marsa 19 P 11
El-Arrouch 20 P 13
El-Harrach 19 P 12
El-Khroub 20 P 13
El-Milia 19 P 13
Foum-Toub 20 P 13
Gouraya 19 P 11
Guelma 20 P 14
Hadjout 19 P 11
Hamma Bouziane 20 P 13
Hammamet 20 P 14
Jijel 19 P 13
Khemis Miliana 19 P 11
Khenchela 20 P 13
Kherba 19 P 11
Lakhdaria 19 P 12
Larba 19 P 12
Mechroha 20 P 14
Médéa 19 P 12
Meskiana 20 P 14
Mila 20 P 13
Miliana 19 P 11
Mostaganem 19 P 11
M'Daourouch 20 P 14
Oued Athmenia 20 P 13
Oued El Kheir 19 P 11
Ouenza 20 P 14
Ouled-Farés 19 P 11
Oum-El-Bouaghi 20 P 13
Qued Zenati 20 P 13
Sedrata 20 P 14
Sendjas 19 P 11
Sidi Lakhdar 19 P 11
Sigus 20 P 13
Skikda 19 P 13
Souk Ahras 20 P 14
Tablat 19 P 12
Tamalous 19 P 13
Tamlouka 20 P 13
Taougrite 19 P 11
Taoura 20 P 14
Ténès 19 P 11
Thenia 19 P 12
Tigzirt 19 P 12
Tipaza 19 P 11
Tizi-Ouzou 19 P 12
Zéralda 19 P 12

E

A Baiuca 18 M 7
A Coruña 18 M 7
A Estrada 18 M 7
A Garda 18 N 7
A Gudiña 18 N 8
A Serra de Outes 18 M 7
Abla 18 P 9
Adanero 18 N 9
Adra 18 P 9
Aguilar de Campóo 18 M 9
Águilas 18 P 10
Ainsa 19 N 11
Alaéjos 18 N 8
Alagón 19 N 10
Alanis 18 O 8

Alaraz 18 N 8
Alatoz 18 O 10
Albacete 18 O 10
Albarracin 19 N 10
Albentosa 19 N 10
Alberique 19 O 10
Albocácer 19 N 10
Albox 18 P 10
Alburquerque 18 O 8
Alcalá de Guadaira 18 P 8
Alcalá de Henares 18 N 9
Alcalá de los Gazules 18 P 8
Alcalá de Xivert 19 N 11
Alcalá la Real 18 P 9
Alcanar 19 N 11
Alcántara 18 O 8
Alcañiz 19 N 10
Alcaracejos 18 O 9
Alcaraz 18 O 10
Alcaudete 18 O 9
Alcázar de San Juan 18 O 9
Alcoi 19 O 10
Alcorisa 19 N 10
Alcúdia 19 O 12
Alcuéscar 18 O 8
Alfaro 19 N 10
Alfarrás 19 N 11
Algar 18 P 8
Algeciras 18 P 8
Algora 19 N 10
Algorta 12 M 9
Alhama 18 O 10
Alhama de Aragón 18 N 10
Alhama de Granada 18 P 9
Alhaurin el Grande 18 P 9
Alicante 19 O 10
Almadén 18 O 9
Álmagro 18 O 9
Almansa 18 O 10
Almarza 18 N 9
Almenar de Soria 18 N 10
Almendralejo 18 O 8
Almeria 18 P 10
Almódovar del Pinar 18 O 10
Almonte 18 P 8
Almoradí 18 O 10
Almudévar 19 N 10
Almuñécar 18 P 9
Almuradiel 18 O 10
Alora 18 P 9
Altsasu 12 M 10
Alzira 19 O 10
Allariz 18 N 7
Allepúz 19 N 10
Amurrio 12 M 9
Andratx 19 O 11
Andujar 18 O 9
Angüés 19 N 10
Anguiano 18 N 9
Anquela del Ducado 18 N 10
Antequera 18 P 9
Aranda de Duero 18 N 9
Aranjuez 18 N 9
Arcos de la Frontera 18 P 8
Archidona 18 P 9
Arenas de San Pedro 18 N 8
Arganda 18 N 9
Arnedo 19 N 10
Arquillos 18 O 9
Arta 19 O 12
Artesa de Segre 19 N 11
Arzúa 18 M 7
Astorga 18 N 8
Atienza 18 N 9
Ávila 18 N 9
Avilés 18 M 8
Ayamonte 18 P 8
Ayerbe 19 N 10
Ayllón 18 N 9
Ayora 18 O 10
Azuaga 18 O 8
Baamonde 18 M 7
Badajoz 18 O 8
Badalona 19 N 11
Baena 18 O 9
Baeza 18 O 9
Bailén 18 O 9
Baiona 18 N 7
Balaguer 19 N 11
Balazote 18 O 10
Balmaseda 12 M 9
Bande 18 N 7
Baracaldo 12 M 9
Barbastro 19 N 11
Barbate de Franco 18 P 8
Barcelona 19 N 11
Barreiros 18 M 8
Baza 18 P 9
Becerreá 18 M 8
Becilla de Valderabuey 18 N 8
Béjar 18 N 8

Belchite 19 N 10
Bembibre 18 M 8
Benabarre 19 N 11
Benasque 19 M 11
Benavente 18 N 8
Benicarió 19 N 11
Berdún 19 M 10
Berga 19 N 11
Bergara 12 M 10
Berja 18 P 9
Bermeo 12 M 9
Betanzos 18 M 7
Beteta 18 N 10
Béznar 18 P 9
Bilbo/Bilbao 12 M 9
Binéfar 19 N 11
Blacos 18 N 9
Boceguillas 18 N 9
Bonete 18 O 10
Borja 19 N 10
Broto 19 M 10
Bueu 18 N 7
Bujaraloz 19 N 10
Burgos 18 N 9
Cabeza del Buey 18 O 8
Cabezuela del Valle 18 N 8
Cabra 18 P 9
Cabreiros 18 M 7
Cáceres 18 O 8
Cádabo 18 M 8
Cádiz 18 P 8
Cala Ratjada 19 O 12
Calahorra 19 N 10
Calañas 18 O 8
Calatayud 19 N 10
Calpe 19 O 11
Calzada de Calatrava 18 O 9
Camariñas 18 M 7
Caminreal 19 N 10
Campillos 18 P 9
Campo de Criptana 18 O 9
Camprodón 19 N 11
Canfranc-Estación 19 M 10
Cangas de Onis 18 M 8
Cangas del Narcea 18 M 8
Cantalejo 18 N 9
Cañaveral 18 O 8
Cañaveras 18 N 10
Cañete 18 N 10
Cañizal 18 N 8
Caravaca de la Cruz 18 O 10
Carballo 18 M 7
Carboneras 18 P 10
Carboneras de Guadazaón
   18 O 10
Cardeña 18 O 9
Cariñena 19 N 10
Carmona 18 P 8
Carrascosa del Campo 18 N 9
Cartagena 18 O 10
Caspe 19 N 10
Castellón de la Plana 19 O 10
Castilblanco 18 O 8
Castro del Rio 18 O 9
Castro Urdiales 12 M 9
Castuera 18 O 8
Cazalla 18 O 8
Cazorla 18 O 9
Ceclavin 18 O 8
Cedeira 18 M 7
Cehegin 18 O 10
Cerezo de Abajo 18 N 9
Cervera 19 N 11
Cervo 18 M 8
Ceuta 18 P 8
Cieza 18 O 10
Cillas 18 N 10
Cintruénigo 19 N 10
Ciria 18 N 10
Cistierna 18 M 8
Ciudad Real 18 O 9
Ciudad Rodrigo 18 N 8
Ciutadella de Menorca 19 O 12
Coca 18 N 9
Cofrentes 19 O 10
Coin 18 P 9
Colmenar 18 P 9
Colmenar Viejo 18 N 9
Constantina 18 O 8
Consuegra 18 O 9
Corconte 18 M 9
Corcubión 18 M 7
Córdoba 18 O 9
Coria/Salamanca 18 O 8
Coria/Sevilla 18 P 8
Crevillente 19 O 10
Cudillero 18 M 8
Cuéllar 18 N 9
Cuenca 18 N 10
Cuevas de Vinromá 19 N 11
Cúllar de Baza 18 O 9

Chantada   ⒠ · ⒠⒮⒯ · ⒡   **Aire-sur-l'Adour**

Chantada 18 M 7
Chelva 19 O 10
Chiclana de la Frontera 18 P 8
Chiva 19 O 10
Daimiel 18 O 9
Daroca 19 N 10
Denia 19 O 11
Don Benito 18 O 8
Donostia/San Sebastian 12 M 10
Dueñas 18 N 9
Écija 18 O 8
El Arahal 18 P 8
El Escorial 18 N 9
El Garrobo 18 O 8
El Molar 18 N 9
El Provencio 18 O 9
Eibar 12 M 10
Eivissa 19 O 11
Ejea de los Caballeros 19 N 10
El Barco de Ávila 18 N 8
El Burgo de Osma 18 N 9
El Cubo 18 N 8
el Pinós 18 O 10
el Vendrell 19 N 11
Elche 19 O 10
Elche de la Sierra 18 O 10
Elda 19 O 10
Épinal 13 K 13
Escalada 18 M 9
Espiel 18 O 8
Estella 12 M 10
Estepa 18 P 9
Estepona 18 P 8
Fábricas de Riópar 18 O 10
Falset 19 N 11
Fermoselle 18 N 8
Fernán Núñez 18 O 9
Ferrol 18 M 7
Figueres 19 N 12
Fisterra 18 M 7
Fornells 19 N 12
Fraga 19 N 11
Fregenal de la Sierra 18 O 8
Frómista 18 N 9
Fuente Alamo 18 O 10
Fuente de Cantos 18 O 8
Fuente el Fresno 18 O 9
Fuente Obejuna 18 O 8
Fuentes de Andalucía 18 P 8
Gálvez 18 O 9
Gandesa 19 N 11
Gandia 19 O 10
Gérgal 18 P 9
Getafe 18 N 9
Gibraleón 18 P 8
Gijon 18 M 8
Girona 19 N 12
Golpejas 18 N 8
Grado 18 M 8
Granada 18 P 9
Grandas de Salime 18 M 8
Granollers 19 N 11
Graus 19 N 11
Guadalajara 18 N 9
Guadalupe 18 O 8
Guadix 18 P 9
Guardo 18 M 9
Guijuelo 18 N 8
Guitiriz 18 M 7
Guntin 18 M 7
Haro 12 M 9
Hellin 18 O 10
Herrera de Pisuerga 18 M 9
Herreruela 18 O 8
Hervás 18 N 8
Higuera 18 O 8
Hijar 19 N 10
Honrubia 18 O 10
Huelma 18 O 9
Huelva 18 P 8
Huércal Overa 18 P 10
Huesca 19 N 10
Huescar 18 O 9
Huete 18 N 9
Igualada 19 N 11
Illescas 18 N 9
Illora 18 P 9
Inca 19 O 12
Infiesto 18 M 8
Irún 12 M 10
Irurzun 12 M 10
Isla Cristina 18 P 8
Iznalloz 18 P 9
Jabugo 18 O 8
Jaca 19 M 10
Jaén 18 O 9
Jaraicejo 18 O 8
Jarandilla 18 N 8
Jerez de la Frontera 18 P 8
Jerez de los Caballeros 18 O 8

Jimena de la Frontera 18 P 8
Jódar 18 O 9
Jumilla 18 O 10
L`Escala 19 N 12
La Alberca 18 N 8
La Albuera 18 O 8
La Almarcha 18 O 10
La Almunia de Doña Godina 19 N 10
La Bañeza 18 N 8
la Boule 18 O 9
La Carolina 18 O 9
La Fuente de San Esteban 18 N 8
La Gineta 18 O 10
la Granadella 19 N 11
La Linea 18 P 8
La Magdalena 18 M 8
La Manga del Mar Menor 18 O 10
La Muela 19 N 10
La Paca 18 O 10
La Palma 18 P 8
La Robla 18 M 8
La Roca de la Sierra 18 O 8
La Roda 18 O 10
la Seu d'Urgell 19 N 11
La Solana 18 O 9
La Torre 18 N 9
La Unión 18 O 10
Lalin 18 M 7
Langreo 18 M 8
Laredo 12 M 9
Lebrija 18 P 8
Lekeitio 12 M 9
Leòn 18 N 8
Lepe 18 P 8
Lerma 18 N 9
Lés 19 M 11
les Borges Blanques 19 N 11
Linares 18 O 9
Logroño 18 N 10
Loja 18 P 9
Lora del Rio 18 O 8
Lorca 18 O 10
Loriol 18 O 9
Los Arcos 12 M 10
Los Navalmorales 18 O 9
Los Palacios y Villafranca 18 P 8
Lozoyuela 18 N 9
Luanco 18 M 8
Luarca 18 M 8
Lucena 18 P 9
Lucena del Cid 19 N 10
Luciana 18 O 9
Lugo 18 M 7
Lumbier 19 M 10
Lumbrales 18 N 8
Lumbreras 18 N 9
l'Hospitalet 19 N 11
l'Hospitalet de l'Infant 19 N 11
Llanes 18 M 8
Llavorsi 19 N 11
Lleida 19 N 11
Llerena 18 O 8
Lliria 19 O 10
Llucmajor 19 O 12
Madrid 18 N 9
Madridejos 18 O 9
Madrigal de las Altas Torres 18 N 9
Maella 19 N 11
Magaz 18 N 9
Mahora 18 O 10
Málaga 18 P 9
Malagón 18 O 9
Malgrat de Mar 19 N 12
Malpica 18 M 7
Mallén 19 N 10
Manacor 19 O 12
Manresa 19 N 11
Mansilla de las Mulas 18 N 8
Manzanares 18 O 9
Maó 19 O 12
Maqueda 18 N 9
Maranchón 18 N 10
Marbella 18 P 9
Marchena 18 P 8
Martos 18 P 9
Matabuena 18 N 9
Mataró 19 N 11
Mazagón 18 O 8
Medina de Rioseco 18 N 8
Medina del Campo 18 N 9
Medina Sidonia 18 P 8
Medinaceli 18 N 10
Meira 18 M 8
Melide 18 M 7
Melilla 18 P 9
Mengibar 18 O 9

Mérida 18 O 8
Miajadas 18 O 8
Mieres 18 M 8
Minglanilla 18 O 10
Miranda de Ebro 12 M 9
Molina de Aragón 18 N 10
Molina de Segura 18 O 10
Mombuey 18 N 8
Monasterio de Rodilla 18 N 9
Mondoñedo 18 M 8
Monforte de Lemos 18 M 8
Monreal del Campo 19 N 10
Monroyo 19 N 10
Montalbán del Campo 19 N 10
Montalbo 18 O 9
Montamarta 18 N 8
Montefrio 18 P 9
Montijo 18 O 8
Montilla 18 O 9
Montoro 18 O 9
Monzón 19 N 11
Mora 18 O 9
Moratalla 18 O 10
Moreda 18 P 9
Morella 19 N 10
Moron de la Frontera 18 P 8
Mota del Cuervo 18 O 9
Motilla del Palancar 18 O 10
Motril 18 P 9
Muelas 18 N 8
Mula 18 O 10
Munera 18 O 10
Murcia 18 O 10
Muros 18 M 7
Nájera 18 N 9
Navalcarnero 18 N 9
Navalmoral de la Mata 18 O 8
Navalvillar de Pela 18 O 8
Navia 18 M 8
Nerva 18 O 8
Nijar 18 P 10
Noia 18 M 7
Novelda 19 O 10
O Barco de Valdeorras 18 N 8
O Castro de Caldelas 18 N 8
Ocaña 18 N 9
Oliana 19 N 11
Oliva 19 O 10
Olmedo 18 N 9
Olot 19 N 11
Olvera 18 P 8
Onda 19 O 10
Ontinyent 19 O 10
Oquillas 18 N 9
Orcera 18 O 9
Ordenes 18 M 7
Orgaz 18 O 9
Orihuela 18 O 10
Orihuela del Tremedal 18 N 10
Oronoz Mugairi 12 M 10
Oropesa/Benicarló 19 N 11
Oropesa/Madrid 18 O 8
Ortigueira 18 M 7
Osera 19 N 10
Osorno 18 N 9
Osuna 18 P 8
Ourense 18 N 7
Oviedo 18 M 8
Padrón 18 M 7
Palafrugell 19 N 12
Palencia 18 N 9
Palma 19 O 12
Palma del Rio 18 O 8
Pamplona Iruña 12 M 10
Pancorbo 12 M 9
Paymogo 18 O 8
Pedrosa del Rey 18 M 8
Pego 19 O 10
Peñafiel 18 N 9
Peñaranda de Bracamonte 18 N 8
Peñarroya-Pueblonuevo 18 O 8
Perales de Alfambra 19 N 10
Piedrahita 18 N 8
Piñor de Cea 18 N 7
Plasencia 18 N 8
Pola de Lena 18 M 8
Pola de Siero 18 M 8
Ponferrada 18 M 8
Pont de Suert 19 N 11
Ponteareas 18 N 7
Pontedéume 18 M 7
Pontevedra 18 N 7
Ponts 19 N 11
Porcuna 18 O 9
Port de Pollença 19 O 12
Portbou 19 N 12
Porzuna 18 O 9
Potes 18 M 9
Pozo Alcón 18 O 9
Pozoblanco 18 O 9

Pozocañada 18 O 10
Pozuelo 18 N 8
Priego de Córdoba 18 P 9
Puebla de Alcocer 18 O 8
Puebla de Don Fabrique 18 O 10
Puebla de Don Rodrigo 18 O 9
Puebla de Sanabria 18 N 8
Puente de Montañana 19 N 11
Puente Genil 18 P 9
Puente la Reina 12 M 10
Puerto de Mazarrón 18 O 10
Puerto de San Vicente 18 O 9
Puerto de Santa Maria 18 P 8
Puerto Lápice 18 O 9
Puerto Lumbreras 18 O 10
Puertollano 18 O 9
Quesada 18 O 9
Quintana de Puente 18 N 9
Quintanar de la Orden 18 O 9
Quintanilla-Sobresierra 18 M 9
Quinto 19 N 10
Quiroga 18 M 8
Redondela 18 N 7
Reinosilla 18 M 9
Requena 19 O 10
Reus 19 N 11
Ribadavia 18 N 7
Ribadesella 18 M 8
Ribes de Freser 19 N 11
Roa 18 N 9
Robleda 18 N 8
Roncesvalles 12 M 10
Ronda 18 P 8
Roquetas de Mar 18 P 9
Rosal de la Frontera 18 O 8
Roses 19 N 12
Ruidera 18 O 9
Rute 18 P 9
Sabadell 19 N 11
Sabiñánigo 19 M 10
Sacedón 18 N 9
Sádaba 19 N 10
Sagunto 19 O 10
Sahagún 18 N 8
Salamanca 18 N 8
Salas de los Infantes 18 N 9
Saldaña 18 M 9
Salou 19 N 11
Sallent de Gallego 19 M 10
San Esteban de Gormaz 18 N 9
San Fernando 18 P 8
San José 18 P 10
San Leonardo 18 N 9
San Martin de Valdeiglesias 18 N 9
San Pedro 18 O 8
Sanlúcar de Barrameda 18 P 8
Sant Antonio de Portmany 19 O 11
Sant Carles de la Rápita 19 N 11
Sant Feliu de Guíxols 19 N 12
Sant Francesc de Formantera 19 O 11
Sant Joan de Labritja 19 O 11
Santa Comba 18 M 7
Santa Eulalia 19 N 10
Santa Eulària des Ríu 19 O 11
Santa Maria de Huerta 18 N 10
Santa Marta 18 O 8
Santa Olalla 18 O 8
Santa Pola 19 O 10
Santa Uxia de Ribeira 18 M 7
Santander 18 M 9
Santanyí 19 O 12
Santiago de Compostela 18 M 7
Santisteban del Puerto 18 O 9
Santo Domingo de Silos 18 N 9
Sanxenxo 18 N 7
Sariñena 19 N 10
Sarriá 18 M 8
Segorbe 19 O 10
Segovia 18 N 9
Serón 18 P 10
Sevilla 18 P 8
Sigüenza 18 N 9
Sisante 18 O 10
Sitges 19 N 11
Solares 18 M 9
Solsona 19 N 11
Sóller 19 O 12
Sorbas 18 P 10
Soria 18 N 10
Soutelo 18 M 7
Sueca 19 O 10
Tábara 18 N 8
Tabernas 18 P 10
Tafalla 19 M 10

Talavera 18 O 9
Talayuelas 19 O 10
Tamames 18 N 8
Tarancon 18 N 9
Tarazona 19 N 10
Tarifa 18 P 8
Tarragona 19 N 11
Tárrega 19 N 11
Tauste 19 N 10
Tembleque 18 O 9
Terminón 18 M 9
Terrassa 19 N 11
Teruel 19 N 10
Tineo 18 M 8
Tobarra 18 O 10
Toledo 18 O 9
Tolosa 12 M 10
Tomelloso 18 O 9
Tordesillas 18 N 9
Torelló 19 N 11
Torija 18 N 9
Toro 18 N 8
Torre de la Higuera 18 P 8
Torre del Mar 18 P 9
Torre Pacheco 18 O 10
Torrebaja 19 N 10
Torrejón el Rubio 18 O 8
Torrelavega 18 M 9
Torremolinos 18 P 9
Torrent 19 O 10
Torrijos 18 O 9
Tortosa 19 N 11
Tossa 19 N 12
Totana 18 O 10
Tremp 19 N 11
Triste 19 N 10
Trujillo 18 O 8
Tudela 19 N 10
Túy 18 N 7
Úbeda 18 N 9
Ugijar 18 P 9
Uña 18 N 10
Usagre 18 O 8
Utiel 19 O 10
Utrera 18 P 8
Valdecilla 18 M 9
Valdepeñas 18 O 9
Valencia 19 O 10
Valencia de Alcantara 18 O 8
Valencia de las Torres 18 O 8
Valverde de Camino 18 O 8
Valverde del Freno 18 N 8
Vall de Uxo 19 O 10
Valladolid 18 N 9
Valls 19 N 11
Vegadeo 18 M 8
Vejer 18 P 8
Vélez Málaga 18 P 9
Vélez Rubio 18 O 10
Vera 18 P 10
Verin 18 N 8
Vic 19 N 11
Vielha 19 M 11
Vigo 18 N 7
Vilafranca del Penedès 19 N 11
Vilagarciade 18 M 7
Vilanova i la Geltrú 19 N 11
Villablino 18 M 8
Villacañas 18 O 9
Villacarrillo 18 O 9
Villacastin 18 N 9
Villadefrades 18 N 8
Villadiego 18 N 9
Villafranca 18 M 8
Villafranca de los Barros 18 O 8
Villafranca del Cid 19 N 10
Villahermosa 18 O 9
Villajoyosa 19 O 10
Villalba 18 M 7
Villalón de Campos 18 N 8
Villalpando 18 N 8
Villamañán 18 N 8
Villamartin 18 P 8
Villanueva de Alcorón 18 N 10
Villanueva de Córdoba 18 O 9
Villanueva de la Serena 18 O 8
Villanueva de los Castillejos 18 O 8
Villanueva de los Infantes 18 O 9
Villanueva del Arzobispo 18 O 9
Villanueva del Rio y Minas 18 O 8
Villapalacios 18 O 9
Villarcayo 18 M 9
Villarejo de Salvanés 18 N 9
Villarreal 19 O 10

Villarrobledo 18 O 9
Villasandino 18 N 9
Villatobas 18 O 9
Villatoya 18 O 10
Villaviciosa 18 M 8
Villena 19 O 10
Vinaros 19 N 11
Virgen de la Cabeza 18 O 9
Vitigudino 18 N 8
Vitoria-Gasteiz 12 M 9
Viveiro 18 M 7
Vivel del Rio Martín 19 N 10
Xátiva 19 O 10
Xinzo de Limia 18 N 7
Yecla 18 O 10
Zafra 18 O 8
Zahara de los Atunes 18 P 8
Zalamea la Real 18 O 8
Zamora 18 N 8
Zaragoza 19 N 10
Zorita 18 O 8
Zuera 19 N 10

EST

Ahtme 10 F 21
Antsla 10 F 21
Elva 10 F 21
Haapsalu 5 F 20
Heltermaa 5 F 20
Häädemeeste 5 F 20
Ihamaru 10 F 21
Jõgeva 10 F 21
Jõhvi 10 F 21
Kalana 5 F 19
Kallaste 10 F 21
Karksi-Nuia 5 F 21
Keila 5 F 20
Kihelkonna 5 F 19
Kilingi Nõmme 5 F 20
Kiviõli 5 F 20
Kohila 5 F 20
Kohtla Järve 10 F 21
Kose 5 F 21
Kuivastu 5 F 20
Kunda 5 F 21
Kuressaare 5 F 19
Kuusalu 5 F 21
Kärdla 5 F 20
Leisi 5 F 20
Lelle 5 F 20
Lihula 5 F 20
Loksas 5 F 21
Mehikoorma 10 F 21
Misso 10 F 21
Mustla 5 F 21
Mustvee 10 F 21
Märjamma 5 F 20
Narva 10 F 22
Nõva 5 F 20
Orissaare 5 F 20
Otepää 5 F 21
Paide 5 F 21
Paldiski 5 F 20
Põltsamaa 5 F 21
Pärnu 5 F 20
Pärnu-Jaagupi 5 F 20
Rakvere 5 F 21
Rannapungerja 10 F 21
Risti 5 F 21
Sindi 5 F 20
Suure-Jaani 5 F 21
Sõru 5 F 20
Sääre 5 F 19
Tallinn 5 F 21
Tapa 5 F 21
Tartu 10 F 21
Tõrva 5 F 21
Türi 5 F 21
Valga 10 F 21
Vasknarva 10 F 22
Viljandi 5 F 21
Virtsu 5 F 20
Võru 10 F 21
Väike Maarja 5 F 21
Vändra 5 F 21

F

Abbeville 12 J 11
Agde 19 M 12
Agen 12 M 11
Agon-Coutances 12 K 10
Aigre 12 L 11
Aiguillon 12 M 11
Aigurande 12 L 11
Aire-sur-l'Adour 12 M 10

Aix-en-Provence 19 M 13
Aix-les-Bains 13 L 13
Ajaccio 20 N 14
Albert 12 K 12
Albertville 13 L 13
Albi 12 M 11
Alençon 12 K 11
Alès 12 M 12
Almuñécar 12 M 11
Ambert 12 L 12
Amboise 12 L 11
Amélie-les-Bains-Palalda
  19 N 12
Amiens 12 K 11
Ancenis 12 L 10
Angers 12 L 10
Angerville 12 K 11
Angoulême 12 L 11
Annecy 13 L 13
Annemasse 13 L 13
Annonay 12 L 12
Antibes 20 M 13
Apt 12 M 13
Arcachon 12 M 10
Arcis-sur-Aube 12 K 12
Arès 12 M 10
Argelès-Gazost 12 M 10
Argentan 12 K 11
Argentat 12 L 11
Argenton-sur-Creuse 12 L 11
Arles 12 M 12
Armentières 12 J 12
Arnay-le-Duc 12 L 12
Arras 12 J 12
Arreau 19 M 11
Aspres-sur-Buëch 13 M 13
Aubagne 19 M 13
Aubenas 12 M 12
Aubigny-s-Nère 12 K 11
Aubusson 12 L 11
Auch 12 M 11
Auray 12 K 9
Aurillac 12 M 11
Auterive 12 M 11
Autun 12 L 12
Auxerre 12 K 12
Avallon 12 L 12
Avignon 12 M 12
Avranches 12 K 10
Ax-les-Thermes 19 M 11
Bagnères-de Bigorre 12 M 11
Bagnères-de-Luchon 19 M 11
Bagnols-sur-Cèze 12 M 12
Baigneux 12 K 12
Bain-de-Bretagne 12 K 10
Bains-les-Bains 13 K 13
Bais 12 K 10
Bar-le-Duc 13 K 13
Bar-sur-Aube 12 K 12
Bar-sur-Seine 12 K 12
Barbezieux-St.Hilaire 12 L 10
Barcelonnette 13 M 13
Barfleur 12 K 10
Barjols 20 M 13
Barrême 13 M 13
Bastia 20 M 14
Baugé 12 K 10
Bayeux 12 K 11
Bayonne 12 M 10
Bazas 12 M 10
Beaucaire 12 M 12
Beaugency 12 K 11
Beaune 12 L 12
Beauvais 12 K 11
Bédarieux 12 M 12
Belfort 13 K 13
Belin-Béliet 12 M 10
Bellac 12 L 11
Bellegarde 13 L 13
Bellême 12 K 11
Belley 13 L 13
Benfeld 13 K 14
Berck 12 J 11
Bergerac 12 M 11
Bernay 12 K 11
Besançon 13 L 13
Béthune 12 J 12
Béziers 19 M 12
Biarritz 12 M 10
Biscarrosse 12 M 10
Bitche 13 K 13
Blaye 12 L 10
Bléré 12 L 11
Blois 12 K 11
Bocognano 20 N 14
Bolbec 12 K 11
Bonifacio 20 N 14
Bordeaux 12 M 10
Bort-les-Orgues 12 L 12
Boulogne-s-M. 12 J 11
Bourbon-Lancy 12 L 12

Bourbonne-les-Bains 13 K 13
Bourg-en-Bresse 13 L 13
Bourg-Lastic 12 L 12
Bourg-Madame 19 N 11
Bourganeuf 12 L 11
Bourges 12 L 11
Bourgoin-Jallieu 12 L 13
Boussens 12 M 11
Brantôme 12 L 11
Breil 13 M 14
Bressuire 12 L 10
Brest 12 K 9
Breteuil 12 K 11
Briançon 13 M 13
Briare 12 K 12
Brienne-le-Château 12 K 12
Brionne 12 K 11
Brioude 12 L 12
Brive-la-Gaillarde 12 L 11
Brou 12 K 11
Caen 12 K 10
Cahors 12 M 11
Calais 12 J 11
Calvi 20 M 14
Cambrai 12 J 12
Candé 12 K 10
Cannes 20 M 13
Cap Ferret 12 M 10
Carcassonne 19 M 11
Carentan 12 K 10
Cargèse 20 N 14
Carhaix-Plouguer 12 K 9
Carmaux 12 M 11
Carpentras 12 M 13
Casamozza 20 M 14
Casteljaloux 12 M 11
Castellane 13 M 13
Castelnau-Magnoac 12 M 11
Castelnau-Médoc 12 L 10
Castelsarrasin 12 M 11
Castillonnès 12 M 11
Castres 12 M 11
Cateraggio 20 N 14
Caudry 12 J 12
Caussade 12 M 11
Cauterets 19 M 10
Cavaillon 12 M 13
Cérilly 12 L 12
Cervione 20 N 14
Chagny 12 L 12
Chalais 12 L 11
Challans 12 L 10
Chalon-sur-Saône 12 L 12
Châlons-en-Champagne
  12 K 12
Châlus 12 L 11
Chambéry 13 L 13
Chamonix 13 L 13
Champagnole 13 L 13
Chantonnay 12 L 10
Charleville-Mézières 13 K 12
Charmes 13 K 13
Charolles 12 L 12
Chartres 12 K 11
Chasseneuil 12 L 11
Château Arnoux 13 M 13
Château Chinon 12 L 12
Château Renault 12 K 11
Château Salins 13 K 13
Château Thierry 12 K 12
Château-du-Loir 12 K 11
Château-la-Vallière 12 K 11
Châteaubriant 12 K 10
Châteaudun 12 K 11
Châteaulin 12 K 9
Châteauneuf-en-Thymerais
  12 K 11
Châteauneuf-sur-Loire 12 K 11
Châteauroux 12 L 11
Châtelguyon 12 L 12
Châtellerault 12 L 11
Châtillon-s.-I. 12 L 11
Châtillon-sur-Seine 12 K 12
Chauffailles 12 L 12
Chaumont 13 K 13
Chauny 12 K 12
Cherbourg-Octeville 12 K 10
Chinon 12 L 11
Cholet 12 L 10
Clamecy 12 L 12
Clelles 13 M 13
Clermont-Ferrand 12 L 12
Clisson 12 L 10
Cognac 12 L 11
Colmar 13 K 13
Colombey-les-Belles 13 K 13
Combeaufontaine 13 K 13
Commercy 13 K 13
Compiègne 12 K 12
Concarneau 12 K 9
Condom 12 M 11

Confolens 12 L 11
Connerré 12 K 11
Corbeil-Essonnes 12 K 11
Corbeny 12 K 12
Corbigny 12 L 12
Corlay 12 K 9
Corte 20 N 14
Cosne-Cours-s-Loire 12 L 12
Coulommiers 12 K 12
Creil 12 K 12
Cressensac 12 M 11
Crest 12 M 13
Culan 12 L 11
Dax 12 M 10
Deauville 12 K 11
Decazeville 12 M 11
Decize 12 L 12
Die 12 M 13
Dieppe 12 K 11
Digne-les-Bains 13 M 13
Digoin 12 L 12
Dijon 13 L 13
Dinan 12 K 10
Dinard 12 K 10
Diou 12 L 12
Dole 12 L 12
Domfront 12 K 10
Douai 12 J 12
Douarnenez 12 K 9
Doullens 12 J 11
Draguignan 20 M 13
Dreux 12 K 11
Dunkerque 12 J 11
Durtal 12 K 10
Ecouis 12 K 11
Elbeuf 12 K 11
Embrun 13 M 13
Epernay 12 K 12
Equisay 12 K 11
Ernée 12 K 10
Espalion 12 M 12
Estagel 19 M 12
Etampes 12 K 11
Eu 12 J 11
Evreux 12 K 11
Facture 12 M 10
Falaise 12 K 10
Fécamp 12 K 11
Feurs 12 L 12
Figeac 12 M 11
Firminy 12 L 12
Flers 12 K 10
Fleurance 12 M 11
Florac 12 M 12
Foix 12 M 11
Fontenay le-Compte 12 L 10
Fougères 12 K 10
Fourmies 12 J 12
Fréjus 20 M 13
Fumay 13 K 12
Fumel 12 M 11
Gaillac 12 M 11
Ganges 12 M 12
Gannat 12 L 12
Gap 13 M 13
Gérardmer 13 K 13
Gex 13 L 13
Gien 12 K 12
Gisors 12 K 11
Givors 12 L 12
Gourdon 12 M 11
Gournay-en-Bray 12 K 11
Gouzon 12 L 11
Gramat 12 M 11
Granville 12 K 10
Grasse 20 M 13
Gray 13 L 13
Grenoble 13 L 13
Grisolles 12 M 11
Gruissan 19 M 12
Guebwiller 13 K 13
Guéret 12 L 11
Guignes 12 K 12
Guillaumes 13 M 13
Guillestre 13 M 13
Guingamp 12 K 9
Guise 12 K 12
Gurs 12 M 10
Haguenau 13 K 14
Hédé 12 K 10
Hennebont 12 K 9
Hesdin 12 J 11
Hossegor 12 M 10
Houeillès 12 M 11
Hourtin 12 M 10
Hyères 20 M 13
l`Isle-Jourdain 12 M 11
l`Aigle 12 K 11
Issoire 12 L 12
Issoudun 12 L 11
Janzé 12 K 10

Joigny 12 K 12
Joinville 13 K 13
Jonzac 12 L 10
L`île Rousse 20 M 14
la Baule 12 L 10
la Boule 12 L 12
la Canourgue 12 M 12
la Chaise Dieu 12 L 12
la Charité 12 L 12
la Châtre 12 L 11
la Ciotat 19 M 13
la Croisière 12 L 11
la Flèche 12 K 10
la Guerche-sur-l'Aubois 12 L 12
la Haye-du-Puits 12 K 10
la Hutte 12 K 11
la Mure 13 M 13
la Réole 12 M 10
la Revaudière 12 L 11
la Roche-sur-Yon 12 L 10
la Rochebeaucourt 12 L 11
la Rochelle 12 L 10
la Seyne 19 M 13
la Tranche-sur-Mer 12 L 10
la Trimouille 12 L 11
Labouheyre 12 M 10
Lacanau-Océan 12 M 10
Lacaune 12 M 12
Lacelle 12 L 11
Lagny-le-Sec 12 K 12
Laharie 12 M 10
Lamballe 12 K 10
Lammotte-Beuvron 12 K 11
Landerneau 12 K 9
Langon 12 M 10
Langres 19 K 11
Lannemezan 12 M 11
Lannion 12 K 9
Lanslebourg 13 L 13
Laon 12 K 12
Lapalisse 12 L 12
Larche 13 M 13
Laruns 12 M 10
Lauzerte 12 M 11
Laval 12 K 10
Lavaur 12 M 11
le Blanc 12 L 11
le Bourg-d'Oisans 13 L 13
le Cateau 12 J 12
le Conquet 12 K 9
le Creusot 12 L 12
le Croisic 12 L 10
le Faouët 12 K 9
le Havre 12 K 11
le Mans 12 K 11
le Mont-Dore 12 L 12
le Mont-Saint Michel 12 K 10
le Perthus 19 N 12
le Puy-en-Velay 12 L 12
le Thillot 13 K 13
le Touquet-Paris-Plage 12 J 11
le Verdon-sur-Mer 12 L 10
le Vigan 12 M 12
Legé 12 L 10
Lempdes 12 L 12
Lens 12 J 12
Léon/Bayonne 12 M 10
les Echelles 13 L 13
les Hayons 12 K 11
les Maisons Blanches 12 L 11
les Sables d`Olonne 12 L 10
les Saintes Maries 19 M 12
Lesparre-Médoc 12 L 10
Levet 12 L 11
Lézignan-Corbières 19 M 12
Libourne 12 M 10
Lille 12 J 12
Lillers 12 J 12
Limoges 12 L 11
Limogne 12 M 11
Limoux 19 M 11
Lisieux 12 K 11
Loches 12 L 11
Locminé 12 K 9
Lodève 12 M 12
Longuyon 13 K 13
Longwy 13 K 13
Lons-le-Saunier 13 L 13
Lorient 12 K 9
Loriol 12 M 13
Loudéac 12 K 9
Loudun 12 L 11
Louhans 13 L 13
Lourdes 12 M 10
Louviers 12 K 11
Luçon 12 L 10
Lunel 12 M 12
Lunéville 13 K 13
Lure 13 K 13
Lussac-les-Châteaux 12 L 11
Luxeuil-les-Bains 13 K 13

Luzy 12 L 12
Lyon 12 L 12
Mâcon 12 L 12
Magny-en-Vexin 12 K 11
Manciet 12 M 11
Mansle 12 L 11
Mantes 12 K 11
Marans 12 L 10
Marennes 12 L 10
Marmanda 12 M 11
Marquise 12 J 11
Mars-la-Tour 13 K 13
Marseille 19 M 13
Martignè - 12 K 10
Martigues 19 M 13
Marvejols 12 M 12
Massat 19 M 11
Matha 12 L 10
Maubeuge 12 J 12
Maubourguet 12 M 11
Mauriac 12 M 11
Mauvezin 12 M 11
Mayenne 12 K 10
Megève 13 L 13
Melle 12 L 10
Melun 12 K 12
Mende 12 M 12
Menton 20 M 13
Metz 13 K 13
Meximieux 12 L 13
Millau 12 M 12
Mimizan-Plage 12 M 10
Mirambeau 12 L 10
Mirande 12 M 11
Mirebeau 12 L 11
Mirepoix 19 M 11
Moissac 12 M 11
Mon Idée 12 K 12
Monosque 13 M 13
Mont-de-Marsan 12 M 10
Montaigu 12 L 10
Montargis 12 K 12
Montauban 12 M 11
Montbard 12 K 12
Montbéliard 13 K 13
Montbrison 12 L 12
Montceau-les-Mines 12 L 12
Montcornet 12 K 12
Montdidier 12 K 12
Montélimar 12 M 12
Montereau 12 K 12
Montesquieu-Volvestre 12 M 11
Montigny-le-Roi 13 K 13
Montlieu-la-Garde 12 L 10
Montluçon 12 L 12
Montmarault 12 L 12
Montmirail 12 K 12
Montpellier 12 M 12
Montreuil 12 J 11
Montsalvy 12 M 12
Morez 13 L 13
Morgat 12 K 9
Morlaix 12 K 9
Mortagne 12 K 11
Mortagne-sur-Sèvre 12 L 10
Morteau 13 L 13
Mouchard 13 L 13
Moulins 12 L 12
Moûtiers 13 L 13
Mulhouse 13 K 13
Murat 12 L 12
Muret 12 M 11
Mussidan 12 M 11
Nancy 13 K 13
Nantes 12 L 10
Nantua 13 L 13
Narbonne 19 M 12
Nemours 12 K 12
Nérac 12 M 11
Neufchâteau 13 K 13
Neufchâtel-en-Bray 12 K 11
Nevers 12 L 12
Nice 20 M 13
Nîmes 12 M 12
Niort 12 L 10
Nogent-le-Rotrou 12 K 11
Nogent-sur-Seine 12 K 12
Noirétable 12 L 12
Noirmoutier-en-l`Île 12 L 10
Nonant-le-Pin 12 K 11
Nort 12 L 10
Nozay 12 K 10
Nyons 12 M 13
Orange 12 M 12
Orléans 12 K 11
Orthez 12 M 10
Oullins 12 L 12
Oyonnax 13 L 13
Paimpol 12 K 9
Pamiers 19 M 11
Paris 12 K 11

Parthenay 12 L 10
Pau 12 M 10
Périgueux 12 L 11
Péronne 12 K 12
Perpignan 19 M 12
Perros-Guirec 12 K 9
Peyrehorade 12 M 10
Peyrolles 19 M 13
Pézenas 19 M 12
Pierre-Buffière 12 L 11
Pino 20 M 14
Pithiviers 12 K 11
Ploërmel 12 K 10
Poitiers 12 L 11
Poix 12 K 11
Poligny 13 L 13
Pons 12 L 10
Pont Audemer 12 K 11
Pont-a-Mousson 13 K 13
Pont-Saint Esprit 12 M 12
Pontarlier 13 L 13
Pontaumur 12 L 12
Pontchâteau 12 L 10
Ponte Leccia 20 N 14
Pontivy 12 K 9
Pontoise 12 K 11
Pontorson 12 K 10
Pornic 12 L 10
Port Navalo 12 K 9
Port Saint Louis 19 M 12
Port Vendres 19 N 12
Porto 20 N 14
Porto - Vecchio 20 N 14
Pradelles 12 M 12
Prades 19 M 11
Pré-en-Pail 12 K 10
Précy-sous-Til 12 L 12
Privas 12 M 12
Propriano 20 N 14
Provins 12 K 12
Puget-Théniers 13 M 13
Puigcerda 19 N 11
Pácy 12 K 11
Quiberon 12 L 9
Quillan 19 M 11
Quimper 12 K 9
Quimperlé 12 K 9
Rambouillet 12 K 11
Recey 13 K 12
Redon 12 K 10
Reims 12 K 12
Remiremont 13 K 13
Remoulins 12 M 12
Rennes 12 K 10
Rethel 12 K 12
Rezé 12 L 10
Ribérac 12 L 11
Riez 13 M 13
Riom 12 L 12
Riom-ès-Montagnes 12 L 12
Roanne 12 L 12
Rochefort 12 L 10
Rodez 12 M 12
Romans-s-Isère 12 L 13
Romilly-sur-Seine 12 K 12
Romorantin-Lanthenay 12 L 11
Roquefort 12 M 10
Roscoff 12 K 9
Rosporden 12 K 9
Roubaix 12 J 12
Rouen 12 K 11
Royan 12 L 10
Roye 12 K 12
Sablé-sur-Sarthe 12 K 10
Sabres 12 M 10
Saint Affrique 12 M 12
Saint Agrève 12 M 12
Saint Amand 12 J 12
Saint Amand-Montrond 12 L 12
Saint André-de-Cubzac
  12 M 10
Saint Armour 13 L 13
Saint Avold 13 K 13
Saint Brévin 12 L 10
Saint Brieuc 12 K 9
Saint Chély-d'Apcher 12 M 12
Saint Claude 13 L 13
Saint Denis 12 K 11
Saint Denis-d'Oleron 12 L 10
Saint Dié-des-Vosges 13 K 13
Saint Dizier 13 K 13
Saint Etienne 12 L 12
Saint Florent 20 M 14
Saint Florentin 12 K 12
Saint Flour 12 L 12
Saint Gaudens 12 M 11
Saint Georges-sur-Loire
  12 L 10
Saint Germain 12 K 11
Saint Gilles-Croix-de-Vie
  12 L 10

I C E · Í N D I C E · N A V N E F O R T E G N E L S E ·
· Z O Z N A M O B C Í · I N D E K S M I E J S C O W O Ś C I

29

EU

Saint Girons (F)·(FIN)·(FL)·(FO)·(GB) **Dungiven**

Saint Girons 19 M 11
Saint Guénolé 12 K 9
Saint Hilaire-du-Harcouët 12 K 10
Saint Jean-de-Maurienne 13 L 13
Saint Jean-d'Angély 12 L 10
Saint Jean-Pied-de-Port 12 M 10
Saint Jouan-de-l'Isle 12 K 10
Saint Julien 13 L 13
Saint Junien 12 L 11
Saint Lô 12 K 10
Saint Maixent-l'Ecole 12 L 10
Saint Malo 12 K 10
Saint Marcellin 12 L 13
Saint Martin-de-Ré 12 L 10
Saint Mathieu 12 L 11
Saint Nazaire 12 L 10
Saint Omer 12 J 11
Saint Palais 12 M 10
Saint Pierre-le-Moûtier 12 L 12
Saint Pol-de-Léon 12 K 9
Saint Pons-de-Thomières 12 M 12
Saint Quay-Portrieux 12 K 9
Saint Quentin 12 K 12
Saint Raphaël 20 M 13
Saint Seine 12 L 12
Saint Sernin-sur-Rance 12 M 12
Saint Sever 12 M 10
Saint Tropez 20 M 13
Saint Yrieix 12 L 11
Saint-Valéry-en-Caux 12 K 11
Sainte Foy-la-Grande 12 M 11
Sainte Hermine 12 L 10
Sainte Maure-de-Touraine 12 L 11
Sainte Menéhould 13 K 12
Saintes 12 L 10
Salbris 12 L 11
Salon-de-Provence 19 M 13
Samatan 12 M 11
Sarlat-la-Canéda 12 M 11
Sarre Union 13 K 13
Sarrebourg 13 K 13
Sarreguemines 13 K 13
Sartene 20 N 14
Saugues 12 M 12
Saulieu 12 L 12
Sault 12 M 13
Saumur 12 L 10
Sauvas 12 M 12
Saverne 13 K 13
Schirmeck 13 K 13
Secondigny 12 L 10
Sedan 13 K 12
Sées 12 K 11
Seiches 12 K 10
Sélestat 13 K 13
Selles 12 L 11
Senlis 12 K 12
Sens 12 K 12
Serres 13 M 13
Sète 19 M 12
Seurre 13 L 13
Seyne 13 M 13
Sézanne 12 K 12
Sigean 19 M 12
Sisteron 13 M 13
Soissons 12 K 12
Solenzara 20 N 14
Sombernon 12 L 12
Sommesous 12 K 12
Soual 12 M 11
Souillac 12 M 11
Soulac-sur-Mer 12 L 10
Stenay 13 K 13
Strasbourg 13 K 14
Surgères 12 L 10
Tarare 12 L 12
Tarascon 19 M 11
Tarbes 12 M 11
Tartas 12 M 10
Tende 13 M 14
Thenon 12 L 11
Thiers 12 L 12
Thionville 13 K 13
Thiviers 12 L 11
Thouars 12 L 10
Til-Châtel 13 K 13
Tonnerre 12 K 12
Tôtes 12 K 11
Toucy 12 K 12
Toul 13 K 13
Toulon/Autun 12 L 12
Toulon/Marseille 20 M 13
Toulouse 12 M 11
Tournon 12 L 12
Tournus 12 L 13

Tours 12 L 11
Tourves 20 M 13
Toury 12 K 11
Troyes 12 K 12
Tulle 12 L 11
Urdos 12 M 10
Ussel 12 L 11
Uzerche 12 L 11
Valençay 12 L 11
Valence 12 L 12
Valenciennes 12 J 12
Valognes 12 K 10
Valras Plage 19 M 12
Vannes 12 K 9
Varzy 12 L 12
Vatan 12 L 11
Vendôme 12 K 11
Verdun 13 K 13
Verneuil 12 K 11
Vernon 12 K 11
Versailles 12 K 11
Vervins 12 K 12
Vesoul 13 K 13
Vichy 12 L 12
Vienne 12 L 12
Vierzon 12 L 11
Vihiers 12 L 10
Villars-les-Dombes 12 L 13
Villefort 12 M 12
Villefranche 12 M 11
Villefranche-de-Lauragais 12 M 11
Villefranche-s-Saône 12 L 12
Villeneuve-Saint-Georges 12 K 11
Villeneuve-sur-Lot 12 M 11
Villers-Bocage 12 K 10
Vire 12 K 10
Vitré 12 K 10
Vitry-le-François 12 K 12
Vittel 13 K 13
Vivonne 12 L 11
Voiron 13 L 13
Vouziers 13 K 12
Wissembourg 13 K 14
Yssingeaux 12 L 12
Zicavo 20 N 14

FIN

Ahola 3 C 22
Alahärma 5 D 20
Alajärvi 5 D 20
Alavus 5 D 20
Anttola 5 E 21
Askola 5 E 21
Autti 3 C 21
Bromarv 5 F 20
Dragsfjärd 5 E 20
Ekenäs 5 F 20
Elimäki 5 E 21
Eno 5 D 23
Enontekiö 3 B 20
Espoo 5 E 20
Eura 5 E 19
Eurajoki 5 E 19
Evijärvi 5 D 20
Forssa 5 E 20
Geta 5 E 18
Haapajärvi 5 D 21
Hailuoto 3 D 20
Hamina 5 E 21
Hammaslahti 5 E 22
Hanko 5 F 20
Harjavalta 5 E 19
Hartola 5 E 21
Haukivuori 5 E 21
Hautajärvi 3 C 22
Heinola 5 E 21
Heinävesi 5 E 22
Helsingfors=Helsinki 5 E 20
Helsinki=Helsingfors 5 E 20
Honkajoki 5 E 19
Hossa 3 C 22
Huittinen 5 E 20
Hukkajärvi 3 D 23
Humppila 5 E 20
Hyrynsalmi 3 D 22
Hyvinkää 5 E 20
Häijää 5 E 20
Hämeenkyrö 5 E 20
Hämeenlinna 5 E 20
Iisalmi 5 D 21
Iittala 5 E 20
Ikaalinen 5 E 20
Ilomantsi 5 D 23
Imatra 5 E 22
Inari/Lieksa 5 D 23
Inari/Virtaniemi 3 B 21

Isojoki 5 E 19
Ivalo 3 B 22
Jaala 5 E 21
Jakobstad=Pietersaari 5 D 20
Jalasjärvi 5 E 20
Joensuu 5 D 22
Joutsa 5 E 21
Joutseno 5 E 22
Joutsijärvi 3 C 22
Juntusranta 3 C 22
Juuka 5 D 22
Juva 5 E 22
Jyrkänkoski 3 C 22
Jyväskylä 5 E 21
Jämsä 5 E 21
Järvenpää 5 E 21
Kaamanen 3 B 21
Kaaresuvanto 3 B 20
Kajaani 3 D 22
Kalajoki 3 D 20
Kangasniemi 5 E 21
Kankaanpää 5 E 19
Kannus 5 D 20
Karigasniemi 3 B 21
Karis 5 E 20
Karkkila 5 E 20
Karleby=Kokkola 5 D 20
Karstula 5 D 20
Kartula 5 D 21
Karvia 5 E 20
Kaskinen 5 E 19
Kauhajoki 5 E 19
Kauhava 5 D 20
Kaukonen 3 C 20
Kaustinen 5 D 20
Kelloselkä 3 C 22
Kemi 3 C 20
Kemijärvi 3 C 21
Kerava 5 E 20
Kestilä 3 D 21
Kesälahti 5 E 22
Keuruu 5 E 20
Kilpisjärvi 3 B 19
Kimito 5 E 20
Kinnula 5 D 21
Kisko 5 E 20
Kitee 5 E 23
Kittilä 3 B 20
Kiuruvesi 5 D 21
Kokkola=Karleby 5 D 20
Kolari 3 C 20
Kontiomäki 3 D 22
Korpilahti 5 E 21
Korpo 5 E 19
Korsnäs 5 D 19
Koskenkylä 5 E 21
Koski 5 E 20
Kotka 10 E 21
Kouvola 5 E 21
Kristinestad 5 E 19
Kuhmalahti 5 E 20
Kuhmo 3 D 22
Kuhmoinen 5 E 21
Kuivaniemi 3 C 21
Kullaa 5 E 19
Kumila 5 E 20
Kuopio 5 D 22
Kuortti 5 E 21
Kurhila 5 E 21
Kurikka 5 D 19
Kuru 5 E 20
Kuusamo 3 C 22
Kuusankoski 5 E 21
Kyyjärvi 5 D 20
Kärsämäki 5 D 21
Kökar 5 F 19
Lahti 5 E 21
Laihia 5 D 19
Laitila 5 E 19
Lammi 5 E 21
Lappeenranta 5 E 22
Lappfjärd 5 E 19
Lapua 5 D 20
Lavia 5 E 20
Lempäälä 5 E 20
Leppäjärvi 3 B 20
Lestijärvi 5 D 20
Lieksa 5 D 22
Liminka 3 D 21
Liperi 5 D 22
Lohiniva 3 C 21
Lohja 5 E 20
Loimaa 5 E 20
Lokka 3 B 22
Loppi 5 E 20
Loviisa 5 E 21
Lumparland 5 E 19
Lusi 5 E 21
Luumäki 5 E 21
Luvia 5 E 19
Maaninkavaara 3 C 22

Maarianhamina 5 E 18
Martti 3 C 22
Mellakoski 3 C 20
Meltaus 3 C 21
Menesjärvi 3 B 21
Merikarvia 5 E 19
Mikkeli 5 E 21
Muhos 3 D 21
Multia 5 E 20
Muonio 3 B 20
Mynämäki 5 E 19
Mäntsälä 5 E 21
Mänttä 5 E 20
Mäntyharju 5 E 21
Mäntyluoto 5 E 19
Naantali 5 E 19
Nagu 5 E 19
Nivala 5 D 20
Nokia 5 E 20
Noormarkku 5 E 19
Nummi 5 E 20
Nurmes 5 D 22
Nuupas 3 C 21
Nykarleby=Uusikaarlepyy 5 D 20
Näljänkä 3 C 22
Orimattila 5 E 21
Orivesi 5 E 20
Oulu 3 C 21
Outokumpu 5 D 22
Padasjoki 5 E 21
Palojoensuu 3 B 20
Pargas 5 E 19
Parkano 5 E 20
Pelkosenniemi 3 C 22
Pello 3 C 20
Perniö 5 E 20
Pieksämäki 5 E 21
Pielavesi 5 D 21
Pietarsaari=Jakobstad 5 D 20
Pihtipudas 5 D 21
Pirttikylä=Pörtom 5 D 19
Pokka 3 B 21
Polmak 3 A 22
Pomarkku 5 E 19
Pori 5 E 19
Porkkala 5 F 20
Porvoo 5 E 21
Posio 3 C 22
Prastö 5 E 19
Pudasjärvi 3 C 21
Pulkkila 3 D 21
Punkaharju 5 E 22
Puolanka 3 D 22
Puumala 5 E 22
Pyhäjoki 3 D 20
Pyhältö 5 E 21
Pyhäntä 3 D 21
Pyhäsalmi 5 D 21
Pälkäne 5 E 20
Pörtom=Pirttikylä 5 D 19
Raahe 3 D 20
Raanujärvi 3 C 20
Raippaluoto=Replot 5 D 19
Raja-Jooseppi 3 B 22
Ranua 3 C 21
Rauma 5 E 19
Rautajärvi 5 D 22
Rautalampi 5 D 21
Rautjärven 5 E 22
Replot=Raippaluoto 5 D 19
Riihimäki 5 E 20
Ristiina 5 E 21
Rovaniemi 3 C 21
Ruovesi 5 E 20
Rymättylä 5 E 19
Rytinki 3 C 22
Saarijärvi 5 D 21
Saarivaara 3 D 22
Salla 3 C 22
Salö 5 E 21
Savitaipale 5 E 21
Savonlinna 5 E 22
Savonranta 5 E 22
Savukoski 3 C 22
Seinäjoki 5 D 20
Siikainen 5 E 19
Siilinjärvi 5 D 22
Simpele 5 E 22
Sinettä 5 C 21
Sirkka 3 B 20
Sodankylä 3 C 21
Somero 5 E 20
Sonkajärvi 5 D 21
Sotkamo 3 D 22
Sottunga 5 E 19
Storby 5 E 18
Sulkava 5 E 21
Suolahti 5 D 21
Suomenniemi 5 E 21
Suomussalmi 3 D 22

Suonenjoki 5 D 21
Suonsalmi 5 E 21
Svettijärvi 3 B 22
Sysmä 5 E 21
Särkilahti 5 E 22
Särkisalmi 5 E 22
Taivalkoski 3 C 22
Taivassalo 5 E 19
Tampere 5 E 20
Tannila 3 C 21
Tepasto 3 B 20
Tervola 3 C 20
Tohmajärvi 5 E 23
Toijala 5 E 20
Tornio 3 C 20
Tulppio 3 B 22
Tuohikotti 5 E 21
Turku 5 E 19
Tuulos 5 E 20
Unari 3 C 21
Urjala 5 E 20
Utajärvi 3 D 21
Utsjoki 3 B 21
Uukuniemi 5 E 22
Uusikaarlepyy=Nykarleby 5 D 20
Uusikaupunki 5 E 19
Vaala 3 D 21
Vaalajärvi 3 C 21
Vaasa 5 D 19
Valkeakoski 5 E 20
Vammala 5 E 20
Vampula 5 E 20
Varkaus 5 E 21
Vartius 3 D 23
Vehmasmäki 5 D 22
Vesanto 5 D 21
Vihanti 3 D 21
Viisarimäki 5 E 21
Viitasaari 5 D 21
Vikajärvi 3 C 21
Vimpeli 5 D 20
Virolahti 5 E 22
Virrat 5 E 20
Virtaniemi 3 B 22
Vuotso 3 B 21
Yli-Näljänkä 3 C 22
Ylikiiminki 3 C 21
Ylitornio 3 C 20
Ylivieska 5 D 20
Ylämaa 5 E 22
Yläne 5 E 19
Äänekoski 5 D 21
Äkäslompolo 3 B 20
Ämmänsaari 3 D 22
Ömossa 5 E 19

FL

Vaduz 13 L 14

FO

Fuglafjørðhur 2 A 1
Klaksvik 2 A 1
Tórshavn 2 A 1
Tvorøyri 2 A 1
Vestmanna 2 A 1

GB

Aberdaron 6 H 9
Aberdeen 7 G 10
Aberraeron 6 J 9
Aberystwyth 6 J 9
Abington 6 G 9
Aboyne 6 G 9
Achnasheen 6 F 8
Aldershot 6 J 10
Alnwick 6 G 10
Alston 6 H 10
Altnaharra 6 F 9
Amlwch 6 H 9
Annan 6 H 9
Appleby 6 H 10
Arbroath 6 G 9
Ardrossan 6 G 9
Arinagour 6 G 8
Arrochar 6 G 9
Ashbourne 6 H 10
Aughnacloy 6 H 8
Aylesbury 6 J 10
Ayr 6 G 9
Bagh 6 G 8
Ballycastle 6 G 8

Ballymena 6 H 8
Balmoral 6 G 9
Banbridge 6 H 8
Banbury 6 J 10
Banff 7 F 9
Bangor/Belfast 6 H 8
Bangor/Birkenhead 6 H 9
Barnard Castle 6 H 10
Barnsley 6 H 10
Barnstaple 6 J 9
Barrow in Furness 6 H 9
Basingstoke/Reading 6 J 10
Basingstoke/Southampton 6 J 10
Bath 6 J 10
Bedford 6 J 10
Belfast 6 H 8
Belford 6 G 10
Berwick-upon-Tweed 6 G 10
Bicester 6 J 10
Birkenhead 6 H 9
Birmingham 6 J 10
Blackburn 6 H 10
Blackpool 6 H 9
Blair Atholl 6 G 9
Bletchley 6 J 10
Bodmin 6 J 9
Bolton 6 H 10
Bonar Bridge 6 F 9
Boston 7 H 11
Bournemouth 6 J 10
Bradford 6 H 10
Braintree 7 J 11
Brecon 6 J 9
Brentwood 7 J 11
Bridgwater 6 J 9
Bridlington 7 H 10
Brighton 6 J 10
Bristol 6 J 9
Brodick 6 G 8
Broughton in Furness 6 H 9
Bude 6 J 9
Builth Wells 6 J 9
Burton-upon-Trent 6 H 10
Bury Saint Edmund`s 7 J 11
Buxton 6 H 10
Caernarfon 6 H 9
Callander 6 G 9
Camborne 6 J 8
Cambridge 7 J 11
Camelford/Cardiff 6 J 9
Camelford/Plymouth 6 J 9
Campbeltown 6 G 8
Canterbury 7 J 11
Cardiff 6 J 9
Cardigan 6 J 9
Carlisle 6 H 9
Carmarthen 6 J 9
Carrbridge 6 G 9
Castle Douglas 6 H 9
Chelmsford 7 J 11
Cheltenham 6 J 10
Chepstow 6 J 9
Chester 6 H 9
Chesterfield 6 H 10
Chippenham 6 J 10
Church Stretton 6 H 9
Cirencester 6 J 10
Clydebank 6 G 9
Colchester 7 J 11
Coleraine 6 G 8
Colwyn Bay 6 H 9
Consett 6 H 10
Corbridge 6 H 10
Corwen 6 H 9
Coventry 6 J 10
Craighouse 6 G 8
Crail 6 G 9
Crawley 6 J 10
Crewe 6 H 10
Crianlarich 6 G 9
Cromer 7 H 11
Croydon 6 J 10
Cushendall 6 G 8
Darlington 6 H 10
Daventry 6 J 10
Derby 6 H 10
Dingwall 6 F 9
Dolgellau 6 H 9
Doncaster 6 H 10
Dorchester 6 J 10
Dover 7 J 11
Downpatrick 6 H 8
Driffield 7 H 10
Drummore 6 H 9
Dumfries 6 G 9
Dunbar 6 G 9
Dundee 6 G 9
Dunfermline 6 G 9
Dungannon 6 H 8
Dungiven 6 H 8

Dunkeld — (GB)·(GE)·(GR)·(H) — **Nagykőrös**

Dunkeld 6 G 9
Durham 6 H 10
Eastbourne 12 J 11
Edinburgh 6 G 9
Elgin 6 F 9
Ellon 7 G 10
Ely 7 J 11
Enniskillen 6 H 7
Evesham 6 J 10
Exeter 6 J 9
Fakenham 7 H 11
Falkirk 6 G 9
Falmouth 6 J 8
Felixstowe 7 J 11
Fionnphort 6 G 8
Fishguard 6 J 9
Folkestone 7 J 11
Forfar 6 G 9
Fort Augustus 6 G 9
Fort William 6 G 8
Fraserburgh 7 F 10
Gainsborough 7 H 10
Gairloch 6 F 8
Galashiels 6 G 9
Garve 6 F 9
Gibraltar 18 P 8
Girvan 6 G 9
Glasgow 6 G 9
Glenbarr 6 G 8
Glenfinnan 6 G 8
Gloucester 6 J 10
Golspie 6 F 9
Grantown-on-Spey 6 G 9
Great Yarmouth 7 H 11
Greenock 6 G 9
Grimsby 7 H 10
Guildford 6 J 10
Harlech 6 H 9
Harlow 7 J 11
Harrogate 6 H 10
Hartlepool 7 H 10
Harwich 7 J 11
Hastings 12 J 11
Havant 6 J 10
Hawes 6 H 10
Hawick 6 G 9
Helmsdale 6 F 9
Hendon 6 J 10
Hereford 6 J 9
Heysham 6 H 9
High Wycombe 6 J 10
Hinckley 6 H 10
Hitchin 6 J 10
Holyhead 6 H 9
Horsham 6 J 10
Huddersfield 6 H 10
Hunstanton 7 H 11
Ilfracombe 6 J 9
Inveraray 6 G 8
Inverness 6 G 9
Inverurie 7 G 10
Ipswich 7 J 11
John o` Groat`s 7 F 9
Keith 6 F 9
Kelso 6 G 10
Kendal 6 H 9
Keswick 6 H 9
Kettering 6 J 10
Kidderminster 6 J 10
Kilkeel 6 H 8
Kilmarnock 6 G 9
King`s Lynn 7 H 11
Kingsbridge 6 J 9
Kingston 7 H 10
Kirkcaldy 6 G 9
Kirkwall 7 F 9
Kyle of Lochalsh 6 G 8
Lanark 6 G 9
Lancaster 6 H 9
Langholm 6 G 9
Larne 6 H 8
Leeds 6 H 10
Leicester 6 H 10
Leominster 6 J 10
Leyburn 6 H 10
Lincoln 7 H 10
Liverpool 6 H 9
Lizard 6 K 8
Llandovery 6 J 9
Llanelli 6 J 9
Llangurig 6 J 9
Loch Baghasdail 6 G 8
Loch nam Madadh 6 F 8
Lochaline 6 G 8
Lochearnhead 6 G 9
Lochgilphead 6 G 8
Lochinver 6 F 8
London 7 J 10
Londonderry 6 H 8
Looe 6 J 9
Loughborough 6 H 10

Louth 7 H 10
Lowestoft 7 J 11
Luton 6 J 10
Lydd 12 J 11
Lyme Regis 6 J 9
Lymington 6 J 10
Lynmouth 6 J 9
Mablethorpe 7 H 11
Machynlleth 6 H 9
Maghera 6 H 8
Maidstone 7 J 11
Mallaig 6 G 8
Malton 7 H 10
Manchester 6 H 10
Mansfield 6 H 10
March 7 H 11
Marlborough 6 J 10
Maryport 6 H 9
Merthyr Tydfil 6 J 9
Middlesbrough 7 H 10
Milford Haven 6 J 8
Moffat 6 G 9
Monmouth 6 J 9
Montrose 6 G 10
Morpeth 6 G 10
Motherwell 6 G 9
Nairn 6 F 9
Newark-on-Trent 6 H 10
Newbury 6 J 10
Newcastle upon Tyne 6 H 10
Newhaven 12 J 11
Newmarket 7 J 11
Newport/Bristol 6 J 9
Newport/Portsmouth 6 J 10
Newquay 6 J 8
Newry 6 H 8
Newton Abbot 6 J 9
Newton Stewart 6 H 9
Newtonmore 6 G 9
Newtown 6 H 9
Norwich 7 H 11
Nottingham 6 H 10
Northampton 6 J 10
Oban 6 G 8
Okehampton 6 J 9
Omagh 6 H 8
Oswestry 6 H 9
Oxford 6 J 10
Peebles 6 G 9
Pembroke 6 J 9
Penrith 6 H 9
Penzance 6 J 8
Perth 6 G 9
Peterborough 7 H 10
Peterhead 7 G 10
Petersfield 6 J 10
Plymouth 6 J 9
Pontypool 6 J 9
Poole 6 J 9
Port Askaig 6 G 8
Port Ellen 6 G 8
Port Nis 6 F 8
Port Talbot 6 J 9
Portadown 6 H 8
Portaferry 6 H 8
Portree 6 G 8
Portsmouth 6 J 10
Preston 6 H 9
Ramsgate 7 J 11
Randalstown 6 H 8
Reading 6 J 10
Ripon 6 H 10
Rochester 7 J 11
Ross-on-Wye 6 J 9
Rothesay 6 G 8
Royston 7 J 11
Saint Austell 6 J 9
Saint Clears 6 J 9
Saint Hélier 12 K 10
Saint Peter Port 12 K 9
Salen 6 G 8
Salisbury 6 J 10
Saxmundham 7 J 11
Scalasaig 6 G 8
Scarborough 7 H 10
Scarinish 6 G 8
Scole 7 J 11
Scourie 6 F 8
Scunthorpe 7 H 10
Settle 6 H 10
Shaftesbury 6 J 10
Sheffield 6 H 10
Shepton Mallet 6 J 10
Shrewsbury 6 H 9
Sidmouth 6 J 9
Silloth 6 H 9
Skegness 7 H 11
Skipton 6 H 10
Sleaford 7 H 10
Sligachan 6 G 8
Slough 6 J 10

Southampton 6 J 10
Southend on Sea 7 J 11
Southport 6 H 9
Spalding 7 H 10
Stafford 6 H 10
Stamford 7 H 10
Steornabhagh 6 F 8
Stirling 6 G 9
Stockport 6 H 10
Stoke 6 H 10
Stonehaven 7 G 10
Strabane 6 H 8
Stranraer 6 H 8
Stratford on Avon 6 J 10
Stromness 7 F 9
Stroud 6 J 10
Sunderland 7 H 10
Sutterton 7 H 10
Swaffham 7 H 11
Swansea 6 J 9
Swindon 6 J 10
Tain 6 F 9
Tairbeart 6 F 8
Tarbert 6 G 8
Taunton 6 J 9
Tavistock 6 J 9
Telford 6 H 10
Tenterden 7 J 11
Thetford 7 J 11
Thirsk 6 H 10
Thornhill 6 G 9
Thurso 6 F 9
Tiverton 6 J 9
Tobermory 6 G 8
Tonbridge 7 J 11
Tongue 6 F 9
Torquay 6 J 9
Troon 6 G 9
Trowbridge 6 J 10
Tynemouth 7 G 10
Uig 6 F 8
Ullapool 6 F 8
Upavon 6 J 10
Wallingford 6 J 10
Walsall 6 H 10
Warrington 6 H 9
Watford 6 J 10
Welshpool 6 H 9
Weston super Mare 6 J 9
Weymouth 6 J 10
Whitby 7 H 10
Whitchurch 6 H 9
Whitehaven 6 H 9
Whithorn 6 H 9
Wick 6 F 9
Winchester 6 J 10
Withernsea 7 H 11
Witney 6 J 10
Wolverhampton 6 H 10
Worcester 6 J 10
Workington 6 H 9
Worthing 6 J 10
Wrexham 6 H 9
Yeovil 6 J 9
York 6 H 10

GE

Avadchara 17 M 27
Aqwa 17 M 27
Bzy'b 17 M 27
Bichvinta 17 M 27
Gagra 17 M 27
Gudauta 17 M 27
Dranda 17 M 27
Lata 17 M 27
Očamčire 17 M 27

GR

Agia 22 O 20
Agia Galini 22 P 20
Agia Marina/Kasos 22 P 21
Agia Marina/Leros 22 P 21
Agia Pelagia 22 P 20
Agia Triada 22 O 19
Agii Deka 22 P 20
Agios Kirikos 22 O 21
Agios Nikolaos/Kriti 22 P 21
Agios Nikolaos/Ioannina 22 N 20
Agnanda 22 O 19
Agrinio 22 O 19
Alexandria/Thessaloniki 22 N 19
Alexandroupoli 22 N 21
Almiros 22 O 20

Amaliada 22 O 19
Amfiklia 22 O 20
Amfilohia 22 O 19
Amfissa 22 O 19
Amorgos 22 P 21
Anatoliko Frangista 22 O 19
Andirrio 22 O 19
Andravida 22 O 19
Andritsena 22 P 19
Andros 22 O 20
Apollonia 22 P 20
Areopoli 22 P 19
Argos 22 O 20
Argostoli 21 O 19
Aridea 22 N 19
Arkasa 23 P 21
Arta 22 O 19
Artotina 22 O 19
Astakos 22 O 19
Astipalea 22 P 21
Astros 22 P 20
Atalandi 22 O 20
Athina 22 O 20
Delfi 22 O 20
Deskati 22 O 19
Diakofto 22 O 19
Didimotiho 22 N 21
Dimitsana 22 O 19
Drama 22 N 20
Edessa 22 N 19
Efzoni 22 N 20
Egina 22 O 20
Egio 22 O 19
Elassona 22 O 19
Elefsina 22 O 20
Eleftheroupoli 22 N 20
Epanomi 22 N 20
Eptahori 22 N 19
Eratini 22 O 19
Ermoupoli 22 P 20
Evdilos 22 O 21
Farsala 22 O 19
Feres 22 N 21
Filakio 22 N 21
Filippiada 21 O 19
Fira 22 P 21
Fiskardo 21 O 19
Florina 22 N 19
Galatas 22 P 20
Gargaliani 22 P 19
Gavrio 22 O 20
Gerolimenas 22 P 19
Geroplatanos 21 O 19
Giannitsa 22 N 19
Githio 22 P 20
Goumenissa 22 N 19
Grevena 22 N 19
Halkida 22 O 20
Hania 22 P 20
Hios 22 O 21
Hrisoupoli 22 N 20
Ierápetra 22 P 21
Igoumenitsa 21 O 19
Ioannina 21 O 19
Iraklio 22 P 21
Istiea 22 O 20
Ithaki 21 O 19
Kalamata 22 P 19
Kalambaka 22 O 19
Kalavarda 23 P 22
Kalavrita 22 O 19
Kamariotissa 22 N 21
Kardamila 22 O 21
Karditsa 22 O 19
Karies 22 N 20
Karistos 22 O 20
Karpathos 23 P 21
Karpenisi 22 O 19
Kastoria 22 N 19
Katerini 22 N 19
Kato Nevrokopi 22 N 20
Kattavia 23 P 22
Kavala 22 N 20
Kavos 21 O 19
Kea 22 O 20
Kefalos 22 P 21
Kerkira 21 O 18
Kilkis 22 N 20
Kimi 22 O 20
Kiparissia 22 P 19
Kissamos 22 P 20
Kithira 22 P 20
Kithnos 22 P 20
Knosos 22 P 21
Komotini 22 N 21
Konitsa 21 N 19
Korinthos 22 O 20
Koroni 22 P 19
Kos 23 P 21
Kozani 22 N 19
Kranidi 22 P 20

Krestena 22 O 19
Lagos/Komotini 22 N 21
Lahanas 22 N 20
Lamia 22 O 19
Langadas 22 N 20
Larisa 22 O 19
Lefkada 21 O 19
Lehonia 22 O 20
Leonidi 22 P 20
Lepoura 22 O 20
Limenaria 22 N 20
Limni 22 O 20
Lindos 23 P 22
Livadia 23 P 21
Livadia/Thiva 22 O 20
Loutra Smokovou 22 O 19
Ierissos 22 N 20
los 22 P 21
Mandoudi 22 O 20
Marathonas 22 O 20
Meg. Horio 23 P 21
Megalopoli 22 P 19
Megara 22 O 20
Mesolongi 22 O 19
Messini 22 P 19
Metsovo 22 O 19
Mikines 22 O 20
Mikonos 22 P 21
Milina 22 O 20
Milos 22 P 20
Mirina 22 O 21
Mitikas 22 O 19
Mitilini 22 O 21
Molai 22 P 20
Monemvasia 22 P 20
Monolithos 23 P 22
Moudros 22 O 21
Nafplio 22 O 20
Naousa 22 N 19
Naxos 22 P 21
Nea Epidavros 22 O 20
Nea Karlovasi 22 O 21
Nea Manolada 22 O 19
Nea Moudania 22 N 20
Nea Zihni 22 N 20
Neapoli/Kozani 22 N 19
Neapoli/Monemvasia 22 P 20
Nemea 22 O 20
Nenita 22 O 21
Nigrita 22 N 20
Olimbia 22 O 19
Orestiada 22 N 21
Orhomenos 22 O 20
Ormos Agiou Ioannou 22 O 20
Palamas 22 O 19
Paleohora 22 P 20
Paleokastritsa 21 O 18
Paramithia 21 O 19
Paros 22 P 21
Patmos 22 P 21
Patra 22 O 19
Pefkohori 22 O 20
Pertouli 22 O 19
Pessani 22 N 21
Petra 22 O 21
Pilos 22 P 19
Pireas 22 O 20
Pirgos 22 O 20
Pirgos/Patra 22 O 19
Plomari 22 O 21
Poligiros 22 N 20
Preveza 21 O 19
Psahna 22 O 20
Ptolemaida 22 N 19
Rafina 22 O 20
Rendina 22 N 20
Rethimno 22 P 20
Rodopoli 22 N 20
Rodos 23 P 22
Sami 21 O 19
Samos 22 O 21
Sapes 22 N 21
Serifos 22 P 20
Serres/ Kavalla 22 N 20
Servia 22 N 19
Sfakia 22 P 20
Sidirokastro 22 N 20
Sigri 22 O 21
Sikia 22 N 20
Sitia 22 P 21
Skala 22 P 20
Skiathos 22 O 20
Skiros 22 O 20
Skopelos 22 O 20
Sofades 22 O 19
Soufli 22 N 21
Sounio 22 O 20
Sparti 22 P 19
Stavroupoli 22 N 20
Stomio 22 O 20
Stratoni 22 N 20

Strofilia 22 O 20
Thasos 22 N 20
Thessaloniki 22 N 20
Thiva 22 O 20
Timbaki 22 P 20
Tinos 22 O 21
Tirnavos 22 O 19
Trikala 22 O 19
Tripoli 22 O 19
Vamos 22 P 20
Veria 22 N 19
Volimes 21 O 19
Volos 22 O 20
Xanthi 22 N 20
Zagora 22 O 20
Zakinthos 22 O 19

H

Acsa 14 K 18
Ajka 14 L 18
Ártánd 15 L 19
Baja 14 L 18
Balassagyarmat 14 K 18
Balatonfüred 14 L 18
Balatonlelle 14 L 18
Balmazújváros 15 K 19
Barcs 14 L 17
Battonya 15 L 19
Békés 15 L 19
Békéscsaba 15 L 19
Beregsurány 15 K 19
Berettyóújfalu 15 L 19
Budapest 14 L 18
Cece 14 L 18
Cegléd 14 L 18
Csoma 14 K 17
Csongrád 14 L 18
Dabas 14 L 18
Debrecen 15 K 19
Dombóvár 14 L 18
Dunaföldvár 14 L 18
Dunaújváros 14 L 18
Eger 15 K 19
Érd 14 L 18
Esztergom 14 K 18
Gödöllő 14 L 18
Gyöngyös 14 K 18
Győr 14 K 18
Gyula 15 L 19
Hajdászoboszló 15 L 19
Hajdúböszörmény 15 K 19
Harkány 14 L 18
Hatvan 14 K 18
Hercegszántó 14 L 18
Heves 15 K 19
Hidasnémeti 15 K 19
Hódmezővásárhely 15 L 19
Jánosháza 14 L 17
Jászberény 14 L 18
Jászladány 15 L 19
Kalocsa 14 L 18
Kaposvár 14 L 18
Kapuvár 14 K 17
Karcag 15 L 19
Kecel 14 L 18
Kecskemét 14 L 18
Keszthely 14 L 17
Kisbér 14 L 18
Kiskőrös 14 L 18
Kiskunfélegyháza 14 L 18
Kiskunhalas 14 L 18
Kiskunmajsa 14 L 18
Kisszállás 14 L 18
Kisújszállás 15 L 19
Kisvárda 15 K 19
Komló 14 L 18
Körmend 14 L 17
Kunmadaras 15 L 19
Kunszentmárton 15 L 19
Lajosmizse 14 L 18
Lepsény 14 L 18
Létavértes 15 L 19
Makó 15 L 19
Mátészalka 15 K 19
Mezőberény 15 L 19
Mezőkövesd 15 K 19
Mezőtúr 15 L 19
Miskolc 15 K 19
Mohács 14 L 18
Monor 14 L 18
Mór 14 L 18
Mosonmagyaróvár 14 K 17
Nagyatád 14 L 17
Nagybajom 14 L 18
Nagyecsed 15 K 20
Nagykanizsa 14 L 17
Nagykáta 14 L 18
Nagykőrös 14 L 18

I C E · Í N D I C E · N A V N E   F O R T E G N E L S E ·
· Z O Z N A M   O B C Í · I N D E K S   M I E J S C O W O Ś C I

31

EU

Nyirábrány (H) · (HR) · (I) **Senigállia**

Nyirábrány 15 K 19
Nyírbátor 15 K 19
Nyíregyháza 15 K 19
Orosháza 15 L 19
Ózd 15 K 19
Pápa 14 L 17
Pásztó 14 K 18
Pécs 14 L 18
Putnok 15 K 19
Rédics 14 L 17
Rétság 14 K 18
Sajószentpéter 15 K 19
Salgótarján 14 K 18
Sárospatak 15 K 19
Sárvár 14 L 17
Sátoraljaújhely 15 K 19
Siófok 14 L 18
Sopron 14 K 17
Sterencs 15 K 19
Szarvas 15 L 19
Szeged 15 L 19
Szeghalom 15 L 19
Székely 15 K 19
Székesfehérvár 14 L 18
Szekszárd 14 L 18
Szentendre 14 K 18
Szentes 15 L 19
Szigetvár 14 L 18
Szikszó 15 K 19
Szin 15 K 19
Szolnok 15 L 19
Szombathely 14 L 17
Tamási 14 L 18
Tapolca 14 L 17
Tass 14 L 18
Tatabánya 14 K 18
Tét 14 L 18
Tiszaföldvár 15 L 19
Tiszafüred 15 K 19
Tiszaújváros 15 K 19
Tiszavasvári 15 K 19
Tokaj 15 K 19
Tótkomlós 15 L 19
Törökszentmiklós 15 L 19
Újfehértó 15 K 19
Vác 14 K 18
Várpalota 14 L 18
Veszprém 14 L 18
Vésztő 15 L 19
Zalaegerszeg 14 L 17
Zirc 14 L 18

(HR)

Beli Manastir 14 L 18
Biograd 21 M 17
Bjelovar 14 L 17
Buševec 14 L 17
Cres 14 M 16
Crikvenica 14 L 16
Čakovec 14 L 17
Daruvar 14 L 17
Delnice 14 L 16
Donji Lapac 14 M 17
Drniš 21 M 17
Đakovo 14 L 18
Đurđevac 14 L 17
Glina 14 L 17
Gospić 14 M 17
Gračac 21 M 17
Hrvatska Kostajnica 14 L 17
Hvar 21 M 17
Imotski 21 M 17
Ivanić Grad 14 L 17
Jablanac 14 M 16
Josipdol 14 L 17
Karlobag 14 M 17
Karlovac 14 L 17
Knin 21 M 17
Kněvci 14 L 17
Koprivnica 14 L 17
Korčula 21 M 17
Krapina 14 L 17
Krk 14 L 16
Kutina 14 L 17
Labin 14 L 16
Letenye 14 L 17
M. Lošinj 14 M 16
Makarska 21 M 17
Našice 14 L 18
Nova Gradiška 14 L 17
Novi Marof 14 L 17
Obrovac 21 M 17
Ogulin 14 L 17
Omiš 21 M 17
Omišalj 14 L 16
Opatija 14 L 16
Opuzen 21 M 18
Orebič 21 M 17

Osijek 14 L 18
Otočac 14 M 17
Pag 14 M 17
Pazin 14 L 16
Plitvica Selo 14 M 17
Ploče 21 M 17
Poreč 13 L 16
Porozina 14 L 16
Požega 14 L 18
Pula 14 M 16
Rab 14 M 16
Rijeka 14 L 16
Rogoznica 21 M 17
Rovinj 13 L 16
Rupa 14 L 16
Senj 14 L 16
Sinj 21 M 17
Sisak 14 L 17
Slatina 14 L 17
Slavonski Brod 14 L 18
Slunj 14 L 17
Split 21 M 17
Stari Grad 21 M 17
Sumartin 21 M 17
Supetar 21 M 17
Šibenik 21 M 17
Trogir 21 M 17
Tušilović 14 L 17
Udbina 14 M 17
Umag 13 L 16
Varaždin 14 L 17
Vela Luka 21 M 17
Vinkovci 14 L 18
Virovitica 14 L 17
Vis 21 M 17
Vrbovec 14 L 17
Vukovar 14 L 18
Zadar 21 M 17
Zagreb 14 L 17
Županja 14 L 18

(I)

Abbasanta 20 N 14
Acerra 21 N 16
Acireale 21 O 17
Ácqui Terme 13 M 14
Adrano 21 O 16
Adria 13 L 15
Agnone 21 N 16
Agrigento 20 P 16
Agrópoli 21 N 17
Alagna-Valsésia 13 L 14
Alatri 20 N 16
Alba 13 M 14
Albano Laziale 20 N 16
Albenga 13 M 14
Álcamo 20 O 16
Alessándria 13 M 14
Alghero 20 N 14
Alife 21 N 16
Altamura 21 N 17
Amalfi 21 N 16
Amandola 20 M 16
Amantea 21 O 17
Amatrice 20 M 16
Ancona 20 M 16
Ándria 21 N 17
Antrodoco 20 N 16
Ánzio 20 N 16
Aosta 13 L 13
Arbatax 20 O 14
Arcidosso 20 M 15
Arezzo 20 M 15
Argenta 13 M 15
Argentera 13 M 13
Ariano Irpino 21 N 17
Arona 13 L 14
Ársoli 20 N 16
Áscoli Piceno 20 M 16
Asola 13 L 15
Asti 13 M 14
Atri 21 M 16
Augusta 21 P 17
Aulla 13 M 15
Auronzo 13 L 15
Avellino 21 N 16
Aversa 21 N 16
Avezzano 20 N 16
Avigliano 21 N 17
Badia 13 L 15
Bagni di Lucca 20 M 15
Bagno di Romagna 20 M 15
Barcellona-Pozzo di Gotto 21 O 17
Bari 21 N 17
Barletta 21 N 17
Bassano del Grappa 13 L 15
Battipáglia 21 N 16

Belluno 13 L 15
Belvedere Maríttimo 21 O 17
Benevento 21 N 16
Bérgamo 13 L 14
Bernalda 21 N 17
Bibbiena 20 M 15
Biella 13 L 14
Bitonto 21 N 17
Bivona 20 O 16
Bologna 13 M 15
Bolognetta 20 O 16
Bonelli 13 M 15
Bono 20 N 14
Borgo Val di Taro 13 M 14
Borgomanero 13 L 14
Borgosésia 13 L 14
Bórmio 13 L 15
Bosa 20 N 14
Bovalino 21 O 17
Bozen (Bolzano) 13 L 15
Bra 13 M 14
Bracciano 20 N 15
Brancaleone Marina 21 O 17
Breno 13 L 15
Brèscia 13 L 15
Brèscia 13 L 15
Breuil-Cervinia 13 L 14
Bríndisi 21 N 18
Brixen (Bressanone) 13 L 15
Buddosò 20 N 14
Busto-Arsizio 13 L 14
Cagli 20 M 16
Cágliari 20 O 14
Cala d'Oliva 20 N 14
Caltagirone 21 P 16
Caltanissetta 20 P 16
Camerino 20 M 16
Campobasso 21 N 16
Canicatti 20 P 16
Canosa 21 N 17
Cáorle 13 L 16
Capo d'Orlando 21 O 16
Capri 21 N 16
Carbónia 20 O 14
Cariati 21 O 17
Carloforte 20 O 14
Carmagnola 13 M 14
Carpi 13 M 15
Carrara 13 M 15
Casale Monferrato 13 L 14
Casalmaggiore 13 M 15
Cassino 20 N 16
Castèl di Sangro 21 N 16
Castèl Volturno 20 N 16
Castelfranco 13 L 15
Castellamare del Golfo 20 O 16
Castelnovo 13 M 15
Castelsardo 20 N 14
Casteltérmini 20 O 16
Castelvetrano 20 O 16
Castiglione della Pescáia 20 M 15
Castrovíllari 21 O 17
Catánia 21 P 17
Catanzaro 21 O 17
Catanzaro Marina 21 O 17
Cattólica 20 M 16
Cavalese 13 L 15
Cécina 20 M 15
Cefalù 20 O 16
Celano 20 N 16
Cento 13 M 15
Cerignola 21 N 17
Cervéteri 20 N 15
Cérvia 21 M 15
Cesena 20 M 15
Cesenático 20 M 15
Cetraro 21 O 17
Chiávari 13 M 14
Chiavenna 13 L 14
Chieti 21 N 16
Chióggia 13 L 15
Chiusi 20 M 15
Chivasso 13 L 14
Cirò 21 O 17
Città di Castello 20 M 15
Civita Castellana 20 N 15
Civitanova Marche 20 M 16
Civitavécchia 20 N 15
Cles 20 L 15
Clusone 13 L 15
Codigoro 13 M 15
Codogno 13 L 14
Cólico 13 L 14
Colle di Tora 20 N 16
Colle di Val d'Elsa 20 M 15
Comácchio 13 M 15
Como 13 L 14
Conegliano 13 L 15
Corigliano Cálabro 21 O 17
Corleone 20 O 16

Corleto 21 N 17
Cortina d'Ampezzo 13 L 15
Cortona 20 M 15
Cosenza 21 O 17
Courmayeur 13 L 13
Crema 13 L 14
Cremona 13 L 15
Crotone 21 O 17
Cúneo 13 M 14
Cuorgnè 13 L 14
Cutro 21 O 17
Desenzano 13 L 15
Dolianova 20 O 14
Domodóssola 13 L 14
Dorgali 20 N 14
Éboli 21 N 17
Édolo 13 L 15
Émpoli 20 M 15
Enna 21 O 16
Faenza 13 M 15
Fano 20 M 16
Fasano 21 N 17
Favignana 20 O 15
Feltre 13 L 15
Fermo 20 M 16
Ferrandina 21 N 17
Ferrara 13 M 15
Fidenza 13 M 15
Finale Lígure 13 M 14
Firenze 20 M 15
Fiumicino 20 N 15
Florinas 20 N 14
FORLI 20 M 15
Fóggia 21 N 17
Foligno 20 M 16
Follònica 20 M 15
Fondi 20 N 16
Fonni 20 N 14
Formazza 13 L 14
Fossacésia 21 N 16
Fossano 13 M 14
Fossombrone 20 M 16
Francavilla Fontana 21 N 18
Frosinone 20 N 16
Gaeta 20 N 16
Gallipoli 21 N 18
Garéssio 13 M 14
Gargnano 13 L 15
Gela 21 P 16
Gemona del Friuli 13 L 16
Génova 13 M 14
Giarre 21 O 17
Gióia del Colle 21 N 17
Gióia di Táuro 21 O 17
Giulianova 21 M 16
Golfo Aranci 20 N 14
Gorízia 13 L 16
Grado/Trieste 13 L 16
Gravina di Púglia 21 N 17
Grosseto 20 M 15
Gúbbio 20 M 16
Gúspini 20 O 14
Iesi 20 M 16
Iglésias 20 O 14
Ímola 13 M 15
Impéria 20 M 14
Irsina 21 N 17
Íschia 20 N 16
Iseo 13 L 15
Isérnia 21 N 16
Ivrea 13 L 14
La Spezia 13 M 14
Lanciano 21 N 16
Lanusei 20 O 14
Larino 21 N 16
Latina 20 N 16
Latrónico 21 N 17
Lauria 21 N 17
Lecce 21 N 18
Lecco 13 L 14
Legnago 13 L 15
Lentini 21 P 16
Lercara Friddi 20 O 16
Lérici 20 M 14
Lévico Terme 13 L 15
Licata 20 P 16
Lido degli Estensi 13 M 15
Lido di Jésolo 13 L 16
Lido di Metaponto 21 N 17
Lido di Óstia 20 N 15
Lignano Sabbiadoro 13 L 16
Lipari 21 O 16
Livorno 20 M 15
Lodi 13 L 14
Loiano 13 M 15
Longarone 13 L 15
Lucca 20 M 15
Lucera 21 N 17
L'Áquila 20 N 16
Macerata 20 M 16
Macomer 20 N 14

Magione 20 M 15
Máglie 21 N 18
Malcésine 13 L 15
Malfa 21 O 16
Manciano 20 M 15
Mandúria 21 N 18
Manfredónia 21 N 17
Mantova 13 L 15
Marcaria 13 L 15
Margherita di Savoia 21 N 17
Marina di Campo 20 M 15
Marina di Castagneto-Donoratico 20 M 15
Marina di Léuca 21 O 18
Marina di Pisa 20 M 15
Marradi 20 M 15
Marsala 20 O 15
Martina Franca 21 N 17
Massa 20 M 15
Massa Maríttima 20 M 15
Matera 21 N 17
Mazara del Vallo 20 O 16
Medicina 20 M 15
Melfi 21 N 17
Mélito 21 O 17
Meran (Merano) 13 L 15
Mesagne 21 N 18
Messina 21 O 17
Milano 13 L 14
Milazzo 21 O 17
Minervino 21 N 17
Mira/Mestre 13 L 15
Mirándola 13 M 15
Mistretta 21 O 16
Módena 13 M 15
Módica 21 P 16
Moena 13 L 15
Mola di Bari 21 N 17
Molfetta 21 N 17
Monasterace Marina 21 O 17
Monastir 20 O 14
Mondovi 13 M 14
Mondragone 20 N 16
Monfalcone 13 L 16
Monópoli 21 N 17
Monsélice 13 L 15
Montalbano 21 N 17
Montalto di Castro 20 N 15
Monte Sant'Angelo 21 N 17
Montepulciano 20 M 15
Montesano 21 N 17
Montevarchi 20 M 15
Monti 20 N 14
Monza 13 L 14
Mortara 13 L 14
Muravera 20 O 14
Muro Lucano 21 N 17
Nápoli 21 N 16
Nardò 21 N 18
Narni 20 M 16
Navelli 20 N 16
Nicastro 21 O 17
Nicosia/Sicilia 21 O 16
Niscemi 21 P 16
Nogara 13 L 15
Nórcia 20 M 16
Noto 21 P 17
Novara 13 L 14
Novi Lígure 13 M 14
Núoro 20 N 14
Ólbia 20 N 14
Omegna 13 L 14
Opi 20 N 16
Orbetello 20 N 15
Oristano 20 O 14
Ortona 21 N 16
Orvieto 20 M 15
Ósimo 20 M 16
Ostiglia 13 L 15
Ostuni 21 N 18
Ótranto 21 N 18
Ovada 13 M 14
Ozieri 20 N 14
Pachino 21 P 17
Pádova 13 L 15
Palazzolo Acreide 21 P 16
Palermo 20 O 16
Palinuro 21 N 17
Pallanza 13 L 14
Palma di Montechiaro 20 P 16
Palmanova 13 L 16
Palmi 21 O 17
Páola 21 O 17
Parma 13 M 15
Partinico 20 O 16
Paternò 21 O 16
Patti 21 O 16
Pavia 13 L 14
Pavullo nel Frignano 13 M 15
Penne 21 N 16
Perúgia 20 M 15

Pésaro 20 M 16
Pescara 21 N 16
Petília Policastro 21 O 17
Piacenza 13 M 14
Piana Crixia 13 M 14
Piazza Armerina 21 P 16
Pieve di Cadore 13 L 15
Pievepelago 13 M 15
Pinerolo 13 M 13
Piombino 20 M 15
Pisa 20 M 15
Pisticci 21 N 17
Pistóia 20 M 15
Pizzo 21 O 17
Póllica 21 N 17
Pompei 21 N 16
Pontassieve 20 M 15
Pontebba 13 L 16
Pontedera 20 M 15
Pontrémoli 13 M 14
Pópoli 20 N 16
Pordenone 13 L 16
Porretta Terme 13 M 15
Porto Azzurro 20 M 15
Porto San Giórgio 20 M 16
Porto Tórres 20 N 14
Portoferráio 20 M 15
Portogruaro 13 L 16
Potenza 21 N 17
Pozzallo 21 P 16
Prato 20 M 15
Primolano 13 L 15
Pula/Cagliari 20 O 14
Quartu-Santa Elena 20 O 14
Ragusa 21 P 16
Randazzo 21 O 16
Rapallo 13 M 14
Ravenna 13 M 15
Réggio di Calábria 21 O 17
Réggio nell'Emília 13 M 15
Rho 13 L 14
Ribera 20 P 16
Riesi 20 P 16
Rieti 20 M 16
Rímini 20 M 16
Riva 13 L 15
Roccadáspide 21 N 17
Roccastrada 20 M 15
Rodi 21 N 17
Roma 20 N 15
Rosarno 21 O 17
Rosignano Maríttima 20 M 15
Rossano 21 O 17
Rovato 13 L 15
Rovereto 13 L 15
Rovigo 13 L 15
Ruvo di Púglia 21 N 17
Sala Consilina 21 N 17
Salemi 20 O 16
Salerno 21 N 16
Salo/Brescia 13 L 15
Salsomaggiore Terme 13 M 15
Saluzzo 13 M 14
Sampierdarena 13 M 14
Sampieri 21 P 16
San Bartolomeo in Galdo 21 N 16
San Benedetto del Tronto 20 M 16
San Bonifácio 13 L 15
San Doná di Piave 13 L 16
San Felice Circeo 20 N 16
San Fratello 21 O 16
San Giovanni in Fiore 21 O 17
San Giovanni Rotondo 21 N 17
San Martino di Castrozza 13 L 15
San Quírico 20 M 15
San Remo 20 M 14
San Severo 21 N 17
San Sosti 21 O 17
San Vito lo Capo 20 O 16
Sanluri 20 O 14
Sannicandro 21 N 17
Sansepolcro 20 M 15
Santa Teresa 20 N 14
Santa Teresa di Riva. 21 O 17
Santéramo 21 N 17
Sant' Ángelo dei Lombardi 21 N 17
Sant' Antíoco 20 O 14
Sapri 21 N 17
Sarzana 13 M 15
Sássari 20 N 14
Sassuolo 13 M 15
Savona 13 M 14
Scalea 21 O 17
Scanzano 21 N 17
Schio 13 L 15
Sciacca 20 O 16
Senigállia 20 M 16

32

EU

I N D E X · O R T S R E G I S T E R · Í N D I C E · I N
P L A A T S N A M E N R E G I S T E R · R E J S T Ř Í K   M Í S

Senise

I · IRL · IS · L · LT · LV · M · MA · MC · MD · MK · MNE · N

Bjørkåsen

Senise 21 N 17
Serra San Bruno 21 O 17
Serri 20 O 14
Sessa Aurunca 20 N 16
Sestri Levante 13 M 14
Sestriere 13 M 13
Siderno 21 O 17
Siena 20 M 15
Siliqua 20 O 14
Siniscola 20 N 14
Siracusa 21 P 17
Sóndrio 13 L 14
Sora 20 N 16
Sórgono 20 N 14
Sorrento 21 N 16
Soverato 21 O 17
Soveria 21 O 17
Spilimbergo 13 L 16
Spinazzola 21 N 17
Spoleto 20 M 16
Spondinig (Spondigna) 13 L 15
Stigliano 21 N 17
Stintino 20 N 14
Stradella 13 L 14
Subiaco 20 N 16
Sulmona 21 N 16
Susa 13 L 13
Taormina 21 O 17
Táranto 21 N 17
Tarquínia 20 N 15
Tarvisio 13 L 16
Taurianova 21 O 17
Témpio 20 N 14
Téramo 20 M 16
Términi Imerese 20 O 16
Térmoli 21 N 16
Terni 20 M 16
Terracina 20 N 16
Terralba 20 O 14
Tertenia 20 O 14
Teulada 20 O 14
Tione di Trento 13 L 15
Tirano 13 L 15
Tívoli 20 N 16
Toblach (Dobbiaco) 13 L 15
Todi 20 M 15
Tolmezzo 13 L 16
Tor Vaiánica 20 N 15
Torino 13 L 14
Torre Mileto 21 N 17
Torriglia 13 M 14
Tortona 13 M 14
Trani 21 N 17
Trápani 20 O 16
Trebisacce 21 O 17
Trento 13 L 15
Treviso 13 L 15
Tricárico 21 N 17
Trieste 14 L 16
Trivento 21 N 16
Troia 21 N 17
Tropea 21 O 17
Údine 13 L 16
Urbino 20 M 16
Valentano 20 M 15
Vallo di Lucánia 21 N 17
Varese 13 L 14
Vasto 21 N 16
Velletri 20 N 16
Venézia 13 L 15
Venosa 21 N 17
Ventimiglia 20 M 14
Vercelli 13 L 14
Verona 13 L 15
Vetralla 20 N 15
Viareggio 20 M 15
Vibo Valéntia 21 O 17
Vicenza 13 L 15
Vieste 21 N 17
Vigévano 13 L 14
Villa San Giovanni 21 O 17
Villacidro 20 O 14
Villasimius 20 O 14
Viterbo 20 N 15
Vittória 21 P 16
Vittório Véneto 13 L 15
Vizzini 21 P 16
Voghera 13 M 14
Volterra 20 M 15

IRL

Arklow 6 H 8
Athlone 6 H 7
Athy 6 H 8
Ballina 6 H 7
Ballybofey 6 H 7
Ballyhaunis 6 H 7
Ballyshannon 6 H 7

Bantry 6 J 7
Belmullet 6 H 7
Bray 6 H 8
Cahersiveen 6 J 6
Carlow 6 H 8
Carrick on Shannon 6 H 7
Carrickmacross 6 H 8
Cashel 6 H 7
Castlebar 6 H 7
Castletown 6 H 7
Cavan 6 H 8
Charleville 6 J 7
Clifden 6 H 6
Clones 6 H 8
Clonmel 6 J 7
Cobh 6 J 7
Cork Corcaigh 6 J 7
Dingle 6 J 6
Donegal 6 H 7
Drogheda 6 H 8
Dublin Baile Atha Cliath 6 H 8
Dun Laoghaire 6 H 8
Dundalk 6 H 8
Durrow 6 H 8
Ennis 6 H 7
Enniscorthy 6 H 8
Ennistimon 6 H 7
Fermoy 6 J 7
Galway 6 H 7
Glenties 6 H 7
Gort 6 H 7
Gweedore 6 G 7
Kells 6 H 8
Kilkee 6 H 7
Kilkenny 6 H 8
Killarney 6 J 7
Kinnegad 6 H 8
Kinsale 6 J 7
Letterkenny 6 H 7
Limerick 6 H 7
Longford 6 H 7
Loughrea 6 H 7
Macroom 6 J 7
Mallow 6 J 7
Maynooth 6 H 8
Midleton 6 J 7
Monaghan 6 H 8
Mullingar 6 H 8
Naas 6 H 8
Nenagh 6 H 7
New Ross 6 J 8
Newcastle West 6 J 7
Port Laoise 6 H 8
Portumna 6 H 7
Rathmullan 6 G 7
Roscommon 6 H 7
Rosslare Harbour 6 J 8
Skibbereen 6 J 7
Sligo 6 H 7
Tarbert 6 H 7
Tipperary 6 J 7
Tobercurry 6 H 7
Tralee 6 J 7
Tuam 6 H 7
Tullamore 6 H 7
Waterford 6 J 8
Westport 6 H 7
Wexford 6 J 8
Wicklow 6 H 8
Youghal 6 J 7

IS

Aðalból 2 C 2
Aðalból 2 C 2
Akranes 2 D 2
Akureyri 2 C 3
Bakkafjörður 2 C 5
Bakkagerði 2 C 5
Bildudalur 2 C 1
Blönduós 2 C 2
Bogarnes 2 D 2
Bolungarvik 2 C 1
Borðeyri 2 C 2
Breiðdalsvík 2 D 5
Buðardalur 2 C 2
Búðir 2 D 1
Burfell 2 D 2
Dalsmynni 2 D 2
Dalvík 2 C 3
Djúpivogur 2 D 5
Drangsnes 2 C 2
Dúfenefsfell 2 D 3
Egilsstaðir 2 C 5
Eskifjörður 2 C 5
Eyjarfótur 2 C 3
Eyrarbakki 2 D 2
Fagurhólsmýri 2 D 4
Fáskrúðsfjörður 2 D 5

Flateyri 2 C 1
Garður 2 D 1
Grenivík 2 C 3
Grindavík 2 D 2
Grundarfjörður 2 D 1
Hafnarfjörður 2 D 2
Hella 2 D 2
Höfn 2 D 4
Hofsós 2 C 3
Hólmavík 2 C 2
Husavík 2 C 4
Hveragerði 2 D 2
Hvolsvöllur 2 D 3
Isafjörður 2 C 1
Keflavík 2 D 1
Kirkjubæjarklaustur 2 D 3
Kolbeinsstadir 2 D 2
Kópasker 2 C 4
Kópavogur 2 D 2
Langholt 2 D 2
Laugarbakki 2 C 2
Laugarvatn 2 D 2
Mosfellsbær 2 D 2
Neskaupstaður 2 C 5
Norðurfjörður 2 C 2
Ólafsfjörður 2 C 3
Ólafsvík 2 D 1
Patreksfjörður 2 C 1
Raufarhöfn 2 C 4
Reyðarjförður 2 C 5
Reykjahilð 2 C 4
Reykjavik 2 D 2
Sandgerði 2 D 1
Sauðárkrókur 2 C 3
Selfoss 2 D 2
Seyðisfjörður 2 C 5
Siglufjörður 2 C 3
Skagaströnd 2 C 2
Stykkishólmur 2 C 1
Suðureyri 2 C 1
þingeyri 2 C 1
þingvellir 2 C 2
þorlákshöfn 2 D 2
þórshöfn 2 C 4
Varmahlið 2 C 3
Vestmannæyjar 2 D 2
Vik 2 D 3
Vopnafjörður 2 C 5

L

Clervau x13 J 13
Esch-s.-Alzette 13 K 13
Ettelbrück 13 K 13
Luxembourg 13 K 13

LT

Alytus 9 H 20
Anykščiai 9 G 21
Ariogala 9 G 20
Biržai 9 G 20
Druskininkai 9 H 20
Dükštas 10 G 21
Dusetos 10 G 21
Garliava 9 H 20
Grinkiškis 9 G 20
Ignalina 10 G 21
Jieznas 9 H 20
Jonava 9 G 20
Joniškis 9 G 20
Jurbarkas 9 G 20
Kaišiadoris 9 H 20
Kalvarija 9 H 20
Kaunas 9 H 20
Kavarskas 9 G 20
Kelmė 9 G 20
Klaipeda 9 G 19
Kretinga 9 G 19
Kupiškis 9 G 20
Kuršėnai 9 G 20
Kėdainiai 9 G 20
Lazdijai 9 H 20
Linkuva 9 G 20
Marijampolė 9 H 20
Mažeikiai 9 G 19
Merkinė 9 H 20
Molėtai 9 G 21
Nemenčinė 10 H 21
Nida 9 G 19
Pabradė 10 H 21
Pakruojis 9 G 20
Palanga 9 G 19
Pandėlys 9 G 21
Panevėžys 9 G 20
Pasvalys 9 G 20
Plungė 9 G 19

Priekulė 9 G 19
Prienai 9 H 20
Radviliškis 9 G 20
Ramygala 9 G 20
Raseiniai 9 G 20
Rietavas 9 G 19
Rokiškis 9 G 21
Rusnė 9 G 19
Salantai 9 G 19
Skaudvilė 9 G 20
Skuodas 9 G 19
Smalininkai 9 G 20
Svėdasai 9 G 21
Šakiai 9 H 20
Šeduva 9 G 20
Šiauliai 9 G 20
Šilalė 9 G 19
Šilutė 9 G 19
Širvintos 9 G 20
Švenčionys 10 G 21
Tauragė 9 G 19
Telšiai 9 G 19
Trakai 9 H 20
Ukmergė 9 G 20
Utena 9 G 21
Užventis 9 G 20
Vabalninkas 9 G 20
Varniai 9 G 19
Varėna 9 H 20
Vievis 9 H 20
Vilkaviškis 9 H 20
Vilkija 9 G 20
Vilnius 9 H 21
Zarasai 10 G 21
Žagarė 9 G 20

M

Rabat 20 P 16
Valletta 21 P 16

MA

Aît-Youssef-ou-Ali 18 P 9
Al Hoceima 18 P 9
Allal-Tazi 18 Q 8
Annual 18 P 9
Ârbaoua 18 Q 8
Asilah 18 P 8
Bab-Taza 18 P 8
Beni-Hadifa 18 P 9
Brikcha 18 Q 8
Chefchaouen 18 P 8
Derdara 18 P 8
El Fendek 18 P 8
El Manzla 18 P 8
Et-Jebha 18 P 9
Ketama 18 Q 9
Ksar-el-Kebir 18 Q 8
Ksar-es-Seghir 18 P 8
Larache 18 P 8
Martil 18 P 8
Mdiq 18 P 8
Mechra-Bel-Ksiri 18 Q 8
Mechra-Ben-Ksiri 18 Q 8
Moulay-Bousselham 18 Q 8
Ouazzane 18 Q 8
Souk-el Arba-du-Rharb 18 Q 8
Souk-el-Arba-des-Beni-Hassan 18 P 8
Souk-el-Arba-du-Gharb 18 Q 8
Souk-Sebt-des-Beni-Gorfat 18 P 8
Souk-Tleta-du-Rharb 18 Q 8
Souk-Tleta-du-Rharb 18 Q 8
Tanger 18 P 8
Targa 18 P 8
Targuist 18 Q 9
Tetouan 18 P 8
Torres-de-Alealá 18 P 9
Zoumi 18 Q 8

MC

Monte Carlo 20 M 13

MD

Basarabeasca 16 L 22
Bălti 16 K 22
Briceni 15 K 21
Cahul 16 L 22
Camenca 16 K 22
Călăraşi 16 L 22
Căuşany 16 L 22
Ceadâr-Lunga 16 L 22
Chiperceni 16 K 22
Chişinau 16 L 22
Cimişlia 16 L 22
Comrat 16 L 22
Congaz 16 L 22
Coteşti 16 K 21
Donduşeni 16 K 22
Drochia 16 K 22
Dubašari 16 L 22

Sigulda 5 G 20
Skrunda 9 G 19
Smiltene 5 G 21
Strenči 5 F 21
Subate 10 G 21
Suntaži 5 G 20
Sãrnate 5 G 19
Špogi 10 G 21
Talsi 5 G 20
Tukums 5 G 20
Ugãle 5 G 19
Valdemārpils 5 G 20
Valka 5 F 21
Valmiera 5 F 21
Varaklãni 10 G 21
Vecpiebalga 5 G 21
Velēna 10 G 21
Ventspils 5 G 19
Viesīte 9 G 21
Viļaka 10 G 22
Viļāni 10 G 21
Vireši 10 G 21
Zilupe 10 G 22

LV

Ãdaži 5 G 20
Ainaži 5 F 20
Aizpute 9 G 19
Aloja 5 F 20
Alūksne 10 G 21
Ape 10 F 21
Auce 9 G 20
Balvi 10 G 21
Bārbele 9 G 20
Bauska 9 G 20
Beļauski 10 G 21
Cēsis 5 G 21
Dagda 10 G 22
Daugavpils 10 G 21
Dobele 9 G 20
Dundaga 5 F 19
Dunte 5 G 20
Eleja 9 G 20
Engure 5 G 20
Ērgli 5 G 21
Grobina 9 G 19
Gulbene 10 G 21
Iecava 9 G 20
Ilūkste 10 G 21
Jaunjelgava 9 G 21
Jaunpils 9 G 20
Jēkabpils 10 G 21
Jelgava 9 G 20
Jūrmala 5 G 20
Kalnciems 5 G 20
Kãrsava 10 G 22
Kekava 5 G 20
Kisa 5 G 20
Kolka 5 F 20
Krãslava 10 G 21
Kuldiga 5 G 19
Lielvãrde 5 G 20
Liepaja 9 G 19
Limbaži 5 G 20
Līvāni 10 G 21
Ludza 10 G 22
Madona 10 G 21
Malta 10 G 21
Nereta 9 G 21
Nica 9 G 19
Nītaure 5 G 21
Olaine 5 G 20
Oviši 5 F 19
Piltene 5 G 19
Pļaviņas 9 G 21
Preiļi 10 G 21
Priekule 9 G 19
Pāvilosta 5 G 19
Roja 5 G 20
Rūjiena 5 F 21
Rézekne 10 G 21
Sabile 5 G 20
Salacgrīva 5 F 20
Salaspils 5 G 20
Saldus 9 G 19
Saulkrasti 5 G 20

MK

Berovo 22 N 20
Bitola 22 N 19
Brod 22 N 19
Debar 21 N 19
Delčevo 22 N 20
Demir Kapija 22 N 19
Dolenci 22 N 19
Gevgelija 22 N 20
Gostivar 21 N 19
Kavadarci 22 N 19
Kičevo 21 N 19
Kočani 22 N 19
Kriva Palanka 22 N 19
Kumanovo 22 N 19
Negotino 22 N 19
Ohrid 21 N 19
Prilep 22 N 19
Radoviš 22 N 19
Resen 22 N 19
Skopje 22 N 19
Štip 22 N 19
Stracin 22 N 19
Struga 22 N 19
Strumica 22 N 20
Tetovo 22 N 19
Veles 22 N 19

MNE

Bar/Podgorica 21 N 18
Berane 21 M 18
Bijelo Polje 21 M 18
Budva 21 N 18
Cetinje 21 N 18
Danilovgrad 21 M 18
Herceg-Novi 21 N 18
Kolašin 21 M 18
Kotor 21 N 18
Mojkovac 21 M 18
Murino 21 M 18
Nikšić 21 M 18
Petrovac 21 N 18
Pljevlja 21 M 18
Podgorica 21 N 18
Risan 21 M 18
Rožaje 21 M 19
Šavnik 21 M 18
Ulcinj 21 N 18
Žabljak 21 M 18

N

Alta 3 B 20
Alta 3 B 20
Alvdal 4 E 15
Andselv 3 B 18
Arendal 4 F 14
Askvoll 4 E 13
Aurlandsvangen 4 E 13
Beiarn 2 C 16
Bekken 4 E 15
Bergen 7 E 13
Berkåk 4 D 15
Berlevåg 3 A 22
Bilto 3 B 19
Bismo 4 E 14
Bjelland 4 F 14
Bjerkreim 7 F 13
Bjerkvik 3 B 18
Bjørkelangen 4 F 15
Bjørkåsen 2 B 17

Edinet 16 K 21
Fãleşti 16 K 22
Floreşti 16 K 22
Grigoripol 16 L 22
Hânceşti 16 L 22
Leova 16 L 22
Leuşeni 16 L 22
Orhei 16 L 22
Rãzeni 16 L 22
Râbniţa 16 K 22
Rãşcani 16 K 22
Rezina 16 K 22
Sãngerei 16 K 22
Slobozia/Tiraspol' 16 L 22
Soroca 16 K 22
Strãşeni 16 L 22
Taraclia 16 L 22
Tighina 16 L 22
Tiraspol 16 L 22
Ungheni 16 L 22
Vulcãneşti 16 L 22

Bodø · N · NL · P · PL · **Człuchów** · EU

Bodø 2 C 16
Bognes 2 B 17
Bonjåkas Tana 3 A 22
Brandal 4 E 13
Brandbu 4 E 15
Breivikbotn 3 A 19
Brekke 4 E 13
Brekken 4 D 15
Brekstad 4 D 14
Brimnes 4 E 13
Brostrud 4 E 14
Bryne 7 F 13
Brønnøysund 2 C 15
Bygdin 4 E 14
Byrkjelo 4 E 13
Båtsfjord 3 A 22
Dal 4 E 15
Dale 4 E 13
Dalseter 4 E 14
Dokka 4 E 15
Dombås 4 E 14
Drammen 4 F 15
Drangedal 4 F 14
Drøbak 4 F 15
Dyranut 4 E 14
Dyrnes (Vestsmøla) 4 D 14
Egersund 7 F 13
Eidfjord 4 E 13
Eidsdal 4 E 13
Eikelandsosen 7 E 13
Elverum 4 E 15
Enden 4 E 15
Enningdal 4 F 15
Ervik 4 E 13
Evje 4 F 14
Fagernes 4 E 14
Fagernes/Tromsö 3 B 18
Fauske 2 C 17
Femundsenden 4 E 15
Festøy 4 E 13
Fillan 4 D 14
Finnsnes 3 B 18
Fiskevollen 4 E 15
Flatebø 7 E 13
Flateland 4 F 14
Flekkefjord 7 F 13
Flesberg 4 F 14
Flisa 4 E 15
Florø 4 E 13
Foldereid 2 D 15
Folldal 4 E 14
Fossby 4 F 15
Fredrikstad 4 F 15
Fyresdal 4 F 14
Førde 4 E 13
Gamvik 3 A 22
Geilo 4 E 14
Gjøvik 4 E 15
Glomfjord 2 C 16
Gol 4 E 14
Gransherad 4 F 14
Grense Jakobselv 3 B 23
Grong 2 D 15
Grotli 4 E 14
Gryllefjord 3 B 17
Grøning 4 E 13
Gudvangen 4 E 13
Gullbrå 4 E 13
Gulsvik 4 E 14
Gvarv 4 F 14
Gåsbu 4 E 14
Hakadal 4 E 15
Halden 4 F 15
Halsvika 4 E 13
Hamar 4 E 15
Hamarøy Oppeid 2 B 17
Hammerfest 3 A 20
Hansnes 3 B 18
Harstad 2 B 17
Hasvik 3 A 19
Hattfjelldal 2 C 16
Hauge 4 E 13
Haugesund 7 F 13
Haukeligrend 4 F 14
Havrysund 3 A 20
Hella 4 E 13
Hellesylt 4 E 14
Hemsedal 4 E 14
Hjelmelandsvågen 7 F 13
Hjerkinn 4 E 14
Holmen 4 E 15
Holøydal 4 E 15
Honningsvåg 3 A 21
Horda 4 E 13
Horten 4 F 15
Hvittingfoss 4 F 15
Hyen 4 E 13
Hægeland 4 F 14
Hønefoss 4 E 15
Jektvika 2 C 16
Jordet 4 E 15

Jostedal 4 E 13
Junkerdal 2 C 17
Kaldfjord 3 B 18
Kalhovd 4 E 14
Kampeseter 4 E 14
Karasjok 3 B 21
Kaupanger 4 E 13
Kautokeino 3 B 20
Kinsarvik 4 E 13
Kirkenes 3 B 22
Kjøllefjord 3 A 21
Kolvereid 2 D 15
Kongsberg 4 F 14
Kongsvinger 4 E 15
Koparnes 4 E 13
Kopervik 7 F 13
Koppang 4 E 15
Kopperå 4 D 15
Korgen 2 C 16
Kragerø 4 F 14
Kristiansand 4 F 14
Kristiansund 4 D 14
Kroken 2 C 16
Kvalsund 3 A 20
Kvanndal 4 E 13
Kvinlog 7 F 13
Kyrksäterøra 4 D 14
Kåfjord 3 A 21
Lakselv 3 A 20
Langeid 4 E 14
Langevåg 7 F 13
Larvik 4 F 14
Leirmoen 2 C 16
Leirvik 7 F 13
Leknes 2 B 16
Leksvik 4 D 15
Lena 4 E 15
Lesjaskog 4 E 14
Levanger 4 D 15
Lillehammer 4 E 15
Lillesand 4 F 14
Lillestrøm 4 F 15
Lom 4 E 14
Lunde 4 F 14
Lutnes 4 E 16
Lyngdal 7 F 13
Lyngseidet 3 B 19
Lærdalsøyri 4 E 14
Løding 4 E 13
Lødingen 2 B 17
Løfallsstranda 7 F 13
Magnor 4 F 15
Malm 4 D 15
Mandal 4 F 14
Mehamn 3 A 22
Melbu 2 B 16
Mjølfjell 4 E 13
Mo i Rana 2 C 16
Moen 4 E 15
Moi 7 F 13
Molde 4 D 13
Mosjøen 2 C 16
Moss 4 F 15
Myre 2 B 17
Myre/Andöya 2 B 17
Mysen 4 F 15
Måløy 4 E 13
Namsos 2 D 15
Narvik 3 B 17
Nedstrand 7 F 13
Neiden 3 B 22
Nes 4 E 14
Nesbyen 4 E 14
Nesflaten 4 F 14
Nesna 2 C 16
Nordfjordeid 4 E 13
Nordfold 2 B 17
Nordkjosbotn 3 B 18
Norheimsund 7 E 13
Notodden 4 F 14
Nybergsund 4 E 15
Nyruti 3 B 22
Nyseter 4 E 14
Nåra 4 E 12
Oanes 7 F 13
Odda 7 E 13
Olderdalen 3 B 19
Olderfjord 3 A 20
Oppdal 4 D 14
Oppsjøhytta 4 E 14
Orkanger 4 D 14
Oslo 4 F 15
Otta 4 E 14
Porsgrunn 4 F 14
Randsverk 4 E 14
Rena 4 E 15
Ringebu 4 E 15
Risør 4 F 14
Rjukan 4 F 14
Rognan 2 C 17
Rosendal 7 F 13

Rossnes 4 E 12
Rødberg 4 E 14
Røros 4 D 15
Rørvik 2 D 16
Røssvassbukta 2 C 16
Røyrvik 2 D 16
Sand/Kongsvinger 4 E 15
Sand/Ølen 7 F 13
Sande 4 F 15
Sandefjord 4 F 15
Sandnes 7 F 13
Sandnessjøen 2 C 16
Sandvika 2 D 16
Sarpsborg 4 F 15
Sauda 7 F 13
Selbu 4 D 15
Seljord 4 F 14
Setermoen 3 B 18
Sinnes 7 F 13
Skarnes 4 E 15
Skarsvåg 3 A 21
Ski 4 F 15
Skibotn 3 B 19
Skien 4 F 14
Skjervøy 3 A 19
Skjolden 4 E 14
Skogmo 2 D 15
Skorovatn 2 D 16
Skudeneshavn 7 F 13
Skånevik 7 F 13
Smedland 4 F 14
Snåsa 4 D 15
Solhom 7 F 13
Solvorn 4 E 13
Sortland 2 B 17
Stathelle 4 F 15
Stavanger 7 F 13
Steine 2 B 16
Steinkjer 4 D 15
Steinsland 2 B 17
Steinstø 4 E 13
Stjørdal 4 D 15
Stor Elvdal 4 E 15
Storforshei 2 C 16
Storslett 3 B 19
Storsteinnes 3 B 18
Stranda 4 E 13
Straumen 2 C 17
Stryn 4 E 13
Stuggudalen 4 D 15
Støren 4 D 15
Sund 7 E 13
Sunde 7 F 13
Sunndalsøra 4 D 14
Surnadalsøra 4 D 14
Svanvik 3 B 22
Svelgen 4 E 13
Svelvik 4 F 15
Svenes 4 F 14
Svolvær 2 B 16
Svullrya 4 E 15
Sykkylven 4 E 13
Sørli 4 D 16
Sørstraumen 3 B 19
Sørvågen 2 B 16
Talvik 3 A 20
Tana bru 3 A 22
Tau 7 F 13
Terråk 2 C 15
Tingvoll 4 D 14
Titran 4 D 14
Tonstad 7 F 13
Tresfjord 4 E 13
Tretten 4 E 15
Trofors 2 C 16
Tromsø 3 B 18
Trondheim 4 D 15
Tvedestrand 4 F 14
Tveitsund 4 F 14
Tyin 4 E 14
Tynset 4 E 15
Tømmerneset 2 B 17
Tønsberg 4 F 15
Ulsberg 4 D 14
Ulsvåg 2 B 17
Ulvik 4 E 13
Vadheim 4 E 13
Vadsø 3 A 22
Varangerbotn 3 A 22
Vardø 3 A 22
Varhaug 7 F 13
Veggli 4 E 14
Veidnes 3 A 21
Verdalsøra 4 D 15
Vestbygd 7 F 13
Vikanes 4 E 13
Vikersund 4 F 15
Vikøyri 4 E 13
Volda 4 E 13
Vormsund 4 E 15

Voss 4 E 13
Våge 7 E 13
Vågåmo 4 E 14
Øksfjord 3 A 19
Ølen 7 F 13
Ørnes 2 C 16
Ørje 4 F 15
Øverbygd 3 B 18
Øvre Rendal 4 E 15
Ådneram 4 F 13
Åfarnes 4 D 13
Åknes 4 F 14
Ålesund 4 E 13
Ålgård 7 F 13
Åmli 4 F 14
Åmot 4 F 14
Åndalsnes 4 D 14
Årdalstangen 4 E 14
Årnes 4 D 15
Åsly 4 D 14

NL

Alkmaar 7 H 12
Amersfoort 7 J 13
Amsterdam 7 J 12
Apeldoorn 7 J 13
Arnhem 7 J 13
Assen 7 H 13
Bergen 7 J 12
Boxmeer 7 J 13
Breda 7 J 12
Delfzijl 7 H 13
Deventer 7 J 13
Doetinchem 7 J 13
Dordrecht 7 J 12
Drachten 7 H 13
den Helder 7 H 12
Ede 7 J 13
Eindhoven 13 J 13
Emmen 7 H 13
Enkhuizen 7 H 13
Enschede 7 J 13
Gorinchem 7 J 13
Gouda 7 J 12
Groningen 7 H 13
Haarlem 7 J 12
Harderwijk 7 J 13
Harlingen 7 H 13
Heerenveen 7 H 13
Heerlen 13 J 13
Helmond 13 J 13
Hengelo 7 J 13
Hilversum 7 J 13
Hoek van Holland 7 J 12
Holwerd 7 H 13
Hoogeveen 7 H 13
Hoogezand-Sappemeer 7 H 13
Kampen 7 J 13
Knokke 7 J 12
Leeuwarden 7 H 13
Leiden 7 J 12
Maastricht 13 J 13
Meppel 7 H 13
Middelburg 7 J 12
Nijmegen 7 J 13
Oostvoorne 7 J 12
Oss 7 J 13
Rotterdam 7 J 12
Sneek 7 H 13
Steenbergen 7 J 12
s-Gravenhage (den Haag)
   7 J 12
s-Hertogenbosch 7 J 13
Terneuzen 12 J 12
Tilburg 7 J 13
Utrecht 7 J 13
Valkenswaard 13 J 13
Venlo 13 J 13
Weert 13 J 13
Winschoten 7 H 13
Winterswijk 7 J 13
Zaandam 7 J 12
Zierikzee 7 J 12
Zutphen 7 J 13
Zwolle 7 J 13

P

Abrantes 18 O 7
Albergaria-a - Velha 18 N 7
Albufeira 18 O 7
Alcácer do Sal 18 O 7
Aljezur 18 P 7
Aljustrel 18 O 7
Almada 18 O 7
Almodôvar 18 O 7

Alpalhão 18 O 7
Alter do Chão 18 O 7
Amadora 18 O 7
Amarante 18 N 7
Arraiolos 18 O 7
Aveiro 18 N 7
Avis 18 O 7
Barca de Alva 18 N 8
Barranco Velho 18 P 7
Barrancos 18 O 8
Barreiro 18 O 7
Baúlhe 18 N 7
Beja 18 O 7
Braga 18 N 7
Bragança 18 N 8
Caldas da Rainha 18 O 7
Caminha 18 N 7
Carregado 18 O 7
Cascais 18 O 7
Castelo Branco 18 O 8
Castelo de Paiva 18 N 7
Castro Daire 18 N 7
Castro Verde 18 O 7
Celorico da Beira 18 N 8
Cercal 18 O 7
Chaves 18 N 8
Coimbra 18 N 7
Comporta 18 O 7
Condeixa 18 N 7
Coruche 18 O 7
Covilhã 18 N 8
Cruzamento Pegões 18 O 7
Elvas 18 O 8
Ericeira 18 O 7
Espinho 18 N 7
Esposende 18 N 7
Estoril 18 O 7
Estremoz 18 O 7
Évora 18 O 7
Faro 18 P 7
Fátima 18 O 7
Ferreira do Alentejo 18 O 7
Figueira da Foz 18 N 7
Galegos 18 O 8
Grândola 18 O 7
Guarda 18 N 8
Guimarães 18 N 7
Lagoaça 18 N 8
Lagos 18 P 7
Lamego 18 N 7
Lavre 18 O 7
Leiria 18 O 7
Lindoso 18 N 7
Lisboa 18 O 7
Loulé 18 P 7
Macedo de Cavaleiros 18 N 8
Mangualde 18 N 7
Marateca 18 O 7
Marinha Grande 18 O 7
Matosinhos 18 N 7
Mealhada 18 N 7
Melgaco 18 N 7
Mértola 18 O 7
Mira 18 N 7
Miranda do Douro 18 N 8
Mirandela 18 N 8
Mogadouro 18 N 8
Moncão 18 N 7
Monchique 18 P 7
Monforte 18 O 8
Monfortinho 18 O 8
Monsanto 18 N 8
Montemor o-Novo 18 O 7
Montijo\Lisboa 18 O 7
Mora 18 O 7
Moura 18 O 8
Mourão 18 O 8
Murça 18 N 8
Nazaré 18 O 7
Odemira 18 O 7
Ourique 18 O 7
Ovar 18 N 7
Pampilhosa da Serra 18 N 7
Penamacor 18 N 8
Peniche 18 O 7
Pinhel 18 N 8
Pombal 18 O 7
Pontão 18 O 7
Ponte de Barca 18 N 7
Ponte de Sor 18 O 7
Portalegre 18 O 8
Portel 18 O 7
Portimão 18 P 7
Pôrto 18 N 7
Póvoa de Varzim 18 N 7
Proença a Nova 18 O 7
Rebordelo 18 N 8
Redondo 18 O 7
Reguengos-de-Monsaraz
   18 O 7
Rio Maior 18 O 7

Sabóia 18 P 7
Sabugal 18 N 8
Sagres 18 P 7
Santa Comba Dão 18 N 7
Santa Luzia 18 O 7
Santarém 18 O 7
Santiago 18 N 7
Santiago do Cacém 18 O 7
Santo Tirso 18 N 7
São Bartolomeu de Messines
   18 P 7
Sao João da Madeira 18 N 7
São Pedro 18 N 7
Segura 18 O 8
Sernancelhe 18 N 8
Serpa 18 O 7
Sertã 18 O 7
Sesimbra 18 O 7
Setúbal 18 O 7
Silvares 18 N 7
Sines 18 O 7
Sintra 18 O 7
Tavira 18 P 7
Tomar 18 O 7
Torrão 18 O 7
Torre de Moncervo 18 N 8
Torres Novas 18 O 7
Torres Vedras 18 O 7
Valença 18 N 7
Venda Nova 18 N 7
Viana de Castelo 18 N 7
Viana do Alentejo 18 O 7
Vieira 18 N 7
Vila Franca de Xira 18 O 7
Vila Nova de Gaia 18 N 7
Vila Pouca de Aguiar 18 N 7
Vila Real/Huelva 18 P 8
Vila Real/PÔRTO 18 N 7
Vila Velha de Rôdão 18 O 7
Vila Verde de Ficalho 18 O 8
Vilar Formoso 18 N 8
Vinhais 18 N 8
Viseu 18 N 7

PL

Annopol 15 J 19
Augustów 9 H 20
Barlinek 8 H 17
Bartoszyce 9 H 19
Barwinek 15 K 19
Bełchatów 14 J 18
Bełżyce 15 J 19
Biała Podlaska 9 J 20
Białobrzegi 15 J 19
Białogard 8 H 17
Białowieża 9 H 20
Biały Bór 8 H 17
Białystok 9 H 20
Bielsk Podl. 9 H 20
Bielsko-Biała 14 K 18
Biłgoraj 15 J 19
Biskupiec 9 H 19
Błaszki 14 J 18
Błonie 9 J 19
Bobolice 8 H 17
Bochnia 15 K 19
Bolesławiec 14 J 17
Braniewo 9 H 19
Brańsk 9 H 20
Brodnica 9 H 18
Brusy 9 H 18
Brzeg 14 J 17
Brzozów 15 K 19
Busko Zdrój 15 J 19
Bychawa 15 J 20
Bydgoszcz 9 H 18
Bytom 14 J 18
Bytów 9 H 18
Chelm 15 J 20
Chełmno 9 H 18
Chełmża 9 H 18
Chodzież 8 H 17
Chojna 8 H 16
Chojnice 9 H 18
Chojnów 14 J 17
Chorzele 9 H 19
Choszczno 8 H 17
Chrzanów 14 J 18
Ciechanów 9 H 19
Ciechocinek 9 H 18
Cieszyn 14 K 18
Cisna 15 K 19
Czaplinek 8 H 17
Czarnków 8 H 17
Czersk 9 H 18
Częstochowa 14 J 18
Człopa 8 H 17
Człuchów 9 H 17

Darłowo   PL · RKS · RO   Suceava

Darłowo 8 H 17
Dąbrowa Białostocka 9 H 20
Dąbrowa Tarn. 15 J 19
Dębica 15 K 19
Dęblin 15 J 19
Dębno 8 H 16
Dobre Miasto 9 H 19
Drawsko Pomorskie 8 H 17
Drezdenko 8 H 17
Drobin 9 H 18
Dynów 15 K 19
Działdowo 9 H 19
Dzierzgoń 9 H 18
Dzierżoniów 14 J 17
Dziwnów 8 H 16
Elbląg 9 H 18
Ełk 9 H 19
Garwolin 15 J 19
Gdańsk 9 H 18
Gdynia 9 H 18
Giżycko 9 H 19
Glinojeck 9 H 19
Gliwice 14 J 18
Głogów 14 J 17
Głowno 14 J 18
Głubczyce 14 J 18
Głuchołazy 14 J 17
Gniezno 9 H 18
Goleniów 8 H 16
Golub - Dobrzyń 9 H 18
Gołdap 9 H 19
Gorlice 15 K 19
Gorzów Wlkp. 8 H 17
Gostynin 9 J 18
Gostyń 14 J 17
Górowo Iławeckie 9 H 19
Grajewo 9 H 19
Grodków 14 J 17
Grójec 15 J 19
Grudziądz 9 H 18
Gryfice 8 H 17
Gryfino 8 H 16
Gubin 14 J 16
Hajnówka 9 H 20
Hel 9 H 18
Hrubieszów 15 J 20
Iława 9 H 18
Iłża 15 J 19
Inowrocław 9 H 18
Izbica 9 J 18
Jalówka 9 H 20
Janów Lubelski 15 J 19
Jarocin 14 J 18
Jarosław 15 K 20
Jasło 15 K 19
Jastrowie 8 H 17
Jawor 14 J 17
Jelenia Góra 14 J 17
Jezewo 9 H 20
Jędrzejów 14 J 19
Kalisz 14 J 18
Kalisz Pomorski 8 H 17
Kamienna Góra 14 J 17
Kamieńsk 14 J 18
Kartuzy 9 H 18
Katowice 14 J 18
Kędzierzyn-Koźle 14 J 18
Kępno 14 J 18
Kętrzyn 9 H 19
Kętrzyn 9 H 19
Kęty 14 K 18
Kielce 15 J 19
Kluczbork 14 J 18
Kłobuck 14 J 18
Kłodzko 14 J 17
Kock 15 J 19
Kolbuszowa 15 J 19
Kolno 9 H 19
Kołbiel 9 J 19
Koło 9 J 18
Kołobrzeg 8 H 17
Komańcza 15 K 19
Koniecpol 14 J 18
Konin 9 J 18
Końskie 14 J 19
Koronowo 9 H 18
Korycin 9 H 20
Kostrzyń nad Odra 8 H 16
Koszalin 8 H 17
Kościan 9 H 18
Kościerzyna 9 H 18
Kozienice 15 J 19
Kraków 14 J 18
Krapkowice 14 J 18
Krasnystaw 15 J 20
Kraśnik 15 J 20
Krosno 15 K 19
Krosno Odrzańskie 8 J 17
Krośniewice 9 J 18
Krotoszyn 14 J 17
Krynica Zdrój 15 K 19

Krynki 9 H 20
Kurów 15 J 19
Kutno 9 J 18
Kwidzyn 9 H 18
Legionowo 9 J 19
Legnica 14 J 17
Leszno 14 J 17
Leżajsk 15 J 19
Lębork 9 H 18
Lidzbark Warmiński 9 H 19
Limanowa 15 K 19
Lipno 9 H 18
Lipsko 15 J 19
Lubaczów 15 J 20
Lubartów 15 J 20
Lubań 14 J 17
Lubin 14 J 17
Lublin 15 J 20
Lubliniec 14 J 18
Lubsko 14 J 16
Lubycza Królowska 15 J 20
Łagów 15 J 19
Łańcut 15 J 19
Łapy 9 H 20
Łeba 9 H 18
Łęczyca 9 J 18
Łochów 14 J 19
Łomża 9 H 19
Łosice 9 J 20
Łowicz 9 J 18
Łódź 14 J 18
Łuków 15 J 19
Maków Maz. 9 H 19
Malbork 9 H 18
Miastko 8 H 17
Miechów 14 J 19
Mielec 15 J 19
Międzychód 8 H 17
Międzylesie 14 J 17
Międzyrzec Podl. 9 J 20
Międzyrzecz 8 J 17
Milicz 14 J 17
Milówka 14 K 18
Mińsk Mazowiecki 9 J 19
Mława 9 H 19
Mogilno 9 H 18
Mońki 9 H 20
Morag 9 H 18
Mrągowo 9 H 19
Mszczonów 15 J 19
Myszyniec 9 H 19
Myślenice 14 K 18
Nakło 9 H 18
Namysłów 14 J 18
Nidzica 9 H 19
Nisko 15 J 19
Nowa Huta 14 J 19
Nowa Ruda 14 J 17
Nowa Sól 14 J 17
Nowe 9 H 18
Nowe Miasto 15 J 19
Nowe Miasto Lubaw. 9 H 18
Nowe Warpno 8 H 16
Nowogard 8 H 17
Nowy Dwór Gdański 9 H 18
Nowy Dwór Maz. 9 J 19
Nowy Korczyn 15 J 19
Nowy Sącz 15 K 19
Nowy Targ 14 K 19
Nowy Tomyśl 8 J 17
Nur 9 H 19
Nysa 14 J 17
Oborniki 8 H 17
Okopy 9 H 19
Olecko 9 H 19
Olesno 14 J 18
Oleśnica 14 J 17
Olkusz 14 J 18
Olsztyn 9 H 19
Olsztynek 9 H 19
Oława 14 J 17
Opatów 15 J 19
Opoczno 14 J 19
Opole 14 J 18
Opole Lubelskie 15 J 19
Orneta 9 H 19
Orzysz 9 H 19
Ostrołęka 9 H 19
Ostrowiec Świętokrzyski
   15 J 19
Ostróda 9 H 18
Ostrów Maz. 9 H 19
Ostrów Wlkp. 14 J 18
Ostrzeszów 14 J 18
Pabianice 14 J 18
Pajęczno 14 J 18
Parczew 15 J 20
Pasłęk 9 H 18
Piaseczno 9 J 19
Piaski 15 J 20
Pilzno 15 K 19

Piła 8 H 17
Piotrków Tryb. 14 J 18
Pisz 9 H 19
Pleszew 14 J 18
Płock 9 H 18
Płońsk 9 H 19
Pniewy 8 H 17
Poddębice 14 J 18
Polanów 8 H 17
Police 8 H 16
Poznań 8 J 17
Proszowice 14 J 19
Prudnik 14 J 18
Pruszcz Gdański 9 H 18
Przasnysz 9 H 19
Przedbórz 14 J 19
Przemyśl 15 K 20
Przeworsk 15 J 20
Przysucha 15 J 19
Puck 9 H 18
Puławy 15 J 19
Pułtusk 9 H 19
Pyrzyce 8 H 16
Rabka Zdrój 14 K 18
Racibórz 14 J 18
Radom 15 J 19
Radomsko 14 J 18
Radziejów 9 H 18
Radzyń Podl 15 J 20
Rawa Mazowiecka 14 J 19
Rawicz 14 J 17
Rogoźno 8 H 17
Różan 9 H 19
Rybnik 14 J 18
Rychwał 9 J 18
Ryki 15 J 19
Rypin 9 H 18
Rzeszów 15 J 19
Sandomierz 15 J 19
Sanniki 9 J 18
Sanok 15 K 19
Sejny 9 H 19
Sępólno Kraj. 9 H 18
Siedlce 9 J 19
Siemiatycze 9 J 20
Sieradz 14 J 18
Sierpc 9 H 18
Skarżysko-Kamienna 15 J 19
Skierniewice 14 J 19
Sławno 8 H 17
Słubice 8 J 16
Słupca 9 H 18
Słupsk 9 H 17
Sochaczew 9 J 19
Sokołów Podlaski 9 J 19
Sokółka 9 H 20
Sopot 9 H 18
Sosnowiec 14 J 18
Stalowa Wola 15 J 19
Starachowice 15 J 19
Stargard Szczecinski 8 H 17
Starogard Gdański 9 H 18
Staszów 15 J 19
Stęszew 8 J 17
Stoczek 15 J 19
Strzegom 14 J 17
Strzelce Kraj. 8 H 17
Strzelce Opol. 14 J 18
Strzelin 14 J 17
Strzelno 9 H 18
Strzyżów 15 K 19
Sucha Beskidzka 14 K 18
Suchorze 9 H 17
Sulechów 8 J 17
Sulęcin 8 J 17
Suwałki 9 H 20
Syców 14 J 18
Szamotuły 8 H 17
Szczecin 8 H 16
Szczecinek 8 H 17
Szczekociny 14 J 18
Szczerców 14 J 18
Szczytno 9 H 19
Szprotawa 14 J 17
Szypliszki 9 H 20
Śrem 8 J 17
Środa Ślaska 14 J 17
Środa Wielkopolska 9 J 17
Świdnica 14 J 17
Świdwin 8 H 17
Świebodzin 8 J 17
Świecie 9 H 18
Świnoujście 8 H 16
Tarnobrzeg 15 J 19
Tarnów 15 J 19
Tczew 9 H 18
Terespol 9 J 20
Tomaszów Lub. 15 J 20
Tomaszów Maz. 14 J 19
Toruń 9 H 18
Torzym 8 J 17

Trzcianka 8 H 17
Trzebiatów 8 H 17
Trzebnica 14 J 17
Tuchola 9 H 18
Turek 9 J 18
Tychy 14 J 18
Ústka 9 H 17
Ustrzyki Dolne 15 K 20
Ustrzyki Górne 15 K 20
Wadowice 14 K 18
Wałbrzych 14 J 17
Wałcz 8 H 17
Warszawa 9 J 19
Wąbrzezno 9 H 18
Wągrowiec 9 H 17
Wejherowo 9 H 18
Węgorzewo 9 H 19
Węgrów 9 J 19
Wieluń 14 J 18
Wieruszów 14 J 18
Wilga 15 J 19
Wisznice 15 J 20
Witków 15 J 20
Władysławowo 9 H 18
Włocławek 9 H 18
Włodawa 15 J 20
Włoszczowa 14 J 18
Wodzisław Śl. 14 K 18
Wolin 8 H 16
Wolsztyn 8 J 17
Wołów 14 J 17
Wrocław 14 J 17
Wronki 8 H 17
Września 9 J 18
Wschowa 14 J 17
Wyrzysk 9 H 17
Wyszków 9 H 19
Wyszogród 9 J 19
Zabrze 14 J 18
Zakopane 14 K 18
Zambrów 9 H 19
Zamość 15 J 20
Zawiercie 14 J 18
Ząbkowice Śląskie 14 J 17
Zblewo 9 H 18
Zduńska Wola 14 J 18
Zgierz 14 J 18
Zgorzelec 14 J 17
Zielona Góra 14 J 17
Ziębice 14 J 17
Złoczew 14 J 18
Złotoryja 14 J 17
Złotów 9 H 17
Zory 14 J 18
Zwoleń 15 J 19
Żagań 14 J 17
Żary 14 J 17
Żnin 9 H 18
Żuromin 9 H 18
Żyrardów 9 J 19
Żywiec 14 K 18

RKS

Besianë 22 M 19
Ferizaj 22 N 19
Gjakovë 21 N 19
Gjilan 22 N 19
Kaçanik 22 N 19
Leposaviq 21 M 19
Mitrovicë 21 M 19
Pejë 21 M 19
Prishtinë 22 M 19
Prizren 21 N 19

RO

Abrud 15 L 20
Adjud 16 L 21
Agnita 15 L 20
Aiud 15 L 20
Alba Iulia 15 L 20
Aleşd 15 L 19
Alexandria/Ruse 22 M 21
Anina 15 L 19
Arad 15 L 19
Avrig 15 L 20
Babadag 16 M 22
Bacău 16 L 21
Baia de Aramă 15 M 20
Baia Mare 15 K 20
Baia Sprie 15 K 20
Balaci 15 M 20
Balş 15 M 20
Băile Herculane 15 M 20
Băileşti 22 M 20
Bălăneşti 15 M 20

Bălăuseri 15 L 20
Bălteni 15 M 20
Bărăganul 16 M 22
Bârlad 16 L 22
Bechet 22 M 20
Beiuş 15 L 19
Beliş 15 L 20
Benesat 15 L 20
Bergeşti-Ciocadio 15 L 20
Bicaz 15 L 21
Biharia 15 L 19
Bistreţ 22 M 20
Bistriţa 15 L 21
Blaj 15 L 20
Bocşa 15 L 19
Borsec 15 L 21
Borşa 15 L 20
Botoşani 15 K 21
Brad 15 L 20
Braşov 15 L 21
Brăila 16 L 22
Breaza 15 L 21
Broşteni/Vatra Dornei 15 L 21
Broţteni/Drobeta-Turnu Severin
   15 M 20
Bucureşti 15 M 21
Budeşti 16 M 21
Buhuşi 15 L 21
Bumbeşti-Jiu 15 L 20
Buru 15 L 20
Buşteni 15 L 21
Buteni 15 L 19
Buzău 16 L 21
Calafat 22 M 20
Caracal 15 M 20
Caransebeş 15 L 19
Carei 15 K 19
Călăraşi 16 M 21
Căpruţa 15 L 19
Câmpeni 15 L 20
Câmpina 15 L 21
Câmpul lui Neag 15 L 20
Câmpulung 15 L 21
Câmpulung Moldovenesc
   15 K 21
Câmpuri 16 L 21
Cârlibaba 15 K 21
Ceica 15 L 19
Cernavoda 16 M 22
Chişineu Criş 15 L 19
Clinen 15 L 20
Cleanov 15 M 20
Cluj Napoca 15 L 20
Cobadin 16 M 22
Cogealac 16 M 22
Comăneşti 15 L 21
Constanţa 16 M 22
Corabia 22 M 20
Corneşti 15 M 21
Covasna 15 L 21
Craiova 15 M 20
Crasna 16 L 22
Crevedia Mare 15 M 21
Cristuru Secuiesc 15 L 21
Curtea-de Argeş 15 L 20
Dej 15 L 20
Deta 15 L 19
Deva 15 L 20
Dobreşti 22 M 20
Dorohoi 15 K 21
Dragomireşti 16 L 21
Drăgaşani 15 M 20
Drăgăneşti Vlaşca 15 M 21
Drăguseni 16 L 22
Drobeta-Turnu Severin 15 M 20
Eforie Sud 16 M 22
Făgăraş 15 L 21
Făget 15 L 19
Fălciu 16 L 22
Fălticeni 15 L 21
Feteşti 16 M 22
Filiaşi 15 M 20
Focşani 16 L 21
Foeni 15 L 19
Galaţi 16 L 22
Găeşti 15 M 21
Gheorgheni 15 L 21
Gherla 15 L 20
Gilău 15 L 20
Giubega 22 M 20
Giurgeni 16 M 22
Giurgiu 22 M 21
Gura Humorului 15 K 21
Halmeu 15 K 20
Haţeg 15 L 20
Hârlău 15 L 21
Hârşova 16 M 22
Horezu 15 L 20
Huedin 15 L 20
Hunedoara 15 L 20
Hurezani 15 M 20

Huşi 16 L 22
Ianca 16 L 22
Iaşi 16 L 22
Ilia 15 L 20
Ineu 15 L 19
Ion Roată 16 M 21
Isaccea 16 L 22
Iveşti 16 L 22
Jebel 15 L 19
Jimbolia 15 L 19
Lăpuşna 15 L 21
Lipova 15 L 19
Luduş 15 L 20
Lugoj 15 L 19
Lunca de Sus 15 L 21
Lupşanu 16 M 21
Ion-Corvin 16 M 22
Ioneşti 15 M 20
Mamaia 16 M 22
Mangalia 16 M 22
Manoleasa 15 K 21
Marghita 15 L 19
Măcin 16 L 22
Măieruş 15 L 21
Mărăşeşti 16 L 21
Medgidia 16 M 22
Mediaş 15 L 20
Micfalău 15 L 21
Miercurea Ciuc 15 L 21
Miercurea Sibiului 15 L 20
Mihăeşti 15 L 20
Mihăileşti 15 M 21
Mizil 15 M 21
Moldova Nouă 15 M 19
Morăşti 15 M 20
Mureşenii Bârgăului 15 L 20
Murighiol 16 M 22
Nădlac 15 L 19
Nănesti 16 L 21
Năşaud 15 L 20
Negreşti 16 L 21
Negreşti Oaş 15 K 20
Nehoiu 15 L 21
Oancea 16 L 22
Ocna-Mureş 15 L 20
Odorheiu Secuiesc 15 L 21
Olteniţa 16 M 21
Oneşti 16 L 21
Oradea 15 L 19
Oravita 15 L 19
Orăştie 15 L 20
Orşova 15 M 19
Orţişoara 15 L 19
Pascani 15 L 21
Petroşani 15 L 20
Piatra Neamţ 15 L 21
Piteşti 15 M 20
Ploieşti 15 M 21
Pogoanele 16 M 21
Poiana Langului 15 L 21
Puchenii Mari 15 M 21
Pucioasa 15 L 21
Puieşti 16 L 22
Raşeşti 16 L 22
Răcăciuni 16 L 21
Rădăuţi 15 K 21
Rădăuţi Prut 15 K 21
Răstoliţa 15 L 21
Râmnicu Sarat 16 L 21
Râmnicu-Vâlcea 15 L 20
Recea 15 M 20
Reghin 15 L 21
Reşiţa 15 L 19
Roman 16 L 21
Românaşi 15 L 20
Roşiori de Vede 15 M 21
Rupea 15 L 21
Salonta 15 L 19
Satu Mare 15 K 20
Săcueni 15 L 19
Sărmaşu 15 L 20
Sângeorz Băi 15 L 20
Sânnicolau Mare 15 L 19
Săvârşin 15 L 19
Sebeş 15 L 20
Seini 15 K 20
Sercaia 15 L 21
Sf. Gheorghe 15 L 21
Sfântu Gheorghe/Sulina
   16 M 22
Sibiu 15 L 20
Sighetu/Marmaţiei 15 K 20
Sighişoara 15 L 20
Sinaia 15 L 21
Siret 15 K 21
Slatina 15 M 20
Slobozia/Bucureşti 16 M 21
Sovata 15 L 21
Strehaia 15 M 20
Stupina 16 M 22
Suceava 15 K 21

Sulina   RO · RSM · RUS   Monastyrščina/Smolensk   EU

Sulina 16 L 22
Şimleu Silvaniei 15 L 20
Ştefăneşti 16 K 21
Ştei 15 L 19
Şugag 15 L 20
Târgovişte 15 M 21
Târtăşeşti 15 M 21
Tăşnad 15 L 20
Târgu Frumos 16 L 21
Târgu Jiu 15 L 20
Târgu Lapuş 15 L 20
Târgu Mures 15 L 20
Târgu Neamţ 15 L 21
Târgu Ocna 15 L 21
Târgu Secuiesc 15 L 21
Târnăveni 15 L 20
Tecuci 16 L 21
Teregova 15 L 19
Timişoara 15 L 19
Tinca 15 L 19
Topliţa 15 L 21
Topolovăţu Mare 15 L 19
Topraisar 16 M 22
Trifeşti 16 K 21
Tulcea 16 L 22
Turda 15 L 20
Turnu Măgurele 22 M 20
Urziceni 16 M 21
Valea lui Mihai 15 K 19
Vaslui 16 L 22
Vatra Dornei 15 L 21
Vălenii de Munte 15 L 21
Vârfurile 15 L 20
Vicovu de Sus 15 K 21
Victoria 15 L 20
Vişeu de Sus 15 K 20
Voineasa 15 L 20
Zalău 15 L 20
Zărneşti 15 L 21
Zimnicea 22 M 21

RSM

San Marino 20 M 15

RUS

Abinsk 17 M 26
Abramovka 11 J 27
Adler 17 M 26
Ageevo 11 H 25
Ahmetovskaja 17 M 27
Ahtyrskij 17 M 26
Aksaj 17 L 26
Aksaj 17 K 28
Alakurtti 3 C 23
Aleksandro-Nevskij 11 H 27
Aleksandrov 11 G 26
Aleksandrovka 17 L 26
Alekseevka 11 J 26
Aleksin 11 H 25
Algasovo 11 H 27
Anapa 17 M 25
Andreapol' 10 G 23
Andrejevo 11 G 27
Androniki 11 F 27
Anna 11 H 27
Antropovo 11 F 28
Apatity 3 B 24
Aprelevka 11 G 25
Apšeronsk 17 M 26
Ardatov 11 G 28
Arefino 11 F 26
Arhangel'skaja 17 L 27
Arhangel'skoe 11 J 27
Arhipo-Osipovka 17 M 26
Arhipovka 10 H 23
Arhys 17 M 27
Arkadak 11 J 28
Armavir 17 M 27
Arsen'evo 11 H 25
Arzamas 11 G 28
Aševo 10 G 22
Atjur'evo 11 H 28
Avilo-Uspenka 17 K 26
Azov 11 L 25
Babaevo 11 F 25
Babynino 11 H 25
Bad 11 G 28
Badinsk 11 H 28
Bagrationovsk 9 H 19
Balahna 11 G 28
Balašov 11 J 28
Baltijsk 9 H 18
Basilevo 11 G 27
Bašmakovo 11 H 28
Batajsk 17 L 26

Bateckij 10 F 23
Baturino 10 G 24
Begunicy 10 F 22
Belaja Glina 17 L 27
Belaja Kalitva 17 K 27
Belebëlka 10 F 23
Belev 11 H 25
Belgorod 11 J 25
Belinskij 11 H 28
Belorečensk 17 M 26
Belyj 10 G 24
Besedino 11 J 25
Beslenej 17 M 27
Betlica 11 H 24
Bežeck 11 F 25
Bibirevo 10 G 23
Bobrov 11 J 27
Bogorodsk 11 G 28
Bogučar 11 K 27
Bokovaja 11 G 29
Bokovskaja 17 K 27
Boksitogorsk 10 F 24
Bol. Ignatovo 11 H 29
Bol'šaja Arja 11 G 28
Bol'šaja Novinka 11 F 26
Bol'šoe Mares`evo 11 G 29
Bol'šoe Muraškino 11 G 28
Bolgatovo 10 G 22
Bolhov 11 H 25
Bologoe 10 F 24
Bologovo 10 G 23
Bol'šakovo 9 H 19
Bol'šaja Džalga 17 L 28
Bol'šaja Orlovka 17 L 27
Bol'šinka 17 K 27
Bol'šoe Alekseevskoe 11 G 26
Bol'šoe Medvedki 11 H 26
Bol'šoe Selo 11 F 26
Bol'šoe Soldatskoe 11 J 25
Bondari 11 H 27
Bor 11 G 28
Borinskoe 11 H 26
Borisoglebsk 11 J 27
Borisovka 11 J 25
Borjatino 11 H 26
Borodinskoe 5 E 22
Boroviči 10 F 24
Borovičič 10 F 22
Borovsk 11 G 25
Brejtovo 11 F 26
Brjansk 11 H 24
Brjuhoveckaja 17 L 26
Bronnicy 11 G 26
Budogošč' 10 F 23
Buj 11 F 27
Buturlino 11 G 28
Buturlinovka 11 J 27
Bytoš' 11 H 24
Caevo 11 F 25
Capel'ka 10 F 22
Čaplygin 11 H 27
Čehov 11 G 26
Čelbasskaja 17 L 26
Cerenskoe 11 F 25
Čerkessk 17 M 27
Černava 11 H 26
Cernjahovsk 9 H 19
Černjanka 11 J 26
Černuha 11 G 28
Čern' 11 H 25
Čerpovec 11 F 26
Cimljansk 17 K 27
Čkalovsk 11 G 28
Čudovo 10 F 23
Čupalejka 11 G 28
Čuvaševa Gora 10 F 25
Dahovskaja 17 M 27
Danilov 11 F 27
Dankov 11 H 26
Davydovo 11 G 26
Demidov 10 G 23
Demjansk 10 F 24
Detčino 11 H 25
Dinskaja 17 L 26
Diveevo 11 G 28
Djatkovo 11 H 24
Dmitriev-L'govskij 11 J 25
Dmitrievka 11 H 27
Dmitrov 11 G 26
Dmitrovsk-Orlovskij 11 H 25
Dneprovskoe 10 G 24
Dno 10 F 22
Dobrinka 11 J 27
Dobrjatino 11 G 27
Dobroe 11 H 26
Dobruči 10 F 22
Dolžanskaja 17 L 26
Dombaj 17 M 27
Domededovo 11 G 26
Doneck 17 K 27
Donskoe/Elec 11 H 26

Donskoe/Stavropol 17 L 27
Donskoj 11 H 26
Dorobino 11 H 26
Dorogobuž 10 H 24
Droskovo 11 H 25
Dubec 11 F 26
Dubna 11 G 25
Dubovka 17 K 28
Dubovskoe 17 L 28
Dubrovka 10 F 22
Dudorovskij 11 H 25
Duhovščina 10 G 24
Dulovka 10 G 22
Duminiči 11 H 25
Dvorki 11 G 26
Dzeržinsk 11 G 28
Džubga 17 M 26
Efremov 11 H 26
Egorlykskaja 17 L 27
Egor'e 11 G 27
Egor'evsk 11 G 26
Ejsk 17 L 26
Elan'-Kolennovskij 11 J 27
Elec 11 H 26
El'cy 10 G 24
El'niki 11 H 28
El'nja 10 H 24
Erahtur 11 H 27
Ermiš 11 H 27
Erši 11 H 24
Eršiči 10 H 24
Esenoviči 10 G 24
Estosadok 17 M 27
Evlanovo 11 J 26
Fatež 11 J 25
Fedorovka 17 L 26
Feofilova Pustyn` 10 F 22
Firovo 10 G 24
Fokino 11 H 24
Fominki 11 G 28
Fumanov 11 G 27
Gagarin 11 G 25
Gajutino 11 F 26
Galič 11 F 28
Gatčina 10 F 23
Gavrilov Posad 11 G 27
Gavrilov-Jam 11 G 27
Gdov 10 F 22
Gelendžik 17 M 26
Gigant 17 L 27
Glazunovka 11 H 25
Glebovskoe 11 G 26
Glubokij/Kamensk-Šahtinskij 17 K 27
Glubokij/Zimovniki 17 L 28
Gluškovo 11 J 24
Golicyno/Moskva 11 G 25
Golicyno/Nižnij Lomov 11 H 28
Golovinka 17 M 26
Gorbačevo 11 H 25
Goreloe 11 H 27
Goricy 11 G 25
Gorjačij Kljuc 17 M 26
Gorka-Voskresenskaja 10 F 24
Gorlovo 11 H 26
Gornjackij 17 K 27
Gorodec 11 G 28
Gorodišče/Staryj Oskol 11 J 26
Gorodnja 11 G 25
Gorodovikovsk 17 L 27
Gorohovec 11 G 28
Goršečnoe 11 J 26
Gračevka 17 L 27
Grajvoron 17 J 25
Grazi 11 H 27
Grebnevo 11 H 27
Gremjač'e 11 H 27
Grjady 10 F 23
Grjaznov 11 G 26
Grjazovec 11 F 27
Gubkin 11 J 26
Gukovo 17 K 26
Gul'keviči 17 L 27
Gusev 9 H 19
Gus'-Hrustal'nyj 11 G 27
Gvardejsk 9 H 19
Hadyžensk 17 M 26
Hahaly 11 G 28
Hiitola 5 E 22
Himki 11 G 26
Hlevnoe 11 H 26
Holm 10 G 23
Holm-Žirkovskij 10 G 24
Homutovo 11 H 26
Hosta 17 M 26
Hot'kovo 11 G 26
Hvaščevka 11 G 25

Hvastoviči 11 H 25
Hvojnaja 10 F 24
Ibnja 11 J 25
Igodovo 11 F 28
Il'inskaja 17 L 27
Il'skij 17 M 26
Il'insko-Zaborskoe 11 G 28
Ilovlja 17 K 28
Il'ino 10 G 23
Il'inskoe 11 G 25
Il'inskoe-Hovanskoe 11 G 26
Inkulino 11 F 28
Insar 11 H 28
Ipatovo 17 L 28
Irklievskaja 17 L 26
Issa 11 F 22
Istobnoe 11 J 26
Ivajtenki 11 H 24
Ivangorod 10 F 22
Ivanovo 11 G 27
Ivanovskaja 17 L 26
Izborsk 10 F 22
Izmalkovo 11 H 26
Iznoski 11 H 25
Izobil'nyj 17 L 27
im. M. I. Kalinia 11 F 29
Jadrin 11 G 29
Jahroma 11 G 26
Jakovlevo 11 J 25
Janiskoskij 3 B 22
Jarcevo 10 G 24
Jaroslavl' 11 F 27
Jaroslavskaja 17 M 27
Jašalta 17 L 27
Jaščera 10 F 22
Jasenskaja 17 L 26
Jasnogorsk 11 H 26
Jaželbicy 10 F 24
Juhnov 11 H 25
Jur`evec 11 G 28
Jurino 11 G 29
Jur'ev Pol'skiy 11 G 26
Juža 11 G 27
Kadom 11 H 28
Kaduj 11 F 26
Kadyj 11 F 28
Kalač 11 J 27
Kalač-na-Donu 17 K 28
Kalevala 3 C 23
Kaliningrad 9 H 19
Kaliningrad/Moskva 11 G 26
Kalinovka 11 J 24
Kaljazin 11 G 26
Kaluga 11 H 25
Kamenka 5 E 22
Kamenka/Kaluga 11 H 25
Kamenka/Ostrogožsk 11 J 26
Kamenka/Penza 11 H 28
Kamenka/Smolensk 10 G 23
Kamennogorsk 5 E 22
Kamensk-Šahtinskij 17 K 27
Kameškovo 11 G 27
Kamyševatskaja 17 L 26
Kandalakša 3 C 24
Kanevskaja 17 L 26
Kantemirovka 17 K 26
Karačaevsk 17 M 27
Karačev 11 H 25
Karginskaja 17 K 27
Karmanovo 11 G 25
Kašary 17 K 27
Kasimov 11 H 27
Kašin 11 G 26
Kašira 11 H 26
Kastornoe 11 J 26
Kastornoe 11 J 26
Kavkaz 17 L 25
Kazanskaja 11 K 27
Kernovo 10 F 22
Kesova Gora 11 F 25
Kesten'ga 3 C 23
Kes' ma 11 F 25
Klimovo 10 J 23
Kikvidze 11 J 28
Kilemary 11 G 29
Kil'dinsroj 3 B 24
Kimovsk 11 H 26
Kimry 11 G 26
Kinešma 11 G 27
Kingisepp 10 F 22
Kiriši 10 F 23
Kirov 11 H 24
Kirovsk/St. Petersburg 10 F 22
Kirsanov 11 H 28
Kiržač 11 G 26
Kletnja 11 H 24
Kletskij 17 K 28
Klimovsk 11 G 26
Klin 11 G 25
Klincy 10 H 23

Knjaginino 11 G 29
Kobona 10 F 23
Kočubeevskoe 17 M 27
Kohma 11 G 27
Kola 3 B 24
Koljubeevo 11 G 25
Kolomna 11 G 26
Kolpino 10 F 23
Kolpny 11 J 25
Kolp' 11 G 27
Kolvica 3 C 24
Kol'čugino 11 G 26
Komariči 11 J 24
Komsomol'sk 11 G 27
Konakovo 11 G 25
Končansko-Suvorovskoe 10 F 24
Kondrat'evo 5 E 22
Kondrovo 11 H 25
Konstantinovsk 17 K 27
Konyševka 11 J 25
Korablino 11 H 27
Korekozevo 11 H 25
Korenovsk 17 L 26
Koroča 11 J 25
Koronevo 11 J 24
Korotin 11 G 29
Kosaja Gora 11 H 26
Kosk 11 H 24
Koski/Roslavl' 10 H 24
Kosorža 11 J 25
Kostomukša 3 D 23
Kostroma 11 F 27
Kotel'nikovo 17 K 28
Kotly 10 F 22
Kotovras 11 J 28
Kotovsk 11 H 27
Kovdor 3 B 23
Kovernino 11 G 28
Kovrov 11 G 27
Kovylka 11 H 28
Kovylkino 11 H 28
Koz`modem`jansk 11 G 29
Kozel'sk 11 H 25
Kr. Karačay 17 M 27
Kr. Rog 11 H 24
Kr. Selo 10 F 23
Krasivka 11 H 28
Krasnaja Gora 10 H 23
Krasnji Baki 11 G 29
Krasnoarmejsk 11 G 26
Krasnoarmejskaja 17 L 26
Krasnoarmejski 17 L 27
Krasnodar 17 L 26
Krasnoe/Elec 11 H 26
Krasnogorodsk 10 G 22
Krasnogvardejskoe 17 L 27
Krasnolesnyj 11 J 26
Krasnolobodsk 11 H 28
Krasnoslobodsk 17 K 28
Krasnozavodsk 11 G 26
Krasnoznamensk 9 H 19
Krasnyi 10 H 23
Krasnyj Holm 11 F 25
Krasnyj Majak 11 G 27
Krasnyj Tkači 11 G 26
Krasuha 11 F 26
Krestcy 11 F 24
Kresty 11 G 25
Kresty/Tovarkovskij 11 H 26
Kriuša/Pervomajsk 11 H 28
Kriuša/Rjazan 11 H 27
Krivandino 11 G 26
Krivorož'e 17 K 27
Kromy 11 H 25
Kronštadt 10 F 22
Kropotkin 17 L 27
Krupec 11 J 24
Krusanovo 11 F 28
Krylovo 9 H 19
Krylovskaja 17 L 26
Krymsk 17 M 26
Kšenskij 11 J 26
Kstovo 11 G 28
Kudever' 10 G 22
Kugul'ta 17 L 27
Kujbyševo 17 K 26
Kukoboj 11 F 27
Kulebaki 11 G 28
Kulevatovo 11 H 27
Kun'ja 10 G 23
Kuolajarvi 3 C 22
Kupreevo 11 G 27
Kurdžinovo 17 M 27
Kurganinsk 17 M 27
Kurgannyj 17 L 28
Kurgolovo 10 F 22
Kurkino 11 H 26
Kurlovo 11 G 27
Kurovskoe 11 G 26
Kursk 11 J 25

Kušalino 11 G 25
Kuščevskaja 17 L 26
Kuševanda 3 C 23
Kuvšinovo 10 G 24
Kuženkino 10 F 24
Kuzovka 11 H 26
Kuz'miniči 11 H 24
Labinsk 17 M 27
Ladožskaja 17 L 26
Lahdenpoh`ja 5 E 22
Lakaš 11 H 27
Lakedemonovka 17 L 26
Lakinsk 11 G 27
Lazarevskoe 17 M 26
Lebedjan 11 H 26
Leningradskaja 17 L 26
Leont`evo 11 F 25
Lesnoe 11 F 25
Ležnevo 11 G 25
Lihoslavl' 11 G 25
Lihovskoj 17 K 27
Liinahamari 3 B 23
Linda 11 G 28
Linec 11 J 25
Lipeck 11 H 26
Lipicy 11 H 25
Lipki 11 H 26
Lipovka 11 J 27
Liski 11 J 26
Livny 11 J 26
Ljady 10 F 22
Ljahi 11 G 27
Ljuban' 10 F 23
Ljubaž 11 J 25
Ljubercy 11 G 26
Ljubim 11 F 27
Ljubytino 10 F 24
Ljudinovo 11 H 24
Ljudkovo 11 H 24
Loknja 10 G 23
Lokot 11 H 24
Lomonosov 10 F 22
Lotošino 11 G 25
Loznicy 10 F 23
Luga 10 F 22
Luh 11 G 27
Luhovicy 11 H 26
Lukaševka 11 J 25
Lukino 11 H 26
Lukojanov 11 G 28
Lukovnikovo 10 G 24
Luvozero 3 D 23
Lyčkovo 10 F 23
Lykošino 10 F 24
Lyskovo 11 G 29
L'gov 11 J 25
L'va Tolstogo 11 H 26
Istra 11 G 25
Majkop 17 M 27
Makarév 11 F 28
Maksatiha 11 F 25
Mal. Privalovka 11 J 26
Mal. Višera 10 F 23
Malino 11 G 26
Maloarhangel'sk 11 J 25
Malojaroslavec 11 G 25
Malye Ramozero 3 B 24
Malye Soli 11 F 27
Malyševo 11 G 27
Mal'čevskaja 17 K 26
Mamonovo 9 H 19
Man'kovo-Berezovskaja 17 K 27
Marevo 10 G 23
Margaritovka 17 L 26
Marino 11 G 29
Mart'janovo 10 G 23
Matveev-Kurgan 17 K 26
Mcensk 11 H 25
Mednoe 11 G 25
Medvenka 11 J 25
Medyn' 11 H 25
Meglecy 10 F 24
Melenki 11 G 27
Meščovsk 11 H 25
Meškovskaja 11 K 27
Mglin 10 H 24
Mičurinsk 11 H 27
Mihajlov 11 H 26
Mihajlovsk 17 L 27
Mihnevo 11 G 26
Mikulino 11 G 25
Miljušino 11 F 26
Millerovo 17 K 27
Mitrofanovka 11 K 26
Mjaksa 11 F 26
Mokšan 11 H 28
Molokovo 11 F 25
Monastyrščina 11 K 27
Monastyrščina/Smolensk 10 H 23

Mončegorsk　　RUS · S　　**Bastuträsk**

Mončegorsk 3 B 24
Morkiny Gory 11 F 25
Morozovsk 17 K 27
Moršansk 11 H 27
Mor'e 10 E 23
Mosal'sk 11 H 25
Mošenskoe 10 F 24
Moskva Odincovo 11 G 26
Mostovskoj 17 M 27
Možajsk 11 G 25
Možajskoe 11 J 26
Msta 10 F 24
Muhtolovo 11 G 28
Murmansk 3 B 24
Murmaši 3 B 24
Murom 11 G 27
Myshako 17 M 26
Myškin 11 F 26
Myt 11 G 28
Mytišči 11 G 26
M'akiševo 10 G 22
Nagor'e 11 G 26
Naro-Fominsk 11 G 25
Naruksovo 11 H 28
Naryškino 11 H 25
Našči 10 F 23
Navašino 11 G 27
Navlja 11 H 24
Navoloki 11 G 27
Nebolči 10 F 24
Nehaevskij 11 J 27
Neja 11 F 28
Nelidovo 10 G 24
Neman 9 G 19
Nerehta 11 G 27
Nerl' 11 G 27
Nerl' 11 G 26
Nesterov 9 H 20
Nesterovo 11 F 26
Nestery 11 H 24
Nevel' 10 G 22
Nevinnomyssk 17 M 27
Neznanovo 11 H 27
Nikel' 3 B 23
Nikitovka 11 J 26
Nikolaevskaja 17 K 27
Nikologory 11 G 27
Nižnedevick 11 J 26
Nižnij Čir 17 K 28
Nižnij Lomov 11 H 28
Nižnij Novgorod 11 G 28
Noginsk 11 G 26
Nosovo 10 G 22
Novaja Kalitva 11 J 27
Novgorod 10 F 23
Novgorodka 10 G 22
Novij Byselki 11 H 28
Novije Čigla 11 J 27
Novoaleksandrovsk 17 L 27
Novoanninskij 11 J 28
Novobokino 11 H 27
Novočerkassk 17 L 27
Novodugino 11 G 24
Novohoperskij 11 J 27
Novokubansk 17 L 27
Novoleuškovskaja 17 L 27
Novomakarovo 11 J 27
Novominskaja 17 L 26
Novominskaja 17 L 26
Novomoskovsk/Tula 11 H 26
Novopetrovskoe 11 G 25
Novopokrovskaja 17 L 27
Novorossijsk 17 M 26
Novoržev 10 G 22
Novošahtinsk 17 K 26
Novoselki 11 G 28
Novosil' 11 H 25
Novosokol'niki 10 G 23
Novotroickoe 17 L 27
Novozybkov 10 H 23
Novyj Oskol 11 J 26
Oblivskaja 17 K 27
Obninsk 11 G 25
Obojan' 11 J 25
Obžeriha 11 G 28
Odoev 11 H 25
Ogibnoe 11 G 29
Ogorel'e 10 F 23
Ol'ginka 17 M 26
Oktjabrs'kaja 11 G 26
Oktjabrs'kij 17 K 28
Oktjabrs'koe 11 J 26
Okulovka 10 F 24
Olenegorsk 3 B 24
Olenino 10 G 24
Ol'hovatka 11 J 26
Opočka 10 G 22
Oredež 10 F 23
Orehovo 11 F 27
Orehovo-Zuevo 11 G 26
Orel 11 H 25

Orlovskij 17 L 27
Ostaškov 10 G 24
Ostrogožsk 11 J 26
Ostrov 10 G 22
Ostrovskoe 11 F 28
Os'mino 10 F 22
Otradnaja 17 M 27
Ovsišče 11 F 22
Ovsiše 11 F 25
Ozernyj 10 G 24
Ozersk 9 H 19
Paleh 11 G 27
Palkino 10 F 22
Pan`kovo 11 F 28
Panino 11 J 27
Parahino-Poddub`e 10 F 24
Pavlovo 11 G 28
Pavlovsk 11 J 27
Pavlovskaja 17 L 26
Paškovskij 17 L 26
Pečenga 3 B 23
Pečory 10 F 22
Penkino 11 G 27
Peno 10 G 24
Pep'evka 11 J 26
Perelazovskij 17 K 28
Pereslavl'-Zalesskij 11 G 26
Pervomajsk 11 H 28
Pervomajsk/Saransk 11 H 29
Pervomajskij 11 H 27
Pervomajskoe 5 E 22
Pesočnja 11 H 24
Pestjaki 11 G 28
Pestovo 11 F 25
Petrodvorec 10 F 22
Petropavlovka 11 J 27
Petropavlovka 11 J 27
Petrovskaja 17 L 26
Petrovskoe 11 G 26
Petuški 11 G 26
Pikalevo 10 F 24
Piscovo 11 G 27
Pitelino 11 H 27
Plavsk 11 H 25
Ples 11 G 27
Pljussa 10 F 22
Ploskoš 10 G 23
Pnevo 10 F 22
Počep 11 H 24
Počinok 10 H 24
Podberez'e 10 G 23
Podol'sk 11 G 26
Pogar 11 H 24
Pogoreloe-Gorodišče 11 G 25
Poim 11 H 28
Pokrov 11 G 26
Pokrovskoe 11 H 25
Pola 10 F 23
Polessk 9 H 19
Poljarnye Zori 3 C 24
Poljarnyj 3 B 24
Polna 10 F 22
Poltavčenskoe 17 L 26
Poreč'e 11 G 26
Porhov 10 F 22
Pošehon`e-Volodarsk 11 F 26
Povorino 11 J 27
Pravdinsk 9 H 19
Prečistoe 11 F 27
Prečistoe/Jarcevo 10 G 23
Pregradnoe 11 J 27
Priazovskaja 17 L 26
Primorsk/Kaliningrad 9 H 19
Primorsk/St. Petersburg
　10 E 22
Primorsko-Ahtarsk 17 L 26
Priozersk 5 E 22
Prirečnyj 3 B 23
Privolžsk 11 G 27
Privol'naja 17 L 26
Prohorovka 11 J 25
Proletarij 10 F 23
Proletarsk 17 L 27
Pronsk 11 H 26
Prževal'skoe 10 G 23
Psebaj 17 M 27
Pskov 10 F 22
Pučež 11 G 28
Puhnovo 10 G 23
Pulozero 3 B 24
Pureh 11 G 28
Puškin 10 F 23
Pustoška 10 G 22
Putjanino 11 H 27
Račevo 11 F 24
Rajda 11 F 25
Rakitnoe 11 J 25
Ramenskoe 11 G 26
Rameški 11 G 25
Rasskazovo 11 H 27

Reboly 3 D 23
Rečane 10 G 23
Rešma 11 G 28
Rjažsk 11 H 27
Rjázan' 11 H 26
Rodničok 11 J 28
Rodniki 11 G 27
Rogačevka 11 J 26
Rogačevo 11 G 25
Rognedino 11 H 24
Romanovka 11 J 28
Romodanovo 11 H 29
Rošal' 11 G 26
Roslavl' 10 H 24
Rossoš' 11 J 26
Rostoši 11 J 27
Rostov 11 G 26
Rostov-na-Donu 17 L 26
Roven'ki 17 K 26
Roždestveno 11 G 25
Rtiščevo 11 J 28
Rudnja 10 H 23
Ruguj 10 F 24
Ruskeala 5 E 23
Rustaj 11 G 28
Ruza 11 G 25
Ruzaevka 11 H 28
Rybinsk 11 F 26
Ryl'sk 11 J 24
Ržaksa 11 J 27
Ržev 11 G 24
Šablykino 11 H 25
Šack 11 H 27
Safonovo 10 G 24
Šahovskaja 11 G 25
Šahty 17 K 27
Šahun'ja 11 G 29
Šajgino 11 F 29
Sakony 11 G 28
Salgana 11 G 29
Saltykovo 11 H 28
Sal'sk 17 L 27
Samarskoe 17 L 26
Sambek 17 L 26
Samet' 11 F 27
Samofalovka 17 K 28
Sampur 11 J 27
Sandogora 11 F 27
Sandovo 11 F 25
Sankt Peterburg 10 F 23
Šapkino 11 J 28
Sapožok 11 H 27
Sarai 11 H 27
Saransk 11 H 29
Sarapovo 11 G 29
Sarov 11 H 28
Sasovo 11 H 27
Šatalorka 11 J 26
Šatki 11 G 28
Šatura 11 G 26
Sazonovo 10 F 25
Ščigry 11 J 25
Sčol'kovo 11 G 26
Šebekino 11 J 25
Sebež 10 G 22
Šehman 11 H 27
Šekino 11 H 26
Šeksna 11 F 26
Seližarovo 10 G 24
Sely 10 G 24
Sel'co 11 H 24
Semeno-Aleksandrovka
　11 J 27
Semenov 11 G 28
Semenovo 11 G 29
Semenovskoe 11 G 25
Semikarakorsk 17 K 27
Semiluki 11 J 26
Semlevo 11 G 24
Serafimovič 17 K 28
Serebrjanye-Prudy 11 H 26
Sereda 11 G 27
Seredka 10 F 22
Seredrjakovo 11 J 26
Sergač 11 G 29
Sergiev Posad 11 G 26
Serpuhov 11 H 26
Sestoreck 10 E 22
Setraki 17 K 27
Severomorsk 3 B 24
Severomorsk III 3 B 24
Severskaja 17 M 26
Sevsk 11 H 24
Šilovo/Dankov 11 H 26
Šilovo/Putjanino 11 H 27
Sima 11 G 26
Simoncevo 11 G 27
Šimsk 10 F 23
Sinegorskij 17 K 27
Sinie Lipjagu 11 J 26
Siverskij 10 F 23

Sknjatino 11 G 26
Skopin 11 H 26
Skorodnoe 11 J 25
Slancy 10 F 22
Slaščevskaja 11 K 27
Slavjansk-na-Kubani 17 L 26
Slavkoviči 10 F 22
Smirnovo 11 G 28
Smolensk 10 H 23
Sobinka 11 G 27
Soči 17 M 26
Sokolovo 11 H 28
Sokolskoe 11 G 28
Solncevo 11 J 25
Solnečnogorsk 11 G 25
Sol'cy 10 F 23
Somino 11 F 25
Sonkovo 11 F 25
Sorokino 10 G 22
Sortavala 5 E 23
Sosnovka/Pervomajskij
　11 H 27
Sosnovka/Rtiščevo 11 J 28
Sosnovo 5 E 23
Sosnovskoe 11 G 28
Sosnovyj 3 C 23
Sovetsk 9 G 19
Sovetskaja 17 K 27
Sovetskaja/Armavir 17 M 27
Sovetskoe 11 J 26
Spas-Demensk 11 H 24
Spas-Klepiki 11 G 27
Spasskoe 11 G 29
Špikulovo 11 J 27
Spokojnaja 17 M 27
Srednegor'e 5 E 22
Srednij Egorlyk 17 L 27
Srednij Ikorec 11 J 26
Staraja Kriuša 11 J 27
Staraja Rudka 11 G 29
Staraja Russa 10 F 23
Starica 11 G 25
Starodub 10 H 24
Staroe Istomino 10 G 24
Staroe Šajgovo 11 H 28
Starojur'evo 11 H 27
Starominskaja 17 L 26
Staroščerbinovskaja 17 L 26
Starotitarovskaja 17 L 25
Staryj Oskol 11 J 26
Stavropol' 17 L 27
Stegalovka 11 J 26
Stepancevo 11 G 25
Stodolišče 10 H 24
Stolpino 11 G 28
Strugi 10 F 24
Strugi Krasnye 10 F 22
Stupino 11 H 26
Sudbišči 11 H 26
Sudimir 11 H 24
Sudislavl' 11 F 27
Sudogda 11 G 27
Sudža 11 J 25
Suhiniči 11 H 25
Suhobezvodnoe 11 G 28
Suhodol'skij 11 H 26
Šuja 11 G 27
Šul'gino 11 J 27
Suraž/Uneča 10 H 23
Surovatiha 11 G 28
Surovikino 17 K 28
Susanino 11 F 27
Suvorov 11 H 25
Suzdal' 11 G 27
Suzemka 11 J 24
Sverero 17 K 27
Svetlogorsk 9 H 19
Svetogorsk 5 E 22
Sviš, čevka 11 H 28
Svjatoslavka 11 J 28
Syrnevo 11 F 27
Syt'kovo 10 G 24
Tacinskij 17 K 27
Taganrog 17 L 26
Tahta 17 L 27
Taldom 11 G 26
Taličkij Camlyk 11 J 27
Talovaja 11 J 27
Talpaki 9 H 19
Taman' 17 L 25
Tarasa 11 H 25
Tatarovo 11 G 27
Tbilisskaja 17 L 27
Teberda 17 M 27
Tejkovo 11 G 27
Temirgoevskaja 17 L 27
Temkino 11 G 25

Temnikov 11 H 28
Temrjuk 17 L 25
Ten'guševo 11 H 28
Teploe 11 H 25
Ternovka 11 J 27
Tihoreck 17 L 27
Tihvin 10 F 24
Tim 11 J 25
Timaševsk 17 L 26
Tokarevka 11 J 27
Tomorovka 11 J 26
Tonkino 11 G 29
Tonšaevo 11 F 30
Torčino 11 G 27
Tormosin 17 K 28
Toropec 10 G 23
Toržok 11 G 25
Tosno 11 F 23
Tovarkovskij 11 H 26
Tregubovo 10 F 23
Troekurovo 11 H 26
Troickoe 11 H 27
Trosna 11 J 25
Trubčevsk 11 H 24
Tuapse 17 M 26
Tufanovo 11 F 27
Tula 11 H 26
Tuma 11 G 27
Tungozero 3 C 23
Tupicyno 10 F 22
Turandino 10 F 24
Turgenevo 11 G 27
Turginovo 11 G 25
Turki 11 J 28
Turki-Perevoz 10 G 22
Tutaev 11 F 26
Tver' 11 G 25
Udomlja 11 F 25
Uglič 11 G 26
Uholovo 11 H 27
Uneča 10 H 24
Upornaja 17 M 27
Ura Guba 3 B 24
Urazovo 11 J 26
Uren` 11 G 29
Urjupinsk 11 J 27
Uruče 11 H 24
Usman 17 J 26
Usman' 11 J 26
Ust`-Džeguta 17 M 27
Ustjužna 11 F 25
Ust' Buzulukskaja 11 J 27
Ust' Labinsk 17 L 26
Usvjaty 10 G 23
Utorgoš 10 F 23
Uvarovo 11 J 27
Uzlovaja 11 H 26
Užovka 11 H 28
Valdaj 10 F 24
Valdimirovka 5 E 23
Valjuki 11 J 26
Varenikovskaja 17 L 26
Varnavino 11 G 29
Vejdelevka 11 J 26
Vekšino 10 F 23
Velikie Luki 10 G 23
Velikij Novgorod 10 F 23
Velikovečnoe 17 M 26
Veliž 10 G 23
Venev 11 H 26
Vereja 11 G 25
Verhnetulomskij 3 B 23
Verhnij Mamon 11 J 27
Verhovina 10 F 24
Vernadovka 11 H 28
Veselyj 17 L 27
Vešenskaja 11 K 27
Ves'egonsk 11 F 25
Vetluga 11 F 29
Vicuga 11 G 27
Virga 11 H 28
Viteml' 11 J 24
Vizimjary 11 G 29
Vjartsilja 5 E 23
Vjazniki 11 G 27
Vjaz'ma 11 G 24
Vladimir 11 G 27
Vladyšnoe 11 F 26
Vohtoga 11 F 27
Vojnica 3 C 23
Voknovolok 3 D 23
Volčki 11 H 27
Volga 11 F 26
Volhov 10 F 23
Volodarsk 11 G 28
Volokolamsk 11 G 25
Volokonovka 11 J 26
Vološino 17 K 26
Volosovo 10 F 22

Volot 10 F 23
Volovo 11 J 26
Voltutino 10 H 24
Vorob'evka 11 J 27
Vorob'evo 11 G 25
Voron`e 11 F 27
Voroncovka 11 J 27
Voronež 11 J 26
Voronok 10 J 24
Vorotynec 11 G 29
Vorsma 11 G 28
Voshod 17 L 27
Voskresensk 11 G 26
Voskresenskoe 11 F 26
Voskresenskoe 11 G 29
Vozdviženskoe 11 G 29
Vozkresenskoe 11 G 27
Voznesenskoe 11 H 28
Vsevoložsk 10 E 23
Vshody 11 H 24
Vtorye Terbuny 11 J 26
Vuorijarvi 3 C 23
Vuva 3 B 23
Vybor 10 G 22
Vydropužsk 11 G 25
Vygoniči 11 H 24
Vyksa 11 G 27
Vyrica 10 F 23
Vyselki 17 L 26
Vyšgorodok 10 G 22
Vyšnij Voloček 10 F 24
Vysock 5 E 22
Vysokoe 10 E 22
Vysokoe/Toržok 11 G 25
Vysokovsk 11 G 25
Zadonsk 11 J 26
Zagolodno 10 F 24
Zaharovo 11 H 26
Zajcevo 10 F 23
Zales`e 11 F 25
Zapadnaja Dvina 10 G 23
Zapal'e 10 F 22
Zapoljarnyj 3 B 23
Zaporožskoe 5 E 23
Zarajsk 11 H 26
Zarečensk 3 C 23
Zarečje 11 H 27
Zarevo 17 J 27
Zavolž`e 11 G 28
Zavolžsk 11 G 27
Ždanovo 10 G 24
Žegalovo 11 H 28
Zelenčukskaja 17 M 27
Zelenoborskij 3 C 23
Zelenogorsk 10 E 22
Zelenograd 11 G 25
Zelenogradsk 9 H 19
Železnogorsk 11 J 25
Zemetčino 11 H 28
Zemljansk 11 J 26
Žerdevka 11 J 27
Zernograd 17 L 27
Žiloj Bor 10 F 24
Zimovniki 17 L 27
Žirjatino 11 H 24
Zlynka 10 J 23
Zmievka 11 H 25
Znamenka 11 H 24
Znamenka 17 K 27
Znamenskoe 11 H 25
Zolino 11 G 28
Zubcov 11 G 24
Žukovka 11 H 24
Élektrostal' 11 G 26
Érivanskaja 17 M 26

Adolfsström 2 C 17
Alberga 4 F 17
Alingsås 4 F 16
Alunda 5 E 18
Alvesta 4 G 16
Ammarnäs 2 C 17
Ammer 4 D 17
Arboga 4 F 17
Arbrå 4 E 17
Areavaara 3 A 20
Arjeplog 3 C 18
Arkösund 4 F 17
Arvidsjaur 3 C 18
Arvika 4 F 16
Asen 4 E 16
Askersund 4 F 16
Avesta 4 E 17
Axmar bruk 5 E 17
Ballasviken 2 C 17
Bastuträsk 3 D 18

Bengtsfors 4 F 15
Bispgården 4 D 17
Bjästa 5 D 18
Björbo 4 E 16
Björkliden 3 B 18
Björna 5 D 18
Blackstad 4 F 17
Blankaholm 4 F 17
Boden 3 C 19
Boliden 3 D 19
Bollnäs 4 E 17
Borgholm 8 G 17
Borlänge 4 E 17
Borås 4 F 16
Botsmark 5 D 19
Bredbyn 5 D 18
Brokind 4 F 17
Bräcke 4 D 17
Brännholmen 3 C 18
Brännås 4 E 17
Brösarp 8 G 16
Burea 3 D 19
Burgsvik 5 G 18
Burträsk 3 D 19
Byske 3 D 19
Byxelkrok 4 G 17
Båstad 8 G 16
Bäckefors 4 F 15
Dalarö 5 F 18
Dannemora 5 E 18
Deje 4 F 16
Dikanäs 2 C 17
Djuramåla 8 G 17
Dorotea 4 D 17
Ed 4 F 15
Edsbyn 4 E 17
Ekenäs 4 F 16
Eksjö 4 F 16
Emmaboda 8 G 17
Enköping 5 F 17
Eskilstuna 4 F 17
Eslöv 8 G 16
Fagersta 4 F 17
Falkenberg 4 G 15
Falköping 4 F 16
Falsterbo 8 G 16
Falun 4 E 17
Filipstad 4 F 16
Finspång 4 F 17
Fjällbacka 4 F 15
Flen 4 F 17
Fredrika 5 D 18
Friggesund 4 E 17
Frövi 4 F 17
Fulunäs 4 E 16
Furudal 4 E 17
Fårösund 5 F 18
Färila 4 E 17
Färjestaden 8 G 17
Gamleby 4 F 17
Gislaved 4 G 16
Glommersträsk 3 C 18
Gnarp 5 E 17
Granö 5 D 18
Grimslöv 8 G 16
Gripsholm 5 F 17
Grisslehamn 5 E 18
Grums 4 F 16
Gränna 4 F 16
Gräsmark 4 F 16
Gullspång 4 F 16
Gysinge 4 E 17
Gäddede 2 D 16
Gällivare 3 C 19
Gävle 5 E 17
Göteborg 4 F 15
Götene 4 F 16
Hablingbo 5 G 18
Hagestad 8 G 16
Hagfors 4 E 16
Hakkas 3 C 19
Hallstahammar 4 F 17
Halmstad 8 G 16
Hammerdal 4 D 17
Handen 5 F 18
Haparanda 3 C 20
Harads 3 C 19
Harg 5 E 18
Haverdal 8 G 16
Hede 4 E 16
Hedemora 4 E 17
Helsingborg 8 G 16
Hennan 4 E 17
Hestra 4 G 16
Hindås 4 F 15
Hjo 4 F 16
Hjältevad 4 F 17
Hofors 4 E 17
Holkekärr 4 F 15
Holmsund/Robertfors 5 D 19
Holmsund/Vännäs 5 D 19
Hotagen 4 D 16
Hudiksvall 5 E 17
Hultsfred 4 F 17
Hållnäs 5 E 18
Hälla 5 D 17
Hällefors 4 F 16
Härnösand 5 D 18
Hässleholm 8 G 16
Höganäs 8 G 16
Högsby 4 G 17
Höljes 4 E 16
Hörby 8 G 16
Hörken 4 F 16
Hörviken 8 G 16
Idre 4 E 16
Ishult 4 F 17
Johannisholm 4 E 16
Jokkmokk 3 C 18
Junosuando 3 C 20
Junsele 4 D 17
Järpen 4 D 16
Järvsö 4 E 17
Jönköping 4 F 16
Jönåker 4 F 17
Jörn 3 C 18
Kalix 3 C 20
Kallsedet 4 D 16
Kalmar 8 G 17
Kapellskär 5 F 18
Karesuando 3 B 20
Karlsborg 4 F 16
Karlshamn 8 G 16
Karlskoga 4 F 16
Karlskrona 8 G 17
Karlstad 4 F 16
Karungi 3 C 20
Katrineholm 4 F 17
Kattisavan 3 D 18
Kinna 4 F 16
Kiruna 3 B 19
Kisa 4 F 17
Klimpfjäll 2 C 16
Klintehamn 5 G 18
Klippan 8 G 16
Kopparberg 4 F 16
Korpilombolo 3 C 20
Kramfors 5 D 18
Kristianstad 8 G 16
Kristinehamn 4 F 16
Krokom 4 D 16
Kumla 4 F 17
Kungsbacka 4 G 15
Kungshamn 4 F 15
Kungälv 4 F 15
Kuollejaure 3 C 18
Kvikjokk 3 C 18
Kåbdalis 3 C 18
Kårböle 4 E 17
Kättilsbyn 4 F 16
Köping 4 F 17
Laholm 8 G 16
Lammhult 4 G 16
Landskrona 8 G 16
Lansjärv 3 C 19
Lappträsk 3 C 20
Laxå 4 F 16
Leipojärvi 3 C 19
Lenhovda 4 G 17
Lerum 4 F 15
Lessebo 8 G 17
Lickershamn 5 F 18
Liden 4 D 17
Lidhult 8 G 16
Lidköping 4 F 16
Lidsjöberg 4 D 17
Lilla Edet 4 F 15
Lillholmsjö 4 D 16
Lillhärdal 4 E 16
Lima 4 E 16
Lindefallet 4 E 17
Lindesberg 4 F 17
Linköping 4 F 17
Linsell 4 E 16
Ljugarn 5 G 18
Ljungby 8 G 16
Ljungdalen 4 D 16
Ljusdal 4 E 17
Loftahammar 4 F 17
Los 4 E 17
Ludvika 4 E 17
Luleå 3 C 19
Lund 8 G 16
Luovos 3 C 18
Lycksele 3 D 18
Lysekil 4 F 15
Långbo 4 E 17
Långträsk 3 C 19
Läckö 4 F 16
Läppe 4 F 17
Lövberga 4 D 17
Lövnäs 3 C 18
Malmberget 3 C 19
Malmö 8 G 16
Malung 4 E 16
Malå 3 C 18
Mariestad 4 F 16
Markaryd 8 G 16
Marsta 5 F 18
Mellerud 4 F 15
Meselefors 2 D 17
Mjöbäck 4 G 16
Mjölby 4 F 17
Mlrdudden 3 C 19
Molkom 4 F 16
Mora 4 E 16
Morjärv 3 C 20
Moskosel 3 C 18
Motala 4 F 17
Mullsjö 4 F 16
Munkedal 4 F 15
Muodoslompolo 3 B 20
Mölle 8 G 16
Mörlanda 4 F 16
Nacka 5 F 18
Naggen 4 E 17
Nattavaara 3 C 19
Nikkaluokta 3 B 18
Njurunda 5 E 17
Nordmaling 5 D 18
Norra Unnaryd 4 F 16
Norrbäck 3 D 18
Norrköping 4 F 17
Norrtälje 5 F 18
Norsjö 3 D 18
Nybro 8 G 17
Nyköping 5 F 17
Nynäshamn 5 F 18
Näsby 8 G 17
Nässjö 4 F 16
Näsåker 4 D 17
Ockelbo 4 E 17
Olofström 8 G 16
Orsa 4 E 16
Osby 8 G 16
Oskarshamn 4 G 17
Oxelösund 5 F 17
Pajala 3 C 20
Pello 3 C 20
Piteå 3 C 19
Porjus 3 C 18
Ramnäs 4 F 17
Ramsele 4 D 17
Robertfors 5 D 19
Roma 5 F 18
Ronneby 8 G 17
Ruskträsk 3 D 18
Råneå 3 C 19
Rätan 4 E 16
Rättvik 4 E 17
Rönnskär 3 D 19
Rönnöfors 4 D 16
Sala 4 F 17
Sandsele 3 C 18
Sandvik 4 G 17
Sandviken 4 E 17
Saxnäs 2 D 17
Simonstorp 4 F 17
Simpnäs 5 F 18
Simrishamn 8 G 16
Sjöbo 8 G 16
Sjötorp 4 F 16
Skara 4 F 16
Skellefteå 3 D 19
Skinnskatteberg 4 F 17
Skog 4 E 17
Skövde 4 F 16
Slite 5 F 18
Slussfors 2 C 17
Smygehamn 8 G 16
Smålandsstenar 4 G 16
Snössvallen 4 E 16
Sollefteå 5 D 17
Sollentuna 5 F 18
Sorsele 3 C 17
Stenungsund 4 F 15
Stocka 5 E 17
Stockholm 5 F 18
Stora Blåsjön 2 D 16
Storfors 4 F 16
Storlien 4 D 15
Storsätern 4 E 15
Storuman 2 C 17
Strängnäs 4 F 17
Strömnäs 2 D 17
Strömstad 4 F 15
Strömsund 4 D 17
Stöde 4 E 17
Stöllet 4 E 16
Sund 4 F 15
Sundbyberg 5 F 18
Sundsbruk 5 E 17
Sundsvall 5 E 17
Sunne 4 F 16
Suorva 3 B 18
Svappavaara 3 B 19
Svartå 4 F 16
Sveg 4 E 16
Svenljunga 4 G 16
Sysslebäck 4 E 16
Säffle 4 F 16
Sälen 4 E 16
Särna 4 E 16
Sävsjö 4 G 16
Söderfors 5 E 17
Söderhamn 5 E 17
Söderköping 4 F 17
Södertälje 5 F 18
Söderåkra 8 G 17
Södra Finnskoga 4 E 15
Sölvesborg 8 G 16
Sörvattnet 4 E 16
Tanumshede 4 F 15
Tierp 5 E 18
Timrå 5 D 17
Tingsryd 8 G 17
Tomelilla 8 G 16
Torekov 8 G 16
Torhamn 8 G 17
Torsby 4 E 16
Torup 4 G 16
Tranås 4 F 16
Traryd 8 G 16
Trelleborg 8 G 16
Trollhättan 4 F 15
Trosa 5 F 18
Tyfors 4 E 16
Tännäs 4 E 16
Tärnaby 2 C 17
Töre 3 C 20
Töreboda 4 F 16
Uddevalla 4 F 15
Ullared 4 G 16
Ulricehamn 4 F 16
Ulvsjön 4 E 16
Umeå 5 D 19
Umfors 2 C 16
Uppsala 5 F 18
Utansjö 5 D 18
Vadstena 4 F 16
Vaggeryd 4 G 16
Valdemarsvik 4 F 17
Vansbro 4 E 16
Vara 4 F 16
Varberg 4 G 15
Vastbacka 4 E 16
Venjan 4 E 16
Vetlanda 4 G 17
Vidsel 3 C 19
Vilhelmina 2 D 17
Vimmerby 4 F 17
Vindeln 5 D 18
Virserum 4 G 17
Visby 5 F 18
Vittangi 3 B 19
Vittjärn 4 E 16
Voxna 4 E 17
Vrena 4 F 17
Vuollerim 3 C 19
Vålådalen 4 D 16
Vårgårda 4 F 16
Vänersborg 4 F 15
Vännäs 5 D 18
Värnamo 4 G 16
Värö 4 G 15
Västermyrriset 3 D 18
Västervik 4 F 17
Västerås 4 F 17
Växjö 4 G 16
Ystad 8 G 16
Ytterhogdal 4 E 16
Åhus 8 G 16
Ålem 4 G 17
Ålshult 8 G 16
Åmadalen 4 E 16
Åmål 4 F 16
Ånge 4 E 17
Ånimskog 4 F 16
Åre 4 D 16
Årjäng 4 F 15
Åsarne 4 D 16
Åseda 4 G 17
Åsele 5 D 17
Åtvidaberg 4 F 17
Älmhult 8 G 16
Älvdalen 4 E 16
Älvkarleby 5 E 17
Älvsbyn 3 C 19
Ängelholm 8 G 16
Ödeshög 4 F 16
Örebro 4 F 17
Öregrund 5 E 18
Örkelljunga 8 G 16
Örnsköldsvik 5 D 18
Örsundsbro 5 F 17
Östavall 4 E 17
Östebymo 4 F 17
Östersund 4 D 16
Överkalix 3 C 20
Övertorneå 3 C 20
Övre Soppero 3 B 19

SK

Bánovce n. Bebravou 14 K 18
Banská Bystrica 14 K 18
Bardejov 15 K 19
Bratislava 14 K 17
Brezno 14 K 18
Čadca 14 K 18
Červená Skala 14 K 19
Dolný Kubín 14 K 18
Dunajská Streda 14 K 18
Galanta 14 K 18
Handlová 14 K 18
Hanušovce 15 K 19
Hlohovec 14 K 18
Hriňová 14 K 18
Humenné 15 K 19
Ilava 14 K 18
Kežmarok 15 K 19
Kľačno 14 K 18
Kolárovo 14 K 18
Komárno 14 K 18
Košice 15 K 19
Kráľovský Chlmec 15 K 19
Kremnica 14 K 18
Krupina 14 K 18
Kúty 14 K 17
Levice 14 K 18
Licince 14 K 19
Liptovský Mikuláš 14 K 18
Lučenec 14 K 18
Makov 14 K 18
Malacky 14 K 17
Martin 14 K 18
Michalovce 15 K 19
Mníšek nad Hnilcom 15 K 19
Nitra 14 K 18
Nova Bystrica 14 K 18
Nové Mesto n. Váhom 14 K 18
Nové Zámky 14 K 18
Pezinok 14 K 17
Piešťany 14 K 18
Poprad 14 K 19
Považska Bystrica 14 K 18
Prešov 15 K 19
Prievidza 14 K 18
Rimavská Sobota 14 K 19
Rožňava 15 K 19
Ružomberok 14 K 18
Salka 14 K 18
Sečovce 15 K 19
Senec 14 K 17
Senica 14 K 17
Sereď 14 K 18
Snina 15 K 19
Spišská Nová Ves 15 K 19
Spišské Podhradie 15 K 19
Stará Ľubovňa 15 K 19
Svidník 15 K 19
Šurany 14 K 18
Tisovec 14 K 18
Topoľčany 14 K 18
Tornaľa 15 K 19
Trenčín 14 K 18
Trnava 14 K 18
Trstená 14 K 18
Turňa nad Bodvou 15 K 19
Vernár 14 K 18
Zlaté Moravce 14 K 18
Zvolen 14 K 18
Žarnovica 14 K 18
Ždiar 14 K 19
Žilina 14 K 18

SLO

Ajdovščina 14 L 16
Bohinjska Bistrica 14 L 16
Celje 14 L 17
Dravograd 14 L 17
Idrija 14 L 16
Jesenice 14 L 16
Kobarid 13 L 16
Kočevje 14 L 16
Koper 13 L 16
Kozina 14 L 16
Kranj 14 L 16
Krško 14 L 17
Litija 14 L 16
Ljubljana 14 L 16
Ljutomer 14 L 17
Lož 14 L 16
Maribor 14 L 17
Metlika 14 L 17
Murska Sobota 14 L 17
Novo mesto 14 L 17
Postojna 14 L 16
Ptuj 14 L 17
Radmirje 14 L 16
Slovenska Bistrica 14 L 17
Trojane 14 L 16
Velenje 14 L 17
Vrhnika 14 L 16
Zidani Most 14 L 17

SRB

Ada 15 L 19
Aleksinac 22 M 19
Bačka Palanka 14 L 18
Bačka Topola 14 L 18
Bajmok 14 L 18
Banatsko Novo Selo 15 M 19
Bečej 14 L 19
Bela Crkva 15 M 19
Bela Palanka 22 M 19
Beograd 15 M 19
Boljevac 22 M 19
Bor 22 M 19
Brza Palanka 15 M 20
Bujanovac 22 N 19
Čačak 21 M 19
Despotovac 22 M 19
Dimitrovgrad/Sofija 22 M 20
Donji Milanovac 15 M 19
Džep 22 M 19
Golubac 15 M 19
Gornji Milanovac 21 M 19
Grocka 15 M 19
Ivanjica 21 M 19
Jagodina 22 M 19
Kanjiža 14 L 19
Kikinda 15 L 19
Kladovo 15 M 20
Klokočevac 15 M 19
Knjaževac 22 M 19
Koceljevo 14 M 18
Kosjerić 21 M 18
Kragujevac 21 M 19
Kraljevo 21 M 19
Kruševac 22 M 19
Kučevo 15 M 19
Kula/Sombor 14 L 18
Kupinovo 15 M 19
Kuršumlija 22 M 19
Kuzmin 14 L 18
Lazarevac 15 M 19
Leskovac 22 M 19
Loznica/Šabac 14 M 18
Ljubovija 21 M 18
Majdanpek 15 M 19
Medveđa 22 M 19
Melenci 15 L 19
Mladenovac 15 M 19
Negotin 15 M 20
Niš 22 M 19
Nova Crnja 15 L 19
Nova Varoš 21 M 18
Novi Pazar/Titova Mitrovica 21 M 19
Novi Sad 14 L 18
Obrenovac 15 M 19
Odžaci 14 L 18
Osečina 14 M 18
Pančevo 15 M 19
Paraćin 22 M 19
Perlez 15 L 19
Petrovac/Požarevac 15 M 19
Pirot 22 M 20
Požarevac 15 M 19
Priboj 21 M 18
Raška 21 M 19
Rogačica 21 M 18
Ruma 14 M 18
Senta 14 L 19
Sjenica 21 M 19
Smederevo 15 M 19
Sombor 14 L 18
Srbobran 14 L 18
Sremska Mitrovica 14 M 18
Stara Pazova 15 M 19
Stepojevac 15 M 19
Subotica 14 L 18
Šabac 14 M 18
Topola 21 M 19
Trstenik 21 M 19
Tutin 21 M 19
Ušće 21 M 19

38

I N D E X · O R T S R E G I S T E R · Í N D I C E · I N
P L A A T S N A M E N R E G I S T E R · R E J S T Ř Í K M Í S

EU

Užice   SRB · TN · TR · UA   Buryn'

Užice 21 M 18
Valjevo 21 M 18
Vasina Okruglica 22 M 19
Velika Plana 15 M 19
Vranje 22 M 19
Vršac 15 L 19
Zaječar 22 M 19
Zemun 15 M 19
Zrenjanin 15 L 19
Žagubica 22 M 19

TN

Babouch 20 P 14
Béchateur 20 P 14
Béja 20 P 14
Binzerte 20 P 14
Bou Salem 20 P 14
Carthage 20 P 15
Dhraa Ben Jouder 20 P 14
El Haouaria 20 P 15
El Marsa 20 P 15
El Oued 20 P 15
El Fahs 20 P 14
El Kebira 20 P 15
El Kef 20 P 14
El Ksour 20 P 14
Enfidha 20 P 15
Gaâfour 20 P 14
Ghar el Melh 20 P 15
Ghardimaou 20 P 14
Grombalia 20 P 15
Haffouz 20 P 14
Hammam Lif 20 P 15
Hammamet 20 P 15
Hergla 20 P 15
Jendouba 20 P 14
Kairouan 20 P 15
Kalla El Khasba/Thala 20 P 14
Kelibia 20 P 15
Korba 20 P 15
Le Krib 20 P 14
Le Sers 20 P 14
M`Saken 20 P 15
Makthar 20 P 14
Mateur 20 P 14
Mejez El-Bab 20 P 14
Menzel Bourgiba 20 P 14
Monastir 20 P 15
Nabeul 20 P 15
Nefza 20 P 14
Pantelleria 20 P 15
Rohia 20 P 14
Sakiet Sidi Youssef 20 P 14
Sbikha 20 P 14
Sidi Bou Ali 20 P 15
Siliana 20 P 14
Sousse 20 P 15
Tabarka 20 P 14
Tajerouine 20 P 14
Tazougrane 20 P 15
Téboursouk 20 P 14
Testour 20 P 14
Thala 20 P 14
Tunis 20 P 15
Zaghouan 20 P 15

TR

Abana 23 N 24
Abide 23 O 22
Acıpayam 23 P 22
Adana 23 P 25
Afyonkarahisar 23 O 23
Akçakoca 23 N 23
Akhisar 23 O 22
Akköy 23 P 21
Akören 23 P 23
Aksaray 23 O 24
Akseki 23 P 23
Akşehir 23 O 23
Alaca 23 N 24
Alaçam 23 N 25
Alanya 23 P 23
Alaşehir 23 O 22
Altınekin 23 O 24
Amasya 23 N 25
ANKARA 23 O 24
ANTALYA 23 P 23
Anamur 23 P 24
Antalya 23 P 23
Araç 23 N 24
Araklı 17 N 26
Armutlu 23 N 22
Arslanköy 23 P 24
Artova 23 N 25
Ayancik 23 N 24

Ayaş 23 N 23
Aydın 23 O 22
Aydıncık 23 P 24
Aydınkent 23 P 23
Ayrancı 23 P 24
Ayvacık 22 O 21
Ayvacık 23 N 25
Ayvalık 22 O 21
Azdavay 23 N 24
Babaeski 22 N 21
Babakale 22 O 21
Bafra 23 N 25
Bakırköy 23 N 22
Balıkesir 23 O 22
Balya 22 O 22
Balâ 23 O 24
Banaz 23 O 22
Bandırma 23 N 22
Bartın 23 N 23
Bayat 23 O 23
Bayat 23 N 24
Bayındır 23 O 22
Bayramiç 22 O 21
Behram 22 O 21
Belcik 23 O 25
Bergama 22 O 21
Beşkonak 23 P 23
Beykoz 23 N 22
Beypazari 23 N 23
Beyşehir 23 O 23
Biga 22 N 21
Bigadiç 23 O 22
Bilecik 23 N 23
Bodrum 23 P 21
Bogaz 23 N 23
Boğaz 23 N 22
Boğazlıyan 23 O 25
Bolu 23 N 23
Bolvadin 23 O 23
Bor 23 O 24
Borlu 23 O 22
Bostan 23 N 24
Boyabat 23 N 24
Bozburun 23 P 22
Bozkır 23 P 23
Bozüyük 23 O 23
Bozyak— 23 P 24
Bucak 23 P 23
Bucakkışla 23 P 24
Buldan 23 O 22
Burdur 23 O 23
Burhaniye 22 O 21
Bursa 23 N 22
Bünyan 23 O 25
Camardi 23 O 25
Cerkezköy 22 N 22
Cevizli 23 P 23
Cide 23 N 24
Cihanbeyli 23 O 24
Çalatlı 23 O 24
Çalköy 23 O 23
Çameli 23 P 22
Çamkonak 23 N 23
Çamlıbel 23 N 25
Çamlıdere 23 N 24
Çamlıyayla 23 P 24
Çan 22 N 21
Çanakkale 22 N 21
Çandır 23 N 24
Çankırı 23 N 24
Çarşamba 23 N 25
Çavdarhisar 23 O 22
Çay 23 O 23
Çaycuma 23 N 23
Çayeli 17 N 27
Çayıralan 23 O 25
Çaykara 17 N 27
Çekerek 23 N 24
Çeltik 23 O 23
Çeltikçi 23 O 23
Çerkeş 23 N 24
Çeşme 22 O 21
Çınarcık 23 N 22
Çifteler 23 O 23
Çiftlik 23 N 24
Çine 23 O 22
Çivril 23 O 22
Çorlu 22 N 22
Çorum 23 N 25
Çubuk 23 N 24
Çumra 23 N 24
Dalaman 23 P 22
Dalyan 22 O 21
Datça 23 P 22
Dazkırı 23 O 22
Demir-~cidere 23 O 22
Demirci 23 O 22
Demirtaş 23 P 23
Demre 23 P 23
Denizli 23 O 22
Dereköy 22 N 21

Derinkuyu 23 O 24
Develi 23 O 25
Devrek 23 N 23
Didim 22 P 21
Dinar 23 O 23
Dinek 23 P 24
Doğanyurt 23 N 24
Dokurcun 23 N 23
Domaniç 23 O 22
Durak 23 P 23
Dursunbey 23 O 22
Düvertepe 23 O 22
Düzce 23 N 23
Eceabat 22 N 21
Edremit 22 O 21
Edirne 22 N 21
Eflani 23 N 24
Eğirdir 23 O 23
Elmalı 23 P 22
Emet 23 O 22
Enez 22 N 21
Erbaa 23 N 25
Erdek 22 N 22
Erdemli 23 P 24
Ereğli 23 P 24
Ereğli 23 N 23
Ermenek 23 P 24
Esenler 23 N 22
Eskipazar 23 N 24
Eskişehir 23 O 23
Espiye 17 N 26
Eşme 23 O 22
Ezine 22 O 21
Ezinepazari 23 N 25
Fatsa 17 N 26
Felahiye 23 O 25
Fethiye 23 P 22
Fındıkpınar 23 P 24
Finike 23 P 23
Foça 22 O 21
Gazipaşa 23 P 23
Gebze 23 N 22
Gediz 23 O 22
Gelibolu 22 N 21
Gemerek 23 O 25
Gemlik 23 N 22
Gerede 23 N 23
Germece 23 N 24
Gerze 23 N 25
Geyve 23 N 23
Giresun 17 N 26
Gölcük 23 N 22
Gölcük 23 O 24
Gölhisar 23 P 22
Gölmarmara 23 O 22
Gölören 23 O 24
Gölpazarı 23 N 23
Gömeç 23 O 25
Gönen 22 N 22
Gördes 23 O 22
Görele 17 N 26
Göynük 23 N 23
Güdül 23 N 23
Güllük 23 P 22
Gülnar 23 P 24
Gülşehir 23 O 24
Gümüşgün 23 O 23
Gümüşhacıköy 23 N 25
Güney 23 O 22
Güneysinir 23 P 24
Güre 23 O 22
Hacılar 23 O 23
Hadim 23 P 24
Hamdi 23 N 24
Hamdi 23 N 24
Hamidiye 23 O 23
Hamidiye 22 N 21
Harmancik 23 O 22
Hatip 23 O 23
Havsa 22 N 21
Havza 23 N 25
Haymana 23 O 24
Hayrabolu 22 N 21
Hierapolis 23 O 22
Himmitdede 23 O 25
Hirfanlar 23 O 24
Ilgaz 23 N 24
Ilgın 23 O 23
Ilica 23 O 22
Ilica 17 N 27
Inecik 22 N 21
Isparta 23 O 23
İgneada 22 N 22
İğdir 23 N 24
İncesu 23 O 25
İSTANBUL 23 N 22
İskilip 23 N 24
İzmir 22 O 21
Kadınhanı 23 O 23
Kadışehri 23 O 25
Kaklik 23 O 22

Kale 23 P 22
Kalecik 23 N 24
Kaleköy 22 N 21
Kalkan 23 P 22
Kalkım 22 O 21
Kaman 23 O 24
Kandıra 23 N 23
Karabiga 22 N 21
Karabük 23 N 24
Karacabey 23 N 22
Karacaköy 23 N 22
Karacasu 23 O 22
Karahamzalı 23 O 24
Karaisalı 23 P 24
Karaman 23 P 24
Karapınar 23 O 24
Karasu 23 N 23
Kargı 23 N 24
Karsantı 23 O 25
Karşıyaka 22 O 21
Kartal 23 N 22
Kastamonu 23 N 24
Kaş 23 P 22
Kaşınhanı 23 O 24
Kavak 22 N 21
Kayac—k 23 P 22
Kayakent 23 O 23
Kaymaz 23 O 23
Kayseri 23 O 25
Kelekçi 23 P 22
Keles 23 O 22
Kemer 23 P 22
Kemer 23 P 22
Kemer/Nazilli 23 O 22
Keskin 23 O 24
Keşan 22 N 21
Kıbrıscık 23 N 23
Kınık 22 O 21
Kırbaşı 23 N 23
Kırka 23 O 23
Kırşehir 23 O 24
Kışlacık 23 N 24
Kızılcahamam 23 N 24
Kızılırmak 23 N 24
Kızılören 23 O 23
Kiraz 23 O 22
Kirikkale 23 O 24
Kirklareli 22 N 21
Kiyiköy 23 N 22
Kocaeli 23 N 22
Konya 23 O 24
Korkuteli 23 P 23
Korucu 22 O 21
Kozaklı 23 O 24
Kösefakılı 23 O 24
Kula/Salihli 23 O 22
Kulu 23 O 24
Kumluca 23 P 23
Kurucaşile 23 N 24
Kuşadası 22 O 21
Küçükbahçe 22 O 21
Küplü 23 N 22
Kürtün 17 N 26
Kütahya 23 O 22
Ladik 23 N 25
Lalapaşa 22 N 21
Lapseki 22 N 21
Lüleburgaz 22 N 21
M.Kemalpaşa 23 N 22
Malkara 22 N 21
Manavgat 23 P 23
Manisa 23 O 21
Marmara 22 N 22
Marmaris 23 P 22
MERSIN 23 P 24
Mecitözü 23 N 25
Menemen 22 O 21
Mengen 23 N 23
Merzifon 23 N 25
Mezrea 23 N 25
Mihalıççık 23 O 23
Milas 23 P 22
Mucur 23 O 24
Mudanya 23 N 22
Mudurnu 23 N 23
Muğla 23 P 22
Mut 23 P 24
Nallıhan 23 N 23
Nazilli 23 O 22
Nevşehir 23 O 24
Niğde 23 O 24
Obruk 23 O 24
Of 17 N 27
Ordu 17 N 26
Orhaneli 23 O 22
Ormanlı 23 N 23
Orta 23 N 24
Ortaca 23 P 22
Ortaklar 23 O 21
Ortaköy 23 O 24
Ortaköy 23 N 25

Osmancik 23 N 24
Osmaneli 23 N 23
Ovacık 23 P 24
Ovacık 23 O 24
Ovacık 23 N 24
Ovacuma 23 N 24
Ödemiş 23 O 22
Ören 23 P 22
Perge 23 P 23
Perşembe 17 N 26
Pinarhisar 22 N 21
Polatlı 23 O 23
Pozantı 23 P 24
Rize 17 N 27
Safranbolu 23 N 24
Sakarya 23 N 23
Salihli 23 O 22
Samsun 23 N 25
Sandıklı 23 O 23
Saratlı 23 O 24
Saray 23 N 24
Saray 22 N 22
Sarayköy 23 O 22
Sarayönü 23 O 24
Sarıcakaya 23 N 23
Sarıgöl 23 O 22
Sarıkaya 23 O 25
Sarıyar 23 N 23
Sariyer 23 N 22
Savaştepe 23 O 22
Seben 23 N 23
Seddülbahir 22 N 21
Seferihisar 22 O 21
Sekili 23 O 24
Selçuk 22 O 21
Selendi 23 O 22
Selimiye 23 P 22
Senirkent 23 O 23
Serik 23 P 23
Seydiler 23 N 24
Seydişehir 23 P 23
Seyitgazi 23 O 23
Sındıran 23 O 24
Sile 23 N 22
Silifke 23 P 24
Silivri 23 N 22
Simav 23 O 22
Sinop 23 N 25
Sivaslı 23 O 22
Sivrihisar 23 O 23
Soma 22 O 22
Sorgun 23 O 24
Söke 23 O 21
Sulakyurt 23 N 24
Sultanhanı 23 O 24
Sungurlu 23 N 24
Susurluk 23 O 22
Sülüklü 23 O 23
Sütçüler 23 O 23
Sütlegen 23 P 22
Şabanözü 23 N 24
Şarköy 22 N 21
Şefaatli 23 O 24
Şereflikoçhisar 23 O 24
Şuhut 23 O 23
Taraklı 23 N 23
Tarsus 23 P 24
Taşcı 23 O 25
Taşköprü 23 N 24
Taşlıca 17 N 26
Taşova 23 N 25
Taşpınar 23 O 24
Taşpınar 23 O 24
Taşucu 23 P 24
Tavas 23 O 22
Tavşanlı 23 O 22
Tayfur 22 N 21
Tefenni 23 P 22
Teke 23 N 22
Tekirdağ 22 N 21
Temelli 23 O 23
Terme 17 N 25
Tire 23 O 22
Tokat 23 N 25
Tomarza 23 O 25
Tonya 17 N 26
Topaklı 23 O 24
Torbalı 22 O 21
Tosya 23 N 24
Trabzon 17 N 26
Truva 22 O 21
Turgut 23 O 23
Turgutlu 23 O 22
Turgutreis 23 P 22
Turhal 23 N 25
Tuzla 23 P 25
Ulubey 23 O 22
Ulukışla 23 O 24
Ulus 23 N 24
Urla 22 O 21
Uşak 23 O 22

Uzunköprü 22 N 21
Uğurlu 22 N 21
Ünye 17 N 25
Ürgüp 23 O 24
Vakfıkebir 17 N 26
Vezirköprü 23 N 25
Yahyalı 23 O 25
Yalova 23 N 22
Yalvaç 23 O 23
Yapraklı 23 N 24
Yarma 23 O 24
Yatağan 23 P 22
Yemişendere 23 P 22
Yenipazar 23 O 25
Yenişehir 23 N 22
Yerköy 23 O 24
Yeşildere 23 P 24
Yeşilhisar 23 O 25
Yeşilova 23 O 22
Yeşilova 23 O 24
Yeşilyazi 23 N 25
Yozgat 23 O 24
Yukarıbey 22 O 21
Yunak 23 O 23
Zile 23 N 25
Zonguldak 23 N 23
İnebolu 23 N 24
İnegöl 23 N 22
İznik 23 N 22

UA

Alčevs'k 17 K 26
Alupka 17 M 24
Alušta 17 M 24
Amrosijivka 17 K 26
Anan'jiv 16 K 23
Andrijivka 17 K 25
Antoniny 15 K 21
Antracyt 17 K 26
Apostolove 17 K 24
Arcyz 16 L 22
Armjansk 17 L 24
Artemivs'k 17 K 26
Avdijivka 11 J 24
Avdijivka/Donéc'k 17 K 26
Bachmač 11 J 24
Bahčisaraj 17 M 24
Balaklija 17 K 25
Balta 16 K 22
Bar/Vinnica 16 K 22
Baranivka 16 J 22
Baštanka 16 L 23
Baturyn 11 J 24
Bazalija 15 K 21
Belogorsk 17 L 24
Berdjans`k 17 L 24
Berdyčiv 16 K 22
Berehove 15 K 20
Berestečko 15 J 21
Berestove 17 L 25
Berezan` 16 J 23
Berežany 15 K 20
Berezivka 16 L 23
Berezna 10 J 23
Beršad' 16 K 22
Beryslav 17 L 24
Bibrka 15 K 20
Bila Cerkva 16 K 23
Bilhorod-Dnistrovs'kyj
   16 L 23
Biljajivka 16 L 23
Bilohir`ja 15 J 21
Bilokorovyči 16 J 22
Bilokurakine 17 K 26
Biloluc'k 17 K 26
Bilopillja 11 J 24
Bilovods'k 17 K 26
Blahodatne 16 K 23
Bobrovycja 16 J 23
Bobrynec' 16 K 23
Bohoduhiv 17 J 25
Bohuslav 16 K 23
Bojarka 16 J 23
Bole'chiv 15 K 20
Bolhrad 16 L 22
Borodjanka 16 J 22
Boromlja 17 J 25
Borova 17 K 26
Borščiv 15 K 21
Boryslav 15 K 20
Boryspiln' 16 J 23
Borzna 10 J 23
Brats'ke 16 K 23
Brody 15 J 21
Brovary 16 J 23
Bucyn 15 J 20
Buky 16 K 23
Buryn' 11 J 24

Bus'k   (UA)   **Žytomyr**   (EU)

Bus'k 15 K 20	Illicivs'k 16 L 23	Kréménčuk 16 K 24	Novoselycja 15 K 21	Selydove 17 K 25	Veselynove 16 L 23
Butenky 16 K 24	Ilovajs'k 17 K 26	Kujbyševe 17 L 25	Novotrojic'ke 17 L 24	Semenivka 10 J 24	Vil'šany 17 J 25
Čaplynka 17 L 24	Inhulec' 16 K 24	Kun'e 17 K 25	Novoukrajinka 16 K 23	Šepetivka 15 J 21	Vil'nohirs'k 17 K 24
Caryčanka 17 K 24	Irpin 16 J 23	Kup'jansk 17 K 26	Novovolyns'k 15 J 20	Seredyna-Buda 11 J 24	Vinnicja 16 K 22
Čerkasy 16 K 23	Ivanhorod 16 K 22	Kurachove 17 K 25	Novovoroncovka 17 K 24	Sevastopol' 17 M 24	Vojkove 17 K 25
Černihiv 10 J 23	Ivano-Frankivs'k 15 K 20	Kurne 16 J 22	Novyj Buh 16 K 24	Ševčenkove 17 K 25	Volnovacha 17 K 26
Černihivka 17 L 25	Izjaslav 15 J 21	Kuzemivka 17 K 26	Nyžnyj Torhaji 17 L 24	Simakivka 16 J 22	Volochiv Jar 17 K 25
Černjachiv 16 J 22	Izjum 17 K 25	Kyjiv 16 J 23	Obolon' 16 K 24	Simferopol' 17 M 24	Volodars'ke 17 L 25
Černomorskoe 16 L 24	Izmajil 16 L 22	Kyrnyčky 16 L 22	Obuchiv 16 J 23	Sivers'k 17 K 26	Volodimir-Volyns´kyj 15 J 20
Červonohrad 15 J 20	Jahotyn 16 J 23	Ladyžyn 16 K 22	Očakiv 16 L 23	Sjeverodonec`k 17 K 26	Volovec' 15 K 20
Charcyz`k 17 K 26	Jalta/Krim 17 M 24	Lazurne 16 L 24	Odesa 16 L 23	Skadovs'k 16 L 24	Volycja 16 J 22
Charkiv 17 J 25	Jalta/Mariupol 17 L 25	Lebedyn 16 J 24	Ohtyrka 17 J 24	Skalat 15 K 21	Vorožba 11 J 24
Cherson 16 L 24	Jasinja 15 K 20	Lenino 17 L 25	Oktjabrs'koe 17 L 24	Skole 15 K 20	Vovčans'k 17 J 25
Chmeliv 11 J 24	Javoriv 15 K 20	Lenkivci 15 J 21	Oleksandrija 16 K 24	Skvyra 16 K 22	Vovčans'ke 17 L 25
Chmel'nyc'kyj 15 K 21	Jelanec' 16 K 23	Letyčiv 16 K 22	Olevs'k 15 J 22	Slavuta 15 J 21	Voznesens'k 16 K 23
Chmil'nik 16 K 22	Jenakijeve 17 K 26	Lisné 16 L 22	Oléksandrivka/Kirovohrad	Slov'janka 17 K 25	Vozsijats'ke 16 K 23
Chorol 16 K 24	Jevsuh 17 K 26	Lityn 16 K 22	16 K 23	Slov'jans'k 17 K 26	Vradijivka 16 K 23
Chotin` 11 J 24	Jur'jivka 17 K 25	Ljubar 16 K 22	Oléksandrivka/Slov''jans'k	Smila 16 K 23	Vylkove 16 L 22
Chotyn 15 K 21	Južne 16 L 23	Ljubeč 10 J 23	17 K 25	Smotryč 15 K 21	Vynohradiv 15 K 20
Chrestyšče 17 K 25	Kača 17 M 24	Ljubešiv 10 J 21	Opišnja 16 K 24	Snihurivka 16 L 24	Vystupovyči 10 J 22
Chust 15 K 20	Kachovka 17 L 24	Ljuboml' 15 J 20	Ordžonikidze 17 K 24	Sokal´ 15 J 20	Vyžnycja 15 K 21
Chyriv 15 K 20	Kaharlyk 16 K 23	Ljubotyn 17 K 25	Orihiv 17 K 25	Sokyrjany 16 K 21	Začepylivka 17 K 25
Cjurupyns'k 16 L 24	Kalančak 17 L 24	Ljubymivka 17 K 24	Orlyne 17 M 24	Sosnove 15 J 21	Zahryzove 17 K 26
Čop 15 K 19	Kaluha 16 L 24	Lochvycja 16 J 24	Oržycja 16 K 24	Šostka 11 J 24	Zaližci 15 K 21
Čornobyl' 16 J 23	Kaluš 15 K 20	Loškarivka 17 K 24	Osmoloda 15 K 20	Spasove 16 K 24	Žaliznyj Port 16 L 23
Čornuchy 16 J 24	Kalynivka 16 K 22	Lozova 17 K 25	Oster 16 J 23	Špola 16 K 23	Zalyščyky 15 K 21
Čortkiv 15 K 21	Kam`janka 16 L 23	Lubny 16 J 24	Ostroh 15 J 21	Špykiv 16 K 22	Zaporižžja 17 K 25
Čudniv 16 J 22	Kamin'-Kašyrs'kyj 15 J 21	Lucgk 15 J 21	Osypenko 17 L 25	Sribne 16 J 24	Žaškiv 16 K 23
Čuhujiv 17 K 25	Kam'janka 16 K 23	Luhans`k 17 K 26	Otynija 15 K 20	Stachanov 17 K 26	Zaturci 15 J 20
Čumaky 17 K 24	Kam'janka- Buz'ka // Bъz'ka	Lypova-Dolyna 16 J 24	Ovruč 16 J 22	Stara Ušycja 15 K 21	Zbaraž 15 K 21
Čutove 17 K 25	15 J 20	Lypovec' 16 K 22	Pavlohrad 17 K 25	Starobils'k 17 K 26	Zboriv 15 K 21
Čyhyryn 16 K 24	Kam'janéc'-Podil's'kyj 15 K 21	Lysyčans'k 17 K 26	Pečenihy 17 K 25	Starokostjantyniv 15 K 21	Zdolbuniv 15 J 21
Čérnivci 15 K 21	Kam''janka Dniprovs'ka	L'viv 15 K 20	Perečyn 15 K 19	Starokozače 16 L 23	Zhurivka 16 J 23
Dašiv 16 K 22	17 K 24	Majaky 16 L 23	Perehins'ke 15 K 20	Staromlynivka 17 K 25	Zin'kiv 16 J 24
Davydiv Brid 16 L 24	Kaniv 16 K 23	Makijivka 17 K 26	Perejaslav-Chmeľnyc'kyj	Staryj Krym 17 L 25	Zlazne 15 J 21
Davydky 16 J 22	Kardamyčeve 16 L 22	Mala Bilozerka 17 L 24	16 J 23	Staryj Saltiv 17 J 25	Žmerynka 16 K 22
Debal'ceve 17 K 26	Karlivka 17 K 25	Mala Vyska 16 K 23	Peremyšljany 15 K 20	Staryj Sambir 15 K 20	Zmijiv 17 K 25
Derhači 17 J 25	Kazanka 16 K 24	Malyn 16 J 22	Pereščepyne 17 K 25	Stavyšče 16 K 23	Znam'janka 16 K 24
Dmytrivka 11 J 24	Kehyčivka 17 K 25	Manevyči 15 J 21	Perha 16 J 22	Štepivka 11 J 24	Zoločiv/Harkiv 17 J 25
Dniprodzeržins'k 17 K 24	Kerč' 17 L 25	Marhanec' 17 K 24	Pervomajs'k 17 K 26	Storožynec' 15 K 21	Zoločiv/L'viv 15 K 20
Dnipropetrovs'k 17 K 25	Kicman` 15 K 21	Mariupol' 17 L 26	Pervomajs'k/Novoukrajinka	Stryj 15 K 20	Zolotonoša 16 K 23
Dniprorudne 17 L 25	Kilija 16 L 22	Markivka 17 K 26	16 K 23	Sudak 17 M 24	Žovka 15 J 20
Dobropilja 17 K 25	Kipti 16 J 23	Mašivka 17 K 24	Pervomajs'kyj 17 K 25	Šuľ'hynka 17 K 26	Žovten 16 L 23
Dobrovelyčkivka 16 K 23	Kirovohrad 16 K 23	Medvyn 16 K 23	Petrivka/Geničensk 17 L 24	Sumy 11 J 24	Žovti Vody 16 K 24
Dokučajevs`k 17 K 26	Kirovs'ke 17 L 25	Melitopol' 17 L 25	Petrivka/Odesa 16 L 23	Svaljava 15 K 20	Zuja 17 L 24
Dolyna 15 K 20	Kiverci 15 J 21	Mena 10 J 23	Petrykivka 17 K 24	Svatove 17 K 26	Zvenyhorodka 16 K 23
Dolyns'ka 16 K 24	Kivšarivka 17 K 26	Merefa 17 K 25	Pidhajci 15 K 21	Sverdlovsk 17 K 26	Žydačiv 15 K 20
Domanivka 16 K 23	Kobeljaki 17 K 24	Mežvodnoe 16 L 24	Pidhorodne 17 K 25	Svitlovods`k 16 K 24	Žytomyr 16 J 22
Donec'k 17 K 26	Kočeriv 16 J 22	Milove 17 K 27	Pidvoloçys'k 15 K 21	Syneľ'nykove 17 K 25	
Dovhe 15 K 20	Kolarivka 17 L 25	Mistky 17 K 26	Piščana 16 K 24	Šyšaky 16 K 24	
Drabiv 16 K 23	Kolky 15 J 21	Mižhir''ja/Chust 15 K 20	Piščanka 16 K 22	Séménivka/Kréménčuk	
Drohobyč 15 K 20	Kolomyja 15 K 21	Mlynok 15 J 21	Pohrebyšče 16 K 22	16 K 24	
Dubno 15 J 21	Komar 16 K 25	Mohyliv-Podil'skyj 16 K 22	Pokrovs'ke 17 K 25	Tal'ne 16 K 23	
Dubove 15 K 20	Kominternivs'ke 16 L 23	Moločansk 17 L 25	Polohy 17 K 25	Taranivka 17 K 25	
Dubrovycja 15 J 21	Kompanijivka 16 K 23	Monastyrs'ka 15 K 21	Polonne 15 J 22	Tarašča 16 K 23	
Dudčany 17 L 24	Komsomols'ke 16 K 22	Moročne 10 J 21	Poltava 17 K 24	Tarutyne 16 L 22	
Dunajivci 15 K 21	Komsomol's'ke 17 K 26	Mošny 16 K 23	Pomična 16 K 23	Tatarbunary 16 L 22	
Dvorična 17 K 26	Komyši 17 J 24	Mostys'ka 15 K 20	Popiľ'nja 16 K 22	Terebovlja 15 K 21	
Dykan'ka 17 K 24	Komyšnja 16 J 24	Motožyn 16 J 22	Portove 17 L 24	Termahivka 16 J 22	
Dymer 16 J 23	Konotop 11 J 24	Mukačeve 15 K 20	Posad-Pokrovs'ke 16 L 23	Ternopil' 15 K 21	
Džankoj 17 L 24	Kon'kove 17 L 26	Murovani-Kurylivci 16 K 22	Pryazovs'ke 17 L 25	Terny 16 K 24	
Dzeržyns'k 17 K 26	Kopyčynci 15 K 21	Mychajlivka 17 L 25	Prykolotne 17 J 25	Terny 11 J 24	
Džuryn 16 K 22	Kopyšče 10 J 22	Mykolajiv/Herson 16 L 23	Pryluky 16 J 23	Tetijiv 16 K 22	
Evpatorija 17 L 24	Korec' 15 J 21	Mykolajiv/L'viv 15 K 20	Prymors'k 17 L 25	Tjačiv 15 K 20	
Fastiv 16 J 22	Korjukivka 10 J 23	Mykolajivka/Pavlohrad 17 K 25	Pryvitne 17 M 24	Tjahynka 16 L 24	
Feodosija 17 L 25	Korop 11 J 24	Myrhorod 16 K 24	Puškari 11 J 24	Tokmak 17 L 25	
Frunzivka 16 L 22	Korosten 16 J 22	Myronivka 16 K 23	Putivl' 11 J 24	Tomakivka 17 K 24	
Gresovskij 17 L 24	Korostyšiv 16 J 22	Myšuryn Rih 16 K 24	Putivl' 11 J 24	Tomašpil' 16 K 22	
Hadjač 16 J 24	Korsun'-Ševčenkivs'kyj	Nadvirna 15 K 20	Pyrjatyn 16 J 24	Torez 17 K 26	
Hajsyn 16 K 22	16 K 23	Narodyči 16 J 22	Péréjaslav-Hmeľnic'kyj	Trojic'ke 16 K 23	
Hajvoron 16 K 22	Kosiv 15 K 20	Nečajane 16 L 23	16 J 23	Trojic'ke 17 L 24	
Halyč 15 K 20	Kostjantynivka 17 K 26	Nechvorošča 17 K 24	P'jatychatky 16 K 24	Trostjanec' 17 J 25	
Hel'mjaziv 16 K 23	Kostopil' 15 J 21	Nedryhajliv 11 J 24	Rachiv 15 K 20	Tuhoľ'ka 15 K 20	
Heničes'k 17 L 24	Kotel'va 17 J 24	Nemyriv 16 K 22	Radča 16 J 22	Tuľ'cyn 16 K 22	
Hirs'ke 17 K 26	Kotovka 17 K 24	Nikolaevka 17 M 24	Radechiv 15 J 20	Turijs'k 15 J 20	
Hlobyne 16 K 24	Kotovs'k 16 K 22	Nikopol' 17 K 24	Radomyšl' 16 J 22	Turka 15 K 20	
Hluchiv 11 J 24	Kovel' 15 J 20	Nižnegorskij 17 L 24	Radyvyliv 15 J 21	Tuzly 16 L 23	
Hlyns'k 16 K 24	Kozača Lopan' 17 J 25	Nižyn 16 J 23	Ratne 15 J 20	Uljanovka 16 K 23	
Hola Prystan' 16 L 24	Kozelec' 16 J 23	Nosivka 16 J 23	Rava-Rus'ka 15 J 20	Uman' 16 K 23	
Holoby 15 J 21	Kozjatyn 16 K 22	Nov. Basan' 16 J 23	Reni 16 L 22	Uspenivka 17 K 25	
Holovanivs'k 16 K 23	Kramators'k 17 K 26	Nova Borova 16 J 22	Rešetylivka 16 K 24	Uspenka 17 K 26	
Holubivka 17 K 25	Krasne 10 J 23	Nova Majačka 16 L 24	Ripky 10 J 23	Ustyluh 15 J 20	
Horlivka 17 K 26	Krasni Okny 16 K 22	Nova Odesa 16 L 23	Rivne 16 K 23	Ust' Čorna 15 K 20	
Horochiv 15 J 20	Krasnoarmijs'k 17 K 25	Nova Praha 16 K 23	Rivne 15 J 21	Užhorod 15 K 19	
Horodec' 15 J 21	Krasnodon 17 K 26	Nova Ušycja 15 K 21	Rohatyn 15 K 20	Uzyn 16 K 23	
Horodenka 15 K 21	Krasnogvardejskoe 17 L 24	Nova Vodolaha 17 K 25	Rokitne 15 J 21	Valky 17 K 25	
Horodnja 10 J 23	Krasnohorivka 16 K 24	Novhorod-Sivers`kyj // Sivйrs`kyj	Romny 16 J 24	Varvarivka 17 K 25	
Horodnycja 15 J 21	Krasnohrad 17 K 25	11 J 24	Roven'ky 17 K 26	Vasylivka 17 L 25	
Horodok/Hméľnyc'kyj 15 K 21	Krasnojil`s'k 15 K 21	Novhorodka 16 K 24	Rozivka 17 L 25	Vasyl'kiv 16 J 23	
Horodok/L'viv 15 K 20	Krasnokuts'k 17 J 25	Novi Jarylovyci 10 J 23	Rubižne 17 K 26	Vatutine 16 K 23	
Horodyšče 17 K 24	Krasnoperekopsk 17 L 24	Novi Sanžary 17 K 24	Rudky 15 K 20	Vel. Bereznyj 15 K 19	
Horodyšče/Čerkasy 16 K 23	Krasnopillja 11 J 25	Novoajdar 17 K 26	Ružyn 16 K 22	Velika Bilozerka 17 L 24	
Hošča 15 J 21	Krasnyj Luč 17 K 26	Novoarchanhel's'k 16 K 23	Ržyščiv 16 J 23	Velika Lepetycha 17 L 24	
Hradyž'k 16 K 24	Krasnyj Lyman 17 K 26	Novoazovs'k 17 L 26	Šachnovščyna 17 K 25	Velika Novosilka 17 K 26	
Hrakove 17 K 25	Krasyliv 15 K 21	Novobohdanivka 17 L 25	Saky 17 L 24	Velikaja Pysarivka 17 J 25	
Hrebinka 16 J 23	Kremenez 15 J 21	Novohrad-Volyns'kyj 15 J 22	Sambir 15 K 20	Velyki Mosty 15 J 20	
Hrušuvacha 17 K 25	Kreminna 17 K 26	Novomoskovs'k 17 K 25	Sarata 16 L 22	Verchnij Rohačyk 17 L 24	
Huljajpole 17 K 25	Krolevec' 11 J 24	Novomykolajivka 17 K 25	Sarny 15 J 21	Verchn'odnipros'k 17 K 24	
Hurivka 16 K 24	Krymne 15 J 20	Novomyrhorod 16 K 23	Ščastja 17 K 26	Verchovyna 15 K 20	
Hurzuf 17 M 24	Kryve Ozero 16 K 23	Novooleksijivka 17 L 24	Ščors 10 J 23	Vertijivka 10 J 23	
Ičnja 16 J 23	Kryvyj Rih 16 K 24	Novopskov 17 K 26	Seljatyn 15 K 21	Vesele 17 L 24